EARLY MOTORCYCLES

Constuction, Operation and Repair

The Curtiss Eight Cylinder Forty-Horsepower Racing Motorcycle, the Fastest Vehicle of This Class Ever Built.

EARLY MOTORCYCLES
Constuction, Operation and Repair

Victor W. Pagé

Dover Publications, Inc.
Mineola, New York

Bibliographical Note

This Dover edition, first published in 2004, is an unabridged republication of the 1924 printing of the second (revised and enlarged) edition of *Motorcycles and Side Cars: Construction, Management, Repair*, originally published by The Norman W. Henley Publishing Co., New York, in 1920. The book's first edition, entitled *Motorcycles, Sidecars and Cyclecars*, was published in 1914.

Library of Congress Cataloging-in-Publication Data

Pagé, Victor Wilfred, 1885–1947.
[Motorcycles, sidecars and cyclecars]
Early motorcycles : construction, operation and repair / Victor W. Pagé.
p. cm.
Originally published: New York : Henley, 1914.
Includes index.
ISBN 0-486-43671-3 (pbk.)
1. Motorcycles. 2. Motorcycles—Conservation and restoration. I. Title.

TL440.P2 2004
629.227'5—dc22

2004052770

Manufactured in the United States of America
Dover Publications, Inc., 31 East 2nd Street, Mineola, N.Y. 11501

PREFACE

The growth of the motorcycle industry has been great during the past few years, and while it has not been as spectacular or imposing as that of its larger brother, the automobile business, it has reached proportions not generally realized except by those in the trade or the veteran riders. At a conservative estimate, several hundred thousand motorcycles are in service in this country, and the demand is increasing as the advantages and economy of this efficient motor vehicle are being better realized. The design and constructional features of the various makes are becoming standardized in some respects, though there is still considerable diversity in specific types. All follow certain rules of practice, however, and instructions for care and operation apply to all standard designs.

The automobilist has been very fortunate in having a large number of books available that cover all phases of motoring for his instruction, and everything desired in that field of knowledge, from deep technical discussions to elementary expositions, have been offered at modest prices. The motorcyclist, at the other hand, who desired a general treatise or instructions on motorcycle construction and operation, has been forced to acquire his knowledge by much research and reading because the books on motorcycling have been in the nature of elementary pamphlets rather than works of any pretensions.

The writer believes that there is a field for a comprehensive treatise dealing with motorcycles and allied subjects, and that some technical as well as practical information will not come amiss, in view of the paucity of such facts relating to motorcycle and sidecar construction, operation and repair. Efforts have been made to discuss the salient points of representative domestic and foreign products and to show clearly the many mechanical points and distinctive constructions that abound in modern practice. The writer has been very fortunate in securing the co-operation of practically all leading manufacturers in the motorcycle industry, and many distinctive drawings and photographs have been furnished especially for his use.

The reader's attention is directed to the very complete information given in the last chapter on motor overhauling which should appeal to the rider-owner as well as the mechanic. Many special photographs, posed in typical repair shops, illustrate this matter.

While some technical information and data are given, the material, for the most part, is of a practical nature that can easily be assimilated and understood by anyone. The instructions given for control, maintenance and repair should be valuable for the novice rider, while the discussions of mechanical principles will undoubtedly appeal to the more experienced riders, dealers and others in the trade.

THE AUTHOR.

NOVEMBER, 1920.

ACKNOWLEDGMENT

The writer wishes to express his appreciation of the valuable assistance offered and consideration shown by the following firms, who had sufficient belief in the distinctiveness and practicability of their product to welcome the light of publicity, and who went to considerable expense and inconvenience to furnish complete details, photographs and working drawings, showing important points of construction and design:

Hendee Manufacturing Company, Springfield, Mass.
Reading-Standard Company, Reading, Pa.
Sterling Motor Company, Brockton, Mass.
Harley-Davidson Motor Company, Milwaukee, Wis.
Excelsior Motor Manufacturing and Supply Co., Chicago, Ill.
F. W. Spacke Machine Company, Indianapolis, Ind.
New Departure Manufacturing Company, Bristol, Conn.
Enfield Cycle Company, London, England.
Rudge-Whitworth, Coventry, England.
F. E. Baker, Ltd., Birmingham, England.
Bowden Wire, Ltd., London, England.
Brown Brothers, Ltd., London, England.
Henderson Motorcycle Company, Detroit, Mich.
Consolidated Manufacturing Company, Toledo, Ohio.
Joerns-Thiem Motor Company, St. Paul, Minn.
Schickel Motor Company, Stamford, Conn.
Triumph Cycle Company, Coventry, England.
Bosch Magneto Company, New York City.

Credit is also due to *Motor Cycling*, an English publication, for a number of illustrations of foreign machines and components and for complete fault-finding table included in last chapter; and to *Motor Life*, an American motoring print, for permission to re-publish an article prepared by the writer dealing with motorcycle troubles. Endeavor has been made to give suitable credit, either in the text or cut lines, for all other illustrations that were not made especially for this treatise. The photographs of foreign cyclecars and motorcycles are by M. Branger or Meurisse, of Paris, France, and were made especially for this work.

The writer also wishes to acknowledge his indebtedness to the Harley-Davidson Motor Co. for permission to reproduce their instructions for operation and repair; also to the Hendee Manufacturing Co. and the Cleveland Motorcycle Co. for valuable new matter.

CONTENTS

CHAPTER I.

Motorcycle Development and Design.

CHAPTER II.

The Motorcycle Power Plant Group.

CHAPTER III.

Construction and Design of Engine Parts.

CHAPTER IV.

Lubrication, Carburetion and Ignition.

CHAPTER V.

Power Transmission System Parts.

CHAPTER VI.

Design and Construction of Frame Parts.

CHAPTER IX.

Harley-Davidson-Remy Electric Lighting And Ignition System.

CHAPTER X.

Motorcycle Troubles And Side Car Attachment.

CHAPTER I.

MOTORCYCLE DEVELOPMENT AND DESIGN.

Why Motorcycles are Popular—How Motorcycles Developed from the Bicycle—Some Pioneer Motorcycles and Influence on Present Design—Causes of Failures in Early Types—Mechanical Features of Early Forms—The Demand for More Power—Essential Requirements of Practical Motorcycles—Motorcycles of Various Types—Light-Weight vs. Medium-Weight Construction—Determining Power Needed—Influence of Road Surface on Traction—How Speed Affects power Needed—Effect of Air Resistance—How Gradients Affect Power Required—Power in Proportion to Weight—Influence of Modern Automobile Practice—The Modern Motorcycle, Its Parts and Their Functions—General Characteristics Common to all Forms—Some Modern Motorcycle Designs.

The motorcycle has been aptly termed the "poor man's automobile" and to one fully familiar with self-propelled vehicles, this term is no misnomer. The modern machine, with its ease of control, its reliability, its power and speed will carry one or two passengers more economically than any other method of transportation. Fitted with a side-car attachment, it becomes a practical vehicle for general use, as the body may be suited for passenger or commercial service. The demand for motorcycles, side cars and delivery vans has created an industry of magnitude that furnishes a livelihood for thousands of skilled workmen, and unmeasurable pleasure for hundreds of thousands who would be deprived of the joys of motoring were it not for the efficiency and low cost of operation of the vehicle that carries them swiftly and comfortably over the highways. The development of the motor bicycle dates back farther than that of the motor car, and it was demonstrated to be a practical conveyance over three decades ago, though it is only within the past six or eight years that this single-track, motor-propelled vehicle has attracted the attention its merits deserve.

Why Motorcycles are Popular.—The automobile attracted the attention of the public for some time before the motorcycle became generally popular, and, as a consequence, the development of the larger vehicle was more rapid for a time. As the early buyers of motor cars were of the class to which money is no object, as long as personal wishes are gratified, most of the manufacturers then building bicycles, to whom the public naturally looked for motorcycles, devoted their energies and capital to the design and construction of automobiles rather than motorcycles, because the prospect for immediate profits seemed greater in catering to the great demand that existed for any kind of automobile that would run at all. The development of the motorcycle was left to people, for the most part, without the requisite engineering knowledge or manufacturing facilities, so, naturally, the growth of the industry was of little moment until an equally insistent demand made itself felt for motorcycles, at which time people with capital began to consider the production of two-wheeled vehicles with favor. The demand for bicycles had been diminishing for several years, and the new type, with motor attached, seemed to offer a field that could be cultivated to advantage.

The evanescent popularity of the bicycle and the rapid rise to almost universal use, with almost as rapid decline was construed as a warning to proceed slowly in building motorcycles, as many thought the future of the motorcycle would be doubtful and that it was merely a passing fad. The bicycle required the expenditure of considerable energy, and, while very valuable as an exerciser, it did not offer pleasure enough for the bulk of our population in proportion to the amount of effort involved in making trips really worth while. The application of mechanical power, however, removed that objection, so the only deterring factor to the ready adoption of the motor-propelled bicycle was a lack of confidence on the part of the public regarding its reliability. It was not long before the endurance and practicability of the motorcycle was established beyond doubt, and as soon as the advantages began to be given serious consideration, a healthy demand, which is growing in importance yearly, stimulated its development from a crude makeshift to a practical and safe method of personal transportation.

The motorcycle and its various combinations with fore cars and side cars appeals to a conservative element who consider the cost of maintenance and operation fully as much as the initial expense of acquiring it. The motorcycle really has many fundamental advantages to commend it, as it has the speed and radius of action of the most powerful motorcar, with a lower cost of upkeep than any other vehicle of equal capacity. As constructed at the present time, the motorcycle is not only low in first cost, but its simplicity makes it an ideal mount for all desiring motor transportation at the least expense. The mechanism of the motorcycle, its control and repair, are readily understood by any person of average intelligence, and with the improved materials and processes employed in its manufacture, combined with the refinement of design and careful workmanship, a thoroughly practical and serviceable motor vehicle is produced which sells at but a slightly higher price than the first high-grade safety bicycles of fifteen years ago. At the present time, the motorcycle is not only popular for pleasure purposes, but it is applied to many industrial and commercial applications that insure a degree of permanency in popular estimation never possible with the bicycle.

How Motorcycles Developed from Bicycles.—Many of the mechanics who turned their attention to motorcycle construction were thoroughly familiar with bicycle practice of the period and, as considerable progress had been made in building light machines that possessed great strength for foot propulsion, it was but natural that the regular form of diamond frame bicycle should be adapted to motor propulsion by the attachment of a simple power plant and auxiliary devices. As a concession to mechanical power, various parts of the machine, such as the front forks, the rims and tires, and in some cases the frame tubes were made slightly heavier, but in essentials the first motorcycles to be made commercially followed bicycle practice, and with power plant removed, it would be difficult to tell them from the heavy built tourist models of pedal cycles. Naturally, the motor and tanks were not always disposed to the best advantage, and for considerable time, as the writer will show, much thought was spent in endeavoring to combine the widely varying principles found in bicycle and motorcycle practice and devise a hybrid machine composed of all the parts of the ordinary bicycle, with the various components of the gasoline or internal combustion power plant disposed about the frame at any point where attachment was possible. The motorcycle of the present day follows automobile principles and is radically different from its earlier prototypes in practically every respect except a general family resemblance owing to the use of two wheels, handle bar control, pedals for starting and placing a saddle so the rider can keep his balance to better advantage by sitting astride as on the bicycle.

Some Pioneer Motorcycles and Influence on Present Design.—As early as 1885, Gottlieb Daimler, who constructed the first practical high-speed internal combustion engine, and who, for this reason,

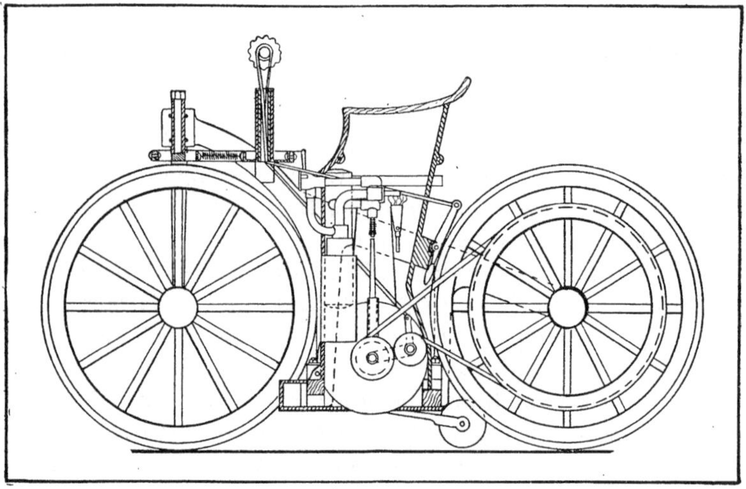

Fig. 1.—Early Model of the Daimler Motorcycle, the Parent of All Present Day Self-Propelled Vehicles.

is known as "the Father of the Automobile," obtained a patent on a two-wheel vehicle shown at Fig. 1. This, while not beautiful in outline, was a practical motor-propelled conveyance, and may be justly regarded as the forerunner of the modern motorcycle. In fact, in general arrangement of parts, this pioneer design is not unlike the modern product. At that time, the only motor vehicles regarded as practical or capable of actual operation for limited distances were types propelled by electric or steam power, and it will thus be apparent that Daimler's crude motor bicycle was not only the foundation of the motorcycle industry but also formed a basis for the development of the automobile which, in its most successful form, employs the internal combustion motor as a source of power.

After numerous designs in which single cylinder motors played a part, in 1889, Daimler patented a double inclined cylinder motor, the first multiple cylinder conception. This original form is that from which the modern V-engine, so widely used at the present time for cycle propulsion, was derived. This creation was also the first to be made in any considerable number and, even at this late day, some of the original Daimler engines are still operated. In this design, the cylinders were inclined but 15 degrees, and eccentric grooves turned in the fly-wheel face were utilized to operate the exhaust valves, instead of the cam motion which is now common. The cylinder was cooled by an enclosed fan wheel which supplied a current of air confined around the cylinder by a jacket, so the first practical high-speed internal combustion engine was cooled by air. This is the method used almost universally in the case of the bicycle motor, even at the present day.

After a time other motors appeared, such as the De Dion motor tricycles, propelled by a small engine based on Daimler lines, and which were more reliable than the first steam coaches and much superior to the early electric vehicles in all important essentials such as radius of operation, cost, reliability and speed. To Daimler must also be given credit for the invention of the first practical carburetor, or device to produce a combustible gas from liquid fuel, also an important factor in the development of the automobile.

The first Daimler machine, which is shown at Fig. 1, with one side of the frame removed, was not unlike the modern loop-frame machine in important respects. While the wheels were placed rather close together, the motor placing was intelligently thought out, and was so installed that the center of gravity was brought closer to the ground than in many of the machines which succeeded it. The drive from the pulley on the motor crankshaft to a larger member on the rear wheel and the use of a jockey pulley or belt tightener to obtain a clutching effect has not been altered in principle since its first application by Daimler. Steering was accomplished by a steering head construction practically the same as on present-day machines. The early form of Daimler motor did not have very much flexibility on account of the sluggish action of the vaporizer and the ignition by hot tubes so the speed was varied largely by allowing the driving belt to slip and by applying the brake. This was done by a controller wheel carried by a standard just in front of the operator's seat. When this was rotated in one direction, the jockey pulley or idler was allowed to drop, so that the belt became loose while a spoon brake, working on the rear wheel tire, was applied progressively as the belt tension was diminished, and consequently the driving power was reduced.

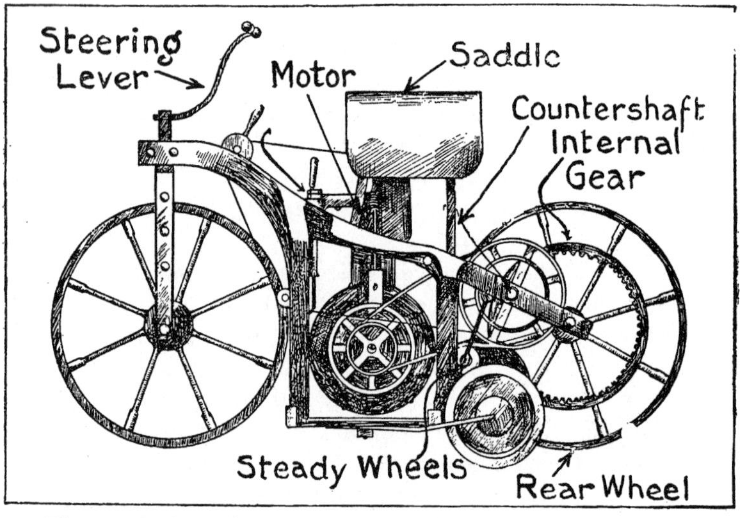

Fig. 2.—Early Daimler Motorcycle With Countershaft Drive.

A later form of Daimler bicycle, in which a countershaft was used, is shown at Fig. 2. The drive from the motor crankshaft to a pulley comprising one member of the countershaft assembly was by belt while a small spur gear provided a further reduction in speed by engaging an internal gear attached to the rear wheel spokes. It will be evident that Daimler not only originated the direct drive motorcycle but that he was also responsible for the first conception of the countershaft drive form. Attention is directed to the use of the auxiliary wheels mounted on each side of the rear driving member to steady the machine and keep it upright when not in motion. The lines of either of the Daimler machines are not unlike the forms we are familiar with, and the resemblance is striking enough, so that the parentage of the modern motorcycle can never be questioned. Daimler, as well as Carl Benz, who was working on a motor-tricycle at the time the former brought out his engine, next directed his energies to the improvement and construction of motor-propelled vehicles of the three- and four-wheel forms instead of the two-wheeler. Although there were spasmodic efforts made by some engineers in motorcycle design, most of them confined their efforts in refining the bicycle, which at that time was just beginning to attract attention because it offered possibilities of almost universal application.

Among the next of the pioneer motor bicycles to attract attention was another German make, shown at Fig. 3. This was constructed by Wolfmueller & Geisenhof, of Munich, Germany. In ordinary appearance it resembled the conventional bicycle design intended for the use of women though the machine had exaggerated dimensions. The saddle was placed low so that the rider could rest his feet on the ground if he desired. The power plant was a peculiar form which was said to develop two horse-power, and which was capable of propelling the 110-pound machine at speeds ranging from three to twenty-four miles per hour. The motor was of the two-cylinder horizontal form having the cylinder heads at the front of the machine while the open ends of the cylinders pointed to the rear. The connecting rods extended to cranks attached to the rear wheel axle, and the drive was direct from the motor cylinders to the traction member as in locomotive practice. Ball-bearings were used at the ends of the connecting rod as well as supporting bearings for the rear wheels. The fuel gas was obtained from a vaporizer of the surface type and the compressed charge was ignited by hot tubes. The cylinders were water-cooled and were surrounded with water jackets, and a supply of water for cooling the engine was carried in a peculiarly shaped tank forming part of the mud-guard over the traction member. The front wheel was used for steering and was mounted in forks in much the same manner as in the machines of to-day. A hand-lever actuated-spoon brake served to retard the speed of the vehicle when desired by frictional contact with the front tire. Both wheels were provided with

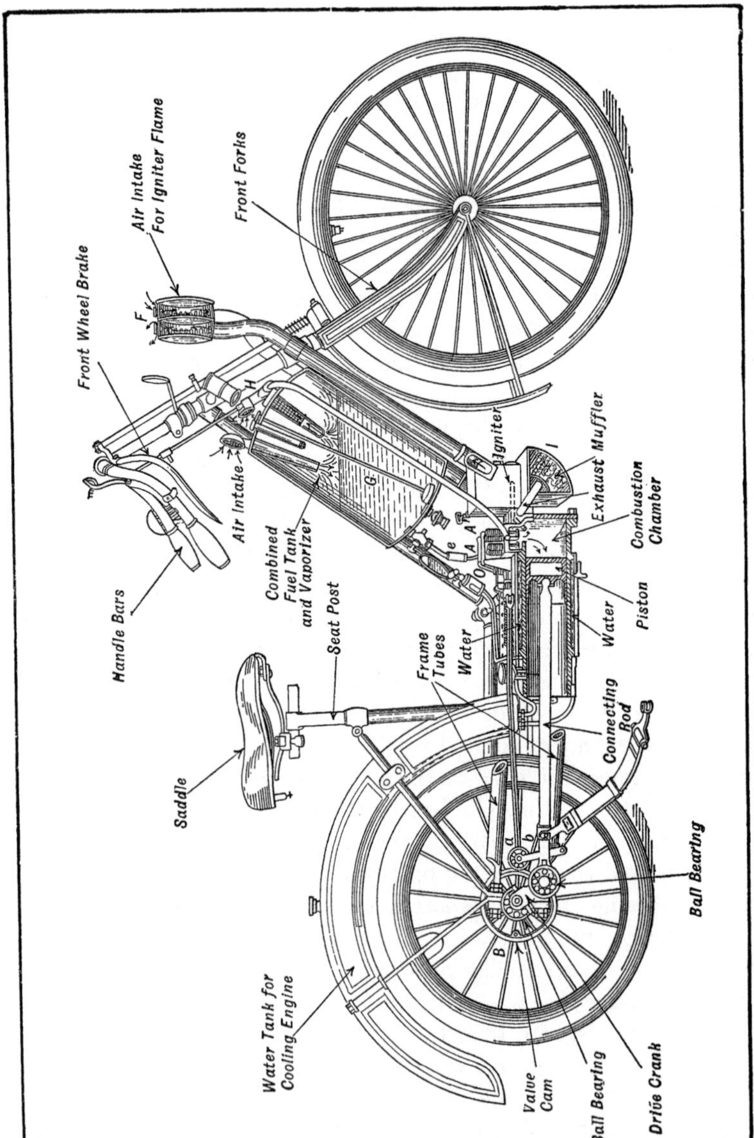

Fig. 3.—The **Wolfmueller Motorcycle, an Early Form of Unconventional Design.**

pneumatic tires. The engine cylinders were $3\frac{9}{16}$ inches in diameter with a stroke of $4\frac{5}{8}$ inches. The driving wheel was 22 inches in diameter while the front wheel was 26 inches in diameter. It is claimed that the fuel supply was sufficient for a run of 12 hours.

One of the earliest of the De Dion-Bouton tricycles is shown at Fig. 4. This had the small air-cooled motor placed back of the rear axle which it drove by suitable gearing. In order to obtain the desired speed reduction, a small spur pinion was mounted on the motor crankshaft which meshed with a large spur gear attached to the differential case. In the tricycle shown, the gasoline vapor was produced by a surface carburetor, and ignition was by hot tube. The machine was provided with pedals and it was possible to drive the

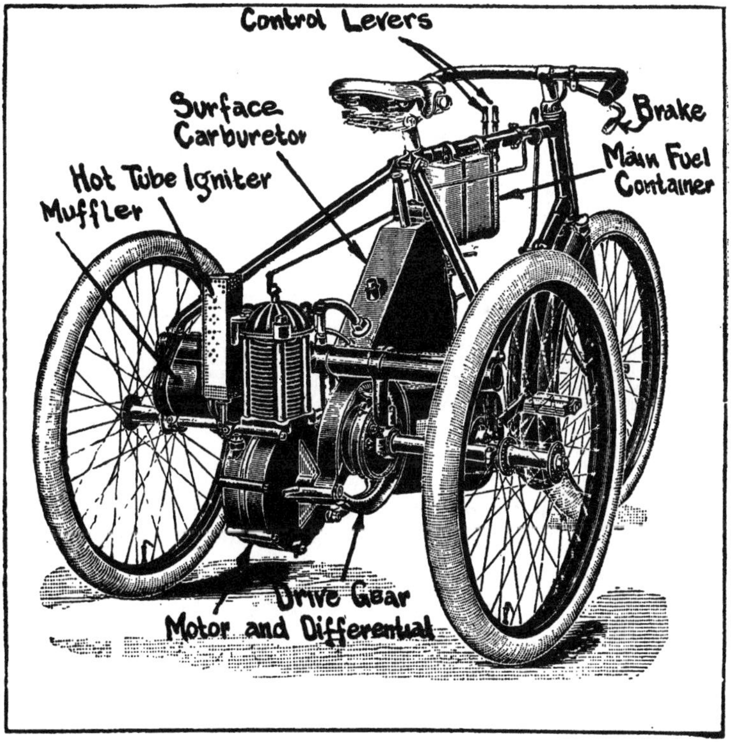

Fig. 4.—One of the First De Dion-Bouton Motor Tricycles.

rear axle by an independent foot-actuated sprocket and chain when desired. This made it possible to set the tricycle in motion by pedaling, and was also intended to provide a means of returning home when the motor became inoperative, which was not an infrequent occurrence. Owing to the limited power of the motor, which was rated at about 1¾ horse-power, the rider often found the pedals of some benefit as an aid to climbing steep grades. Some of these tricycles were converted into four-wheelers or quadricycles, as shown at Fig. 5, by the addition of a fore carriage which provided accommodations for a passenger. A later form of motor tricycle, in which electrical ignition

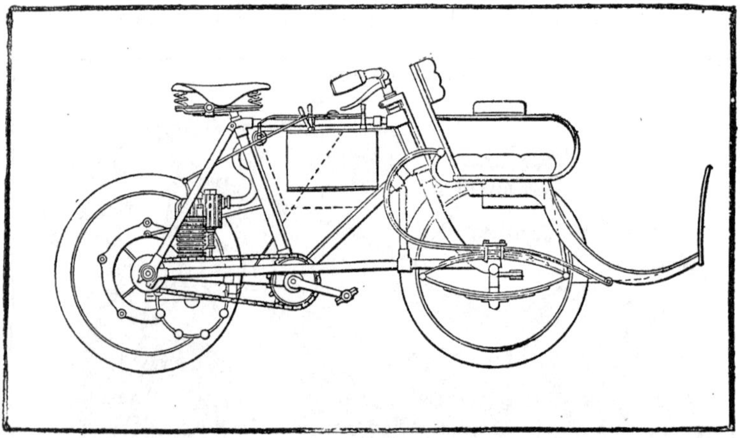

Fig. 5.—Motor Tricycle With Two Wheel Fore Carriage to Carry Passenger.

replaced the hot tube method, is shown at Fig. 6. By careful study of this side view and the rear end shown at Fig. 4, it will not be difficult to understand the construction of the earliest form of motor tricycles to be used successfully.

All of the pioneer designers did not devote their attention to tricycle construction, as some carried on experiments with the two-wheeled forms. One of the ingenious efforts to adapt the safety bicycle to motorcycle service is shown at Fig. 7. The power plant, which included a small gasoline engine with its auxiliary devices was mounted on a fixed axle at the center of the rear wheel, and remained stationary while the wheel revolved around it to drive the bicycle. Owing to the limited amount of space provided for the power plant, which meant that an engine of small power only could be used, this form of construction did not prove as practical as those in which the motor and its auxiliary devices were attached to the frame.

One of the problems that confronted the pioneer designer was the proper location of the power plant. The diversified designs in which the early designers attempted to solve this problem are clearly shown at Fig. 8. At *A*, an early form of De Dion motor bicycle is shown in

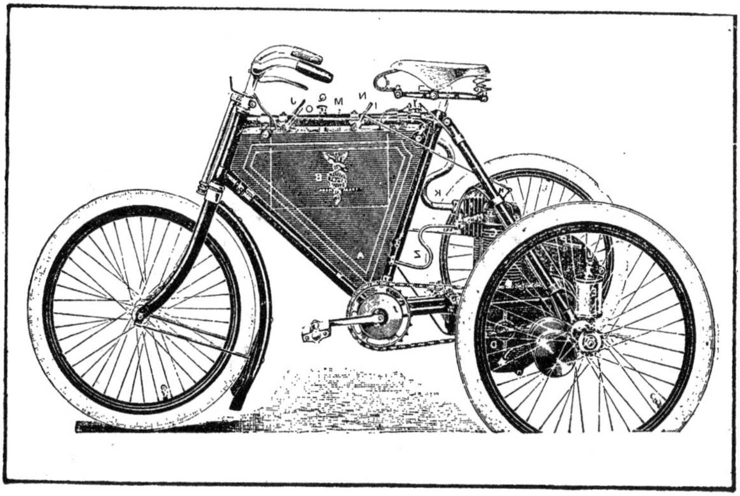

Fig. 6.—Side View of the Ariel Motor Tricycle, a Pioneer Form Using Electrical Ignition.

outline, and in order to obtain a low center of gravity, the power plant was placed back of the seat-post tube and crank hanger while the crank case was attached to the rear-fork stays. In the machine shown at *B*, which was known as the "Pernoo," the motor was placed on extended stays behind the rear wheels and drove that member by direct belt connection. Another motorcycle which was brought out about this time is shown at *C*, and was designed by a man named Werner. In this construction, the motor was carried on an extension of the front-fork crown, and the object desired by the inventor was to permit one to convert an ordinary bicycle into a motorcycle by the addition of the modified front forks to which the engine was attached. Power was transmitted by means of a belt from a small pulley on the motor crankshaft to a larger member attached to the wheel. It is apparent that the designer had in mind an equal distribution of the load on the two wheels in the construction shown at *A*. In both the forms, shown at *B* and *C*, the weight was not distributed as it should be, as in one case practically all of the weight came on the rear wheels, which made steering difficult, while in the other, the proportion of the weight carried by the front wheel was productive of skidding at the rear end when the machine was used on wet roads. The machines

Fig. 7.—Early Motorcycle Design With Power Plant Enclosed in Interior of Rear Wheel.

shown were evolved in the period ranging from 1894 to 1898, and were adaptations of the diamond frame safety bicycle, which at that time had been demonstrated to be a thoroughly practical vehicle.

During this period, American inventors were by no means idle. In 1898, Oscar Hedstrom, an expert constructor of light racing bicycles, turned his attention to the design and construction of motor-propelled tandems which were used in bicycle racing as pacemakers. His products were very successful, and their consistent performances on the track, as well as the speed developed, attracted the attention of George M. Hendee, who owned a large interest in the Springfield

Fig. 8.—Some Early Designs of Motorcycles Showing Diversity of Opinion Regarding Placing of Power Plant and Auxiliary Devices.

Coliseum, a very prominent bicycle race-track of the period. Mr. Hendee, who was engaged in building bicycles, determined that there would be a great future for the motorcycle if a satisfactory machine for roadwork could be evolved. Negotiations began between Messrs. Hendee and Hedstrom, and in January, 1901, Mr. Hedstrom became associated with the Hendee Manufacturing Company, and the development of the Indian motorcycle began. It is said that in four months' time, he not only designed the model machine, but built every part of it with his own hands. Many of the original features incorporated in the first Indian machine are retained in the modern forms, and have not been changed in principle since used on the pioneer creation built thirteen years ago.

The earliest Indian motorcycle to be manufactured in quantities is shown at Fig. 9, with all parts clearly outlined. The general lines of the diamond frame bicycle were followed in this as in other early forms, though a decided innovation was made by placing the motor in the frame in such a position that it formed a continuation of the seat-post tube, which was attached to the top of the cylinder. The motor crankcase was supported by the crank hanger which was located at approximately the same position as in bicycles intended for foot propulsion. This permitted the inventor to dispose of the auxiliary parts of the power plant so that the bicycle lines were not interfered with to any extent. The gasoline tank was mounted over the rear wheel and was partially supported by the mud-guard, while a smaller container between the rear forks and the seat-post tube served as a reservoir for the lubricating oil used in the engine. The carburetor was designed by Mr. Hedstrom, and with but few changes and refinements in minor detail, is used to-day, and is considered to be one of the most efficient of the many vaporizers used on motorcycles. The drive from the motor crankshaft was to a large sprocket, carried by a countershaft extending from the crank hanger, and this, in turn, imparted motion to a smaller sprocket which drove the rear wheel through the medium of a chain connection with a sprocket on the rear wheel hub, which was a modified form of bicycle coaster brake.

Ignition was by battery and spark coil, and control of the power plant was obtained by varying the time of ignition and regulating the

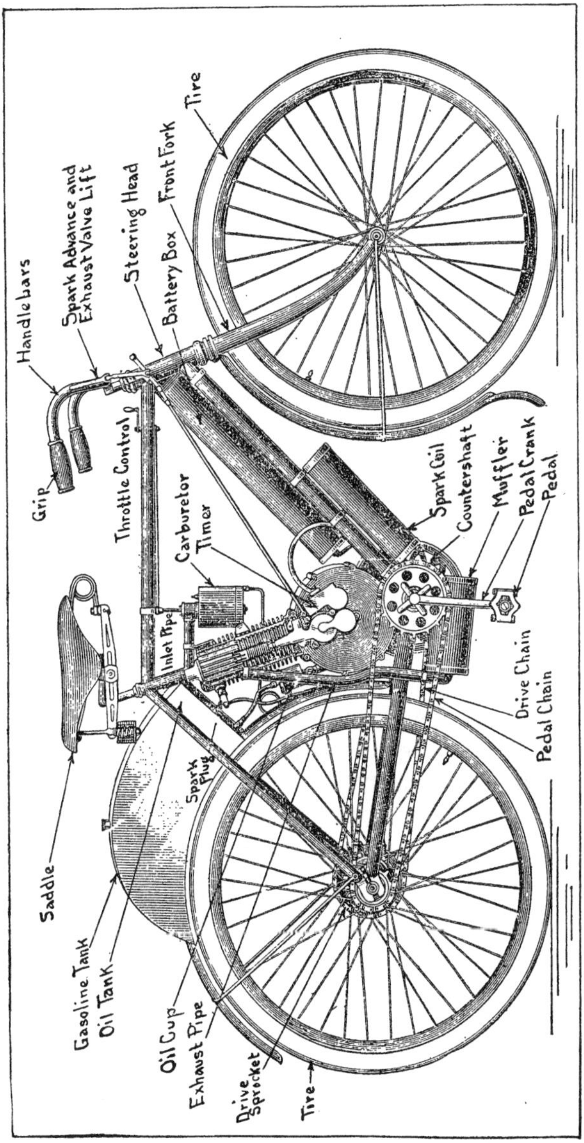

Fig. 9.—The First Indian Motorcycle to be Produced in a Commercial Way.

supply of gas admitted to the carburetor in much the same way as on modern machines.

A feature of even the earliest Indian model was ease of control, as while other contemporary manufacturers were producing machines having levers at all points of the frame, the Indian had the grip control that is now famous and almost universally used in America. By turning the grip on the right hand side of the handle-bar in one direction, it was possible to raise the exhaust valve so that the engine would be inoperative, while a twist in the other direction allowed the exhaust valve to close, thus permitting the motor to function, and a further movement advanced the ignition timer to speed up the engine. While throttle control on the early form of machine shown was by a small crank attached to the top frame tube near the steering head, it was not long before the left grip was also used in controlling the motor by being attached to the carburetor throttle. Owing to the excellence of the Hedstrom motor and carburetor, the neatness of design and the ease of control, the Indian motorcycle was eagerly accepted by the public, and the American motorcycle industry was fairly under way.

It must not be inferred that no other successful American machines were built at this time because there were quite a number of practical motorcycles evolved by other bicycle firms. Four of the early types are outlined at Fig. 10, and as the general construction and location of parts is clearly shown it will not be necessary to describe these machines in detail. This applies equally as well to the types shown at Figs. 11 and 12. A point that will strike the observant reader is the diversity of ideas as relates to power plant installation, as opposed to the very general acceptance of one method of installation at the present time. For instance, in the group at Fig. 10, the Thomas and Holley machines have the motor mounted with the cylinder center line coinciding with that of the seat-post tube, while the Orient and the Mitchell had the motor placed well forward in the frame with the cylinder inclined toward the steering head instead of toward the rear of the machine. In every case, the drive was by means of belts. In the Thomas, a combination steel and leather belt was used, while in the other three forms flat belts were employed. Two of the machines, the Mitchell and the Orient, did not use belt idlers or jockey pulleys, while the Thomas and the Holley found the idler pulley of sufficient merit to

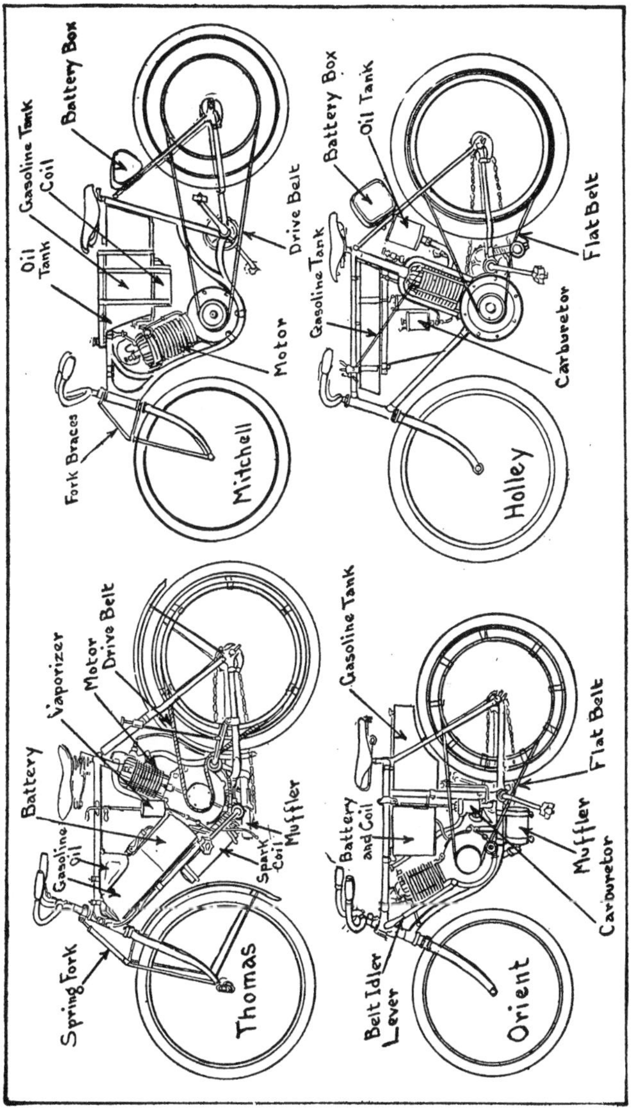

Fig. 10.—Examples of Early American Motorcycle Design, All of Which Were Manufactured on a Commercial Scale.

incorporate it in their construction. We find the same diversity of practice in the motorcycles shown at Fig. 11. In two of these, the Merkel and the Yale-California, the motors had the cylinder inclined toward the steering head, while the other two, the Pope-Columbia and the Marsh, utilized the opposite placing of the power plant. In the Columbia machine, the motor was carried back of the seat-post tube, while in the Marsh, the cylinder formed a continuation of that member. The general trend of former constructors to belt drive as opposed to the present tendency in the other direction is also clearly shown in this group, as but one of the machines, the Pope, utilized the double chain drive which is now the leading form of power transmission.

At the top of Fig. 12 is depicted a machine that in many respects resembles the accepted types of the present day. This was designed by Glenn Curtiss, now a famous aviator and builder of aerial craft. In this, the motor was placed with the cylinder vertical instead of inclined as in all the other machines shown. The business-like disposition of the auxiliaries, such as the gasoline tank, battery box, muffler, carburetor, the long wheel base and the general neat appearance of the machine are all commendable. The only thing needed to make this early form of machine an equal in appearance and performance to those of the present day was the addition of magneto ignition. The Wagner machine, which is shown in the center of the plate, incorporated for many years a distinctive form of frame construction, inasmuch as a separate loop member to carry the motor was added below the lower frame member of the conventional diamond frame. The Royal machine was also distinctive owing to the ingenious manner in which the power plant was housed in a nest formed by four tubes branching from the seat-post tube to the crank hanger. The Royal machine was also distinctive in the system of drive employed, because, while practically all of the contemporary machines, with the exception of the Pope and Indian, utilized belt drive, this employed a countershaft speed reduction and chain drive to the rear wheels. Instead of employing a sprocket and chain reduction, as did the Pope and the Indian, the drive from the motor crankshaft to the countershaft and the main reduction in speed was through spur gearing. A single chain served for both motor and pedal drive, as an ingenious clutching

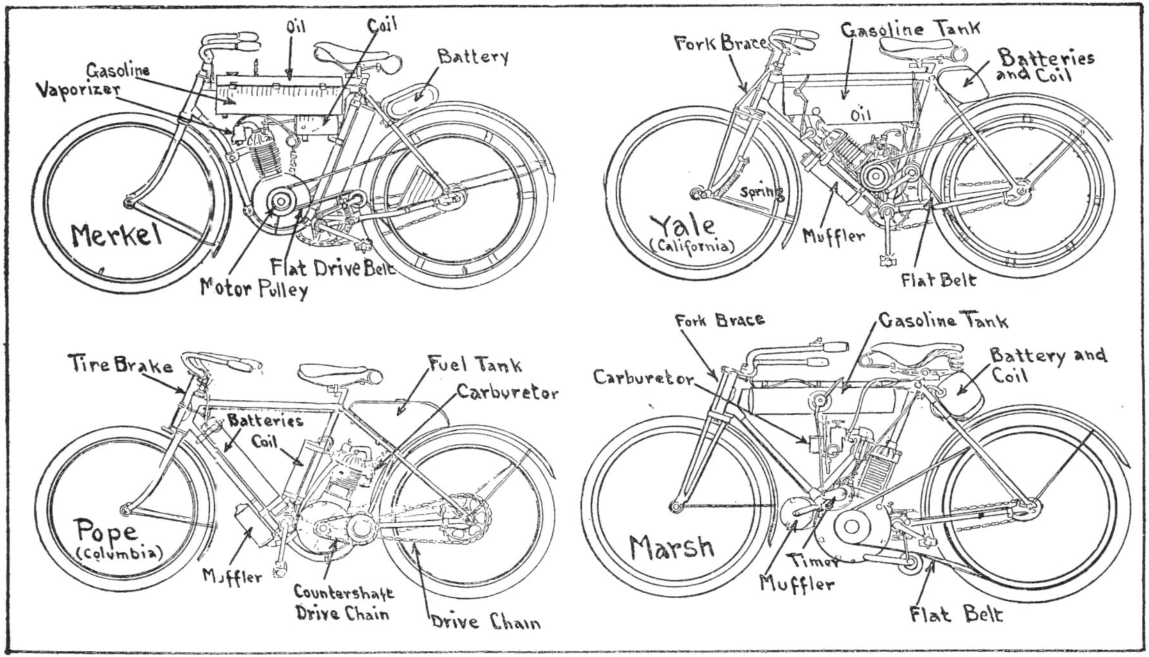

Fig. 11.—Some Early American Motorcycles Which Show a Wide Diversity of Opinion Regarding Essentials of Design Which are Standardized at the Present Time.

arrangement was provided by which the pedals could be brought into engagement for propelling the machine and starting the motor, and then the drive was taken by the same chain from the motor crankshaft, and the pedals automatically uncoupled by an overrunning clutch.

Another form of machine developed by American engineers, which was called the "New Era," on account of the number of advanced features incorporated in its design, is shown at Fig. 13. This was one of the first American machines to furnish a two-speed gear as regular equipment, and to substitute foot-boards instead of the usual form of pedaling gear. As the pedals were eliminated, it was not necessary to supply a seat of the usual form which is needed to permit the rider to pedal a machine when starting, and a more comfortable form seat, very much of the same nature as used in agricultural machinery, was provided for the rider. This seat was supported by springs, and as it conformed to the figure it proved to be very comfortable. The motor, which was a single-cylinder type was placed directly under the form seat, and the planetary two-speed gear was located on the engine shaft. The high and low-speed clutches were controlled by foot levers conveniently disposed on the running board, while another pedal provided control of the band brake acting on the rear wheel. The form shown was one of the earlier models in which ignition was by battery and coil, but other machines were made of more modern form employing a magneto. The fuel tank was carried over the rear wheel, as was common practice on many machines of that period and the drive was by single chain direct from the driving sprocket on the motor crankshaft to a larger member on the wheel. This machine was evidently too far in advance for its time, as the riders did not seem to take kindly to its unconventional lines which forced the company manufacturing them out of business. It is interesting to note that in this early form of machine, we find incorporated so many of the improvements and refinement usually associated only with machines of the present day.

The Demand for More Power.—When the first attempts were made to convert the bicycle into a motorcycle by the addition of a power plant, it was the intention of many of the constructors of the early types of machines to depend to some extent upon the rider to

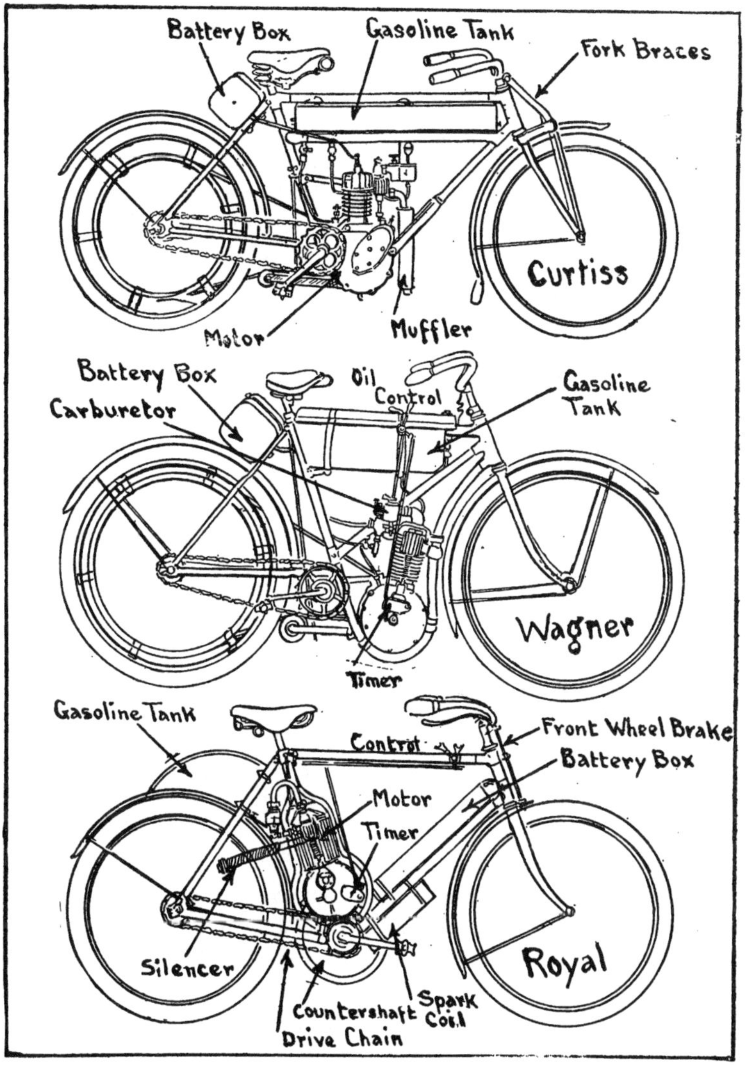

Fig. 12.—Some Pioneer Forms of American Motorcycles That Were Successfully Used Under Actual Service Conditions.

assist the motor at times when the resistance to motion was too great to be overcome by the small power plant provided. In order not to stress the frame tubes of the usual bicycle construction too much, the gasoline motors employed were of extremely low power, when judged in the light of our present day knowledge. Many of the successful motors were not over 1.25 horse-power, and a machine with a power plant rated at 2.50 horse-power was considered to be much heavier and more powerful than was absolutely necessary. The method of figuring the horse-power required on the early machines was very simple, as it was assumed that if a man, who was commonly given a rating of one-eighth to one-twelfth of a horse-power could propel a bicycle satisfactorily, and attain fair speed, that a motor of one and one-quarter horse-power should certainly prove sufficiently powerful to take the machine anywhere the rider wanted to go. Of course, it was not considered a serious disadvantage if one was forced to assist the motor up a moderate hill or over a stretch of sandy road by vigorous pedaling.

It did not take the early rider or motorcycle manufacturer long to discover that a frame structure that was entirely suitable for a foot-propelled machine was not necessarily strong enough to withstand the vibrations imposed by mechanical power. This vibration came, not only from the nature of the prime mover employed but was also due, in a measure, to the increased speeds made possible by the application of mechanical energy. As it was obviously necessary to increase the weight and strength of the frame to take care of the added stresses, it was also important to augment the power proportionately. Another factor that made it necessary to install more powerful motors was the demand for speed that soon became manifest after the machines had been mastered by their riders. To one not accustomed to motorcycling, a speed of 20 or 25 miles per hour was very fast, but after the first few rides had been taken, and the rider had confidence in his machine and ability to control it, many sought for machines having greater power, and consequently more all around ability. This demand was met by the manufacturers, and the horse-power of motorcycle power plants has increased over 800 per cent., as on makes that formerly utilized one and a quarter to two horse-power motors a decade or so back, we find on the modern forms

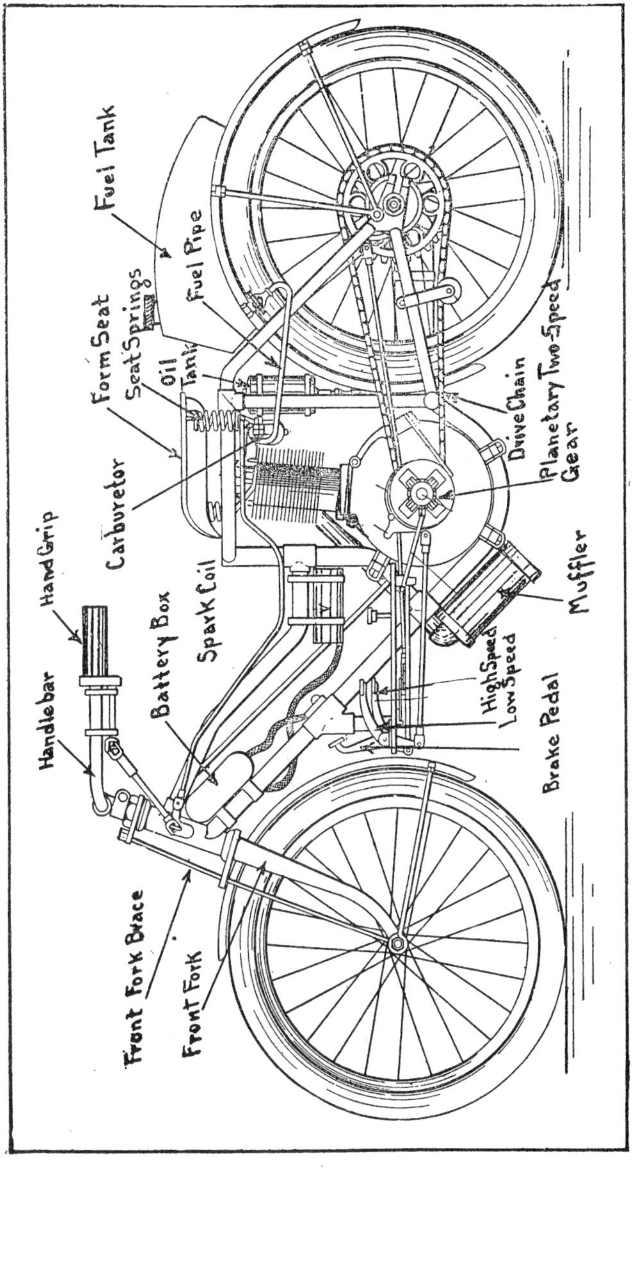

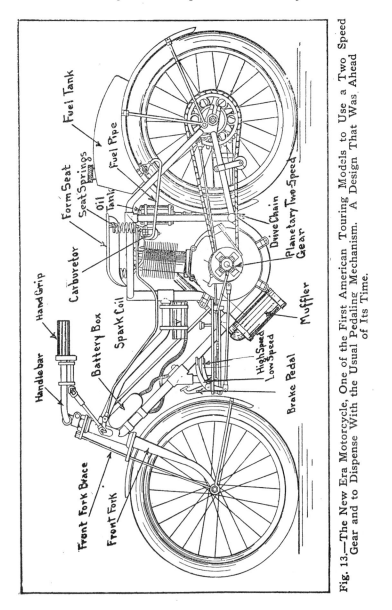

Fig. 13.—The New Era Motorcycle, One of the First American Touring Models to Use a Two Speed Gear and to Dispense With the Usual Pedaling Mechanism. A Design That Was Ahead of Its Time.

powerful motors which are capable of easily developing 12 to 15 horse-power.

Essential Requirements of Practical Motorcycles.—Before describing the parts of motorcycles, their functions or features of construction, it may be well to review a few of the essentials that are necessary in the practical motorcycle.

First, the machine should not only be simple and strong in construction but it should have a soundly designed and well-made framework as well as a powerful motor. The power plant should be so installed that it may be easily reached for inspection and the various components should be so accessibly located that any of the parts liable to give trouble can be reached without dismantling the entire machine. Most designs of the present day embody this important requirement.

Second, every provision should be made for the comfort and safety of the rider. This means that the saddle should be placed so a low riding position obtains in order that the rider may be able to put his feet on the ground to steady himself when necessary. Comfortable foot-rests or foot-boards should be provided in addition to the usual pedaling mechanism, and all the control levers should be placed conveniently so the rider may reach them, preferably without removing his hands from the handle-bars.

Third, the modern machine should be provided with wheels and tires of ample size, and should also include some form of spring fork and resilient frame construction to absorb vibration and to relieve the rider of all road shocks. The machine should not only be provided with an efficient power transmission system but should also include adequate brakes.

Fourth, the weight should be so distributed that the center of gravity, even with the rider in position, should come as near the ground as possible, in order to promote stability, and the load carried should also be proportioned so that the traction or driving wheel will carry more than the front or steering wheel. The machine should also be fitted with some method of free engine control so that the power plant may be kept running even if the machine must stop as in traffic. While a two-speed gear or other variable speed mechanism is the most desirable, it is not absolutely necessary, as very good results have been obtained with machines having a free engine clutch or its mechanical equivalent.

Fifth, the pleasure and convenience of the rider should be given some consideration, as, in addition to comfort and safety, it is desirable to make operation of the machine as simple as possible. For example, some form of automatic or mechanical oiling system is much to be preferred to the usual hit or miss oil pump system of lubrication. A fairly capacious fuel container should be provided in order to insure a reasonable touring radius. An efficient muffler should be provided so that the machine will be silent in operation. The machine work on the engine, and the fitting of the various parts, should be accurately done so the power plant will retain oil and the machine be a clean one to handle. A fairly long wheel base and large wheels are fully as desirable as the use of spring forks or frames to secure easy riding. The proportion of power to weight should be such that an actual surplus of power is held in reserve under normal operating conditions for use in any emergency.

Practically all of the essential requirements enumerated can be found in modern machines, though the average purchaser would be guided to a large extent in selecting a mount by a number of personal preferences, and it cannot be expected that any one type of machine will satisfy all riders.

Motorcycles of Various Types.—Three forms of power have been successfully adapted to vehicle propulsion, and among the many diversified types of automobiles we find some propelled by gasoline engines, while others depend upon the energy derived from a steam boiler or electric battery. While either of the three main forms of prime movers may be used in a practical way on motor cars, attempts that have been made by motorcycle designers to adapt steam or electric power to the two-wheel vehicle have rarely met with success. The electric motorcycle is impractical on account of the weight of the storage battery necessary to produce power, and also because its radius of action and possible speed would be limited. Some early inventors adapted the electric battery to the propulsion of three-wheelers or tricycles, and it was not very long ago that an announcement was made that an electric motorcycle would soon be available. To date, this promise has not been realized, and it is difficult for one to see how electric power could be applied to advantage on a two-wheeler and obtain the same desirable features that are so easily secured by the use of the gasoline motor.

Some experiments were tried in this country to apply steam power to motorcycles, but none of these ever proceeded far beyond the experimental stage. In England, however, there is a steam-propelled motorcycle that is not radical in appearance and which must be a commercial success because it is said that it has been on the market for three years. The drawing at Fig. 14 shows the general appearance of this machine which is known as "the Pearson and Cox," presumably because it is made by this firm in Shortlands. Despite the unconventional means of propulsion, this motorcycle is not so much different than those we are accustomed to that it would attract attention except of those well versed in motorcycle construction.

The power is supplied by a single cylinder, single-acting steam engine with a bore of 1¾ inches and a stroke of 2½ inches. This is mounted in the frame back of the seat-post tube and immediately in front of the rear wheel. The power plant is supported by the rear forks. The engine is given a nominal rating of 3 horse-power, but it is said that the boiler has capacity enough to furnish steam pressure sufficiently high so the engine will generate 6.50 horse-power. The power is delivered to the rear wheel through the medium of a single roller chain which connects sprockets mounted on the engine crankshaft and on the rear wheel hub. Owing to the fact that the steam power is always in reserve and that the steam engine may be put in motion by simply opening a throttle valve, it will be evident that no clutch or variable speed gear is necessary. When climbing hills, one merely admits more steam to the engine cylinder and its power is increased proportionately as the steam pressure is augmented.

The water is converted into steam in a flash boiler which is a coil composed of about 65 feet of pipe heated by the burner flame. The boiler is called a "flash generator" because as soon as water is pumped into the coil by the plunger pump driven from the engine for that purpose, it is converted instantaneously into steam having the high pressure of 1,000 pounds per square inch, and a temperature of 800 deg. Fahr. As the pump that supplies the water to the flash coil is driven directly from the engine, the amount of water supplied and consequently the steam generated is proportional to the demands of the engine. At very low speeds, when the steam consumption is small, a by-pass valve opens so some of the steam passes back into the water tank and is condensed into water. This valve is controlled from one of the grips on the handle-bar. The boiler, or rather, steam generator is located directly under the front diagonal frame tube and is protected from dirt by a liberal sized mud-guard on the front wheel. The whole of the diamond of the usual type camel-back frame is filled by the water and fuel container. In order to prevent waste of water which would make frequent refilling of the tank necessary, the exhaust steam is condensed by a suitable device and is pumped back into the water tank where it is used over again.

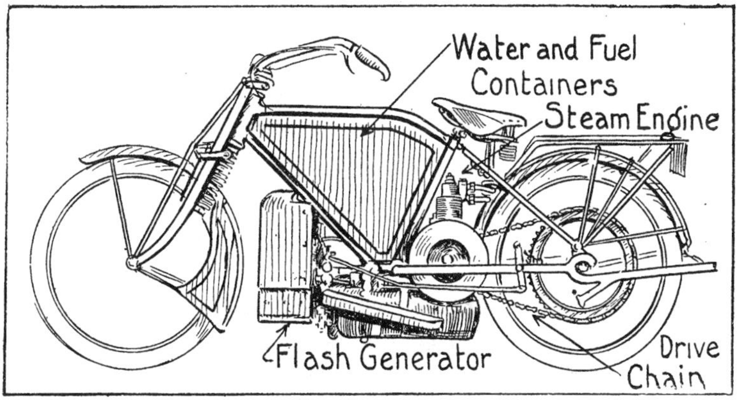

Fig. 14.—The Pearson and Cox Motorcycle. An Unconventional English Design Using Steam as Motive Power.

The heat to flash the water into steam is produced by a burner that utilizes crude oil, the cheapest form of oil fuel. Even though about twice as much of the cheap fuel is needed, as the amount of gasoline consumed by a gas motor of similar capacity, it is claimed that the fuel cost per mile is less than on the internal combustion engine propelled forms. The operation of starting the generator is not unlike that of starting the familiar gasoline torch. A certain amount of the oil is allowed to drip into a suitable shallow pan, and this puddle is ignited and heats the oil contained in the vaporizing coil that forms part of the burner to a high enough point to generate gas, at which time the main fire may be lighted

After the burner fire has been started, a small amount of water is injected into the hot flash coil by an auxiliary hand water pump, and the requisite steam pressure is obtained for starting the engine. Of course, after the vehicle is once set in motion the generation of steam is automatic. The speed and power of the engine may be controlled by a simple throttle valve in the steam line between the generator and engine cylinder which may be operated very easily from one of the grips. While this machine has had some sale in England, it is doubtful if the ease of control and smooth operation permitted by steam power offers enough advantages over the gasoline motor to make steam power a factor in motorcycle design. There is an added disadvantage in connection with steam power that the average rider will not take kindly to, and that is the possibility of a disastrous fire occurring, should the fuel tank spring aleak and allow the liquid fuel or fumes due to its evaporation to come in contact with the naked flame at the generator.

The use of the gasoline motor as a source of power for motorcycles is, therefore, general and it can be stated with truth that the internal combustion engine is really the only practical form of power plant for motorcycle use. The modern forms of gasoline engine are not only simple in construction, easy to understand, reliable and economical, but are also flexible enough and have sufficient reserve power so that there really would be no advantages of moment obtained by using steam or electricity that would outweigh the complication, weight and lack of efficiency that are common attributes of either of these indirect systems of power generation. In a gasoline engine, the fuel gas is converted into power directly in the engine cylinders, whereas with a steam engine it is necessary to convert water into steam and direct the steam to the engine cylinder to produce the power. Obviously the efficiency or amount of useful power obtained by burning a given quantity of fuel would be greater if it was utilized directly in the cylinder or by the internal combustion process than if burned under a steam boiler where a large part of the heat would be wasted in the form of exhaust gas through the boiler flues.

While motorcycles cannot be classified into types by the form of power used, as is possible with automobiles, they may be grouped into various classes depending upon their weight, the amount of power provided, the type of gasoline engine used, the method of power transmission, or the use to which the machine is adapted.

For example, motorcycles are constructed even at the present day that have engines of lower power, and which are correspondingly light as a result. Such machines are called "light-weights," a typical example of which is shown at Fig. 15. A light-weight motorcycle is not much heavier, as far as the frame is concerned, than the usual form of roadster bicycle, and the power plant need not be over 2.50 horse-

Fig. 15.—The Motosacoche. A Typical European Lightweight Type.

power. A light-weight motorcycle provided with a two-wheeled front axle instead of the conventional single wheel is shown at Fig. 16. A tricycle of this type is intended for elderly persons, women, or young people who do not desire to travel at high speeds, yet who wish to experience the pleasures of motorcycling, with maximum safety. Light-weights may be of two forms, according to the type of power plant used. They may be either single or double cylinder and the gasoline engine employed may operate on either the two-cycle or four-cycle principle. The next class of machine is the medium-weight, while the third classification is composed of the powerful touring motorcycles which are usually termed "heavy-weights," on account of the strong construction and large power plants used.

Either the medium-weight or heavy-weight machine may be divided into three general groups depending upon whether the machine is used for pleasure, business or racing. The medium-weight machines may be "singles," on account of using one-cylinder engines, or "twins"

Fig. 16.—Lightweight European Tricycle With Motosacoche Power Plant.

because two-cylinder power plants are utilized. A single may be either belt or chain drive, or the engine may be two-cycle or four-cycle. A heavy-weight machine may employ any one of three types of power plant, as some are provided with large single-cylinder motors while others utilize powerful two or four-cylinder power plants. Then again, all machines may be grouped into two general classes, "single geared," if only a free engine clutch is provided, and "two speed" or "variable speed," if some form of change speed mechanism, as well as a clutch is included in the design. It is, therefore, extremely difficult for one to classify motorcycles intelligently, though for the purpose of description they may be grouped into, the light, medium, or heavy-weight types without considering the form of power plant used, the method of drive of any of the individual characteristics of the various designs.

Light=weight vs. Medium=weight Construction.—Of the three classes, machines that might be included in the true heavy-weight class are so rare that there are really only two distinct types to be considered. Fully 90 per cent. of the motorcycles in general use may be grouped in either the light-weight or medium-weight classification. The light-weights are obtainable in various forms as we find in the domestic and foreign market machines that range in capacity from 1.75 to 2.75 horse-power, some of which use single cylinder motors while others employ small two cylinder engines. The light-weights usually range between 80 pounds and 140 pounds. Practically all light-weight machines, even if they utilize variable speed gearing, retain the pedalling gear. Where the roads are good, the light-weight has much in its favor. In initial cost, it is comparatively inexpensive and is economical of maintenance on account of the large mileage possible on small quantities of fuel and lubricating oil. A light-weight machine is easy to ride, start and control in traffic. A light-weight machine may be carried up or down a short flight of steps into a house without much trouble, and in the event of a serious breakdown the lighter forms may be propelled by foot power without undue exertion if the transmission system is thrown out of action. The light-weight machine, however, has the disadvantages incidental to the use of low-powered engines. These are lack of speed, hill climbing ability and lack of capacity for rough road work. The light-weight type appeals to people of conservative taste, or to the middle-aged and it is also a very suitable form of machine for those who are active and not very far advanced in age to start on. It is claimed by many authorities that motorcycle manufacturers have reached the extreme in catering to the riders demanding speed and power, and it is certainly true that the most powerful machines are difficult to handle, and are more expensive to maintain than the simpler and lighter forms.

The most important class of motorcycle is the medium-weight machine which, for the most part, is provided with engines ranging from 3.50 to 6 horse-power. While these machines are generally intended for carrying a single passenger and are not well adapted for the attachment of side cars or delivery vans, still they have sufficient power to carry a tandem attachment on fair roads, that are not too hilly. Of course, if fitted with a free engine clutch and two-speed gear, medium-weight machines may be used in connection with side car or delivery van work, if the gear ratio is intelligently selected. If not more than 4 or 5 horse-power is desired, a single-cylinder engine

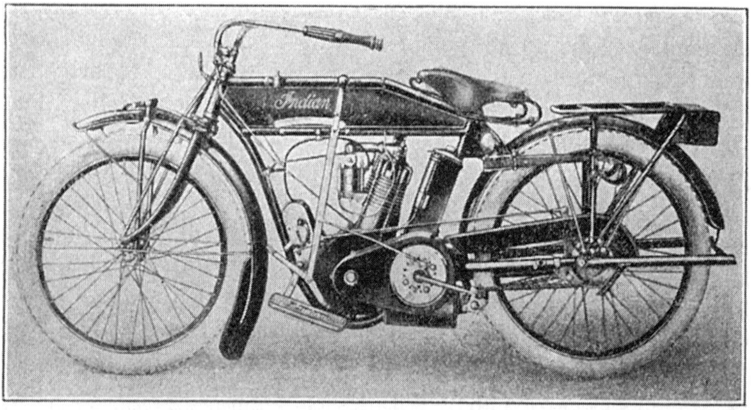

Fig. 17.—Standard 1914 Model Single Cylinder Indian Motorcycle.

will prove very satisfactory, and while the greater part of the demand, at the present time, seems to be for powerful twins, it is evident to one who analyzes the situation carefully that there will eventually be a reaction in favor of the one-cylinder type on account of its economy, simplicity, and ease of operation. To be thoroughly practical and capable of surmounting difficulties ordinarily met with, the machine of the future must include a variable speed gear as well as free engine clutch. The single-cylinder motorcycle shown at Fig. 17 is a representative American type that is a good example of the single-cylinder medium-weight class. At Fig. 18 a medium-weight single-cylinder machine of English design with its important parts outlined is clearly

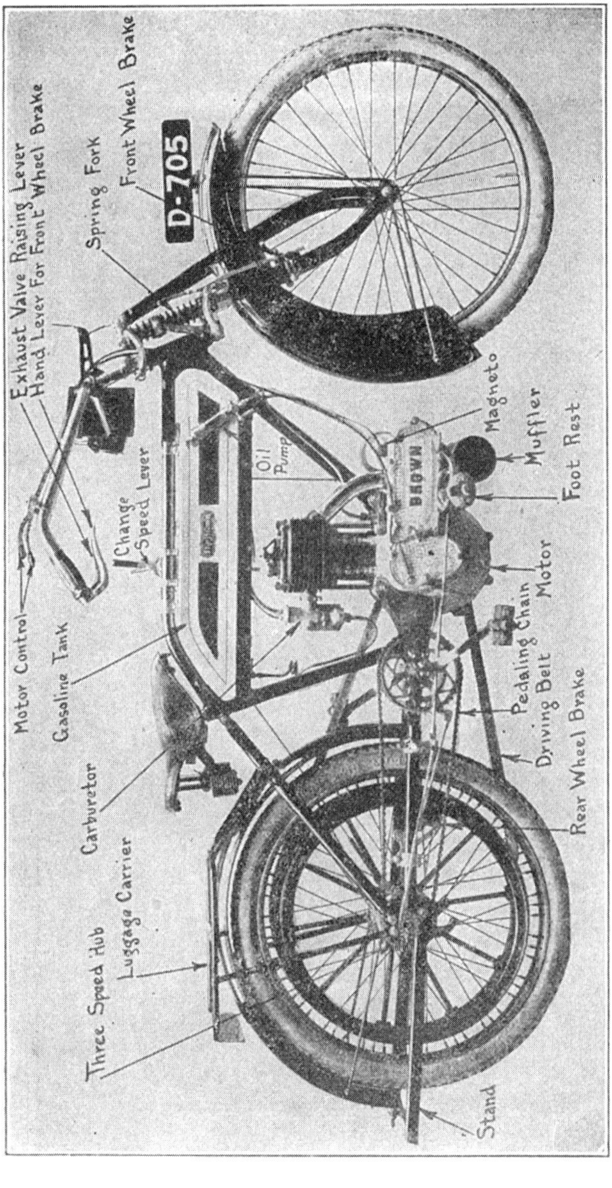

Fig. 18.—The Brown (English) Motorcycle With Important Parts Clearly Indicated.

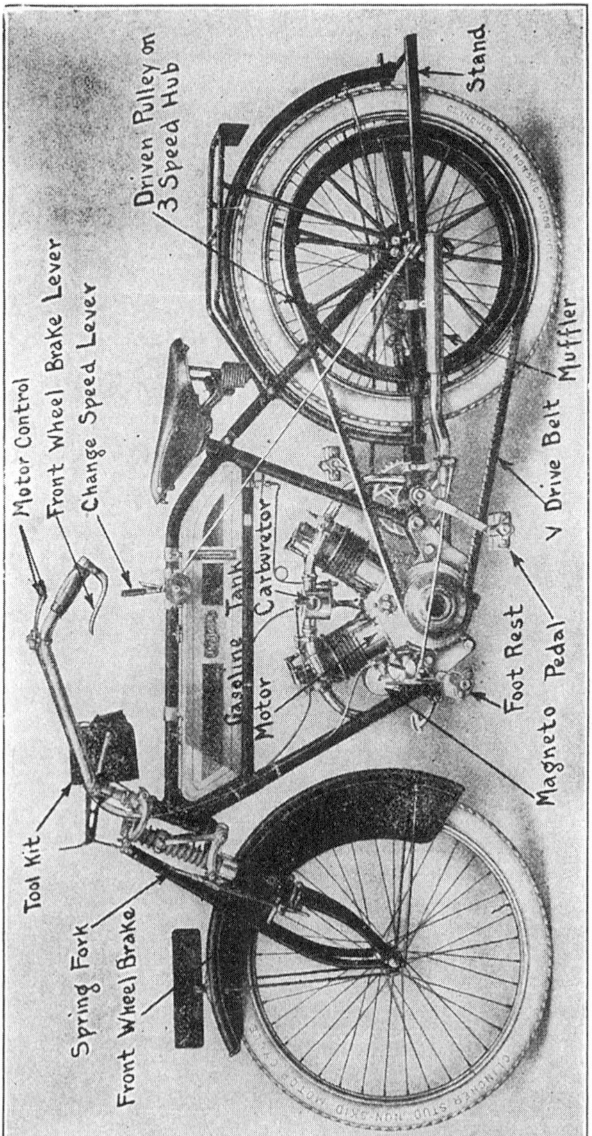

Fig. 19.—The Brown Light Twin Motorcycle.

depicted. An example of the medium-weight machine with small twin-cylinder engine and three-speed variable gear in the rear hub is shown at Fig. 19. It will be observed that the American machine is of the chain drive type, whereas the English designs employ V-belts for power transmission. The medium-weight machine answers practically all of the requirements of the average rider, as it is sufficiently fast and powerful to make it a good touring machine and its construction is heavy enough to enable it to withstand the stresses incidental to operation on rough roads. At the other hand, the medium-weight machine can be handled by any person of average strength, and very satisfactory mileage is obtained from lubricating oil, gasoline and tires.

In the heavy-weight classification, we have the powerful twins and four-cylinder machines rated at from 7 to 10 horse-power, which have ample capacity to handle a side car or delivery van, and which, for the most part, are provided with variable speed gears, and seldom with single-cylinder engines. It is hard to define sharply the distinguishing line between the medium and heavy-weight classes, though most medium-weight machines weigh less than 210 pounds, while the heavy-weight machines will vary between that minimum and a maximum of about 300 pounds with full equipment. A typical machine that may be considered as being on the border line between the heavy-weight and medium-weight classes is shown at Fig. 20. This is an American design and is fitted with a motor rated at from 7 to 9 horse-power, and a variable speed gear. A machine of the true heavy-weight class which is equipped with a four-cylinder power plant is shown at Fig. 21.

On this machine it will be noticed that the usual form of pedaling gear is omitted entirely, because the machine is so heavy that it would be practically impossible to pedal it for any distance in event of breakdown of the power plant. Fortunately, the gasoline engine has been developed to a point where serious derangements are practically unknown, and on most of the medium-weight machines the usual pedaling gear is provided only to facilitate starting and to provide for brake operation rather than as a means of propulsion. A machine of the type shown at Fig. 21 is practically a two-wheeled automobile and demonstrates clearly how radically different the modern motor-

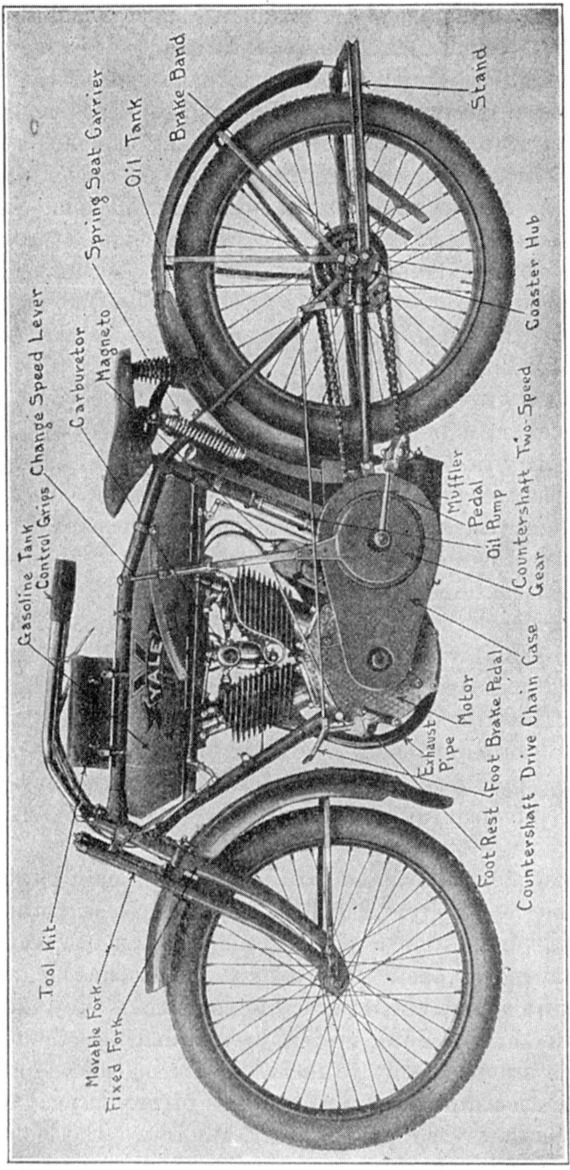

Fig. 20.—The Yale Two Speed Twin Cylinder Model for 1914.

cycle is in construction when compared to the bicycle that formed the basis for the first design.

In the various classes enumerated, one will find machines that have been designed for certain specific purposes, for example, at Fig. 22 is shown a stock racer which is a type of machine that is stripped down to as light weight as possible, and which is geared high in order to obtain the maximum possible speed. The dropped handle-bar makes it easy for the rider to assume a crouching position, which, as we shall see later, makes for minimum air resistance, whereas the elimination of unnecessary weight also makes possible the attaining of high speeds with the same amount of power as would be utilized

Fig. 21.—The Henderson Four Cylinder Motorcycle With Tandem Attachment.

in a touring machine. Obviously a machine of this type would not be as comfortable for road use as the regular model, on account of the elimination of the spring fork, the upturned handle-bar, the mud guards, foot rests, and other auxiliaries which increase the comfort of the rider. A special form of machine which, while of unconventional appearance, is nevertheless practical, is depicted at Fig. 23. This is intended for the use of women, as it not only has the usual form of open frame, but also carries the power plant far enough forward and has it well protected so as not to interfere with the skirts of the rider. The tri-car shown at Fig. 24 shows the application of the

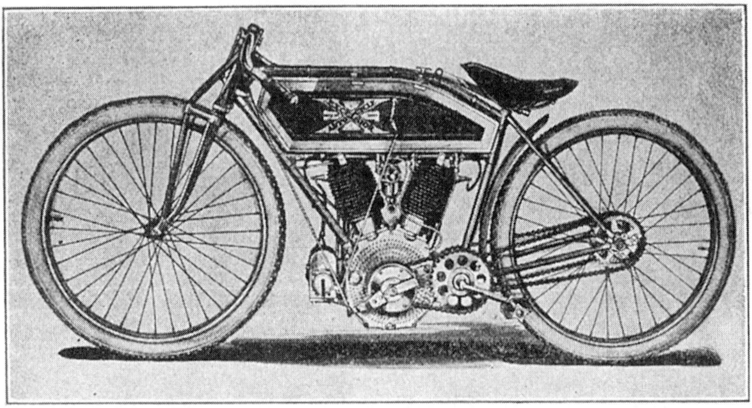

Fig. 22.—The Excelsior Standard Stock Racer.

motorcycle to commercial work, and the vehicle outlined is really a composite form, composed of a two-wheel fore-carriage attached to a twin-cylinder motorcycle. This motorcycle truck weighs complete but 530 pounds and will carry 600 pounds in addition to the weight of the driver. The application of side cars will be considered in a

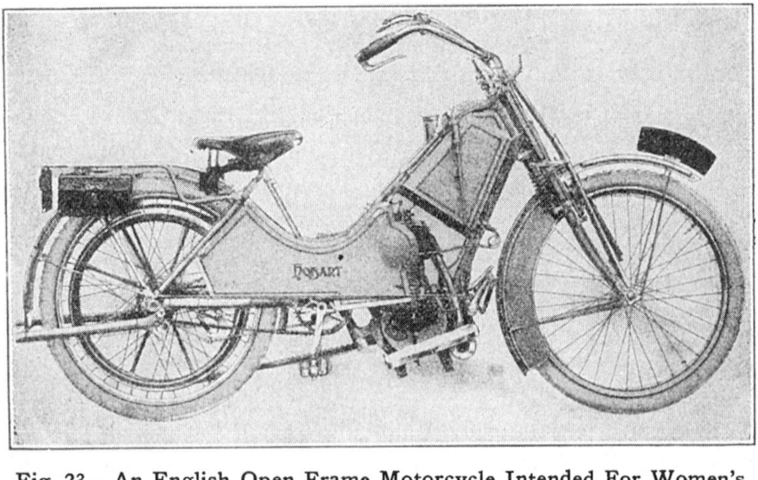

Fig. 23.—An English Open Frame Motorcycle Intended For Women's Use.

chapter devoted to that form of construction. Summing up, it is apparent that no one class of motorcycle will suit everybody. A machine that might be eminently satisfactory to one individual might fail entirely in fulfilling the requirements of another. The low-powered motorcycle is suitable for those who do not care to travel fast or far and who wish an economical machine that is easily handled. The machine of medium weight and moderate power will suit the average individual who wishes a strong machine capable of keeping up a good average on a long trip, and that will have power enough to

Fig. 24.—The Harley-Davidson Motorcycle Truck, a Commercial Application That Has Proven Thoroughly Practical.

climb average hills and negotiate our ordinary roads. The heavy powerful machine is the mount for the enthusiast or expert who has graduated from the light-weight or medium-weight class, and who does not object to weight or expense as long as his machine is capable of high speeds with a sufficient margin of power to surmount the steepest hills or negotiate the most unfavorable roads.

Determining Power Needed.—The amount of power needed to propel a motorcycle depends upon a number of factors, all of which are variable. The chief resistance to motion of self-propelling vehicles, such as automobiles and motorcycles, when operated on a level road at low and moderate speeds consists of the rolling resistance at the point of contact between traction member and the ground and friction in driving, power-transmitting and supporting elements. At high speeds one must take into account the factor of air resistance, though at low speeds this can be neglected because of its low value. When a motorcycle is to be propelled up a gradient, one must take into consideration the added resistance due to gravity, and the amount of power required to drive the machine depends upon the weight of machine and rider, steepness of the hill and the speed it is desired to maintain. Obviously, when descending hills, less power is needed than when running up hill or on the level. It takes more power to drive a heavy machine than a light one, other conditions being equal. A smooth-running construction is easier to push than one in which considerable friction exists, and much more power is needed on machines intended for high-speed work than on types where the operating speeds are moderate. No matter how powerful the power plant is, the only available means of determining the capacity of the vehicle is a consideration of the amount of push available at the contact point of traction member and road, so while it is imperative to supply enough power, it is equally important to so distribute the weight as to insure adequate adhesion between traction member and road surface and to have as efficient delivery of power from motor to rear wheel as possible.

Influence of Road Surface on Traction.—The resistance offered by various roads depends primarily on the character of the surface, but it is also controlled to a limited extent by the size of wheels, character of tires and speed. The traction coefficients as given by Norris follow:

On rails or plates..............	5.16	pounds per ton
Asphalt or hardwood..........	12.24	pounds per ton
Macadam.....................	30.60	pounds per ton
Loose gravel..................	140 to 200	pounds per ton
Sand.........................	400	pounds per ton

The influence of tires provided may be summed up concisely by saying that the resistance of iron and solid rubber tires is approximately the same, while with well-inflated pneumatic tires, it will be 25 to 30 per cent. less. The figures given above are for pneumatic tires, though the amount of air pressure in the tires influences the traction resistance to a degree. Hard tires have much less resistance than softer ones. A generally accepted value for well-inflated pneumatic tires is 50 pounds per ton on hard, level asphalt, and this is the basis commonly used in automobile engineering practice. A value of 80 pounds per ton for macadam and hard dirt roads will provide a desirable margin, and can be followed to advantage because motorcycle wheels are relatively small, commonly ranging from 26 to 30 inches in diameter, with 28-inch wheels predominating. Larger diameter wheels, such as used on automobiles, are more capable of rolling over minute obstructions and bridge small hollows easily and with less effort than would be required of supporting members of less diameter. The traction resistance would, therefore, be higher with low wheels than high ones, if the road surfaces were not absolutely smooth. The total effort required to overcome traction resistance R may be approximated by considering the following formula, in which W is total weight of motorcycle and load:

$$\frac{W \times 80}{2{,}000} = R \text{ or } \frac{W \times 4}{100} = R.$$

How Speed Affects Power Needed.—The value obtained by formula is but one of the factors to be considered in determining the horse-power required, therefore it is important to consider velocity of cycle as well. This value is generally taken in feet per minute, so if V is the speed in miles per hour, then

$$\frac{V \times 5{,}280}{60} = 88\ V$$

is the speed in feet per minute, and the horse-power required to overcome traction resistance of a certain vehicle and passengers at a known speed may be derived by the following:

$$\text{H.P.} = \frac{W \times 4}{100} \times 88\ V \times 1/33{,}000.$$

Consider, for example, that it is desired to approximate the power necessary to overcome traction resistance of a motorcycle and passengers weighing 500 pounds at a speed of 40 miles per hour, and that air resistance is neglected for the moment. Substituting known values in the above formula, we have

$$\text{H.P.} = \frac{500 \times 4}{100} \times 88 \times 40 \times \frac{1}{33{,}000} \text{ or}$$

$$\text{H.P.} = \frac{20 \times 3{,}520}{33{,}000} = \frac{70{,}400}{33{,}000} = 2.10 \text{ H.P.}$$

This would indicate that the torque corresponding to 2 horse-power applied at point of contact of traction wheel and ground would be capable of driving 500 pounds at the rate of 40 miles per hour over smooth macadam or dirt road. Let us consider a condition where the road surface would offer a greater resistance to traction and yet permit of the same speed as previously considered, or 40 miles per hour. If the road surface is loose gravel, the resistance will be 200 pounds per ton, and the formula for traction resistance would be:

$$\frac{W \times 200}{2{,}000} = R \text{ or } \frac{W}{10} = R.$$

The complete formula, taking speed into consideration, is:

$$\text{H.P.} = \frac{W}{10} \times 88 \times 40 \times \frac{1}{33{,}000} \text{ or}$$

$$\text{H.P.} = \frac{500 \times 88 \times 40}{10 \times 33{,}000} \text{ or } \frac{1{,}760{,}000}{330{,}000} = 5.33 \text{ H.P.}$$

As the motorcyclist would be apt to meet loose gravel or dirt, the amount of power needed must be figured using the unfavorable roads as a basis. It is not likely that the rider could negotiate a soft road safely at 40 miles per hour, so the amount of power obtained above is somewhat higher than actually needed, because the speed would be reduced as the traction resistance increased. It would be possible to run at 20 miles per hour, however, so figuring power needed on this basis, we have:

$$\text{H.P.} = \frac{W}{10} \times 88 \times 20\, 1/33{,}000 = \frac{500 \times 20 \times 88}{10 \times 33{,}000} = 2.69 \text{ H.P.}$$

It will be seen that the reduction in vehicle speed has made it possible to drive the motorcycle over a gravel road at 20 miles per hour, with but little more power than that needed to drive it over a macadam road at 40 miles per hour. The factor of air resistance must be taken into consideration at a speed of 40 miles per hour, however, so the power needed to overcome air resistance must be added to that required for traction.

Effect of Air Resistance.—A commonly used formula for approximating power needed to overcome the air resistance at various speeds as given by Brooks in which V is velocity of vehicle in feet per second, and A the projected area of front of cycle and rider, is

$$H.P. = \frac{V^3 \times A}{240{,}000}.$$

This formula assumes still air, so if the cycle is to be driven against a wind of known velocity, this should be added to the cycle velocity. We will assume for simplicity that the motorcycle is to attain a speed of 40 miles per hour in still air. This is equal to a speed of 58.6 feet per second. The projected area will vary with the size and position of the rider, and even with a large rider sitting upright on the average motorcycle, it is not apt to exceed 5 square feet, whereas, if the rider crouches along the tank or rides low, the projected area of machine and rider will not exceed 4 square feet.

This was determined experimentally by photographing a standard machine and medium-weight rider as shown at Fig. 25, having the rider assume two positions. At A he is sitting in the usual road-riding posture or upright, and it is reasonable to assume that this is the position that offers the maximum exposed area against which air resistance becomes effective. The view at B shows the position assumed by most riders on the track, in which the operator's body rests on the tank, and this may be taken as the position that offers a minimum exposed area to air resistance.

As the basis for figuring is the projected area, rather than actual exposed area, it was possible to draw outlines corresponding to the two positions on squared plotting paper as at Fig. 26. The photographs were of such a size that each square represents one square inch in area. Therefore, by counting the squares, it was not difficult to

Fig. 25.—Showing Position of Rider For Road Work at A and When Minimum Air Resistance is Desired at B.

approximate the area of the rider and machine in the two positions. As a check upon this simple method, the areas were computed with a planimeter and were found to agree very closely with the areas obtained by counting the squares.

Using the Brooks formula and substituting known values, we have:

$$\text{H.P.} = \frac{58.6^3 \times 5}{240{,}000} = \frac{201{,}050 \times 5}{240{,}000} = 4.14 \text{ H.P.}$$

To overcome the resistance of air at speeds of 60 miles per hour, or 88 feet per second, with rider in crouching position, we have the following:

$$\text{H.P.} = \frac{88^3 \times 4}{240{,}000} = \frac{681{,}472 \times 4}{240{,}000} = 11.3 \text{ H.P.}$$

From the example previously considered, this means that it will require 2.1 horse-power to overcome traction resistance of a 500-pound motorcycle and load at 40 miles per hour, and 4.14 horse-power to overcome the air resistance, this making a total of 6.24 horse-power to propel a 500-pound motorcycle and load on a level road at a speed of 40 miles per hour. If only level roads were to be considered, or highways having a good surface, a 7 horse-power motorcycle power plant would be ample for all requirements up to a speed of 40 miles per hour, and would carry two passengers easily under these conditions, if there was no loss in power transmission elements. Owing to this loss, the power plant should be capable of delivering that amount of power to the rear wheel after all losses have been deducted.

How Gradients Affect Power Required.—A motorcycle must be capable of surmounting any gradient apt to be met *en tour* if it is to be considered a practical conveyance, so another item that must be reckoned with in determining power required is the ability to climb hills. The amount of power needed depends on all the factors previously considered, such as condition of road surface, the speed it is desired to attain, weight of machine and passengers, and in addition one must take cognizance of the steepness or pitch of the grade.

The ability of a motorcycle to climb hills depends upon correct application of power to the traction member as well as ample power plant capacity. An engine of relatively small power may be suitable

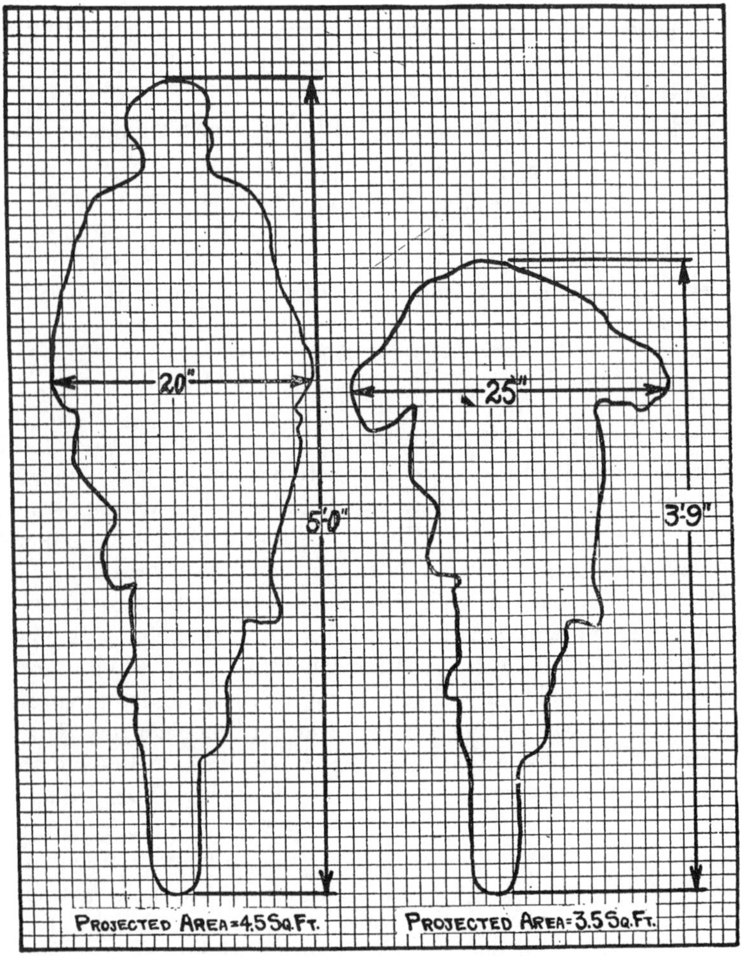

Fig. 26.—Diagram Illustrating Method of Estimating Projected Area of Motorcycle Rider in Two Positions.

to push a motorcycle up a very steep hill if the gear ratio between engine shaft and rear wheel is low enough; at the other hand, an engine of twice the power would not enable one to climb a hill if the gear ratio was too high. With a one-gear machine, it is necessary to use a gear ratio that is a compromise between the two extremes, in order not to sacrifice speed too much on the level, as when the gear ratio is low; or hill-climbing ability, as when the ratio of drive is high. If a two-speed machine is used, one can have a high gear that will permit of any speed within the capacity of the power plant and yet have a gear suitable for ordinary running conditions without going into the low speed. The lower ratio will permit the rider to negotiate sand or hills at a low speed, and yet the engine can be run fast enough to develop its full power.

It is necessary to exert an effective push between traction member and the ground equal to 1 per cent. of the total load for each 1 per cent. rise or pitch. For example, to climb a hill having a rise of 20 per cent. or one foot rise for every five feet in horizontal distance, it will be necessary to add an effective push at traction member equal to 20 per cent. of the total weight to the power ordinarily required on the level road having the same character of road surface as the hill to be surmounted.

Considerable difference of opinion obtains as to the methods of calculating grade percentages, and some confusion may exist in the mind of a non-technical reader regarding the difference between the percentage and angle of a grade. A diagram is given at Fig. 27, which shows the method in vogue graphically. If it is assumed that the base of the triangle represents a line 1,000 feet long, and that the first sloping line represents a road having a rise that brings it 50 feet above the starting point, this would be considered as a rise of 50 feet in 1,000 feet or 1 to 20, and would correspond to a 5 per cent. grade. The rise is based on the length of the base line, not of the hypotenuse of the triangle, which is represented by the inclined roadway. A grade which represents 100 per cent. corresponds to an angle of but 45 degrees, not perpendicular, as is commonly supposed. When the grade becomes steep enough so the angle of inclination is over 30 degrees, gravity overcomes traction and some positive method of drive, such as gear wheels running on toothed tracks, is necessary to climb greater gradients than 30 degrees angle.

The following table gives the percentages and corresponding angles of inclination for gradients ordinarily met with, except in the very mountainous sections of the country:

TABLE OF GRADIENTS.

Grade.		Equal to Angle of	Rise or Fall in One Mile Feet.
Per Cent.	Units.		
20	1 in 5	11 deg. 19 min.	1,056
17	1 in 6	9 deg. 26 min.	880
14	1 in 7	8 deg. 9 min.	754
12.5	1 in 8	7 deg. 8 min.	635
11	1 in 9	6 deg. 17 min.	586
10	1 in 10	5 deg. 43 min.	528
9	1 in 11	5 deg. 11 min.	480
8	1 in 12	4 deg. 46 min.	440
7.75	1 in 13	4 deg. 24 min.	406
7	1 in 14	4 deg. 5 min.	337
6.5	1 in 15	3 deg. 49 min.	352
6.25	1 in 16	3 deg. 35 min.	330
6	1 in 17	3 deg. 22 min.	310
5.5	1 in 18	3 deg. 11 min.	293
5	1 in 20	2 deg. 52 min.	204

We have seen that a torque or push corresponding to 7 horse-power, at point of contact of traction wheel and ground, would be capable of propelling 500 pounds at the rate of 40 miles per hour over a smooth dirt road not having any rise, air resistance included. At this speed, the 28-inch traction wheel would be making a little less than 500 revolutions per minute. This is equal to a torque that can be easily obtained by the following simple formula:

$$\text{Torque or T} = \frac{\text{H.P.} \times 63{,}024}{\text{R.P.M.}}$$

Substituting known values in above equation, we find that

$$\text{T} = \frac{7 \times 63{,}024}{500} = 882.3 \text{ inch-pounds at center of wheel.}$$

To find torque at point of contact between rear wheel and ground, the turning moment at center of wheel must be divided by wheel radius, or 14, giving a value of 63 pounds push. To climb a 20 per cent. grade, one would need an additional effective push of 100 pounds, which is 20 per cent. of the total weight to be moved of 500 pounds. To maintain a speed of 40 miles per hour up a 20 per cent. grade, an engine of very high power would be needed. To illustrate, if the engine was running at 2,500 revolutions per minute, a ratio of 5 to 1 would permit the rear wheel to turn 500 times per minute. From

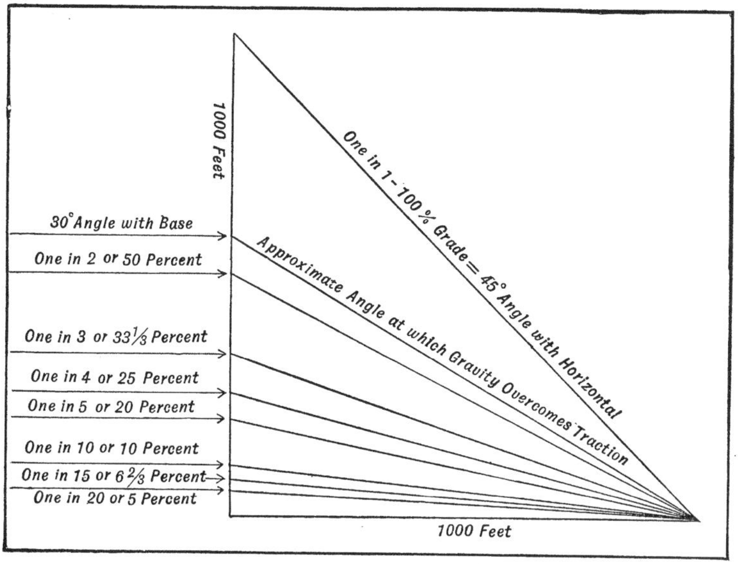

Fig. 27.—Diagram Showing Method of Calculating Grade Percentage.

the data at hand, it will not be difficult to figure the motor horsepower needed. To the push of 63 pounds necessary to overcome traction and air resistance, an additional push of 100 pounds must be added. This will be a total push of 163 pounds at 14 inches radius, which is equivalent to 2,282 inch-pounds at wheel center. This torque could only be obtained by expenditure of 18.1 horse-power. Obviously, it would not be practical to use engines of this capacity, so the speed would have to be reduced when climbing any hill of magnitude to correspond to the severity of the ascent, and the gear ratio must be selected carefully in order to enable the engine to run sufficiently fast to develop its maximum horse-power.

If the speed is reduced to 20 miles per hour, as could be easily done by using a slow-speed gearing giving a rear-wheel speed of half that needed to cover 40 miles per hour, without cutting down engine speed, much less power would be needed to move the same weight. At 20 miles per hour, air resistance would be so slight it could almost be neglected, requiring less than 0.5 horse-power to overcome it. The formula for finding power necessary to overcome traction resistance would be:

$$\text{H.P.} = \frac{500 \times 4}{100} \times 88\text{V} \times \frac{1}{33{,}000}$$

Substituting known values, we have:

$$\text{H.P.} = \frac{20 \times 88 \times 20}{33{,}000} = \frac{35{,}200}{33{,}000} = 1 \text{ H.P.}$$

This would be equal to a torque of 252 inch-pounds at wheel center or a push of 18 pounds at tire. Add to this 100 pounds to overcome resistance of gradient, and we obtain a torque of 118 pounds at 14 inches radius, or 1,652 inch-pounds at wheel center. This torque could be easily delivered by a 6.5 horse-power motor, neglecting losses in transmission which, however, would be geared down 10 to 1 on account of the interposition of slow speed gearing.

If we had a machine with a gear of 5 to 1, the motor should be capable of delivering 6.5 horse-power to the traction wheel at a speed of 1,250 revolutions, instead of at 2,500 revolutions per minute which would call for a considerably heavier and larger power plant on account of the greater piston displacement necessary to develop the same power at the lower speed.

Power in Proportion to Weight.—The amount of power used by motorcycle designers does not vary materially for similar weights of machine, though the amount of useful energy available for traction depends on many other conditions besides nominal horse-power of motor. The average single-cylinder machine, equipped with a 4 to 5 horse-power engine with full equipment of accessories, will weigh less than 200 pounds; this is 1 horse-power for every 40 to 50

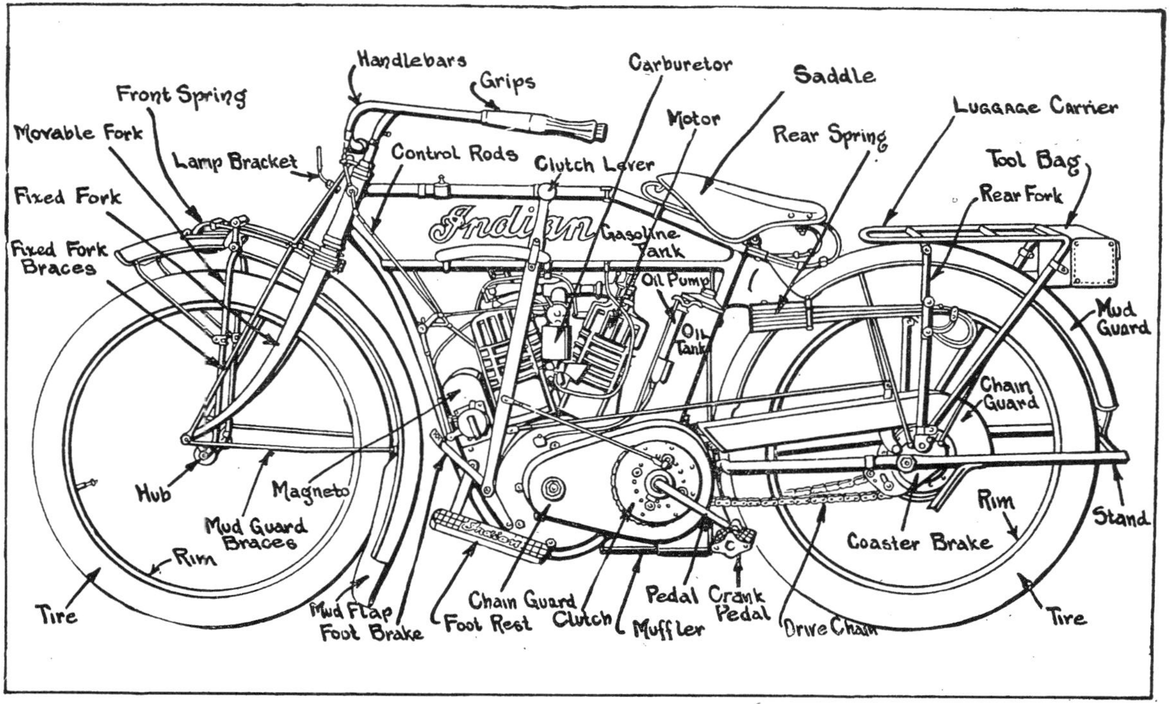

Fig. 28.—Side View of Standard Indian Twin Cylinder Model with All Important Parts Clearly Indicated.

pounds vehicle weight. Several prominent light-weight machines of European build have engines rated at 2½ horse-power and weigh well under 100 pounds. The average twin-cylinder motorcycle, with high gear ratio to permit of speed, must have more engine power in ratio to weight than a machine intended for touring, in order that it may have some hill-climbing ability. The weight of a number of prominent twin machines as determined by the writer varies between 250 to 300 pounds with full equipment. The engine power given by the makers, which is a purely nominal rating figured by the simple empirical formula of the S.A.E., is much under the actual capacity of the engine because this determination is made by using a piston speed constant that is much less than that possible in motorcycle engines. The nominal ratings vary from 7 to 9 horse-power, the power plant of lesser capacity being furnished for the lighter machines. This would make the nominal power ratio to weight about 1 horse-power for each 35 pounds motorcycle weight. The actual ratio is much higher than this, as engines rated at 7 to 9 horse-power have developed twice this in brake tests, so the true ratio of power to weight in twin machines of American design is about 1 horse-power for every 20 pounds.

As will be apparent, the addition of one cylinder to a motorcycle engine will practically double its power without a corresponding increase in weight. The engine is no heavier, save for the added cylinder and its internal mechanism, and the increase in size of frame parts, transmission elements and tires to provide adequate resistance to the stresses imposed by the larger power plant does not increase the weight materially. The average practice seems to be to provide about 1 nominal horse-power for each 50 pounds weight in touring motorcycles with a gear ratio that will not permit of high speeds and 1 nominal horse-power for each 35 pounds weight in fast, twin-cylinder machines. The foreign rating, because of the uniformly better roads in England and France, as well as general use of variable speed gears, is somewhat different, the average being about 1 nominal horse-power for each 50 pounds cycle weight.

Influence of Modern Automobile Practice.—When the motorcycle was first conceived, it was clearly the intention of the inventors to follow bicycle lines in their entirety, and to change the design only as much as was necessary to apply the internal combustion motor and its auxiliary devices. The first aim was simplicity, as it was believed that most of the recruits to the motorcycle would come from the vast army of wheelmen and that, unless one conformed very closely to the construction with which they were all familiar, they would not take kindly to the power-propelled forms. This same impression was current among early automobile designers, and for the first few years motor-propelled vehicles did not differ much in appearance from the horse-drawn carriages of the period. It did not take automobile designers long to realize that the requirements of the two forms of conveyances were radically different, and the true development of the automobile dates back to the time when the rules of practice applying to animal-drawn conveyances were discarded, and the problem of motor vehicle design studied from an entirely new angle. The same is true of motorcycle development, because, while undoubtedly the bicycle industry contributed much to the first motorcycle designers, there is now a tendency to depart from the rules of practice found desirable in bicycle construction and to base motorcycle design upon entirely new principles which apply only to self-propelled vehicles.

The modern motorcycle, therefore, may be considered more of an automobile than a bicycle, because in the latest forms we have practically all of the features found in automobile construction. The motorcycle of to-day uses a free engine clutch and change speed gearing, a positive power transmission system and forms of power plant not unlike those used in automobiles. The general construction throughout is stronger and heavier, and larger tires are used. Spring forks and spring frames contribute much to the comfort of the rider, and are really developed from the automobile, which always has carried the load on resilient members, whereas the majority of bicycles depended solely on pneumatic tires to cushion the road shocks. The general rules upon which modern motorcycles are based are those of automobile design rather than the bicycle art, and this is the best insurance of reliability and efficiency that the motorcyclist of to-day has. So long as the development of the motorcycle follows lines that have been demonstrated to be correct in automobile practice, though, of course, changed in detail to make them suitable for the lighter con-

Fig. 29.—Side View of the Eagle Chain Drive Twin Cylinder Motorcycle.

struction, we can hope for material progress and refinement and perhaps the attainment of practical perfection.

The Modern Motorcycle, Its Parts and Their Functions.—Before describing the construction or features of design of motorcycle components, it will be well to outline the principal parts of the motorcycle, and describe their functions so the matter that follows will be intelligible to the non-mechanical reader who is not experienced with the motorcycle mechanism. The foundation of any form of vehicle must necessarily be a frame to which the various parts are attached and which also serves to join the front and rear wheels on which the weight is carried. In general aspect, the frame of the conventional form of motorcycle does not differ from that of the bicycle, though in some constructions a departure is made in utilizing springs as a portion of the framework. This is true of the machine which is shown at Fig. 28 with all important parts clearly outlined. One important difference between the motorcycle frame and that of the bicycle is the use of heavily reinforced tubing, and a departure from the usual diamond frame structure. The lower diagonal bar which goes to the crank-hanger of the motorcycle is often in the form of a loop in which the motor is supported. To provide greater strength than would be secured by but one tube at the top of the frame, practically all motorcycles have two tubes which extend from the steering head to the seat-post mast or tube. In order to obtain a low saddle position, the top frame tube drops appreciably at a point about one-third of its length away from the seat post. The space between the frame bars is usually occupied by fuel and oil tanks.

Next in importance to the frame structure, which includes the wheels, handle bars, saddle, mud guards, luggage carrier, rear wheel stand and foot rests as well as the frame itself is the power plant, and then comes the transmission system. The power plant is composed of a gasoline engine and a number of auxiliary devices upon which its action depends. The driving system includes the clutch, the variable speed gearing and the method of final drive. The direction of travel of a motorcycle is controlled in the same manner as that of a bicycle as the front wheel is mounted in a fork member, swiveled in the steering head of the frame. The fork stem is usually provided with ball-bearings so it will turn easily, and the long leverage ob-

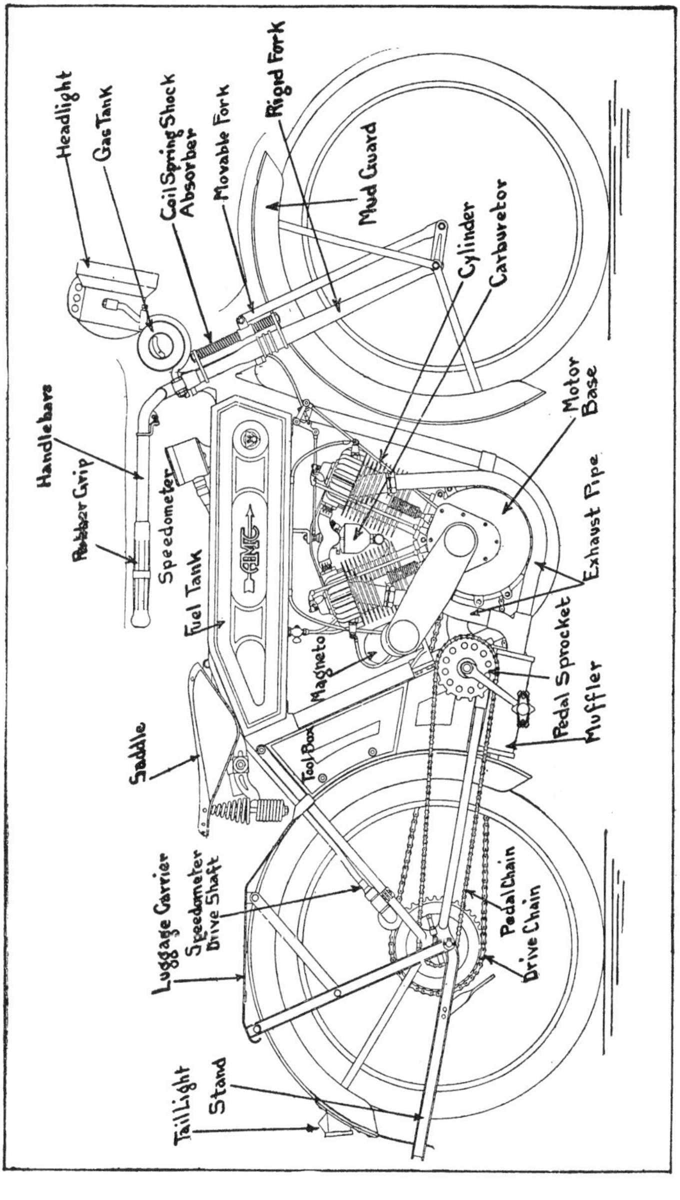

Fig. 30.—The AMC Twin Cylinder Motorcycle With Full Equipment.

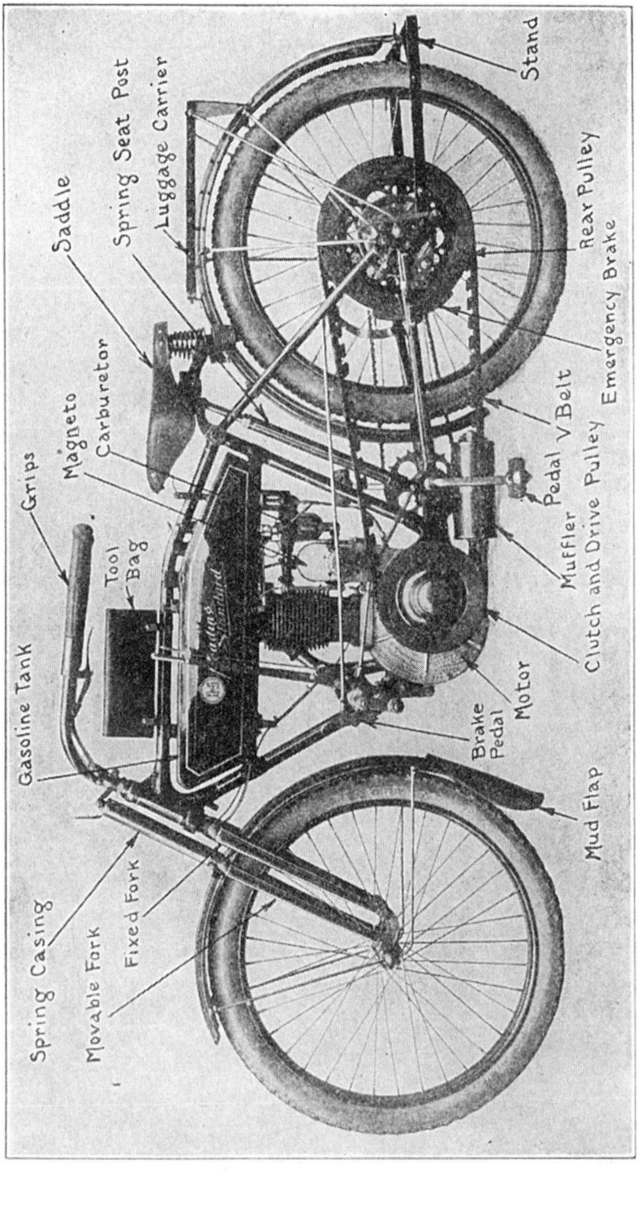

Fig. 31.—Showing Principal Parts of the Reading-Standard Motorcycle, a Representative American Design.

tained by the conventional handle bars insures positive control of the front wheel under any road condition. In order to make for easier riding, the front wheel is carried in a supplementary movable fork member which is attached to links extending from the fixed fork at its lower end and to a laminated leaf spring at its upper end. The base portion of the spring is securely attached to the fixed fork member so that while the front wheel is free to move up and down under the influence of road irregularities, the main stress is taken by the fixed fork member which is capable of only the oscillating motion necessary to steer. The rear end of the frame of the machine shown

Fig. 32.—The Schickel Motorcycle is a Distinctive Design Employing a Two-Cycle Power Plant.

at Fig. 28 is also carried by a leaf spring and the rear wheel is mounted in a movable fork member that operates in just the same way as that at the front end.

The power of practically all motorcycles is derived from burning gasoline vapor in the cylinders of a small heat engine which is termed a gasoline motor on account of having been designed primarily for use with that fuel, though at the present time these engines will work on practically any hydrocarbon liquid. Grouped with the motor are the auxiliary devices consisting of a carburetor to supply the explosive vapor to the cylinders and a magneto which furnishes the electrical energy used for exploding the gas in the combustion chambers. The fuel tank, oil pump, and oil tank may also be considered part of the power plant. In the machine shown, the power of the engine is delivered from a small sprocket on the motor crankshaft to a large sprocket forming a part of a clutch casing. The driven members of the clutch are attached to a small sprocket, which in turn delivers its power to a larger member attached to the rear-wheel hub. The clutch is a simple device used to disconnect or connect the engine power to the rear wheel at the will of the rider. If the clutch is out, the engine will operate without moving the rear wheel, though if the clutch parts are in engagement the power will be delivered from the engine crankshaft to the rear wheel, and the engine cannot operate without producing a forward motion of the machine to which it is attached. The wheels used on a motorcycle resemble very much, in general appearance, those commonly employed on bicycles. The rims are heavier and made of steel, while the spokes are of much greater strength to sustain the greater load. The tires are of the double-tube form universally used in automobile and motorcycle practice in which the inner air tube of very flexible rubber is protected from abrasion and depreciation incidental to road contact by a tougher, stronger, but less resilient casing or shoe. The general appearance of motorcycles of various designs and the relation of important components to each other will be readily ascertained by careful examination of the illustrations Figs. 28 to 39, inclusive.

General Characteristics Common to all Forms.—While motorcycles may differ from each other in various essentials of design, there are a number of characteristics which are common to all modern forms. Among these may be stated the method of control, the location of the power plant, the general design of the frame, the placing of the rider's seat, and a number of other points of likeness, which can be easily ascertained by inspection. The use of spring forks, and either spring frames or resilient saddle supports, is general, because the rider demands these refinements at the present time. No matter what form of final driving system is used, the modern machine is not complete without the free engine clutch or variable speed gear, and in most forms these two are provided in one unit. Machines that are built in America follow certain general features which are common to all, and are readily distinguishable from machines of foreign design

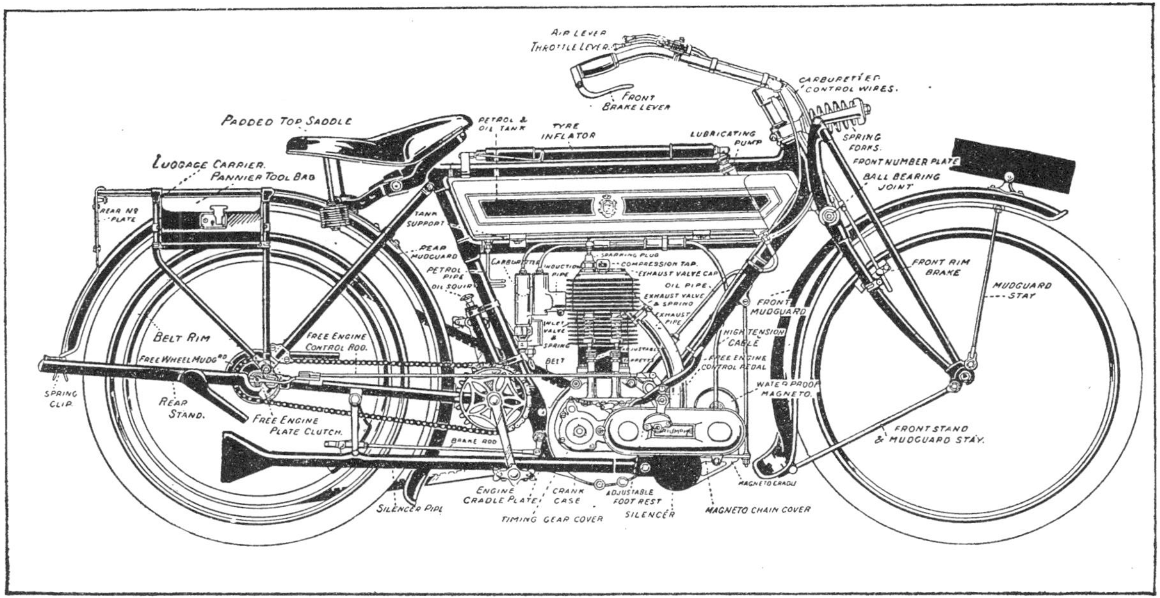

Fig. 33.—Showing the Important Parts of the Triumph Single Cylinder Motorcycle, a Typical English Design.

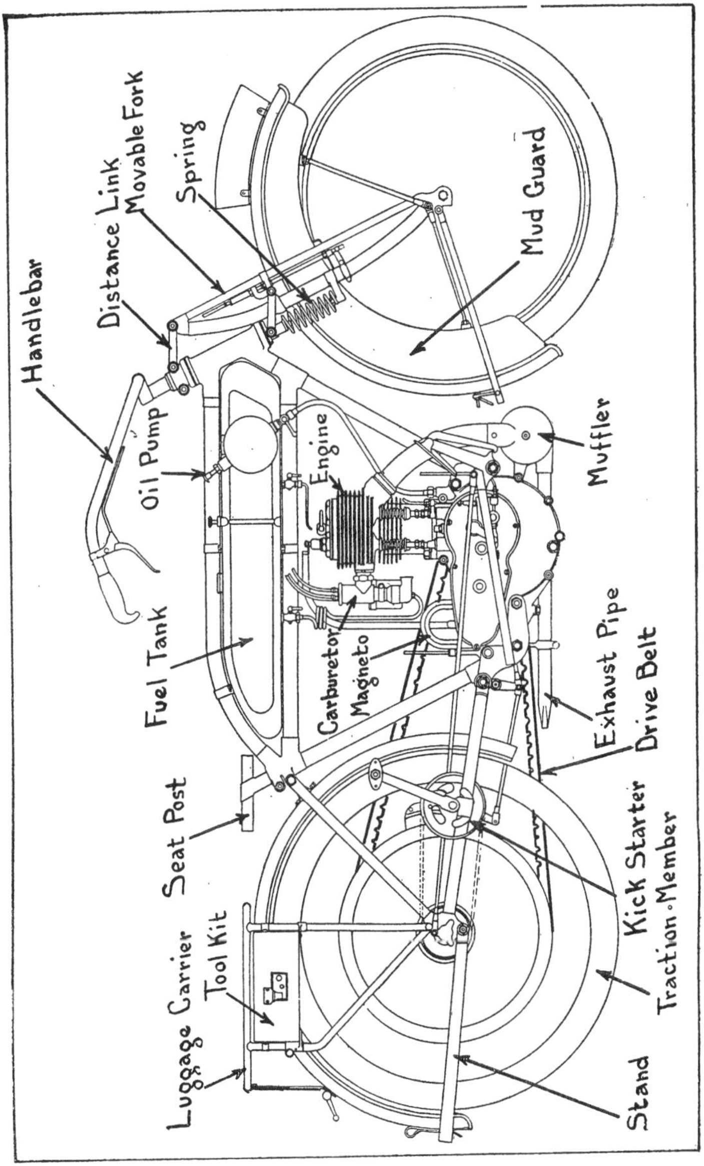

Fig. 34.—Side View of Single Cylinder Motorcycle of English Design With Important Parts Marked For Easy Identification.

which, in turn, have other peculiarities of construction which are distinctive. It is the general opinion of those versed in motorcycle practice that the American machine is much simpler in appearance and much easier to control, and withal fully as efficient as the more complicated foreign designs.

Some Modern Motorcycle Designs.—The illustration at Fig. 29 depicts a successful American motorcycle which has a particularly pleasing appearance. It is provided with a twin-cylinder power plant, and utilizes double chain drive. It incorporates the modern improvements such as spring forks and spring seat post, a free engine clutch, and handle bar control, as not only is the motor speed capable of being varied by the control grip, but the clutch action as well. The wheel base is sufficiently long to insure easy riding, the power plant is carried low to promote stability, and large tires make for easy riding and for minimum depreciation.

The machine shown at Fig. 30 is another American design which is shown fully equipped with various necessary accessories. An efficient single cylinder machine employing a novel system of transmission is shown at Fig. 31. Belt drive is employed, though the arrangement of the under-geared clutch and drive pulley permits the use of a large driving member, which is much more favorable to efficient power transmission by belt than the smaller pulleys attached directly to the engine crankshaft. The machine at Fig. 32 is a distinctive American design employing a single-cylinder, two-cycle engine as a source of power. This is practically the only motorcycle on the American market equipped with a two-cycle power plant. There are a number of other distinctive features such as the spring fork construction and the use of a large hollow aluminum casting which not only acts as a fuel container but which also serves as the main member of the cycle frame, inasmuch as it includes the steering head at the front end and the seat-post supporting tube at the rear.

The machine depicted at Fig. 33 is a representative English design and is a motorcycle that has received wide application abroad. If one compares the general construction of this design with the American machines, it will be noted that the latter are much simpler in appearance, on account of concealed control members for one thing, and the elimination of the front rim brake and its necessary mechan-

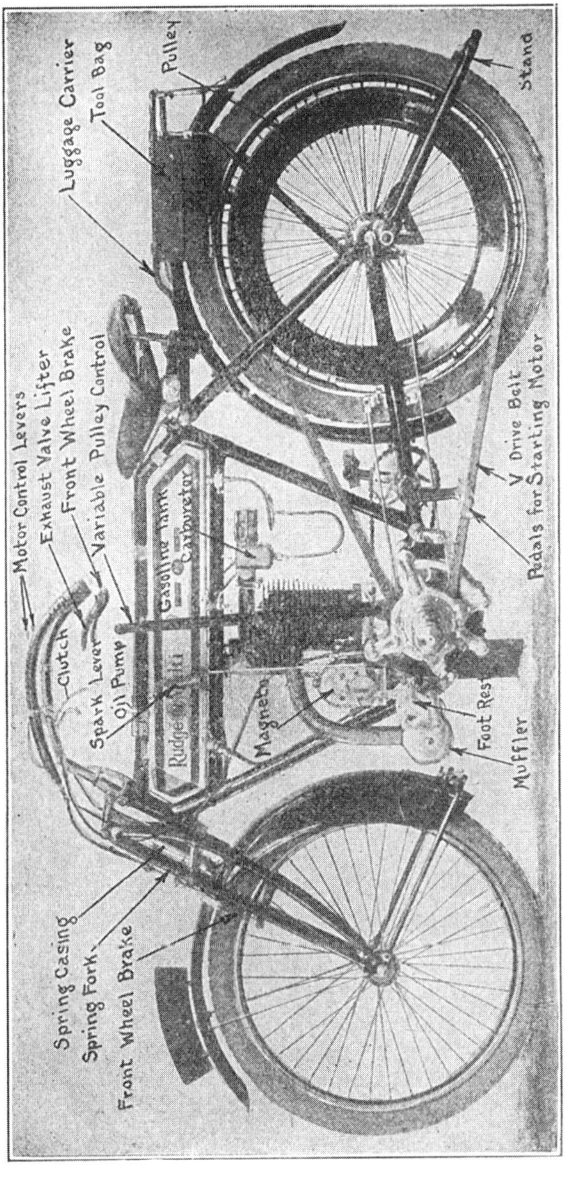

Fig. 35.—The Rudge-Multi Single Cylinder Motor cycle.

Fig. 36.—The Scott Two Cylinder Motorcycle, an English Design That Incorporates Many Distinctive Features. Such as a Water-Cooled Two Stroke Motor and Open Frame.

ism, as well as a simpler design of spring fork. While the foreign machines are unconventional to American eyes, they are very efficient, and for the most part are said to be considerably more economical to operate than our American machines. Owing to the uniformly better roads found in England and France than are generally provided in this country, the construction is lighter and power plants of lesser capacity are the rule. In the illustration at Fig. 33, all important parts are clearly outlined, and from what has been presented previously it should not be difficult for the reader to understand their functions. Other representative English machines of the single-cylinder type are shown at Figs. 34 and 35.

A machine of very unconventional appearance, yet one that should not be too hastily judged because of the wide variance from our preconceived American notions of what a motorcycle should look like, is shown at Fig. 36. This bristles with original features, and it has demonstrated its practicability beyond doubt by winning one of the most important of all English motorcycle competitive events, the Tourist Trophy race, for two years in succession. The power plant is a two-cylinder, two-cycle, water-cooled motor which furnishes the same steady pull as a four-cylinder, four-cycle with a materially diminished number of working parts. It is mounted on the bottom frame tube with the cylinders inclined toward the steering head. The cooling water is carried in a combined water-tank and radiator which is placed above and forward of the engine cylinders and just back of the steering head. The frame is a peculiar open girder construction, and it is claimed that the elimination of the top frame tube makes it very easy to mount or dismount from the machine. No pedals are provided, as the engine is started with a hand crank in the same manner as an automobile motor, and as a two-speed and free engine gear is provided, the motorcycle may be readily started from a standstill. The fuel tank is of approximately oval section, and at the back end it provides a support for the rear fork stays to which the front end of the luggage carrier and the saddle supporting member are attached. The machine is provided with foot boards and a front wheel stand, following general European practice. One point that will impress the American motorcyclist is the multiplicity of control levers mounted on the handle bars, and the general appearance of

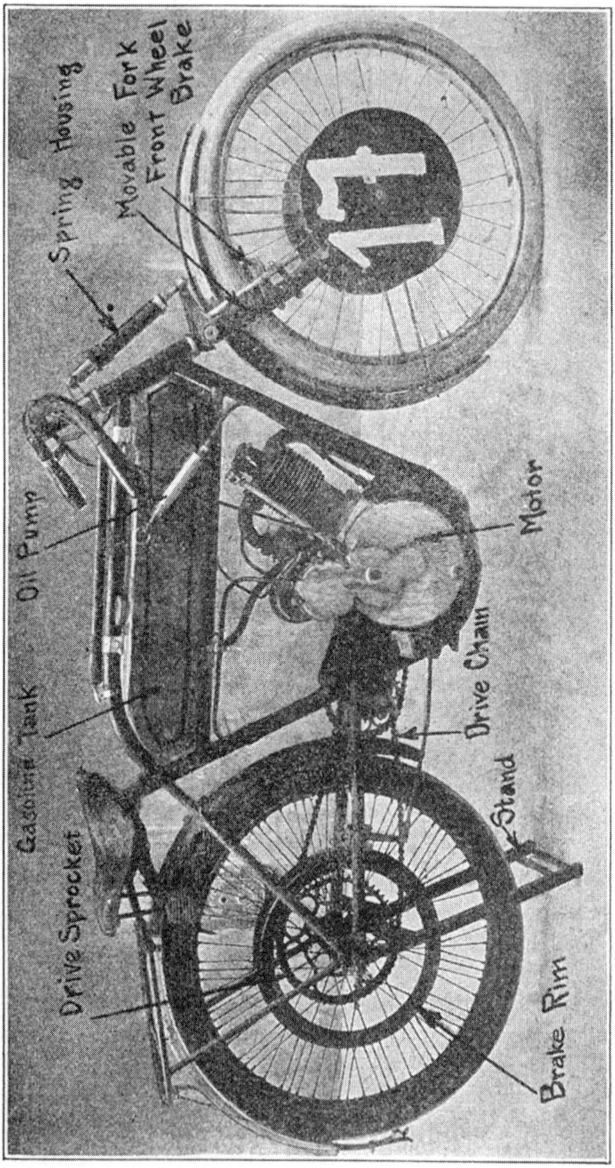

Fig. 37.—An Example of French Motorcycle Design.

Fig. 38.—The Clement Twin Cylinder Motorcycle, Another Example of French Design.

Fig. 39.—Peugeot Twin Cylinder Model, One of the Leading French Motorcycles.

complication is much intensified by the number of control wires extending from the handle bars to the various portions of the mechanism they are intended to regulate.

The motorcycles shown at Figs. 37 to 39, inclusive, are of French design, and it will be apparent that these follow English practice more than American, though they are not as well finished in detail as either the English or American machines. A single-cylinder motor with a double chain drive is utilized for power in the motorcycle shown at Fig. 37, which is the simplest of the three forms. Two-cylinder motors are used on the remaining two designs, one using a single chain final drive, while the other employs a V-belt. The spring fork of the Clement machine, shown at Fig. 38, is of English design, though the similar members of the other two are undeniably of French derivation. The utility of the front wheel stand which is provided on a number of the foreign machines is clearly outlined at Fig. 38, and it will be apparent that it is possible to remove both front and rear wheels from the machine in question without depriving it of means of support that will keep it upright, and in the proper position for the easy replacement of the wheels. This is a valuable feature, as it is often desirable to rotate the front wheel as when adjusting the wheel bearings, testing the wheel for truth of running and in making tire repairs. If both front and rear wheels are removed from an American machine, there is nothing to support the front end, and it requires considerable patience to find the necessary odds and ends such as cobbles, bricks or pieces of wood to support the motor weight by filling up the space between the bottom of the frame and the ground, in order to raise the front wheel clear for removal or to keep the frame in proper position for wheel replacement. In essentials, the English and French motorcycles do not differ from those we are familiar with, though, of course, one must expect to find the individuality of the foreign designer expressed in some ways. It is apparent to anyone who will consider the merits of the various designs shown, without prejudice, that the American designer produces neater motorcycles than his foreign contemporary, and machines that are really more practical because of the simplicity of control and the general strength of parts demanded by our severe operating conditions.

CHAPTER II.

MOTORCYCLE POWER PLANT GROUP.

The Gasoline Engine and Auxiliary Devices—Features of Two Main Engine Types—Operating Principles of Four-Cycle Engines—How Two-Cycle Engine Works—Methods of Figuring Rated Horse-Power—How Actual Horse-Power is Tested—Relation of Torque to Horse-Power and Its Meaning—Reason for Cooling Engine—Air of Water Cooling—Efficiency of Air-Cooled Motors—Methods of Air Cooling—Water-Cooling Methods—Features of One-Cylinder Motors—Advantages of Multiple-Cylinder Forms—Types of Two-Cylinder Power Plants—Four-Cylinder Forms—Power Plant Support and Location—Motorcycle Engine Parts and Their Functions.

The Gasoline Engine and Auxiliary Devices.—To the uninformed, a motorcycle or automobile power plant seems to consist essentially of a gasoline motor, but to the initiated it is known that while the internal combustion engine is a very important component of the power plant it is of little more value than so much metal when one of the important auxiliary devices which are distinct in construction from the engine fails to function properly. A complete motorcycle power plant with all auxiliary devices clearly outlined is illustrated at Fig. 40, and it will be apparent that in addition to the gasoline engine various other devices are included in the power-producing assembly.

In the first place, it is necessary to provide some method of storing the fuel, or a gasoline tank, and then of supplying it to the cylinder in the form of an inflammable gas. The latter is the function of the carburetor to which the gasoline from the tank is first directed. This device mixes the gasoline vapor and air in proper proportions, and supplies the vapor to the inlet valve cage of the motor. Some means of exploding the charge of gas in the cylinder is necessary, so an ignition system is used which is composed of a high-tension magneto, a suitable length of conductor and a spark plug in the cylinder. The

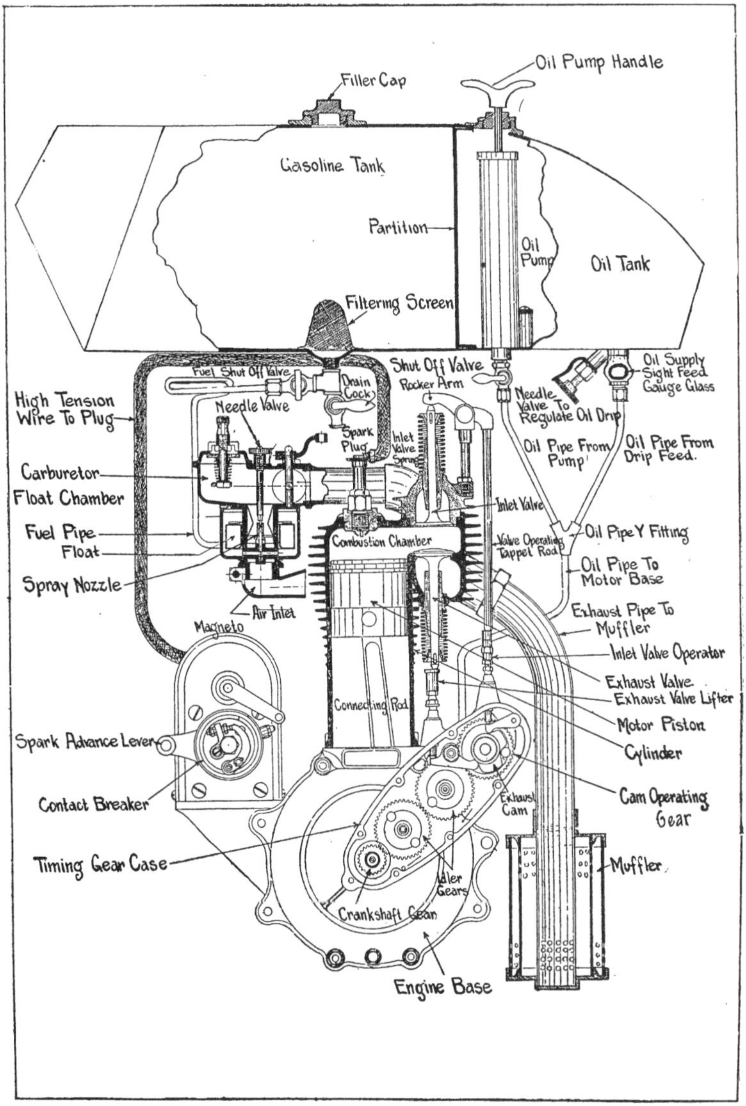

Fig. 40.—Complete Motorcycle Power Plant, Showing the Relation of All Auxiliary Components to the Gasoline Engine.

wire conveys the electricity generated by the magneto to the spark plug inserted in the combustion chamber. In order to prevent annoyance, due to noisy operation, a silencing device or "muffler" is attached at the end of the pipe through which the exhaust gases leave the engine cylinder. As it is important that any piece of machinery should be properly oiled, if it is desired that it work efficiently, a portion of the gasoline tank is partitioned off to form a supplementary oil tank to hold an adequate supply of lubricant. Some means of supplying the oil to the engine must be provided so, in the simple form of power plant outlined, one may inject the oil directly to the engine base through the medium of a hand-operated oil pump. This may be either built into or attached to the side of the tank. Another means of supplying oil besides the hand-pump is provided on most motorcycle power plants, and this may be either a mechanically operated pump or a gravity sight-feed system in which the oil flows to the engine because of its weight. The amount of lubricant is regulated by a suitable needle valve that controls the passage leading from the oil tank to the gauge glass chamber. In addition to the gasoline engine itself, it is therefore necessary to include a carburetor or gas maker, a magneto or spark producer, a muffler to silence the exhaust gases, some system of lubrication, and suitable containers for fuel and lubricating oil. Another type of power plant with all parts clearly shown, excepting the fuel and oil containers, is presented in Fig. 41.

Features of Two Main Engine Types.—Two types of gasoline engines have been applied generally to furnish power for transportation purposes. These differ in construction and operating cycle to some extent, though in all forms power is obtained by the direct combustion of fuel in the cylinders of the engine. In all standard engines, a member known as the piston travels back and forth in the cylinder with what is known as a reciprocating motion, and this in turn is changed into a rotary motion by suitable mechanical means to be described fully in proper sequence. Gas engines may operate on either the two-cycle or four-cycle principle, the former being the simplest in action, though the latter is easiest to understand.

The sectional view of a two-cycle engine depicted at Fig. 45 shows the three moving parts employed. The gas is introduced into the cylinder, and expelled from it through ports cored into the cylinder

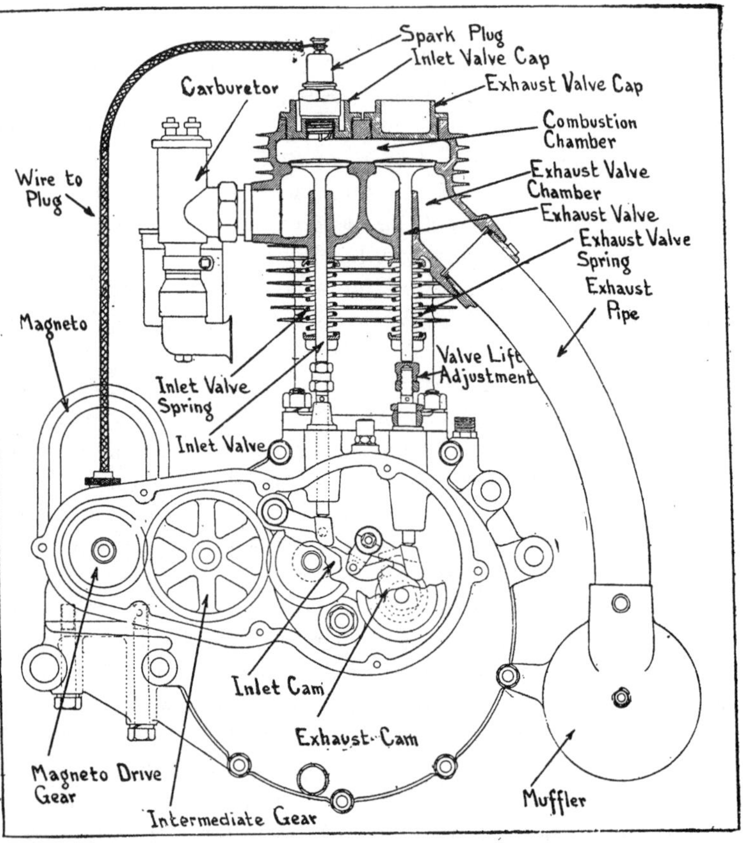

Fig. 41.—Complete Single Cylinder Motorcycle Power Plant of English Design, Showing Location of Carburetor, Magneto and Muffling Device.

walls, which are covered by the piston at a certain portion of its travel and uncovered at other portions of the stroke. The three moving parts are the piston, connecting rod and crankshaft. If this type of power plant is compared with the four-cycle engine shown at Fig. 42, it will be apparent that it is much simpler in construction.

In the four-cycle engine, the gas is admitted into the cylinder through a port at the head closed by a valve, while the exhaust gas is expelled through another port controlled in a similar manner.

These valves must be operated by mechanism distinct from the piston. In addition to the three main moving parts used in the two-cycle engine, there are a number of auxiliary moving members that are part of the valve-operating mechanism. The four-cycle engine is more widely used because it is the most efficient type. The two-cycle engine is simpler to operate and very smooth running, but it is not as economical as the four-cycle because a portion of the fresh gas taken into the cylinder is expelled through the open exhaust port with the burnt gases before it has a chance to ignite. As the four-cycle engine is more generally used, its method of operation will be described first.

Operating Principles of Four-cycle Engines.—The action of the four-cycle type will be easily understood if one refers to the illustrations at Figs. 42 and 43. It is called a four-stroke engine because the piston must make four strokes in the cylinder for each explosion or power impulse obtained. The principle of a gas engine is similar to that of a gun, i. e., power is obtained by a rapid combustion of some explosive or other quick-burning substance. The bullet is driven out of a gun barrel by the powerful gases liberated when the charge of powder is ignited. The piston of a gas engine is driven toward the open end of a cylinder by the similar expansion of gases resulting from combustion.

The first operation in firing a gun or securing an explosion in the cylinder of a gas engine is to fill the combustion space with combustible material. The second operation is to compress this, and after compression, if the charge is ignited, the third operation of the cycle will be performed. In the case of the gun, the bullet will be driven out of the barrel, while the piston of the gas engine will be forced toward the open end of the cylinder. As the bullet leaves the mouth of the gun, the barrel is automatically cleared of the burnt powder gases which escape to the outer air because of their pressure. The gun must be thoroughly cleared before the introduction of a new charge of powder. In a gas engine, the fourth operation or exhaust stroke is performed by the return stroke of the piston.

The parts of a simple engine have been previously indicated, and, in order to better understand the action, it will be well to consider briefly the various parts and their functions. The cylinder is an im-

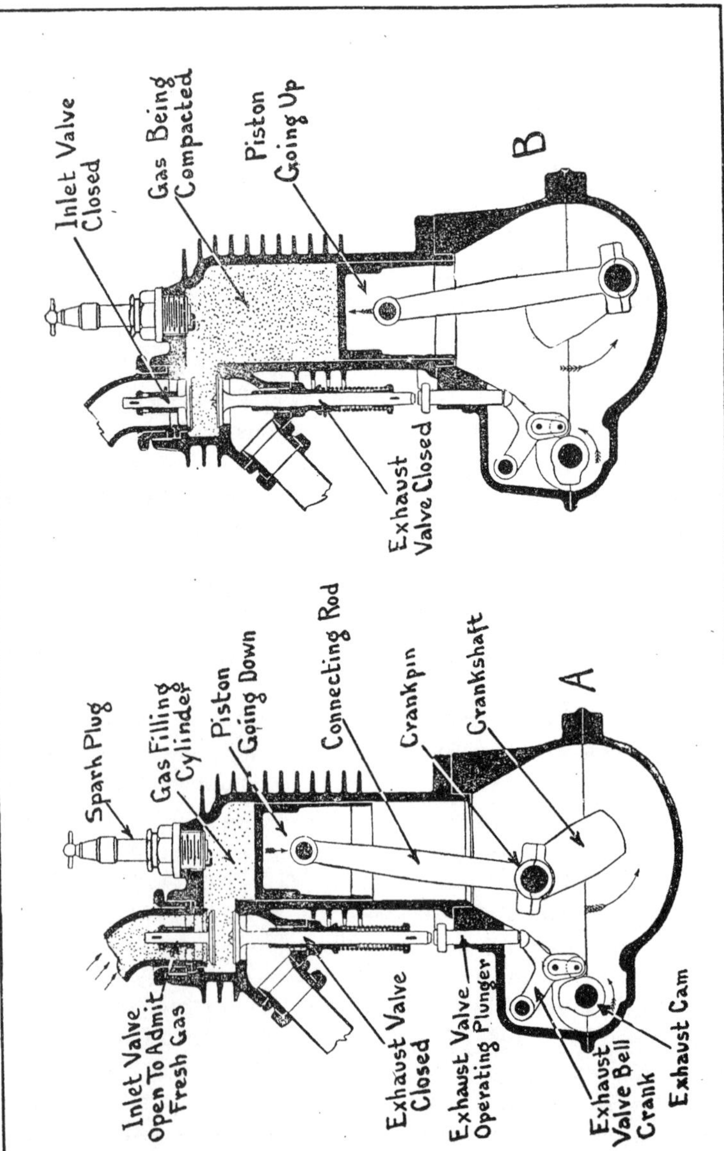

Fig. 42.—Diagrams Illustrating Action of Four-cycle Motorcycle Power Plant. A—Piston Starting on Induction Stroke. B—Piston Starting on Compression Stroke.

portant member because it is in this portion that practically all the work is accomplished. The cylinder is provided with three ports at the combustion end, one through which the gas is admitted, controlled by an inlet valve, another through which the burnt gas is expelled, closed by the exhaust valve, and the third in which the spark plug used to ignite the compressed gas is screwed. The reciprocating motion of the piston, which is the member moving up and down in the cylinder, is transformed into a rotary motion of the crankshaft by a connecting rod and crank pin.

In the simple engine shown at Figs. 42 and 43, the inlet valve is an automatic one, while the exhaust member is raised from its seat by a mechanism including the cam-shaft, cam, valve-operating bell crank and plunger. At Fig. 42-*A*, the piston is starting to go down on the first stroke of the four necessary to produce a complete cycle of operations. As the piston descends, it creates a suction in the combustion chamber, the automatic valve is drawn down from its seat and a fresh charge of gas is inspired into the cylinder through the inlet pipe which communicates with the gas-supply device or carburetor. The inlet valve will remain open until the piston reaches the bottom of its stroke. As soon as the pressure inside the cylinder is equal to that outside, which condition obtains as soon as the piston has reached the end of its downward stroke and the cylinder is filled with gas, the inlet valve is closed and the piston starts to return on the next stroke, as shown at Fig. 42-*B*.

As both valves are closed, the combustible gas with which the cylinder is filled is compressed into a much smaller volume. The reason for compression is that any agent which gives out energy through the expansion of gases is rendered more efficient by confining it in a restricted space and directing the whole energy against some one spot. A tuft of guncotton could be ignited while lying loosely in the hand and it would burn freely but without explosion. If it is confined in a gun barrel and exploded, it will drive the bullet out with a great amount of force, or burst the metal walls of the container. Gasoline vapor and air will ignite and burn freely at atmospheric pressure, and a gasoline engine could be made to run without compression. The expansion of the unconfined gases would not be great enough to do effective work, however, and the fullest efficiency of the

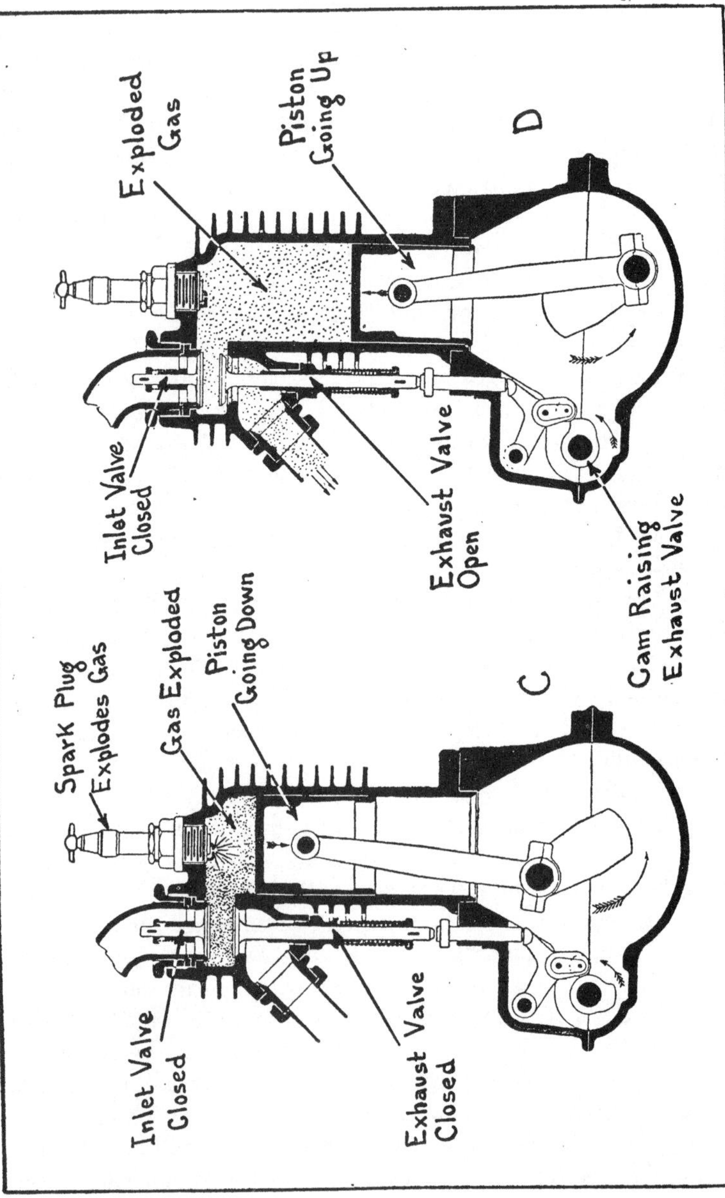

Fig. 43.—Diagrams Illustrating Action of Four-cycle Motorcycle Power Plant. C—Position of Piston at Start of Power Stroke. D—Piston Starting on Scavenging Stroke.

fuel is obtained by compacting it into the smallest possible space and then igniting it at the instant when it is compressed the most.

Any chemical action requires close contact between the materials producing it, if it is to occur under the most favorable conditions. That which occurs when a mixture of gasoline vapor and air are brought into contact with the flame or arc of the electric spark is practically instantaneous if the gases are crowded together. If the gas is not properly compressed, the action becomes more dilatory, extending to a slow combustion wherein the temperature is not raised enough to expand the gases efficiently as the degree of compression is lessened. A good example of slow combustion is the decay of wood, while the phenomenon that we call "burning" may be taken as an illustration of quick combustion. It is said that the same amount of heat is produced by either combustion, but only the latter produces it quickly enough to be noticeable.

The comparatively slow combustion of the gases in the engine cylinder, when at atmospheric pressure would not permit the energy derived from the heat to act all at once. When the gases are compressed, the particles of vapor are in such intimate contact that combustion is practically instantaneous, and the gases give off maximum energy by expanding their utmost, due to the high temperature developed. The piston is also in a position to be acted upon most readily as the force due to pressure of the gas is directly against it and not exerted through a cushion of elastic half-ignited gas as would be the case if the charge was not compressed before ignition.

When the piston reaches the top of its second stroke, the compressed gas is exploded by means of an electric spark between the points of the spark plug, and the piston is driven down toward the open end of the cylinder, as indicated at Fig. 43-*C*. At the end of this down stroke, the pressure of the gases is reduced to such a point that they no longer have any value in producing power. At this time, the cam, which is operated in timed relation to the crankshaft travel, raises the exhaust valve from its seat, as at Fig. 43-*D*, and the burnt gases are expelled through the open exhaust port until the cylinder is practically cleared of the inert products of combustion, the natural scavenging action, due to gas pressure, being assisted by an upward movement of piston. The piston once more begins to descend, as shown at Fig. 42-*A*, and the inlet valve opens to admit a new charge. The rest of the cycle of operations follow in the order indicated, and are repeated as long as the cylinder is supplied with gas and this is ignited.

When a two-cylinder engine is employed the action is practically the same, except that the two cylinders are accomplishing different operations of the cycle simultaneously. For example, in the engine shown at Fig. 44, which is of the two cylinder V-type so widely used in motorcycle and cycle car practice, we find at *A* that while the piston in the left hand cylinder is going down and drawing in a charge, the piston in the right hand cylinder has just reached the end of its compression stroke, and is starting to go down under the influence of the expanding ignited charge of gas. When the pistons reach the bottom of the stroke, before starting up again it will be seen at *B* that the cylinder on the left hand side is full of fresh gas and the inlet valve is closed, while that on the right side is still filled with the flaming gases due to the previous explosion. The position of the pistons at the end of the next stroke is depicted at *C*. Here the cylinder on the left side, the piston of which has just compressed a charge, has its combustion chamber full of burning gas, while the cylinder on the right side is just being cleared of the inert gases produced by the previous explosion through the open exhaust valve member. At *D*, the beginning of the last or exhaust stroke in the left side cylinder is indicated. As the piston is about to go up and the exhaust valve is opened, the burnt gases can be properly discharged. The right hand cylinder is filling with gas through the open inlet valve as the suction stroke in that cylinder is not yet fully completed.

It will be evident that while the piston in one cylinder is just beginning to go down on an inlet stroke, that in the other cylinder is just completing a compression stroke. When the piston in the left-hand cylinder is just beginning its compression stroke, that in the right-hand cylinder is completing its explosion stroke. When the piston in the left-hand cylinder is being forced down by exploded gas, the similar member of the right-hand cylinder is just finishing its exhaust stroke. When the piston in the left-hand cylinder is starting on its exhaust stroke, that in the right-hand cylinder has just completed its suction stroke. By having two cylinders performing differ-

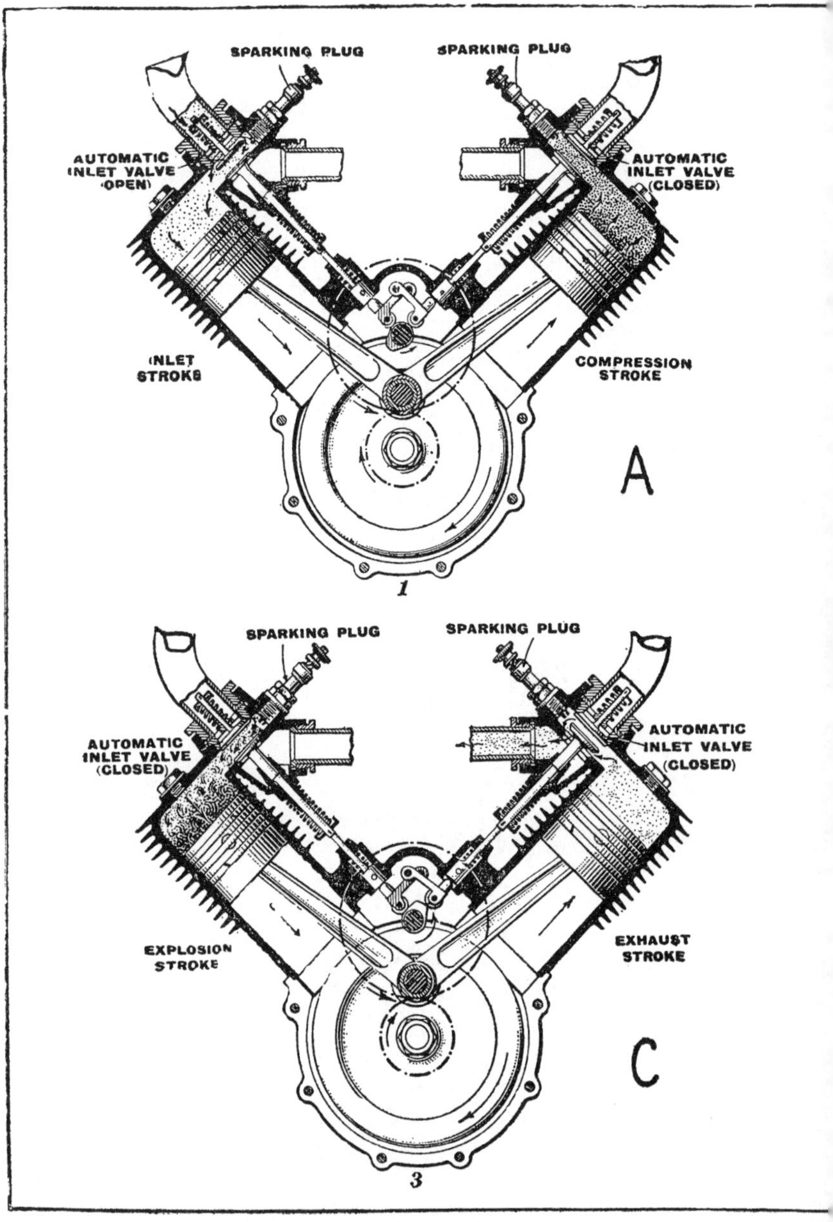

Fig. 44.—Diagram Showing Action

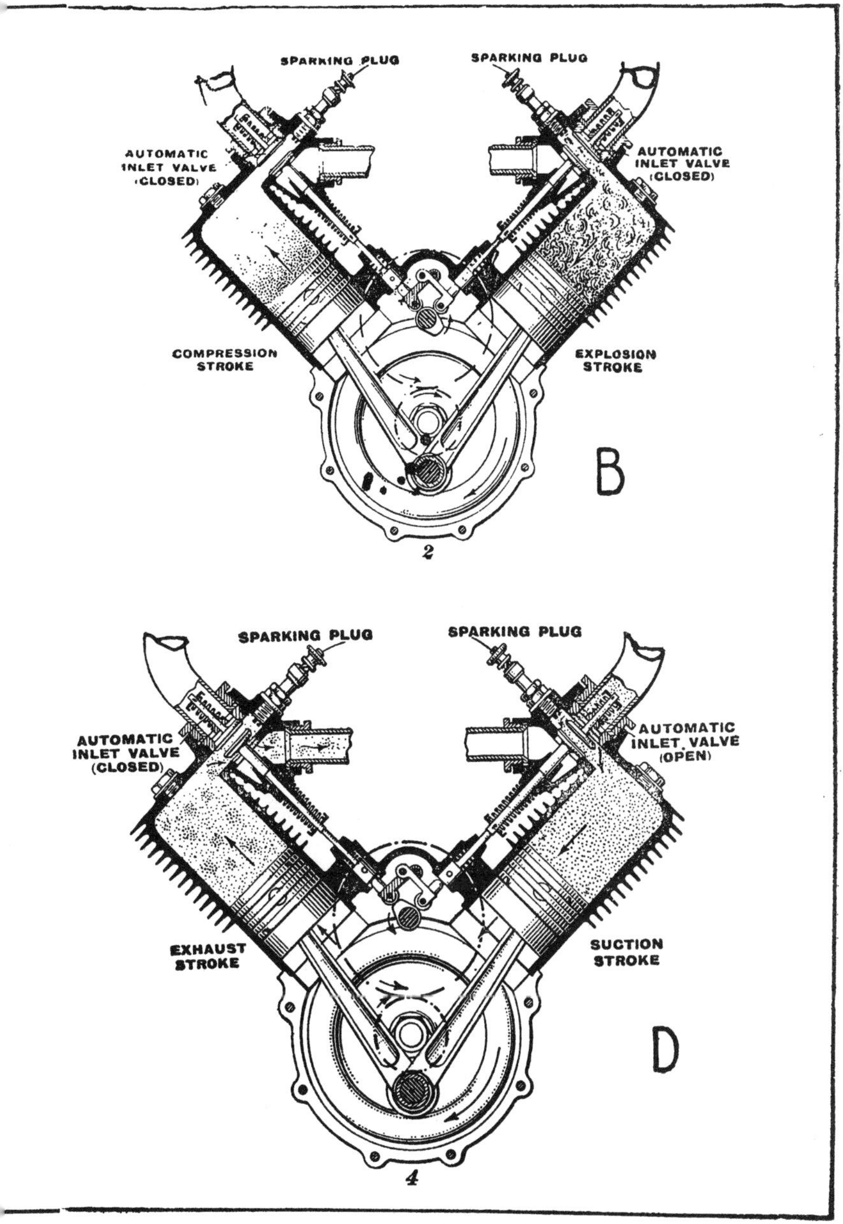

of Twin Cylinder, Four-cycle Motor.

ent functions simultaneously, it is possible to obtain one explosion for each revolution of the fly-wheel, whereas in a single-cylinder engine it takes two revolutions of the crankshaft to obtain one useful power stroke.

How Two-cycle Engine Works.—The two-cycle engine works on a different principle, as while only the combustion chamber end of the piston is employed to do useful work in the four-cycle engine, both upper and lower ends are called upon to perform the functions necessary to two-cycle engine operation. Instead of the gas being admitted into the cylinder, as is the case with the four-cycle engine, it is first drawn into the engine base, where it receives a preliminary compression, prior to its transfer to the working end of the cylinder.

The views at Fig. 45 show clearly the operation of a two-port, two-cycle engine. Assuming that a charge of gas has just been compressed in the cylinder and that the upward movement of the piston while compressing the gas above it has drawn in a charge through the automatic intake valve in the crank-case, it will be apparent that as soon as the piston reaches the top of its stroke, and the gas has been properly compressed, the explosion of this charge by an electric spark will produce power in just the same manner as it does in the four-cycle motor. As the piston descends, due to the impact of the expanding gases, it closes the automatic inlet valve in the crank-case and compresses the gases confined therein.

When the piston reaches the bottom of the cylinder it uncovers the exhaust port cored in the cylinder wall and the burnt gases leave the cylinder because of their pressure. A little further and the downward movement of the piston uncovers the intake port, which is joined to the crank-case by a by-pass passage, at which time a condition exists as indicated at Fig. 45, B. The piston has reached the bottom of its stroke, and both exhaust and inlet ports are open. The burnt gases are flowing out of the cylinder through the open exhaust port, while the fresh gases are being transferred from the crank-case, where they had been confined under pressure to the cylinder. The fresh gas is kept from passing out of the open exhaust port opposite the inlet opening by a deflector plate cast on the piston head, which directs the entering stream of fresh gas to the top of the cylinder.

As the piston goes back on its up stroke, the exhaust and inlet ports are closed by the piston wall, and the charge of gas is compressed prior to ignition. As the piston travels up on its compression stroke, the inlet valve in the crank-case opens, due to the suction produced by the piston, and admits a charge of gas through the open crank-case intake port. It will be seen that an explosion is obtained every two strokes of the piston instead of every four strokes, as is the case with a four-cycle engine. In the two-cycle form, one explosion is obtained for each revolution of the crankshaft, while in the four-cycle two revolutions of the crankshaft are necessary to obtain one power impulse.

The operating principle of the three-port two-cycle engine is just the same as that previously described except that the gas from the carburetor is admitted to the crank-chamber through a small port in the cylinder wall, which is open when the piston reaches the top of the stroke. The three-port method of construction makes it possible to dispense with the automatic inlet valve shown in Fig. 45, and an engine of this kind is therefore a true valveless type. The two-cycle motor, while it offers many advantages in theory, has some weaknesses, because if it did not have any disadvantages, it would soon entirely supplant the more complicated four-cycle engine. The two-stroke type has already proven practical in the Scott motorcycle, a British design, and the Schickel motorcycle, an American construction. At the present time, there is considerable interest manifested in this type of power plant in England, and a number of very efficient light-weight machines of two and three horse-power have been evolved that employ small two-cycle power plants. The only form of two-cycle engine to have received any application in motorcycle service is the valveless three-port type. The two-port system has received some application in marine service, but it is not capable of as high speed, and is not apt to function so regularly as the three-port, owing to check valve trouble. In the latter form, all valves are eliminated.

As the exhaust port opens first and closes last, considerable burnt or inert gas will mix with and dilute each new charge, and as the exhaust port is still open after the inlet port closes it is apparent that even the best designed deflector will not provide positive insurance that none of the fresh charge will be discharged with the hot gas and escape to the outer air through the muffler without ever being exploded

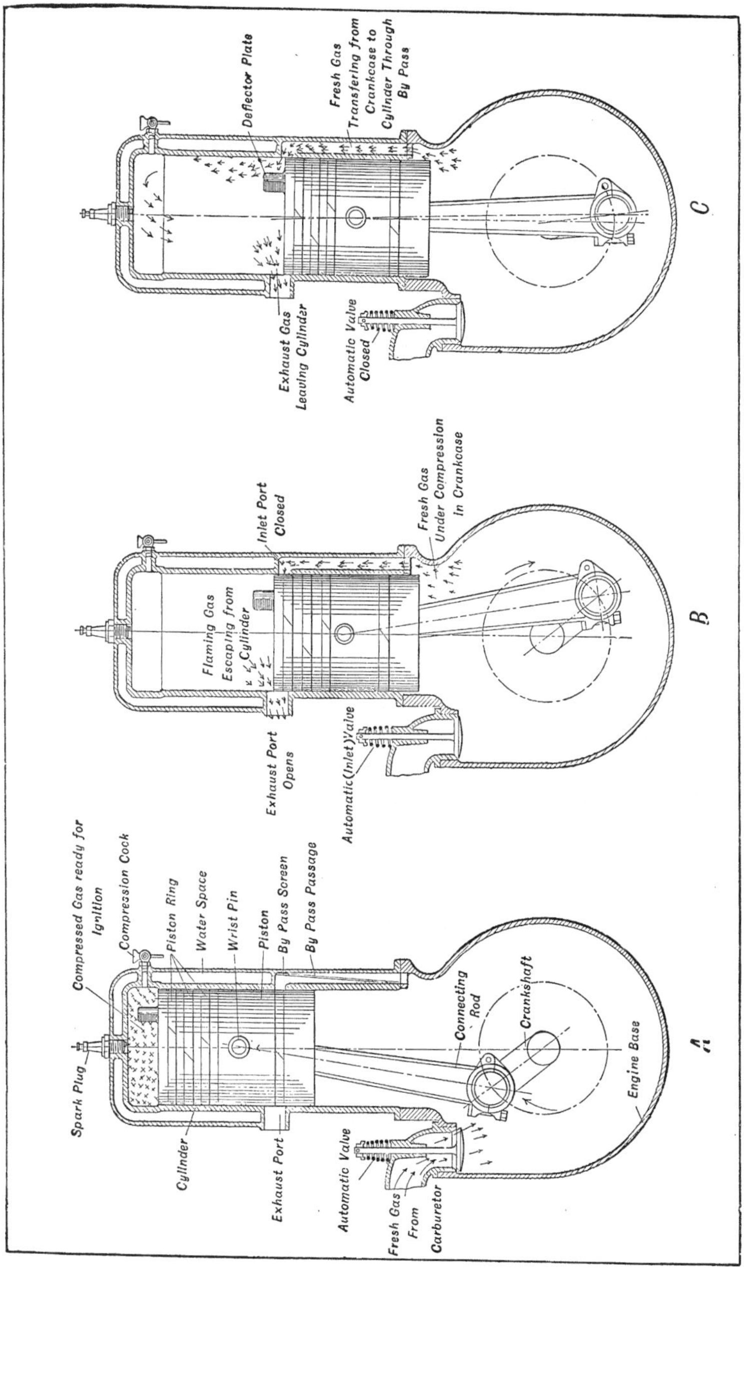

Fig. 45.—Diagrams Defining Action of Two-Stroke Motor.

at all. The efficiency of a two-cycle motor is considerably lower than that of a four-cycle, as while theoretical considerations would indicate that with twice the number of explosions one should double the power for a given cylinder volume, the actual increase over a four-cycle of the same size is but fifty per cent. Of course, the two-cycle engine has some real merits to offset the grave defects. Its extreme simplicity insures that nothing can go wrong with the engine itself because the piston, connecting rod and crankshaft are the sole moving parts. A two-cycle engine will continue to develop its rated power, and actually improves in power output as it continues in service. In a four-cycle engine, however, if the valve timing changes, as is very apt to occur when the valve-operating mechanism wears or gets out of adjustment, its efficiency is materially reduced. Barring accidents due to deliberate neglect, practically the only condition that can develop in the cylinder that will reduce the power output of a two-cycle engine is carbonization, and it is not a difficult matter to scrape off the carbon deposits from a simple cylinder with no valve chamber in the head, as employed in two-cycle engines. Of course, the bearings at the crank-case may wear to such a point that there will be a loss in crank-case compression, but this will not occur until the engine has been in service for a long period, and when bearing depreciation does materialize it is not a difficult proposition to refit the brasses, and restore the engine to its former efficiency. It is claimed that the two-cycle motor will not carbonize as quickly as the four-cycle because, while the latter is lubricated for the most part by haphazard hand pump supply, on most of the two-stroke engines lubrication is very easily accomplished by mixing the lubricating oil with the gasoline. The two-cycle construction is peculiarly well adapted for this system of lubrication, which would soon put a four-cycle engine out of commission because the fresh charge, which contains the oil emulsion, is first drawn into the crank-case where considerable of the oil will be deposited on the mechanical parts before the charge is directed into that portion of the cylinder above the piston. The two-cycle engine is not anywhere near as flexible as the four-cycle power plant, but it is capable of a high-power output at low speeds. Owing to the frequently recurring explosions an even pull or torque is obtained from a two-cycle motor, which promotes efficiency and lessens wear of the transmission system, including speed-changing gear as well as final drive, and which also materially augments the life of the tire on the traction member.

Methods of Figuring Rated Horse-power.—To calculate the horse-power of any four-cycle motor, the following general formula may be used, this giving the output of a single cylinder, and must be multiplied by the number of cylinders for multiple cylinder engines:

$$\frac{P\ L\ A\ R}{33{,}000 \times 2} = \text{H.P.}$$

In which

P = Pounds per square inch.
L = Length of stroke in feet.
A = Piston area in inches.
R = The number of revolutions per minute.

The following can be used for either four-cycle or two-cycle motors, depending on the constant used as a divisor:

$$\frac{D^2 \times L \times n \times \text{M.E.P.} \times \text{R.}}{550{,}000} \text{ I.H.P. 4-cycle}$$

Constant for two-cycle engines, 275,000.

D^2 = Bore of cylinders in inches squared.
L = Stroke of piston in inches.
R = Revolutions per minute of crankshaft.
n = Number of cylinders.
M.E.P. = Mean effective pressure.

The formula below is a simple one for four-cycle engines, though the results can be multiplied by 1.50 to obtain power rating of average two-cycle engine of the same dimensions:

H.P. = PLD^2R with three decimal places pointed off.

In which

P = Mean effective pressure.
L = Stroke in inches.
D = Diameter in inches.
R = Number of cylinders.

The mean effective pressure can be assumed or taken from tables. A speed of 1,000 revolutions per minute is the only assumption made, and the formula takes into consideration pressure, bore and stroke, and is the simplest form to which the writer has yet been able to reduce the horse-power fomula, still retaining all the essentials.

The pressure in any engine is assumed to be a mean effective pressure or average pressure throughout the stroke, and is written M.E.P. For gasoline engines of the usual four-cycle type, this pressure can be assumed at between 75 and 100 pounds, it, of course, varying with the general design. The actual mean effective pressure

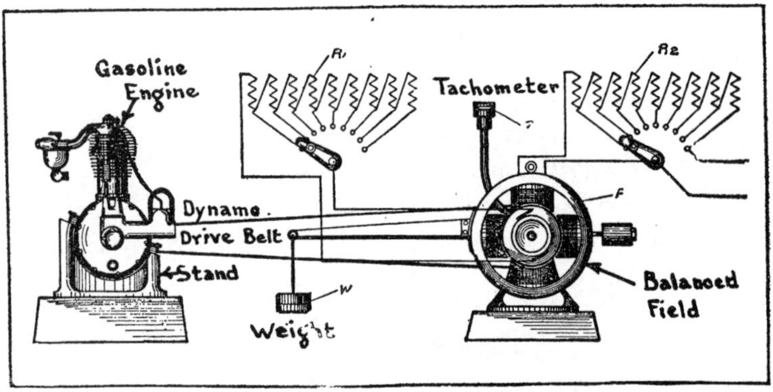

Fig. 46.—Method of Testing Power of Motorcycle Engine With Cradle Dynamometer.

of an engine which has already been built can be determined by the manograph, which records by means of a streak of light the outline of the indicator card, which, if desired, can be permanently retained by means of a photographic plate. It can also be determined at speeds under 500 revolutions per minute by diagrams produced by ordinary steam engine indicators, but these are not accurate when used with high-speed gasoline engines, the manograph being far superior.

Mean effective pressure increases as the compression, and decreases as the revolutions per minute augment. The thermal efficiency of a motor is the ratio between the work done and the thermal energy contained in the fuel consumed, and is between 15 to 30 per cent. The mechanical efficiency, by which is understood the ratio between the work actually done to the energy expended on the piston by the expanding gases, is approximately 85 per cent.

For easy comparison of one machine with another, and for facilitating handicapping at hill-climbs and race meets, the following formulæ have been given out by clubs and associations. For the sake of uniformity, let:

D^2 = Square of piston diameter in inches.
L = Stroke in inches.
R = Revolutions per minute.
N = Number of cylinders.

S.A.E. formula.......... H.P. $= \frac{D^2N}{2.5}$

Roberts formula......... H.P. $= \frac{D^2LNR}{1{,}800}$

Royal Auto Club......... H.P. $= \frac{(D + L)^2N}{9.92}$

TABLE OF HORSE-POWER FOR USUAL SIZES OF MOTORCYCLE MOTORS, BASED ON S. A. E. FORMULA.

Bore.		Horse-power.		
Inches.	M/M	1 Cylinder.	2 Cylinders.	4 Cylinders.
2½	64	2½	5	10
2⅝	68	2¾	5½	11
2¾	70	3	6	$12\frac{1}{10}$
2⅞	73	$3\frac{5}{16}$	6⅝	13¼
3	76	$3\frac{3}{5}$	$7\frac{1}{5}$	$14\frac{2}{5}$
3⅛	79	$3\frac{15}{16}$	$7\frac{13}{16}$	15⅝
3¼	83	4¼	8½	....
3⅜	85	$4\frac{9}{16}$	9⅛	....
3½	89	$4\frac{9}{10}$	$9\frac{4}{5}$	....
3⅝	92	5¼	10½	....
3¾	95	5⅝	11¼	....
3⅞	99	6	12	....

To simplify reading of the above, the horse-power figures are approximate, but correct within one-sixteenth.

How Actual Horse-Power is Tested.—While it is possible to arrive at some estimate during the preliminary designing or construction of a motorcycle power plant of the amount of power that can be expected, the only true indication of actual engine capacity is some form of dynamometer or brake test. A typical method of testing is illustrated at Fig. 46 and the general arrangement of parts can be readily understood by referring to the diagram. The apparatus used for this test is known as a "cradle-dynamometer" and power is measured by an electro-magnetic pull, the value of which increases as the engine capacity augments. The motor drives the armature of what is really an electric generator by a belt, and an electric current is produced which is dissipated or absorbed by the resistance R1. This current sets up a magnetic attraction which tends to pull the field around with it. This field ring is not only very carefully balanced but is supported by ball bearings in the pedestals which permit it to oscillate with but slight magnetic pull. The amount of magnetic attraction may be measured by the weight W carried at the end of the long lever attached to the oscillating field. The pull depends upon the amount of current flowing through the field, and this is usually supplied from an independent source and is controlled by the rheostat R2. In calculating the power developed, it is necessary to know the number of revolutions the armature is making, so this is determined by the revolution counter or tachometer T which is driven from the armature shaft by suitable gearing and a flexible shaft.

In making a test, a number of resistance coils in the rheostat R1 are put in circuit for absorbing the armature output, and enough electric current from some extraneous source is allowed to flow through the field by means of the rheostat R2 to hold the motor down to the required speed. Weights are placed on the arm at W until the field ring balances. The number of revolutions as indicated by the tachometer is noted and the horse-power obtained under these conditions may be readily computed. If it is desired to test the horse-power at lower or higher speeds, the weights are removed and the amount of current flowing through the field is altered to obtain the desired speed. If the current is increased the speed becomes less, while decreasing the current will allow the motor to run faster. When the proper number of revolutions are obtained, the weights are changed until the field ring again balances. The horse-power is very easily found by a simple formula which can be expressed as follows if one assumes that the distance from where the weight is supported to the center of the armature shaft is one foot:

$$\text{H.P.} = \frac{\text{Weight} \times \text{R.P.M.} \times 2 \times 3.1416}{33{,}000}$$

For example, if the motor pulls 29 pounds at 2,400 revolutions per minute, we would have substituting known values in the above formula:

$$\frac{29 \times 2{,}400 \times 2 \times 3.1416}{33{,}000} = 13.25 \text{ H.P.}$$

If the field current is strengthened so that the motor is slowed down to 1,500 revolutions per minute and the torque is indicated as 36 pounds, we have:

$$\frac{36 \times 1{,}500 \times 2 \times 3.1416}{33{,}000} = 10.\ 28 \text{ H.P.}$$

The actual horse-power of an engine may be determined by other forms of dynamometers, of which the Prony brake is a widely used form. This differs from the electric devices described, as the power delivery is obtained by a friction brake that, in its simplest form, may consist of a rope passed around a fly-wheel or pulley attached to the motor shaft or driven by it and having its free ends attached to spring balances or one attached to a fixed point while the other is weighted. The usual form of Prony brake consists of a band of leather or steel to which a number of hardwood blocks are fastened, and the whole is bent around the fly-wheel of the enginc to be tested to form a brake band, which may be made to bear against the fly-wheel with any degree of pressure desired by the operator. A lever is attached to one side of the brake hand, and the tendency of the revolving fly-wheel to carry the lever around with it when the band is tightened, is resisted by weights or spring balances. The method of determining the power with the mechanical brake is just the same as that followed when the electric cradle dynamometer method is employed.

Another simple and effective method of determining the horse-power is to have the engine run a generator of electricity and absorb the current delivered by any suitable resistance such as banks of incandescent lamps. The current output from the generator may be measured, and for every 746 watts of current obtained, the engine is delivering about 1.10 horse-power. While 746 watts is the electrical equivalent of a horse-power, there is a certain loss in energy in converting the mechanical power into electric current, and this must be considered in determining the engine power. Still another method of obtaining the actual horse-power of a gasoline engine is by driving a large air fan which has movable vanes or plates attached to the arms so that these may be placed at any point on the length of the arm. As it takes a certain amount of power to overcome air resistance, if the area of the plates is known, one can determine the amount of power delivered by the engine by considering the distance the blades travel in a given time.

Relation of Torque to Horse-Power and Its Meaning.—In considering the power capacity of various types of prime movers, "torque" is a technical term that receives considerable application, and like most of the simple mechanical expressions, it does not mean much to the average reader of semi-technical or mechanical works. As it is a very simple way of expressing power delivered to or by a rotating member, such as an engine crankshaft, pulley, sprocket or wheel, it seems desirable that a more general understanding of this term should exist. The writer has used this expression previously, and as it will be employed in a number of the chapters to follow, in exposition of power generation and transmission systems, the appended brief explanation may serve to promote a proper understanding of its meaning.

It is generally known that power is expended in doing work, and that as the amount of work or resistance is increased, the amount of power or energy required augments proportionately. The power delivered by an engine crankshaft can be expressed very well as "torque" which generally is considered in pounds-inches or pounds-feet, or simply as a certain pull or push having a definite value in pounds.

The relation between torque and horse-power is simply that the former is produced by or can produce the latter. The amount of torque is directly proportional to the power producing it, and it increases as the power augments, if the rotative speed remains constant.

For example, we desire to find the useful driving force or power delivered by a gasoline engine of certain proportions. If the engine was used in motorcycle propulsion, it would be desirable to know the amount of pull that would be present at the pitch line of the driving sprocket, in order to ascertain if the engine could overcome the resistance of traction wheel movement. This pull would be a torque of so many pounds value depending upon the speed and power of the engine and the distance between the sprocket pitch line and a point at crankshaft center. In ascertaining the value of the turning effort or torque, it is desirable to find the amount present at one inch radius from shaft center first, then the actual pull may be readily determined by dividing the torque in inch-pounds by the distance in inches from the crankshaft center to the point where the power is exerted.

The following simple example will clearly define the practical application of the formula previously used to this case. The formula expressed as a rule is: Torque is equal to the product of the horse-power multiplied by 63,024, divided by the revolutions per minute of the shaft. This rule is almost universally employed in determining the value of the pull available from a given power at a definite point of one inch from shaft center. Assuming that the engine in question was capable of delivering 10 horse-power to its crankshaft, at a speed of 2,000 revolutions per minute, and that we wish to find the pull available at the driving face of a 6-inch diameter, flat belt pulley, attached to the engine crankshaft, we can substitute known values and have the following expression:

$$\frac{10 \times 63{,}024}{2{,}000} = \frac{630{,}240}{2{,}000} \text{ or 315 inch-pounds.}$$

Dividing this value by the radius of the pulley, or 3 inches, gives us a pull equivalent to 105 pounds at the pulley surface. If this could be transmitted without loss directly to the 18 inches diameter driving pulley on the rear wheel, we would have a pull of 105 pounds on the surface of that member at 9 inches radius from traction wheel center. Owing to the difference in size between the pulleys, the driven member would turn at but one-third the speed of the driving member on the engine shaft, or 666.66 revolutions per minute. Even though the wheel turns slower, the torque, one inch from the traction wheel center, would be equivalent to 10 horse-power, as while it would be 945 inch-pounds, the speed of the rear wheel is but one-third that of the engine shaft, and therefore the torque should be three times as much. If the amount of power remains constant, the torque or pull increases as the speed is reduced, and diminishes as the speed of rotation is augmented. Torque or pull is always greatest near shaft center, as for example, at one-half inch radius it is twice as great as at one-inch radius, all other conditions remaining equal. It is usually based on one inch radius to facilitate calculation. An engine capable of exerting a torque or pull of 315 inch-pounds would only exert 26.20 pounds pull at 12 inches radius under the same speed and power conditions. The torque of large engines is measured in foot-pounds in order to simplify figuring, while that of smaller capacity power plants is more often expressed in inch-pounds.

When actual horse-power tests are made, there is a point in every horse-power diagram where the torque and horse-power curve lines intersect, and an engine is not exerting its greatest torque at its highest rotative speed. It will be noted that the horse-power curve in the diagrams at Fig. 47 attains its maximum value at a certain point, and from there it drops as the speed increases. This falling off in power is on account of the higher mechanical losses in the power plant at high speeds due to the increased friction of the parts and also thermal losses because of difficulties in scavenging or clearing out the cylinder properly and taking in a full charge of fresh gas. As one would expect, the torque is greatest at low speeds, and gradually becomes less as the speeds of rotation increase. The relation of torque and horse-power lines to each other when plotted on charts is clearly shown in the diagrams at Fig. 47. In the upper one, the test of a single cylinder engine rated at 5 horse-power is shown, while in the lower one the results obtained by testing a 9 horse-power nominal rating twin-cylinder engine are plotted.

Such diagrams are not difficult to read, and they are especially valuable in presenting a large volume of information in a small space.

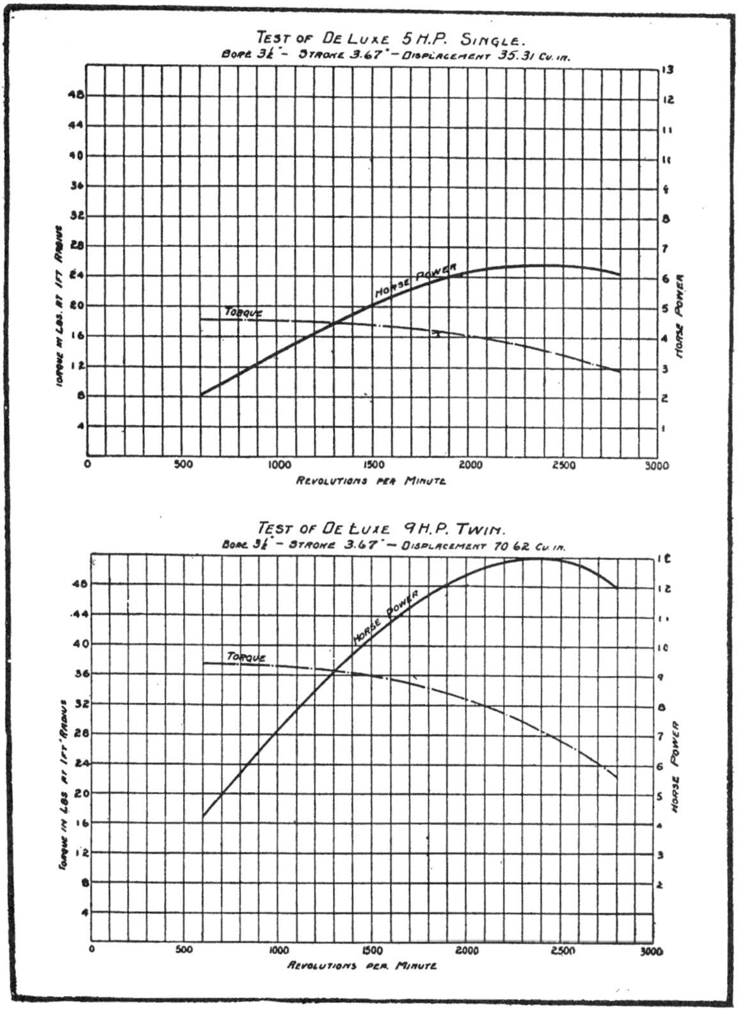

Fig. 47.—Curves Showing Horse Power of Gasoline Motors at Various Speeds of Crankshaft Rotation.

To read these diagrams, it is merely necessary to trace a vertical line denoting the speed in revolutions per minute desired to the point where it intersects the horse-power curve, and then following out the horizontal line to the right of the chart, where the horse-power delivered at that speed will be clearly indicated. The same procedure is followed in reading the torque, only that the horizontal line is followed to the left of the diagram where the torque in pounds at one foot radius is outlined. For example, considering the upper chart, it will be apparent that if we follow the vertical line indicating 1,300 revolutions per minute upward, we will find that it intersects both the torque and horse-power curves. Following an imaginary horizontal line from this point on the diagram to the right, we find that the engine in question is developing approximately 4.50 horse-power while the torque is about 18 pounds. It will be observed that the power plant rated at 5 horse-power will develop 6.33 horse-power at 2,400 revolutions per minute.

Another diagram that gives some interesting data pertaining to the relation of motorcycle speed in miles per hour and the engine power developed is presented at Fig. 48. It will be observed that the maximum engine power represented by the highest point in the curve is obtained at a vehicle speed of approximately 47.5 miles per hour, and that from this point to 65 miles per hour the power curve drops appreciably. At 47.5 miles, the engine is delivering 13.9 horse-power, whereas at a rear wheel speed corresponding to 65 miles per hour the engine is developing but 9.3 horse-power. The horse-power obtained by this test is different than that secured by trial of the engine alone, and the object was not to ascertain the brake horse-power of the engine but the actual power available at the rear wheel for traction, which, on account of mechanical losses in the power transmission system, would be fully 20 per cent less than the amount of power that would be shown by the engine on a brake or dynamometer test where the power of the engine crankshaft would be measured instead of that proportion of it delivered at the rear wheel.

A simple rule for finding the torque at one-inch radius from center, exerted by a shaft rotated with a given amount of power that can be easily memorized, if one assumes a speed of rotation of 1,000 revolutions per minute, is: Multiply the horse-power by 63, which will give the pull in inch-pounds, and then divide this product by the distance in inches from shaft center to the point of power application, and the result is the torque or pull available at that point directly in pounds.

Reason for Cooling Engine.—It is apparent that power is produced in an internal-combustion engine by a series of explosions in the cylinder. As the temperature of the explosion is over 2,000 deg. Fahr. in some cases, the rapid combustion and continued series of explosions would soon heat up the metal parts of the combustion chamber to such a point that they would show color unless cooling means were provided. Under these conditions, it would be impossible to lubricate the cylinder, because even the best quality of lubricating oil would be burnt. The piston would expand sufficiently to seize in

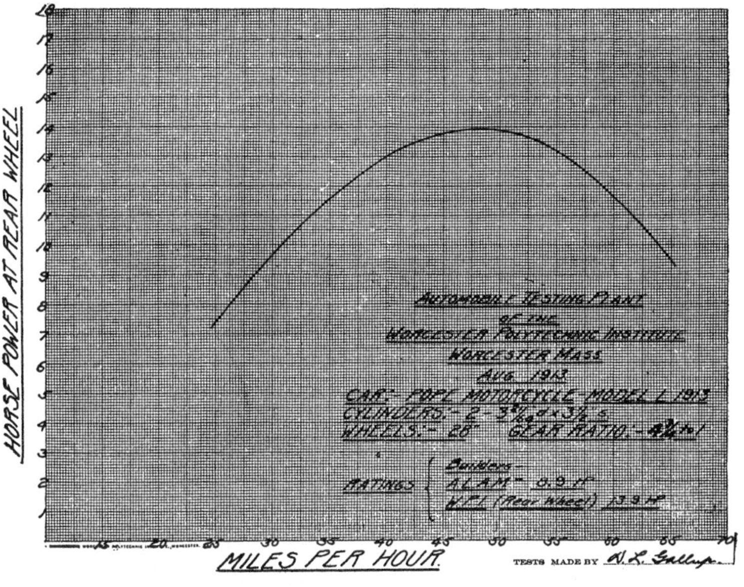

Fig. 48.—Chart Showing Horse Power at Rear Wheel of Motorcycle at Various Speeds.

the cylinder and the valves would warp so that they could no longer hold compression. Premature ignition of the charge would probably take place long before the engine was put out of commission by the distortion of the parts.

The fact that the ratio of engine efficiency is dependent upon the amount of useful work delivered by the heat generated from the ex-

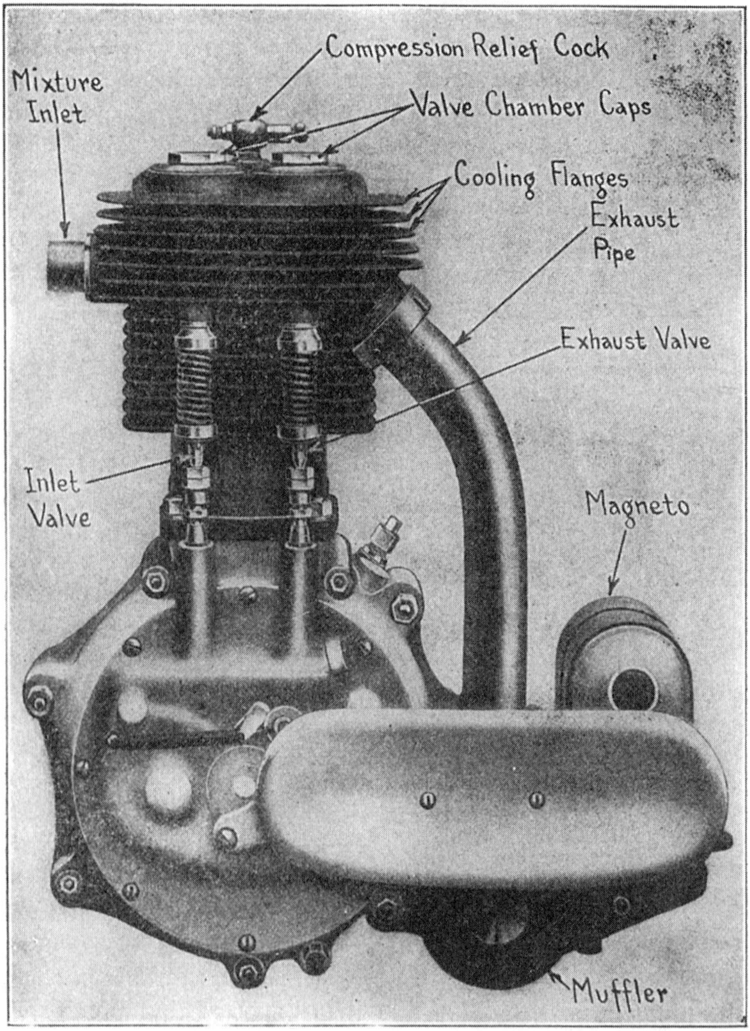

Fig. 49.—Typical Single Cylinder Motorcycle Power Plant, Showing Arrangement of Cooling Flanges to Increase Radiating Surface of the Cylinder.

plosion makes it important that the cylinders be cooled to a point where the cylinder will not be robbed of too much heat. The losses through the water jacket of the average water-cooled automobile power plant are over 50 per cent of the total fuel efficiency. While it is very important that the engine should not get too hot, it is equally desirable that it is not cooled too much. The object of cylinder cooling is, therefore, to keep the heat of the cylinder metal below the danger point but at the same time keep the engine hot enough to obtain maximum power from the gas burnt.

Air or Water Cooling.—The method of abstracting the heat from the cylinder generally employed in the small motors used in motorcycle propulsion is by means of direct air cooling, though on the larger motors, sometimes used in cycle car and light automobile service, the heat is absorbed by water circulated around the cylinders through a suitable jacket which keeps it confined against the heated portions. In an air-cooled engine, the application of the air to the cylinders is direct, and there is no intermediate transfer of heat from the cylinder wall to the radiating surfaces by means of water. Any water-cooling system must, of necessity, be indirect, as after the water is heated it must pass through a radiator where it is subjected to the cooling influence of air currents to reduce its temperature, and make it available for further use. In a motor which employs a water-cooling system, there is a certain loss of heat to the water jacket which is called "Jacket Loss," and the amount of heat wasted in this manner depends upon the difference in temperature between the heat of the explosion and the heat of the cylinder wall. As water loses its cooling efficiency when it boils, the temperature of the water jackets, and consequently the wall of the water-cooled cylinder, must be maintained at a point below 212 deg. Fahr. which is the boiling point of water. The temperature of the cylinder wall of an air-cooled motor may be readily and safely maintained at a temperature nearly 150 degrees higher. This would indicate that, with a reduced heat loss, an air-cooled motor would be more efficient than a water-cooled form. Then, of course, the features of simplicity that are so necessary in motorcycle design cannot be readily obtained if the water-cooling system is employed because in its simplest form it requires a radiator to cool the water, and suitable piping to conduct the water from the engine cylinder water jacket to the point where the heat is radiated into the air. As an air-cooled engine can be made considerably lighter than a water-cooled form, and as the direct system of cooling has demonstrated that it is thoroughly practical for the small engines used in motorcycle work, it does not seem necessary to provide motorcycle motors with water jackets. All of the American motorcycles use the air-cooling method, though several foreign machines have water-cooling systems.

Efficiency of Air-Cooled Motors.—The air-cooled motor is more efficient than the water-cooled forms, because in any internal combustion engine it is the heat energy of the fuel that is converted into useful work. This transformation is brought about by the rapid combustion or burning of the fuel which is often called "an explosion." The rapidly burning gases develop high pressures which produce power, as we have seen, by acting on the piston and the reciprocating parts. The temperature and pressure of the explosion both fall very rapidly, on account of the rapid escape or transfer of heat through the walls of the cylinder and the piston head. A certain amount of heat loss is a necessary evil that cannot be avoided in any internal combustion engine, and as previously stated, efficient lubrication cannot be obtained if the cylinders get much hotter than 400 deg. Fahr. A cylinder may be allowed to heat up to 350 deg. Fahr. and still be on the safe side as far as effective lubrication is concerned. In comparing the efficiency of air and water cooled motors, a good method of doing this is to base the values on the amount of mileage possible on a given fuel consumption. An air-cooled engine will use a maximum of 0.80 of a pound of gasoline for each brake horse-power hour at half load, and 0.60 of a pound of gasoline for each brake horse-power hour developed at full load. The average water-jacketed automobile engine will use from 1 to 1.50 pounds of fuel at half load, and from 0.90 to 1.20 pounds per brake horse-power hour at full load. From the foregoing, it will be apparent that the air-cooling system is more efficient and economical than the water-cooling methods, and in view of its simplicity it is not difficult to understand why it is almost universally used in motorcycle power plants of American design.

Air-Cooling Methods.—Air cooling may be obtained by two methods: either simple radiation, or combined radiation and convection. The former system is used only on motors of a stationary type that are not provided with a cooling fan. The most widely used system is a combination of radiation and convection. Radiation simply means that the heated air rises from the hot cylinder because it is lighter than the cooler air which takes its place. Convection means cooling by air in motion, and, obviously, wherever convection is used there must, of necessity, be included the radiation principle. The method generally used on motorcycles where the power plant is exposed to the air, and where the cylinder is swept by air drafts or currents created by the rapid travel of the machine, is to augment the normal available radiating surface of the plain cylinder by providing cooling flanges as indicated at Figs. 49 and 50.

These flanges not only surround the entire cylinder exterior but also cover the valve chamber and the cylinder head. By the use of these members, the area of radiating surface is largely increased, and while air has considerably less capacity for absorbing heat than water, the surface from which the heat is radiated may be increased to such a point by judiciously placed flanges so the heat will be dissipated fast enough to keep the cylinder from overheating. The cooling flanges may be of the same diameter the entire length of the cylinder, as shown at Fig. 49, or they may become less in diameter as the cylinder temperature decreases, as shown at Fig. 50. They are widest at the combustion chamber, and taper down in diameter to but little more than that of the cylinder at the bottom of that member. On some types of flange-cooled engines, the designers drill holes through the flanges as indicated at Fig. 51, and while these materially reduce the effective radiating surface it is claimed that there is more opportunity for the cooling-air current to pass around and between the flanges, and thus superior cooling is obtained. The air-cooling flanges on most motorcycle power plants are placed horizontally, or at right angles to the cylinder center line, though in some forms, where the cylinder is inclined, the flanges are disposed at an angle to the cylinder wall so that they will be approximately horizontal when the power plant is in position. On some forms of double cylinder opposed engines, the flanges run the length of the cylinder, in order to promote free circulation of air. Where air-cooled motors are protected by a hood or bonnet, as in cyclecars and light automobiles, it is customary

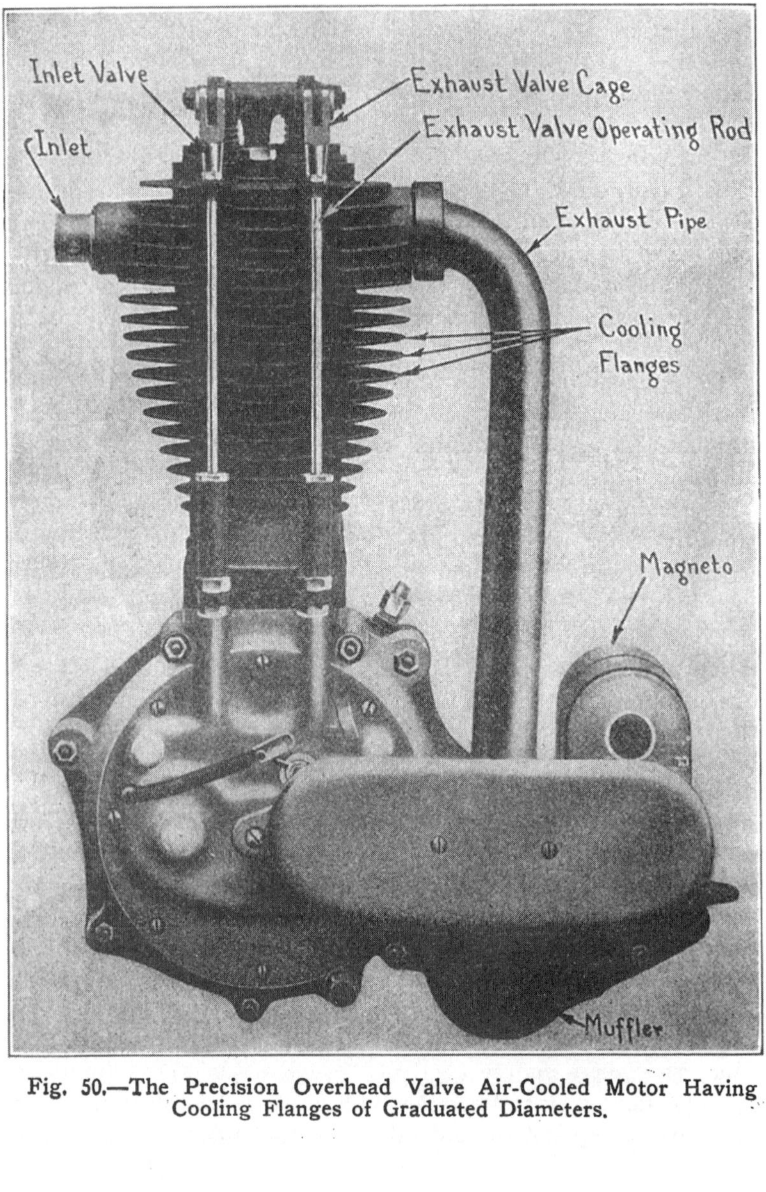

Fig. 50.—The Precision Overhead Valve Air-Cooled Motor Having Cooling Flanges of Graduated Diameters.

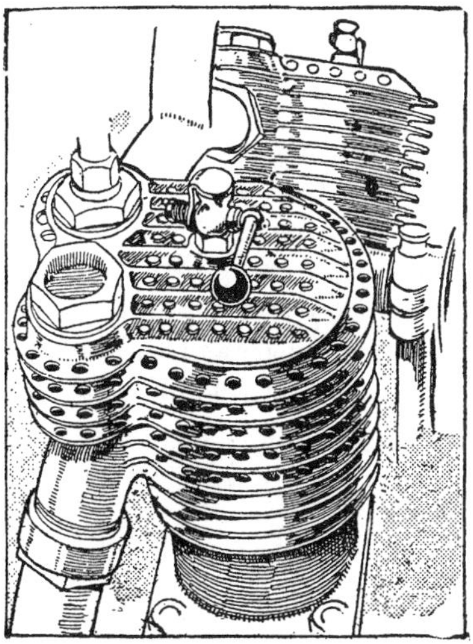

Fig. 51.—Showing Method of Perforating Flanges to Facilitate Air-Cooling.

to provide a cooling fan driven from the engine crankshaft to keep a constant draft of air in motion around the engine cylinders. In some automobile power plants the cylinders have been encased in sheet metal jackets, and air currents from a blower are made to circulate through these jackets and around the cylinders, but this is not necessary on motorcycles. Copper-plating the cylinders increases the rate of heat transfer to the air. Radiation may also be augmented by painting the cylinders with a dull black stove polish.

Water=Cooling Methods.—When a liquid is employed for cooling it is circulated through jackets which surround the cylinder castings, and when the excess heat is absorbed, the hot liquid is led to a cooler where the heat is abstracted from it by means of air currents. The cooled liquid is then taken from the cooler and again circulated around the cylinders of the motor. The view of a typical one-cylinder motor at Fig. 53 shows the arrangement provided for water cooling by radiators attached to the engine cylinder.

Two methods of keeping the cooling liquid in motion are used. The simplest system is to utilize a natural principle that a hot liquid being lighter than a cold one will tend to rise to the top of the cylinder when it becomes heated, while cool water takes its place at the bottom of the water jacket. The more complicated system is to use a positive circulating pump of some form which is driven by the engine to keep the liquid in circulation.

Some eminent motorcycle designers contend that the rapid circulation of liquid obtained by means of a pump may cool the cylinders too much and the temperature of the engine may be reduced to a point where its efficiency will be somewhat lower than if the engine were allowed to run hotter. For this reason, some foreign engineers use the natural method of water circulation. The cooling liquid is applied to the cylinder jackets below the boiling point and the water issues from the top of the jacket after it has absorbed enough heat to raise it just about to the boiling point. The simplicity of the thermo-syphon system of cooling makes it specially adapted to motorcycles and other light vehicles. With this system of cooling, it is necessary to use more liquid than with pump-circulated systems, and the water jackets of the cylinders, as well as the water spaces in the radiator and the water inlet and discharge manifolds, should have greater capacity and be free from sharp corners that might impede the flow of liquid.

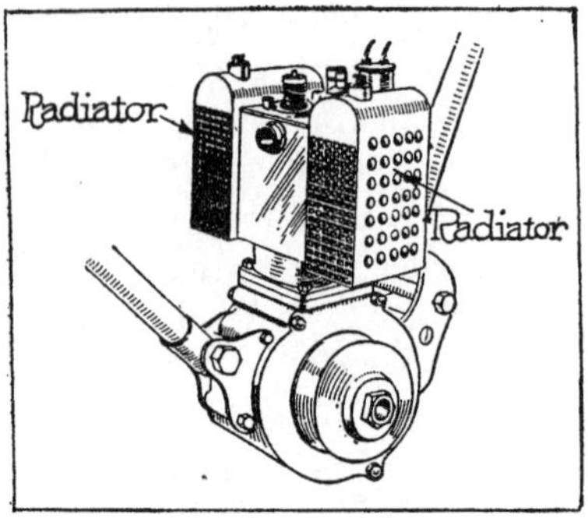

Fig. 52.—View of Green-Precision Motor With Radiators Attached to the Sides of the Water Jacket.

A system of cooling in which a pump is depended on to promote circulation of water is sometimes employed in cyclecar practice. The radiator is generally carried at the front end of the frame, and serves as a combined water tank and cooler in most cases. It is usually composed of upper and lower water tanks, joined together by a series of pipes, which may be round and provided with a number of corrugated flanges to radiate the heat, or which may be flat in order to have the water pass through in thin sheets and cool more easily. The cold water which settles at the bottom of the cooler is drawn from the lower part of the radiator by a gear-driven pump and is forced through a manifold to the water jackets surrounding the exhaust valve chamber of the cylinder. As the water becomes heated, it passes out of the top of the water jacket into the upper portion of the radiator, but as a general rule the rate of circulation is dependent upon the power and speed of the pump rather than the degree of temperature of the water. On account of the more rapid flow of liquid, the radiator and piping may be of less capacity than when the simple thermo-syphon is employed.

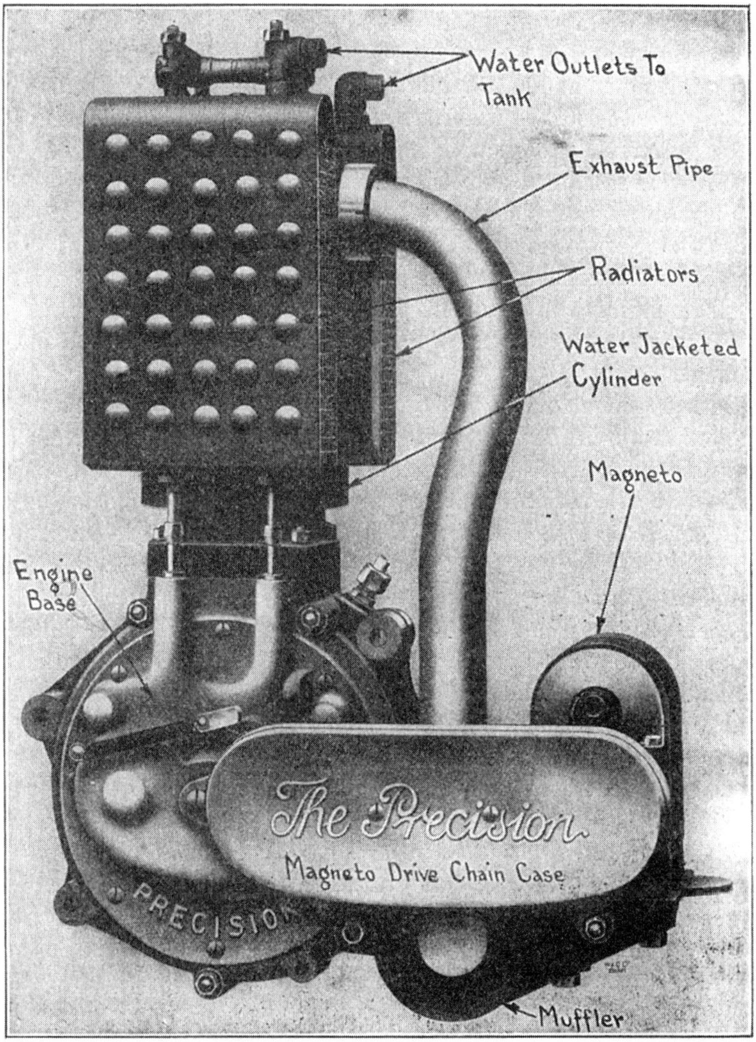

Fig. 53.—Complete Water-Cooled Power Plant With Radiators Integral.

Some typical water-cooled motors that have been designed for motorcycle use abroad are shown at Figs. 52 to 54 inclusive. The engine shown at Fig. 52 in place on the motorcycle frame is the same as that depicted at Fig. 53, and it will be observed that the radiators which serve to cool the water are attached directly to the sides of the water jacket. There is ample opportunity for the air currents to pass through the radiators, and it is possible to carry a reserve supply of water in a tank attached to the top frame bar which may be used as an auxiliary source of supply by connecting it to the water outlets at the top of the radiator that are clearly depicted at Fig. 53. On very small engines, it will be unnecessary to provide any water container, as the radiators themselves may hold enough water to secure adequate cooling.

Both of the engines depicted at Fig. 54 are of the two-cycle form and are shown in the position they occupy in the motorcycle frame to which they are fitted. That at A is the Rex motor, and it will be observed that the radiator is placed at the front end of the machine just back of the steering head and follows the diagonal tube extending from the steering head to the motor crank-case. The bottom of the radiator is connected directly to the bottom of the water jacket, and the heated water from the top of the cylinder passes through suitable pipes to the top of the radiator. The cooling system depicted at B is that of the Scott motorcycle, and the disposition of the radiator and arrangement of water piping is practically the same as in the example previously considered.

The engine depicted at Fig. 53 is a four-cycle form while those outlined at Fig. 54 are two-cycle engines which are said to be more difficult to cool successfully by air than the conventional form of four-stroke engine in which one entire stroke of the piston is devoted to clearing out the burnt gases from the cylinder while another full stroke is utilized in drawing in a cool charge of fresh gas. The Shickel engine, an American two-cycle form shown at Fig. 58, is cooled successfully by air, and in view of the fact that air cooling has been applied successfully to motor truck engines having 4.50-inch bore and operating on the two-cycle principle, it is apparent that it should be more successful and practical on the smaller two-stroke engines employed as motorcycle power plants.

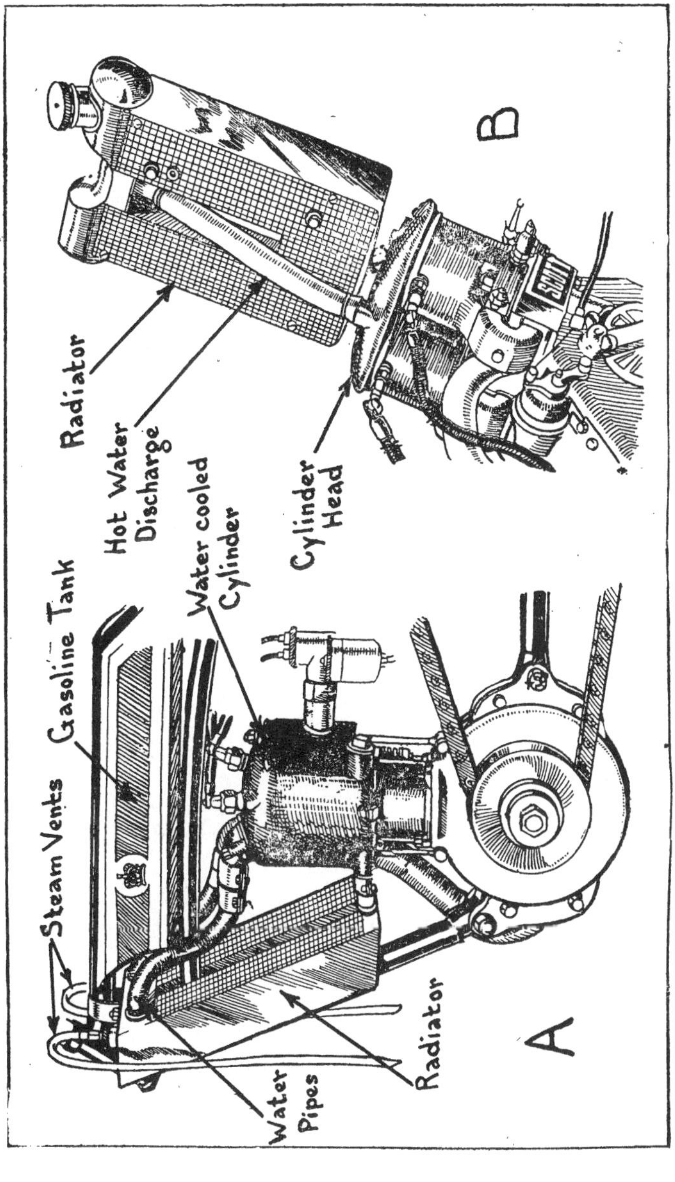

Fig. 54.—Water-Cooled Motorcycle Power Plants of English Design, Showing Arrangement of Radiators and Water Connections.

Features of One-Cylinder Motors.—The single-cylinder engine offers a main advantage of extreme simplicity. This is of considerable importance in the lighter motorcycles that are to be operated by inexperienced riders. Among some of the disadvantages that may be cited against the single-cylinder power plant are greater weight in proportion to power developed, lack of even power application because only one stroke out of four made by the piston is effective. A one-cylinder engine lacks the even turning moment and steady running qualities that a multiple-cylinder power plant possesses. If run faster

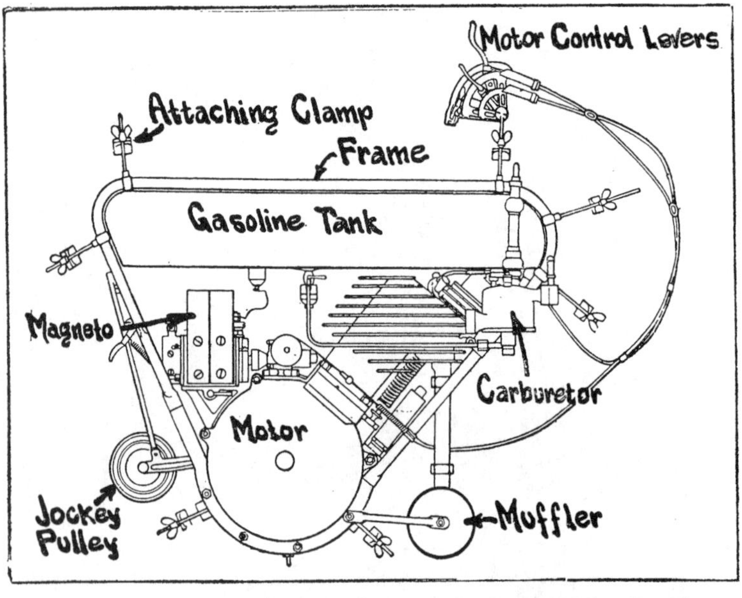

Fig. 55.—Typical Complete Power Plant Unit Adapted for Attachment in Standard Diamond Frame Bicycle.

or slower than the critical speed for which it was designed, there will be considerable vibration. Despite these faults, the single-cylinder engine is very practical in applications to light and medium-weight machines, and ample power may be obtained to cope with any condition ordinarily met with in road service. Typical one-cylinder engines are illustrated at Figs. 55 to 57, inclusive.

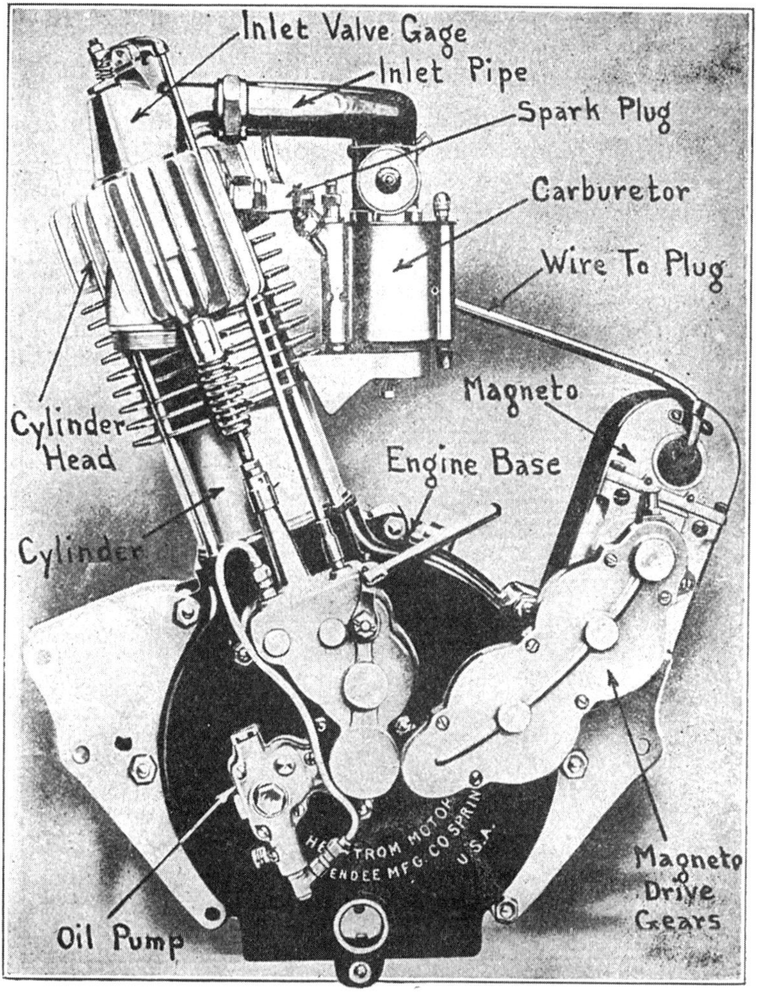

Fig. 56.—Power Plant of Single Cylinder Indian Motorcycle.

If of the two-cycle type, one will obtain the same even torque and steady application of power with one cylinder as provided by a two-cylinder opposed four-cycle engine, and steadier running than provided by most V-twins, though one must sacrifice some of the flexibility and quick get-away of the four-cycle power plant to obtain the advantages of the simpler two-stroke motor. The Schickel two-cycle motor construction is shown at Fig. 58.

Advantages of Multiple-Cylinder Motors.—Power is obtained in the multiple-cylinder motor by using a number of cylinders instead of one large member. The cylinders are arranged in such a way that any multiple-cylinder motor may be considered as a number of single-

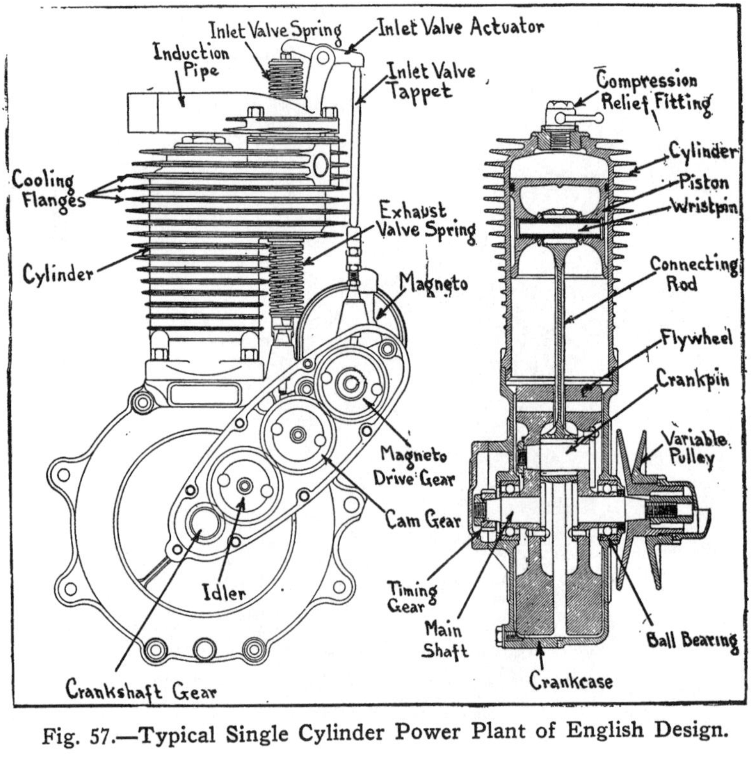

Fig. 57.—Typical Single Cylinder Power Plant of English Design.

cylinder engines joined together so that one cylinder starts to deliver power to the crankshaft where the other leaves off. By using a number of smaller cylinders, instead of a large one, all of the revolving parts may be made lighter, and the reciprocating members are easier to balance because the weight of the parts in one cylinder often

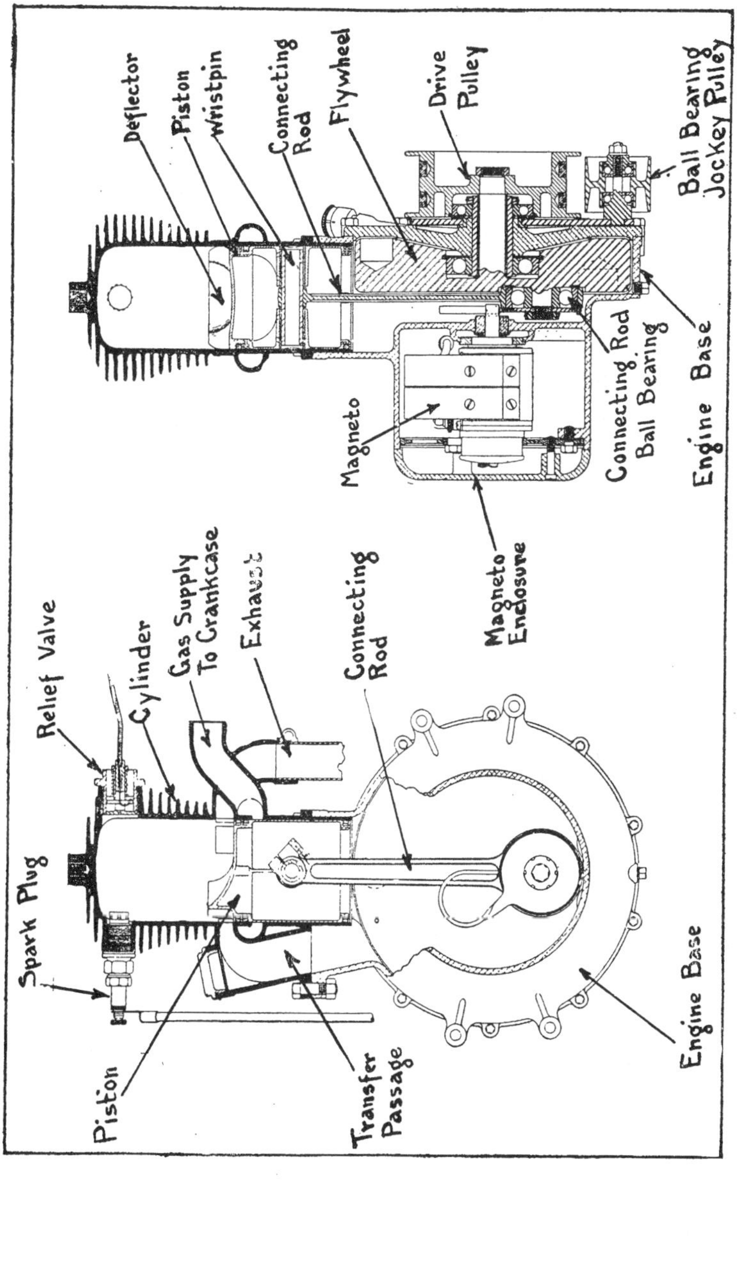

Fig. 58.—Sectional Views of the Schickel Motor, an American Two Stroke Power Plant.

counter-balances the reciprocating mass in the other that works in connection with it.

Multiple-cylinder engines may be run faster than single-cylinder ones of the same power, are not so heavy in proportion to the power developed and produce a more even turning effect at the crankshaft. No matter how well designed the single-cylinder power plant is, the power impulses will come in jerks, and a very heavy fly-wheel member or pair of fly-wheel members is needed to equalize the intermittent power strokes. In a multiple-cylinder engine, where the explosions follow each other in rapid succession, the power application is obviously much more even. A single-cylinder engine will give but one useful power stroke when of the four-cycle type, to every two revolutions of the crankshaft. A two-cylinder motor will give one explosion every revolution, though these are not always evenly spaced, the regularity and evenness of firing being largely dependent upon the arrangement of the cylinders.

Types of Two=Cylinder Motors.—Most two-cylinder motorcycles employ engines of the V-type, i. e., with the two cylinders placed at an angle, and converging to a point at which they contact with the crank-case of the motor. In England, there are a number of machines which employ horizontal cylinders, and one or two makes have been evolved in which the two-cylinder engine has vertical or upright cylinders. We have seen that in a single-cylinder engine considerable dependence is placed upon a fly-wheel which stores up energy and which tends to even up or equalize the intermittent power application derived from but one explosion every two revolutions. We have also learned that multiple-cylinder engines produce more uniform torque because explosions follow each other more rapidly. Where two-cylinder motors are employed, the arrangement of the cylinders and the crank throws with relation to each other has material influence upon the evenness of operation.

For example, in an engine where one of the cylinders fires during one-half of a revolution and the second cylinder produces a power impulse directly after it or while the first cylinder is on its exhaust stroke, it is evident that the engine crankshaft will have to describe almost a continuous revolution before it can receive another power impulse. While the crankshaft receives what would be equivalent to a power impulse each revolution, in reality it receives two power impulses in one revolution and none during the second. When the cranks are arranged as shown at A, Fig. 60, and the cylinders are vertical, the explosions will follow each other without any appreciable interval, and the only advantage obtained is that the cranks, connecting rods and pistons balance much better than in some other forms. While the vibration due to poor mechanical balance is eliminated to some extent with this construction, a certain unevenness of running obtains on account of the way the explosion occurs.

When the cranks are set on the same plane as shown at B, and both of the pistons move up and down together, it is possible to obtain a

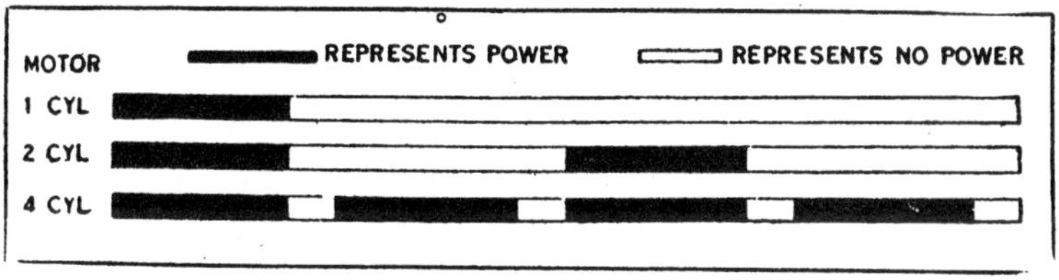

Fig. 59.—Diagram Showing the Advantages of Multiple Cylinder Engines in Obtaining Uniform Power Delivery.

good firing order, i. e., an explosion would occur the first part of the first revolution in one cylinder and the first part of the second revolution in the other cylinder. The explosions are separated by equal intervals of time, and the power application is much more uniform than obtained from the type shown at A. The disadvantage of this method of construction is that the mechanical balance is far from ideal, and counter-weights must be provided to reduce the vibration incidental to both pistons moving up and down together.

With the double opposed motor which is shown at C, the crank-pins are arranged at 180 degrees, and the explosions occur at regular intervals and with the same firing order as prevails in the construction shown at B. This form of motor also has a good mechanical balance. With the V-type of motor it is apparent that the smaller the angle between the cylinders the more evenly spaced the firing sequence becomes, though the mechanical balance is more difficult to obtain when the degree of angularity is small. In a motor with the cylinders

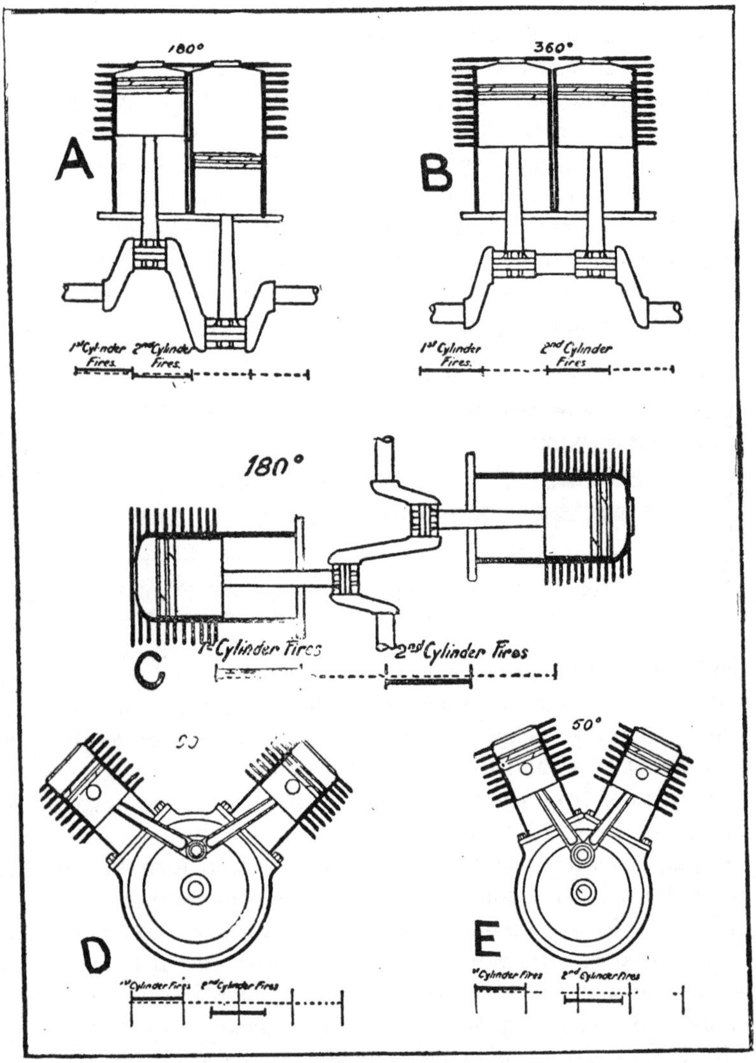

Fig. 60.—Diagrams Illustrating Various Arrangements of Crankshafts on Two Cylinder Motorcycle Power Plants.

at an angle of 90 degrees to each other and with the two connecting rods working on the same crank-pin, the mechanical balance is good but the impulses occur very close together. The better mechanical balance is obtained because the pistons partially balance each other, and a slightly better firing order prevails than in the arrangement shown at A, as there is an interval corresponding to about one-quarter of a revolution between the explosions. When the cylinders are set at an angle of 50 degrees, as indicated at E, the impulses are almost equally divided between the blank spaces as indicated in the diagram. It is possible to have the cylinders set so the explosions are spaced even more regularly, as with the cylinders at 41 degrees, which is said to be the prevailing angle in this country.

The same difficulties are met with in securing good mechanical balance as in the form shown at B, as it is imperative that counter-weights be fitted to balance the reciprocating mass to some extent and reduce vibration. The great advantage of the V-twin motor is that it is a form that may be easily installed in the motorcycle frame, and while the balance is far from perfect it is sufficiently good if the counter-weights are intelligently applied, so a very practical power plant is secured. The original twin-cylinder motorcycle power plant, and one of the first multiple-cylinder gasoline engines, is depicted at Fig. 61, C, and is an adaptation of the single-cylinder form evolved by Daimler, and clearly outlined at A and B. The cylinders in this Daimler motor were placed at an angle of approximately 15 degrees, which is considerably less than present practice.

The engine shown at Fig. 62 is utilized on the Triumph, an English design, and the crank pins are disposed at an angle of 180 degrees. The motor is set in the frame with its crankshaft at right angles to the top frame tube, and not parallel with it as might be expected. The crankshaft carries an outside fly-wheel at one end and a sprocket for chain drive at the other. The inlet valves are at the front of the cylinders and the exhaust valves are at the rear. Both are operated by a camshaft which is driven by a spiral gear from the crankshaft. A typical twin-cylinder V-engine of American design, that may be considered a good example of established practice and which has received wide application, is shown at Fig. 63.

One of the most efficient of the British light-weight motorcycles is

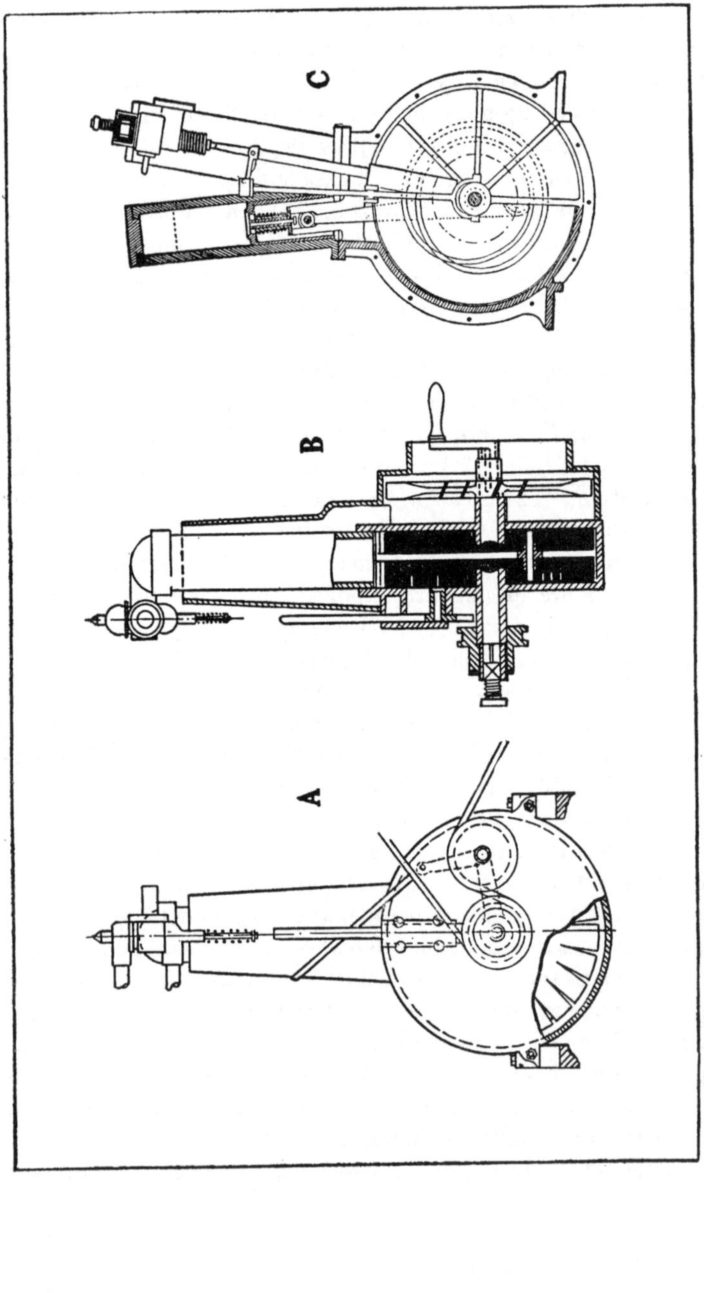

Fig. 61.—Views Showing Construction of Early Daimler Motors, the First Practical High Speed Internal Combustion Power Plants.

provided with the two-cylinder power plant shown at Fig. 64 in which the cylinders are placed horizontally and opposed to each other. The crankshaft, which is depicted in the sectional view of the crank-case at the left of the illustration, has two crank-pins placed at an angle of 180 degrees, and is mounted on ball bearings to insure free running. A distinctive feature of the design is the method of mounting the valves in valve chambers that are inclined so the valves may be actuated from the lower portion of the cam gear case. The method of ribbing the cylinders to secure more effective cooling permits the air draft induced by cycle motion to reach practically all parts of the cylinders, which would not be possible if the flanges were applied in the conventional manner that proves so effective on vertical cylinders. This is a very compact engine that is capable of delivering a uniform torque, and that operates with very little vibration, as the even spacing of the explosions and large external fly-wheel make for very easy running. The method of magneto and valve-operating cam drive may be readily ascertained as well as other ingenious details of design by studying the reproduction of the maker's engineering drawing that so clearly outlines all details of construction.

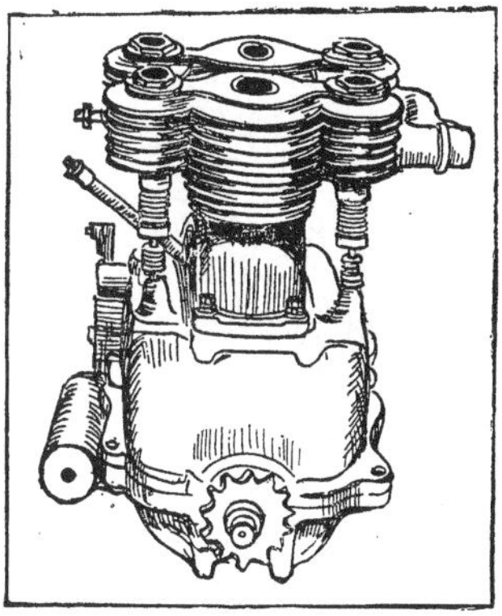

Fig. 62.—The Triumph Two Cylinder Motorcycle Power Plant, an Unconventional English Design.

One of the most distinctive of the unconventional power plants used for motorcycle propulsion is the Scott two-cycle, depicted at Fig. 65. This shows an early model in which a combined air and water cooling system was employed, the liquid being depended on to keep the water-jacketed head cool while the cylinders were provided with cooling flanges of generous proportions. The cylinders are mounted side by side, one each side of the engine center line, which coincides with the center line of the machine. Attention is directed to the small size of the crank-cases, which is necessary to

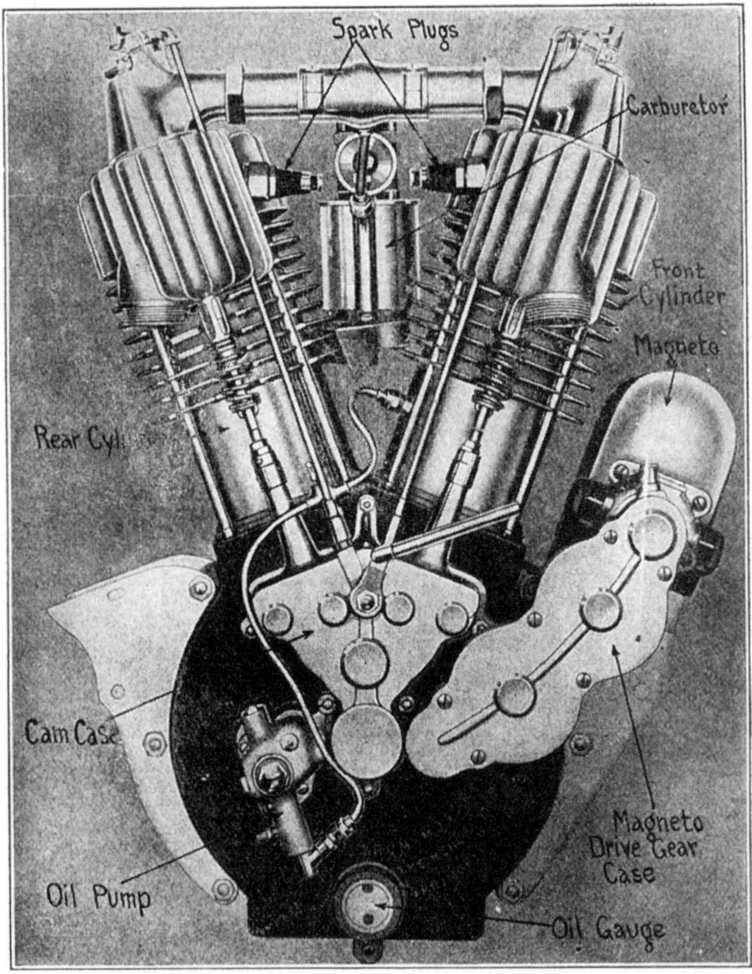

Fig. 63.—Complete Power Plant Assembly Employed on Two Cylinder Indian Motorcycle.

insure adequate preliminary compression of the charge before it is transferred from the engine base to the cylinders. The fly-wheel is mounted between the two cylinders, and carries the driving sprockets on its hub which also forms a connecting coupling between the two

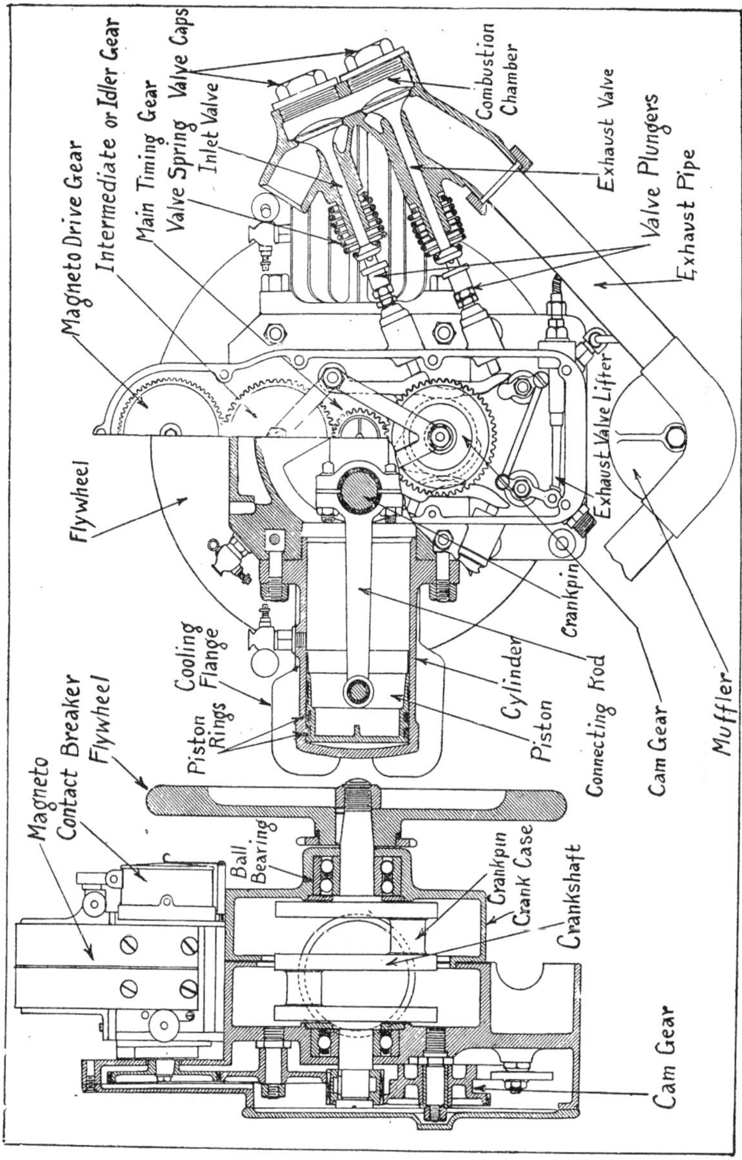

Fig. 64.—Part Sectional Views of the Douglass Opposed Cylinder Motorcycle Motor.

cranks, the assembly forming a built-up crankshaft with the crank-pins at the extreme ends. The arrangement of the ports for the passage of the gases in and out of the cylinder and the method of controlling them by the piston movement is clearly shown in the side sectional view through one of the cylinders. With the piston in the position shown, the exhaust ports are fully open for discharging the burnt gases and the inlet ports at the opposite side are also uncovered to permit the gas compressed in the engine base to by-pass into the cylinder through the transfer passage. The piston is provided with a deflector to direct the entering fresh gas to the top of the cylinder, and prevent it passing out of the open exhaust ports opposite the point where it first enters the cylinder. When the piston reaches the top of its stroke, another row of ports is opened by the bottom of the piston and the crank-case is charged with gas. When one piston is up, the other member is down and the pistons balance each other. An explosion is obtained in each cylinder every revolution, which indicates that this engine should provide the same even torque as obtained from a four-cylinder engine of the four-stroke pattern, inasmuch as the crankshaft receives two impulses each revolution.

Four=Cylinder Forms.—The real value of a multiple-cylinder motor is more apparent when four or six cylinders are used, because in the former one obtains a power impulse every half revolution of the fly-wheel, while in the latter three power strokes are delivered every revolution. The diagram presented at Fig. 59 compares in a graphic manner the useful power impulse of engines having one, two and four cylinders respectively. The shaded parts represent periods where power application obtains, while the unshaded portions represent no power. In the one-cylinder engine, it will be evident that less than one-quarter of the cycle represents useful energy. In the two-cylinder engine the explosions may be evenly spaced, but are separated by appreciable spaces where no power is developed.

Even in the four-cylinder engine there are periods (corresponding to the early opening of the exhaust valves on the power stroke) where no useful energy is directed against the crankshaft. The torque or power application is uniform enough for all practical purposes, except where the utmost refinement is desired, as in high-grade motor car power plants. In the six-cylinder engine there are no periods in the

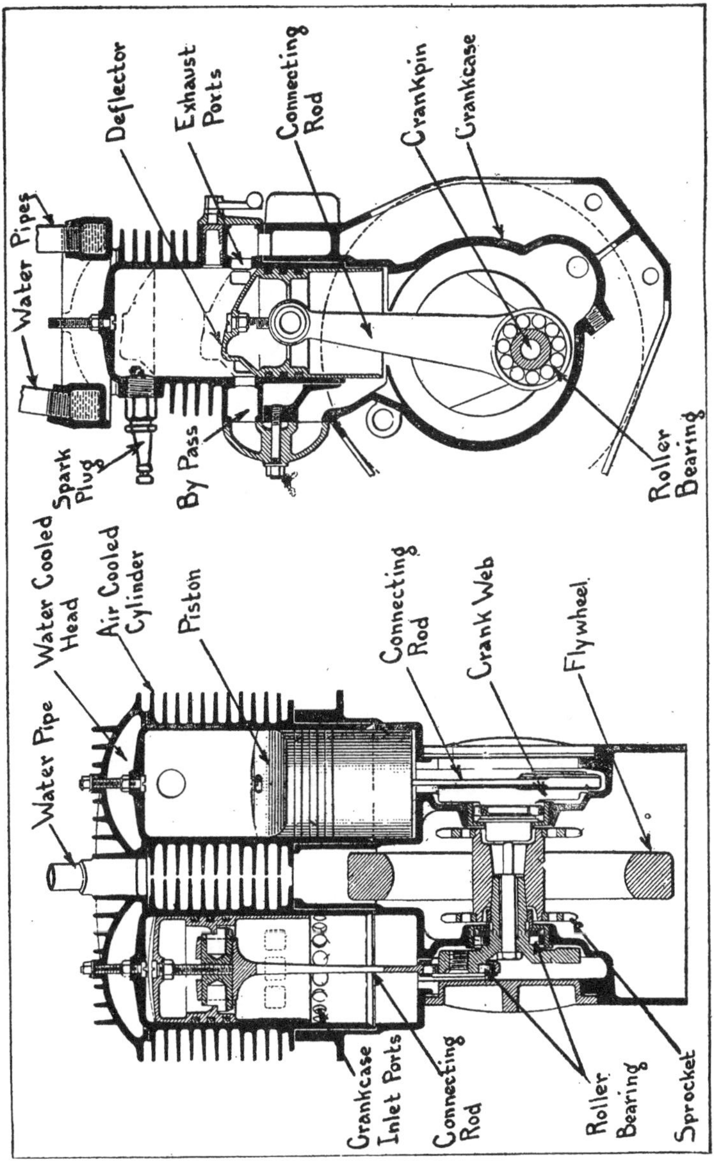

Fig. 65.—Sectional View Showing Arrangement of Parts in Scott Two-cycle Power Plant.

cycle of operation where the crankshaft is not positively driven. In fact, the explosions overlap each other, and a very smooth-acting power plant is obtained. For motorcycle service, however, a four-cylinder motor will prove to be very satisfactory, and will operate with minimum vibration, and, in view of the very satisfactory operation of the ordinary V-twin power plant, it is open to question if the four-cylinder motor offers marked enough advantages to compensate

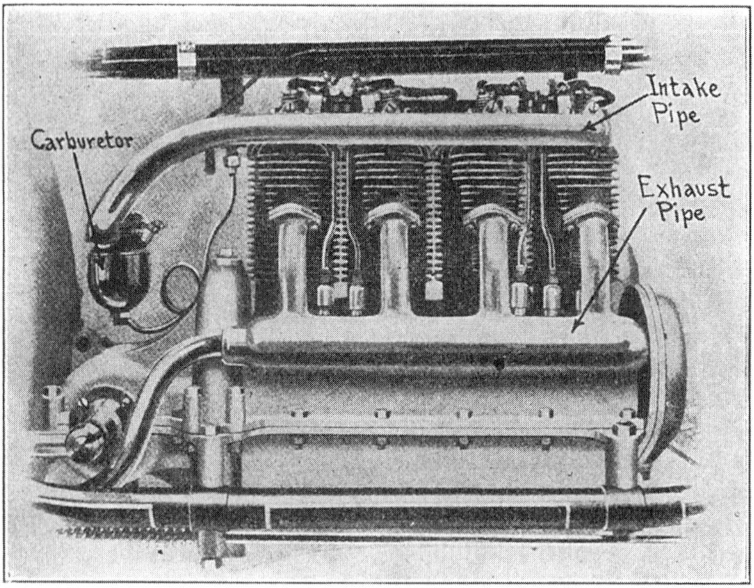

Fig. 66.—Manifold Side of the Henderson Four Cylinder Motorcycle Power Plant.

for its added complication. Of course, there are riders who want the best there is, regardless of cost, and where maximum silence, freedom from vibration and even power application are desired, it is evident that the four-cylinder power plant best fulfills the requirements.

The four-cylinder motor utilized in the Henderson motorcycle, an American design previously illustrated, is shown installed in the frame at Fig. 66 when viewed from the valve side, and in section to show practically all the details of construction at Fig. 67. In general

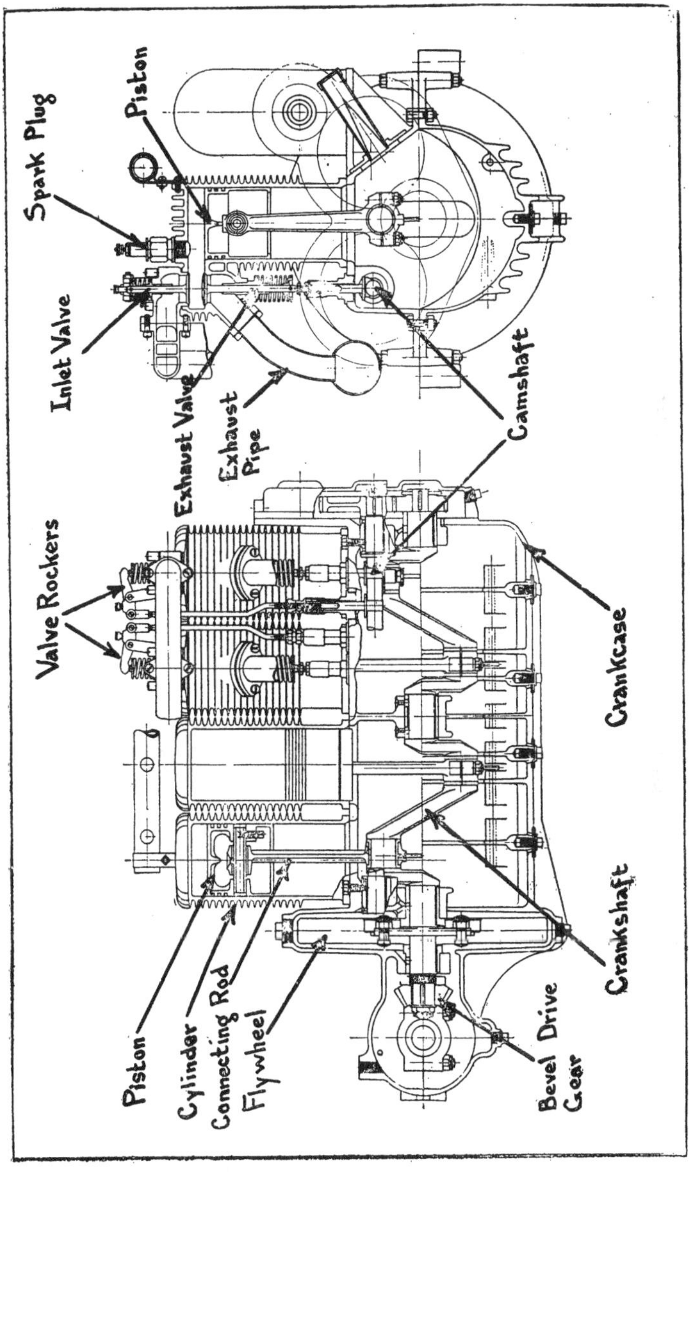

Fig. 67.—Sectional Views Defining Internal Construction of Henderson Four Cylinder Motorcycle Power Plant.

arrangement of parts, this power plant follows the lines established in automobile practice. A sectional view of the F. N. four-cylinder engine, which shows the practical application of a five-bearing crankshaft and the arrangement of the crank-pins, so two pistons are going down while the other two are on their up stroke, is presented at Fig. 68. It will be noticed that the Henderson crankshaft, while it has four crank throws, is a three-bearing form, having one main journal at the center and one at each end, whereas the F. N. design has a

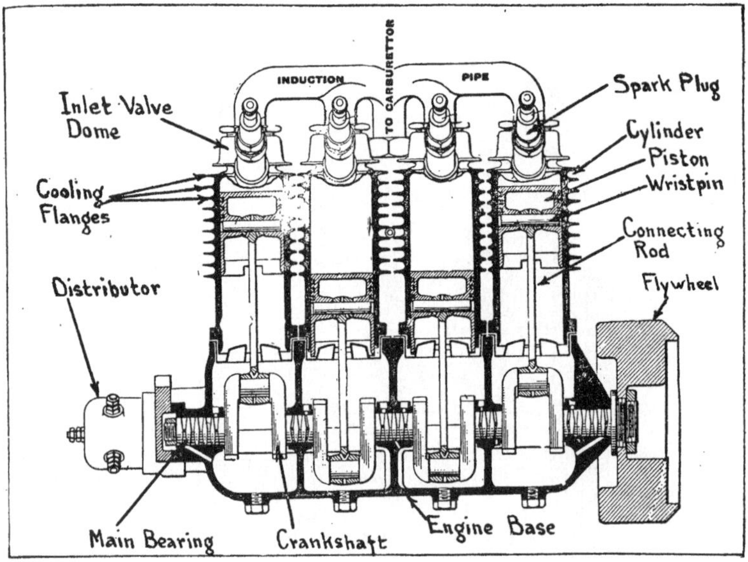

Fig. 68.—Sectional View of the F. N. Four Cylinder Motor.

bearing between all crank throws as well as at the ends of the crankshaft.

Power Plant Support and Location.—We have seen that in the early days the designers considered the gasoline motor an attachment to the bicycle, and that it was disposed of in numerous ways, few of which were really satisfactory and effective. The average rider who is familiar with present practice may not consider that power plant location or support is much of a problem, and in view of the remarkable unanimity of opinion regarding power plant placing in modern machines, this view is, to a certain extent, justified, though those who have been identified with motorcycle construction long enough know that considerable experimentation was necessary before the designers of power-propelled cycles were able to place the power plant to the best advantage. As soon as designers realized that the power plant was an important component part of the vehicle and that it should

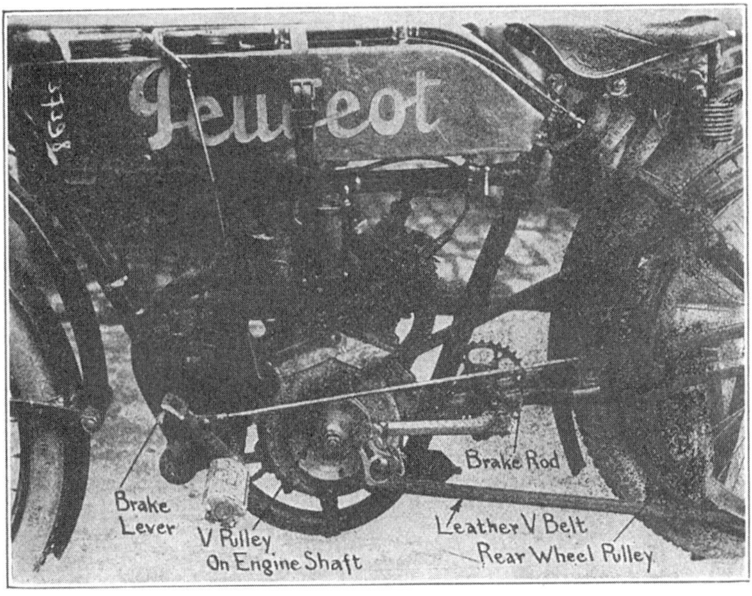

Fig. 69.—The Peugeot (French) Motorcycle Power Plant Installed in Frame.

be incorporated in the design, the diamond frame was abandoned, and special frame constructions evolved, in which provision was made for the secure anchorage of the engine base.

The non-technical reader has no comprehension of the amount of stress present at the points of motor support and why these must be amply strong, but some idea may be gained if one considers that all the time the motor is driving the rear wheel there is a reaction or pull on the engine fastenings that tends to loosen it from its supports. This force is equal to that exerted by the motor to drive the motorcycle. In addition to the torque reaction, as this force is called, there is an added twisting stress due to the common system of taking the power from one side of the motor only, which tends to turn the motor on a vertical axis, whereas the torque reaction tends to rotate the power plant on a horizontal axis at the center line of the crankshaft. Besides securing ample strength in the design of motor supports, it is also important to mount the power plant in a way that

Fig. 70.—Valve Side of the Excelsior Twin Cylinder Power Plant.

will permit of its ready removal from the frame for repairs. It is also desirable to have the motor fastened securely enough so the frame structure will resist its tendency to vibrate at all speeds except at the critical speed for which the balance weights were calculated, therefore some makers anchor the cylinders to the frame tubes as well as the engine base.

The loop frame design is widely employed because the motor may be removed from the frame without disturbing the integrity of the frame structure. Designers who favor this method of motor support also contend that the engine base is better protected when mounted above a substantial frame tube than when suspended so it forms part of the frame. The installation of the Peugeot engine in a loop frame of substantial design is shown at Fig. 69, and in this construction it is not believed necessary to anchor the cylinders to the frame in any way. When the cylinders are not secured to the frame and a loop

Fig. 71.—Valve Side of the Yale Twin Cylinder Power Plant. Note Design of Cooling Flanges, Which Permit an Unobstructed Flow of Air Over the Cylinders.

frame is employed, it is possible to remove a cylinder from the crank-case, in many cases, without removing that member from the frame. The crank-case may be made lighter when it is not an integral part of the frame, and should the frame weave there is no strain imposed on the cylinder as that member is free to move slightly even though the crank-case is securely held.

In the Excelsior machine, the power plant forms a part of the frame, and is depended upon to give the frame strength, as that member would not be very strong with the engine base removed. Of course, the makers contend that there is no need for strength when the motor is not in place because at such times the motorcycle is out of commission, but there is always the liability of springing the lower portions of the tubes when they are not supported if the frame is carelessly handled when the motor is not in place. A loop frame is much stronger than the forms shown at Figs. 70 and 71, when the motor is removed, and there is no possibility of distorting the frame. The Excelsior motor is supported at five points, and, when in place, the structure is very strong. As the lower portion of the crank-case is exposed, it is made heavier and stronger than in the forms where it is protected by the frame tube loop, and this added strength has a favorable bearing on general rigidity of the assembly. The motor is supported at three points on the crank-case, two being at the rear and one at the front, and each of the cylinders is attached to the frame member below the tank by substantial clips. This method of attachment is very valuable in open-frame machines where there is some opportunity for frame weaving, especially if the power plant retaining bolts loosen even a slight amount.

While the attachment of the cylinders steadies the motor wonderfully, and holds it in place, some who do not favor this construction contend that the expansion of the cylinders when heated renders it imperative to have the upper end of the cylinders free to move under its influence. This objection seems to be more theoretical than real because machines with the cylinders anchored have given just as good service in practical application as those that were free to expand unhindered.

The Yale power plant, shown at Fig. 71, is anchored to the frame in much the same manner as the Excelsior, as the rear end of the engine base is attached to substantial plate members firmly secured to the crank hanger, while the front portion is provided with a lug fitting between the jaws of the fork attached to the lower end of the diagonal frame tube. The water-cooled power plant of the Regal-Green motorcycle, an English design depicted at Fig. 72, also forms part of the frame assembly and is fastened in much the same manner as the Excelsior and Yale power plants. The method of installing

Fig. 72.—Showing the Application of the Precision Water-Cooled Motor on Regal-Green Motorcycle.

a four-cylinder power plant is exemplified at Fig. 66 which shows the fastenings that hold the Henderson motor in place. The lower portion of the frame is composed of two parallel tubes which converge at the front end to the steering head, and as there is sufficient space between them for the comparatively narrow crank-case possible with the small four-cylinder design, this member may be provided with suitable lugs or arms cast integral which rest on the frame tubes and be securely

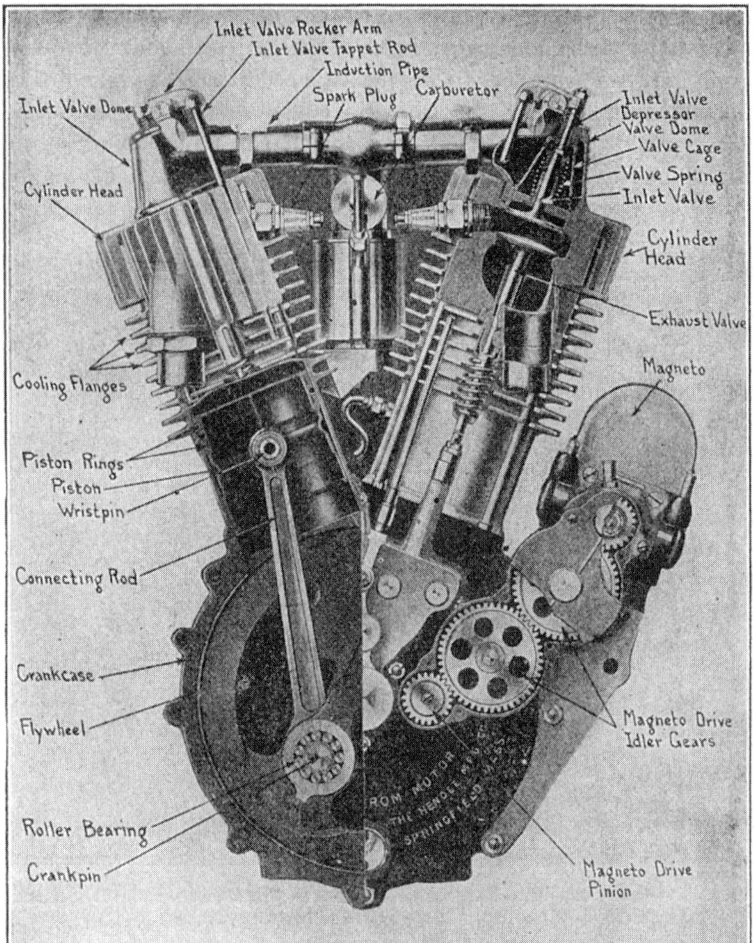

Fig. 73.—Part Sectional View Showing Arrangement of Important Internal Parts of Two Cylinder Indian Motorcycle Power Plant.

retained by bolts or studs passing through the tube and crank-case extensions. A very secure four-point suspension system is obtained in this manner, and owing to the smooth running and lack of vibration, incidental to the employment of a four-cylinder engine, it is not necessary to anchor the cylinders to the frame in any way except by the necessary bolts which keep them in place on the engine base.

Motorcycle Engine Parts and Their Functions.—In order that the non-technical reader may become thoroughly familiar with the principles of operation and appearance of the various parts of motorcycle power plants a number of forms will be described and the functions of the various parts made clear. The engine at Fig. 73 is shown in part section as the crank-case and the lower part of one of the cylinders is cut away, while the other cylinder is sectioned through the valve chamber. The engine consists of an engine base, which also serves as a crank-case to which the two cylinders and all other parts are attached. The members inside the cylinders that reciprocate up and down, and which receive the force of the explosion, are termed "pistons," and there is one in each cylinder. The reciprocating movement of these pistons is converted into a rotary movement of the crank-pin by means of connecting rods which oscillate at their upper ends on wrist pins that pass through suitable bosses in the piston. The inlet valve, which is the member through which the gas is admitted into the cylinder is carried in a valve cage which in turn is installed in an air-tight dome which is utilized to press the valve cage firmly against the seating in the cylinder head. The inlet valve is normally kept seated by a valve spring, and is opened at the proper time by the inlet valve depresser, which is worked by the inlet valve rocker arm. The rocker arm is operated by a tappet rod which extends to the top of the cylinder from the timing gear case. The exhaust valve is the member controlling the port through which the burnt gases leave the cylinder, and this is raised from its seat at the desired period in the cycle of operations by a push rod that bears against the lower portion of the valve stem. The exhaust valve is kept seated in the same manner as the inlet valve though the spring is stronger.

The spark plugs which are inserted in the combustion chambers are employed to explode the gas with a spark derived from the magneto which is driven by a train of gearing from the crankshaft. The cylinder heads, as well as the cylinders, are provided with cooling flanges and are held in place on the cylinders by bolts extending to the crank-case which also serves to hold the cylinders firmly by clamping them between the heads and engine base. The fly-wheels are

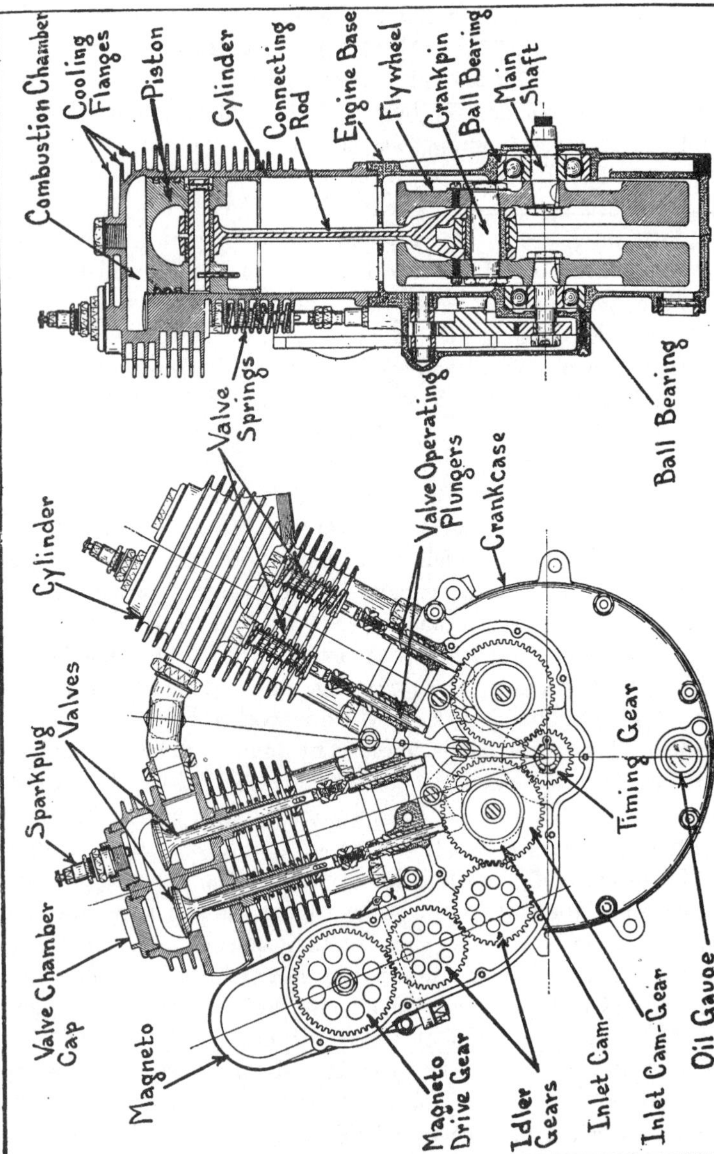

Fig. 74.—Sectional View Outlining Construction of the Reading-Standard Twin Cylinder Power Plant.

employed to steady the action of the engine, and to store up power during the idle strokes in order to keep the engine parts in motion at such times as there is no useful pressure exerted against the piston tops. The carburetor that supplies the explosive gas to the cylinders is securely attached to an induction pipe that joins the inlet valve domes of the two cylinders.

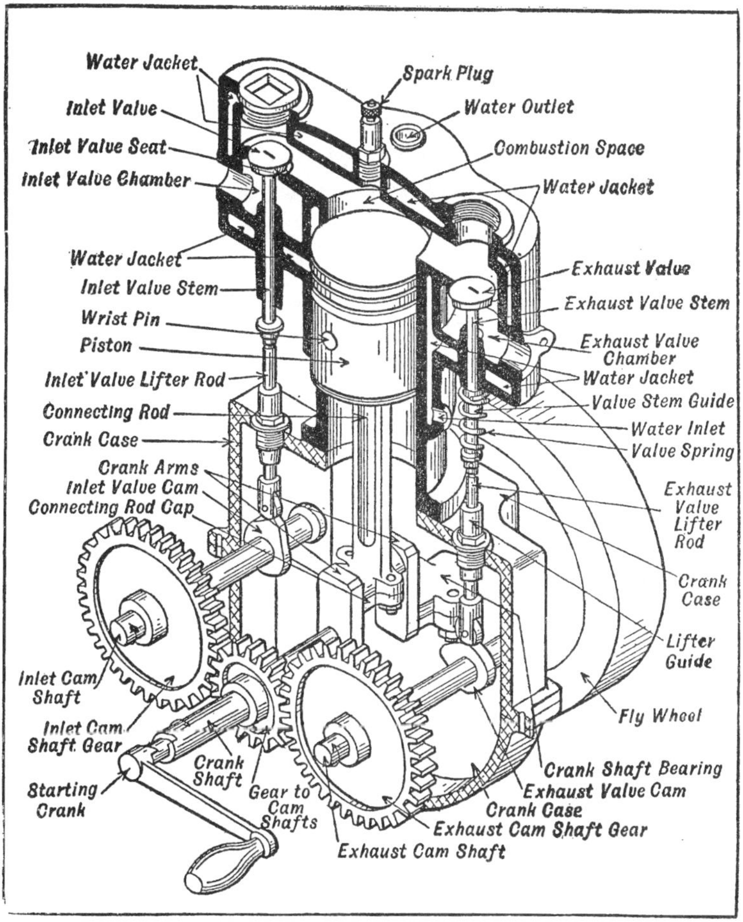

Fig. 75.—Diagram Showing Principal Parts of Single Cylinder Water-Cooled T Head Power Plant.

The twin-cylinder power plant, shown at Fig. 74, is practically the same in operation as that previously described though the cylinder design and location of valves is very much different. In the side view, the valve-operating mechanism and the magneto drive gears are clearly outlined, while in the sectional view at the right, the arrangement of the fly-wheel and crankshaft assembly and the method of supporting it on ball bearings is outlined. The engine at Fig. 75 is a simple T-head form with water jacket, and is a type that is used to some extent on light cars and cyclecars. All parts are clearly indicated, and in view of the explanations previously given regarding the duties of these parts, the reader should have no difficulty in understanding the relation they bear to each other in the complete power plant, and the part they play when the engine functions.

CHAPTER III.

CONSTRUCTION AND DESIGN OF ENGINE PARTS.

Methods of Cylinder Construction—Advantages of Detachable Heads—Material Employed and Methods of Finishing—Combustion Chamber Design—Relation of Valve Placing to Engine Efficiency—Bore and Stroke Ratio—Influence of Compression on Power Developed—Offset Cylinders—Automatic and Mechanical Valves—Valve Design and Construction—How Valves are Operated—Valve Timing—Pistons and Rings—Wrist-Pin and Connecting Rod Arrangements—Crankshaft Forms and Fly-wheels—Engine Base Design and Construction—Plain and Anti-Friction Engine Bearings.

Methods of Cylinder Construction.—There are two general designs of cylinder construction followed by motorcycle designers, namely, the one-piece and the two-piece types. A typical cylinder of the one-piece pattern is depicted at Fig. 76 in connection with the piston, its wrist-pin and one of the piston rings. The cylinder in place on a single-cylinder power plant of Spacke make is shown at Fig. 77, while the part sectional view at Fig. 78 shows clearly the one-piece construction. In the early days, before the development of satisfactory cylinder-head packing, and when sheet asbestos and copper were the only packing mediums known for obtaining a gas-tight joint between the cylinder and cylinder head, there was considerable trouble experienced due to loss of compression and power through leaky packings. It was found that the sheet asbestos did not have sufficient strength to resist the high pressure, and the sheet metal packings were too hard to conform to any irregularities that might exist in the seating between the combustion chamber and cylinder when these were separate castings held together by clamping bolts. The complaints voiced by the riders against the two-piece construction led many manufacturers to cast their cylinders and valve chambers in one piece instead of depending upon any kind of a packing, as necessary in the two-piece construction.

While the one-piece cylinder offers advantages of some moment, in reducing the liability of leakage by eliminating a packed joint, it has the disadvantage of rendering the piston considerably more inaccessible than was the case where the cylinder head could be removed from the cylinders and expose the piston top so carbon deposits could be removed easily without taking the cylinder off of the engine base. With a one-piece construction, it is, of course, necessary to remove

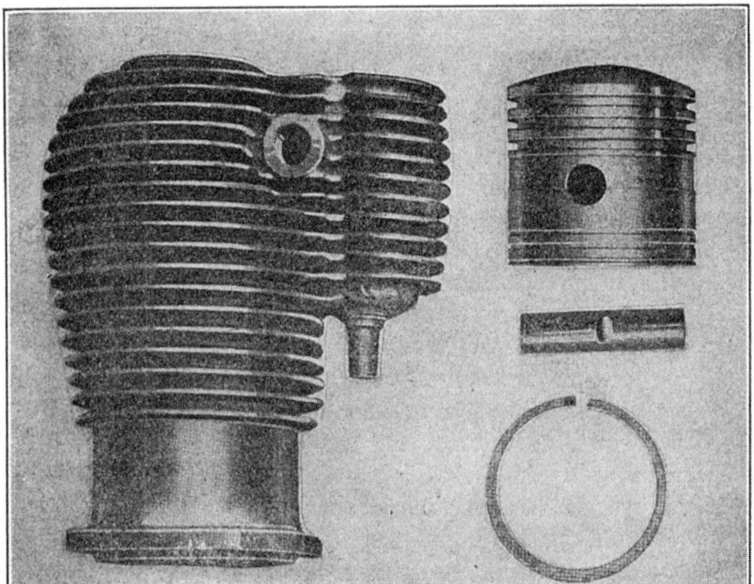

Fig. 76.—One-Piece Cylinder Construction, Also Dome Head Piston, Wrist Pin and One of the Eccentric Piston Rings Used With It.

the cylinder. Another advantage possessed by the detachable combustion head construction is that it is possible to grind the valves in very easily when that member is removed, as it can be taken to the bench and placed in a vise where it can be held securely and worked on to advantage. In grinding the valves, particularly the exhaust, in most cylinders of the one-piece pattern, if one does not wish to take the entire cylinder assembly from the crank-case to gain access to

Fig. 77.—Exterior View of the De Luxe Single Cylinder Motorcycle Power Plant, Showing Practical Application of One-Piece Cylinder.

the cylinder from the engine, the work must be done with that member in place, and there is always a possibility of having some of the abrasive used in valve grinding find its way into the cylinder interior, where it would do considerable harm by causing scratches that run the length of the cylinder, and which interfere materially with retaining proper compression. Of course, it is not necessary for the rider to get the abrasive into the cylinder, but at the same time many inexperienced persons, when grinding valves, have not realized the importance of keeping the emery from the cylinder interior, and trouble has been experienced owing to unintentional neglect of this essential precaution.

The inlet valve of most motorcycle engines is carried in an easily detachable cage which incorporates the valve seat, and it is, therefore, easy to grind this member at the bench. There are cylinder forms, however, of the T or L design where both inlet and exhaust valves seat directly in the valve chamber. In cases of this kind there would, of course, be just as much liability of emery getting into the cylinder while grinding the inlet valve as when fitting the exhaust member. The one-piece cylinder construction has the material advantage of considerably simplifying the motor construction as it eliminates the extra piece or casting that is necessary if the combustion chamber is separate from the cylinder.

Advantages of Detachable Cylinder Heads.—The sectional view of the engine depicted at Fig. 79 shows clearly the construction of a detachable head and the method of holding it in place on the cylinder casting. It will be observed that the cylinder head not only includes the combustion chamber but also incorporates the extension in which the valves are located. The cylinder is a simple ribbed cylindrical member which can be easily handled in casting and machining. It is held in place against a seating on the engine base by long bolts or studs which screw into the crank-case at the lower end, and which have nuts at the upper end to clamp the detachable head firmly in place. In the engine shown, three bolts are used, but owing to their disposition but one of the bolts shows in this view. It will be evident that the cylinder acts as a spacer between the detachable head and the crank-case, and that the retention bolts serve to draw the head and crank-case together, thus clamping the cylinder firmly

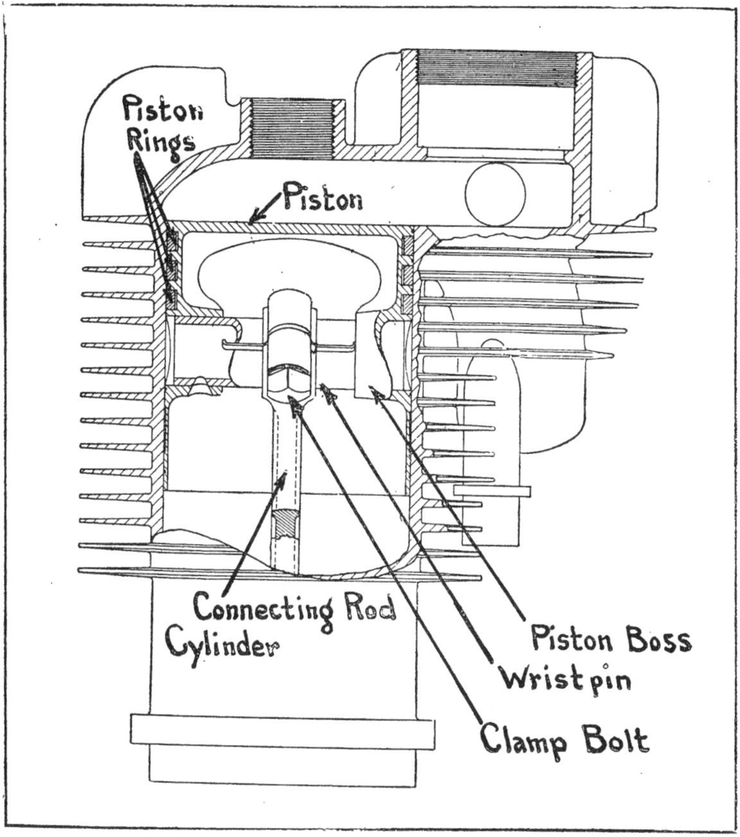

Fig. 78.—Part Sectional View of One-Piece Cylinder, Defining Construction of Piston, Wrist Pin, and Upper End of Connecting Rod.

in place. The two-piece construction is quite practical at the present time because great improvements have been made in the construction of gaskets or packings.

The sheet asbestos formerly used had the advantage of being compressible and thus forming a very good packing, though the light rings of this soft material were very fragile and could not be used more than once, as they were invariably destroyed when the cylinder head was removed from the cylinder. The hard copper did not bed itself properly, and unless the retaining bolts were tightened down practically the same at the three points on the cylinder head there was very apt to be a compression and explosion leak because the inflexible material did not permit the head to bear down against the gasket resting on the cylinder. As both forms of packing had their merits, it occurred to some designers to try a combination of the two materials and a gasket or packing ring was evolved that consisted of sheet asbestos ring enclosed in a shell of very light sheet copper or brass. The metal held the asbestos in place firmly and provided an item of strength that was desirable. At the other hand, the light gauge of the copper used did not interfere materially with the flexible properties of the asbestos, and the gasket readily conformed to any slight irregularity or roughness on the cylinder or cylinder head seat. This form of gasket practically eliminated the troubles which were present in the old detachable head engine, and many designers continued to use the two-piece construction.

In addition to the big feature of providing a degree of accessibility to the piston top and combustion chamber interior for removing carbon deposits without dismantling the entire engine, there was retained the added advantage of having a cylinder head available that permitted grinding in the exhaust valves without danger of abrasive matter getting into the cylinder. Another feature of merit in connection with the detachable head construction is that cylinder replacements are less expensive than is the case when a one-piece cylinder is employed. As will be evident, practically all of the depreciation will exist at that portion of the cylinder that is traversed by the piston. Therefore, with the one-piece construction when the cylinder became worn to a point where it was desirable to replace it because the thinness of the metal in most motorcycle cylinders does not permit of reboring or grinding to remove deep scratches, it was necessary to throw away a perfectly good combustion head and valve seatings, which had depreciated but slightly in service. With the detachable cylinder construction if that member wears it can be cheaply renewed, and the combustion head can be used just as well with the new cylinder as with the old one. It is also possible to machine the interior of the combustion chamber more easily with the separable head con-

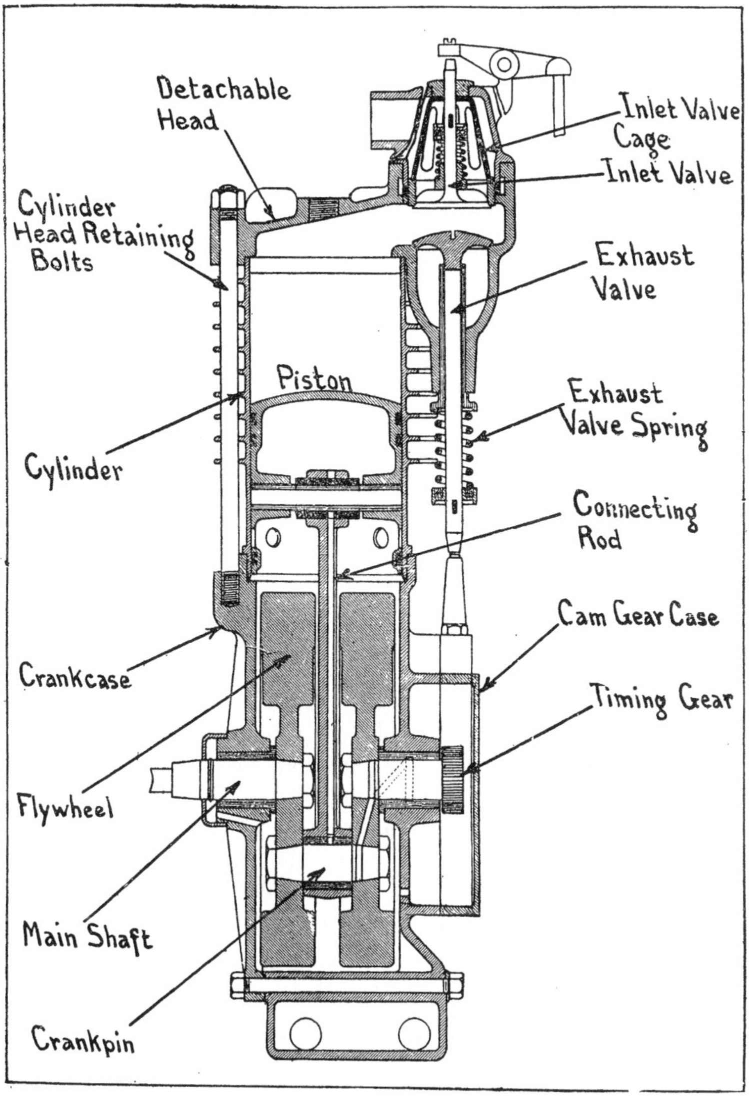

Fig. 79.—Sectional View of Single Cylinder Motor of English Design Using Detachable Cylinder Head.

struction. This is a feature of some importance, especially in overhead valve types.

Materials Employed and Method of Finishing.—Cylinders are invariably made of close grain gray iron which contains considerably more phosphorus than is usually found in the ordinary grades of cast iron because the metal must be capable of flowing readily and filling the mould. It would be rather difficult to use the ordinary casting metal because it would not flow readily into the small spaces left in the sand when the flanges are moulded, but the metal containing phosphorus in larger proportions fills these spaces completely, and makes it possible to obtain cylinder castings with perfectly formed cooling flanges. Some of the cast irons used in cylinder construction also contain some tungsten, and this alloying element produces an iron that has a high degree of resistance to heat.

The common method of finishing cylinders of the simple form, i. e., without a cylinder head is to bore these out with a roughing cut and then to anneal the castings and allow them to age for a time before the finishing processes take place. The reason for the annealing and aging is to remove any internal stresses that may have been left in the cylinder casting when the moulten metal cooled, and usually removing the scale as is done by the roughing cut, permits the cylinders to distort appreciably. If the finishing process is continued right after the rough boring without the annealing, just as soon as the cylinder was put in service it would be apt to distort sufficiently under the high heat to produce some friction between the piston and cylinder walls. In annealing the cylinders, they are placed in a furnace and heated to a higher temperature than will ever be produced by the explosions after they are in service. This tends to not only relieve the strains produced in casting but after the cylinders are cooled they have distorted as much as they ever will. The aging process is a simple one as it consists of allowing the cylinders to remain undisturbed after they cool for several weeks.

There are two methods of finishing the cylinders followed by most engine builders. One of these consists in taking a finishing cut or of removing enough metal from the cylinder bore, so the size is very close to standard, after which the remaining metal is removed by reaming. The other method is to grind out the surplus metal by high speed emery wheels mounted on a spindle that is adapted to traverse the length of the cylinder. Those who favor reaming contend that the grinding process will deposit small particles of emery in the open pores of the cast iron, and that this material is only dislodged after the engine is placed in service, at which time it will cause trouble by producing scratches on the cylinder walls. Those who favor grinding contend that the reaming process does not produce as true and smooth a bore as grinding, because if a reamer blade strikes a hard spot in the metal of the cylinder wall it will spring away from the hard portion and cut a little deeper than it should in the softer portions opposite. Some makers follow the reaming process with a lapping operation, which is done by revolving the cylinder in a suitable fixture, and at the same time having a dummy piston made of some soft metal, charged with abrasive and oil, reciprocate rapidly up and down in the cylinder while it revolves. Engines that have the cylinders finished by the lapping process do not need to be run in as long on the block as those in which the cylinders are either reamed or ground to a standard size.

Combustion Chamber Design.—One of the important considerations in the design of the internal combustion motor, and one that has material bearing on its efficiency, is the shape of the combustion chamber, and this is especially true of the air-cooled forms of cylinders which operate at considerably higher temperatures than the water-cooled forms. The endeavor is made to use a form of combustion chamber that will provide for the least heat loss, and that will not interfere with a balanced design of a cylinder. Theoretically, any cylinders having pockets at the side to hold the valves are not as desirable as those forms in which the valves are placed directly in the head, and where the cylinder is uniform in diameter at all points. It is contended by designers favoring valve-in-the-head location that the expansion and contraction of the cylinder will be uniform because the metal is evenly distributed whereas on most patterns, having extensions at the side, the irregular placing of the metal will mean that one portion of the cylinder becomes hotter than the other part, and as it will not cool as fast, the cylinder will not expand and contract evenly at all points. The greater the amount of metal to be heated, the more the heat loss and the less efficient the engine. The im-

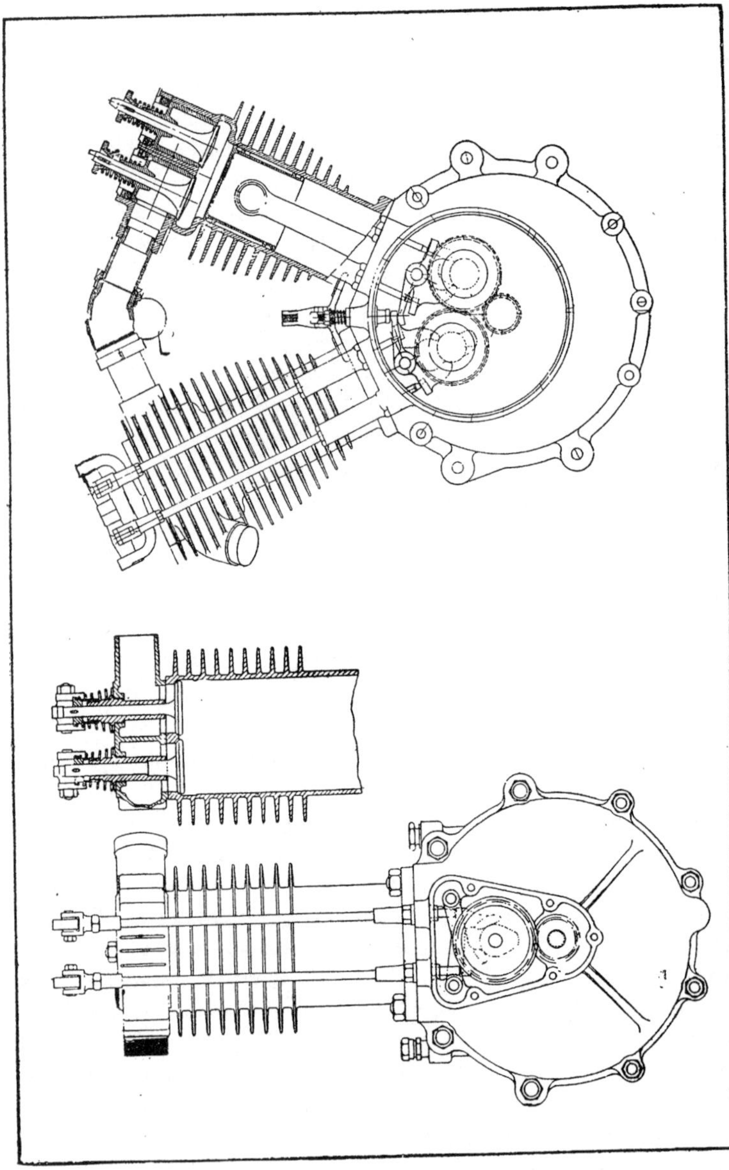

Fig. 80.—Typical Valve-in-the-Head Motors, Showing Methods of Installing the Valves so They Will Open Directly Into the Combustion Chamber.

portant factor that has to do with the form of the combustion chamber used is that of valve placing, and there is considerable diversity in practice as relates to location of the members that control the ingress and egress of gas to or from the cylinders.

Relation of Valve Placing to Engine Efficiency.—The fundamental consideration that determines valve location is that the gas be admitted to the cylinder as quickly as the speed demands, and that after it has been properly compacted and exploded that the inert products of combustion should be exhausted or discharged from the cylinder with as little back pressure as possible. While this is an imperative condition if one is to obtain satisfactory operation from any type of gasoline engine, either air or water-cooled, imperfect operation of the valves will be manifested much sooner in the small high-speed air-cooled motorcycle power plants. For example, if the form of the combustion chamber is such that the entrance of fresh gas is impeded, the cylinder will not fill thoroughly with mixture at high speeds, whereas if the exhaust gas flow is impeded to any extent a part of the burnt gases will be retained in the cylinder, and these will reduce efficiency by diluting the fresh charge and making it slower burning, and thus cause lost power and overheating.

Another factor that has a decided bearing upon the rotative speeds of small internal combustion engines is the sizes of the valves, and some valve locations permit the use of larger valves than do other positions. As will be seen by reference to illustrations, Figs. 80 to 85, inclusive, there are many ways of installing the valves, and that each method outlined must possess some points of merit is best proven by the fact that practically all of the forms illustrated are used by reputable manufacturers of motorcycles.

The valve in the head system, which is shown in two forms at Fig. 80, possesses important advantages from a theoretical point of view, and actual performance has indicated that it is a very desirable form of construction. When the valves are placed directly in the head, the inflow is direct, and the discharge is obtained with minimum back pressure. The inside of the combustion chamber may be machined, making a very good construction for an air-cooled cylinder. The cylinder casting is simple, and large valves may be employed which can be easily removed if either the cage or the removable head construction are used. The machined combustion chamber is advantageous for several reasons, one of the most important of which is that there are no sharp edges or corners to become hot and cause pre-ignition of the charge, and it is also difficult for carbon deposits to lodge on perfectly smooth machined surfaces. The combustion

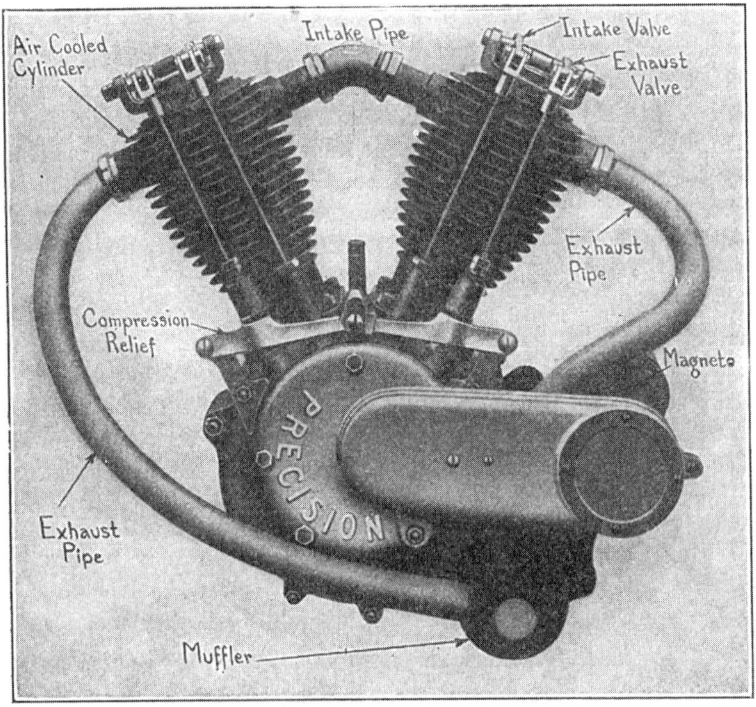

Fig. 81.—The Precision Twin Cylinder Valve-in-the-Head Motorcycle or Cyclecar Power Plant.

chamber is uniform in shape, and expansion will be even when the cylinder is heated.

When the valves are placed in the head there are two main methods of construction followed. In one of these, the head casting is removable, and the valves seat directly in that member. In the other construction, the valves are carried in cages inserted into openings provided for their reception when the cylinder is a one-piece member. The valve-in-the-head motor shown at Fig. 81 is the same as that outlined in section at Fig. 80, and the method of operating the valves when at the top of the cylinder may be readily understood. The valves are not always placed with the stems vertical, so that they are

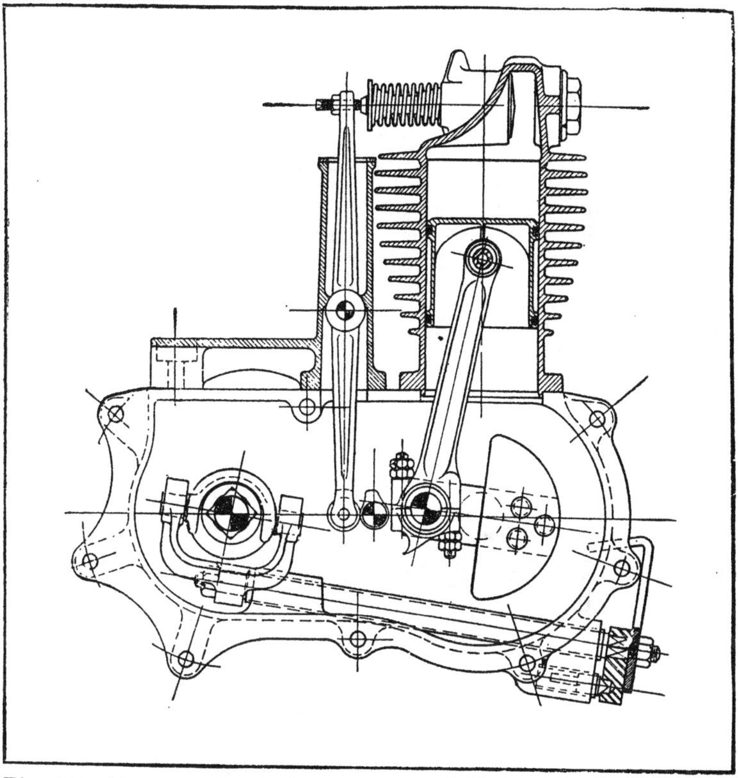

Fig. 82.—Unconventional Arrangement of Valves in the Precision Junior Motorcycle Power Plant.

pushed down by rocker arms when it is desired to admit gas into the cylinder or to open a port for its discharge, as in some cases the valves are placed with their stems horizontal as shown at Figs. 82 and 83. The former shows a light English power plant in which the valves seat directly in the cylinder head. They are actuated by long rocker

Fig. 83.—An Unconventional American Motorcycle Power Plant of Early Design in Which the Horizontal Valves Open Directly Into a Vertical Combustion Chamber.

arms fulcrumed at approximately their central point, and have a roll at the lower end to follow cam profiles, while an adjustable set screw at the upper end imparts motion to the horizontal valve stem. The valves may be readily exposed for grinding by removing the valve cap at the front of the cylinder. The valves are placed side by side, and both are mechanically operated.

The peculiar method of valve placing shown at Fig. 83 was used with some degree of success on one of the earlier American motorcycles known as the Royal. In this, the valves were carried in cages that bolted to an extension from the top of the cylinder that formed a narrow combustion chamber. The valves were placed horizontally, and were operated by bell cranks pivoted on the valve cage extension, and these were actuated by tension rods instead of the usual form of compression or push rod. The valves were opened by a downward movement or pull of the rod instead of by an upward motion as is now conventional practice. The engine described proved very satisfactory in practical service, and many machines were made using this unconventional power plant before the manufacture of these machines was discontinued.

The usual arrangement of the valves is as depicted at Figs. 84 and 85. In this system, which is the oldest in use, as it was originated by Daimler, the inlet valve is located directly above the exhaust member, and is usually carried in a valve cage held in place by a suitable dome or other retaining means. The dome on the Indian motor, which is shown at Fig. 85, is secured in place by an ingenious bayonet lock arrangement so it can be easily removed by moving it over from the position shown about half a turn and lifting it out. The form of combustion chamber made possible has considerable merit, especially in air-cooled motors, as the fresh, cool gases from the carburetor strike the exhaust valve head, and have a very beneficial effect as they assist in reducing the temperature and by preventing the valve head from overheating, the valve or its seating is not so apt to warp and pit as would be the case if it were not adequately cooled. The inlet valve may be of either the automatic or mechanically operated type, though, at the present time, practically all inlet valves are actuated by positive mechanical means. The cylinder is an easy form to machine, and the casting, even when the combustion chamber is integral with the cylinder, is not a difficult one to make.

One of the disadvantages of this construction is that if large valves are employed, the pocket must be of corresponding size, and considerable heat loss will result, due to the irregular form of the com-

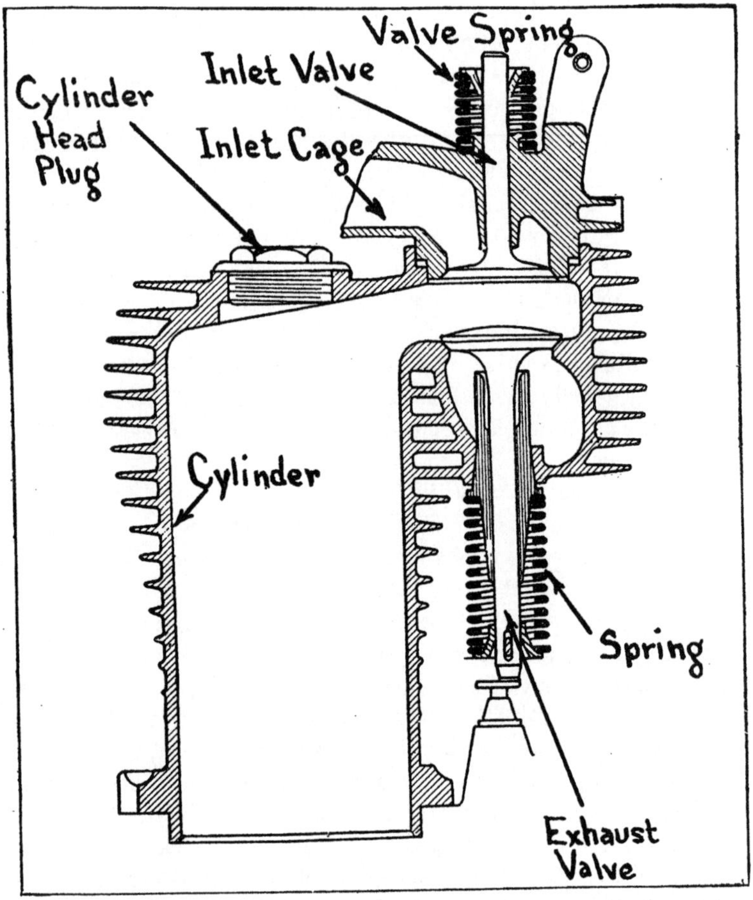

Fig. 84.—One-Piece Motorcycle Cylinder, Showing the Valve Arrangement Generally Employed.

bustion chamber. The gases cannot be discharged as directly as when the valves are placed in the head, as there is a sharp corner that must be turned whether the gas is flowing in or out of the cylinder. This feature is not one that is of sufficient importance to be advanced as a positive disadvantage, because so many of the very efficient motorcycle power plants have the valves arranged in the manner shown that the practicability of this arrangement cannot be questioned. It is customary, when the valves are arranged in the manner described, to locate the spark plugs in the side of the combustion chamber so the points or electrodes will be swept by the incoming gases. This tends to keep the temperature down and to keep them free of oil to some extent.

The form of cylinder shown at Fig. 88 is known as the L-cylinder, because of its shape. The valves are side by side and are located in a common extension from the combustion chamber, and in multiple cylinder tandem forms, it is possible to operate all valves from a common single cam shaft. The valve chamber is closed by threaded plugs at the top, and the valves may be easily reached by removing these members. A very simple valve-operating system is possible, and the springs and valve adjustments are easily reached when desired. The chief disadvantage advanced against this form of cylinder is that a very large pocket is necessary unless the valves are restricted in size. If considered from a purely theoretical point of view, this form of cylinder has the same disadvantages as the T-head form, in which the valves are placed at opposite sides of the cylinder, each in a separate extension, though to a somewhat lesser degree. The combustion chamber form that is most effective is that in which the valves are placed directly in the head, and next in order comes that shown at Fig. 85, in which the valves are placed one above the other with the extension of just the size necessary for the one valve. In the form in which the valves are placed side by side the efficiency is a little greater than in the T-head form, where the combustion chamber is of a shape that permits of considerable heat loss.

The T-head construction has an important advantage in that large valves can be used, and a better balanced cylinder casting is possible than if the L-head construction is used. There are two valve chambers, usually of equal size, so the expansion is apt to be more uniform when the cylinder is heated than in those constructions having a valve chamber at but one side of the cylinder. Wherever the pocket construction is used, in addition to heat loss and the uneven cylinder expansion, it must be obvious that the passage of the gases will be impeded to some extent. For instance, consider a cylinder of the L form. When the piston goes down on its suction stroke, the

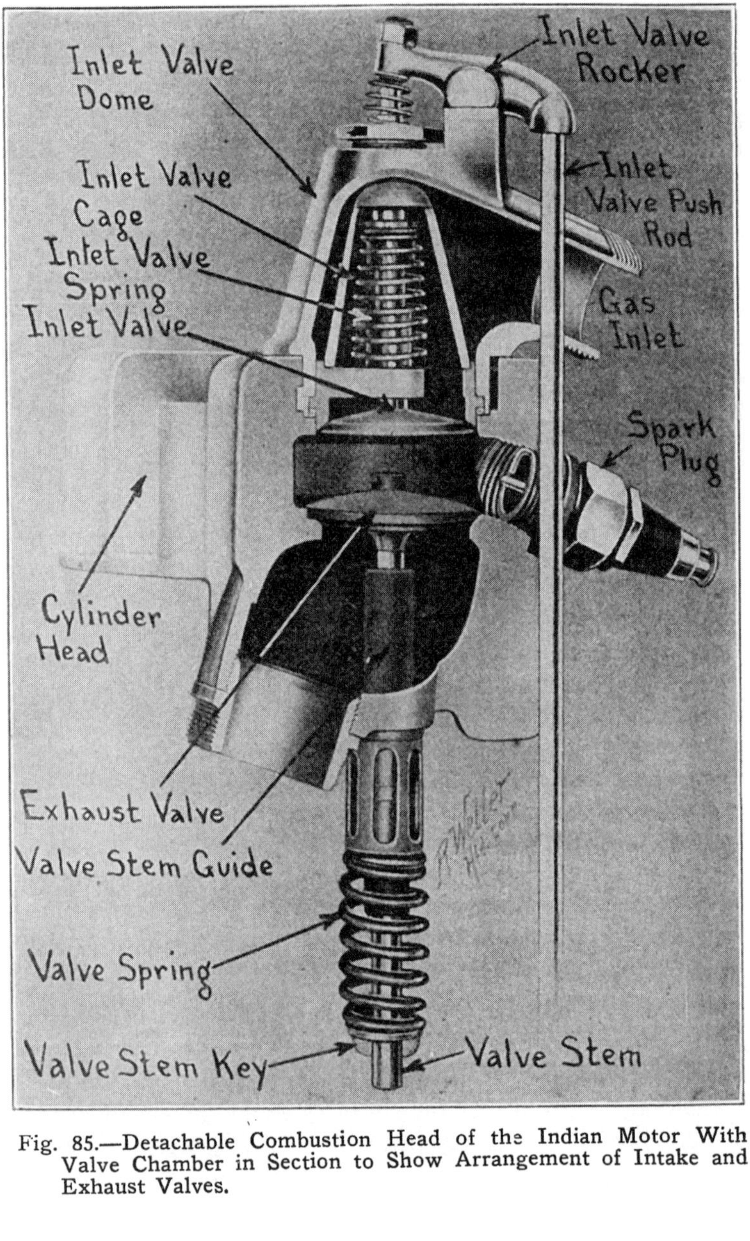

Fig. 85.—Detachable Combustion Head of the Indian Motor With Valve Chamber in Section to Show Arrangement of Intake and Exhaust Valves.

inlet gases rushing in through the open inlet valve will impinge themselves sharply upon the valve cap, and then the direction of flow changes abruptly at a sharp angle to permit the gases to enter the cylinder. The same applies to the exhaust gas, except that the direction of flow is reversed. When the valve-in-the-head type of cylinder is employed the only resistance offered to the passage of the gas is

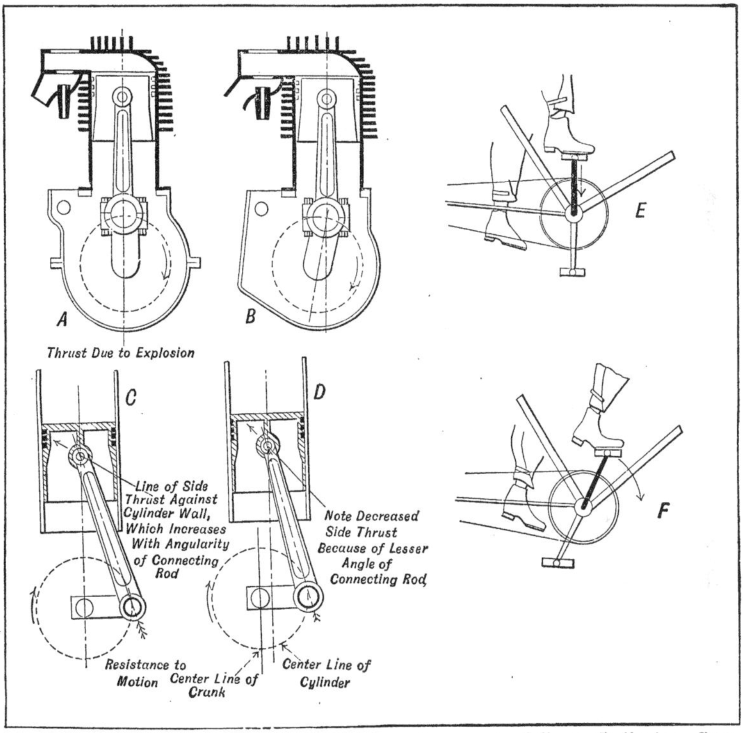

Fig. 86.—Diagrams Illustrating Advantages of Offset Cylinder Construction.

in the manifold, and if these are properly proportioned the velocity of gas flow will not be reduced much. Experience has shown that a valve-in-the-head motor is more flexible and responsive than the other forms, and in most cases it will be somewhat more efficient and deliver more power than others of the L or T form that have the same piston displacement.

Bore and Stroke Ratio.—A question that has created considerable discussion among automobile engineers is the proper relation of the bore to the stroke, and recent developments indicate that long-stroke motors, which are those forms where the piston travel is 1.5 or 1.75 times the diameter of the cylinder bore, have many advantages to commend them. While the long stroke principle is well adapted to motors designed for low and moderate speed, it is not suited as well for the small high-speed motors used as motorcycle power plants. The stroke seldom exceeds the bore by any material amount, and the usual ratio is 1 to 1.25. For example, an engine with a 3.5-inch bore would not be likely to have more than 4-inch stroke. The reason that the length of the stroke or the amount of piston travel does not exceed the diameter of the bore by any great amount is the endeavor to keep within proper limits as regards piston speed.

In an air-cooled motor, the question of lubrication is the main governing factor, which determines the velocity of piston motion, and the greater its speed, the more difficulty there is in securing proper oiling of the reciprocating member. Most automobile engineers endeavor to keep the piston speed to about 1,000 feet per minute, though in motorcycle engines satisfactory service is obtained with piston speeds as high as 1,200 feet per minute in machines built for road work and even higher if the engines are designed with the requirements of racing service in mind.

Let us consider what is meant by piston speed and how this influences the number of revolutions possible. Assume that we have an engine with a stroke of 6 inches, it is evident that during 2 strokes the piston will have covered a distance of 1 foot. As there are 2 strokes per revolution of the fly-wheel or crankshaft, it will be seen that a normal speed of 1,000 revolutions per minute is permissible for an engine with a 6-inch stroke without exceeding the limits established by engineers. If the piston had a stroke of 4 inches, 1,500 revolutions would mean a piston travel of 1,000 feet per minute, and with a 3-inch stroke, the safe speed of 1,000 feet would not be exceeded if the engine crankshaft revolved 2,000 times per minute. There is no arbitrary rule that can be cited as establishing the factor of piston speed or relation of bore to stroke definitely and in races, engines have been used where the piston speed was over twice that considered good practice.

Influence of Compression on Power Developed.—The relation of compression ratio to the amount of power obtained when the charge of gas is exploded is such that more power is obtained with high compression than where the gas is not compacted to such a degree. With water-cooled engines, such as used in general automobile practice and a few motorcycles, it is possible to use higher compressions which mean a smaller combustion chamber in relation to the volume swept by the piston than is permissible with air-cooled engines. This is because more heat is developed with a high compression prior to ignition and it is possible to compress the gas to a point where the engine would overheat rapidly owing to the limitations of the air-cooling system. An engine with a high compression is not so well adapted for general service as one with a medium compression because the engine will not be as flexible or operate as smoothly under normal service conditions. The general practice in motorcycle engines intended for road use is to use a compression pressure of about 60 pounds gauge indication which means that the gas in the cylinder and combustion chamber is compressed to about one-fourth the volume it occupies before it is compacted. In an air-cooled motor, if the compression pressure exceeds 75 or 80 pounds, the engine will heat up rapidly and the cylinder head will soon become hot enough to fire the gas without the aid of the electric spark. This results in pounding, and while the engine is more powerful than a type with lower compression, it cannot be used for any extended periods without incurring the danger of preignition.

The following table shows the maximum explosion pressure, in pounds per square inch, obtained with various degrees of compression. In this case, the compression ratio means the volume the gas occupies after compression based on an initial pressure of about 15 pounds per square inch, which is that present in the cylinder when the piston reaches the end of its suction stroke, and when the cylinder is full of gas, and, therefore, has the same pressure as the atmosphere. A compression ratio of 3 means about 45 pounds compression. A ratio of 4 about 60 pounds, etc. The actual amount of compression is not the pressure that one would obtain by multiplying the atmospheric pressure directly by the ratio of reduction in volume because compressing the charge increases the temperature, and this in turn produces an increase in pressure so that the actual compression is somewhat higher than would be obtained by a simple calculation. This variation is not sufficiently great however, so that it must be considered at length in a practical discussion; so we will assume, in comparing the results of the table appended, that the compression pressure is that of the atmosphere multiplied by the compression ratio indicated.

MAXIMUM EXPLOSION PRESSURE.

Compression Ratio.	Maximum Explosion Pressure (Pounds per square inch)
3	230
3.2	250
3.4	274
3.6	298
3.8	321
4.0	344
4.2	368
4.4	392
4.6	414
4.8	437
5.0	460

It will be evident that as the compression increases, the amount of pressure obtained when the charge is exploded augments as well, and that if there were no other consideration involved, the engine with the highest compression would give the most power.

Offset Cylinders.—In some constructions, the cylinder is placed on the engine base so its center line is to one side of the center line of the crankshaft, and diagrams are presented at Fig. 86 which make clear the advantages obtained by this method of cylinder placing. The view at A is a section through a simple motor having the conventional cylinder arrangement and the center-lines of both crankshaft and cylinder coincide. The sectional view at B shows the cylinder placed to one side of center so its center line is distinct from that of the crankshaft and at some distance from it. The amount of offset to be allowed is a point upon which considerable difference of opinion exists, the usual offset being from 15 to 25 per cent. of the stroke.

The advantages of the offset are shown at C and D. If the crankshaft turns in the direction of the arrow, there is a certain resistance to motion proportional to the resistance offered by the load which is always less than the amount of energy exerted by the engine as long as the vehicle is in motion. There are two thrusts acting against the cylinder wall to be considered, one of these due to the expansion of the gas against the piston top and the other being produced by the force that resists the motion of the piston. These thrusts may be represented by arrows, one of which acts directly in a vertical direction on the piston top, the other on a straight line through the center of the connecting rod. Between these two thrusts, a third line may be drawn to represent a resultant force that serves to bring the piston in forcible contact with one side of the cylinder wall. This angular resultant is generally termed "side thrust." In the engine shown at C which is one in which the center line of cylinder and crankshaft coincide, the crankshaft is at 90 degrees or about one-half stroke, and the connecting rod is at approximately 20 degrees angle. A shorter connecting rod would increase the diagonal resultant and side thrust, while a longer one would reduce the angle of the connecting rod, and correspondingly diminish the side thrust. With an offset construction depicted at D, it will be noted that the same connecting rod length as shown at C, and with the crankshaft in the same position, the connecting rod angle is but 14 degrees, and the side thrust is reduced proportionately.

Another important advantage is that greater efficiency is obtained from the explosion with an offset crankshaft, because the crank-pin is already inclined when the piston is at top center, and all of the energy imparted to the piston by the explosion may be utilized directly and will produce a useful turning effort. With the cylinder placed directly on a line with the crankshaft, as shown at A, some of the force produced by the explosion will be exerted in a straight line, and until the crank moves, the pressure that might be employed in obtaining useful turning effort is wasted by producing a direct pressure upon the lower half of the main bearing and the upper half of the crank-pin bushing. If one will compare the illustrations at E and F, this important advantage offered by the offset construction may be readily understood. This shows a bicycle crank hanger, and it is apparent that the effort of the rider is not as well applied when the crank is at position E as when it is at position F. In fact, practically all riders instinctively place the pedal as shown at F when starting out, because it is much easier to start the bicycle under these conditions than when the crank is straight up and down. Apparently, position E corresponds to the construction shown at A where the cylinder and crankshaft centers coincide, while that at F is comparable to the conditions present when an offset cylinder is employed.

It is advanced by those who do not favor the offset cylinder placing that while side thrust is diminished on the explosion stroke it becomes greater than in the other construction on the compression and exhaust strokes. This is true, but it would seem to the writer that it is more desirable to reduce side thrust under conditions where the maximum pressure is exerted against the piston top, as obtains during the explosion stroke, even if a little sacrifice is made on the upstroke against the much lighter pressures that are present on the compression or exhaust stroke.

Automatic and Mechanical Valves.—The first motorcycle engines evolved, as was also true of the early forms of automobile motors, had but one of the valves in each cylinder operated by mechanical means. The inlet valves could be controlled by the suction of the piston as it descended on its inlet stroke, because the difference in pressure between the cylinder interior and that of the outside air was such that a partial vacuum existed in the cylinder, and as the valve head had more pressure on its upper side than on that adjacent to the combustion chamber it would, of course, open automatically. The spring on the valve stem needed only to be heavy enough to return the valve to its seat at the end of the inlet stroke. When the pressures above and below the valve heads had become equalized through the cylinder filling with fresh gas, it was approximately at atmospheric pressure at the end of the stroke. When the piston started to go up on the compression stroke, the pressure of the gases

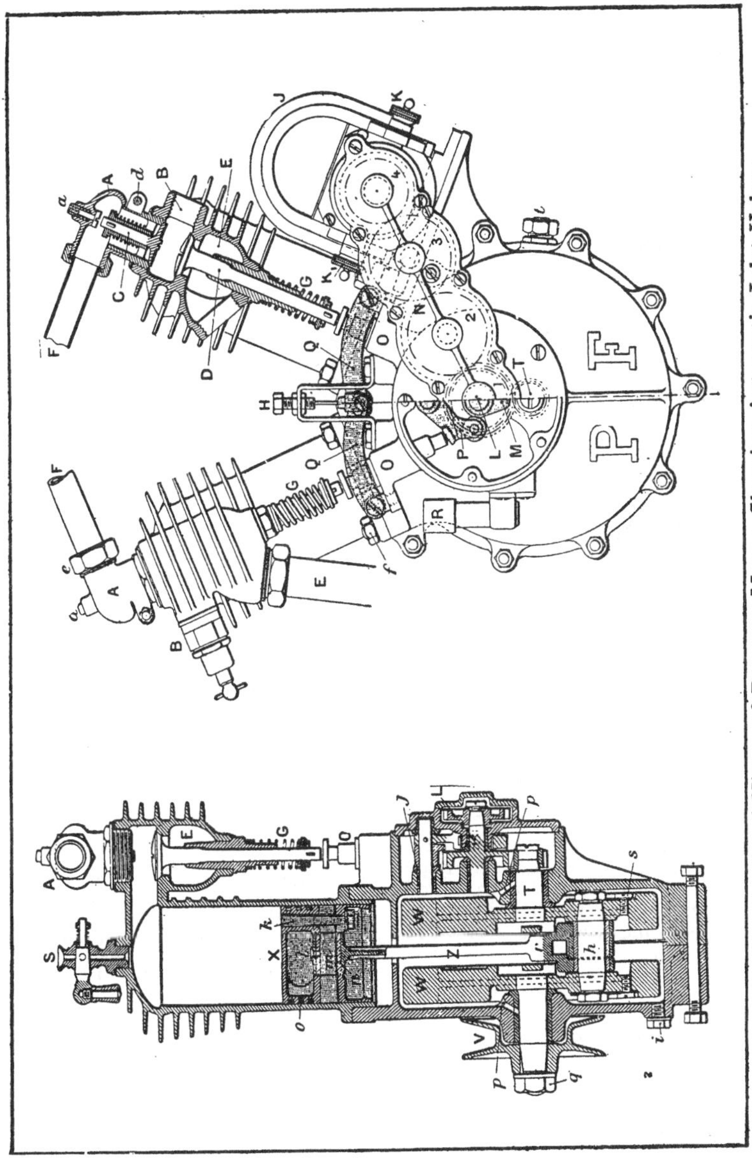

Fig. 87.—Sectional Views of Peugeot Motor, Showing Automatic Inlet Valves.

increased from that of the atmosphere to three and five times this value when the piston had reached the end of its upward movement. This compressed gas and the explosion that followed as well as the pressure in the cylinder during the exhaust stroke were always greater than that of the atmosphere, so the inlet valves remained seated, and only opened when there was a partial vacuum in the cylinder.

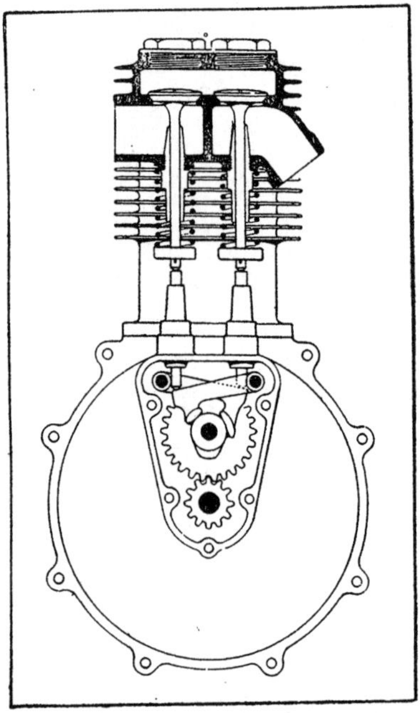

Fig. 88.—Sectional View of L Head Cylinder, Showing Arrangement of Valves When Duplicate Members are Used for Inlet and Exhaust Port Control.

The automatic valve had an important advantage and that was its simplicity, as it did not require any external operating mechanism. At the other hand, a motor fitted with automatic inlet valves was not as satisfactory, after it had been in service for a time, as the form in which the inlets were actuated mechanically. Automatic valves were apt to flutter at low engine speeds, and were not only noisy but also prevented drawing in a full charge of gas into the cylinders. Accumulations of congealed oil or carbon between the valve head and seat would tend to make these members stick, which would prevent prompt starting as well as making the valve late in opening. The light springs that were employed to reseat the valves did not have pressure enough to crush any small particles of carbon that lodged between the valve head and its seat, and, as a result, the automatic valve was apt to leak on the slightest provocation. On twin-cylinder engines used for motorcycles or on the four-cylinder types adapted for automobiles, the use of automatic valves did not conduce to smooth running because the only way of insuring that each cylinder would receive the same amount of gas was to carefully go over the inlet valves periodically to see that the tension of all the springs was the same; that each valve opened the same amount, and that all were properly cleaned. If one cylinder was lubricated more than the others, the valve in that member was apt to stick while the others would function properly. There was no uncertainty regarding exhaust valve operation because these members have, of necessity, always been actuated mechanically, so after rather unsatisfactory experiences with the automatic inlet valve, motorcycle engine designers decided to operate both valves mechanically.

The mechanical valve is positive in action, the spring used to return it to its seat can be made strong enough so that this function is performed correctly several thousand times per minute, and the valve is not susceptible to sticking owing to accumulations of oil or to remain open either partially or completely because of the interposition of some minute piece of foreign matter between the valve head and its seating. A typical motorcycle power plant of the twin-cylinder form, in which automatic inlet valves are employed, is depicted at Fig. 87. Attention is called to the inlet valve depressors mounted at the top of the inlet valve cages A. These were used to open the valves when starting the motor to make sure that they were free, and not stuck to the seat. The sectional view of the valve chamber depicted at Fig. 88 shows one application of mechanical valves, and in this form it will be apparent that the valves are duplicates, which means that the intake and exhaust valves are interchangeable, and only one spare valve need be carried as a replacement.

Valve Design and Construction.—One of the most important considerations in valve design is to have these of ample size, and many factors are to be considered before the size can be determined. Among these may be stated the location in the cylinder, the method of operation, the material employed, the degree of lift or free opening desired, the speed of rotation of the engine, and the method of cooling the engine cylinder. It will be apparent from our review of the various possible valve locations that if these members are placed directly in the cylinder head, we are not only able to obtain an ideal combustion chamber form but we can also use valves of fairly large size. The method of operation also has some bearing on the size of the valves. For example, when automatic inlet valves were used, it was the general practice to obtain the required area of valve opening by using valves of large diameter, but with less lift or movement than is ordinarily allowed for mechanical valves. For this reason, automatic valves were 15 to 20 per cent. larger in diameter than mechanically operated members. When both valves are mechanically operated,

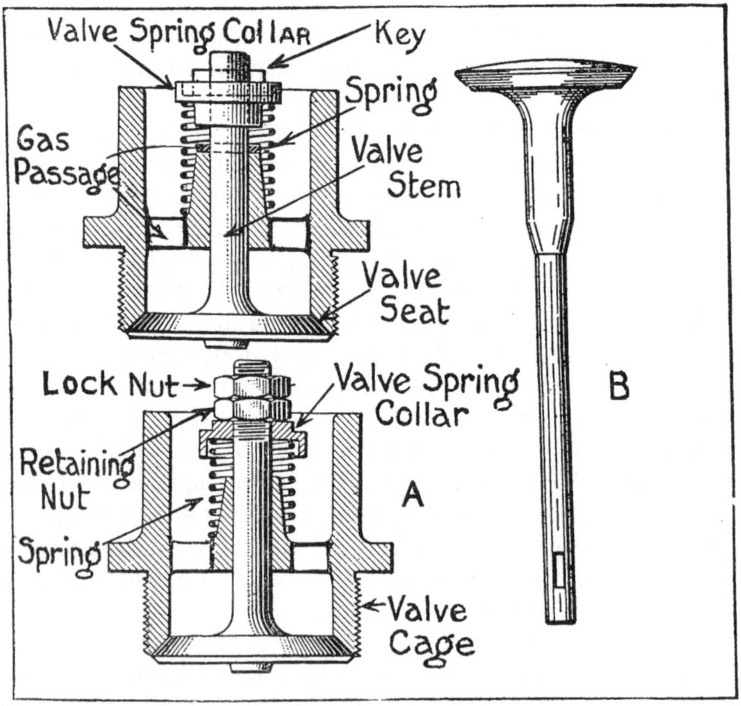

Fig. 89.—Typical Motorcycle Valves. A—Automatic Inlet Valves. B—Usual Construction of Exhaust Valves.

it is an advantage of some moment if they are made of the same size and interchangeable, as this not only greatly simplifies manufacture but is appreciated equally well by the rider if replacements are necessary.

The relation of the valve diameter to the cylinder bore is one upon which considerable difference of opinion exists. The writer has always been of the opinion that, in air-cooled engines designed for high speed, the valves should be nearly half the diameter of the bore in width, whereas others do not favor diameters in excess of one-third the bore. The larger the area of the valve the less lift required, and this is an important factor where extreme speed is desired, because the valve is more silent in operation, and there is less wear on the parts. A valve with a small lift can be opened to its maximum point by a cam with a low profile, whereas one with a small diameter and requiring greater lift will, of course, require a higher cam that will be somewhat more abrupt in action. A large valve is more subject to warping than one of lesser diameter, and this is a factor that must be considered in connection with the design of exhaust valve. The exhaust valve becomes very hot, especially if the engine is run with a rich mixture and a retarded spark, and it is necessary to make these of materials that are not apt to be affected by heat as well as proportion them so the diameter and distribution of metal around the head will tend to prevent deformation under heating.

The mushroom or poppet valve has become generally accepted in motorcycle practice, though in automobile engineering considerable attention is being paid to development of various types of sleeve, sliding ring, reciprocating piston or rotary forms of valves. The flat seat valve is seldom used in motorcycle practice, though it has been applied to some extent on automobile engines. The usual construction is to use types in which the face of the valve is beveled to fit an angular seating. This form has important advantages, one being that the wedging action of the valve head in its seating not only tends to make a tighter seat but that it is drawn in place positively by the spring pressure. Even if the valve stem guide is worn appreciably the valve will center itself when the beveled head seats. The method of valve construction generally employed is to make that member in one piece, though formerly the head was sometimes made of one substance such as cast iron and riveted onto another material, such as a steel stem. These valves did not prove satisfactory owing to difficulty of keeping the head tight on the stem, as the constant hammering action of the valve head against the seat in combination with the heat caused internal stresses that produced distortion and loosening of the head relative to stem.

At the present time valves are generally machined from forgings of alloy steel and are made in one piece, though valves in which a nickel steel head is electrically welded to a carbon steel stem have received some application. For high-speed air-cooled engines a new tungsten alloy steel has been adopted to some extent. While nickel steel valves have much higher resistance to heat than the ordinary grades of steel or cast iron, the tungsten alloy is unquestionably superior. Tungsten is extensively used in making high-speed steels for lathe tools, and in this service a tungsten alloy metal will retain its cutting edge even when brought to a red heat by the combination of heavy cuts and high speed. These qualities make this alloy especially well suited to air-cooled engine service, and it is contended that a properly treated tungsten valve will retain its toughness and resistance to deformation at temperatures over 500 degrees higher than those ordinarily present in motor cylinders.

The two forms of valves ordinarily used are shown at Fig. 89. The two at the left of the illustration are inlet valves, while that at the right is an exhaust-port controlling member. Inlet valves are usually made lighter than the exhaust, especially if of the automatic form, and the sections can be thinner because the inlet valve is kept much cooler by the flow of the comparatively cool gas, whereas the exhaust valves are subjected to intense heat when the inert products of combustion are discharged as a flaming gas around them. It is good practice, even on inlet valves, to have a large fillet between the valve head and stem because this strengthens the stem at its weakest point, and prevents distortion of the head as well as preserving its proper alignment with the stem.

The two common methods of holding the valve-spring collar in place are depicted. In the upper view, the valve stem is slotted, and a key is passed through it which is prevented from moving sideways by the chambered head of the valve-spring collar. As that member is always pressed securely against the key by the valve spring, the key must stay in place as long as the spring performs its functions. The collar of the valve in the lower portion of the illustration is held in place by a nut and lock nut which fit the threaded end of the valve stem.

The exhaust valve, which is shown at the right of the illustration,

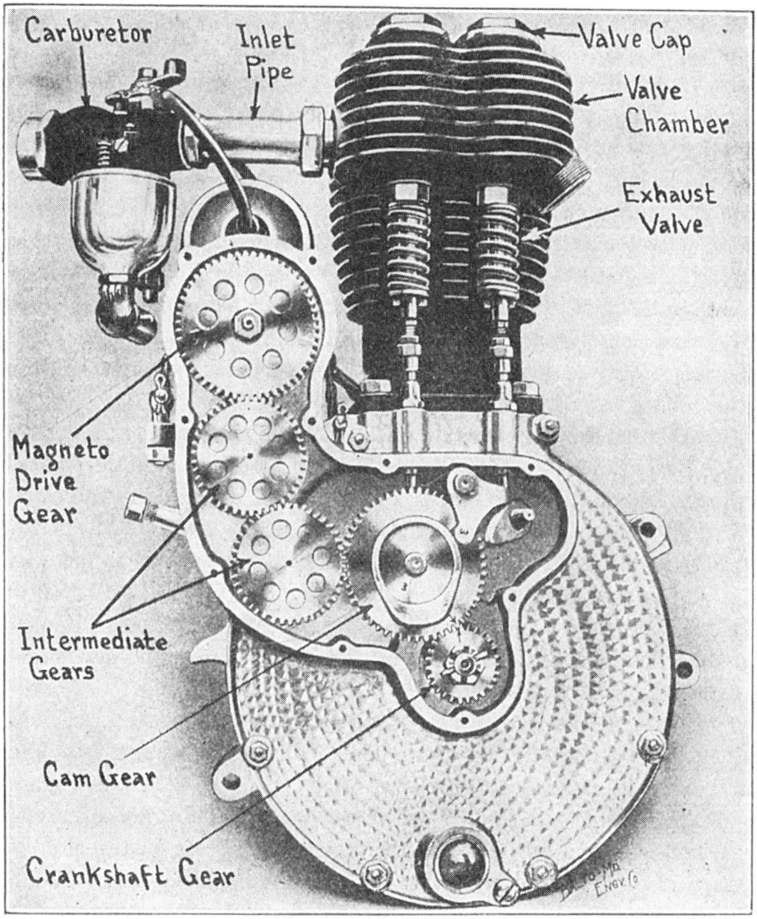

Fig. 90.—View of Reading-Standard Single Cylinder Motor With Timing Gear Case Cover Removed to Show Valve Operating Mechanism.

is an example of excellent valve design. The head is domed, which is preferable to the perfectly flat form, and it is also smooth and without the slotted boss shown on the inlet valves in the same illustration. The slotted boss is necessary on a thin valve head, because it is by inserting a screw driver in this that the valves are turned for grinding.

If a slot was cut directly in a light valve head, it might weaken the construction to some extent. With the domed head, it is a simple matter to cut a screw-driver slot in the arched portion without weakening the head construction. The exhaust valve outlined is a well-proportioned one-piece valve, as there are no sharp corners to become heated, the head is of such shape that it will not warp, and the enlargement of the valve stem near the head not only has a tendency to deflect gases flowing in or out of the cylinder but also strengthens the stem at a point that is normally weak. As the exhaust gas strikes the valve stem immediately below the head when that member is open, and as considerable heat is present that tends to scale and burn away the valve stem, especially if ordinary carbon steel is used, the extra metal is of great value.

How Valves are Operated.—The method of operating the valves of a motorcycle engine is determined by their location, and the general arrangement of the cams employed to raise or depress the valves, as the case may be. When the valves are placed side by side in the cylinder head, as shown at Fig. 90, it is possible to operate them by very simple means as all that is needed is some form of push rod or plunger arrangement supported by suitable guides that will be lifted by small levers riding on the cams, and in turn raise the valve stems against which they bear.

The operation of the cam is not difficult to understand, as most cams consist essentially of a circle having a raised point at one portion of its outer circumference. All portions of the circle are, of course, the same radius from the center except at the point raised to form the cam. As long as the cam rider or follower rests on the circular portion, it will not move, because the point against which it bears on the cam surface is always the same distance from the cam center. When the raised portion of the cam comes in contact with the lever, it will cause that member to move, and this movement may be made to occur at any portion of the crankshaft or piston travel, or exactly when it is needed. The height of the raised portion is one of the contributing factors that determine the amount of valve opening, the others being the proportions or leverage of the cam riders and the adjustment of the valve plungers.

In motorcycle engines, it is now common practice to make the cams integral with the gear driving them. This gear is always driven at half crankshaft speed, and very often it is one of the members that drives the gear train that produces motion of the magneto armature.

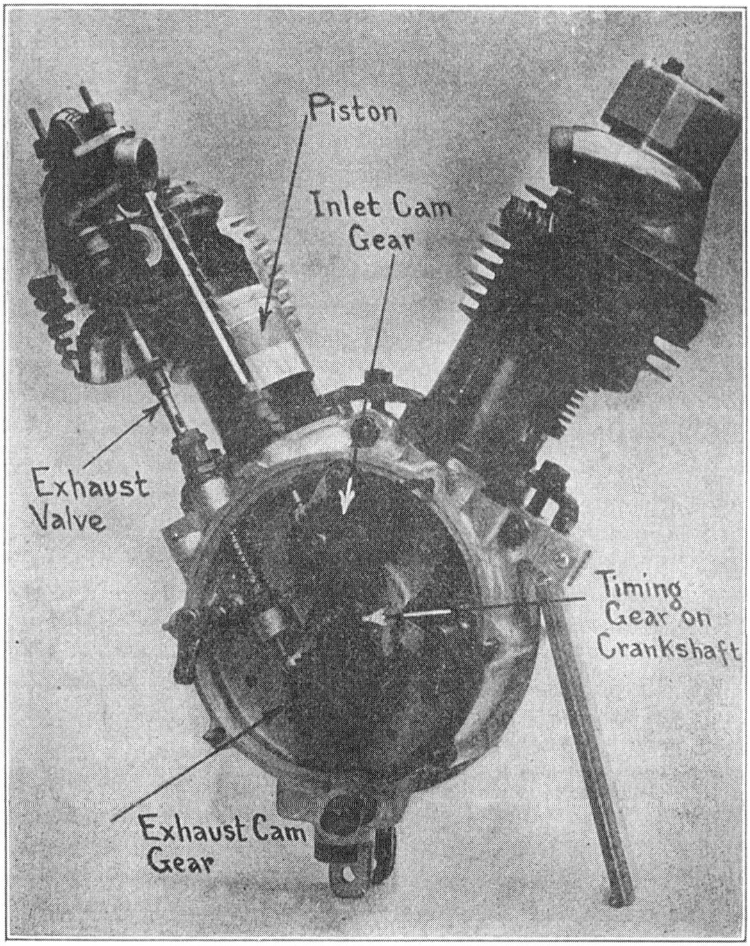

Fig. 91.—Part Sectional View of the Royal Enfield (English) Twin Motor, Showing Application of Two Separate Cam Gears, One for the Inlet Valves, the Lower One for Operating the Exhaust Members.

Sometimes two separate cams are used, each driven by its own gear. An example of this construction is outlined at Fig. 91. In this, the inlet cam and mechanism employed in actuating the inlet valves is mounted above the timing gear on the crankshaft while the exhaust cam and its driving gear is mounted below it. On the multipe-cylinder engines, of which the form shown at Fig. 92 is an example, cylinders of the T-head type are used. In this case, the inlet valve is mounted at one side of the cylinder and the exhaust valves are mounted on the other side. This means that each set of valves must have an independent cam-shaft driven from a common crankshaft gear, and that one cam must be provided on each of these shafts for each valve to be operated. In engines of this type, the valve-operating mechanism is much more direct than in other forms where there may be several cam riders interposed between the cam and the valve stem in addition to the usual valve-operating push rod. In the cylinder, depicted at Fig. 92, the valve-operating push rod is lifted directly by the cam without the interposition of any auxiliary levers, as a roll at the lower end of the tappet rides on the cam and, of course, follows the contour very accurately. This type of construction is much more common in automobile practice than it is on motorcycle engines, because the high-speed power plants used in the latter form of vehicle demand an entirely different treatment as far as the method of valve operation is concerned than do the slower-acting automobile motors.

For instance, where the tappet rod is actuated directly from the cam, there is a certain amount of side thrust present between the tappet and its guide all the time that the tappet roller is being raised by the incline on the cam profile. At high speeds, this thrust action is very noticeable and, as it contributes to wear, high-speed engines soon become noisy if the direct system of valve operation is employed. When a lever or cam follower is interposed between the cam and the valve stem, that member will be subjected to thrust instead of the valve-operating plunger. As an example of the direct method of valve operation, the cross-sectional view at Fig. 92 is excellent, and the two forms of operating the valves that are commonly used may be clearly understood by referring to Fig. 93 where they are well defined. The exhaust valve is operated directly by means of a plunger which bears upon a cam rider which is lifted by a suitable member on the cam-

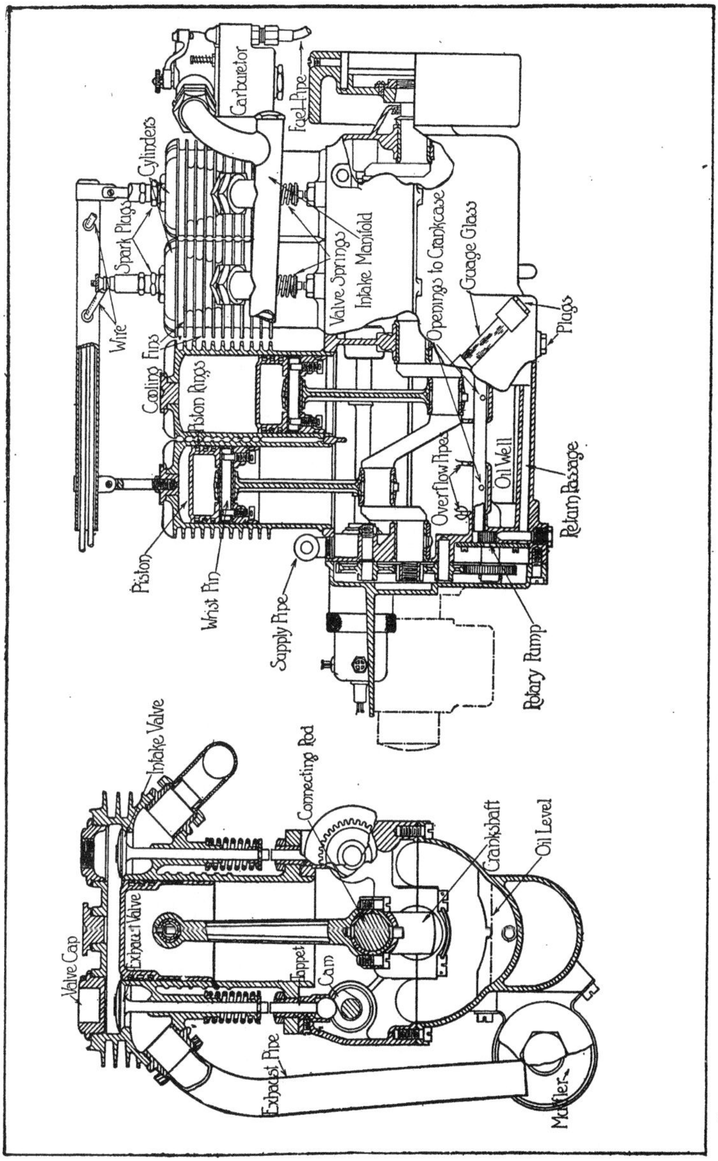

Fig. 92.—Sectional Views Showing Construction of the Pierce Four Cylinder Motorcycle Power Plant in Which Independent Cam Shafts are Employed to Operate the Valves.

shaft below it. The upward movement of the valve-operating plunger results in a direct corresponding motion of the valve, which, of course, must be raised from its seat in order to permit the gas to flow through the exhaust port. The inlet valve, which must be depressed to open, works in a direction opposite to that of the valve plunger movement. While the valve plunger is being raised, the inlet valve stem must be depressed. This is easily accomplished by the use of a rocker arm or simple lever fulcrumed approximately at its center, and having one portion bearing against the valve stem while the cther is in contact with a tappet rod extending from the valve-operating plunger. As will be evident, an upward movement of one end of the lever will result in a corresponding movement in the other direction at the other end.

When valves are placed directly in the head, both members are actuated by rocker arms and tappet rods. The view of the valve-operating mechanism at Fig. 94 shows a rather unconventional system in which face cams are used to operate the bell cranks, which, in turn, raise the valves. The usual form of cam has the raised portion on its outer periphery instead of on the face. When face cams are used, considerable end thrust is present on the cam-shaft; and in the engine shown, all end movement of the cam-shaft, due to the side thrust of the spiral gears employed in driving the cam-shaft or magneto or the side thrust against the cams, caused by the valve springs, is taken by a pair of ball-thrust washers which always keep the cam-shaft in perfect alignment, and which prevent any friction because of this side thrust. Plain thrust bearings in the form of hardened steel or fiber washers have been tried at similar points, but these have not proven satisfactory, because too much friction was present between the plain bearing faces at high engine speeds, especially where lubrication was not always adequate. The use of thrust bearings of the anti-friction type means that the cam-shaft will operate for extended periods without any perceptible bearing looseness. With the old forms of plain bearings, when these wore there was considerable end movement possible in the cam-shaft, and considerable strain was imposed on the driving gears and valve-actuating mechanism. The use of ball bearings has entirely cured any trouble due to side movement of the shaft. This motion not only produced considerable noise by

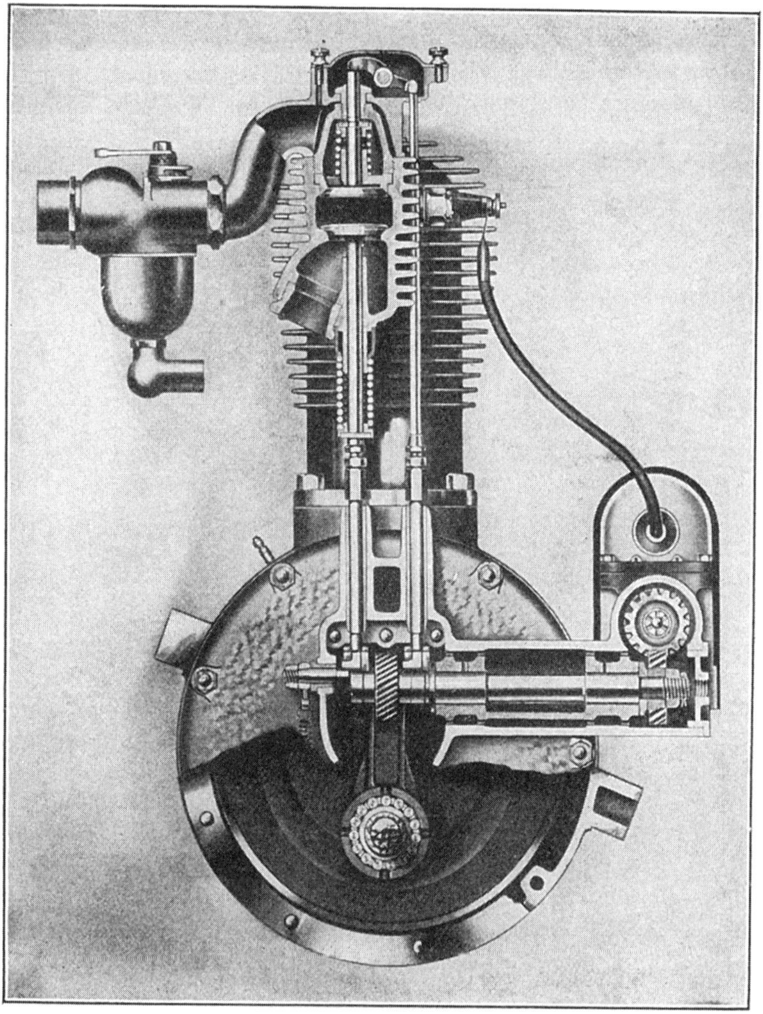

Fig. 93.—Valve Operating System and Magneto Drive of the De Luxe Single Cylinder Motorcycle Engine. Note Also Roller Bearings in Connecting Rod Big End.

permitting the gears to grind, due to poor alignment, and also promoted a metallic knock due to side slap of the cam-shaft, but it also interfered with engine efficiency by altering the valve timing.

The complete valve-operating mechanism used in the Indian motor is shown at Fig. 95, while the method of relieving the compression to permit of prompt starting is clearly outlined at Fig. 96. The inlet

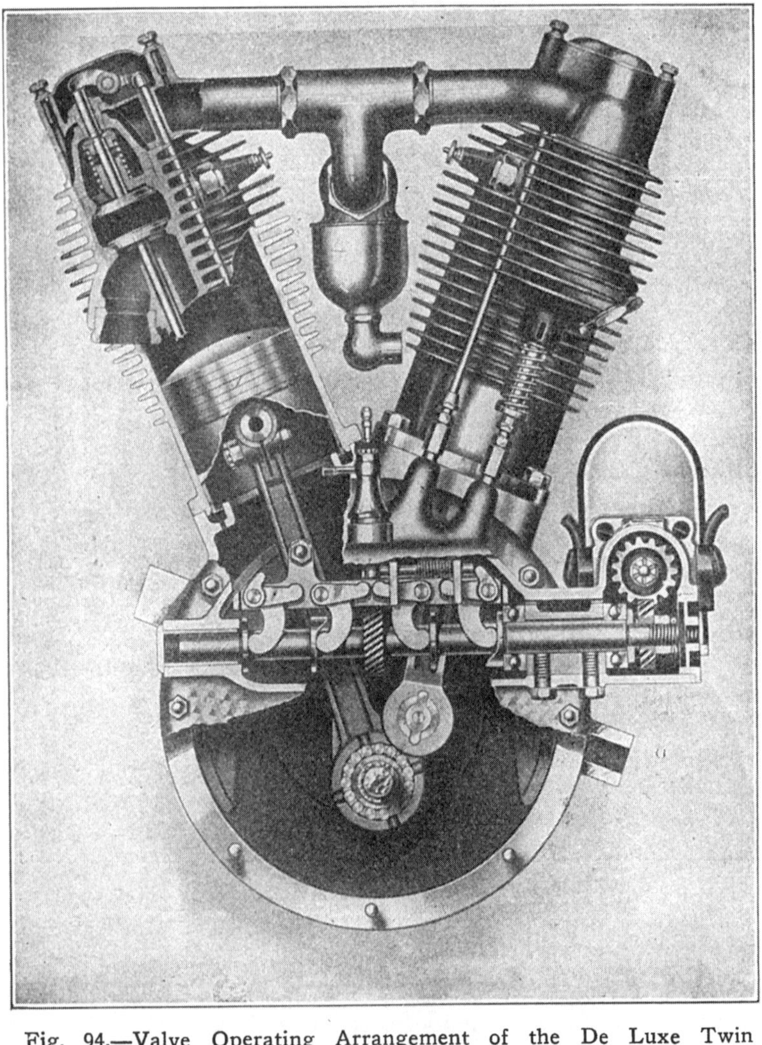

Fig. 94.—Valve Operating Arrangement of the De Luxe Twin Cylinder Motor.

and exhaust cams are integral and are operated by a common cam-shaft. The inlet cam followers are in the form of simple forged bell cranks which bear against the inlet valve lift lever in the manner indicated. A motion of the lower end of the bell crank will be transmitted to the inlet valve lift lever which bears against it. It is claimed for this valve-operating mechanism that the action is quiet at the highest engine speeds, that the system is positive in action, and that it is not subject to rapid depreciation. All of the bell cranks and valve lift levers are of hardened steel, and the entire mechanism is

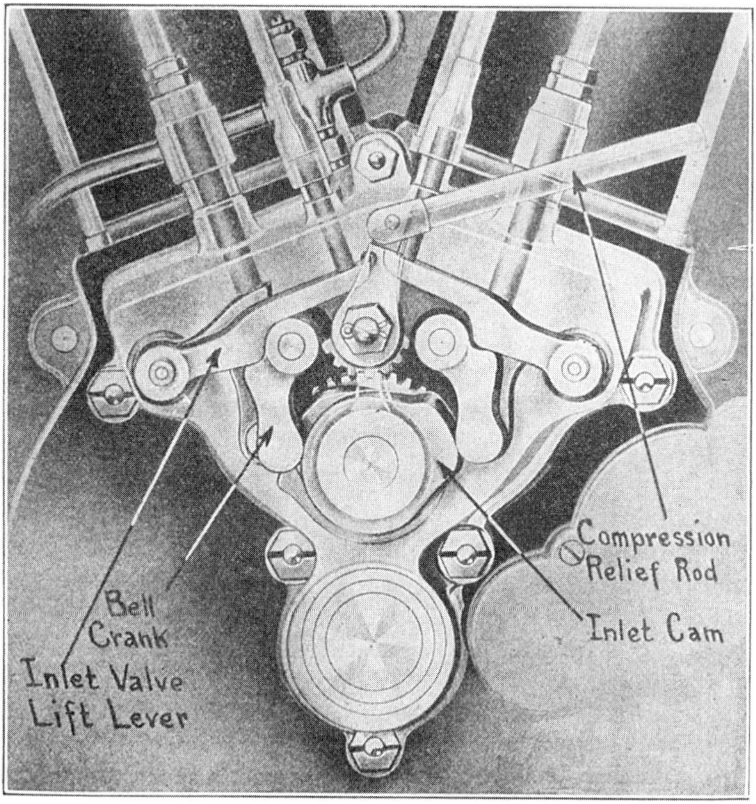

Fig. 95.—Valve Operating Mechanism of the Indian Twin Cylinder Motor.

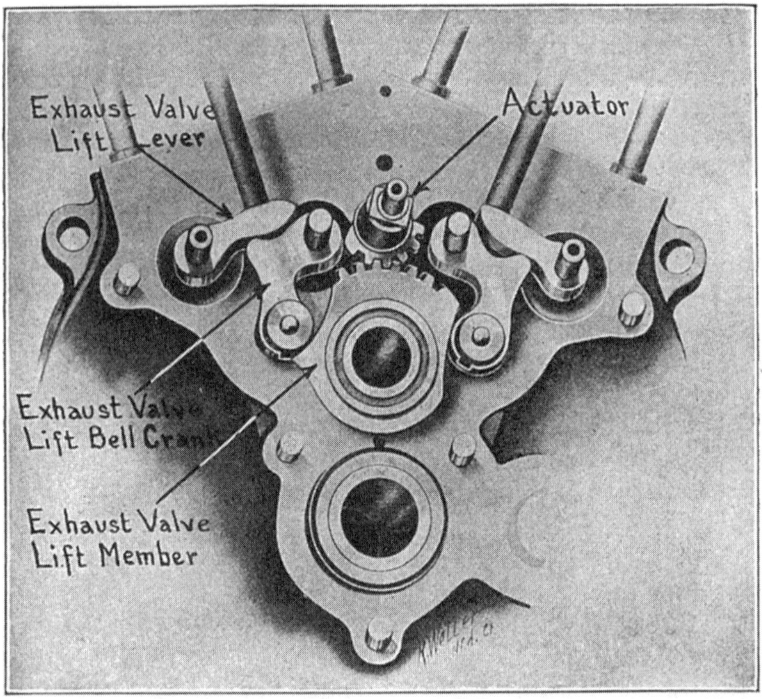

Fig. 96.—Method of Raising Exhaust Valves to Relieve Compression in Cylinders Employed on Indian Twin Motors.

well encased so that it will operate in oil and at the same time be kept clean and free from dirt.

In order to promote easy starting in motorcycle engines, it is customary to provide some system of relieving the compression in the cylinders so the engine may be turned over with minimum exertion on the part of the rider. This is generally accomplished by partially raising the exhaust valves by an auxiliary actuater controlled by hand and independent of the usual exhaust cam. The system used on the Indian motor and shown at Fig. 96 is not only simple, but it is effective and positive as well. A thin double cam member having a series of teeth in the upper portion is placed between the two exhaust valve lift bell cranks. This may be rocked by a toothed segment connected to the grip on the handle bar. When the double cam is rocked, it will raise the exhaust valve lift bell crank regardless of the exhaust cam position, and these members, in turn, will raise the exhaust valve by the short exhaust valve lift levers they bear against.

The views at Fig. 97 show a simple and effective valve-operating mechanism used on the Precision engines, which are of English design. Both of the mechanisms described are employed on single-cylinder engines. The view at Fig. 97, A, is of the gears assembled on the cam case, and it will be apparent that the engine shaft-gear is mounted between the inlet cam drive gear and the exhaust cam drive gear. The view at B, which shows the assembly in the cam case, makes clear the type of valve-operating bell crank and unconventional cams employed. These are internal instead of external forms, and they are formed integral with the half time or speed reduction gears. The valve-lifting plungers are provided with adjustments so the distance between the top of the plunger and the valve stem will be very closely regulated.

The valve-operating mechanism at Fig. 98 is employed in another form of Precision engine in which the valves are placed side by side in an extension from the cylinders, both being of the same type and interchangeable. The view at A shows the appearance of the assembly when viewed from the front, and the method of housing the cam-gear case attached to the engine base. The gear used to drive the cam is twice the size of that on the engine shaft, and therefore drives the cam-shaft at one-half engine speed, as is customary. The valves are raised by plungers which rest on the ends of levers that carry the cam-riding rolls. The arrangement of these members, and form of cams used, are depicted at Fig. 98, B. Each of these levers is fulcrumed at its extreme end and carries a cam roller which follows the cam contour with minimum friction.

One objection that has been advanced against valve-in-the-head motors, is that the overhead valve-operating mechanism was subject to rapid depreciation on account of the presence of grit and dirt at the somewhat limited bearing point on the rocker arms. In order to prevent the accumulation of foreign matter, some makers of motorcycle engines are enclosing the inlet valve-gear so it is not only protected from deposits of dirt but makes the engine appear considerably

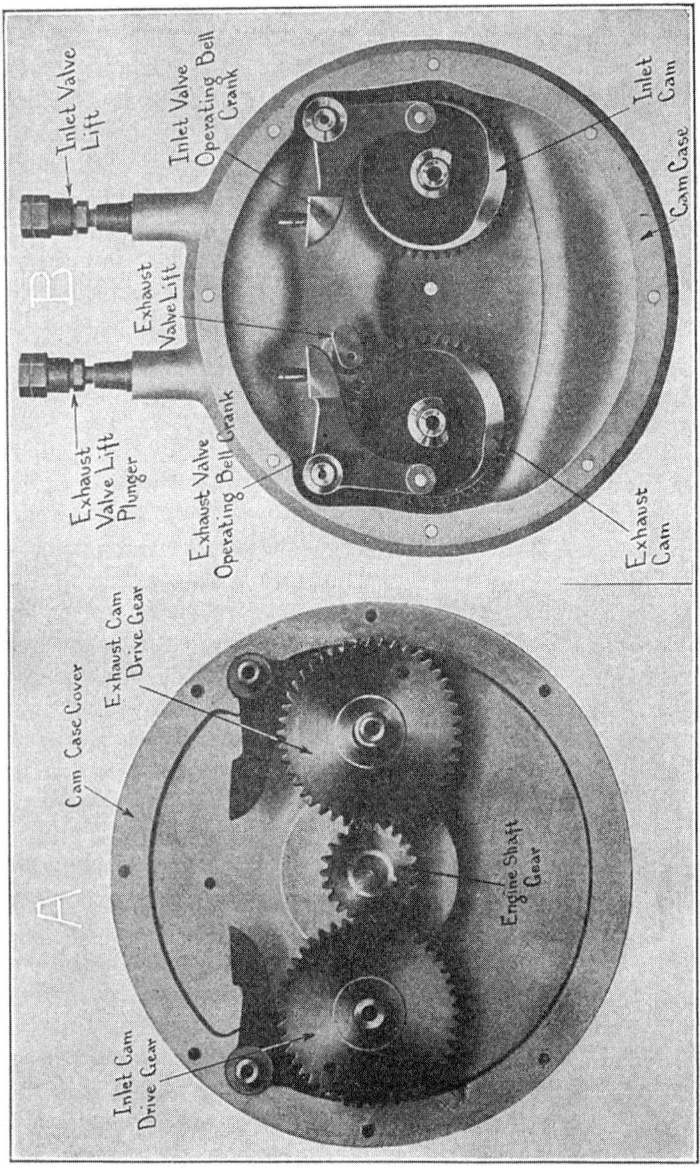

Fig. 97.—Valve Operating Mechanism of Precision Overhead Valve Motors. A—Showing Cam Drive Gear Arrangement. B—Form of Valve Operating Bell Crank and Internal Cams Used.

simpler and actually decreases the noise. The external view of the twin-cylinder power plant at Fig. 99 shows the smooth appearance of the inlet valve-cage, while the method of closing in the rocker arm with a pressed steel cap held in place by two screws can be understood by reference to Figs. 93 and 94.

Valve Timing.—Another important consideration that has material bearing on the power, speed and flexibility of the motorcycle power plant is the valve timing. It is imperative that the valves not only open to their full extent but also that they open in correct relation to the movement of the piston, in order to insure a full charge of fresh gas or thorough expulsion of the exhaust. In the first gas engines which were built to operate at low speed, the usual practice was to open the inlet valve just as soon as the piston started to go down on its suction stroke, and to open the exhaust valve when the piston had reached the end of its power stroke. The inlet valves were closed promptly at the end of the first down stroke of the piston, while the exhaust valve was seated just before the inlet valve opened or at the end of the exhaust stroke. It will be evident that the valves were each opened a period corresponding to one-half revolution of the flywheel, or 180 degrees crankshaft travel.

In endeavoring to secure greater speed and flexibility from the internal combustion motor, which was imperative before it could be applied with any degree of success to vehicle propulsion, the designers, reasoning from well-established steam practice, began to consider giving the exhaust valves a "lead," or to open them before the pistons had reached the end of the explosion stroke. As the exhaust gases had considerable pressure, a large portion of this residue would escape through the open exhaust valves before the piston had reached the end of its power stroke, and during the next up stroke the cylinder would be thoroughly cleared out by the displacement of gas, due to the upward movement of the piston. The control of the valve timing is by altering the relation the timing gears and adjustment of the valve-lifting push rods or tappets bear to the piston travel.

In the engine shown at Fig. 100, the cover has been removed from the cam gear case so the various gears employed in operating the valve-lifting cams and the magneto are shown in proper relation. It will be observed that the timing gear is attached to the crankshaft,

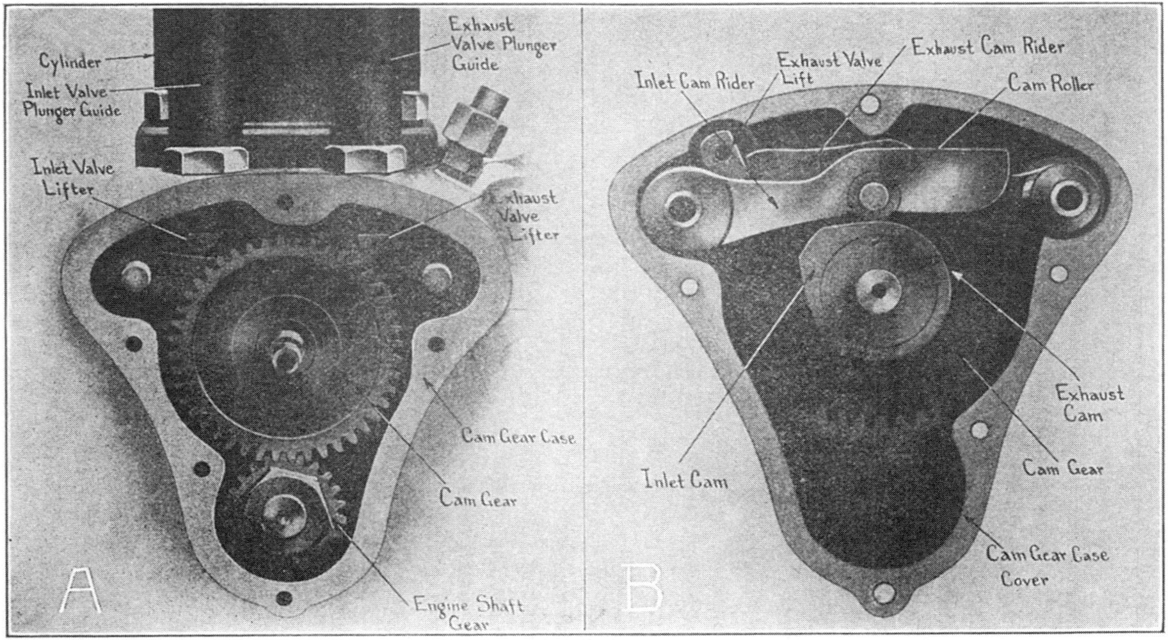

Fig. 98.—Arrangement of Valve Operating Gear of Single Cylinder L Head Precision Motors. A—Timing Gear Case With Cover Removed, Showing Method of Driving Cam Gear From Crank Shaft. B—Outlining Cam Gear With Inlet and Exhaust Cams Integral and Design of Valve Raising Levers.

and that this meshes with cam gears, one of these being employed for each cylinder. In timing the motor after the adjustment of the gears has been disturbed it is necessary to place the distinguishing marks on the various gears as indicated in the illustration. One gear is

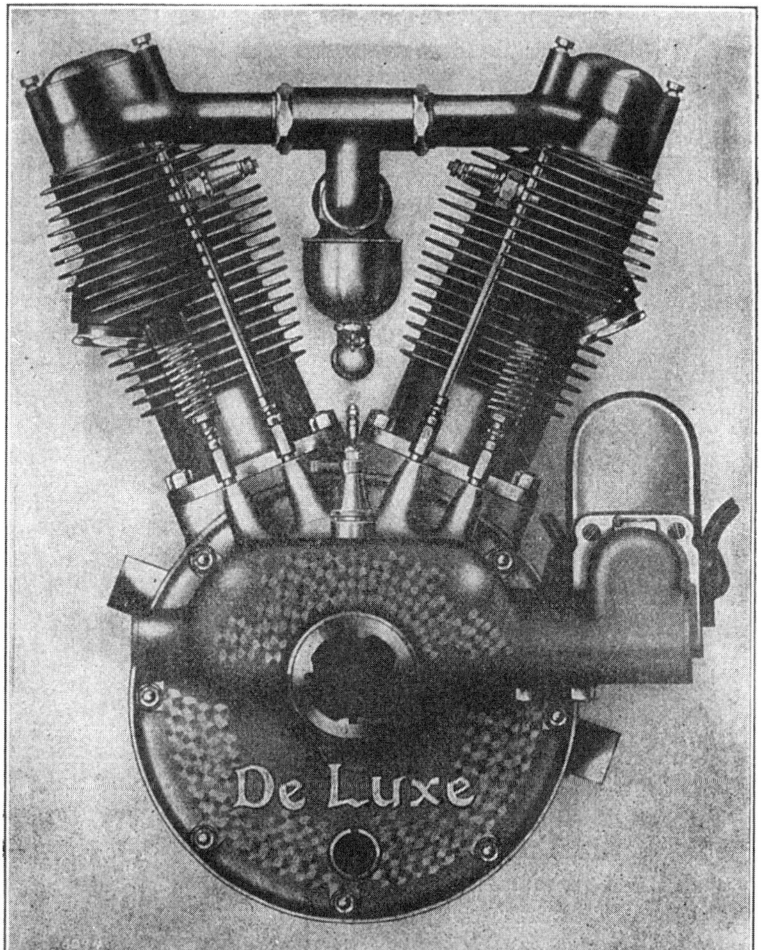

Fig. 99.—The De Luxe Twin Cylinder Motorcycle Power Plant With Enclosed Inlet Valve Operating Gear.

marked F and has an arrow pointing to one of the teeth immediately under the letter. The other cam gear is marked R, and has a similar arrow extended to the gear teeth. The cam and gear assembly marked F is employed for the front cylinder, that marked R is utilized for the rear cylinder. Two arrows are placed on the crankshaft gear, and to secure proper valve timing it is required that the cam gears be replaced so the arrows on the side will register with those on the crankshaft gear. An arrow is also marked on the magneto-drive gear, and when the arrows on the timing gears are in proper register, that on the magneto gear should coincide with a corresponding mark on the timing gear case. The idler or intermediate gears may be replaced without any regard to the way they are meshed, as these will not affect the timing provided that the remainder of the gears are in proper relation to the marks provided as an index for proper resetting.

The view at Fig. 101, which represents a single-cylinder engine with one-half of the cylinder and crank-case removed, shows the position of the piston when the exhaust valve is about to open, and the sectional view through the valve chamber shows the exhaust valve still seated, but its operating mechanism which is indicated in the timing gear case is just about to ride on the point of the cam and open the valve. The exhaust valve in this specific instance opens when the piston is about 7/16 of an inch away from the bottom of the cylinder, measuring from that point to the bottom of the piston. In this case, the exhaust valve starts to open when the crankshaft has traveled 135 degrees from the position at the time the gas was ignited, and the crank-pin must cover an arc of 45 degrees before the fly-wheel will have completed the half revolution corresponding to the downward travel of the piston during the expansion stroke. The exhaust valve should close when the crank-pin has traveled a distance of 193 degrees on the exhaust stroke, which means that the crank will have reached its top center and the piston has started to go down again a distance corresponding to 13 degrees movement of the crank-pin. This represents a downward movement of the piston of but 1/16 of an inch. Just as soon as the exhaust valve closes, the inlet valve opens as shown at Fig. 102. The inlet valve remains open a period corresponding to 10 to 20 degrees movement of the crank-pin after the piston has reached the bottom of the suction stroke, or has covered approximately 3/32 of an inch upward movement on the compression stroke.

The actual duration of the exhaust period is therefore the sum of 45 degrees and 193 degrees, or 238 degrees. The inlet valve remains open a period corresponding to 180 to 190 degrees crank-pin travel.

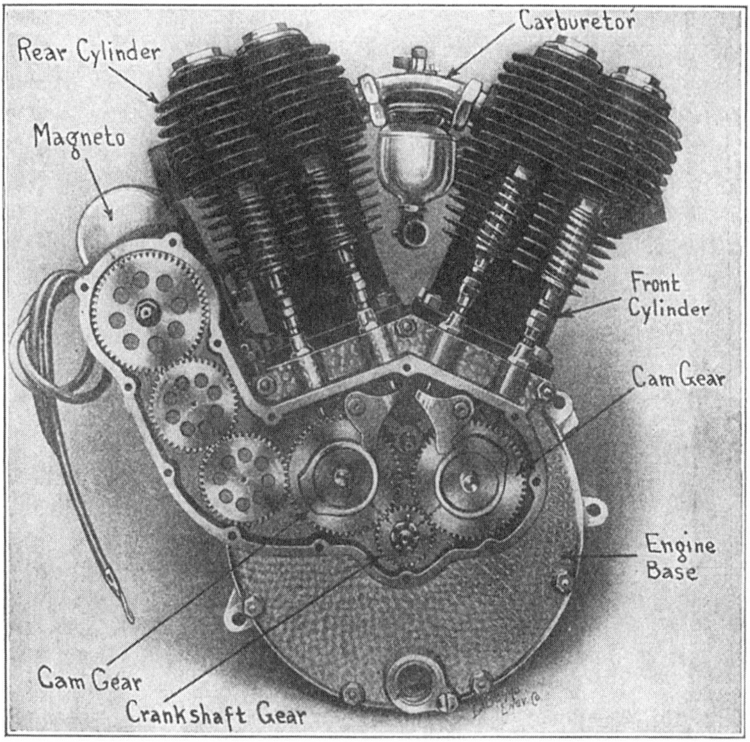

Fig. 100.—Reading-Standard Twin Cylinder Motor With Cover Removed From Timing Gearcase to Show Designs of Cams and Marks on Gears to Indicate Correct Setting as Determined by the Factory.

The reason that the inlet valve is allowed to lag and that the exhaust valve does not close exactly on center is that the gas has acquired a certain degree of momentum during the upward stroke of the piston, and this may be taken advantage of in securing more thorough charging or scavenging if the valve remains open for a time after the piston reaches the top of its stroke. The exact duration of the inlet and exhaust periods depends upon a number of factors, and will vary in practically all engines by a few degrees crank-pin travel.

It is generally recognized, however, that it is imperative to open the exhaust valve early if high speed and efficiency are to be obtained,

Fig. 101.—Sectional View Showing Point in Crank Pin Travel at Which Exhaust Valve Opens on Thiem Single Cylinder Motor.

and that some benefit is derived by deferring the opening of the inlet valve until a condition of partial vacuum exists in the cylinder. If the inlet valve opens late, the gas will tend to rush into the cylinder faster than would be the case if it opened just after the piston had reached the top of its scavenging stroke. The valve opening may be varied very accurately by suitable adjusting members on the valve-operating plungers, or by a threaded adjustment of the tappet rod, or the use of a small screw at the end of the rocker arm to contact with the valve stem. The proper position of a rocker arm on a valve-in-the-head motor, when the valve is closed, is shown at Fig. 103, A. There should be 0.010 inch clearance between the valve stem and the end of the rocker arm when the valve is fully closed, in order to provide for lengthening of the valve stems due to expansion from heat. The position of the rocker arm with the valve half open is shown at B,

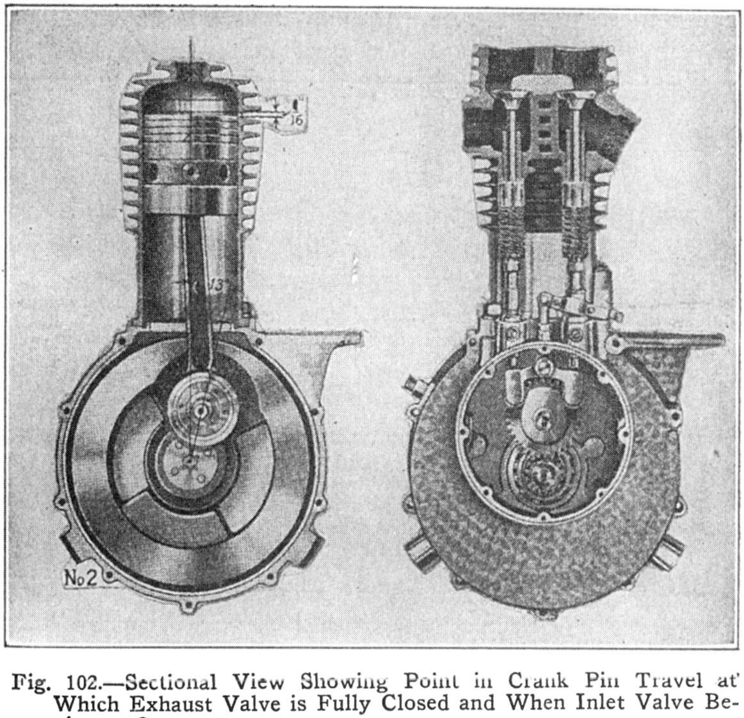

Fig. 102.—Sectional View Showing Point in Crank Pin Travel at Which Exhaust Valve is Fully Closed and When Inlet Valve Begins to Open.

and the angle assumed by the valve lever when the valve is fully opened is shown at C. If the fulcrum is exactly at the center of the rocker arm, the opening or lift of the valve may be readily ascertained by measuring the travel of the tappet rod center line which is indicated in the illustration by the distance between the diverging center lines.

Pistons and Rings.—Pistons are invariably made of cast iron in motorcycle power plants, though steel has been employed to a limited extent in aeroplane and very high-speed automobile and cycle motors. The piston is always less in diameter than the bore of the cylinder, in order to provide space for an oil film between the piston and cylinder walls. In order to prevent leakage of the gas, elastic or spring packing members called piston rings are inserted in grooves in the piston. It is common practice to provide three rings which are usually placed above the wrist-pin. In some constructions, two rings are placed at the top and one at the bottom of the piston, and

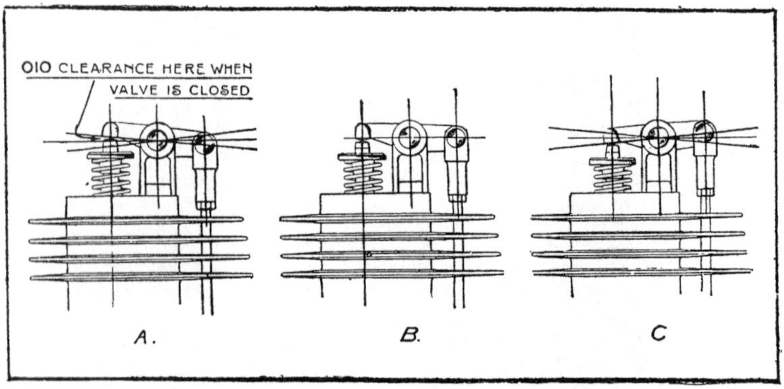

Fig. 103.—Positions of Rocker Lever Used in Depressing Overhead Valves. A—Showing Clearance When Valve is Closed. B—Valve Half Opened. C—Rocker Arm Position With Valve Fully Opened.

it is contended that this makes for steadier support of the piston as well as preventing, as much as possible, the leakage of compression.

The most popular form of piston is the flat-top type depicted in the assembly of engine parts at Fig. 104 and very clearly outlined in the various sectional views of complete power plants previously presented. In some engines, domed-head pistons are employed, while those used in two-cycle motors have a projecting ridge or raised portion to deflect the fresh gas coming in from the transfer passage to the top of the cylinder. The piston rings are of two general forms, one termed "eccentric" because the ring is thicker at one portion, and the "concentric" in which the ring is of uniform thickness and the circles representing the inner and outer peripheries of the ring are concentric to each other. In order to permit of installation of the piston rings on the piston, they are split at one point, and have sufficient elasticity so that they may be snapped in place in the grooves made to receive them on the piston wall. Two forms of joints are used in piston rings; one is the diagonal cut, the other is termed the "stepped" joint. Some makers provide a small pin in the ring groove

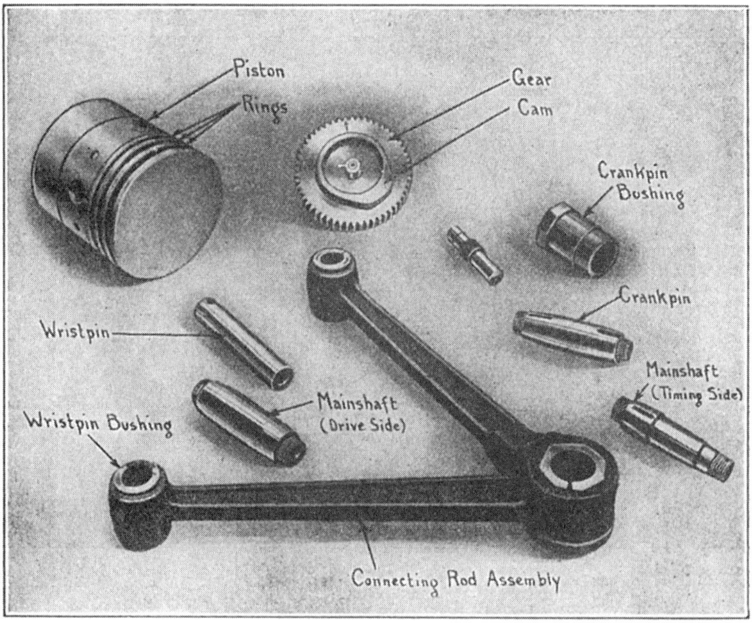

Fig. 104.—Group Showing Some of the Internal Parts of the Reading-Standard Twin Cylinder Motor. Note Arrangement of Connecting Rod Assembly.

to keep them from working around, because if the slot in the three rings should happen to get in line, there is apt to be a loss of compression with the diagonally split rings. With the stepped joint, it is not so important to use the stop pins as the character of the joint is such that leakage is reduced appreciably, and it is considered good practice to have the rings free to move, because it makes for more even wear on the cylinder wall. The piston rings fit their grooves snugly but yet are free to move circumferentially though not up and down in the groove.

The argument advanced in favor of the dome piston top is that the arched construction is stronger, and that the liability of accumulations of oil being deposited on the arched head is less than with a flat head which in some cases may actually have a slight depression at its center. The flat top form is easier to machine.

Wrist Pin and Connecting Rod Arrangements.—The upper

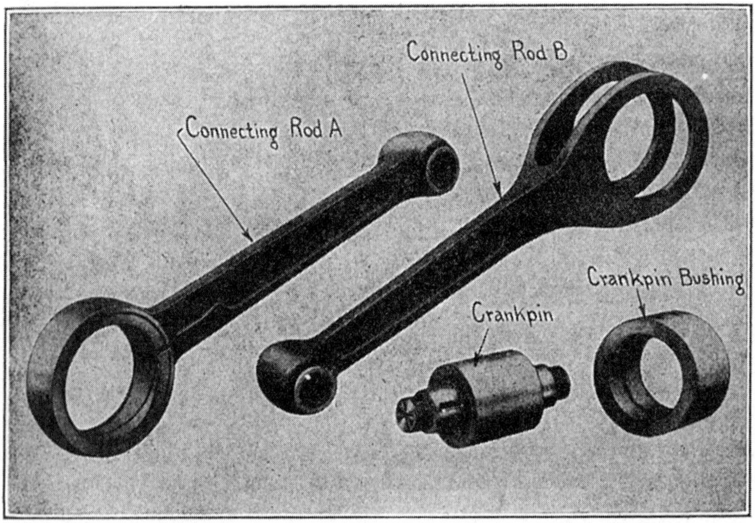

Fig. 105.—Components of Twin Cylinder Connecting Rod Assembly Taken Down to Show Design of Connecting Rod Big End.

end of the connecting rod oscillates on a short steel shaft that passes through suitable bosses in the piston. Wrist pins are usually of hardened steel and may be of solid cylindrical or tubular section. The tubular section is preferred because oil may accumulate in the interior of the hollow wrist pin which acts as a reservoir for its retention, and from which it may be directed to the wrist-pin bushing, usually of phosphor bronze. The retention of the wrist pin is by positive means, because if this member is permitted to move sideways in the piston it is apt to wear a wide groove in the cylinder wall, as the hard and sharp edges of the wrist pin act the same as a planer tool when the piston reciprocates in the cylinder. These grooves generally ruin the cylinder, because they are so deep that there would not be enough metal left for strength if the cylinders were rebored. The commonest method of wrist pin retention is to use a set screw which passes through the boss of the piston and into the wrist pin. If that member is hollow, a small split pin may be passed through the end of the set screw projecting into the wrist pin interior to prevent it from backing out. In some cases, the set screw is kept from backing out by a lock nut.

The wrist pin does not always have a bearing in the upper end of the connecting rod, as sometimes the connecting rod is clamped to the wrist pin member so this member must oscillate in suitable bushings pressed into the piston bosses. This method of construction has an important advantage, inasmuch as considerably more bearing surface is obtained than when a bushing is forced into the upper end of the connecting rod, which must be comparatively narrow in order to fit between the bosses on the piston. Another advantage is that the wrist pin is positively clamped and is thus prevented from end movement. The various common methods of wrist pin retention may be clearly understood by referring to the many sectional views of typical motorcycle power plants presented in this and the preceding chapter.

Connecting rods are invariably steel drop forgings and are made in two main types. The simplest of these is the one-piece rod which is used on engines having built-up crankshafts, while the other is necessary on multiple-cylinder engines using one-piece crankshafts, and is a two-piece form because the lower end is divided so a portion forms a cap for the bearing. Half of the main bearing is attached to the connecting rod, while the other half of the bushing is firmly secured to the connecting rod cap. The cap and connecting rod are joined together by substantial bolts.

The connecting rod of a single-cylinder engine is very simple, and is of the general form indicated at Fig. 105, A. In the majority of twin-cylinder engines, one of the connecting rods is forked at the lower end, as shown at B, Fig. 105, and the rod that works in connection with it has a single end which fits between the fork members of the other. Both rods work on a common crank pin. Connecting rod A, at Fig. 105, is provided with a bushing having a sufficiently large bore so that it will work freely on the outside of a large bushing that is forced tightly in place in the fork sides of connecting rod B. The bushing that fits the forked rod is adapted to bear directly on the crank pin. It will be apparent that the bushing in connecting rod A is employed on an oscillating bearing, whereas that in connecting rod B revolves with the crank pin, and is therefore subject to wear on its inside by the friction of the crank pin and on its exterior by the bushing of connecting rod A.

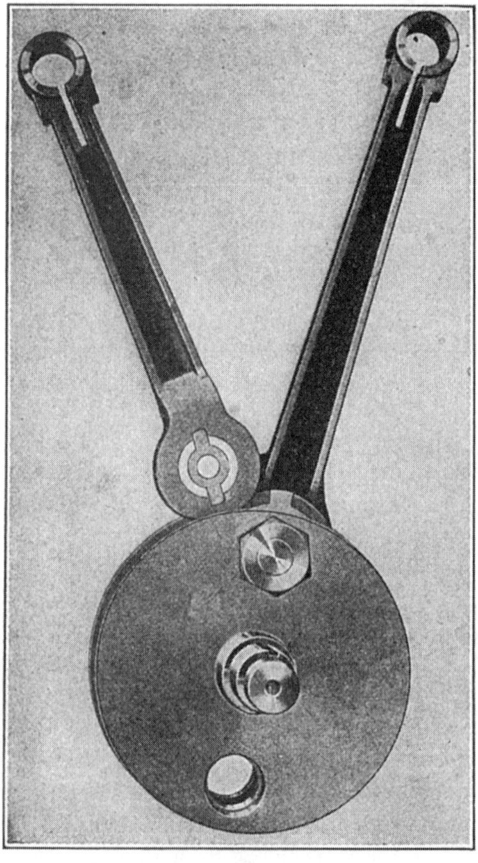

Fig. 106.—Connecting Rod and Crankshaft Assembly of the De Luxe Twin Cylinder Motor.

Another method of double connecting rod arrangement is shown at Fig. 106. In this, the main connecting rod encircles the crank pin and carries a lug above the crank pin to which a shorter rod is attached. The long member is usually called the "master" connecting rod.

The connecting rod arrangement of the Premier (English) engine differs considerably from conventional practice because the arrangement of the rods is such that both pistons move together in their respective cylinders, and reach the ends of the up and down stroke simultaneously. With the connecting rod arrangement commonly employed on twin-cylinder V-motors, one of the pistons reaches the end of its stroke in advance of the other, and it is impossible to obtain an even sequence of explosions, i. e., to have them separated by equal intervals. With reference to the Premier connecting rods assembly, which is depicted at Fig. 107 in connection with the fly-wheel assembly and at Fig. 108 in the engine interior, rod A conforms to conventional practice and its lower end encircles the usual form of crank pin joining the fly-wheels to form a crankshaft assembly. Rod B, however, is a forked member that fits bosses cast on the fly-wheel. The arrangement of these bosses is such that as the fly-wheel assembly revolves the pistons will move exactly the same distance, and it is, therefore, possible to have the explosions just as evenly spaced as when a double cylinder opposed engine is used or a twin-cylinder tandem arrangement with both connecting rods attached to a common crank pin.

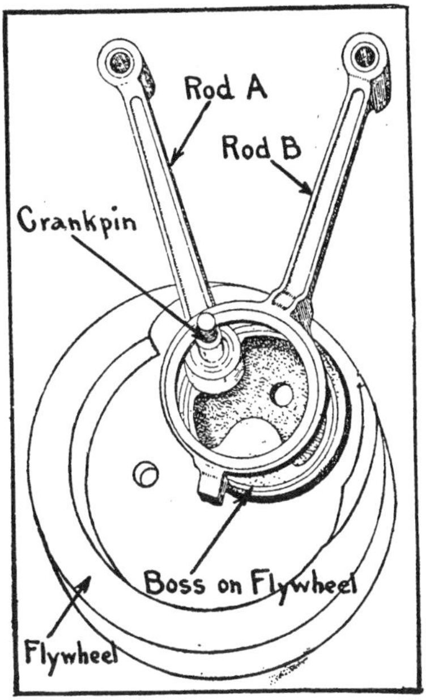

Fig. 107.—Unconventional Connecting Rod Arrangement Utilized in Premier Two Cylinder Motor.

Crankshaft Forms and Fly-wheels.—The common construction of the crankshafts of one and two cylinder motorcycle power plants is a built-up type in which the fly-wheels form an important part of the assembly. In the four-cylinder forms, the crankshaft is a four-throw, one-piece pattern just as in automobile practice. A typical built-up crankshaft and fly-wheel assembly is outlined at Fig. 109. In this, the crank-pins are pressed into suitable bosses at the center of the fly-wheel webs. The crank-pin is a tight fit, and is forced in place with an arbor press. To prevent loosening, a key is added as a further precaution, and the end of the pin is riveted over. The crank pin is provided with a threaded portion at each end, and clamping nuts are used to draw the two fly-wheels tightly in place against a shoulder on the crank pin. The assembly is therefore composed of two fly-wheel castings, which in this case are duplicate members,

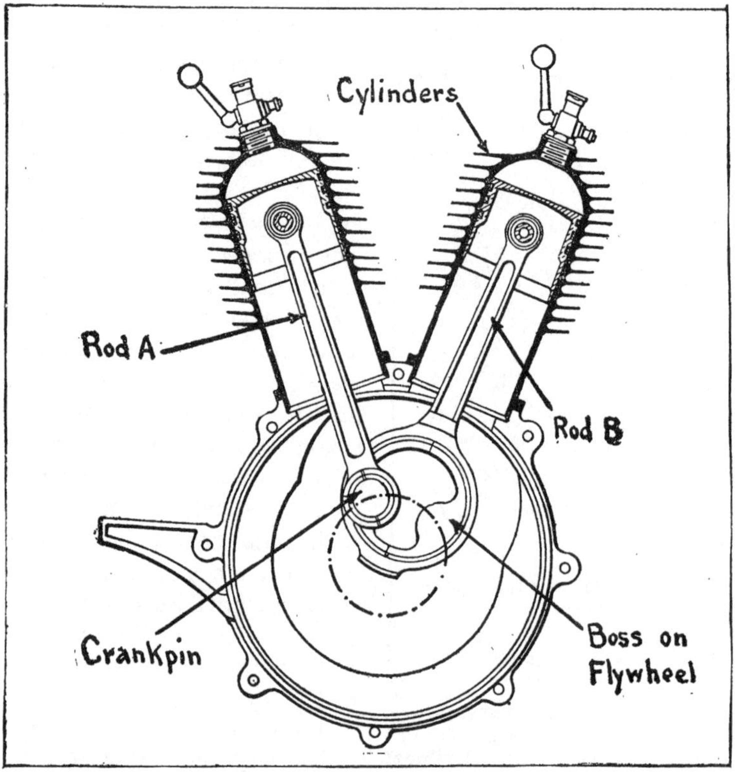

Fig. 108.—Diagram Showing How Premier Connecting Rod Arrangement Permits Both Pistons to Reach the Top or Bottom of the Stroke Simultaneously.

except that one is a right and the other is a left; the crank-pin and the two portions of the main shaft that are riveted in the fly-wheel hubs. In taking this assembly apart, the fly-wheel and main shaft relation is not disturbed because the two fly-wheels may be easily separated to release the crank-pin and connecting rod by loosening and removing the clamping nuts on the crank pin. Other forms of built-up crankshafts similar in general design to this one are shown in sectional views of power plants in various portions of this treatise.

The crankshaft outlined at Fig. 110 is the one used on the new Triumph (English) two-cylinder vertical tandem motor. The crankshaft is a one-piece pattern similar to that employed in automobile practice, and the connecting rods are of the two-piece form with a removable lower cap portion to permit their assembly on the one-piece shaft. The crankshaft shown at Fig. 111 is that used on the Iver-Johnson twin motor, and employs a double crank-pin which is arranged so the cylinders fire at equal intervals the same as in the double cylinder opposed type. The construction is such that the fly-wheel castings are securely attached to the drop-forged crank which has the crank pins in staggered relation. With this arrangement, the cylinders are not exactly in the same plane, i. e., their center lines do not coincide with the center line of the crank-case as is common practice. One cylinder is set to the right and the other to the left of the engine center, in order to allow for the double crank-pin arrangement.

The crankshaft arrangement of a typical four-cylinder engine with one of the connecting rods and its piston in place is shown at Fig. 112. This crankshaft has four crank-pins joined together by a series of web members and three main journals. The entire assembly is forged in one piece, and follows automobile practice in all respects except that of size. Two of the crank-pins are on the same plane so that two of the pistons travel up and down together. The usual arrangement is to have the two center pistons move in conjunction and the two end ones to go up while the center ones are going down and *vice versa.*

The method of fly-wheel attachment on the four-cylinder crankshaft depicted is clearly outlined at Fig. 92. The fly-wheel hub is tapered to fit the taper on the crankshaft, and is also keyed in place to prevent the fly-wheel from turning. A substantial clamp nut on the threaded end of the crankshaft serves to keep the fly-wheel pressed firmly on the taper. The endeavor of the designers is to make the fly-wheels as large as the design of the engine permits and to have the rims reasonably heavy because the farther away the weight is

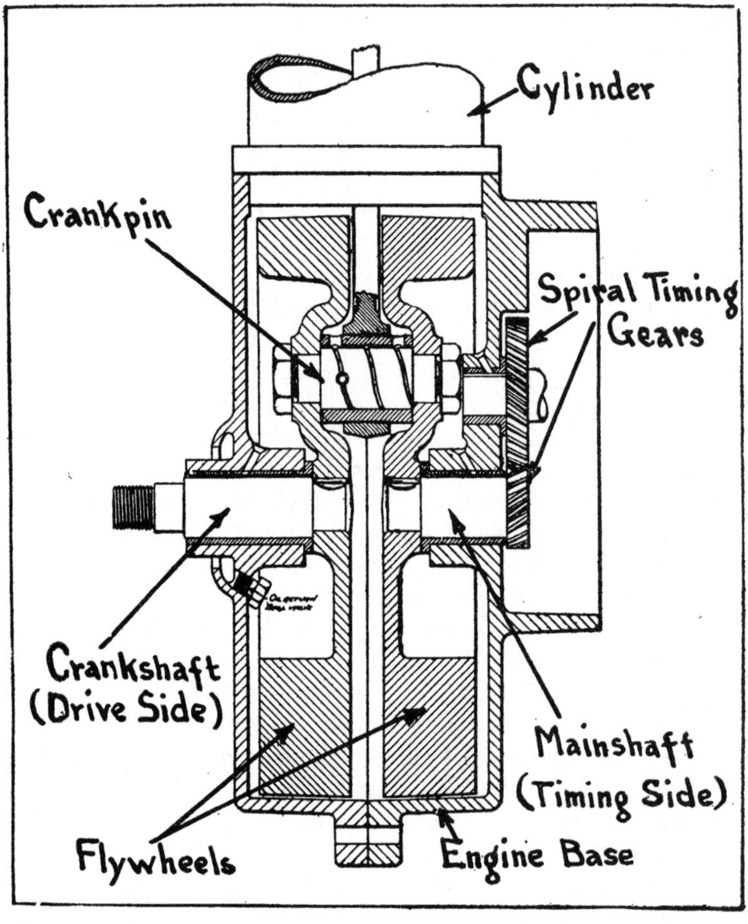

Fig. 109.—Sectional View of Crank Case of AMC Motor, Showing One Method of Assembling Built Up Crank Shaft in Which the Flywheel Webs are Utilized for Supporting the Crankpin.

carried from the crankshaft center the more effective does the fly-wheel become as an evener of engine movement. As has been previously explained, the momentum acquired by the fly-wheel during the expansion or power stroke of the engine is depended on to keep the pistons, valves, etc., in operation during the strokes in which no power effort is being applied to the crankshaft, and under conditions where a decided resistance may be offered to piston movement, as during the compression stroke. Heavy fly-wheels permit an engine to run steadily at low speed and also reduce vibration. The size and weight of the fly-wheel rim depends upon the size of the cylinder and the amount of compression. While most fly-wheels used in motorcycle engines are of cast iron, some makers employ steel forgings even in the built-up form of crankshaft. The fly-wheel of a single-cylinder or a two-cylinder V-engine usually has incorporated with it the counter-weights provided to balance that of the reciprocating parts and to promote smooth running.

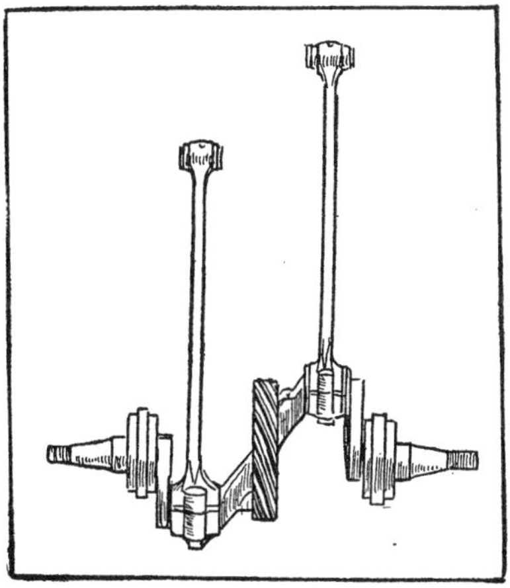

Fig. 110.—Crankshaft Arrangement of Triumph Two Cylinder Vertical Engine.

Engine Base Design and Construction. — The conventional method of constructing the crank-case of a one or a two cylinder motorcycle power plant is to form that member in two pieces, which join together on the engine center lines. The two halves are made of aluminum alloy, and the joints are of the matched form, in order to make the crank-case oil-tight. The timing gear chamber is usually cast integral with one of the halves of the crank-case. The two portions are clamped tightly together by through bolts, extending from one side to the other. The timing gear case is sometimes known as the distribution chamber, and is either provided with a cover or is in itself removable, in order to gain access to the timing gears and valve-operating mechanism. The aluminum crank-case is preferred, though on some cheap engines cast iron has been employed. The only objection against the cast iron is that it weighs nearly three times as much as the lighter alloy commonly used. The cast iron is equally strong and will hold threads better than the softer metal. This method of crank-case construction is shown at Fig. 74.

Another form in which the crank-case member itself is the full width of the engine and not divided vertically in the center is shown at Fig. 77. In this, a removable side plate enables one to gain access to the engine interior and is securely held in place against the crank-case proper by a series of studs.

When multiple-cylinder engines are used, as at Fig. 92, automobile practice is followed in that the crank-case is made in two portions and is split horizontally. The upper portion serves as a base for attaching the cylinders and also carries the main bearings, and the lower portion is utilized as an oil pan and is not subjected to any strain. The engine is supported in the frame by lugs cast with the upper half of the crank-case.

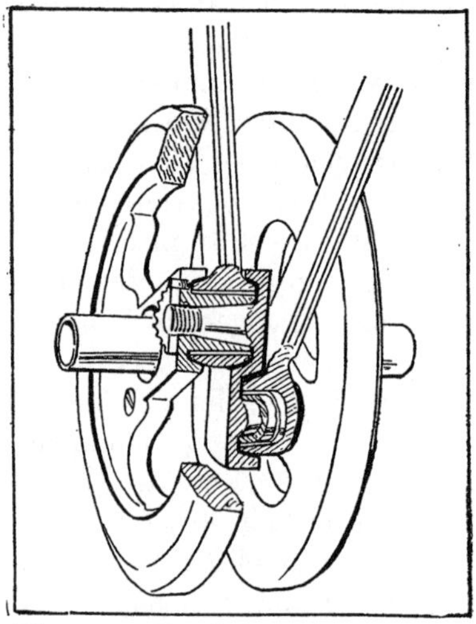

Fig. 111.—Crankshaft Arrangement of Iver-Johnson Twin Motor.

The crank-cases of most engines are provided with some form of gauge glass, in order that the rider may be able to ascertain the amount of oil present in that member. In single and double cylinder engines, a non-return ball check valve is often screwed into the crank-case to permit the air compressed therein, each time the piston moves down, to escape, and usually a small piece of copper tube directs the escaping air to a point underneath the crank-case to insure that the oil with which the air is saturated will not soil the machine. The bearings used in the crank-case may be of two forms, the plain bushing, made of phosphor bronze or other suitable bearing metal, or anti-friction bearings of the ball or roller type. The four-cylinder power plant depicted at Fig. 92 uses plain bushed bearings while that at Fig. 74 has anti-friction bearings of the ball type to support the crankshaft assembly. The engine at Fig. 79 is a plain bearing form throughout as the main bearings, as well as those at the upper and lower end of the connecting rod, are in the form of bronze bushings forced in place in the crank-case bosses.

Plain and Anti-Frictional Engine Bearings.—Decided advantages are obtained when ball or roller bearings are used to support the crankshaft, because these not only simplify the lubrication problem but they also reduce friction to a minimum, which makes the engine freer running. It is claimed that engines fitted with anti-friction bearings are more "lively," and are faster than the plain bearings forms. Anti-friction bearings are well adapted to this work, and the successful application of ball and roller bearings in racing

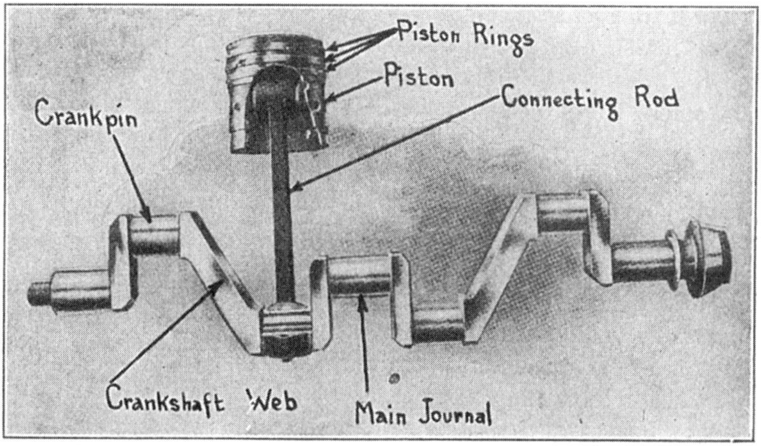

Fig. 112.—Four Cylinder Crankshaft of the Three Main Bearing Type.

motors has demonstrated forcibly the advantages of substituting rolling for sliding friction at all points where copious lubrication is questionable. To use bearings with rolling members successfully, it is necessary to not only make proper size selections but to install them correctly as well as make provision for adequate lubrication, though bearings of this form will run with considerably less oil than plain bushings. As much less heat is evolved through the reduction of internal work due to friction, anti-friction members will prove more enduring and be capable of more extended periods of operation with materially less lubricant, which is depended on in a plain bearing for separating the metal surfaces and at the same time to conduct away the heat evolved at high speeds due to rubbing of surfaces over each other.

In order to prove that space limitations, to which motorcycle designers adhere so closely, make it difficult to use properly designed journals of the plain bearing type, the reader is asked to study the following brief analysis of the loads present upon a typical connecting-rod assembly using plain bearings and depicted at Fig. 113, and the bearing area provided to resist them. In this, rod *A* is the member attached to the main bushing encircling the crank-pin, while rod *B* is a forked member with the big ends bearing upon the outer surface of the main bronze bushing. The bore of the main bushing is 1¼ inches, its length is 1½ inches. The outside diameter is 1¾ inches, and the width of the forked connecting rod members is 7/16 inch each side. The projected area of the bushing serving rod *A* can be represented by a rectangle 1¼ inches by 1½ inches, which has an area of 1.875 square inches. The projected area of the bearing surfaces serving rod *B* can be represented by a rectangle ⅞ inch by 1¾ inches and has an area of 1.53 square inches.

Before considering the application of anti-friction bearings, let us first briefly review some of the conditions governing plain bearing construction, and then we can understand how the motorcycle designer is forced to make his bearing design, especially as relates to connecting-rod big ends, a compromise that will endeavor to reconcile widely differing factors. Some of the essentials considered in plain bearing designs, are: Proportions and dimensions of bushing as relates to diameter and length; selection of suitable bearing metal; the amount of clearance to be allowed between shaft and bearing, and provisions for lubricating. Considering first the proportions, these depend upon various conditions, such as: Size of the shaft, which must be strong and stiff and which must be of sufficient diameter to obtain this strength, and enough length so the bearing pressures will not exceed a certain value in order to retain an oil film. Contrasted to these are the opposing conditions that circumferential or rubbing speed must be low to reduce the work of friction (which calls for small diameters) and also that the bushing length be held to a point where there can be no concentration of pressure from deflection (which calls for short bearings) on any limited area of the bushing surface. As to proportions, most engineering authorities recommend that engine bearings be at least 1.5 times as long as the diameter of the shaft where space considerations permit. In the main bearing of the connecting-rod assembly described, the ratio is considerably less than this as the length is but 20 per cent. greater than the diameter, and in the bearings of rod *B*, the length is but half the diameter. Here we have the first departure from good engineering practice.

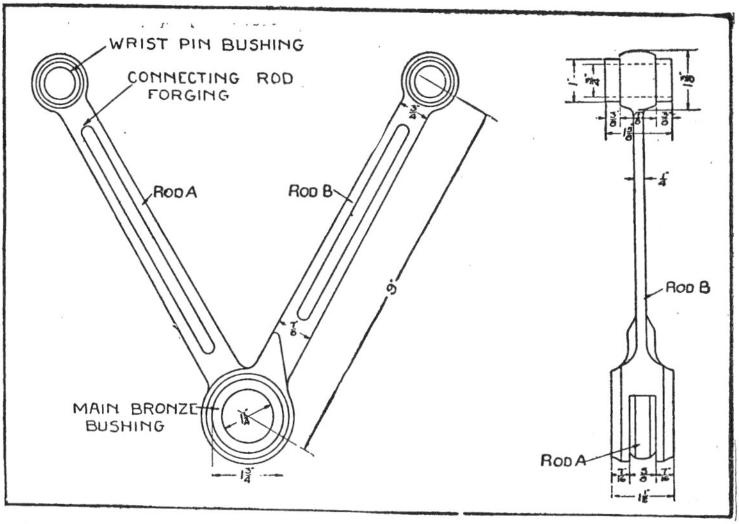

Fig. 113.—Usual Arrangement of Connecting Rods of Twin Cylinder Motorcycle Power Plant. This Working Drawing Gives the Principal Dimensions of an Assembly Used on a Nine Horse-power Motor.

The bearing metals are well selected in reference to the loads they are to carry and the bronze used has a high degree of resistance to deformation, and on the main bearing at least it is working in combination with a hardened steel crank-pin. Conditions are not so favorable at the forked oscillating bearing, however, as here the rod ends are comparatively soft where they bear against the outside surface of the bronze bushing. The value for safe working stress on crank-pin bearings is given as 1,280 pounds per square inch projected area for hard steel and bronze in combination, and as 800 pounds per square inch for unhardened steel on bronze.

The main crank bushing of the connecting rod assembly at Fig. 113 bears against a hardened steel pin so the higher value applies, but the oscillating member, which is soft enough so it can be cut with a file bears against bronze, so the lower value must be used. The pistons used are 3½ inches bore; which means that the piston top area is 9.62 square inches. If we assume an explosion pressure of 300 pounds per square inch, which value may obtain at times in all power plants, this gives us a value of 2,886 pounds as the force of the explosion on the piston top. At a speed of 2,000 revolutions per minute, it should be considered that the main crank-pin bushing, which takes the explosion pressure of each cylinder is subjected to this force 2,000 times per minute as an explosion is obtained for each revolution, and both pistons must impart their pressure directly against the one crank-pin. We have seen that the projected area of the main crank-pin bushing is 1.87 square inches, so we can find the unit stress per square inch bearing surface by dividing the total pressure by the available projected area. This gives us a value of 1,543 pounds per square inch and shows that the main bearing would be overloaded nearly 300 pounds per square inch if only the explosion pressure was considered.

There are other loads on the bearing that must be added, one of these being the load due to centrifugal force of the rapidly rotating connecting-rod big ends as well as the inertia loads produced by the reciprocating members. To discuss these would be to complicate the discussion so that it would be difficult of comprehension by the average reader and it would serve no useful purpose because the load due to explosion pressure alone brings an overload on the bearings. Considering the load on the forked big end, we find that the projected area of 1.53 square inches is subjected to a load of 2,886 pounds at instant of explosion. This means a unit stress of 1,886 pounds per square inch on a bearing suited only for 800 pounds per square inch, and means an overload of 1,086 pounds or over 125 per cent.

This insufficient bearing area is obviously the reason for some of the trouble experienced with plain journals, as it is apparent that high unit pressures will squeeze the lubricant from between the surfaces and produce an actual metallic contact at times between bushing and crank-pin. The overload on the bearing is not serious enough to deform either bearing metal, but it certainly does promote cutting and scoring the bushing and crank-pin through the failure of lubrication. The lubricant forced from between the surfaces is thrown off of the rapidly revolving crank-pin by centrifugal force, and, unless new oil is supplied in a positive manner, the surfaces will be in actual metallic contact from time to time. Under the conditions outlined, it is not strange that plain bushings subjected to such severe service should depreciate rapidly.

The problem of main bearing design is not a serious one, as these can always be made sufficiently large, and there is no force tending to throw the oil out to any injurious degree when the fly-wheel assembly they support revolves. Another important point is that two bearings can be used to support the load that one crank-pin bushing of less than half their projected area must take. This condition alone is much more favorable to endurance, because the film of lubricant remains between crankshafts and bushings, and unit pressures are not high enough to squeeze it out.

Two forms of anti-friction bearings are used in connecting-rod big ends, and for crankshaft support. The roller bearing has advantages of moment in this application, but it has more friction than a properly applied ball bearing. The crank-pin, which is hardened and ground, forms an ideal surface for the bearing rollers to work on, and as the big end of the connecting rod can be hardened and ground very accurately a free running bearing can be obtained that will not be materially larger in diameter than a plain form, except for the difference in thickness between the bronze bushing and the roller members. The error commonly made is to make the rollers too small in diameter, and, while it is very desirable to keep the dimensions of the big end bearings down as much as possible, it is a harmful tendency when carried to extremes. Rollers are ordinarily about 3/8 inch in diameter, whereas, if proportioned in accord with the loads upon them, they should be 1/2 inch in diameter, at least.

If comparison is made between ball bearings and the rollers ordinarily used, it will be well to state that a roller bearing of sufficient capacity would be nearly as large, though some space would be saved by the elimination of the outer race member needed with the ball bearing. The rollers bear directly against the metal of the connecting rod but the balls run in a separate hardened race member which has a groove of proper curvature for the balls to run in, and which is retained by the connecting rod big end. Either form indicated will give good service, though where the design permits, the most efficient bearing, which is the ball type, will prove more enduring.

The writer knows that considerable trouble obtained with the early ball bearings used for this purpose but in practically all cases, it could be ascribed to the desire to use bearings of small size, fostered to some extent by the wishes of designers more familiar with bicycle practice than with the requirements of self-propelled vehicles, and also to the competition between the manufacturers of such bearings. If one manufacturer recommended a larger bearing than a competitor, the business went to the maker selling at the lowest price, regardless of the merits of the bearing or its capacity for the work. The ultimate consumer was not the only one who suffered by this policy as the failure of such bearings reacted against the motorcycle builder, who promptly shifted the blame to the bearing manufacturer, who had to take it whether it belonged to him or not. This created the erroneous impression in some quarters that ball bearings were not as well suited to the work as roller bearings, whereas when properly selected and installed, these bearings answer all requirements besides running with minimum friction.

While a roller bearing is somewhat less in diameter than a ball bearing of the same capacity, it is wider and will contain nearly the same amount of metal. If the connecting rod big end wears it increases in bore, and either larger rollers or a new rod are needed. With a ball bearing, the outer race is an integral part of the bearing, it can be ground and fitted to the balls very accurately, as well as made of proper material. Ball bearing race members are usually of chrome steel, which has superior resistance while the drop forged rods are usually of a low carbon steel and must be carbonized at the bearing point, and treated before a sufficient degree of hardness can be obtained. With a ball bearing, the outer race is not only of proper stock treated independently, but the rod does not need other than a toughening treatment, if any, which does not call for carburizing.

While the writer does not mean to imply that roller bearings are wanting in reliability, or other features, out of justice to the ball bearing it is necessary to outline their advantages over the other types.

One of the conditions that has materially interfered with efficient ball bearing service has been the methods employed in installing them. A sectional view of the engine base of a power plant of European design is shown at Fig. 114, and this depicts the method of mounting

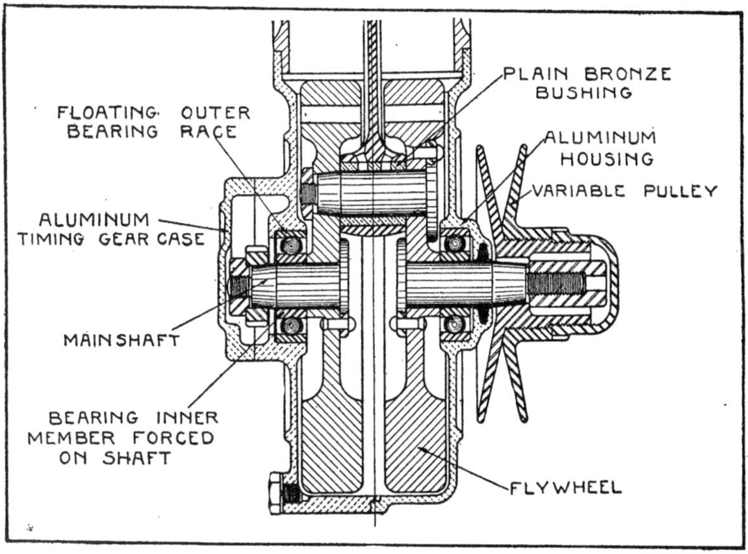

Fig. 114.—Sectional View of Crank Case, Showing Application of Single Row Ball Bearings in Supporting Flywheel Assembly.

usually employed. If the work of fitting is carefully done, the mounting will give satisfaction, though in the rush incidental to regular manufacturing, bearing inner race members are apt to be pushed on shafts machined a trifle small rather than forced on. The outer races rest directly in the housing of soft material, usually cast aluminum. While the bearing does not loosen up at once, still the constant succession of shocks due to explosion pressure tends to pein out the stressed metal supporting the outer race member. This enlargement of the bearing housing permits the outer race to turn, and soon it is a very poor fit in the crank-case. The same applies to the inner race, which becomes loose on the shaft, so loose in fact, that the shaft will become scored and appreciably reduced in diameter. This condition is not exaggerated one iota, the crank-case of several ball bearing machines under the writer's observation have worn in just the manner indicated, and the bearing supporting shafts also.

Of course, bearings of standard bore and diameter cannot be used for replacement purposes, and the only remedy is to bush the housings with a steel or bronze member after it has been bored out enough to accommodate it, providing there is metal enough in the bearing housing walls. If the shaft is scored, it can be turned down enough to permit a steel bushing being forced on, this being machined so the outside diameter corresponds to the bearing bore. An alternate method, the more costly and satisfactory one, is to replace the defective members with new parts.

Installing the ball bearings in this manner is not the best practice, and no less an authority than Riebe, in a recent address before an engineering society, condemned the common practice as shown at Fig. 114, and advised the positive retention of bearing inner races by clamping members, as well as the housing of the outer races in bushings of harder material than the aluminum commonly used for crank and gear cases. As this engineer is one of the pioneers in the design of ball bearings, such advice cannot be passed by lightly.

The writer desires to submit a suggestion for the design of a twin-cylinder crank-case at Fig. 115, in which the bearing installation is on correct engineering lines as advised by leading authorities. To begin with, the design is different from that usually followed in that the cylinder centers are placed one to each side of the crank-case center line or in staggered relation. This point, no doubt is open to criticism, inasmuch as it makes for a slightly wider crank-case and more expensive construction. At the other hand, it would appear that if the front cylinder is set a little to one side, that the rear cylinder will receive some effect from the air draft created by cycle movement, and that more complete cooling will result. This placing of the cylinders independently of the crank-case center line makes it possible to use

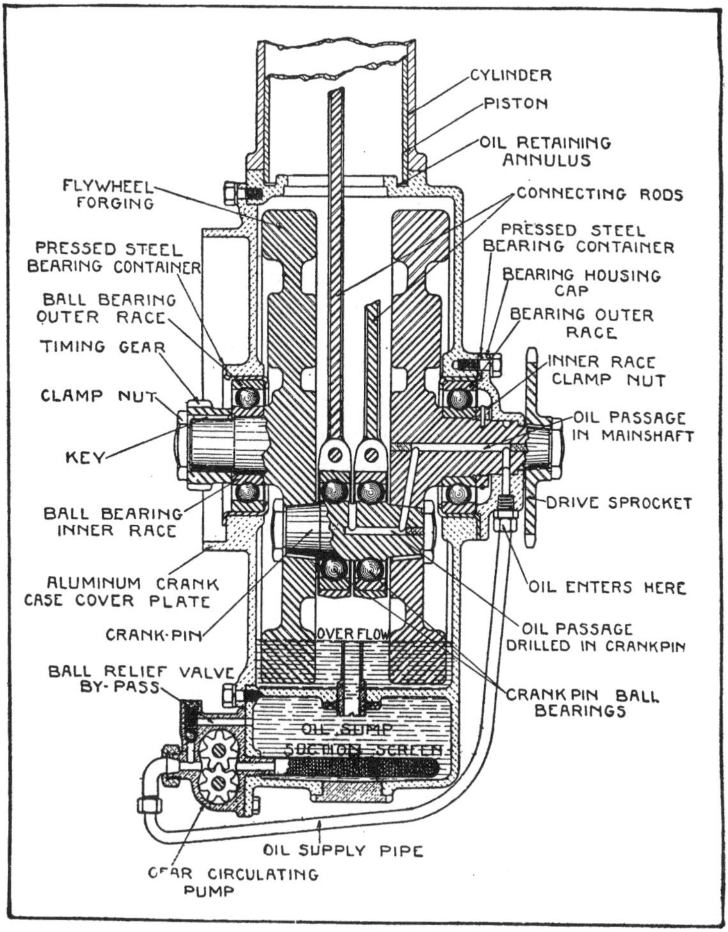

Fig. 115.—Design Drawing Showing Correct Application of Ball Bearings to Connecting Rod Big Ends as Well as Main Bearings of Twin Cylinder Motorcycle Power Plants. Note Automatic Lubrication System Provided.

ball bearings of correct proportions on the crank-pin, as each connecting rod has its independent anti-friction bearing.

The ball bearings are special in that they are assembled on the crank-pin, which takes the place of the bearing inner race members, but as the balls, separators, outer races and even curvature of the inner ball races on the crank-pin conform to standard practice, such a bearing should not cost appreciably more than the regular standard product and a remarkable saving is effected in bearing diameter by forming the ball races on the crank-pin in the manner indicated. The outer races are kept from side movement by a clamping bolt passing through a slotted boss just above the bearing. As the outer race members may be ground within .0002 inch plus or minus, it will be apparent that but little bolt movement will suffice to hold the outer race firmly in place in connecting rod big ends.

Special attention is directed to the main bearings and the method of retention. Both are housed in supplementary pressed steel container, forced into the soft aluminum crank-case, these members of hard material resisting deformation due to alternate shock stresses much better than the softer alloy they protect. The bearing on the drive side has a clamped inner race, held tightly against a shoulder on the fly-wheel by a threaded clamping nut and the outer race, while not tightly clamped by the housing cap, is held so it will not have any more than .01 inch end movement. The inner race of the bearing at the timing gear end is clamped between shoulders on the fly-wheel shaft and timing gear, which member is firmly pressed against the inner race by the threaded retention nut. The outer race is allowed to float in its pressed steel container.

CHAPTER IV.

LUBRICATION, CARBURETION AND IGNITION.

Theory of Lubrication—Forms of Lubricants—Devices for Supplying Oil—Sight Drip Feeds—Simple Splash System with Hand-Pump—Mechanical Oilers—Lubricating Two-Cycle Engines—Motorcycle Fuel, Its Derivation and Use—How Fuel is Carried—Principles of Carburetion Outlined—What the Carburetor is for—Early Vaporizer Forms and Their Defects—Elements of Carburetor Design—Features of Automatic Carburetors—Typical Motorcycle Carburetors—Foreign Carburetor Designs—Methods of Carburetor Adjustment—Typical Mufflers and How They Operate—Use and Abuse of the Muffler Cut-out Valve—How Compressed Gas is Ignited—Parts of Simple Battery System—High Tension Magneto Action—Operation of Standard High Tension Magneto—Magneto Driving Means—Ignition Timing—Detection of Faults.

Theory of Lubrication.—All bearing surfaces, no **matter** how smooth they appear to be to the naked eye, have minute projections, and, when examined under a microscope, the surface of even a finely finished bearing appears rough. If bearings were run without oil, the microscopic projections on the shaft and on the bushing or box in which the shaft revolves would tend to interlock, and a great amount of friction would result. This would mean that much of the power developed by the engine would be utilized in overcoming this resistance. Without some means of minimizing this loss, considerable heat would be generated if the bearings were run dry, and, as a result, the overheated bearings would soon depreciate and would give signs of distress long before they failed by becoming firmly burned together.

The reason a lubricant is supplied to bearing points will be readily understood if one considers that the close-fitting surfaces of the shaft and bushings are separated by this elastic substance, which not only fills up the minute depressions, thus acting as a cushion, but which absorbs the heat generated by friction as well. In properly lubricated bearings, the oil takes all the wear that would otherwise come on the metallic bearings. The grade of oil and amount to use depends entirely on the bearing points where it is to be applied. An oil that would be entirely suitable for lubricating the interior surfaces of the gas-engine cylinder would not be suitable for bearings in some cases if these were subjected to heavy pressures. At the other hand, the semi-fluid oil or grease which cushions the teeth of the driving and change speed gearing so well could not be used in the cylinders of the engine.

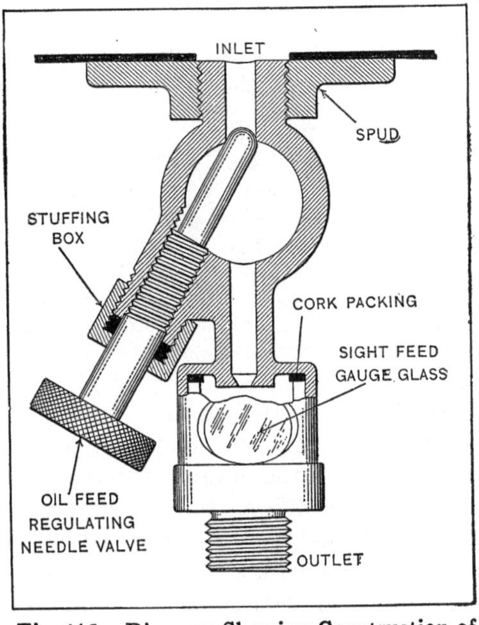

Fig. 116.—Diagram Showing Construction of Drip Feed Lubricator.

When used for air-cooled engine lubrication, an oil must be capable of withstanding considerable heat, in order that it will not be evaporated or decomposed by the hot metal of the cylinder. The oil used for cylinders or bearings should have a low cold test, i. e., it should not thicken up at low temperatures so that it will not flow freely. All authorities contend that lubricants must be free from acid which will corrode the metal surfaces to which the oil is applied. A lubricant must have sufficient body to prevent metallic contact of the parts between which it is depended upon to maintain a resilient film. It should not have too high a body or too much viscosity because a lubricant that is too thick will have considerable friction in itself, and will not flow readily between bearing surfaces.

If the lubricant is to be used in gearing where great cushioning qualities are desired in addition to positive lubrication, it must have a heavy body and the semi-solid graphite greases are the best materials to use for this purpose. The grease or oil should also be free from injurious adulterants of either vegetable or animal origin, because these invariably contain fatty acids that will decompose and attack metal surfaces or gums which will coagulate or oxidize by exposure to air and retard the action of the bearings. The best lubricants for motorcycle use are derived from a crude petroleum base with the exception of graphite which is a form of pure carbon that is a good lubricating medium for certain purposes.

Forms of Lubricants.—Oils of organic origin, such as those obtained from animal fats or vegetable substances, will absorb oxygen from the atmosphere which may cause them to become rancid. As a rule, these oils have a very poor cold test, because they solidify at comparatively high temperatures. Their flashing point and fire test are also so low that they are not suitable at points where considerable heat exists, such as the interior of a gas engine. The only oil that is used to any extent in lubricating gas engines that is not derived from a petroleum base is castor oil, which is obtained by pressing the seeds of the castor plant. This has been used on high-speed racing motorcycle engines and on aeroplane power plants, where it is practically pushed right up past the piston and out of the combustion chamber with the exhaust gases, so fresh oil must be supplied all the time to replace that ejected from the engine. Obviously this method of oiling would not be considered economical, and would not be suitable on either business or pleasure automobiles or motorcycles.

Among the solid substances that have been used for lubrication to some extent may be mentioned tallow, which is obtained from the fat of certain animals, such as cattle and sheep, and graphite, which is a natural mineral product. Tallow is usually employed as a filler for some of the greases used in transmission gearing, but should never be utilized at points where it will be exposed to much heat, and even under these conditions pure mineral greases are to be preferred. Graphite is obtained commercially in two forms, the best known being flake graphite, where it exists in the form of small scales or minute sheets, and the deflocculated form, where the graphite has been ground or otherwise divided into a dust. It is usually mixed with oil of high viscosity and used in connection with lubrication of change speed or power transmission gear parts, though it has been mixed with cylinder oil and applied to engine lubrication with some degree of success. Graphite is not affected by heat or cold, acids or alkali, and has a strong attraction for metal surfaces. It remains in place better than an oil, and, as it mixes readily with oils and greases, their efficiency for many applications is increased by its use.

Any oil that is to be used in the gasoline engines must be of high quality and for that reason the best grades are distilled in a vacuum so the light distillates will be separated at a much lower temperature than ordinary distilling practice permits. When distilled at the lower heat, the petroleum is not so apt to decompose and deposit free carbon. A suitable lubricant for gas-engine cylinders has a vaporizing point at about 200 deg. Fahr., a flash point of 430 deg. Fahr., and a fire test of about 600 deg. Fahr. Cylinder oil is one lubricant that must be purchased very carefully. A point to remember is that the best quality oils, which are the most efficient, can only be obtained by paying well for them. The few cents saved in using a cheap oil is not of much moment when compared to the repair bill that may accrue from its use. The cheap oil will not only deposit carbon very freely in the cylinder heads but is liable to gum up the piston rings and valves, and detract much from the smooth operation and power capacity of the motor.

Devices for Supplying Oil.—When the internal combustion engine was first evolved, the importance of adequate lubrication to secure efficient engine action was not as fully realized as it is at the present time. Practically all of the early forms of engines were slow acting and the problem of lubrication was not as serious as that which confronts the present-day designer of high-speed power plants. The earliest system of oil supply was by filling the crank-case to a certain level, and depending on the rotating parts to pick up the oil and throw it around the interior of the motor. Later, the sight feed devices that have been used for lubricating bearings of steam engines and other machinery were applied to the gasoline engine. These consisted essentially of a glass cup held in place between bronze castings to form the top and bottom of the oil container, respectively. The amount of oil supplied the bearing points was regulated by a suitable needle valve, and the oil supply could be observed through a small glass window in the bottom of the cup, before it reached the interior of the engine. Modern practice calls for a positive supply of the lubricating medium by mechanical means and the most effective of the methods of lubrication now in use are those in which the operator is depended on only to keep the oil container filled up.

Sight Drip Feeds.—An example of the fitting employed to regulate the oil flow when the lubricant is supplied by gravity is clearly shown at Fig. 116. Fittings of substantially this design have received wide application on motorcycles. They are usually screwed directly into the bottom of the oil tank, and as that member is always carried higher than the engine, when included in the fuel container, the oil will tend to flow by its own weight. The device consists of a simple casting member carrying at its lower end a small chamber adapted to receive a sight feed gauge glass through which the oil feed may be readily observed. The pipe connecting the sight feed fitting to the engine base is attached directly to the bottom of the chamber carrying the gauge glass. The oil enters the device through the opening in the bottom of the tank, and the amount of flow can be regulated within a wide range by the use of the oil feed regulating needle valve which also serves as a shut-off valve when lubrication is not desired. The oil collects in the globular portion of the casting and drips through the constricted opening above the sight feed gauge glass.

Simple Splash System with Hand Pump.—While the customary manner of lubricating the first engines was by supplying the crank-case directly with oil, there were certain defects to this system that made it imperative to add some device for directing the oil to the engine base without need of the rider dismounting. On the earlier motorcycles, it was common practice to supply a small oil cup just below the oil tank that held a certain amount of lubricant. The arrangement was such that this cup could be filled from the main container, and the instructions of the manufacturers were usually explicit in stating that every eight or ten miles of average riding that it would be necessary for the rider to supply the engine base with another cup full of oil. This meant that it was necessary for the rider to dismount and fill the cup from the main tank before permitting its contents to flow to the engine interior. The next improvement to be made was the addition of a hand-operated plunger pump to supply the oil, and this was usually placed convenient to the rider so it could be operated without stopping the machine. A popular location was directly at the side or in the interior of the oil container. This system of lubrication is used on a number of motorcycles, even at the present time, either alone or in combination with some form of a drip feed fitting.

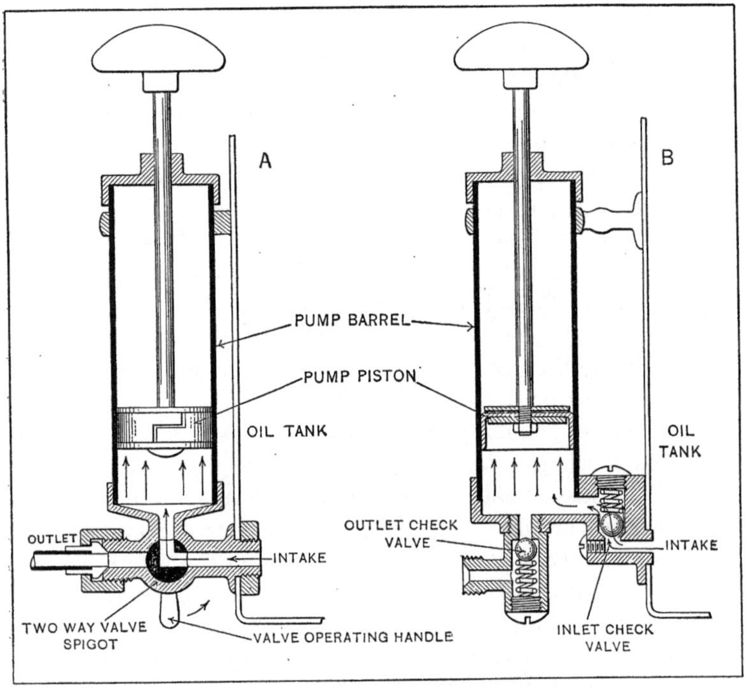

Fig. 117.—Types of Plunger Pumps Utilized in Forcing Oil to Engine Crank Case.

The plunger pumps are of two general types, as shown at Fig. 117. That outlined at *A* has manual control of the oil flow while that at *B* has automatic control. In the former, a two-way valve is provided in the bottom of the pump chamber, the spigot of which can be placed in three different positions. When placed as shown, with the valve operating handle pointing straight down, the interior of the pump is directly in communication with the oil container, and an upward stroke of the plunger will fill the pump barrel or cylinder with lubricant. When the pump plunger is nearly to the top of its stroke, the valve-spigot operating handle is moved around in the direction of the arrow, so that it lies parallel with the intake passage. Under this condition, the two-way valve spigot was moved around so that the oil in the pump barrel may be forced through the outlet pipe because the oil tank is shut off by the solid wall of the spigot. If the valve-operating handle is turned a half revolution from the position assumed when discharging lubricant from the pump barrel, both orifices, that at the bottom of the pump, as well as the intake from the oil tank, are shut off, and no oil will flow either to the pump or to the engine until the valve-operating handle is moved as indicated. The arrows show the direction of flow of the oil when the pump piston ascends.

Another popular form of pump is shown at Fig. 117-*B*, and one reason for its popularity is that it is automatic in action, and requires no other attention on the part of the rider than raising and depressing the pump piston. When the pump piston moves upward, it creates a partial vacuum in the pump barrel, and this lifts the inlet-check valve from its seating and permits oil to flow into the pump interior. As soon as the pump cylinder is full, the inlet-check valve is reseated by a suitable spring, and, as the pump handle is moved down, the pressure of the oil tends to keep the intake check more firmly seated. The other check valve, however, is installed so it will open under the influence of the oil pressure, and this permits the lubricant to flow from the pump to the outlet pipe. The action of a pump of this nature may be easily understood by remembering that the intake-check valve will open only when the piston is going up, while the outlet-check valve will leave its seat only when the piston is going down.

Some trouble is apt to materialize in a pump of this character, owing to the check valves becoming clogged up by gum or wax in the oil, and if this occurs the pump will not operate satisfactorily. For this reason, the check valves are usually housed in such a way that they may be easily removed for cleaning. Those who favor the manually operated valve contend that the elimination of the check valve makes the action of the pump positive, and therefore best adapted to the requirements of the ordinary rider.

The oil injected into the engine base fills the crank-case to a certain height, as indicated at Fig. 118, and, as will be apparent, the revolving fly-wheel will pick up the lubricant and throw it about the interior of the engine liberally. The oil supply to the motor shown is by a hand-operated plunger pump which injects a charge directly to the

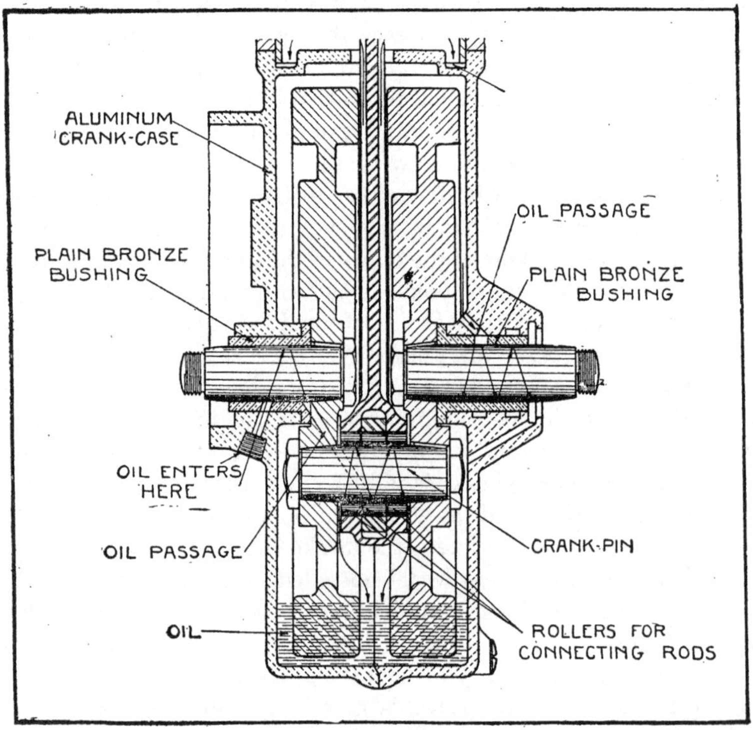

Fig. 118.—Application of Simple Splash System to Motorcycle Engine Lubrication.

crank-case as well as by a drip-valve fitting connected beneath the timing gear case.

This oiling system has given excellent satisfaction on a prominent machine, the Excelsior. Even though anti-friction bearings are used in the connecting rod big ends, every precaution has been taken to supply oil to the roller bearings in a positive manner. The lubricant enters beneath the timing-gear case, and is directed to the main bearing shaft from which it is conducted to the crank-pin by a passage drilled in the fly-wheel web, and communicating with a similar passage in the crank-pin so the oil is discharged at the central point of the bearing. Before it can be thrown off by centrifugal force, it must lubricate the roller bearings at either side. The oil mist always present in the crank-case and cylinder interior lubricates the piston, cylinder walls and main bearings positively.

Mechanical Oilers.—The problem of gas engine lubrication has always been a vital one when plain bearings are used, and, while the simple splash system has the advantage of lack of complication, the motor is always operating in a state of either feast or famine as regards lubrication of parts. Main shaft bearings, cylinders, and all reciprocating parts will receive plenty of oil by the splash system, providing the oil level is high enough so the fly-wheels will pick up the lubricant as they rotate. The connecting rod big ends, which are attached to a rotating member, and one that turns very fast at that, cannot receive adequate quantities of oil because they throw it off as fast as it collects between the surfaces, except in some engines where the oil is supplied to the connecting rod big ends first. The writer does not mean to imply that the rod ends do not get oil, but from the way they wear out and the condition of the surfaces, it is apparent that they do not get enough oil at all times. Then again, when one considers that this is the bearing that takes the greatest stress, and that the projected area of the bushing is seldom conducive to maintenance of an oil film, it is not strange that anti-friction bearings are being used so generally to replace big end plain bushings.

One of the first lessons learned by automobile engineers was that oil must be supplied in a positive manner if connecting-rod bushings were to endure, so in all automobile engines designed for racing or other exacting work and in most pleasure cars, force-feed lubricating systems are employed, and the lubricant is directed to the bearings through passages in the crankshaft by pressure produced by some positively driven force pump. If this precaution is considered desirable on automobile power plants, where bearing surfaces do not need to be restricted in size, and which operate at about half the speed of a motorcycle engine, then it is apparent that positive lubrication is not only very desirable but indispensable in small, high-speed engines of the air-cooled forms used to propel motorcycles.

The oil pump used on the Indian motorcycle, and the method of application are clearly outlined at Fig. 119. The phantom view shows the simplicity of the pump mechanism very clearly, as well as defining the method of reciprocating the plunger. A small worm gear is driven

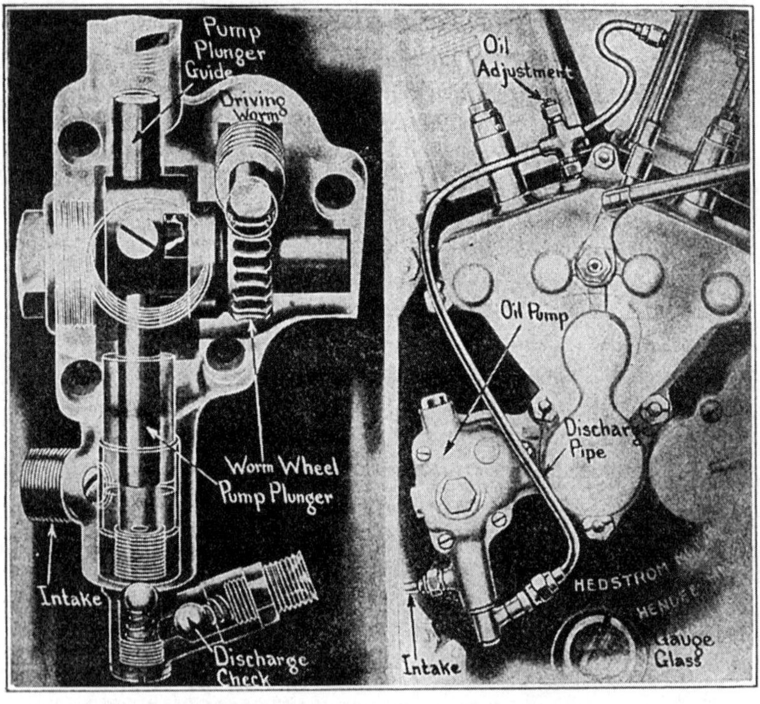

Fig. 119.—Mechanical Oil Pump Used on the Indian Motorcycles and Method of Application to the Power Plant.

from the timing gear, through the medium of a small spur pinion on the end of the driving worm shaft that projects into the engine interior. This worm rotates a worm wheel that works the crank employed to reciprocate the pump plunger. As the pump plunger is raised, oil flows in to fill the barrel through the intake which is coupled directly to the tank, and on the down stroke the oil is discharged through the outlet-check valves to the front cylinder, from which it drips into the interior of the engine. The oil level in the engine base can be readily ascertained by a gauge glass or window in the side of the crank-case. The oil is supplied to the front cylinder to insure that that member will receive an adequate supply. The tendency of the fly-wheels as they rotate is to throw the oil into the rear cylinder

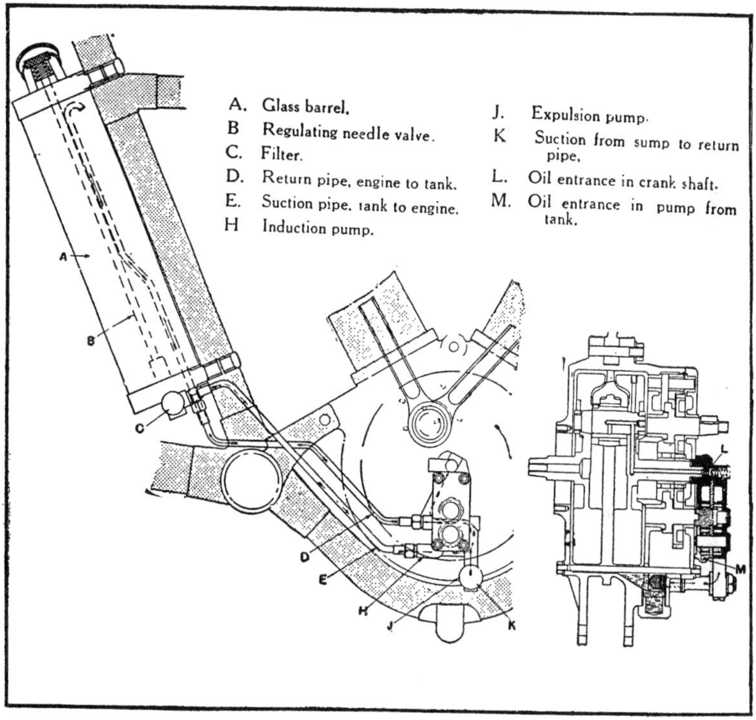

Fig. 120.—Lubricating System Employed in the Royal Enfield Motorcycle.

rather than the front one, because that member is approximately in line with the oil spray as it is discharged tangentially from the rapidly revolving fly-wheel rim. This would result in the rear cylinder securing better lubrication than the front one if no provision was made for directing the oil from the mechanical pump to the front cylinder. In most cases, a mechanical oil pump is supplemented by a hand-operated type which is used in emergencies when it is necessary to supply more lubricant than the pump will deliver, as in fast riding.

The oiling system of a prominent English machine, the Royal Enfield, is outlined at Fig. 120. The oil is carried in the tank at the back of the seat-post tube, and one of two pumps fitted outside of the timing-gear case draws the lubricant from the tank to the engine. The second pump, called the expulsion member, forces the oil from the engine base back again into the tank. Obviously, as long as the engine is running, there is a continuous circulation of oil. The diagram clearly outlines the whole system and the path followed by the oil from the tank A to the engine and back again. The supply of lubricant is regulated by a needle valve B which has a knurled top, and from that point passes through a filter C along the suction pipe E to the induction pump H. This pump discharges into the hollow end of the crankshaft L, forcing the oil along this shaft through an aperture in the fly-wheel, into the crank-pin bearing, from which point it is distributed by centrifugal force to the other engine parts. The oil then drips back into a sump integral with the crank-case, and any excess which has not passed through the engine shaft also reaches this sump through a by-pass or release valve. The expulsion pump J draws the oil from the sump K and passes it back again to the tank through the return pipe D. A filter in the sump retains any residue contained in the oil, and insures that only clean lubricant will be pumped back into the tank.

The lubricating system used in the four-cylinder Pierce motorcycle is somewhat similar, except that but one pump is utilized instead of two. This system is clearly shown at Fig. 121. The oil flows by gravity to the base of the crank-case, from an oil tank forming part of the large front frame tube, and passes through the working parts as it flows. This flow is rapid and is started when a valve at the top of the tank is given a quarter turn. As soon as the engine starts, a rotary pump of the gear type sucks the oil from the oil well or sump at the bottom of the crank-case and forces it through a discharge manifold into chambers in which the lower ends of the connecting rod dip. With this system it is necessary to shut off the flow of oil at the tank whenever the machine is stopped, in order to prevent flooding the motor.

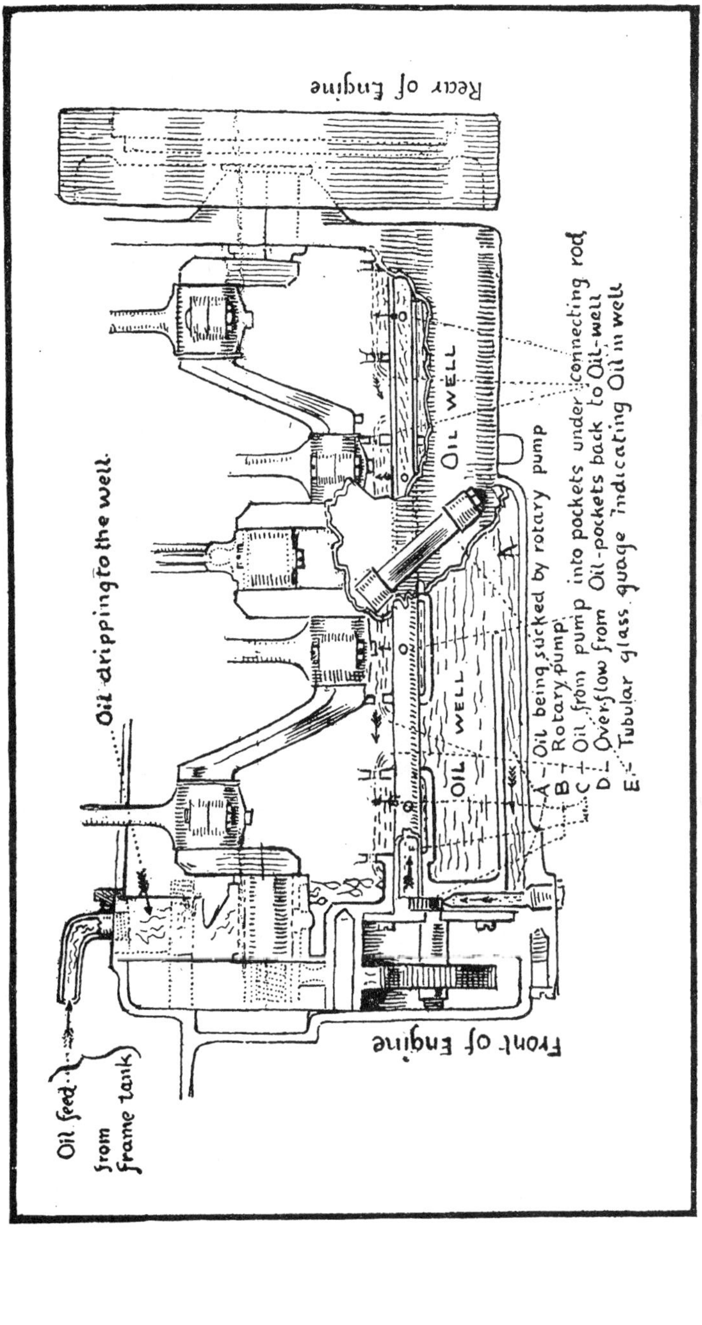

Fig. 121.—Lubricating System Used in Pierce Four Cylinder Motorcycle Power Plant.

A modification of this system is shown at Fig. 122 applied to a single-cylinder engine. The usual form of pump drive by spiral gears is employed to draw oil from the container or sump integral with the engine base, but it is discharged from the oil supply pipe into a passageway that communicates with the interior of a hollow crank-pin. From here, it passes through an oil tube attached to the connecting rod and lubricates the wrist pin. The oil thrown from the rapidly revolving fly-wheel lubricates the cylinder and piston walls thoroughly.

The lubrication system outlined at Fig. 115 insures that the bearings will receive copious oiling and is a form that has given excellent service on thousands of automobiles, as well as having been successfully applied to four-cylinder motorcycle engines. The pump draws oil from a sump cast integral with the crank-case through a filter screen. The oil level in the crank-case proper is kept at a certain predetermined height by an adjustable overflow pipe so the fly-wheels will pick up lubricant as they revolve, as in conventional systems. The advantage of the adjustable overflow is that this can be easily changed at any time to permit of more or less oil in the crank-case. For example, if the engine is to be run at high speeds, as in racing, the level can be made higher. When the machine is new, or after new rings have been fitted to the piston, it may also be desirable to furnish more oil than would be required under normal operating conditions. The standpipe adjustment can be readily altered to suit conditions.

The gear pump discharges the lubricant at some pressure and this is piped to a point at the bottom of the bearing housing cap at the drive side, where it communicates with a groove in the crankshaft. This groove is connected to a drilled passage in the shaft by another hole drilled at right angles to that in the shaft. The passage extends through the fly-wheel to the crank-pin center, from which a discharge hole directs the oil to a point between the crank-pin ball bearing races. The centrifugal force assists in distributing the lubricant, and the crank-pin bearings receive all they need. The oil spray thrown off by the revolving crank-pin supplements that picked up by the fly-wheels, and all interior parts receive positive lubrication. As the oil may be kept to the correct level automatically to insure adequate lubrication by splash, the rider's responsibility ceases when he has

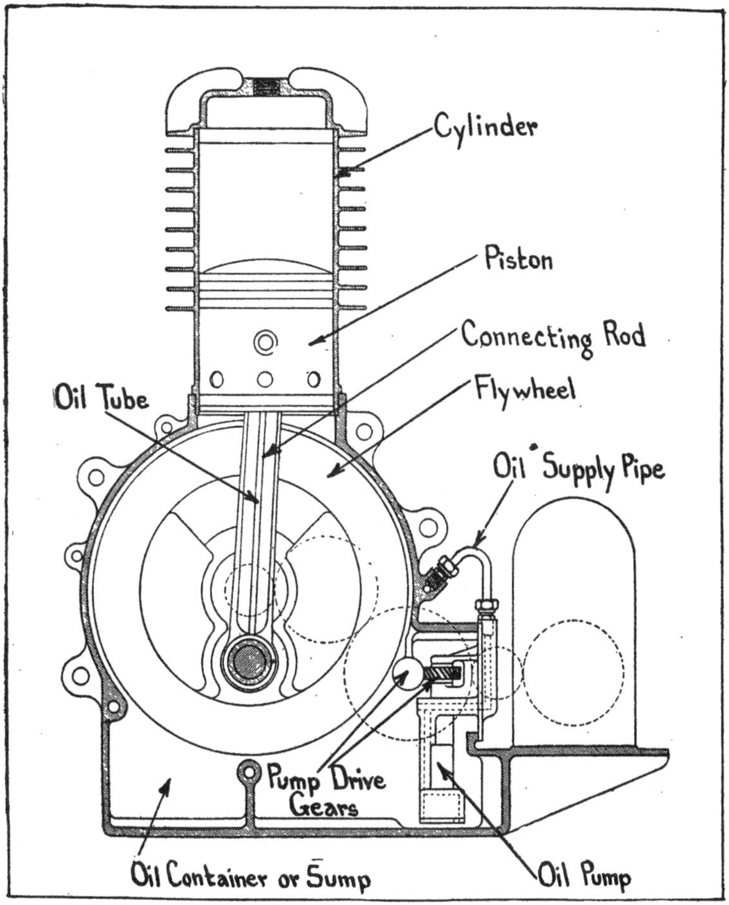

Fig. 122.—Mechanical Oiling System Applied to Single Cylinder Motor.

placed sufficient good oil in the sump. He may even be relieved of this duty by having an oil tank attached to the sump in such a manner that oil will be automatically supplied by the air lock system.

Lubricating Two-Cycle Engines.—An advantage of some moment that is obtained by the use of a two-stroke power plant is the very simple method of lubrication employed in which all pumps, sight feed or drip devices and piping may be eliminated. The method of supplying the lubricant consists merely of mixing a certain amount of oil with the gasoline by pouring it directly into the gasoline tank. Owing to the construction of a two-cycle motor, which decrees that the explosive mixture must go into the engine base before it can pass into the cylinder it is possible to supply oil in the manner indicated. The oil is not dissolved by the gasoline but still its viscosity or body is reduced to such a point that it will pass through the spray nozzle of the carburetor without any difficulty. It separates from the explosive vapor in the engine base and condenses in the form of minute globules of oil on all interior parts of the engine. A certain amount of the condensing oil vapor finds its way to the bottom of the engine crank-case, and is distributed by the fly-wheel just as in other splash systems. The amount of oil used is approximately one-half pint per gallon of gasoline, i. e., if two gallons of gasoline were poured into the fuel tank, it would be necessary to add a pint of oil to insure that the engine would be adequately lubricated. The proportion may also be expressed as, one part of oil to sixteen parts of gasoline by volume.

Attempts have been made to lubricate four-cycle engines in this manner, but have not been successful on account of the mixture being supplied directly to the cylinder interior instead of to the engine base. The oil deposited in the combustion chamber interfered materially with correct valve action and promoted carbonization and caused ignition trouble by short-circuiting the spark plugs. In the two-cycle motors, the oil is well separated from the mixture before the gas charge is transferred to the cylinder interior from the crank-case.

Motorcycle Fuel, Its Derivation and Use.—The great advance of the internal combustion motor can be attributed more to the discovery of suitable liquid fuel than to any other factor. The first gas engines made, utilized ordinary illuminating gas as a fuel, and, while this is practical for use with stationary power plants, wherever it is available, such as the natural gas fields of the Middle West, or in cities and towns having a central gas producing plant, it is obvious that it could not be very well applied to portable self-propelling power plants used for cycle propulsion. When it was discovered that certain of the liquid fuels belonging to the hydro-carbon class, which includes petroleum and its distillates, benzol and benzene, which are coal tar products and alcohol, could be carbureted or mixed with air to form an explosive gas, the gas engine became widely used as a prime mover for all classes of vehicles.

The liquid fuels have the important advantage that a quantity sufficient for an extended period of engine operation can be easily carried in a container that will not tax the capacity of the engine, and that requires but comparatively little space in any out-of-the-way portion of the frame. When used in connection with a simple vaporizing device, which mixes the liquid with sufficient quantities of air to form an inflammable gas, the fuel is automatically supplied to the engine without any attention being demanded from the operator as long as the supply in the tank is sufficient to produce a flow of liquid through the pipe joining the mixing device and fuel container.

Up to date, the most important fuel used in connection with motorcycle and automobile engines has been one of the distillates of crude petroleum, known generally to the trade as "gasoline." This liquid, which is a clear white, very light-bodied substance, evaporates very rapidly at ordinary temperatures. This feature made it especially adaptable for use with the early forms of mixing valves, because it mixed so readily with air to form an explosive gas. Fifteen years ago, there were very few industrial uses for gasoline and it sold for less than five cents a gallon in some cases. During the past decade, the demand for it has increased by leaps and bounds, and it now sells for four times as much as it did when the gasoline engine was first introduced.

The specific gravity of gasoline varies from sixty to seventy-six degrees, though very little of the latter is now obtainable except by special arrangement with the oil-producing company. It was formerly thought that gasoline any heavier than seventy-six degrees would not work satisfactorily in the cylinders of the gas engine, and, while this is true of the early crude and inefficient vaporizers, modern mixing devices have been evolved which handle gasoline of sixty-two degrees specific gravity and even heavier. The percentage of gasoline produced from crude oil in proportion to the other elements is very small, and as the demand has increased to such proportions, the tendency of the producer has been to make gasoline heavier or of lower specific

Fig. 123.—Showing Location of Fuel and Oil Containers on the Eagle Motorcycle. This Arrangement is Representative of Standard Practice.

gravity by distilling off some of the heavier oils with it to increase the bulk produced.

Experiments are being tried with kerosene and alcohol in automobile carburetors, but these fuels are not considered seriously in connection with the motorcycle, on account of the small fuel consumption of all motorcycle power plants. When a gallon of gasoline will suffice for 50 or 60 miles' travel, fuel expense is not a serious item, even considering the present price of gasoline.

How Fuel is Carried.—The conventional method of carrying both the fuel and lubricating oil is clearly shown at Fig. 123, which gives a view of the Eagle motorcycle with the side of the tank broken away to show its division into two parts. The larger portion serves as a container for gasoline and is connected directly to the float chamber of the carburetor by the gasoline feed pipe. The oil container also houses the plunger pump used to supply oil directly to the crank-case and is provided at the bottom with a drip feed of the type previously described. The location of the motorcycle fuel tank is practically the same on all machines at the present time, though in the early days, as can be very clearly understood by referring to the views of pioneer forms of motorcycles given in the first chapter, it was attached to the frame at any convenient point. The popular location was overhanging the rear wheel. At the present time, the tank is invariably placed above the motor, and, while most makers favor the detachable construction by which a removable tank is placed between the top frame tubes, some manufacturers incorporate the tank as part of the frame structure. This is true of the Schickel motorcycle, in which the tank is an aluminum casting that also has the steering head and suitable projecting lugs for anchorage of the frame tubes cast integral. In the Pierce motorcycle, the frame is made of large tubing, and this serves to contain the fuel and lubricating oil as well as forming the frame structure. While the fuel tanks are usually made of steel, they are either galvanized or copper or brass plated in the interior to prevent corrosion due to moisture or acids in the gasoline. The endeavor of most designers is to attach the tank to the frame in a positive manner, and yet have the tank retaining brackets or clips accessible so that member can be easily removed for repair if it becomes damaged. The best material for tanks is heavy gauge copper as it is easier to solder than steel, and is not affected by moisture or other agents that would have a chemical action on steel.

Principles of Carburetion Outlined.—Carburetion is a process of combining the volatile vapors evaporating from the hydrocarbons previously mentioned with enough air to form an inflammable gas. The amount of air needed varies with the character of the liquid fuel and some mixtures burn much quicker than others. If the fuel and air mixture is not properly proportioned, the rate of burning will vary, and either an excess of fuel or air will reduce the power obtained from combustion materially. The proportions of air and liquid needed vary according to the chemical composition of the liquid.

Gasoline, which is that commonly used at the present time, is said to comprise 84 per cent carbon and 16 per cent hydrogen. Oxygen and nitrogen form the main elements of the air, and the former has a great attraction for the main constituents of hydrocarbon liquids. What we call an explosion is merely an indication that the oxygen of the air has combined chemically with the carbon and hydrogen of gasoline. In figuring the proper amount of air to mix with a given quantity of fuel one takes into account the fact that eight pounds of oxygen are required to burn one pound of hydrogen, and that two and one-third pounds of oxygen are necessary to insure the combustion of one pound of carbon. As air is composed of one part of oxygen and three and one-half portions of nitrogen by weight, for each pound of oxygen one needs to burn either hydrogen or carbon, four and one-half pounds of air must be allowed. About sixteen pounds of air must be furnished to insure combustion of one pound of gasoline, the hydrogen constituent requiring six pounds of air, while the carbon component needs ten pounds of air.

Air is not usually considered as having much weight, but at a temperature of 62 deg. Fahr. fourteen cubic feet of air will weigh a pound. Two hundred cubic feet of air will be needed to burn a pound of gasoline according to theoretical considerations. The element nitrogen, which is the main constituent of air, is a deterrent to burning as it does not aid combustion or burn itself. Therefore, it is usual practice to provide four hundred cubic feet of air to each pound of gasoline. Mixtures varying from one part of gasoline vapor to from four to thirteen parts of air can be ignited, but the best results are obtained when five to seven parts of air are combined with one of gasoline vapor. This mixture produces the most rapid combustion, the highest temperature, and, consequently, the most pressure.

What the Carburetor is for.—Any device which will supply gasoline and air in measured quantities so inflammable mixtures of the proper proportions will be supplied the engine is called a "carburetor." In its simplest form, a carburetor would consist of a pipe open at one end for the admission of air, and joined to the cylinder at the other, and having a spray nozzle or opening through which gasoline could be injected into the air stream placed at some intermediate point in the pipe between the air inlet and the gas outlet to the cylinder.

Early Vaporizer Forms.—The surface carburetor was the first device to be used in combining air with gasoline to form an explosive vapor. Before the motorcycle or automobile became popular, the gasoline available was of very high volatility, i. e., it evaporated much more readily than the heavier fuels available to-day. A typical surface carburetor, such as used on one of the earliest practical motorcycles, the Wolfmueller, is shown at Fig. 124. The operation of this device is easily understood. The carburetor was filled with fuel to a definite height which was so regulated that the surface of the liquid was just below the lower main air pipe opening. The air entered through a funnel-shaped member which deflected it over the surface of the fuel. Here it became mixed with the vapor given off by the volatile liquid and the mixture passed through a safety screen to a mixing valve on top of the carburetor. The vapor given off was very rich, and, in order to dilute it, extra air was admitted through an auxiliary air cone attached to the mixing valve. The gas supply to the engine was regulated by a simple throttle as was also the amount of air from the auxiliary air entrance. A separate throttle was provided to regulate the quantity of gas supplied as the only function of the mixing valve or chamber was to regulate the quality of the gas.

Another form of surface carburetor that received wide application on the early motor tricycles of De Dion-Bouton manufacture is outlined at Fig. 125, A. In action, it is very similar to that previously described, except that it was improved in some details. For example, a plate was attached to the bottom of the main air supply tube, and this insured that all the air currents would pass over the surface of the liquid and become saturated with vapor. It was necessary to use a mixing valve at the top of this carburetor, in order to dilute the rich vapor, so as to secure an explosive mixture of proper proportions.

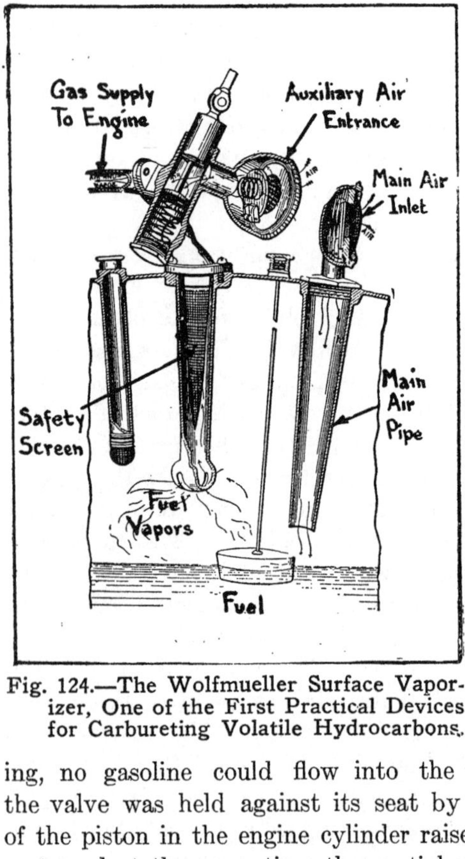

Fig. 124.—The Wolfmueller Surface Vaporizer, One of the First Practical Devices for Carbureting Volatile Hydrocarbons.

The simple form that is really the parent of our present float feed carburetors is shown at Fig. 125, B. In this, the gasoline was supplied from a container to a fuel inlet on the side of the main casting. A regulating needle valve was placed in the passage that provided communication from the fuel inlet to the jump valve seat. The air entered below the jump valve which was normally spring retained against the seating so that the mixing device was divided into two parts, one below, the other above the valve. As the valve covered the spray opening, no gasoline could flow into the mixing device as long as the valve was held against its seat by the spring. The suction of the piston in the engine cylinder raised the jump valve from its seat, and at the same time the partial vacuum caused the gasoline to spray out of the opening and mix with the current of air drawn in through the main air inlet and into the upper portion or mixing chamber of the device. The amount of liquid supplied the mixture was regulated by the needle valve, while the proportion of

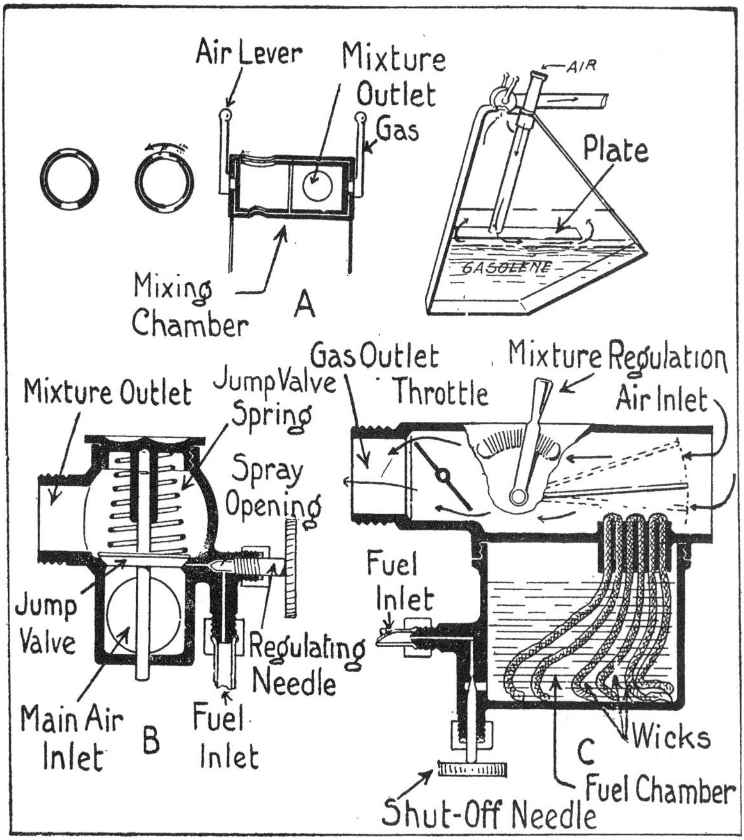

Fig. 125.—Early Types of Gasoline Carburetors. A—De Dion Bouton Surface Vaporizer. B—Simple Spraying Device With Automatic Jump Valve. C—Diagram of Wick Carburetor.

air could be altered at will by limiting the movement of the jump valve.

A third form that received limited application is known as "the wick feed carburetor," and is illustrated at C, Fig. 125. In this device, the liquid was drawn to the top of the container by the capillary attraction of the wicks, and as the top of these were brushed over by the main air current, the vapors given off were mixed with it to form an explosive gas. The mixture proportions were regulated by a simple shutter which could be swung on an arc so that it could be brought very close to the wicks or moved away. This shutter deflected the entering main air current against the wicking, and when in its uppermost position, practically no air would enter the mixture without passing over the surface of the wicks and becoming saturated with fuel vapor. When the shutter was in an intermediate position, part of the entering air stream would pass over the wicks while the remaining portion would flow directly into the column of gas and dilute it if too rich. The fuel inlet from the tank to the fuel chamber of the mixing device was controlled by a shut-off needle and the amount of mixture supplied the engine could be varied by a simple throttle of the damper type.

Defects of Simple Vaporizer Forms.—The simple mixing valve forms have disadvantages of some moment, the main defect being that they are somewhat erratic in action, and that the mixture cannot be as well regulated as when float feed carburetors are used. While the primitive forms gave fairly good results with high grade gasoline, they do not carburet the lower grades of fuel used to-day properly, and do not supply enough gas of proper consistency for the present types of engines. The most efficient modern power plants utilize float feed carburetors instead of simple mixing valves. The advantage of the float construction is that the gasoline is maintained at a constant level regardless of engine speed. In the simple forms of generator valves in which the gasoline opening is controlled by a poppet valve, a leak in either valve or valve seat will allow the fuel to flow continuously whether the engine is drawing in a charge or not. During the idle strokes of the piston when there is no suction effect exerted to draw in gasoline vapor, the liquid fuel will collect around the air opening, and when the engine does draw in a charge it is excessively rich because it is saturated with globules of liquid fuel.

With a float feed construction, a constant level of gasoline or other fuel is maintained at the right height in the standpipe, and will only be drawn out of the jet by the suction effect of the entering air stream. The objection to the simple surface or wick feed is that the tendency is to draw off only the more volatile constituents of the fuel, and that after a time the heavier elements included in gasoline will remain in the vaporizer and will not be changed to gas. Obviously the engine is not capable of utilizing all of the fuel. With a float controlled spray nozzle, the spray is composed of all the constituents of the liquid, and the lower grade portions that are mixed with those having higher evaporation points are drawn into the cylinder and burnt instead of settling to the bottom of the carburetor.

Elements of Carburetor Design.—The float-feed carburetor, with concentric float and mixing chambers, is the standard American type, and preference is given to automatic carburetors. In England, the practice is different, as the carburetors have separate float and mixing chambers for the most part, and are manually controlled instead of having automatic compensation for speed variation as is general in this country. In float-feed carburetors, the principle of mixing the gasoline vapor and air is the same as in the early forms of mixing devices, but the method of fuel supply is different. The device consists of two parts, a float chamber and a mixing chamber. The standpipe in the mixing chamber is connected to the float chamber, and the arrangement is such that the level of liquid in the float chamber is kept to a height equal to that of the spray nozzle. The fuel pipe from the tank or main container is coupled to the inlet pipe of the float chamber, and the opening is closed by means of a needle point carried by a hollow metal or cork float. The length of the needle is such that its point shuts off the gasoline supply when the level of gasoline in the float chamber coincides with the top of the standpipe. Whenever the fuel is drawn out of the float chamber sufficiently fast so the level is reduced, the float will sink with the decreasing liquid, and the passage in the fuel supply pipe is opened, allowing gasoline to flow into the float chamber until the liquid is at the proper height. Just as soon as the proper level is reached, the float and the needle it actuates are moved until the valve shuts off the flow of gasoline from the tank.

The concentric float chamber feature insures a constant level of fuel at the nozzle. When the nozzle is carried at one side of the float chamber, if the carburetor tilts, as is possible when climbing or descending a grade, if the float chamber is higher than the nozzle, the carburetor will flood. If conditions are reversed, the level of fuel in the spray nozzle will not be high enough, and the mixture will be too thin. With the spray nozzle placed at the central point of the device no reasonable amount of tilting will change the height of the liquid at that point, and a mixture of constant proportions is insured under all abnormal as well as normal operating conditions. The advantages of this construction do not seem to be properly appreciated by European designers, though generally accepted by American engineers.

Features of Automatic Carburetors.—The simple form of float feed spraying carburetor has disadvantages that made improvements in construction necessary before it became really efficient. One of these was that as the engine speed increased, the suction effect augmented in proportion, and as more gasoline was sprayed into the mixture because of the higher degree of vacuum created in the cylinder, the mixture became too rich at high speed. This is the main reason for the introduction of the modern automatic carburetor, such as shown at Fig. 128. In this device, the needle valve is mounted concentric with the float, i. e., the mixing chamber passes through the center of the carburetor, while the bowl, in which a horse-shoe shaped float is placed, surrounds the mixing chamber. The air pipe is constricted around the spray nozzle in order to get the proper air speed to insure positive suction of liquid at low engine speeds. At high engine speeds, when the mixture would be too rich in the simple form of carburetor, an automatic auxiliary air valve, which is carried to one side of the mixing chamber, opens and admits air to the mixture to dilute it. In the English carburetors, it is necessary to regulate the air supply with every change in engine speed, as it is believed that this is the only way to secure maximum economy. An automatic carburetor obviously must give average results, and intelligent hand regulation means that the best mixture for any engine speed can be selected by trial instead of approximated by an initial setting of the carburetor.

Typical Motorcycle Carburetors.—One of the most popular of all motorcycle carburetors, and the type which has undoubtedly received the widest application because it has been a standard fitting on the Indian motorcycle since its inception, is illustrated at Figs. 126 and 127. The external view at Fig. 126 will assist in making clear the action, while the arrangement of internal parts can be readily ascertained by consulting the sectional drawing at Fig. 127. This design originated through a desire of its inventor, Oscar Hedstrom, who was then building motor-pacing tandems, to eliminate the continual shifting of an air valve every time the throttle was moved, as was true of the early carburetors and even present-day foreign designs. The Hedstrom was the first automatic carburetor to receive general approval, and was also one of the first to incorporate the concentric arrangement of float and mixing chambers that is so common at the present time. The automatic compensation feature was secured by a conical sleeve working in the mixing chamber, and actuated through a suitable connecting rod and crank arrangement attached to the throttle barrel. A manually regulated air shutter was provided to get a correct mixture when starting the machine, and when this has been set to provide a proper running mixture, the carburetor automatically took care of mixture variations and proper compensation was made between the air and the gasoline as the throttle was moved. In the latest form of Hedstrom carburetor, a pilot jet is provided in a separate mixing chamber which facilitates starting the motor and insures steady running at low engine speed. This carburetor was one of the contributing causes that made the Indian machine superior to the earlier forms of foreign and domestic manufacture, because it provided a much better and more uniform mixture than the mixing valves and surface vaporizers that were generally employed, and permitted greater engine speeds and flexibility.

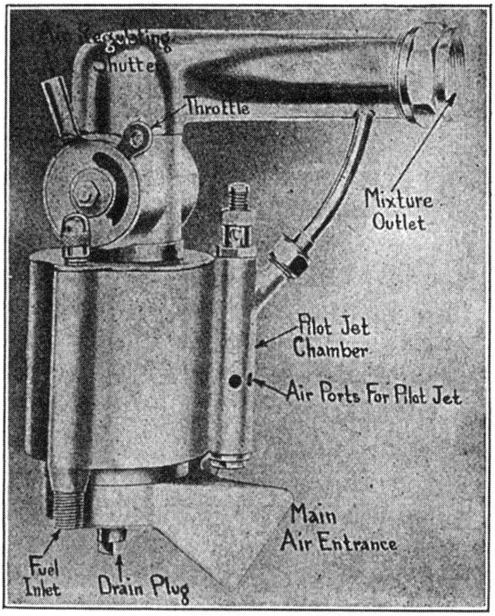

Fig. 126.—The Hedstrom Automatic Carburetor Used on Indian Motorcycles.

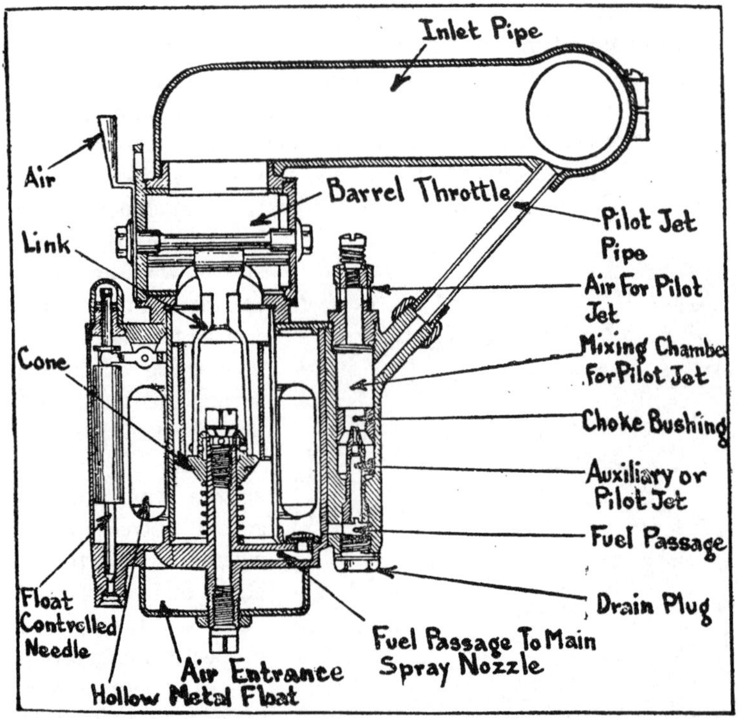

Fig. 127.—Sectional View Showing Interior Arrangement of Hedstrom Automatic Carburetor.

Sectional views showing the construction of the Schebler motorcycle carburetor are presented at Fig. 128. This is a concentric form, and a feature of merit is the method by which the fuel supply is augmented as the throttle is opened. The adjusting needle valve is carried on a bell crank which can be rocked by a cam forming part of the throttle linkage. This cam is so arranged that as the throttle is opened a spring, bearing against the bell crank member, will raise the needle from its seating in the spray nozzle and permit more gasoline to enter the mixture. The auxiliary air supply is regulated by altering the tension of the spring used to keep the air valve seated. In the Hedstrom carburetor, the float is of hollow metal, whereas in the Schebler a cork float is utilized. The method by which the float shuts off the flow of fuel from the tank when it reaches the right height in the float chamber is practically the same in all carburetors. A lever of the first class transmits the upward motion of the float to the needle, which moves in the opposite direction, and which shuts off the fuel inlet when the liquid reaches the proper level in the float chamber.

In the Kingston carburetor, shown at Fig. 129, the concentric float and mixing chamber are retained, as this construction may be said to represent standard American practice. A feature of the device is the use of a series of balls of varying weight to control the auxiliary air ports. As the throttle is opened, and the suction becomes greater,

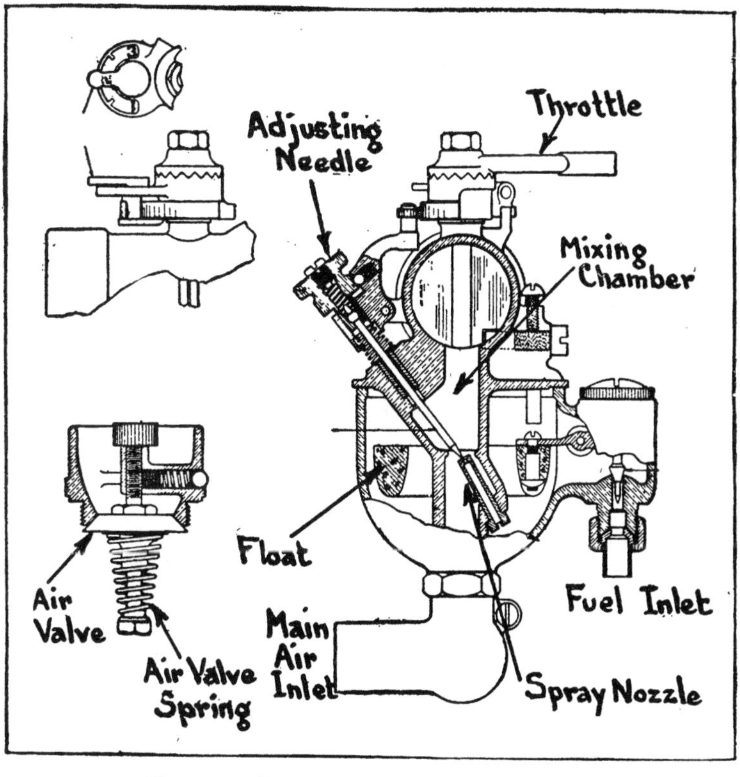

Fig. 128.—Schebler Motorcycle Carburetor.

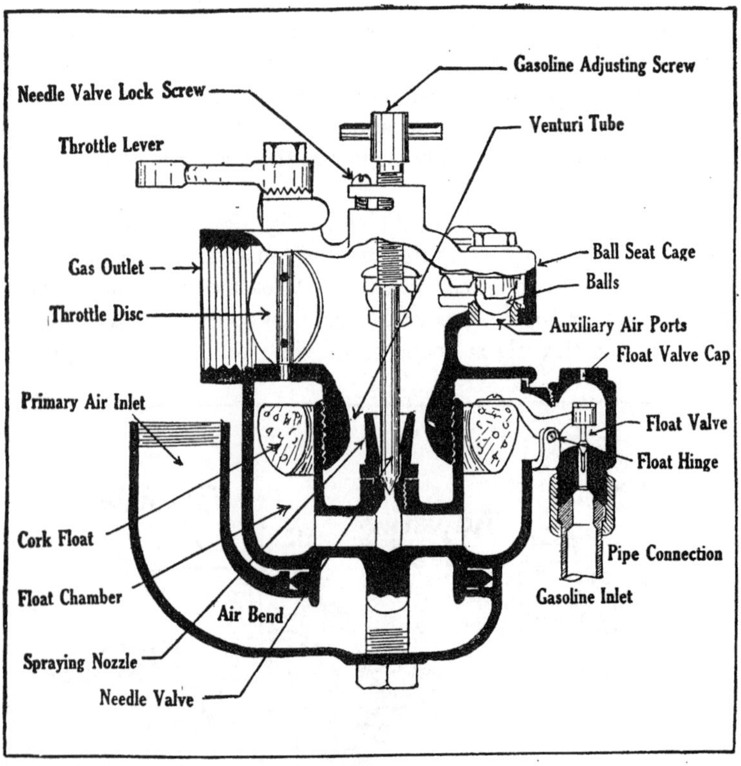

Fig. 129.—The Kingston Automatic Carburetor With Auxiliary Air Control by Ball Valves.

the balls open progressively and admit more air to the mixture. In this carburetor, no provision is made for altering the amount of auxiliary air under the control of the rider, but, instead, mixture proportions are altered by a needle valve which determines the amount of fuel sprayed from the stand pipe.

At Fig. 130, sectional views of the Breeze carburetor are depicted and in this form automatic regulation of the fuel supply is possible, as the throttle is opened because of a direct mechanical interconnection between the throttle lever and the regulating needle valve, as outlined at Fig. 131. The auxiliary air supply is regulated by means of a flat seated air valve provided with the usual adjustable reseating spring.

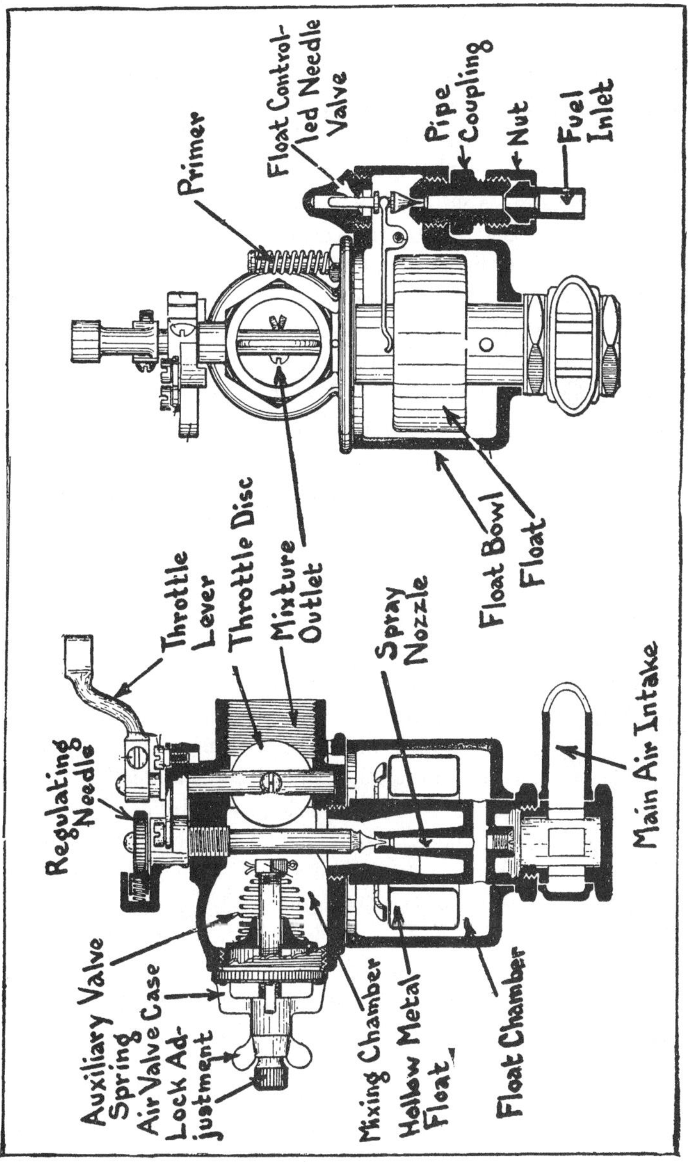

Fig. 130.—Sectional Views Showing Construction of Breeze Motorcycle Carburetor.

The manner in which the mechanical interlock between the needle valve and throttle lever works can be readily determined by observing the relative positions of the numbers on the regulating needle valve top with the throttle in the closed and opened position. It will be observed that in the closed position, the figure 1 is approximately in line with the center line of the carburetor, whereas when the throttle is opened the needle valve has opened sufficiently so the numeral 3 now registers with the carburetor center line. Practically all carburetors include a "tickler" or primer provided so the float can be depressed several times to cause gasoline to overflow the spray nozzle and thus provide a rich mixture for starting.

Foreign Carburetor Designs.—Carburetors of English and French design are considerably different from those of American manufacture because the automatic feature is seldom utilized, and also because the float chamber is usually distinct from and set at one side of the mixing chamber. European carburetors are not only more bulky than our American forms but would not meet with much favor in this country on account of the constant manipulation of the air valve necessary every time the throttle is moved.

The Longuemare, a popular French carburetor, is shown at Fig. 132, while two representative English types are outlined at Fig. 133. The feature of the Longuemare carburetor is the design of the spray pipe which includes an ingenious method of regulating the quantity of fuel spray by a conical plug provided with a number of passages so the fuel is atomized in a number of fine streams instead of one large stream as is the case when a spray nozzle having but a single central opening is used. The small streams are more quickly vaporized and are more easily absorbed by the entering air than the one large stream would be. The amount of gasoline is varied by changing the depth or number of the passages cut on the face of the tapered plug. If the mixture is too rich, one or more of the grooves may be filled in with solder, whereas if it is not sufficiently rich, the grooves provided may be made deeper and thus allow more liquid to flow into the mixture. The form shown is provided with a heating jacket and when used, in connection with an air-cooled motor, a portion of the exhaust gas is usually deflected through this chamber to furnish heat. It is not customary to provide these heating chambers on motorcycle carburetors.

The English carburetors shown at Fig. 133 are practically the same in principle, the only difference being in details of construction. For example, that on the left employs a counter-weighted float arrangement, while that at the right is considerably simpler because the float needle which regulates the main fuel inlet is attached directly to the float and moves in the same direction. The method of auxiliary air regulation, and also the throttle control in the device at the left, is by semi-circular slides which are normally pressed down by springs,

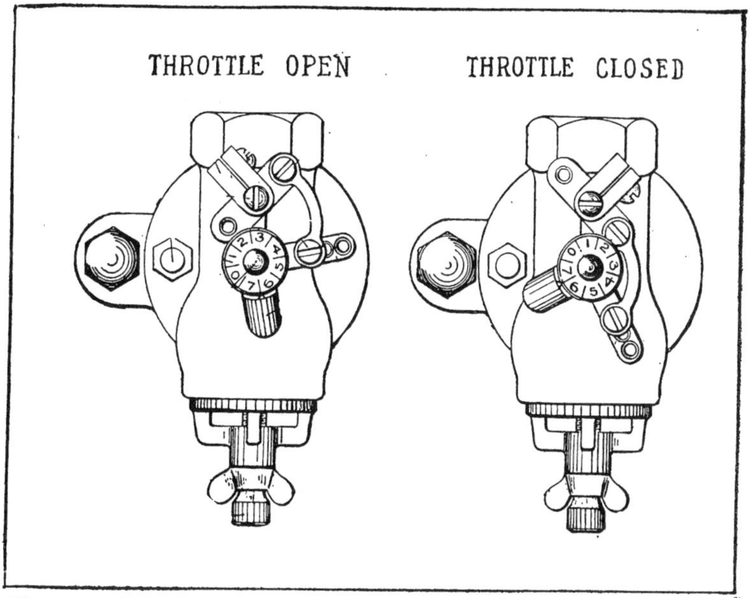

Fig. 131.—Top Views of Breeze Motorcycle Carburetor, Showing Mechanical Interlock Between Throttle and Mixture Regulating Needle.

so as to regulate the size of the extra air opening or that leading to the engine. These slides are adapted to be worked from the handle bars through Bowden wire control. In the device at the right, concentric slides are utilized to regulate the proportion of air admitted the mixture, and the quantity of gas supplied the motor. The outer slide is the member controlling the extra air, while the inner member regulates the supply of gas. In the American carburetors having a needle valve pointing directly into the spray nozzle, an advantage of some moment is gained by breaking up the entering fuel stream into a spray. In the English device, at the right of Fig. 133, a small spraying cone is attached to the throttle slide that is intended to perform the same function.

It is desirable to interpose some form of strainer or filter in the gasoline line between the tank and the carburetor in order to prevent

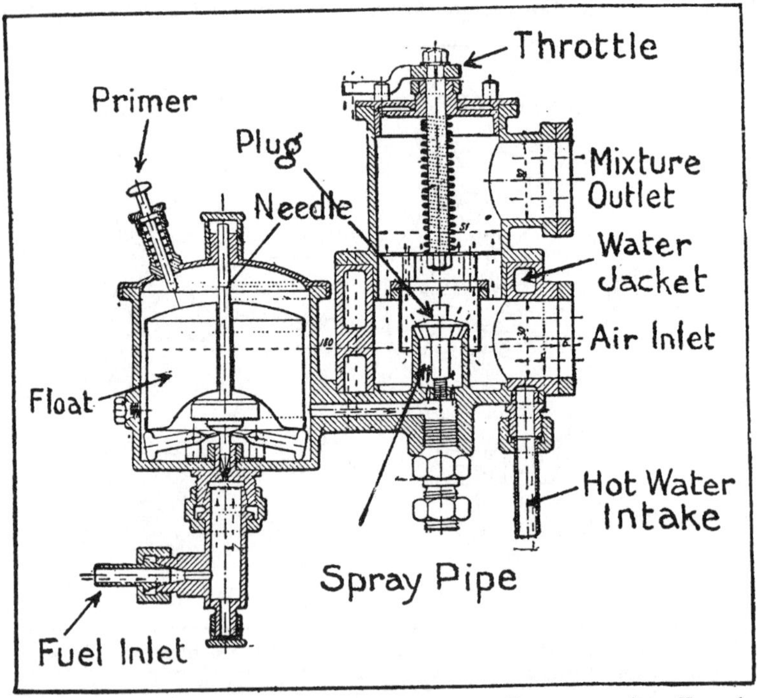

Fig. 132.—The Longuemare Carburetor, a Representative French Design.

dirt or water from reaching the interior of that device. Two typical straining devices are outlined at Fig. 134. In both of these, a gauze screen is used to separate the dirt from the gasoline, and a settling chamber is provided in which all dirt or water collects instead of flowing to the carburetor. Suitable drain cocks are provided so the settling chamber may be cleaned out when necessary.

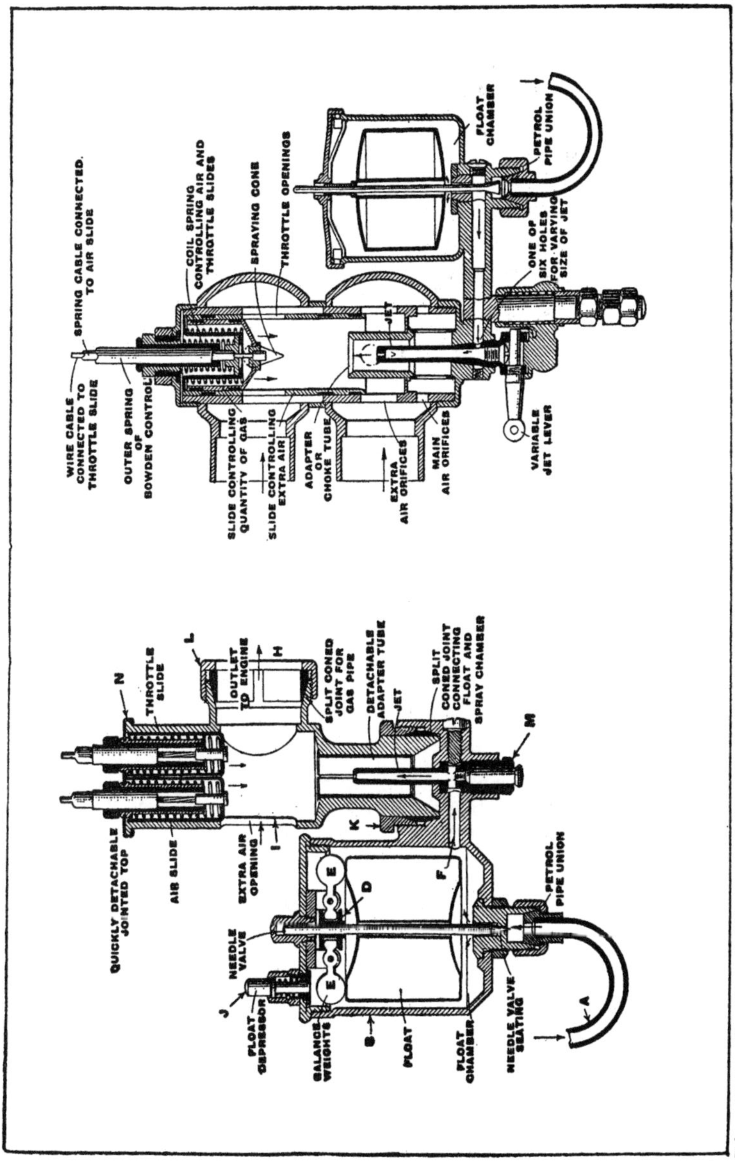

Fig. 133.—Sectional Views of Typical English Carburetors, Showing the Placing of the Float Chamber at One Side of the Mixing Chamber and the Air Regulation by Hand Operated Valves.

Another point that needs to be carefully observed to secure proper carburetion, in addition to the design of the vaporizer, is to proportion the intake manifold so the gas flow will not be obstructed and the charge will reach the cylinders promptly. The inlet manifold used on motorcycles is very simple when applied to twin-cylinder engines and in most cases endeavor is made to have the carburetor attached to the inlet pipe in such a way that it may be readily detached without disturbing the remainder of the piping, or the inlet pipe itself is fitted with suitable threaded connections at the ends so it can be removed from the valve chambers. Various forms of inlet pipes used in con-

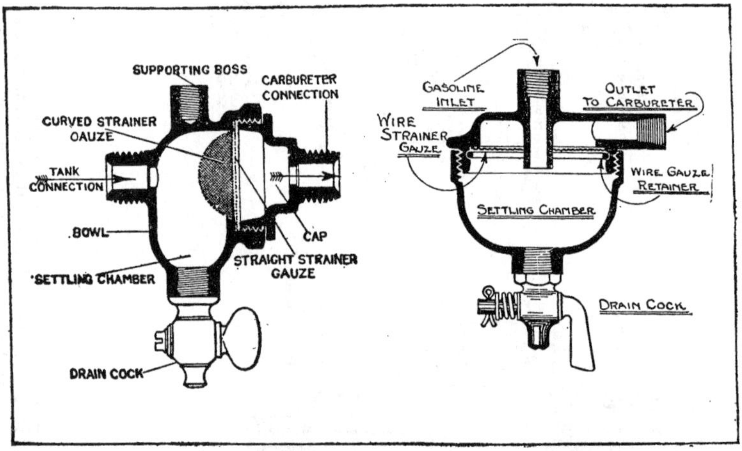

Fig. 134.—Strainers of Breeze Design to be Interposed Between Gasoline Tank and Carburetor for Preventing Passage of Water or Sediment to the Mixing Device.

nection with twin-cylinder engines are shown at Fig. 135. At A, the inlet valve dome castings have extensions to which a very short fitting carrying the carburetor is attached. At B, the manifold is a one-piece member attached to the inlet valve domes by easily removable retaining couplings. The construction at C is similar to that shown at B, except that it has a more pronounced curvature. In the manifold shown at A, the intake pipe is straight, whereas in those shown at B and C the gas passages are laid out with curves that are intended to provide an easy path from the carburetor to the cylinder

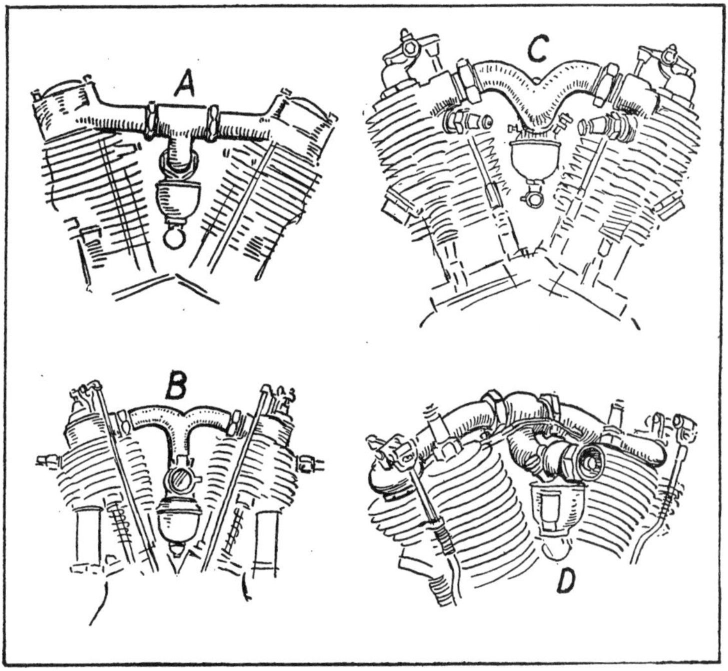

Fig. 135.—Design of Inlet Manifold for Twin Cylinder Motorcycle Power Plants. A—De Luxe. B—Emblem. C—Monarch. D—Fielbach.

interior. The form shown at D is also laid out in curves, but instead of the manifold rising from the carburetor to the valve chamber the pipes leading from the central fitting to which the carburetor is attached have a pronounced drop to the top of the cylinder.

The design of a suitable inlet manifold for a four-cylinder engine is one that calls for considerable judgment, as it is not practical to use the same type of a manifold as is employed on automobile motors owing to lack of space, and also because the carburetor must be carried at one end instead of at the side of the engine. It is possible to design an inlet manifold for a four-cylinder automobile motor that will give practically the same length of passage from the carburetor to any one of the four cylinders, and each cylinder receives the same quantity, and presumably the same quality of explosive mixture. As an example of a four-cylinder manifold, that used on Pierce engines is shown at Fig. 136. Viewed from the exterior, it would appear that the intake pipe was a simple tubular member having a branch leading to each cylinder, but when one examines the sectional view it will be seen that a partition wall is placed in the interior, and that this compensates in a degree for the difference in distance between the inlet valve of the first cylinder and the carburetor carried at the rear of the motor.

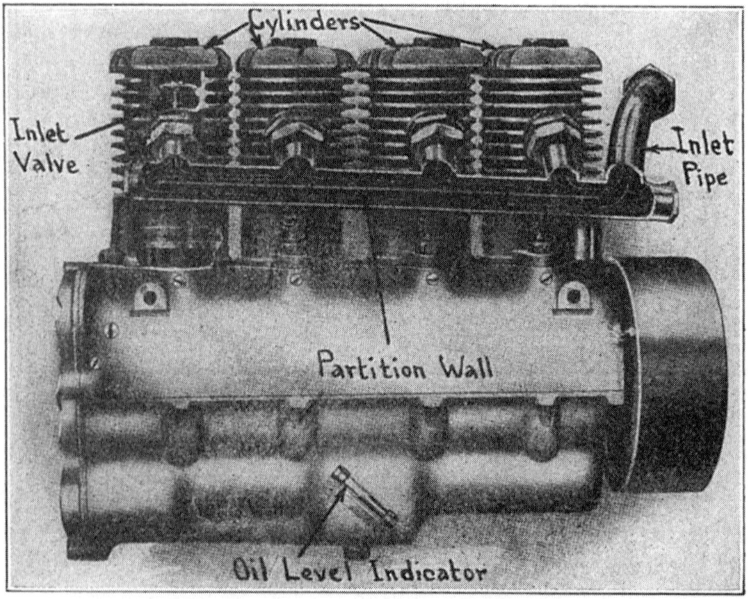

Fig. 136.—Inlet Manifold for Four Cylinder Motorcycle Power Plant.

Typical Mufflers and How They Operate.—After the charge of gas compressed in the cylinder has been ignited, and even when the piston reaches the bottom of its stroke, the exhaust gas still has considerably more pressure than the atmosphere. It is said that the pressure of the exhaust gases discharged through the exhaust valve when that member is first opened is about 40 to 45 pounds, and if the gas is discharged directly into the air, the vibration caused by the violent ejection of the gases produces a noise comparable to a gunshot. The function of the muffler is to silence the exhaust by permitting the gas to expand to approximately atmospheric pressure before it reaches the air. One of the difficulties incidental to muffler design is to provide a form that will be effective as a silencer, and yet not offer appreciable resistance to the flow of the gases as this produces a back or negative pressure on the piston top when rising on the exhaust stroke which reduces the power output of the engine. This problem is not a difficult one for automobile designers to solve, because they have plenty of space available and can make the expansion chambers large enough so that there is ample space for the gas to expand before leaving the muffler interior. It is only necessary to provide an expansion chamber of a little more than three times the cubical capacity of one of the cylinders, and to break up the entering gas stream to facilitate its expansion, and one obtains a very effective muffler that offers no appreciable back pressure. In motorcycle practice, it is necessary that the muffler should be small and not occupy much space, so it is seldom that the motorcycle muffler will have more than the cubical capacity of the cylinder to which it is applied. When one considers that the gases are being discharged into a silencer at a velocity of 6,000 to 7,000 feet per minute, with the

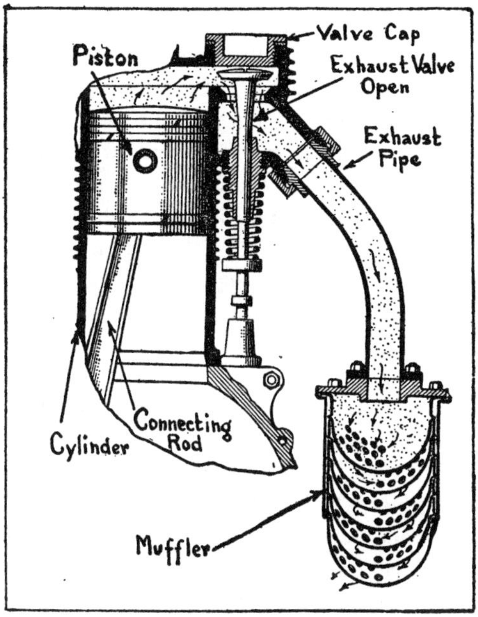

Fig. 137.—Showing the Use of Muffler to Receive and Silence the Exhaust Gases Before They are Discharged to the Atmosphere.

motor running 2,000 revolutions, it will be apparent that it is a problem of some magnitude to dissipate the current of gas rapidly enough to break up its acoustic powers without producing a negative pressure against the piston.

The construction of a typical motorcycle muffler of English design is shown at Fig. 137. The principle of silencing involved is to break up the gas into a large number of small streams by the medium of perforated baffle plates through which the gas must pass before it is discharged to the air. The general practice is to provide one muffler for both cylinders because but one is exhausting at a time. Some of the foreign motorcycle builders provide a separate muffler for each cylinder as indicated at Fig. 138. The somewhat novel and effective silencing arrangement used on Iver-Johnson motorcycles is shown at Fig. 139. This consists of what is practically an extension of the exhaust pipe, perforated with a large number of holes. It is said to be reasonably silent, and as there are no baffle plates interposed to hinder the flow of gas, it offers minimum back pressure.

An efficient muffler of American design is shown in the sectional view at the bottom of Fig. 139. In this, the gas enters a large chamber which is separated into six compartments by four baffle-plate members and an inner cylinder. Before the gas can pass out, as indicated by the arrows, it must first pass through the perforated baffle plates into an intermediate expansion chamber which communicates with a concentric cylindrical expansion chamber extending the length of the muffler. This has suitable perforations in its wall.

The endeavor of designers is to make mufflers that can be easily taken apart for cleaning which is a desirable feature in view of the oily character of the exhaust gas discharged from the average motorcycle power plant. In the form at Fig. 139, the various components are held together by a through bolt and the muffler can be easily disassembled by loosening one of the clamping nuts at the end of the bolt. The various parts may be removed from the main head fitting, and after all deposits of oil and carbon have been removed, it is a simple matter to replace the perforated cones around the central expansion chamber and clamp these members between the muffler heads by the retaining bolt. If cleaning is neglected, the openings in the baffle plates may become choked with carbon, and, as the area of the passages is decreased, considerable back pressure will be present which may cause the engine to overheat.

Use and Abuse of the Cut-Out Valve.—Many mufflers are provided with a cut-out valve designed so that gas can be discharged directly from the exhaust pipes to the outer air instead of into the muffler interior. It is an advantage to include a cut-out with the muffler as this can be opened when full efficiency of the engine is desired as in speed work or hill climbing. The cut-out also affords an

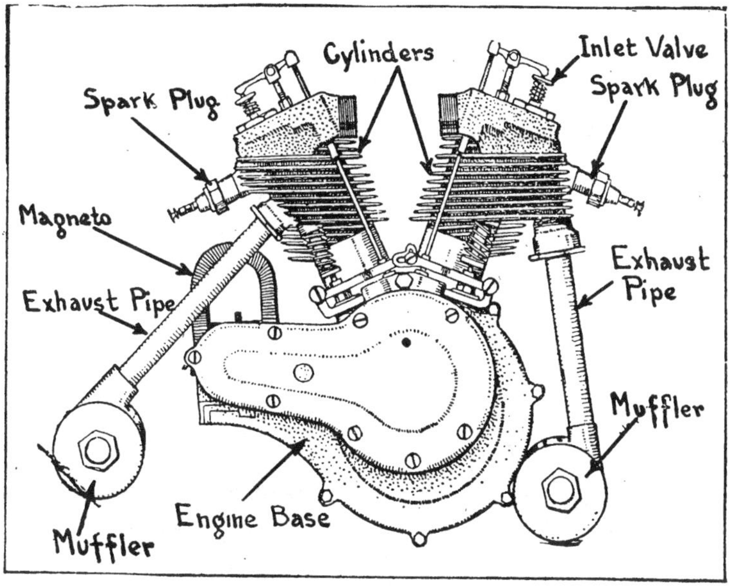

Fig. 138.—Premier Motorcycle Power Plant Which Utilizes Two Mufflers, One for Each Cylinder.

opportunity to judge the regularity of engine running, because the explosions can be heard easily with a cut-out opened. While the cut-out is a useful fitting, it has been abused in many instances by riders who leave it open in passing through towns or when using the motorcycle in traffic. In fact, the practice of running with an open muffler has been so general in the past that the impression conveyed to the layman has been that in silence of operation a motorcycle and a rapid fire gun are synonymous. Practically all of the motorcycles on the market to-day are provided with effective and efficient silencers, and there is no excuse for running with a cut-out open in average touring work. Some manufacturers are successfully combating the open muffler evil by eliminating the cut-out fitting altogether which makes it imperative that all exhaust gases be discharged through the muffler. The arrangement of the cut-out and muffler of the Excelsior motorcycle is clearly outlined at Fig. 140. The muffler head has the branches, in

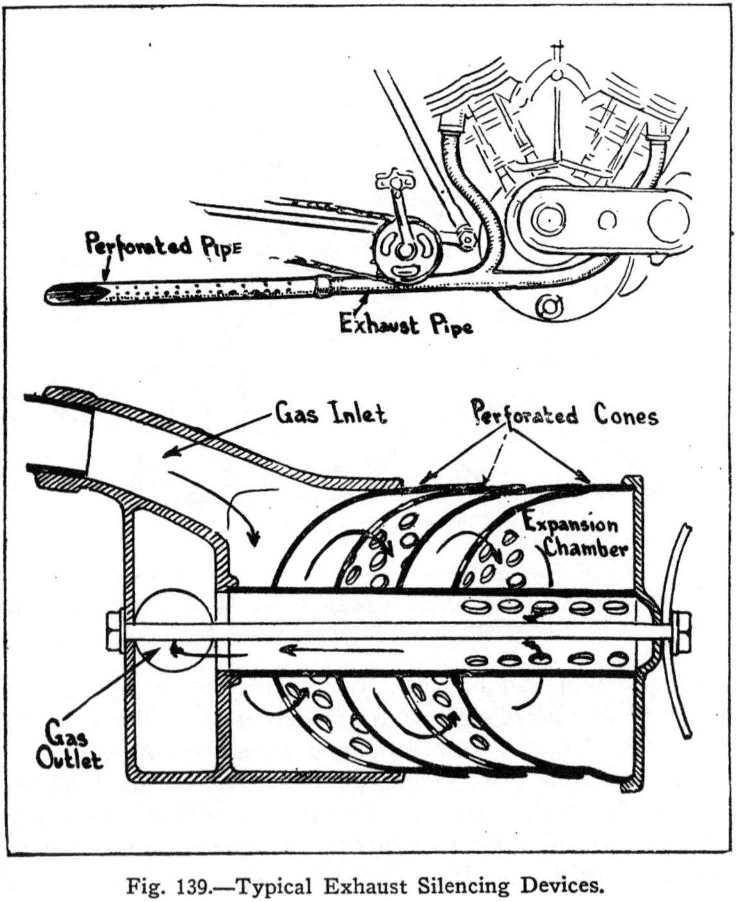

Fig. 139.—Typical Exhaust Silencing Devices.

which the exhaust pipes are secured, cast integral, and, at one side of the head, an opening is provided in this casting which is closed by a suitable damper or shutter easily worked by a small lever or crank to which it is attached. This crank can be moved easily with the foot, and can be opened or closed while riding as conditions dictate, and will stay in either the open or closed position.

How Compressed Gas is Ignited.—When the gas engine was first developed, the compressed gas was exploded by means of a naked flame which was permitted to communicate with the combustion

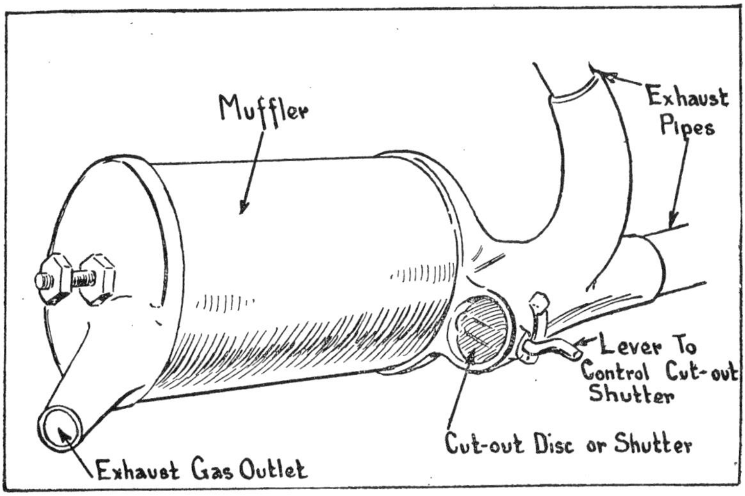

Fig. 140.—Method of Utilizing Exhaust Cutout Valve in Connection With Excelsior Muffler.

chamber interior by means of a slide valve which moved at the proper time to permit the flame to ignite the gas back of the piston. This system of ignition was practical only on the primitive gas engines where the charge was not compressed to any degree. When it became desirable to compress the gas before firing it, the hot tube system of ignition was used. This method involved the use of an incandescent platinum, porcelain or nickel tube in the combustion chamber, the tube or ignitor being kept in a heated condition by a flame burning in it. Another method depends upon the property of gases firing themselves if compressed to a sufficient degree, provided that a certain amount of heat was stored in the cylinder head to insure complete vaporization of the gas, and help produce the proper kindling temperature.

Practically all of the gas engines in use at the present time, except those employed for stationary power that operate on the Diesel system, utilize electrical ignition systems. In all motorcycle and automobile power plants, the compressed gas is exploded by a minute electric arc or spark in the cylinder, the current for which is produced by some form of chemical or mechanical generator of electricity. The early forms of ignition systems had a disadvantage in that they were not flexible and could be used successfully only on constant speed engines. None of these methods are practical in connection with motorcycle power plants because they do not permit the flexible engine action that is so desirable and necessary.

While electrical ignition systems are somewhat more complicated than the other simpler types, they are the most efficient, and as their peculiarities are now generally understood, there is no difficulty in applying them successfully. Two forms of electric ignition systems have been used, the most popular being that in which a current of electricity under high potential or pressure is forced to leap an air space between the points of a spark plug which is screwed into the cylinder. The other system, which is used to a limited extent on marine engines, is known as the low tension system because a current of comparatively low voltage is utilized instead of the high pressure current used in the more popular systems. Whereas the spark is produced in the high tension system by the current heating up the air particles between the points of the spark plug, it is produced in the combustion chamber when the low tension method is employed by moving electrodes which come in contact with each other, and which produce a spark as they separate.

The essential elements of any electrical ignition system are: First, a simple and practical method of current production; second, suitable timing apparatus to cause the spark to occur at the right point in the cycle of engine action; third, some form of igniter to produce the spark in the combustion chamber; fourth, apparatus to transform the low tension current obtained from batteries or dynamo to one of greater

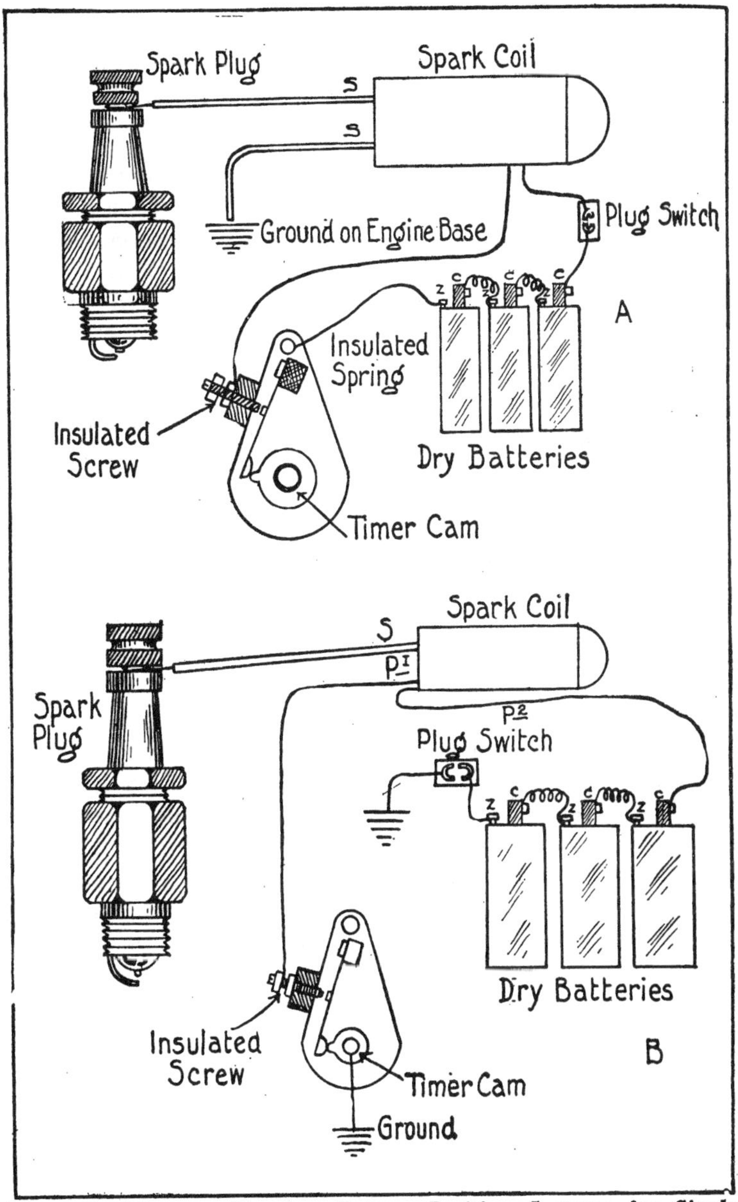

Fig. 141.—Diagram Showing Battery Ignition Systems for Single Cylinder Engines.

value before it can produce a spark in the cylinder; and fifth, suitable wiring, switches and other apparatus to convey the current produced by the generator to the auxiliary apparatus, and from these to the spark-producing member in the cylinder head.

There are two common means for obtaining the electrical current used to produce the spark in the cylinder, one of these depending on a chemical action, the other an electro-magnetic action. The first class includes the various forms of primary and secondary batteries, while the second group includes the various mechanical appliances, such as dynamos and magnetos. The simplest method of current generation is by means of a simple chemical cell, generally known as the "dry battery." These belong to the primary cell class because a current of electricity is generated by the oxidation of one of the elements of which the cell is composed by the electrolyte. Any primary battery consists of three main elements: First, a plate of some material which will be acted on by the electrolyte; second, an electrolyte which may be a solution of a salt or acid in water, which will have a chemical affinity for the active element; third, a neutral plate which serves to collect the electricity produced by the chemical combination of the electrolyte and active elements.

The dry battery is so called because the electrolyte is in the form of a paste instead of a liquid. The dry cell consists of a zinc can filled with electrolyte and a depolarizing chemical in the center of which a carbon rod or plate is placed. The function of the depolarizer is to keep the cells active for a longer period than would be the case if only a simple electrolyte was used. The zinc can serves as a container for the electrolyte and also forms the active member. The carbon rod is the neutral or collecting member. A terminal is attached to the zinc can and is known as the negative, commonly indicated by a minus sign thus (—) while the terminal attached to the carbon is known as the positive connection (commonly indicated by a plus sign +). It is to these terminals that the wires forming the external circuit of the cell are attached, the internal circuit being completed by the electrolyte and depolarizer.

A single dry cell does not have enough power to produce a spark, so a number of these are generally joined to form a battery. The common method of connecting dry cells is in series; this means that the positive terminal of one cell is always coupled to the negative terminal of its neighbor. When cells are coupled in this manner, the battery has a voltage equal to that of one cell times the number of cells so joined. For instance, three dry cells would have a potential or current pressure of four and one-half volts, as one dry cell has a pressure of one and one-half volts. The amount of current produced by the batteries is measured in amperes and the battery capacity will depend upon the size of the active element and the strength of the electrolyte. The ordinary No. 6 dry cell which is six inches high by two and one-half inches in diameter will indicate a current strength of about twenty amperes. When cells are joined in series, the amperage of the set is equal to that of but one cell.

When dry batteries are used for motorcycle ignition purposes, they are always coupled together in a series connection to obtain the proper voltage and current strength. The dry battery has a number of advantages, chief among which are its cheapness, ease of installation, compactness and simplicity. It has the disadvantage of being limited in capacity and not suited for continuous work, which it shares with all other forms of primary battery. When dry cells are exhausted, there is no method of renewing them to efficiency, and they must be replaced. They are seldom used on modern machines.

The coming of electrical self-starting and lighting systems on motorcycles has created some degree of interest in storage batteries, and in one machine, the Indian, which can be obtained with full electrical equipment, the battery current is employed for ignition purposes as well as for lighting and for starting the motor.

The storage battery is a chemical current producer that is capable of being recharged when it is exhausted by passing a current of electricity through it in a reverse direction to that of the current given out. Storage batteries are composed of elements of practically the same material, and can only become active when a current of electricity is passed through them. The materials generally used are grids of lead filled with a paste composed of lead oxides. When the current of electricity passes through these plates, they become enough different in nature so that a difference of electrical condition exists between them, and when the cell is fully charged, a current may be drawn from it in just the same way as from a primary battery.

Storage batteries have the advantage that they may be used for continuous current production, and as they may be recharged when exhausted, it is not necessary to replace them with new members when they will no longer produce current. The storage battery is called a "secondary cell" because it can only give out energy after a current of electricity has passed through it, whereas a primary battery in good condition will produce electricity as soon as it is completed. The storage battery uses an electrolyte composed of dilute sulphuric acid and water, while a dry battery uses an alkaline electrolyte composed largely of sal-ammoniac.

The average form of storage battery used for ignition, lighting or starting purposes is really composed of a number of separate cells, which are placed in a common carrying case of wood or hard rubber. The connection between the cells is made by plates of lead which are burned to the elements, leaving but two terminals free, one of which is a negative member while the other leads from the positive plates. To prevent spilling of the electrolyte, the top of the cell or battery is sealed with a hard rubber plate over which is poured a pitch and rosin compound. The electrolyte is renewed through a small vent in each cell which is covered by a removable hard rubber cap. These vents also allow for the escape of the gases evolved when the cell is being charged or when it is delivering a current of electricity.

Parts of Simple Battery Systems.—The first system of ignition to be applied after the hot tube method had been abandoned was the various electrical systems in which batteries furnished the current. The wiring of two ignition systems for single-cylinder motorcycle engines is shown at Fig. 141, while a diagram showing the arrangement of parts and the method of joining them in a two-cylinder ignition system is outlined at Fig. 142. In the simple system depicted at A, Fig. 141, three dry cells are joined together in series to form a battery capable of delivering about 4.5 volts. This voltage would not be sufficient to leap the air gap or space between the points of the spark plug because it requires a pressure of several thousand volts to produce a spark between the plug points. Therefore, an important element of all battery systems is the transformer or induction coil employed to raise the voltage of the current so it will overcome the resistance offered by the air gap. It is not necessary to go deeply into the theory of induction coil action at this time because none of the present day motorcycles, with the exception of the Hendee Special Model Indian, utilize these members or batteries for ignition. In its simplest form, the induction coil consists of a core composed of soft iron wire around which is wound two or three layers of No. 16 or 18 magnet wire. This is thoroughly insulated from another coil of very fine, thread-like wire comprising several thousand turns which is wound around the coil of coarse wire. The coarse wire is termed "the primary winding," because the energizing current from the battery flows through it. The fine wire, which is not in electrical connection with the battery, but which is excited by induction, is termed "a secondary coil" for this reason. In addition to the windings and core, a condenser is also included in the assembly which is contained in torpedo-shaped casings of hard rubber. Each time a current of electricity passes through the primary coil, an induced current of considerably higher voltage flows through the secondary coil. In order to insure that this rush of secondary current will only take place at such times that a spark is needed in the cylinder, a mechanically-operated switch termed the "timer," which is driven by the crankshaft of the engine, is interposed in the circuit between the batteries and the primary coil.

Considering first the four terminal coil shown at A, we find that two of the leads are insulated more heavily than the other two. The two wires with the thick insulation are secondary wires, and one is grounded while the other goes to the insulated terminal of the spark plug. The flow of secondary current is completed because the plug body, which carries one of the electrodes, is also grounded by being screwed into the cylinder casting. When a four-terminal coil is used, both terminals of the timer are insulated from each other, and the circuit is completed only when the platinum points on the timer spring and insulated contact screw are in contact. One of the primary wires, therefore, is attached directly to the insulated screw of the timer, while from the insulated contact spring another wire makes connection with the zinc terminal of the battery. The other primary terminal is connected to one side of a plug switch, while the wire from the carbon terminal of the battery is connected to the other. Before starting the engine, it is necessary to bridge the gap between the plug switch members by a suitable metallic connector, and then, as the engine is rotated, the timer cam will bring the platinum points on the insulated spring and screw together, and close the primary circuit when the piston reaches the end of its compression stroke, and when the gas is fully compacted preparatory to explosion. Vibrator coils, which are very popular in automobile and marine service, are seldom used in motorcycle ignition systems, because with the high speed of the engine a single quick contact not only produces the required spark but means a considerable reduction in battery consumption. It is necessary to regulate the contact screw of the timer very carefully to secure the best results from the engine, and a difference of an eighth of a turn is often all that is needed to increase or reduce the engine speed appreciably.

The wiring diagram presented at B is practically the same as that outlined above it, except that one of the secondary terminals is joined inside of the coil to one of the primary leads which goes to the battery. The primary wire P-1 goes to the insulated screw on the timer, and the primary wire P-2 goes to the carbon terminal of the dry cell battery. The zinc terminal of the battery is attached to one of the segments of the plug switch while the other member is grounded. The timer cam, which is attached to a metal shaft, is also grounded, and the current flow from the plug switch to the timer cam is through the metal parts of the engine and frame. But one secondary wire, S, projects from the coil, and this, of course, goes directly to the insulated terminal of the spark plug.

When a two-cylinder engine is to be served by a battery ignition system, it is necessary to use two coils, one for each cylinder, and a two-point timer. The two induction coils are invariably housed in a single casing and are connected together inside in such a way that but five leads or wires extend from the coil case. Two of these are secondary wires, one from coil A and the other from coil B. The remaining two secondary leads are joined together inside of the coil casing and connected to the primary wire common to both coils. Two primary wires extend from the coil case that are electrically insulated from each other, as each of these serves an individual coil. The primary wire from coil A goes to the insulated contact at one side of the timer, while the primary wire from coil B is attached to the in-

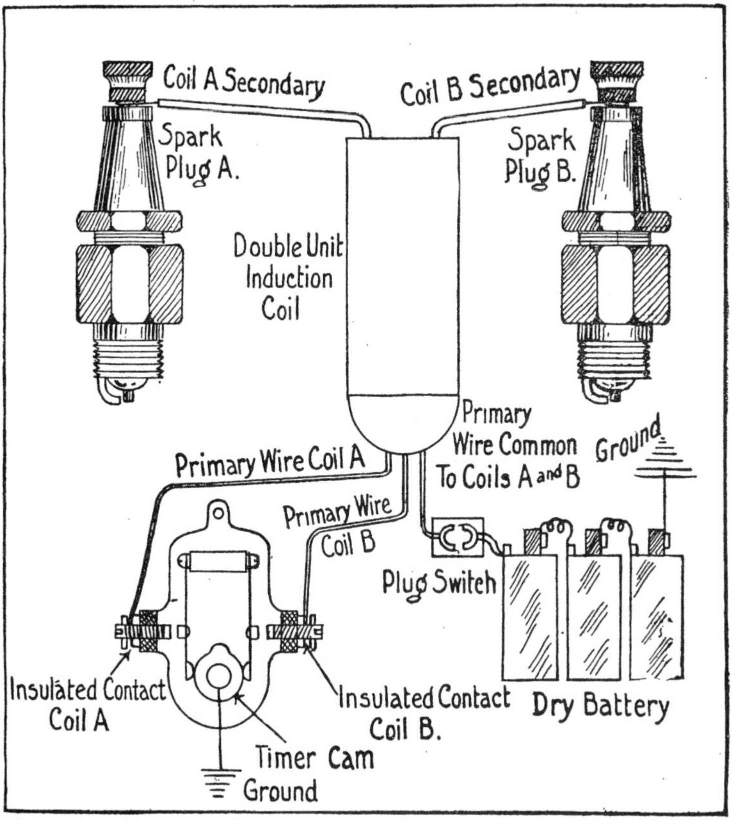

Fig. 142.—Diagram of Battery Ignition System for Two Cylinder Engine.

sulated contact at the other side. One end of the battery circuit is grounded as is also the timer cam. As the cam revolves, connection is made first between one pair of insulated contacts and then between the other. The spacing of the springs that are actuated by the cam is such that the explosions occur at the proper time in the cylinders and depend upon the method of placing the cylinders and design of the crankshaft. In the timer shown at Fig. 142, the explosions are separated by even intervals because the cam contact blocks on the timer springs are opposite each other and separated by a space equal to 180 degrees or half a revolution of the timer-cam travel.

A timer used for single-cylinder engines is shown at Fig. 143 with all parts clearly indicated and one for two-cylinder power plants at Fig. 144. The basis of the timer is often a block of fiber to which suitable binding posts are attached to support the vibrating spring and the contact screw. In the form outlined, these members are attached to terminals secured to the timer base by means of internal wires or suitable metallic connections. The wires comprising the outer circuit are attached to these terminals. The cam of the timer, shown at Fig. 143, is different in form from that at Fig. 144. The former normally keeps the spring out of contact with the platinum-pointed contact screw, and an electrical connection is established only when the cam rider or block on the end of the vibrator spring falls into the notch cut into the periphery of the cam. In the form at Fig. 144, the cam has a raised portion which lifts the springs into engagement, and establishes a connection by positive mechanical means instead of depending upon the spring tension as in the other construction.

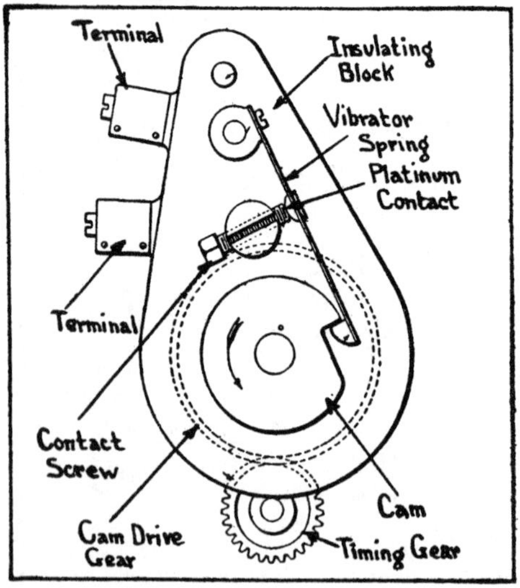

Fig. 143.—Timer Used in Connection With Battery Ignition System for One Cylinder Motor.

In order to produce a spark in the combustion chamber and yet have no leakage of gas, it is necessary to use a special fitting termed "the spark plug" between the points of which the ignition spark takes place. A typical spark plug is shown in section at Fig. 145. The central rod to which the terminal is attached passes through a porcelain body which insulates it from the steel portion that screws into the cylinder. Electrodes extend from the plug body to within a thirty-second of an inch of the central rod, and it is between these members that the spark takes place. Most of the motorcycle plugs are insulated with mica instead of porcelain, but the general principles of construction are the same in all. The only differences are in points of minor detail such as the size of the thread at the bottom of the plug body and the form of insulation and number of electrodes. Motorcycle spark plugs are provided in two thread sizes, the standard being the metric, which is considerably smaller and finer than the other, which is the regular half inch standard iron pipe thread. The spark plug is usually located in the combustion chamber in such a way that the points are in the path of the fresh gases as they enter through the open inlet valve as shown at Fig. 146. Combination insulations, such as a mica core pressed in a porcelain shell, are used on some plugs, while others are lava or steatite for separating the central electrode from the remainder of the assembly.

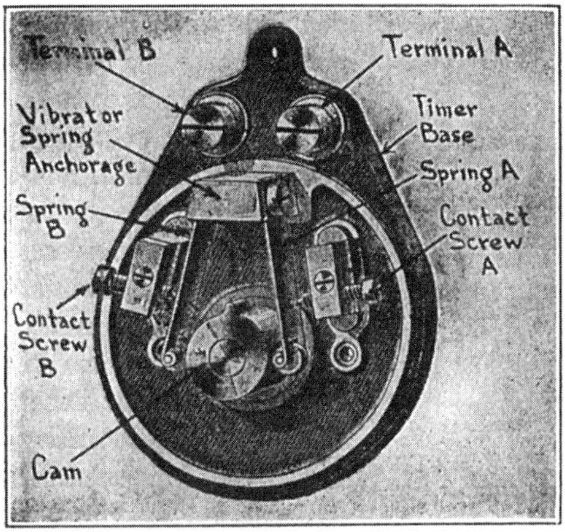

Fig. 144.—Form of Timing Device Employed in Battery Ignition System for Twin Cylinder Motor.

High Tension Magneto Action.—Taking electricity from either a dry or storage battery is comparable to drawing a liquid from a reservoir filled with a certain definite supply. As the demands upon the reservoir increase, its capacity and the amount of liquid it contains become less in direct proportion. Batteries cannot maintain a constant output of electricity for an indefinite period, and their strength is reduced according to the amount of service they give. A mechanical generator of electricity produces current without any actual deterioration or depreciation of chemicals and plates, as is true of a battery. There is some wear present in a mechanical generator, but this is so small compared to the amount of service it will give that its effect is practically negligible as regards current output.

A simple analogy that will enable one to appreciate the merits of the mechanical generator may be made with a pump system of drawing a liquid from a practically inexhaustible reservoir. As long as the pump is turned it will supply liquid. The same thing is true of a mechanical generator of electricity which will supply current as long as the rotating parts are turned. With batteries, when the engine speed increases, and the demands upon them become greater, the current strength decreases at a time it should be strong. With a mechanical generator of electricity, the current output increases as the speed, and as these devices are usually driven directly from the engine, when this member demands more electricity the mechanical generator will supply it automatically because it is being driven faster.

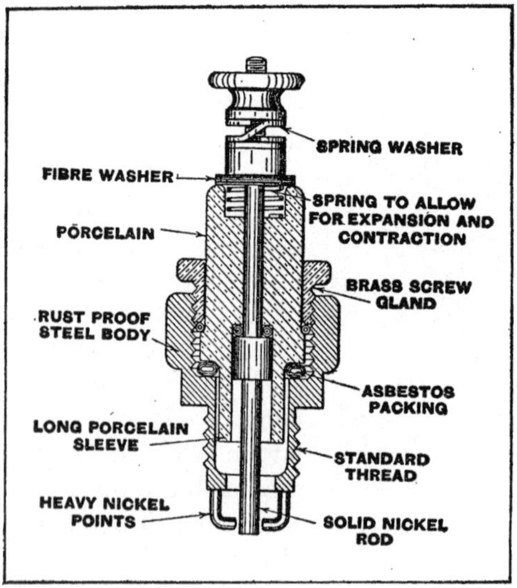

Fig. 145.—Sectional View of Spark Plug With Porcelain Insulation.

The high tension magneto is the form that is generally used in motorcycle ignition systems, and its popularity is increasing among other gas engine users as well. The main advantage of the true high-tension magneto is that it comprises in one device all the elements of the current generating and intensifying devices and all that is needed in connection with a high tension magneto are the spark plugs and the wires by which they are connected to the instrument. A high-tension magneto for a four-cylinder engine is but very little more complicated than one used on a two-cylinder power plant. The only difference is in the number of contacts in the distributor, and the speed at which the device is driven.

A typical high-tension magneto utilized in connection with a single-cylinder engine is outlined in its simplest form at Fig. 147; and at Figs. 148 and 149, the parts and their proper relation are clearly shown. The armature is a two-pole type having an approximately H section, and it is wound with two coils of wire. One of these is a

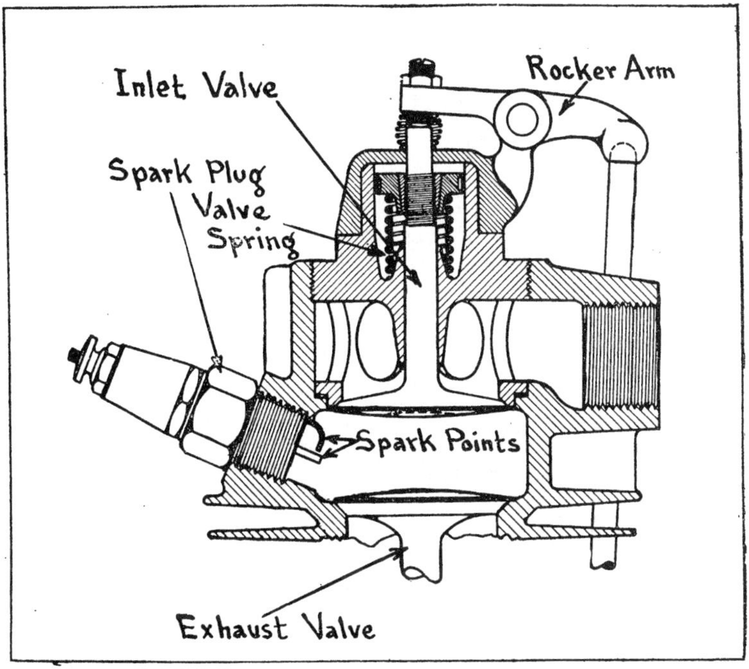

Fig. 146.—Diagram Showing Method of Locating Spark Plug so Points Will be in the Path of the Inlet Gases.

comparatively coarse one corresponding to the primary winding of an induction coil, while the other is a fine winding having many turns that performs the same function as the secondary coil. The armature shaft is mounted on ball bearings to insure easy rotation. The magnetic field is produced by means of two horseshoe magnets attached to iron pole pieces which form the armature tunnel. Mounted on and turning with the armature is a condenser which is placed in shunt connection with the contact points in the magneto breaker box. The armature is driven by positive chain or gear drive, and it is timed in such a way that the contact points of the magneto contact breaker separate only when a spark is desired in the engine.

The contact breaker, which corresponds to the timer of a battery ignition system, consists of a fixed member which carries one of the platinum contact screws while the movable bell-crank lever carries

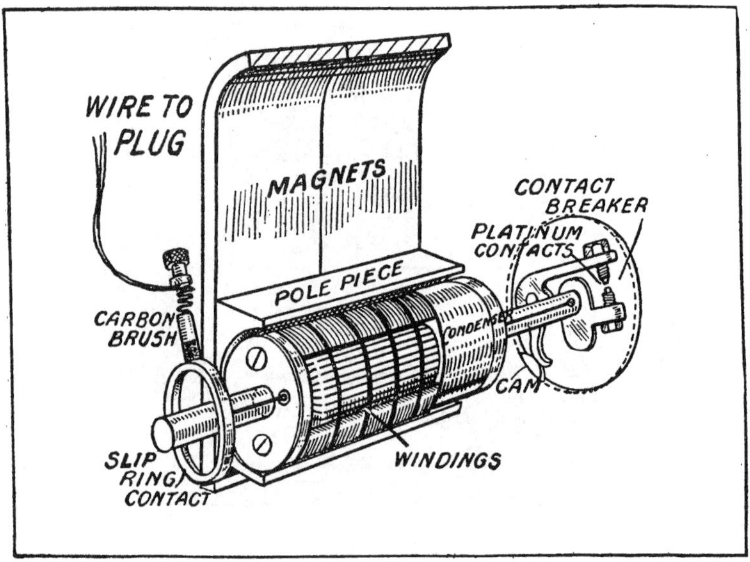

Fig. 147.—Simplified Diagram Showing Arrangement of the Principal Components of True High Tension Magneto.

the other platinum contact. The condenser is used to absorb a surplus current which is due to self induction between the various windings of wire and to prevent the excess current so generated from producing a spark that would tend to burn the contact points as they separate. The safety spark gap is interposed between the high-tension brush and the ground in such a way that any excess current that might injure the windings, if it was allowed to go through the instrument in the regular manner, will be allowed to flow to the ground without passing through the external circuit. This device performs the same function for the magneto as a safety valve does for a steam boiler, in that it provides a means of escape for excess pressure that might injure the device if no means were provided for its disposal other than the regular channels of distribution.

On a four-cylinder motor, the magneto is driven at crankshaft speed, the contact breaker cams being arranged in such a manner that the contact points separate twice during each revolution of the armature. Every time the contact points are separated a current of electricity leaves the armature by means of a high-tension brush

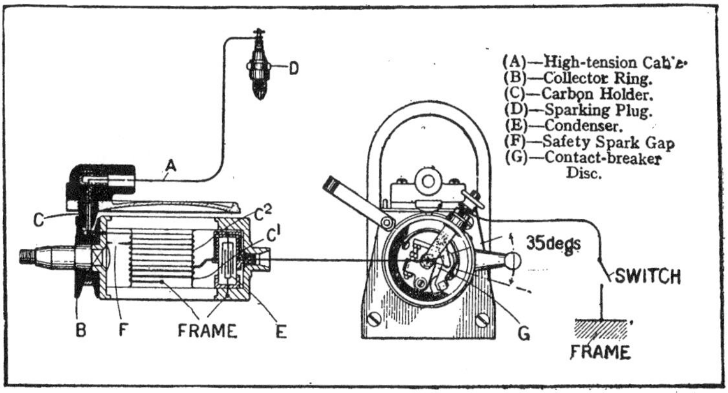

Fig. 148.—Wiring Diagram Showing Method of Connecting Components of the Bosch Magneto.

which bears on the insulated contact ring carried at one end of the armature shaft, and is led to a distributing brush at the center of the secondary current distributing member. The spark plugs are attached to wires which lead to the segments in the distributor, there being one segment for each spark plug. The distributor shaft is revolved at half armature speed by means of gears, and the revolving contact brush makes contact with one of the segments each time that the spark points separate, so the current of electricity is directed to the plug which is in the cylinder about to fire. It will be seen that this device includes the current generating and commutating means as well as the timing mechanism.

Operation of Standard High-Tension Magneto.—Some magnetos intended for twin engines of the V-type have a special arrangement of the pole pieces, as indicated at Fig. 150, so the period of maximum current production will correspond to the point where ignition is desired. The armature of the magneto is driven at the same speed as the cam shaft, and the direction in which the armature is to rotate is indicated by the makers. The angle between the cylinders

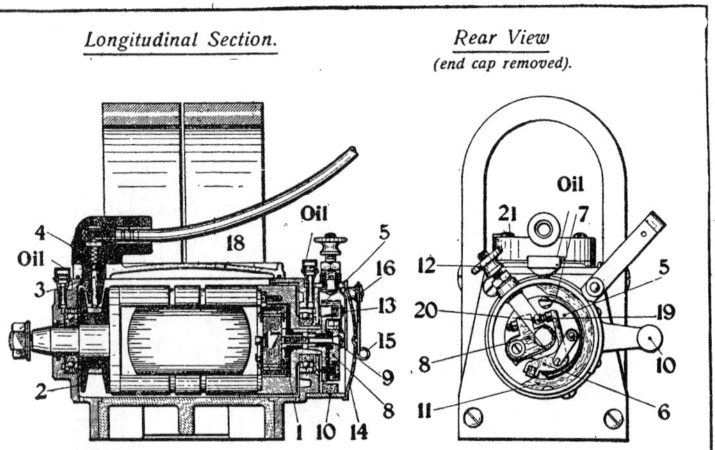

1. Brass plate.
2. Slip ring.
3. Carbon brush.
4. Carbon holder.
5. Interrupter disk.
6. Interrupter lever.
7. Spring.
8. Contact piece.
9. Screw.
10. Timing arm.
11. Steel segment.
12. Binding post.
13. Spring.
14. Cover.
15. Spring.
16. Bolt for spring 15.
17. Condenser.
18. Dust cover.
19. Short platinum screw.
20. Long platinum screw.
21. Conical fastening screw for carbon holder 4.

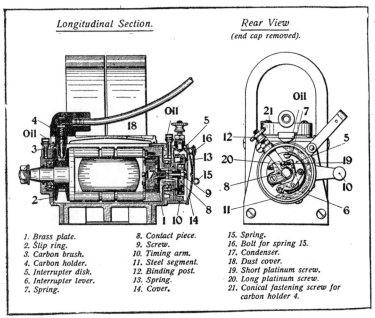

Fig. 149.—Longitudinal Section and Rear View of Bosch Motorcycle Magneto.

of the engine for which the magneto is intended is also indicated, and a magneto cannot be used for the reverse direction to that in which it is stamped or for an angle different from that indicated. As has been previously outlined in the operation of a twin-cylinder V-type four-cycle engine, each cylinder fires once during every two revolutions of the crankshaft, but the two firing strokes are not evenly spaced in the two revolutions, i. e., there is an interval of more than one revolution between the firing strokes of cylinder 1 and cylinder 2, and an interval of less than a revolution between the firing stroke of cylinder 2 and the following firing stroke of cylinder 1. The revolutions of the crankshaft are therefore divided into a long period and a short period, and, as a rule, cylinder 1 is considered to be that which fires at the beginning of the long period, while No. 2 is that in which a spark takes place at the beginning of the short period. An examination of the interrupter or breaker box of such a magneto, which is clearly shown at Fig. 151, will show that the two segments are marked with the characters 1 and 2, and it will be observed that the dust cover of the magneto also bears these numerals which in that case refer to the two high-tension terminals which are also clearly shown at Fig. 151. When the steel segment marked 1 is operating the interrupter, the carbon brush marked 1 will be in connection with the current-distributing segment on the slip ring, and the secondary current produced at that instant will pass from the magneto to the spark plug connected to that brush. When the engine is installed in a motorcycle, cylinder 1 is the member nearest to the rear wheel and is the one by which the magneto timer is set. The brushes are usually carried in easily removable members as at A, Fig. 152, which shows the brush for a one-cylinder magneto, or at B and C which show the exterior views and section of one of the brushes intended for a two-cylinder magneto.

Magneto Driving Means.—As the magneto will produce current sufficient to overcome the resistance of the air gap at the spark plug only at a certain definite armature position, and as the contact-breaker points must separate coincidently with the attainment of the position of maximum current generation, it is imperative that the magneto be positively driven by the motor to which it is fitted, and by a method of drive that will obviate any possibility of slipping. In this respect, the magneto is different from a dynamo or, in fact, forms of magnetos which deliver a current of low voltage, and which require auxiliary timing and current intensifying appliances before the electrical energy is available for ignition. When the timing device forms part of the magneto, and is attached to the magneto armature, it is imperative that the contact-breaker points separate always at the same time in the cycle of operation.

A simple method of driving a magneto is shown at Fig. 153. In this, a chain extends from a sprocket on the cam-gear shaft to a member of the same size on the magneto armature shaft. The cover of the gear case and chain case is removed to show the relation of the parts to each other. As the chain is protected from abrasive material in the form of dust or grit, and as it is always thoroughly oiled, there will be but little wear or stretching. In this country, the general practice is to drive the magneto through a train of intermediate gears interposed between the cam-timing gears and a suitable member attached to the magneto armature. Some makers, notably Spacke and Pope, drive the magneto by means of worm or spiral gears, and, in some instances, this device may be driven by beveled gearing. It is important to have the drive as direct as possible, because in a system with a large number of gears there is apt to be some back lash develop between the various gear members after the engine has been used for a time, and this may interfere with the accuracy of the spark timing.

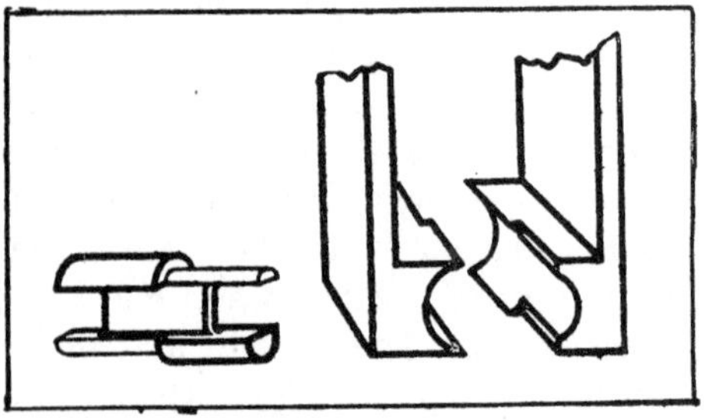

Fig. 150.—Arrangement of Pole Pieces and Armature in Some Magnetos Intended for Two Cylinder V Engine.

Ignition Timing.—An important point in connection with successful operation of the magneto ignition system is that the break between the magneto contact points takes place just when it is desired to obtain a spark in the cylinder. Therefore, in timing a twin-cylinder motor, the engine should be turned over until the piston in cylinder 1 is at the top dead center or upper end of the compression stroke. The position of the piston may be determined by a wire passed through a pet cock or any other opening in the cylinder head, or by a suitable mark on the driving pulley provided by the maker of the engine to indicate that the piston has reached the top of its stroke. The magneto is then bolted to the base prepared for it with the driving gear loose on the armature shaft and the dust cover over the armature removed. The timing control lever attached to the contact breaker is placed in the full retard position which is done by moving it as far as it will go, in the same direction as the armature is driven. The armature should then be rotated by hand until the cam is separating the interrupter points. The armature should be held firmly in this position and the driving gear is then tightened on the armature shaft. It is imperative that there should be no slippage during this operation. Carbon brush 1 is connected to spark plug of cylinder 1

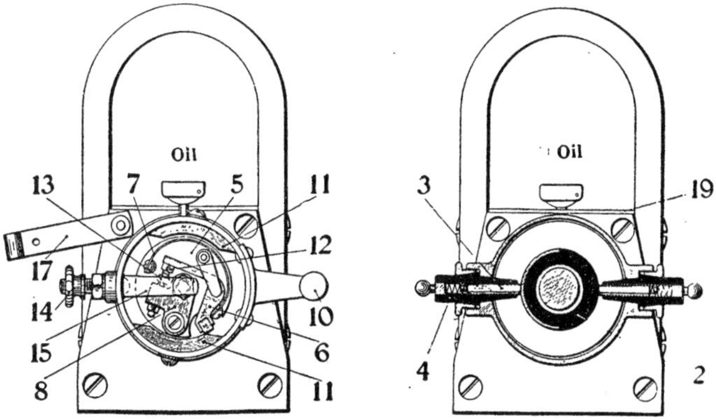

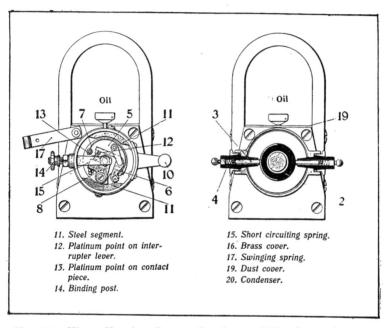

11. Steel segment.
12. Platinum point on interrupter lever.
13. Platinum point on contact piece.
14. Binding post.
15. Short circuiting spring.
16. Brass cover.
17. Swinging spring.
19. Dust cover.
20. Condenser.

Fig. 151.—Views Showing Contact Breaker and Distributor Arrangement of Bosch Magneto for Two Cylinder Engines.

and carbon brush 2 to the spark plug in the remaining cylinder. Before starting the engine to verify the timing, the dust cover should be replaced over the armature. Timing a single-cylinder engine is, of course, somewhat simpler as there is but one secondary lead from the magneto to the spark plug.

The position of the piston in the cylinder of the Precision engines is shown at the top of Fig. 154, and it is at this point that the contact points should be just separating, provided that the lever on the contact-breaker case is fully advanced. With the lever fully advanced, the spark points separate before the piston reaches the top of its compression stroke, whereas if the lever on the contact breaker is placed in the retard position the points should not separate until the piston has reached the top of its stroke.

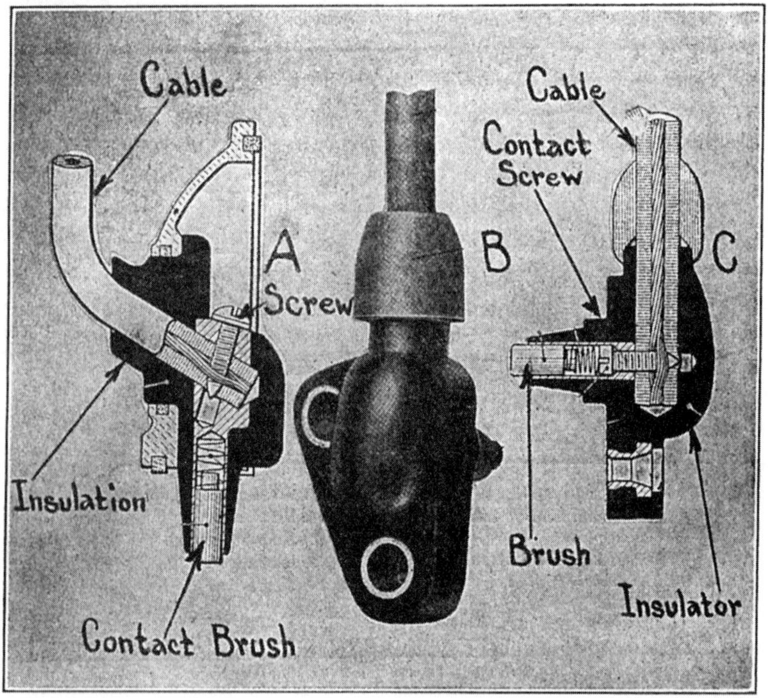

Fig. 152.—Carbon Brush Holders Used in Bosch Magneto, Showing Methods of Making Connections With Secondary Cable.

If a two-cycle engine is to be timed, and the cranks are arranged at 180 degrees, as shown at Fig. 155, the explosions will be separated by equal intervals, and a form of magneto with regular type pole pieces may be employed. The contact breaker arrangement is such that the points are separated at equal intervals because there is no long period or short period as is the case with a V-type, four-cycle engine. The arrangement of the pistons of a twin-cylinder four-cycle motor in which the explosions are evenly spaced is shown at the top of Fig. 156. A magneto of the same type would also be used with a double-cylinder opposed motor. In the V-type engine, shown at the bottom of Fig. 156, the explosion in cylinder 1 occurs at the beginning

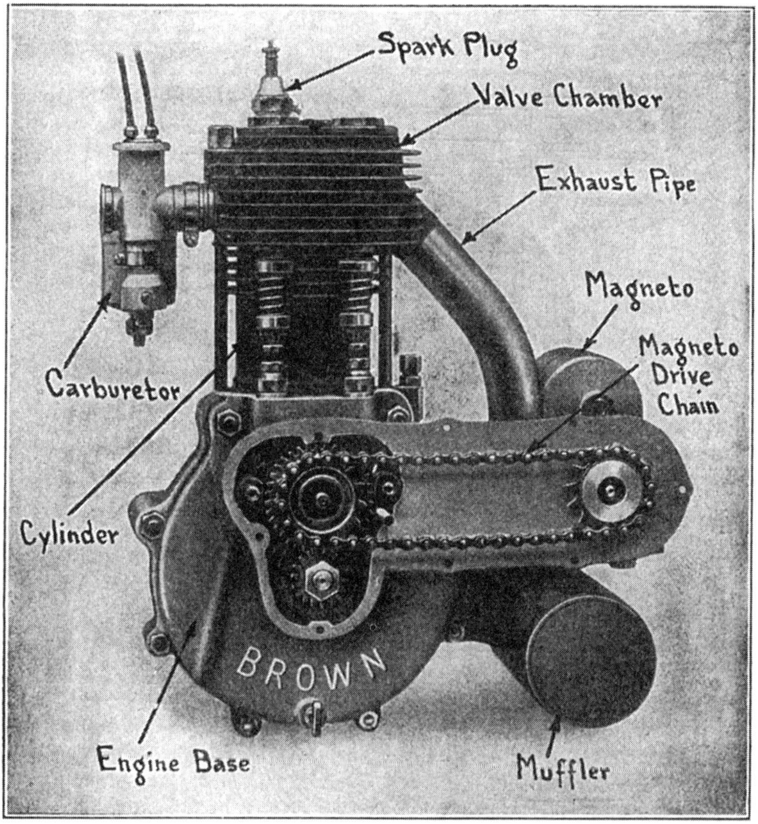

Fig. 153.—Depicting Application of Roller Chain to Magneto Drive.

of the period that is equal to one complete revolution plus the angle A between the cylinder center lines while the explosion in cylinder 2 occurs one revolution minus the angle between the cylinders after the explosion in cylinder 1.

The arrangement of the contact breaker and distributor parts of a four-cylinder magneto is shown at Fig. 157. Just as the cam R is about to separate the contact points, the metal distributing segment of the distributor should be in communication with one of the insulated brushes that are connected to the plugs in the various cylinders; in this case, it would complete the circuit between the

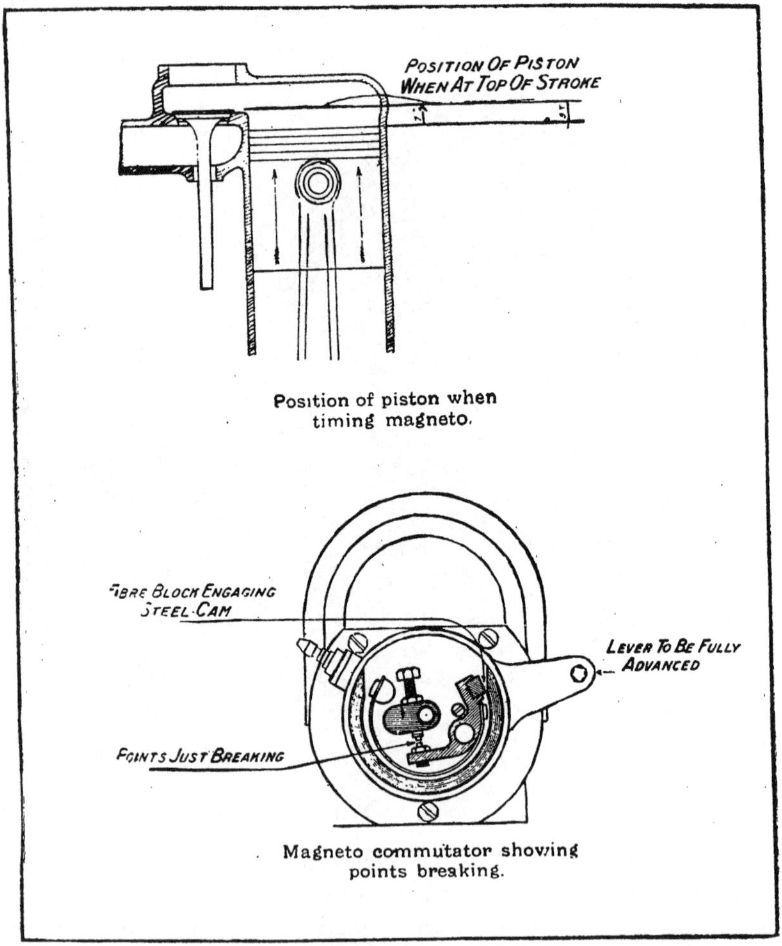

Fig. 154.—Ignition Timing Diagram.

central distributing member and the brush connected to the cylinder about to fire.

In order to cut off the ignition, the primary circuit of the magneto must be grounded, and this may be accomplished by either of two methods. The one most commonly used in this country is retarding the ignition to an extreme point, at which position of the interrupter housing, a flat spring attached to the primary binding post is brought in contact with a grounded pin located on the magneto end plate. Another method is to connect the binding post to the ground through

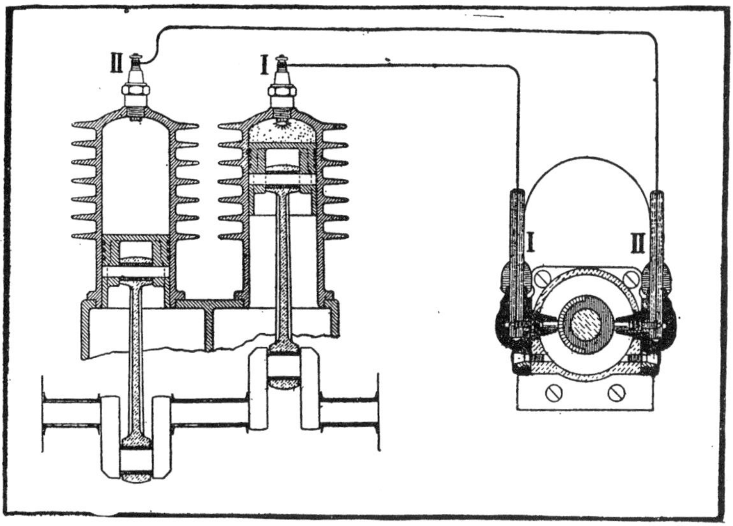

Fig. 155.—Arrangement of Cranks in Two Cylinder Two-cycle Engine to Secure Even Firing Intervals.

the medium of some form of switch, one wire being connected to the binding post and the other switch wire being led to any convenient part of the engine or frame. A cut-out switch adapted for location on the handle bars of a motorcycle is shown at Fig. 158. A block of fiber serves to insulate the contact spring from the handle bar, and when it is desired to ground the circuit, a contact is established between the end of the spring and the handle bar by pressing on the hard rubber knob at the free end of the spring. The action of a

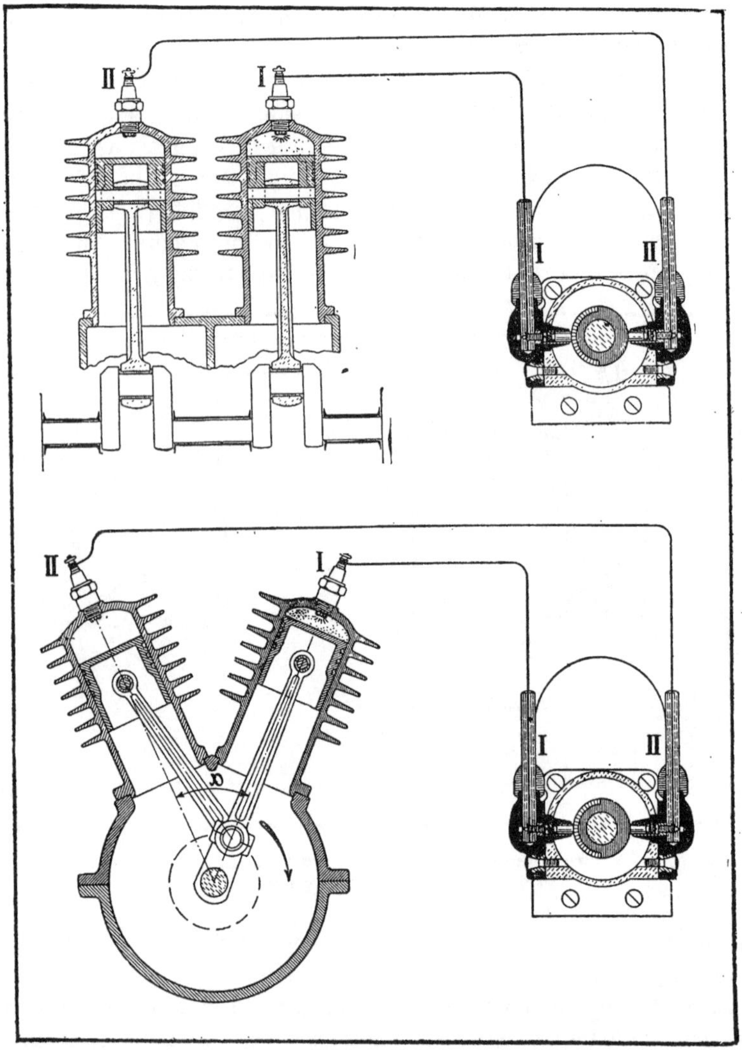

Fig. 156.—At Top, Arrangement of Crank Pins in Two Cylinder Vertical Engine to Secure Even Periods of Time Between Explosions. Below, Usual Arrangement of Crankpin in Two Cylinder Motorcycle Powerplant.

magneto switch is radically different from that of the type employed for battery ignition. With the latter, the current will not flow unless the primary circuit is completed, whereas with a magneto, completing the primary circuit means a discontinuation of current generation. What would be the "on" position in a battery switch is the "off" position in a magneto system.

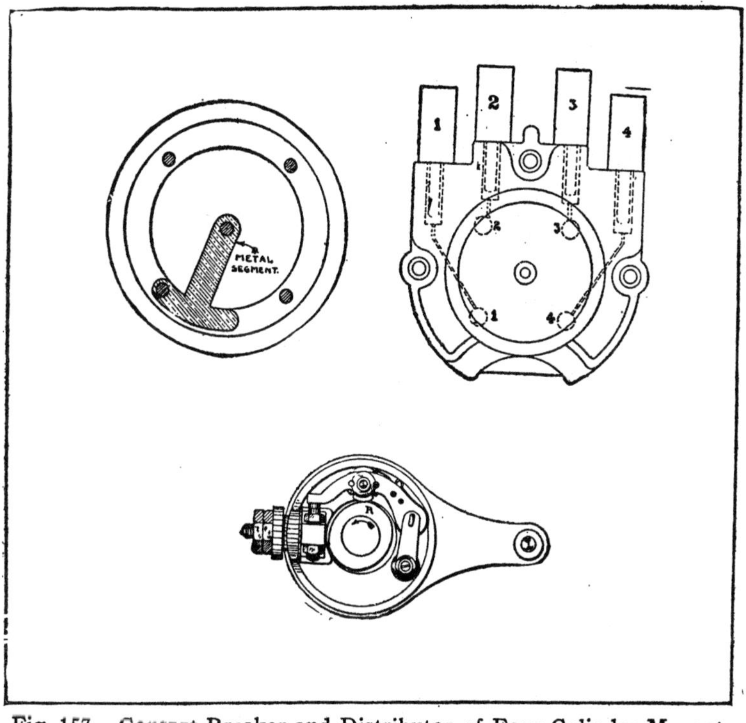

Fig. 157.—Contact Breaker and Distributor of Four Cylinder Magneto.

Detection of Faults.—The following instructions are issued by the makers of the Bosch magneto, and as they cover the ground thoroughly, they are reprinted verbatim:

In case of a fault in the ignition system, the firing will become irregular or will cease entirely. In case of irregular firing, the fault is almost invariably due to a defective spark plug, and if this condition is noticed the spark plugs should be changed.

To locate the cylinder that is misfiring, disconnect the cable from spark plug 1 and crank the engine. If the engine operates on cylinder 2 under these conditions, it shows that the ignition of that cylinder is correct and locates the defect in cylinder 1. However, should no ignition occur, the spark plug of cylinder 2 is defective and must therefore be replaced.

The more common defects of spark plugs are as follows:

First.—Fouling of the plugs, due to the carbonization of the insulation. A fouled plug may be cleaned by the use of a stiff bristle brush dipped in gasoline.

Second.—Too large a gap between the electrodes of the spark plug. The normal spark plug gap should be from 0.5 to 0.6 millimeter (about 1/64 inch), smaller or larger gaps being detrimental to good ignition. If the gap between the spark plug electrodes is too great, the current will discharge across the safety spark gap on the magneto. When the plug is unscrewed from the cylinder, however, the spark will jump across the plug electrodes instead of across the safety spark gap. This does not signify that the distance between the spark plug electrodes is correct, for when the spark plug gap is subjected to the compression that exists in the cylinder the resistance between the points of the gap is greatly increased.

The distance between the spark plug electrodes must therefore be much less than is required when the spark passes in the open air.

Third.—Short circuiting of the spark plug by metallic beads formed across the spark plug gap by the intense heat of the magneto current. The removal of these metallic beads will correct the difficulty.

If ignition fails suddenly, there will probably be a short circuit in the cable connected to binding post 170 and leading to the switch. A difficulty of this sort may be determined by disconnecting the cable from the magneto and testing to see whether ignition is resumed. Should ignition still prove faulty and irregular, the interrupter should be inspected to ascertain if the interrupter lever moves freely, and if the platinum points make good contact.

Should ignition be irregular in both cylinders, the contact points should be examined, which may be done by swinging spring 17 to one side and removing cover 16 (Fig. 151).

The following points should be observed: Screw 9 should be screwed tight into position; the platinum-pointed screws 12 and 13 should make contact when the interrupter lever 6 is not touching the steel segments 11; the distance between the platinum-pointed screws should be about 0.5 millimeter when the interrupter lever 6 is resting on one of the steel segments 11, and the metal blade, pivoted to the adjusting wrench that is supplied, may be used as a gauge for this distance.

If the parts of the interrupter appear to be in order, screw 9 may be withdrawn and the contact-breaker disk removed complete. The platinum points should be examined, and if they are rough or worn—but only in this event—they should be trued with a fine flat file, or

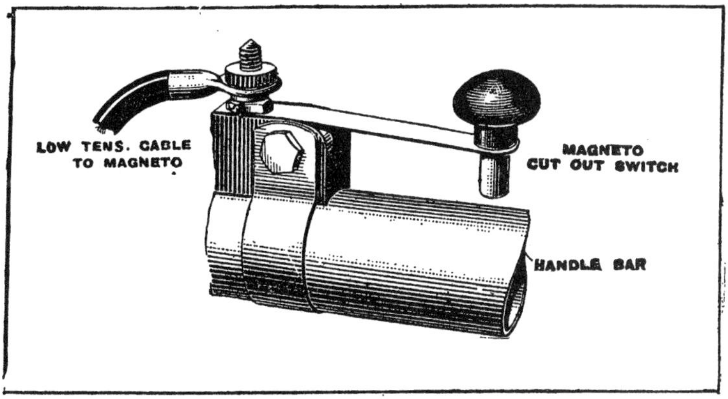

Fig. 158.—Magneto Cutout Switch for Attaching to Motorcycle Handlebars.

with fine emery cloth. If they are oily and dirty, they should be cleansed with gasoline. The surface between spring 15 and the screw 9 should be kept clean.

An investigation as to the cause of trouble may be summarized as follows: First, change the spark plug; second, examine the spark plug cable; third, test for trouble in the switch or switch cable by operating the magneto with the cable disconnected from binding post 170; fourth, examine the interrupter lever for free movement; fifth, dismount the interrupter to examine platinum contacts.

The armature is supported on ball bearings and should be lubricated with a few drops of light oil every 300 to 500 miles, applied to the oil holes, which can be found at each end of the magneto, covered by hinged brass plates.

The other parts of the apparatus require no lubrication, and care should be taken to prevent the introduction of oil into the interrupter parts. These operate without lubrication, and oil will interfere with their action.

CHAPTER V.

POWER TRANSMISSION SYSTEM PARTS.

Utility of Clutch Defined—Theory of Friction Clutch Action—Types of Clutches—Materials Employed in Clutches—Clutch Location—Typical Motorcycle Clutches—Why Change Speed Gearing is Desirable—Value of Variable Speed Gearing—Variable Speeds by Slipping Clutch—Change Speed Gear Location—Variable Speed Pulleys—Engine Shaft Gear—Countershaft Gears—Rear Hub Gears—Three Chain Systems—Planetary Countershaft Gears—Sliding Gear Type—Power Transmission Methods—Belt Drive Systems—Types of Belts—Standard Belts—Advantages of Drive by Chains—Single Chain Direct Drive—Double Chain Drive—Types of Driving Chains—Combination Chain and Belt Drive—Bevel and Worm Gear Final Drive—Relation of Engine Power to Gear Ratio.

The power transmission group is next in importance to the energy producing elements and much depends upon correct application of the various devices utilized in transmitting the engine energy to the traction member. The efficiency of the motorcycle as a whole depends largely on that of the power transmission system. An extremely powerful and effective motor is of little avail if a large proportion of the power it produces is consumed by friction or transmission losses before it can be applied to the rear wheel to produce useful work. The principal elements of the transmission system of a simple motorcycle are first, a clutching device that permits of releasing the engine from the driving medium or applying the power at will, and second, some system of transmitting the engine power from the clutch to the rear wheels. Many of the 1914 motorcycles include still another element, the variable speed gear, in the power transmission system.

Utility of Clutch Defined.—Practically every motorcycle produced at the present time is fitted with a free engine and clutching device that will permit of running the engine without driving the vehicle. In the early days of motorcycle development, the drive was direct from the engine crankshaft to the rear wheels without any engine releasing device. It was necessary to start all motorcycles by a preliminary pedaling process which meant that the entire machine had to be pushed along briskly regardless of character of road surface or gradients so the motor would be turned sufficiently fast to start. It was not possible to put the machine on a stand, as is done at the present time, because the absence of the free engine device made it imperative that the machine should acquire a certain amount of momentum before the power was applied. The result was that it required a very strong person to start a powerful twin-cylinder motor fitted to a heavy machine, because, while the machine might start in ten feet, it might require vigorous pedaling for half a city block before the engine was started. When the engine did start, it was apt to race or take hold suddenly because very often the spark would be well advanced or the throttle would be opened to secure easy starting. The sudden application of power was not favorable to the power transmission system and snapped chains or broken belts were not an uncommon result when the power was suddenly applied in this manner.

When a free engine clutch is employed, it is possible to place the machine on a stand and start the power plant with comparative ease because the only resistance to overcome is that offered by the motor itself instead of the rider having to furnish the power to move the heavy machine along the road. After the engine is started, it is possible to release the clutch and disconnect the power from the rear wheels. This enables the rider to take the machine off the stand, keep the engine running, and start off very gradually by utilizing the power of the motor which is delivered to the rear wheel in gradually increasing increments if the friction clutch is let in slowly. Another advantage of the clutch is that it permits of ready control under unfavorable riding conditions such as in traffic, climbing hills, or overcoming poor highway surfaces. Instead of controlling the machine by continually interrupting the motor action, as was the case in the old direct drive days, a twist of the grip on the handle bar or an easy movement of a conveniently placed lever will release the clutch, interrupt the drive and permit the rider to bring his machine to a standstill, if necessary, without stopping the motor.

The control of modern machines is very similar to that of an automobile, and is such an improvement over the old system that its importance is not apt to be realized except by those of us whose experience dates back far enough so we can qualify as veteran motorcyclists. With the old forms of machines, when a patch of sand was encountered or a gradient that did not permit one to "rush" the hill by putting on full speed before reaching the bottom and depend largely on momentum to assist in overcoming the resistance, it was necessary to either get off and push the machine or to endeavor to assist the engine by vigorous pedaling. If perchance one was unfortunate enough to become stalled in the middle of a hill, it was practically impossible to make a new start without returning to the bottom and making another rush to overcome the unfavorable conditions. At the present time, if an engine tends to slow down, due to a patch of sand or other resistance, the rider can slip the clutch a trifle, enable the engine to pick up speed so that it will not stall, and yet deliver enough power to the rear wheel to obtain positive drive.

Theory of Friction Clutch Action.—Clutch forms that are applied to motorcycles are invariably of the friction type, as no progress has been made in utilizing the various hydraulic, pneumatic, or magnetic clutches that have been offered at various times by over-sanguine inventors. The friction clutch has proven to be the most satisfactory, and has received wide practical application in its various forms. The important requirement of a clutch is that it will be capable of transmitting the maximum power of the motor without any loss due to slipping when fully engaged. A clutch should be operated easily and require but minimum exertion on the part of the operator. A clutch should be gradual in action, i. e., when it takes hold, the engine power should be transmitted to the driving member in a gradual and uniform manner or the resulting shock may result in serious injury to some part of the driving mechanism. It is also imperative that a clutch release at once when desired, and that there be no continued rotation of parts, which insures that the drive will be interrupted positively when the clutch is disengaged. In considering the design of a clutch, it is very desirable that this component be located in an accessible manner, which is a good feature, as it permits of easier removal for inspection, cleaning and repair. It is imperative that some form of adjustment be provided so a certain amount of wear will be compensated for, without replacing any expensive parts. A simple design with a minimum number of operating parts is more to be desired than a more complicated form which may have some minor advantages, but which is much more likely to cause trouble.

To illustrate the transmission of power by frictional adhesion of various substances with each other, one can assume a simple clutch form consisting of two metal discs or plates in contact, the pressure keeping them together being due to the weight of one member bearing upon the other. If the discs are not heavy, it will be found easy to turn one upon the other, but if weights are added to the upper member a more decided resistance will be felt which will increase directly as the weight on the top disc and consequently the total pressure augments. It is possible to add enough weight so it will be difficult to move one plate without producing a corresponding movement of the other. If one of these plates is mounted on an engine shaft, and the other applied to the transmission member so that a certain amount of axial movement is possible, and the pressure maintaining contact was obtained by springs instead of weights, one would secure a combination capable of transmitting power, inasmuch as the spring pressure applied to one disc would force it against the other, and one shaft could not revolve without producing motion of the other.

Types of Clutches.—Three main forms of friction clutches have been employed in motorcycles, and these, in the order of their importance, are disc, plate, band and cone designs. The disc clutch is the most popular because it is a compact form, and in its simplest design it would consist of a casing driven by the engine with a series of discs attached to it, and another member carrying another set of discs that was connected to the driving wheel by suitable gearing. The discs attached to the case are distinct from those carried by the driven member, and driving contact is maintained between the two by steel springs. It is possible to house a multiple disc clutch in an oil-tight casing, which means that it is possible to slip this form of clutch much more than the cone or band types, which for the most part operate without lubricant. A large number of small diameter discs are employed to transmit the power, and the required contact area

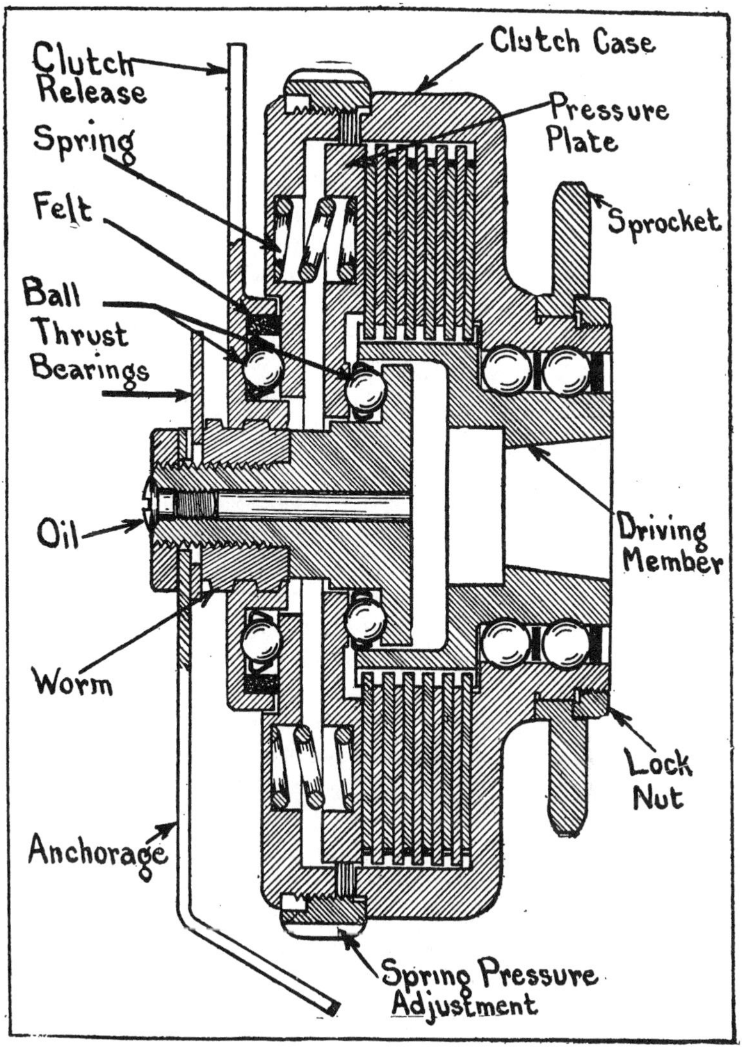

Fig. 159.—Sectional View of the Eclipse Engine Shaft Multiple Disc Clutch.

is obtained by the use of a number of comparatively small surfaces, instead of two larger ones, as is the case with the cone or band clutch.

The type of multiple disc clutch that is the most widely adopted is shown at Fig. 159, and, while the form outlined uses discs of the same material, in some forms of clutches one set of discs will be of steel while the other will be of phosphor bronze. The drive from the engine shaft is taken by a driving member keyed to it, and one set of plates is securely fastened to this member. The remaining plates are attached to the clutch case and revolve with it and the drive sprocket that goes to the rear wheel is also secured to the clutch case. The pressure to maintain the plates in frictional contact is obtained from a series of coil springs which act against a pressure plate which, in turn, bears against the disc assembly. The use of oil in this form of clutch is of advantage because it not only promotes easy engagement by interposing an elastic cushion between the metal plates and thus prevents too rapid engagement, but it also reduces depreciation when the clutch is released or the discs are slipping by each other because of its value as a lubricant. Owing to the small diameter of multiple disc clutches, the inertia of the driven member or tendency to rotate when disengaged is less than in a cone clutch or band form of larger diameter. The spring pressure is usually sufficient to squeeze the oil from between the plates as soon as the clutch is fully engaged, and a metal to metal contact is then obtained. In fact, if the lubricant was retained between the surfaces, the clutch would slip, but as it is gradually forced out and there is a certain amount of slipping as long as any of the lubricant remains, this feature insures that the power will be applied in a gradual manner even if the clutch is carelessly operated.

The cone clutch in its simplest form consists of a female member in the form of a saucer-shaped metal piece, and a male member, which is a truncated cone, which fits into it, and a spring or leverage to maintain frictional contact between the surfaces. The male member is usually faced with some frictional material to secure better driving power through superior frictional adhesion. Band clutches may be of two forms. The one that is most generally used in connection with planetary speed change gearing consists of a steel band lined with frictional material that contracts against a drum or an internal band which is expanded inside of the drum. The internal form is generally used when it is desired to keep both parts in motion, as for instance in transmitting power between the shaft on which the expanding band is attached to the drum against the inside periphery of which it bears. The constricting band clutches are generally used in the form of a brake to restrain the motion of a planetary gear carrying member in order that the gears will transmit power.

Materials Employed in Clutches.—One of the important points in clutch design is to secure as much frictional adhesion between the parts as possible. The transmitting efficiency of a clutch will vary with the coefficient of friction (which means the amount of adhesion) under pressure and, of course, the more friction between the surfaces for a given amount of spring pressure the more suitable the clutch will be for transmitting power. A metal usually forms one frictional surface in all forms of clutches, and some types, notably the multiple-disc forms, have all friction surfaces of metal. The metallic materials generally used are cast iron, aluminum and bronze castings, and sheet steel and bronze in the form of thin stamped discs. The non-metallic frictional materials often employed are leather, asbestos fabrics, textile belting and cork. Leather is the best lining or facing for clutches where the friction area is large and where the clutch is not apt to be slipped much. When used, it must be kept properly lubricated and soft because, if it becomes dry, it will engage very suddenly and promote harsh clutch action. Care must be taken not to supply too much oil, because the co-efficient of friction will be reduced to a low point and the surfaces will slip by each other. Chrome-tanned leather is generally used because it has good wearing qualities and, in addition to being a very resilient material, it possesses a very satisfactory degree of frictional adhesion when pressed against a cast iron member. Oak-tanned leather is also used for clutch facings. A clutch for motorcycle use should be faced with asbestos fabric rather than leather, unless it formed a part of a two-speed gear, which would not require slipping the clutch to any extent. These asbestos fabrics, of which raybestos is one of the best known, are used to some extent as a facing in multiple disc clutches of the dry plate type. Cork is sometimes used in connection with metal surfaces in the form of inserts which are compressed into suitable holes machined to receive them. Cork has a high coefficient of friction, and is not materially affected either by excessive lubrication or lack of oil. The cork inserts promote gradual engagement and possess very desirable wearing qualities. Metal to metal surfaces are the rule in multiple disc or plate clutches of small diameter where a multiplicity of surfaces are depended on for driving, but when a lesser number of plates of larger diameter are used, cork inserts or an asbestos fabric facing are invariably provided on one set of plates.

Clutch Location.—There are three points in a motorcycle where it is possible to apply a friction clutch, these being on the engine crankshaft, on a countershaft, or in the rear wheel. The faster the parts of a clutch turn, the smaller in diameter they can be to transmit the same amount of power, and for this reason the engine shaft is favored by a number of makers. Sometimes the clutch is attached directly to the crankshaft extension, to which the sprocket would normally be fastened in a direct or countershaft drive construction, and at the present time the engine shaft location is growing in favor. The most general location, which may be considered typical of standard practice, is at the crank hanger, which involves the use of a larger clutch on account of the lessened speed of that member. If the clutch is housed in the rear hub it must be even larger, i. e., it must have a greater number of discs if it uses the same spring pressure as either an engine shaft or countershaft clutch or it must employ higher spring pressure if it uses the same number of discs as would ordinarily be used in either of the other locations. It is contended by those who favor the rear wheel location, that while the clutch parts must be larger, they are also more substantial and stronger, and owing to the reduction in speed the surfaces are not apt to wear as rapidly when they slip by each other with the clutch partially released as would be the case in an engine-shaft clutch or even the countershaft type. The latter form is a compromise between the two extremes, the engine-shaft clutch on one hand and rear hub form on the other.

Typical Motorcycle Clutches.—The multiple disc clutch shown at Fig. 159 is the engine-shaft type, and is very compact as well as effective. When the springs are compressed to release the clutch by drawing the pressure plate away from the disc assembly; the outer casing which carries the driving sprocket revolves on a double row ball bearing, the inner race of which is formed by the driving member attached to the engine shaft. To release the clutch, a suitable lever, provided with an internal spiral thread, is rocked on a fixed member which has an external spiral thread. This fixed member communicates with the pressure plate through the medium of a ball thrust bearing, and as the clutch release lever is moved, the spiral thread or worm produces a lateral displacement of the pressure plate.

Another form of engine-shaft clutch is shown at Fig. 160. In this,

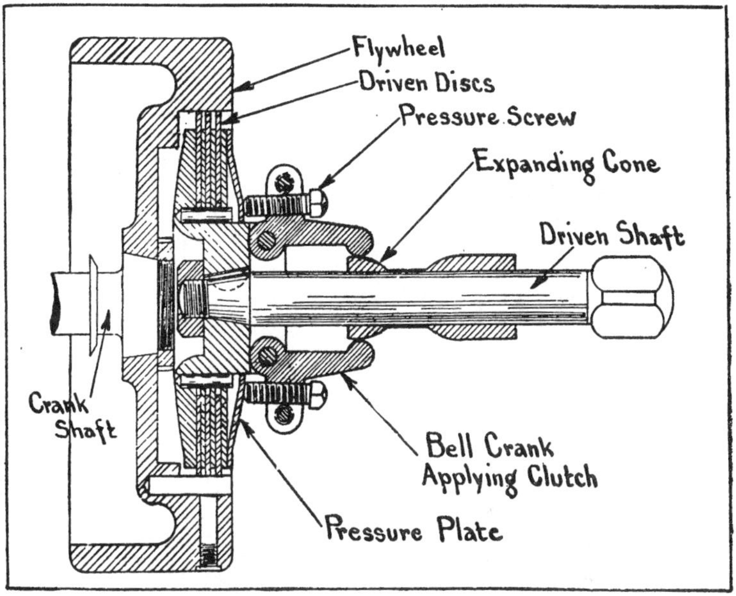

Fig. 160.—Sectional View of the Pierce Cone Actuated Multiple Disc Clutch.

the clutch is applied by a series of bell cranks which are provided at one end with an adjustable pressure screw bearing against the pressure plate of the disc assembly, and a bearing portion at the other end which works against a movable cone member that applies the clutch by spreading out the bell cranks and squeezing the driven and driving disc assemblies together.

The Eclipse countershaft clutch shown at Fig. 161 has been widely specified, and is the same in general construction and principle of operation as the form shown at Fig. 159, except that the drive from the engine goes to a sprocket attached to the clutch casing while the driving sprocket is secured to the inner member, which in this case is the driven instead of the driving portion of the clutch. The releasing means is similar to that previously described and is by spirally threaded members.

The countershaft clutch shown at Fig. 162 is used on Indian motorcycles, and while it is a multiple disc form it employs friction facing

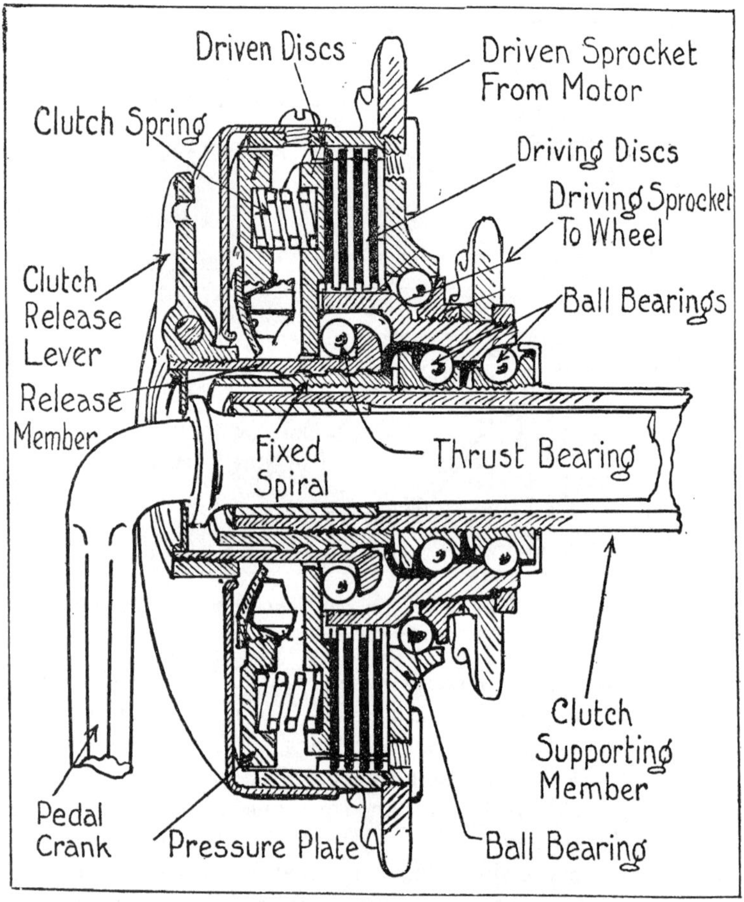

Fig. 161.—Sectional View of the Eclipse Countershaft Type Free Engine Clutch.

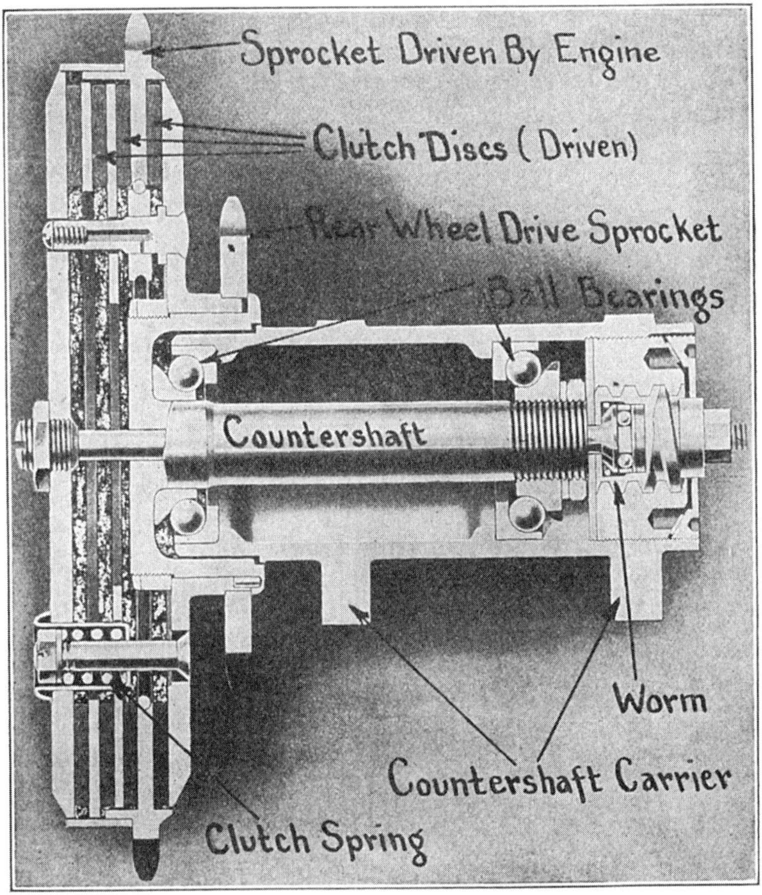

Fig. 162.—Countershaft Type Multiple Disc Clutch Used on Indian Motorcycles.

on part of the discs instead of utilizing the metal-to-metal contact. This view is valuable also, in showing the method of application of a countershaft clutch assembly in a carrier member adapted to fit the crank hanger box of the frame. The method of releasing this clutch is similar to that employed in the other forms as it involves a movable worm operating in a fixed, internally threaded member. The angle of the threads on the worm is such that as it is rocked in the nut it advances and pushes against a rod passing through the center of the countershaft and securely attached to the pressure plate which forms the outer member of the clutch case. The pressure plate is normally kept in contact with the clutch disc assembly by small coil springs which exert their pressure against cups carried by the pressure plate. The springs are compressed to a suitable degree by adjustable nuts carried on bolts that hold the inner and outer clutch members together and which tend to clamp the disc assembly between them. The large sprocket is driven by the engine, while the small one is employed to drive the rear wheel.

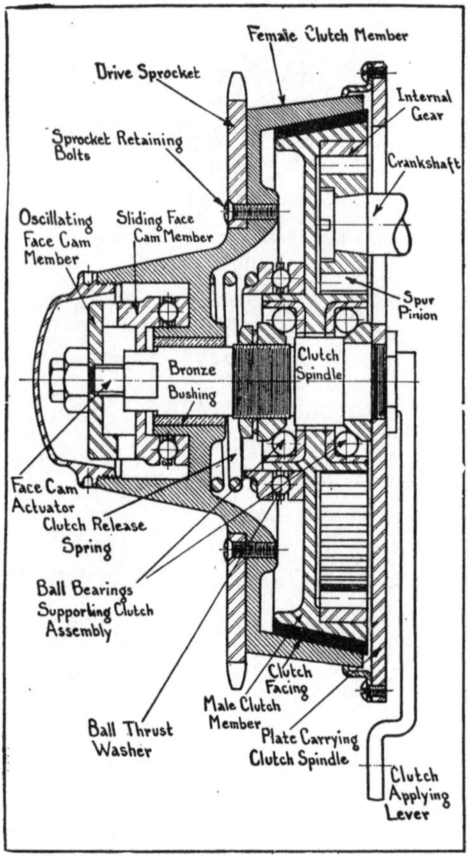

Fig. 163.—Sectional View of the Reading-Standard Cone Clutch.

The cone clutch used on the Reading-Standard motorcycle is outlined at Fig. 163. As all important parts are clearly depicted, the reader should have no difficulty in following the method of operation. In this clutch the spring is a releasing member and not an actuating member, as is true of the forms previously described. The clutch assembly is mounted on a spindle which is securely attached to a plate or anchorage member fastened to the engine base. The drive from the crankshaft to the male clutch member is through a spur pinion attached to the crankshaft which meshes with a larger internal gear member that drives the male clutch casting. The female clutch member carries the drive sprocket that is connected to the rear wheel by a suitable chain, and in some models it drives a V-belt pulley.

Contrary to the usual cone clutch practice, the male clutch member does not move axially because it is held positively in place on the clutch spindle by two cup and cone bearings that prevent any endwise movement. To apply the clutch, the female clutch member is moved axially by a face cam arrangement. The oscillating face cam member, which has a series of inclined planes on its surface, is attached to a shaft that is moved by the clutch applying lever. A sliding face cam member that cannot rotate because it fits a squared portion of the clutch spindle is moved against the ball thrust bearing and presses the female clutch member firmly against the male clutch member as the pressure-applying lever oscillates the movable face cam member. When the clutch-applying lever is moved in a direction opposite to that necessary to apply the clutch, the face cam members separate and the clutch release spring pushes the female clutch member, which is movable, away from the male clutch member that is mounted on bearings that permit only a rotary movement. It is advanced by those who favor this form of clutch construction that much more gradual application is possible as the pressure is at the control of the rider than if obtained by means of the usual spring. It is claimed that should conditions demand it sufficient pressure may be exerted to lock the two portions of the clutch together into practically a single unit, whereas springs sometimes become weakened, and as the driving pressure is not positively maintained there is no way of remedying the slipping due to weakened springs except by replacing them or making a suitable adjustment of the pressure plate so the springs are compressed more tightly. The male clutch member is faced with frictional material in order to secure greater adhesion between the driven and driving members.

An example of a free engine clutch of the multiple disc type installed in the rear hub is shown at Fig. 164. This hub is used on Rex motorcycles which are of English manufacture. The driving member forms an inner hub that is independent of the outer hub shell except for the driving connection that exists when the discs are pressed together. The flanged driving member B is attached to the driving pulley by suitable spokes and revolves on ball bearings P. The outer hub shell, which carries one set of discs is mounted on bearings N. When the clutch assembly K is pressed together by the springs J, the main hub A and the driving member B are securely locked together and ball bearings N do not revolve. When the internally threaded member E is moved on the externally threaded member or worm F,

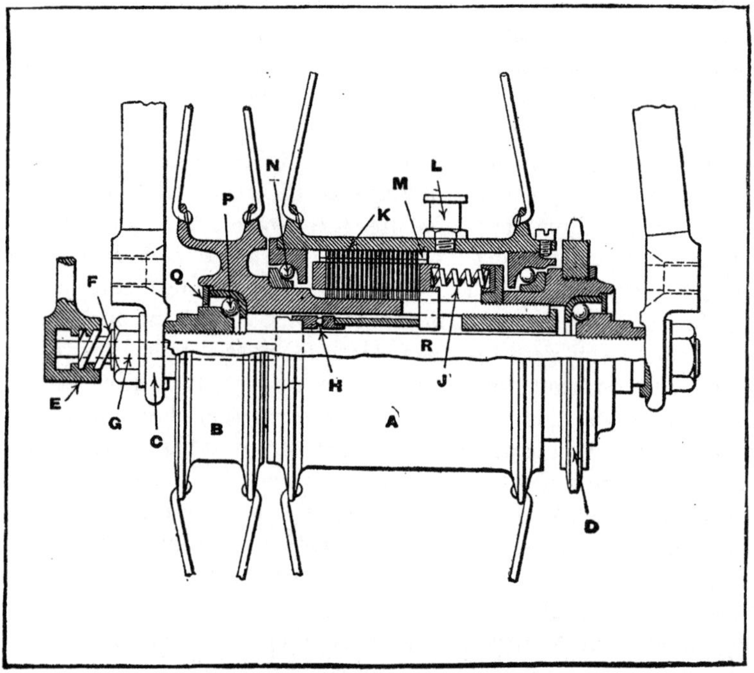

Fig. 164.—Detailing Construction of the Rex (English) Free Engine Clutch Forming Part of the Rear Hub.

it exerts pressure against the transfer rod G passing through one end of the axle R and pushes against a ball thrust bearing H which compresses the springs J by moving the pressure plate away from the disc assembly. When the discs are free, outer hub A can turn on ball bearings N independently of the member B, which continues to revolve as long as the engine is in motion.

Why Change Speed Gearing Is Desirable.—While the introduction of the friction clutch was a great step in advance, and made for rapid development of the motorcycle industry because it made it possible for people to operate motorcycles who would find it extremely difficult to manipulate the old directly connected types, still there is something lacking in a machine that is equipped only with a free engine clutch. We have previously considered the effect of the varying conditions upon the power needed to propel a motorcycle, and the writer has endeavored to make clear the relation the gear ratio must bear to the resistance. Under favorable conditions of operation,

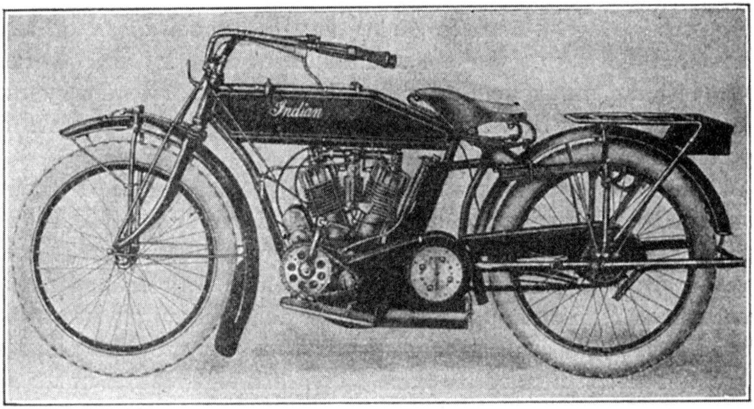

Fig. 165.—Indian Motorcycle With Two Speed Countershaft Gear.

when there is no undue influence to retard the progress of the machine, it is possible to drive the motorcycle without the expenditure of the entire energy the power plant is capable of. This makes high speeds possible and enables the engine to turn over at a number of revolutions that will permit it to exert the power necessary or even an actual surplus of energy. In a direct connected machine, as the resistance to motion increases, the tendency of the power plant is to slow down, which means that the power output is diminishing at a time that more is needed. If, therefore, some form of auxiliary gearing is provided that will permit the engine to run at its maximum speed and yet reduce the rear wheel and vehicle speed proportionate to the resistance encountered, it will be possible for the engine to exert its full power at those times when the full capacity is needed, and, what is more important, the interposition of positive reduction gearing means that the power will be transmitted to the traction member where it can do useful work instead of being dissipated by heating the friction members of a slipping clutch.

Value of Variable Speed Gears.—If a two-speed or other variable gear did not permit of any other advantages besides enabling one to surmount gradients steeper than could be taken with a single-geared machine, this alone would justify its existence and make it profitable to install them in the modern motorcycles. When one considers that they permit of easy starting under any road condition or on any grade, and that they also make possible increased safety and superior control of the motorcycle in traffic, it will be understood why the general demand of the discriminating rider is for two-speed gears or equivalent devices.

A two-speed gear makes it possible to provide a smaller power plant without reducing the actual ability of the motorcycle in the least. It will climb any grade a single-geared motorcycle of greater capacity would surmount, and would be able to overcome many gradients and unfavorable road surfaces that the larger and more powerful machine could not be operated on. It provides positive control in traffic, a smooth running, and lack of vibration under all conditions that obviously could not be obtained with an engine having a larger piston displacement and proportionately greater force to the explosions. The small engine will also provide a satisfactory speed on the level, because on the direct drive or high gear the ratio may be sufficiently high to permit of high speed, owing to the provision of the reduction gearing to permit use of the lower ratio at such times as the resistance becomes too great to be overcome by the direct drive. The reduction of power plant capacity made possible by the two-speed gear will promote several other improvements in motorcycle design that will appeal to many of conservative temperament. The most important of these is undoubtedly the reduced cost, both in initial expense and maintenance of the lighter machine. If the power plant capacity can be reduced, then the weight of the motorcycle may be lessened, owing to the materially diminished stresses on the frame, power transmission and supporting members. It costs less to drive a lighter machine, there is less depreciation and wear and tear if vibration is reduced. Smaller tires, less gasoline and oil consumption, greater comfort, and improved control are all desirable factors that will increase the pleasure of motorcycling, and augment the ranks of motorcyclists, and thus directly benefit the entire industry.

Variable Speed by Slipping Clutch.—Many motorcyclists are under the impression that the friction clutch in its various forms will permit of sufficient variation in the gear ratio to provide a margin of reserve power for hill climbing not obtained with a rigid drive machine. The free engine clutch is a very desirable improvement in motorcycles and has many advantages, inasmuch as it will permit the motorcycle to be started from a standstill, and enables the rider to stop his machine in traffic without stopping the power plant. It also provides for superior control in traffic, but is not an effective substitute for a variable speed gear of the positive type.

As any reduction in rear wheel speed, relative to that of the power plant, can only be obtained by slipping the clutch, it is obvious that the power lost in slippage between the friction surfaces can serve no useful purpose at the contact point of rear wheel and ground, and, in fact, if enough power is allowed to waste in this manner, sufficient heat may be generated by friction to seriously injure the mechanism comprising the clutch. As it is the rear wheel horse-power that counts in climbing hills or in pulling through sand, the variation in ratio between the engine shaft revolutions and rear wheel speed obtained by slipping the clutch does not increase the torque or pull at the rear wheel to any extent, and therefore is ineffective.

Consider a case where we have a motor capable of delivering 12 horse-power at 2,500 revolutions per minute. Almost any of our modern twin engines with a nominal rating of 8 to 10 horse-power can produce this energy. Assume that our gear ratio is 4 to 1, this means that with the clutch locked in positive engagement, that the rear wheel will be driven at 625 revolutions per minute, and that the rear wheel pull or effective power is equal to the capacity of the power plant minus the loss in transmission. If we assume 20 per cent. loss in transmission, we have an effective torque such as produced by 9.5

horse-power, and our rear wheel is revolving at 625 revolutions per minute.

Suppose we have a two-speed gear that will reduce the rear wheel speed to half that obtaining on the high or direct drive. If our engine runs at 2,500 revolutions per minute and our rear wheel turns at 312.5 revolutions per minute, we have practically the same effective torque as at the higher rear wheel speed, which obviously could not be used in climbing gradients because the increased resistance and the decrease in vehicle speed must be proportionate, if only the same amount of power is available at the motor. Of course, there would be a further loss due to the gearing, which would be compensated for by the lessened wind resistance due to the lower motorcycle speed. It will be evident that the introduction of a speed-reducing gear cannot increase the effective horse-power of the motor except that it permits the power plant to attain the same speed as with the higher ratio, whereas the motorcycle speed is reduced because the ratio of drive between rear wheel and engine is now actually 1 to 8.

Consider the result obtained by a slipping clutch in comparison with that secured by the interposition of intermediate speed-reduction gearing. The resistance to motion is such that the rear wheel cannot turn any faster than 312.5 revolutions per minute, and yet the horse-power required is just as great as though the rear wheel was turning at 625 revolutions per minute. The clutch is slipped sufficiently so the engine can run at its maximum speed of 2,500 revolutions per minute. The gear ratio between the clutch and rear wheel remains the same regardless of how much the clutch is slipped or 4 to 1.

Therefore, in order to get a rear wheel speed of 312.5 revolutions, the clutch-driven members must turn at 1,250 revolutions. The difference between that speed and that of the plates driven by the engine (assuming that the clutch is mounted on the engine shaft) is 1,250 revolutions per minute, which means that the clutch is slipping sufficiently to permit of the loss or actual waste of 50 per cent. of the power of the motor. The effective power output cannot be based on the number of engine revolutions but upon the revolutions per minute of the member driving the wheel. If the engine is delivering 12 horse-power to its crankshaft, but half that or 6 horse-power is being taken by the drive sprocket attached to the clutch member turning at 1,250 revolutions per minute. The actual torque or horsepower available at the rear wheel must be based on the lower figure less the losses in transmission. Therefore, under conditions where the entire power capacity of the machine is needed to overcome resistance to motion, no form of slipping clutch can be effective because the diminution in rear wheel speed can only be obtained by wasting power represented by the revolutions of the engine lost in slip between the clutch members. At the other hand, the intermediate reduction gearing of the two-speed gear transmits power rather than losing it because it is positive and not flexible, and, while no gearing will work

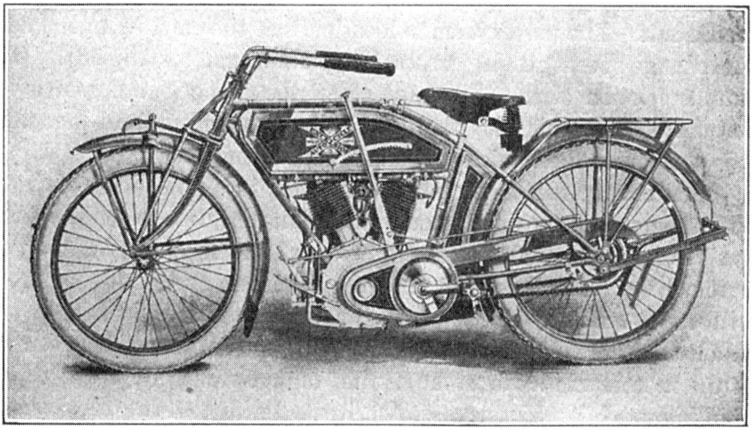

Fig. 166.—Showing the Location of the Planetary Two Speed Gear on the Excelsior Motorcycle.

without friction, the loss of energy through this added resistance is not to be compared with that wasted through clutch slip. While a friction clutch will provide variation of speed between rear wheel and engine shaft, it does this only at the expense of lost power, and a friction clutch is only effective for maximum power transmission when the clutch members are locked together and when clutch slipping is at a minimum. A reduction gearing reduces the speed without slip or loss other than that produced by the friction of gears and their bearings. It will be obvious that any claims where the friction clutch is given the same value as the reduction gear for obtaining varying effective reduced speed ratios are absurd. The ideal combination is that of the reduction gearing and friction clutch, because with the two, we are able to obtain all the good features desired. We can slip the clutch on the level to slow up the machine, yet, when a hill or poor road confronts us, the reduction gearing may be brought in action to transmit power positively.

Change-Speed Gear Location.—As most forms of change-speed gearing are combined with a clutch, the usual method of location is the same as that which obtains with the friction clutches previously described. The simpler forms such as variable speed pulleys and some forms of planetary gearing are usually attached to the engine crankshaft. The most common location is at the crank-hanger where the change-speed gearing takes the place usually occupied by the simpler friction clutch. In some cases, the change-speed gear is incorporated as a unit with the power plant, though in most machines it is a separate mechanism distinct from the engine.

When change-speed gearing is employed, it is possible to dispense with the usual pedal starting gear, though it must be replaced by some equivalent device such as a kick starter or hand crank such as used on automobiles. The Indian motorcycle is made in one model "de luxe" with an electric self-starter very similar in action to those employed in automobiles. When the pedaling gear is eliminated, the control of the motorcycle is the same as that of an automobile, as the drive is interrupted by shifting a clutch instead of by raising the exhaust valves or interrupting the ignition as was formerly the practice with direct drive single-gear machines. The application of a kick starter to a modern two-speed motorcycle is clearly shown at Fig. 155, and in this construction the change-speed gearing replaces the usual crank-hanger. In the machine shown at Fig. 166, the variable speed gearing is used in connection with the pedal-starting lever, and is mounted as a countershaft, replacing the conventional friction clutch assembly widely used at that point.

In the Harley-Davidson motorcycle, shown at Fig. 167, the two-speed gearing is incorporated in the rear hub instead of being attached to either the crank-hanger or the engine shaft. The same reasons that are given for friction clutch location apply just as well as the two-speed gear, and the slower the parts turn the larger and more substantial they must be to transmit the same amount of power. An engine shaft gear can have much smaller parts than a rear hub type, but, as is true of friction clutch design, a compromise between these two extremes is favored by most designers, and the speed gearing is installed at the crank-hanger in the form of countershaft where the speed of rotation is about half that of the engine shaft, and in some cases nearly twice as much as the rear wheel velocity.

Variable Speed Pulleys.—The simplest form of variable speed gear which involves the use of belt drive is the expanding V-pulley. A simple form in which the variation is obtained only when the pulley

Fig. 167.—The Harley-Davidson Eight Horsepower Twin Cylinder Motorcycle, With Two Speed Gear in the Rear Hub.

is adjusted by the rider is shown at Fig. 168. In this, a fixed flange is attached to a hub that is provided with one large thread to receive the adjustable flange, and with a thread of smaller diameter to fit the locking member. The main portion is secured to the engine crankshaft. When the pulley is assembled, the nearer the flanges are together the higher the gear ratio, because the belt is forced to drive at the top of the flanges. As the flanges are spread apart, the belt can drop lower, and as it fits a portion of the pulley of lesser diameter, the ratio of drive will, of course, be lower than when it is at the top of the pulley. The adjustment of the flange is a simple matter, as it involves merely the release of the locking member and the movement of the flange on its thread to the desired point. When the proper degree of adjustment has been secured, the locking member is set up tightly against the adjustable flange and maintained in position by it.

At Fig. 169, a pulley is shown that is said to compensate automatically for increased resistance at the driving wheel by providing a lower gear ratio. In this, the movable flange member is forced

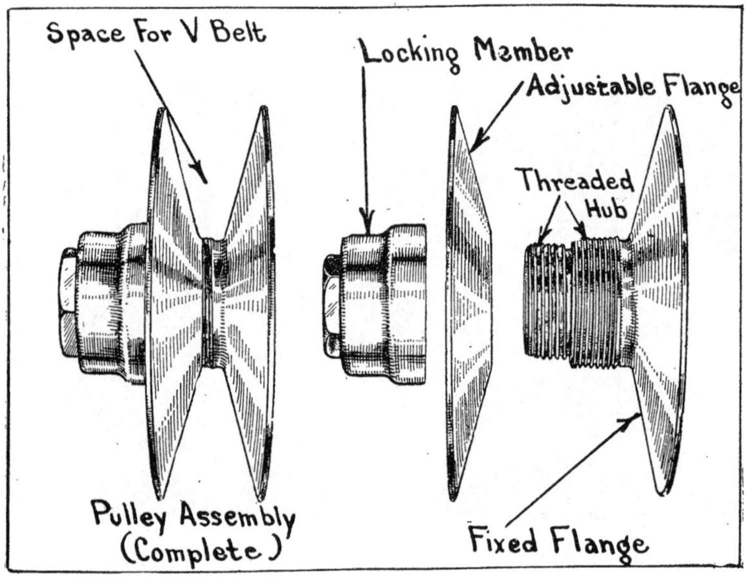

Fig. 168.—Construction of Simple Adjustable Pulley for V Belts.

toward the fixed flange by a series of coil springs, and it is claimed that as the resistance increases the belt tension becomes greater and forces the flanges apart until a point is reached where the ratio of drive has been reduced to the proper value. Variable pulleys of this form are provided with an auxiliary operating means which can be used to provide a lower gear ratio or a free engine independent of the resistance if desired.

The complete installation of the Auto-Varia, which is of English design is shown at Fig. 170. A pulley control roll is mounted at the lower portion of a control handle, the upper end of which works in a sector attached to the frame. The function of the roll is to force the movable flange of the pulley outward when it is desired to obtain the lower ratio, and to spread the flanges so far apart that the belt

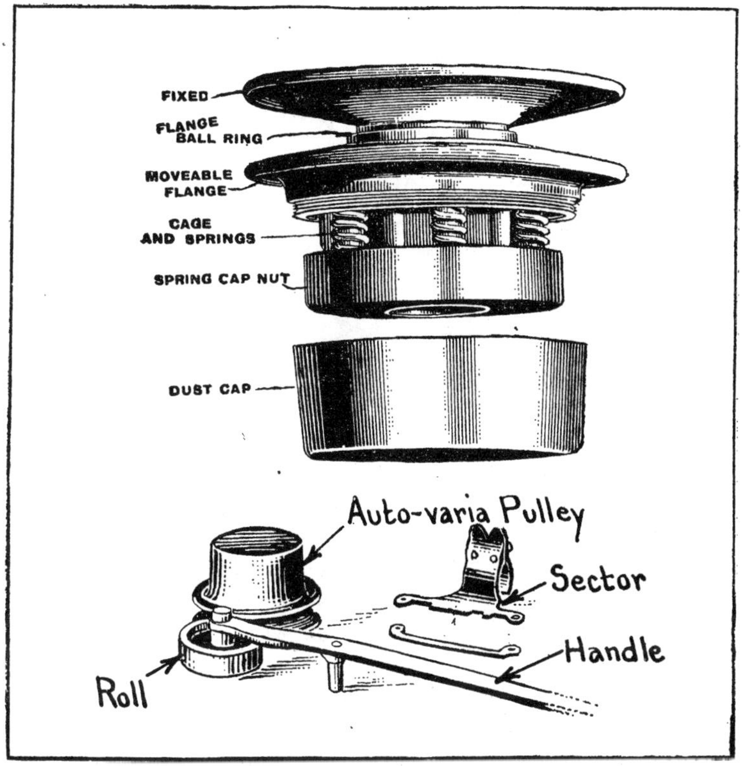

Fig. 169.—The Auto-Varia Pulley for V Belts.

will ride on a free, ball bearing supported ring at the bottom of the pulley when a free engine is desired. A variable pulley with which a friction clutch is included is shown at Fig. 171. This is a Rudge-Whitworth design and is said to give very satisfactory results. The action is the same as that of the simpler forms, means being provided for actuating the clutch that are independent of those available for

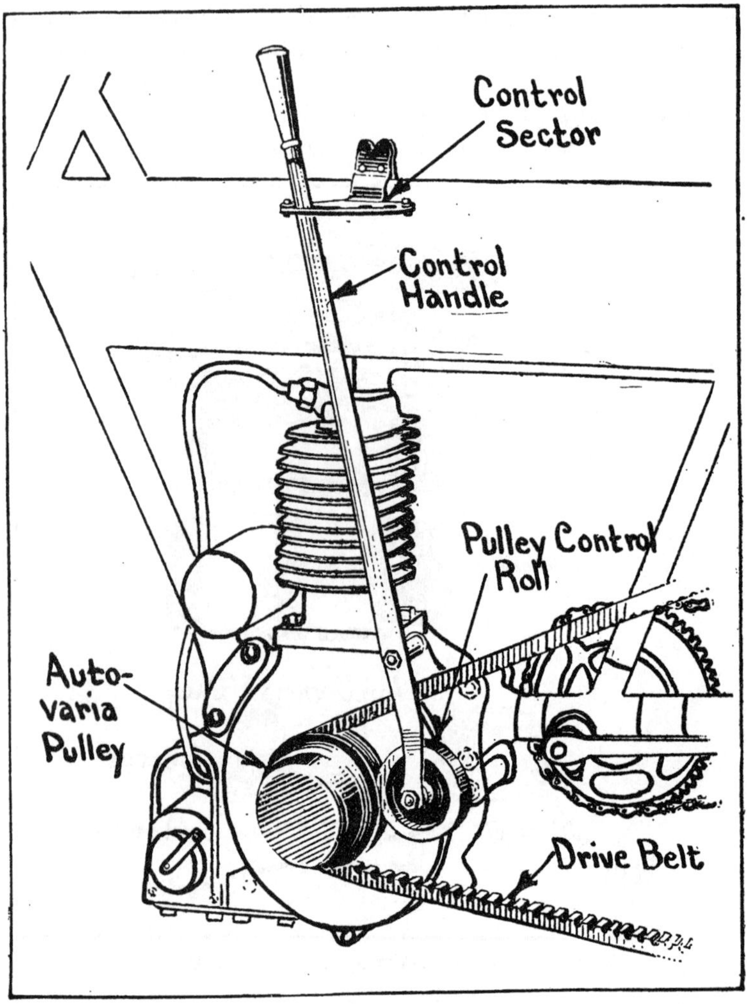

Fig. 170.—Showing Practical Application of the Auto-Varia Pulley and Control System.

varying the position of the movable pulley flange. With the driving belt in the position shown the flanges are spread apart as far as they will go, and the lowest ratio of drive is obtained. This device is rather more complicated than some of the simpler forms that are said to give fully as good results in practice.

Engine Shaft Gear.—A two-speed and free engine planetary gear of English design, and sold under the trade name of "Fits all," is shown at Fig. 172. While the arrangement is such that the drive is by means of V-belt, it is possible to replace the belt pulley with a

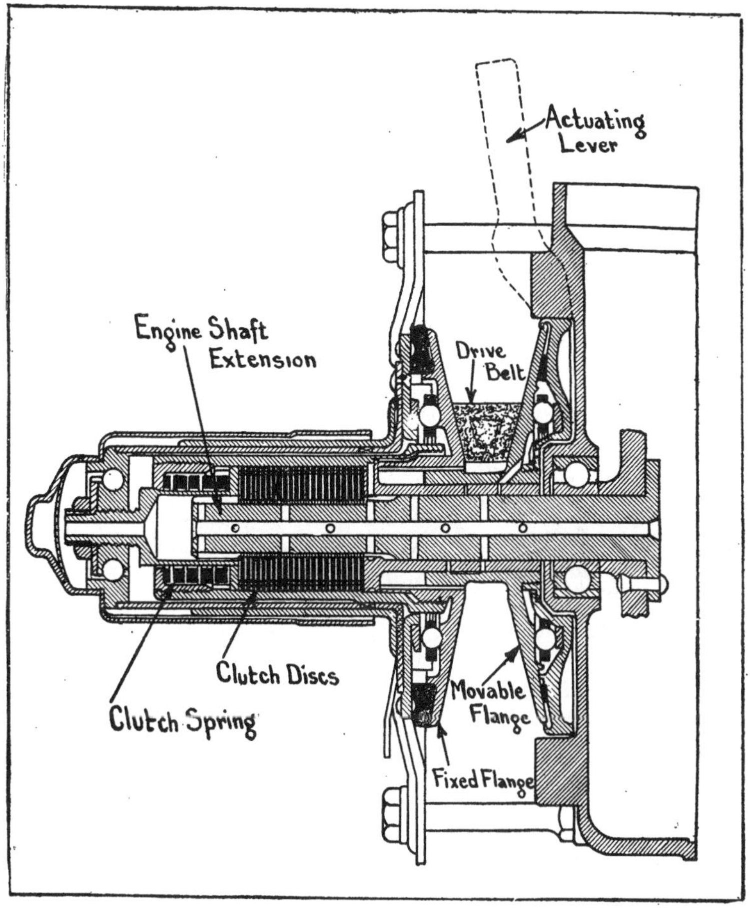

Fig. 171.—Variable Pulley and Free Engine Clutch Combination Used on the Rudge-Multi Motorcycle.

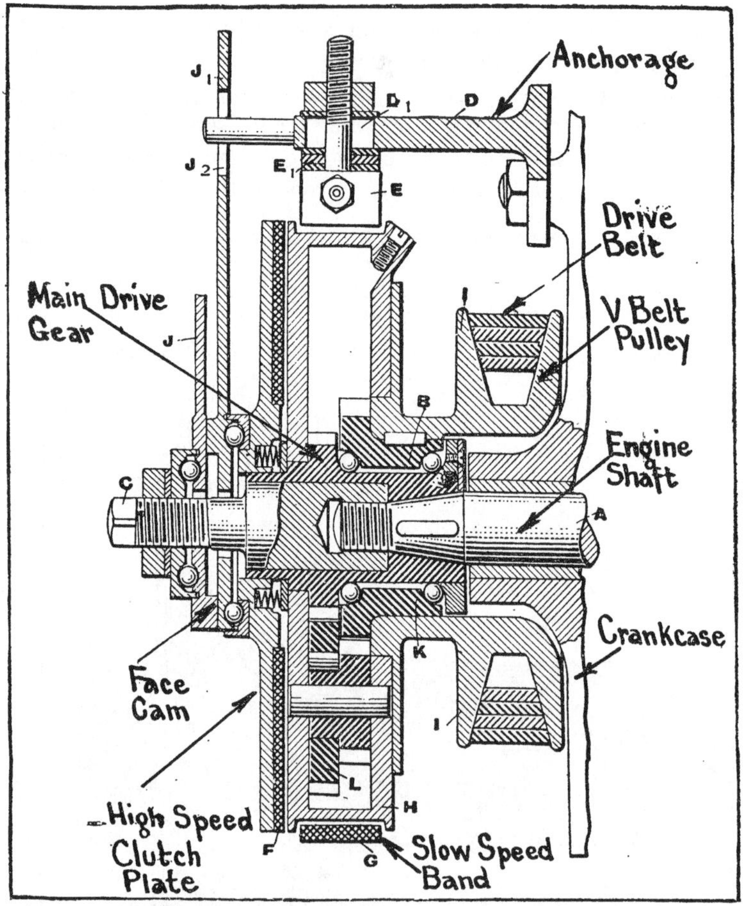

Fig. 172.—Sectional View of Typical Planetary Two Speed Gear, Adapted for Application to Engine Shaft.

sprocket, and obtain chain drive. The action of this gear is simple, and, if thoroughly understood, it will serve to make clear the principles underlying speed reduction by all forms of planetary gear sets. A main driving member that carries the assembly is securely keyed to the engine shaft A and is held firmly in place by a threaded shaft extension that forms an auxiliary support for the gear assembly. When the parts are in the position shown in the sketch, the engine may turn without driving the rear wheel because the main driving gear will rotate the planetary reduction gears L around on the bearing stud on which they rotate without producing any movement of the pulley I. If the friction band G is clamped around the drum H to keep it from turning, while the planetary pinion assembly L will turn on the stud, the pinion carrier H cannot rotate and the planetary pinions therefore serve as an intermediate gearing connecting the main drive gear with the pulley drive gear B. The main drive gear is about the same size as the larger gear of the planetary pinion assembly and therefore turns it at about the same speed. The small gear of the planetary pinion assembly is smaller than the driving gear B with which it meshes so a reduction in speed is possible between the belt pulley I and the engine shaft A due to the difference in size between gears B and the small member of the assembly L. While but one spur pinion assembly is shown, most planetary gears use two or more sets spaced equally around the casing H in order to equalize the driving strain and prevent wear on the bearings that would be unavoidable if but one set of intermediate pinions was employed. When it is desired to obtain the direct drive, the brake band G is released and the high speed clutch plate F is firmly pressed against the side of the drum H by a face cam and ball thrust arrangement, controlled by the rider, and the entire assembly is thus locked together as a unit so the drive is direct from engine shaft A to the drive pulley I.

Countershaft Gears.—Countershaft gears are made in infinite variety, and they may form part of the power plant unit or be attached to the crank-hanger. The views of the De-Luxe motor at Figs. 173 and 174 show clearly the external appearance of a two-speed gear of the countershaft type when it forms part of the power plant. This makes it possible to utilize the regular pedal-starting gear, if desirable, as the change-speed gearing is placed forward of the crank-hanger and is independent of it. Where the change-speed gearing is not a part of the engine case and must be supported from the crank-hanger, it is sometimes impossible to utilize the pedal gear for starting the engine, so an auxiliary starting-crank arrangement, such as shown at Fig. 175, must be used to turn the engine crankshaft over and start the motor.

The arrangement may be easily understood from the illustration.

The view at A shows the starting crank in place with the jaw clutch making a suitable connection between the starting-handle shaft and the main gear shaft, as soon as the engine starts the handle is automatically released, and a coil spring will force the starting clutch out of engagement so that the member to which the starting crank is attached does not rotate except when it is pressed into engagement with the clutch member by suitable end pressure on the starting handle.

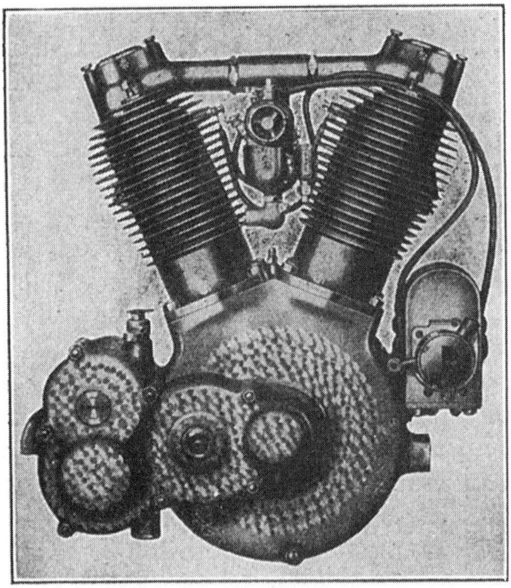

Fig. 173.—Carburetor Side of Spacke Two Cylinder Motor With Two Speed Gear Integral With Power Plant.

The arrangement of the clutch and change-speed gearing in the Michaelson unit power plant is outlined at Fig. 176. In this, the multiple disc clutch of the usual pattern is attached to an extension of the engine crankshaft, and drives an intermediate gear assembly consisting of two gears, one larger than the other, which in turn transmit the crankshaft motion to a suitable spur gear on the main driving shaft of the two-speed gearing. The arrangement of the gears in this variable speed member is practically the same as those shown at Fig. 179. A shifting clutch member clutches either of the gears to the sprocket-drive shaft. The use of the intermediate gear member provides for a first-speed reduction gear completely enclosed and running in oil. This power-transmitting element takes the place of the usual short chain that joins the engine crankshaft to the conventional countershaft gear arrangement such as outlined at Fig. 178. The engine is started by a small sprocket member that drives a suitably formed clutching member at one side of the gear case and which engages the main shaft of the change-speed gearing. This position is preferable to a direct application to the engine crankshaft because the engine is started through the intermediate gears, which insures that the crankshaft B can be maintained at a higher rate than would be possible by direct application of the starting handle, owing to the geared-up drive between the starting means and the crankshaft. In order to start the average motorcycle power plant promptly, it is necessary to rotate it at a fairly high rate of speed. This was always an important advantage in connection with the usual pedal-starting gear, because the rear wheel could be turned over fast enough by the feet to revolve the engine crankshaft at a higher rate of speed than is possible with most kick starters or equivalent devices. There are conditions where it is important to turn the engine over fast to secure prompt starting, such as in cold weather when the gasoline does not vaporize readily. The application of the geared-up starting crank gives practically the same rotative speed as would be obtained through the conventional pedal-gear arrangement.

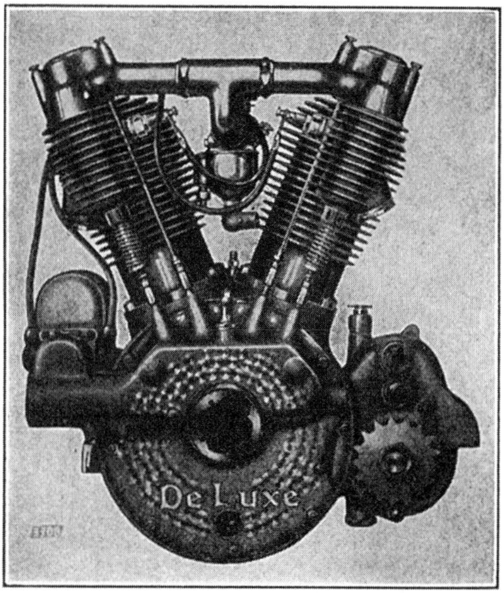

Fig. 174.—Valve Side of De Luxe Unit Power Plant Showing Driving Sprocket on the Gear Box.

The Minneapolis power plant which is shown at Fig. 177 is similar in general arrangement to the Michaelson, but employs a distinctive means of speed changing. The transmission is of the planetary type using positive clutches for both high and low speed which, of course, is made possible by utilizing a master clutch on the engine crankshaft. A jaw clutch member is adapted to slide on a bushing surrounding the main shaft, and this may be engaged either with the member carrying the planetary reduction or it can be moved over to push a clutch member in engagement with the driving gear of the transmission shaft. When in the position indicated, the gear that drives the transmission shaft is clutched to that member. If the jaw clutch is moved to the other extreme, a series of projections extending from

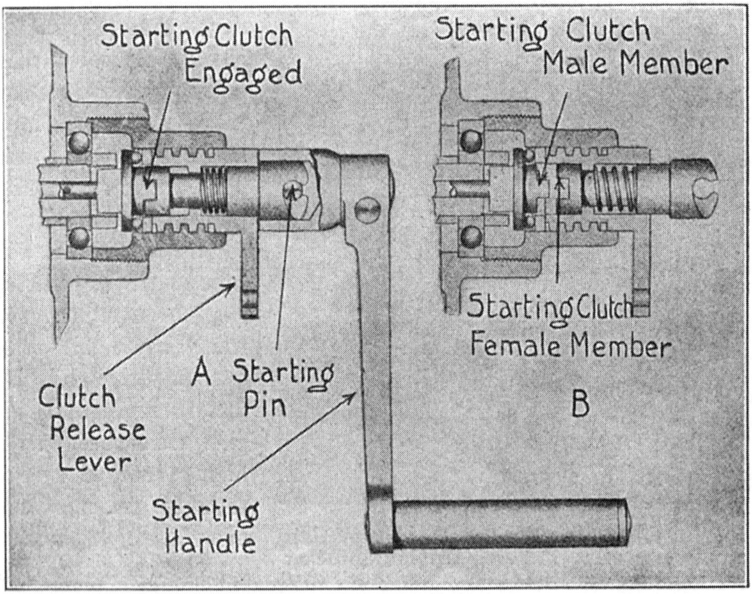

Fig. 175.—Starting Handle Clutch Arrangement Used in Connection With Jardine Two Speed Gears.

the face of the clutch shifter engage suitable depressions in the planetary gear-carrying plate, and keep that member from rotating because the jaw clutch shifter is securely anchored to a through bolt, extending from one side of the gear case to the other, which keeps it from rotation. When used in connection with planetary gearing, it takes the place of the usual band clutch, and the drive is then to the member carrying the driven spur gear inside of the case, and threaded

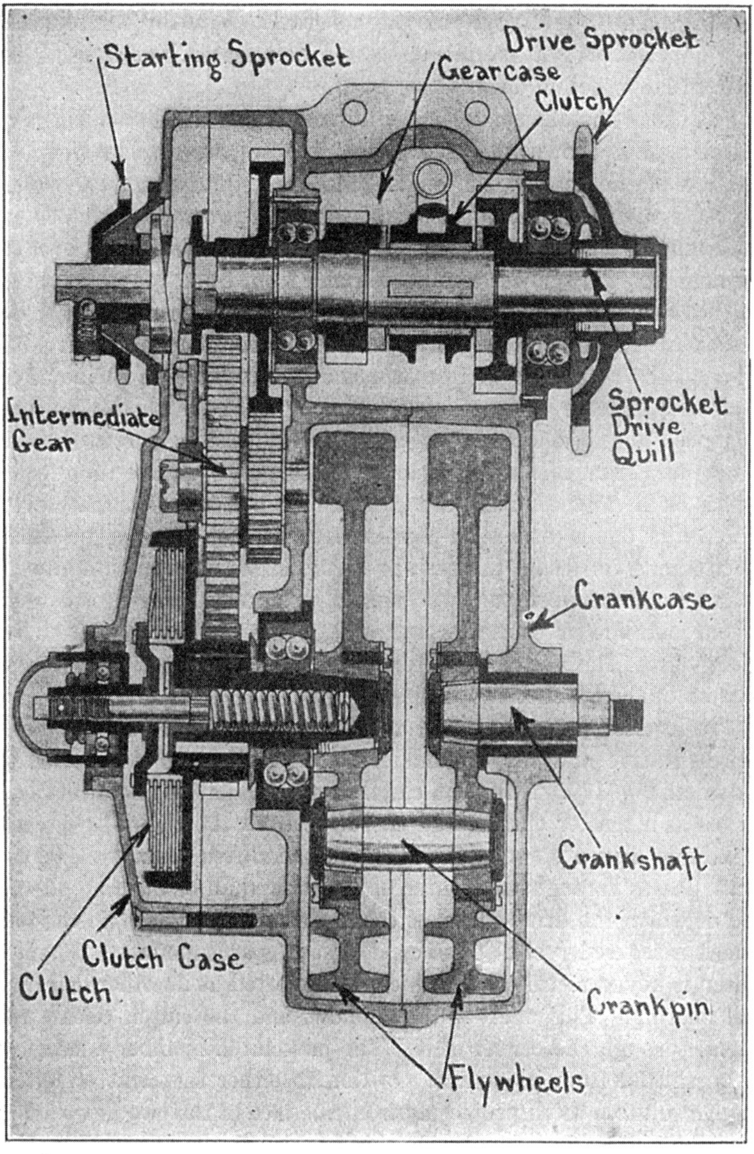

Fig. 176.—Showing Arrangement of Change Speed Gearing in Michaelson Unit Power Plant.

on the outside to receive the driving sprocket. With this construction, it is imperative that the master clutch be released before either the high or low speed is engaged.

The usual installation of a countershaft gear of the shifting jaw clutch type is shown at Fig. 178. At the bottom or plan view, the relation of the gear to the engine base, and the method of driving from the engine crankshaft, is clearly shown. A compensating clutch at the engine crankshaft is utilized to prevent depreciation of the chain through unsteady power application and from the sprocket mounted on that member, the drive is by chain to the sprocket attached to the main clutch member that forms part of the countershaft gear. The drive to the rear wheel is from the smaller sprocket on the countershaft to a suitable member on the rear hub. The method of shifting the speed is also depicted, the jaw clutch controlling the two speeds is operated from a small lever attached to the top frame tube which works on a notched quadrant providing three stops for the lever. The center one is in neutral position, and at such times as the small lever stands vertically, the shifting clutch in the transmission interior is at a point between the two engaged positions. Moving the lever to one extreme or the other will engage the high or low speed respectively. The clutch is shifted by a foot pedal attached to the bottom of the bracket supporting the power plant.

The interior arrangement of the Indian two-speed gear, which is representative and the original of all the shifting clutch forms, is shown at Fig. 179. A friction clutch of the regulation Indian pattern serves as a master clutch, and the drive from the engine is directly to a large driven sprocket attached to the clutch casing. A driven shaft passes through the center of a hollow quill or bushing, at one end of which the drive sprocket that transmits the power to the rear wheels is secured, while at the inside a spur gear is mounted. The jaw clutch is keyed to this shaft which is supported at its other end by a ball bearing. This shaft is also hollow, and the clutch release rod passes through the center of it. The jaw clutch member is adapted to be shifted from its central position to either the right or left to engage suitable teeth projecting from the face of the two gears. The gear that is attached to the bushing carrying the sprocket meshes with a smaller member carried on a countershaft to one side of the

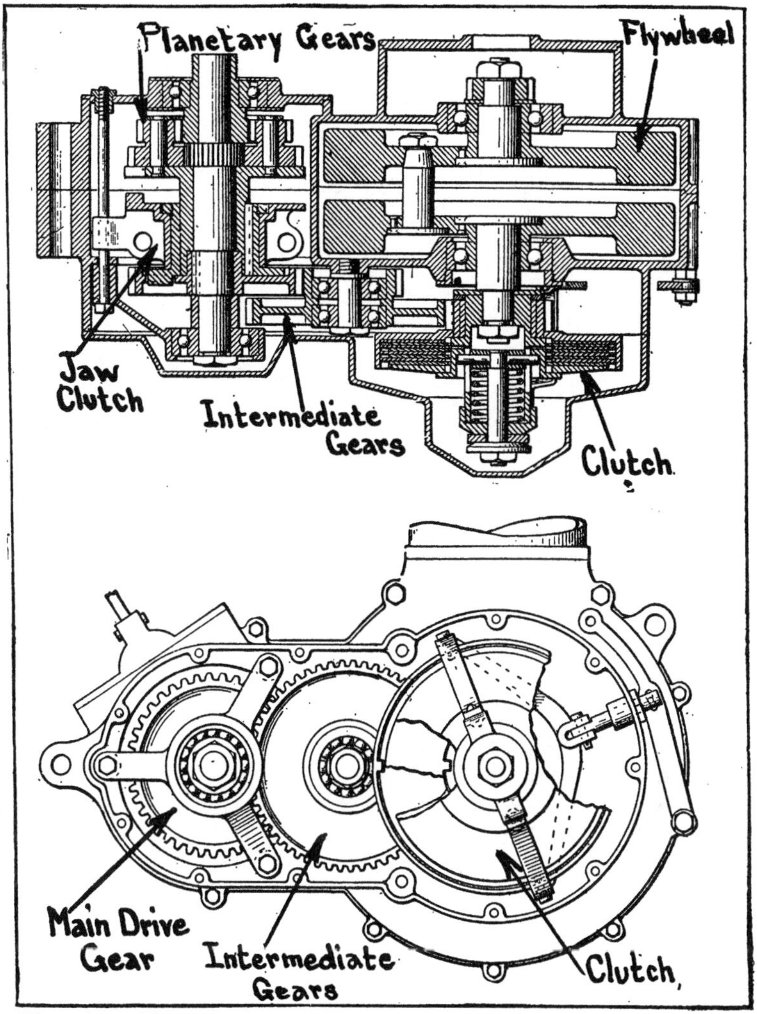

Fig. 177.—Views Depicting Construction of the Minneapolis Unit Power Plant and Gearset.

main shaft. A larger gear on the countershaft meshes with a smaller member that is normally free to revolve on the main shaft, and which is independent of it at all times except when the jaw clutch is moved over to engage with the teeth on its face.

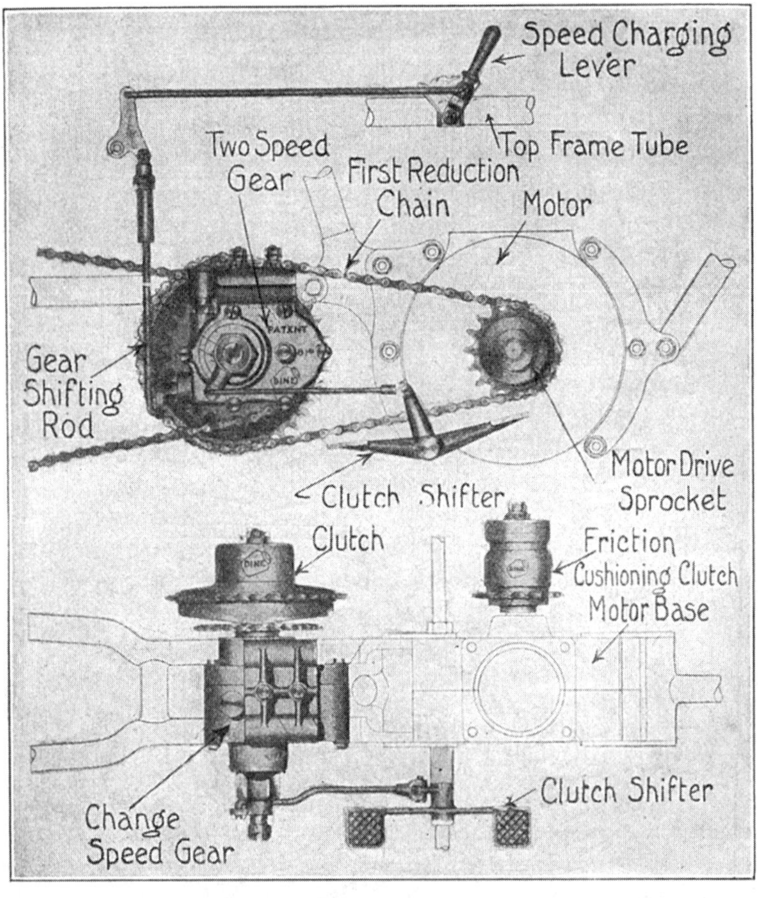

Fig. 178.—Methods of Installing the Jardine (English) Countershaft Type Two Speed Gear.

With the jaw clutch in the position shown, even if the master clutch is engaged, the rear wheel will not turn because the sleeve carrying the drive sprocket does not rotate. To obtain the low speed ratio, the jaw clutch is moved to the right to make fast to the shaft the smaller of the gears mounted on that member. The drive is then from the clutch to the small gear, which, in turn, drives the large gear on the countershaft at a lower rate of speed. The other gear member on the countershaft is smaller than the sprocket drive gear, and a further reduction of speed is possible between these two. The driving sprocket is turning in the same direction as the main shaft, but at a lower rate of speed on account of the reduction gears interposed between the sprocket and the clutch-driven shaft. To obtain the high-speed ratio, the jaw clutch is moved to the left, and makes the sprocket-drive gear fast to the main shaft. This means that the driving sprocket would turn at the same speed as the main shaft to which the clutch is attached. The master clutch is shifted by a

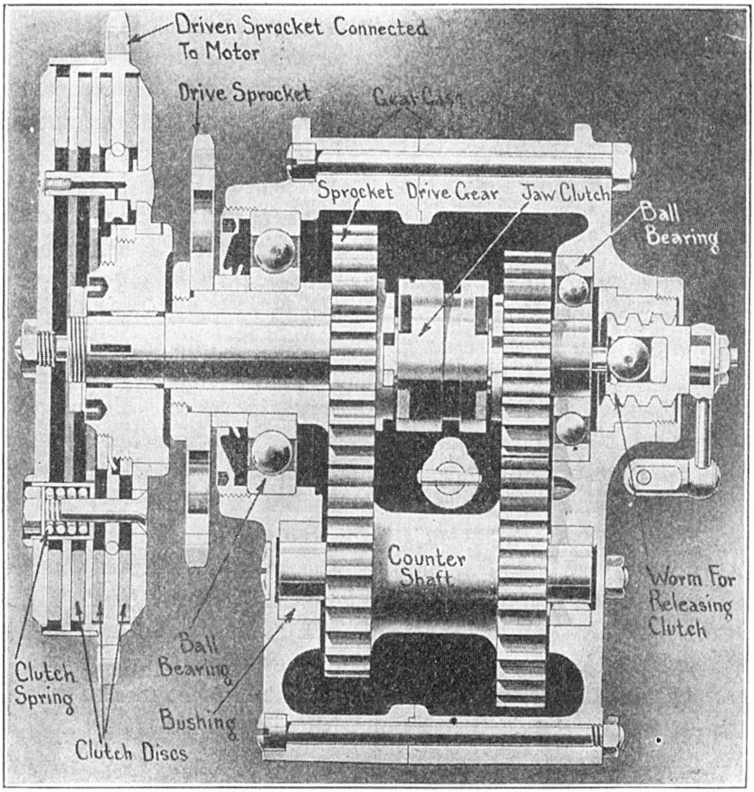

Fig. 179.—Sectional View Showing the Two Speed Individual Clutch Gear and Master Clutch of the Friction Type Employed on the Indian Motorcycle.

releasing worm that exerts pressure against a rod passing through the center of the main shaft, and attached to the outermost clutch plate. When this plate is moved to the left, the clutch springs are compressed, and the driving pressure between the plates is interrupted. It is necessary to release the master clutch at all times that the jaw clutch member is shifted, because if the positive clutch is moved with the friction clutch engaged it will start the motorcycle so suddenly that the parts of the transmission system may be stressed to the breaking point.

Another form of countershaft variable speed gear is shown at Fig. 180. This differs from the type previously described, in that it is a sliding gear form and provides three forward speeds instead of two as is common practice. The power from the engine is delivered to the clutch case by the sprocket A, and the inner member of the clutch is attached to and drives the main shaft B of the transmission. A sliding gear D is mounted on the main shaft, and is provided with clutch projections E on both sides. When the member D is moved to the extreme right of the gear case, the projecting teeth E clutch corresponding members on the small spur gear G, thus locking the gear G to the main shaft. The gear G is considerably smaller than the gear L mounted on the countershaft H, and turns that member at a lower rate of speed. The driving sprocket M is attached to a bushing to which the sprocket-driving gear is securely fastened. The constant mesh gear on the countershaft H that meshes with the gear F is smaller than that member, and thus a further reduction in speed is obtained. The driving sprocket M turns at a considerably lower speed than the main driving shaft B, owing to the two reductions obtained, one between the gears G and L, and the other between the small constant mesh gear on the countershaft and the sprocket gear F. If the sliding member B is engaged with the member K on the countershaft there is but one reduction in speed, and that is between the constant mesh gears, because the gears D and K are practically the same size. This is an intermediate ratio that is not as slow as the low speed, and yet is slower than the direct drive.

If the sliding member D is moved to the extreme left, the clutch teeth E-1 will engage suitable members projecting from the gear F, and will lock the sprocket drive gear directly to the main shaft and obtain a direct drive. With this form of transmission, it is even more important to release the master clutch before speed changes are effected than it is with the sliding clutch forms in which the gear teeth are always in mesh. If the sliding member D is moved into mesh with the gear K, with the clutch engaged, it will be apt to produce serious damage to the teeth of the two gears, because it is almost impossible to mesh spur gears when both are in motion. A kick starting

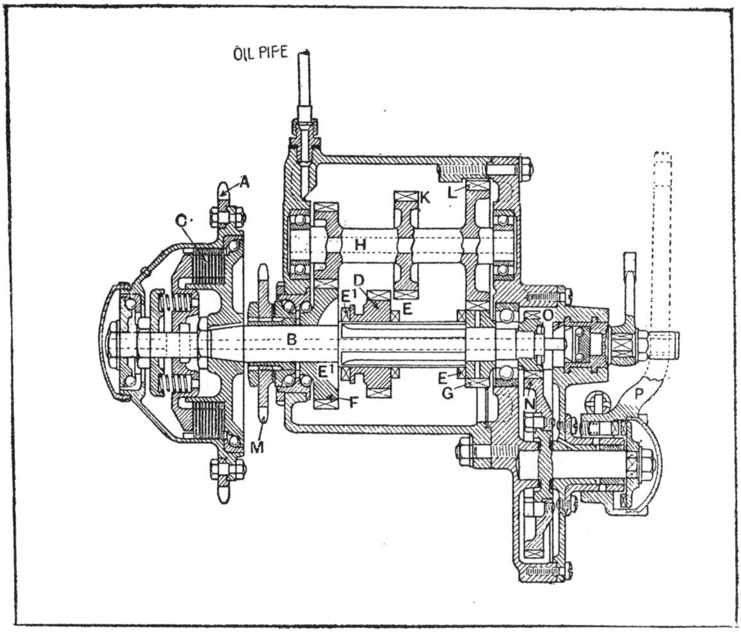

Fig. 180.—English Three Speed Countershaft Change Speed Gearing of the Sliding Type.

gear is incorporated with this gear-set. The pedal crank P which is adapted to be pushed by the foot of the rider is clutched to the gear N which meshes with a much smaller gear O attached to the main shaft B. Even if the pedal P is only moved through a small portion of a revolution, the engine shaft will be turned several times on account of the gearing of the starter as well as the step-up between the large sprocket A on the clutch and the smaller member on the engine shaft.

Rear Hub Gears.—Several forms of rear hub gears have been applied, and these are practically all of the planetary type. That shown at Fig. 181*a*, in cross section, and at Fig. 182, in partial disassembly, is used on the Thiem motorcycle, which is an American design. The gear itself is patterned very closely after a popular English two-speed hub. The method of obtaining the low speed by the use of planetary reduction gears is practically the same as that employed in the engine shaft gear shown at Fig. 172. A suitable brake band clutches a drum securely fastened to the axle, and one

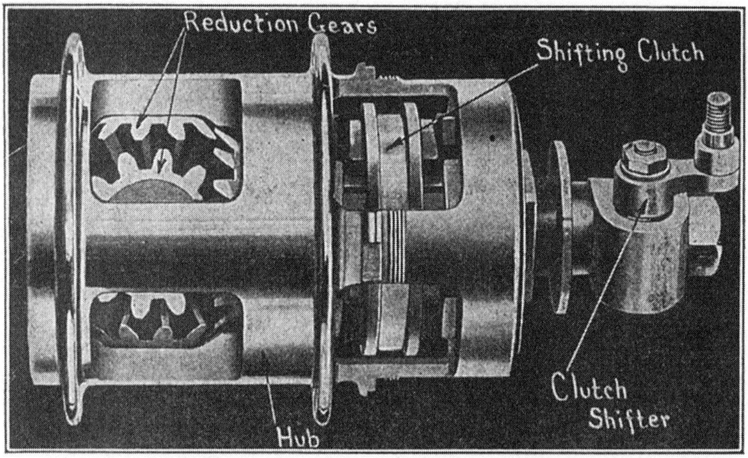

Fig. 181.—Novel Method of Speed Reduction by Bevel Gearing Incorporated in the Harley-Davidson Two Speed Hub.

of the main gears of the planetary reduction is also keyed to the axle. The other sun gear, as the central main member is called, is attached to the hub member proper. The drive from the motor is by V-belt to a pulley rim laced to the drum carrying the planetary reduction gears by the conventional wire spokes. When it is desired to apply the low speed, the brake band that works on the outer drum is constricted and holds that drum and the axle to which it is fastened stationary. The planetary pinions are free to revolve on their retaining studs and drive the hub shell because they must turn it in the same direction, though at a slower rate of speed, than the pulley rim

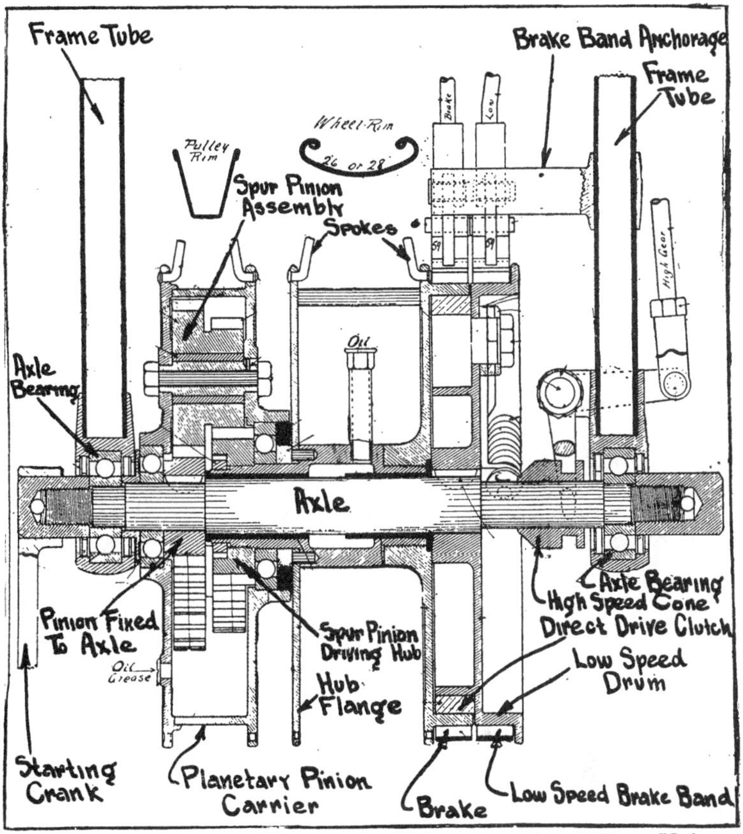

Fig 181a.—Sectional View of the Thiem Two Speed Rear Hub.

travels on account of being forced to roll around the spur gear keyed to the axle. To obtain a high speed, an expanding band clutch is engaged by leverage actuated by a shifting cone, and the entire hub assembly is locked to, and must turn with the axle. The principle of this gear may be more easily grasped if one remembers that the axle travels forward with the road wheel when in high speed or direct drive position; that it is held stationary when in low speed and that it will revolve backward when in the neutral or free engine position. The inner brake band serves as a running brake, and will retard the hub positively whether the gearing is in use or not.

A distinctive form of reduction gear mounted in the rear hub is that used in connection with the Harley-Davidson motorcycle. The gearing is of the bevel form and operates on the planetary principle. A shifting dog clutch is employed in addition to the master clutch which is of the friction type. When moved in one position, the master clutch drives the hub directly, and when it is pushed to the other position it drives the hub through the medium of the bevel-speed reduction gear. The complete device is not shown in the illustration (Fig. 181), as a clutch assembly and a friction brake must be added to the simple hub shown to complete the mechanism.

Fig. 182.—The Thiem Two Speed Hub Partially Disassembled to Show Arrangement of Mechanism.

Forms of hub gears working on the planetary principle have been evolved abroad which provide three forward speeds, but these are so complicated that they have received practically no application in America. There seems to be no good reason for the use of three-speed gears unless the motorcycle power plant lacks capacity, and, as the best American practice seems to be to provide a two-speed gear more for emergency use and to use power plants that will have sufficient power to overcome practically all normal resistance on the direct drive or high gear, the low gear is to be used only for starting, in hill climbing or in negotiating unfavorable highway surfaces. Practically all of the time the motorcycle is in use it may be operated on the

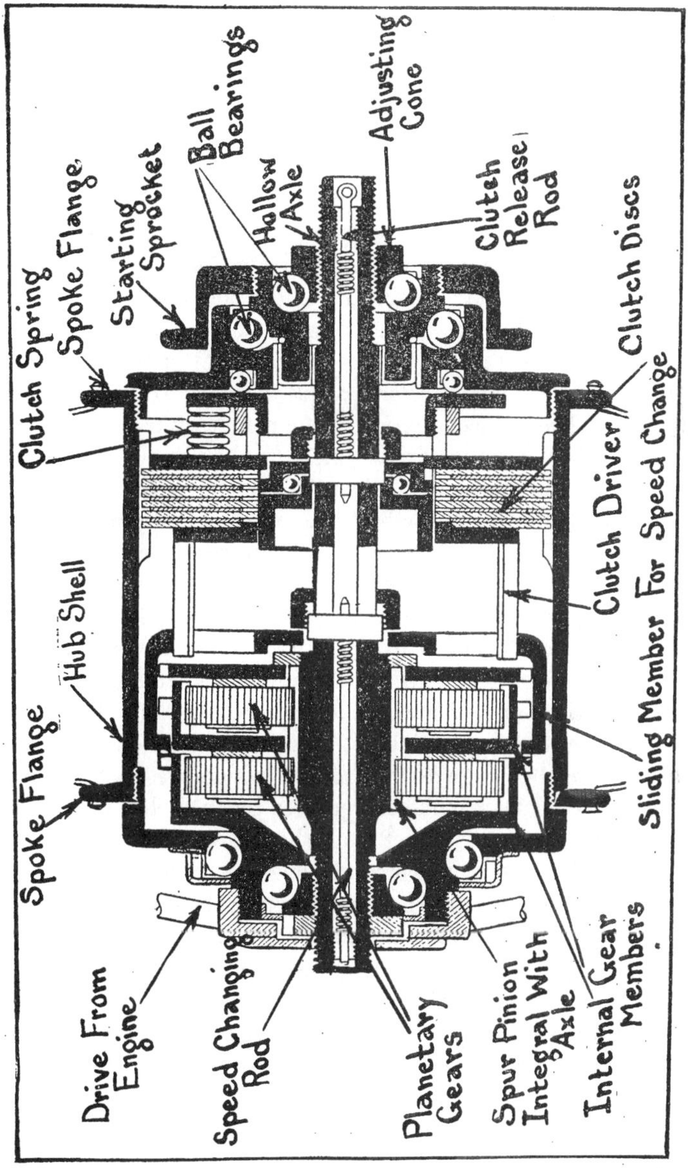

Fig. 182a.—Sectional View Showing Construction of the Sturmey-Archer Three Speed Planetary Rear Hub Gear.

direct drive or high speed. Fitting an intermediate ratio between the high and the low is not necessary when the power plant is of suitable proportions, though it might be of some value if the machine was under-powered, and the direct drive could only be used under exceptionally favorable operating conditions.

The Sturmey-Archer is a typical example of a three-speed hub, and it is said that the lowest gear ratio is to be used only when extremely high resistance must be overcome. The internal construction can be clearly understood by referring to Fig. 182*a*. When on the high gear, all parts of the hub are locked together solidly as the hub shell is driven directly from the driving member. On the second or intermediate gear, the drive is obtained from an internal gear member which rolls planetary pinions around a stationary central gear integral with the axle. The reduced motion of the planetary pinions is transmitted to the wheel hub by a driving member that clutches extensions from the friction clutch carrier. When the lowest gear of all is brought into action, the drive is through still another set of pinions and a further reduction in speed is effected. The direct drive is obtained by a plate clutch in the hub interior. It is said that a reduction of 47 per cent. in speed is obtained on the intermediate speed, and that a further reduction of 40 per cent. is secured on the low speed. The various speed changes are effected by moving a laterally shiftable member to the right or left, and the lowest speed ratio is obtained as the member is moved to the right. When on the high gear, the cup-shape driven member engages projections which are on the rim of the circular or internal gear member driven by the belt pulley. This means that the high gear is direct from the drive pulley carrier to the plate clutch. When the intermediate speed is desired, the sliding member engages with the internal gear carrying the first set of planetary pinions, and this internal gear meshes with and drives the second train of planetary pinions. On the lowest speed, the driven member engages with the carrier of the second set of planetary pinions.

Three Chain Systems.—A form of two-speed gear that has been used with some degree of success on European motorcycles is that shown at Fig. 183, in which a double sprocket is attached to the engine crankshaft, and two chains extend to the sprockets on the countershaft. Each of these sprockets may revolve independently of the other or both may revolve free of the smaller driving sprocket used for driving the rear wheels. It is said that an advantage of this type of gear is that both speeds are direct and the friction and power loss due to the use of gear pinions is not present. It is also advanced that this system is extremely quiet in action, and that the clutches, which are of the internal expanding type may be used to give a free engine on either gear ratio.

The original form is undoubtedly the Phelon & Moore, which is

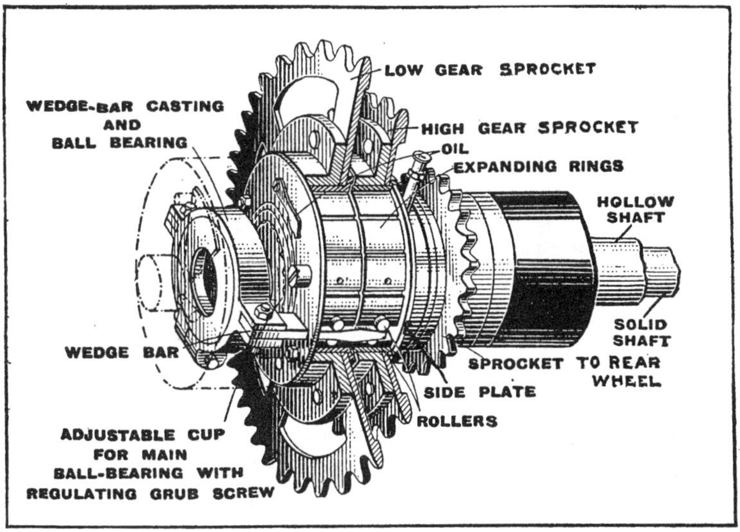

Fig. 183.—Phelon & Moore Two Speed Individual Clutch Countershaft Gear.

shown at Fig. 183. The low-gear sprocket, which is the largest, is the outside member, while the high-gear sprocket, which is the smaller of the two large ones, is the inside member. The clutch members act as bearings on which the sprockets revolve when the gear is in neutral position, but when expanded the shoes grip the interior of the drum carrying the sprockets very tightly and transmit the power to the small sprocket to which the brake shoes are fastened. The internal clutches are brought into engagement by sliding a wedged-shaped member to the right or left as the case may be, and spreading out the brake shoes. In the form shown at Fig. 183, if the wedge bar is moved to the right, the brake shoe that clutches the high speed sprocket will be expanded, and the drive will be from the engine shaft to the countershaft through that member, while the low gear or larger sprocket will revolve freely on the brake shoes that are not expanded and which therefore act as a bearing for that member. If the wedge bar is moved to the left, the outside sprocket will be clutched to the driving member, and the smaller or high-gear sprocket will revolve freely on its brake shoes. It would seem that there would be considerable wear due to the movement of the sprocket carrier over the brake shoes, but the successful use of this form of change-speed gear for a number of years indicates the large surface of the bearing and the provisions made for lubricating them are adequate to prevent untimely depreciation.

The two-speed gear used on the Enfield (English) motorcycle is of the same pattern and is clearly outlined at Fig. 184. Either gear ratio may be brought in action by expanding the hardened steel bands A into one of the drums B, also of hardened steel, to which the chain wheels C are secured. The change in gear ratio is obtained in the same manner as in the Phelon & Moore by driving through the large sprocket for low speed and through the smaller sprocket for high speed. The expanding bands A are carried on internal drums D which take the drive, and which are keyed on the ball bearing shaft E that is employed to drive the sprocket F that connects with the rear hub. The clutches are engaged by cams cut into the block G, which is capable of sliding in either direction according to which gear is desired. The action of the cam is to force one of the pegs H against the split roller I, which forces open the band A until it engages with B, which is rotated by the engine. The object of splitting the roller I is to permit the clutch to pick up smoothly. The block G which contains the cam is moved by the rack J and the pinion K, which is operated by a vertical shaft and lever at the top of the crank. Three pairs of cams numbered 1, 2, and 3 are cut in G, each of these being .005 inch higher than the one preceding it. Should the band A wear to such a point that cam A is not sufficiently high to operate it, the member G may be turned around so the next larger cam will be used to expand the brake band. The practical application of

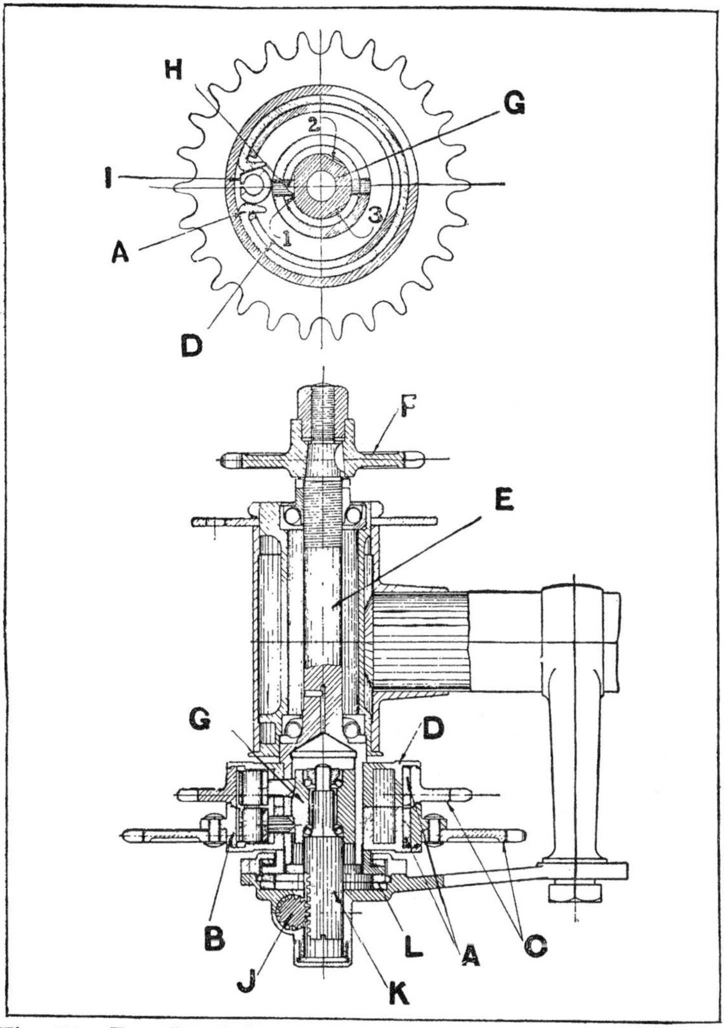

Fig. 184.—Two Speed Countershaft Gear Used on the Royal Enfield Motorcycle.

this gear to a Clement (French) motorcycle is clearly outlined at Fig.185.

Planetary Countershaft Gear.—Several of the American motorcycles employ a planetary reduction gear mounted on an extension projecting from the crank-hanger. A successful form, which is used on the Excelsior motorcycle is shown at Fig. 186. The drive from the motor is to the sprocket B attached to the planetary gear carrier A which also forms the male member of the friction clutch employed for direct drive. When it is desired to obtain a low speed ratio, the female member of the high speed clutch is pulled out of engagement with the male member, which is fixed and the V-shape bronze brake

Fig. 185.—Three Chain Speed Changing and Driving System Used on Clement Motorcycle.

band M is tightened around the carrier I, to which is attached the gear H. As this gear is held stationary, the planetary pinions must rotate on their studs as they are carried around by the member A, and, as they turn at the same time, they drive the gear E, which is securely keyed to the bushing to which the sprocket G is fastened. To obtain a high gear ratio, the member M is released and the female member J, of the cone clutch, is brought into engagement with the male member so the drive is direct from the sprocket B through the clutch members to the member F to which the wheel driving sprocket G is keyed. The member J is actuated by the operating worm K which is oscillated by the lever L. The entire construction is mounted on ball bearings so but little friction is present, and the liability of bearing depreciation is proportionately reduced. The practical installation of this gear, and the method of operation by a single handle, is clearly shown at Fig. 166. If the handle is moved in one direction the low speed is applied, and in the other position the high speed will

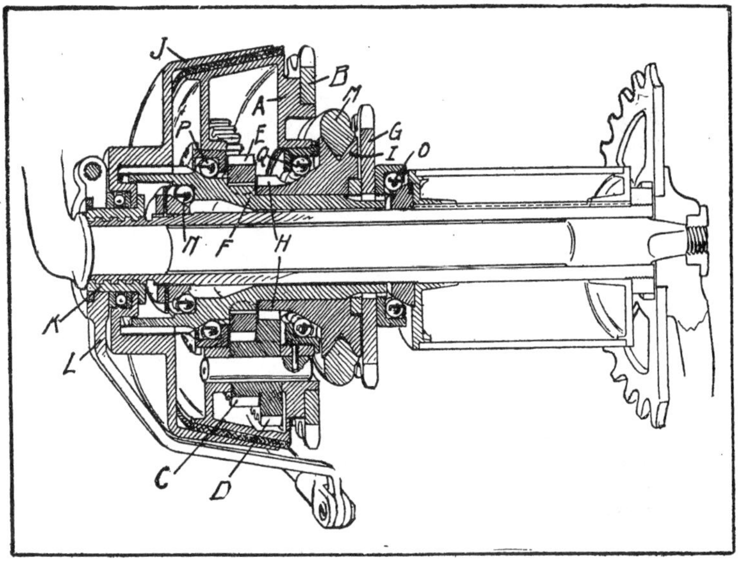

Fig. 186.—The Substantial Two Speed Planetary Gearset of the Countershaft Type Used on Excelsior Motorcycles.

be engaged. When in the position shown or approximately at the center of the notched quadrant, the gear is in the free engine position as neither the high-speed clutch J nor the low-speed friction band M is in engagement with their respective co-acting members.

Sliding Gear Type.—The sliding gear forms which have been so generally used in automobile practice have received but limited application in motorcycles. This is not as popular among motorcycle designers as the individual clutch systems are, because considerable damage may result to the transmission gear when handled by the inexperienced rider. If attempt is made to change the speeds without releasing the main clutch member, the gear teeth will be burred or destroyed entirely. These pieces may get into the transmission and wreck the entire construction. It is contended by those who favor this construction that there is no more reason for the motorcycle rider to damage a transmission than there is for the automobile operator. As a general rule, the motorcycle is not intended to be

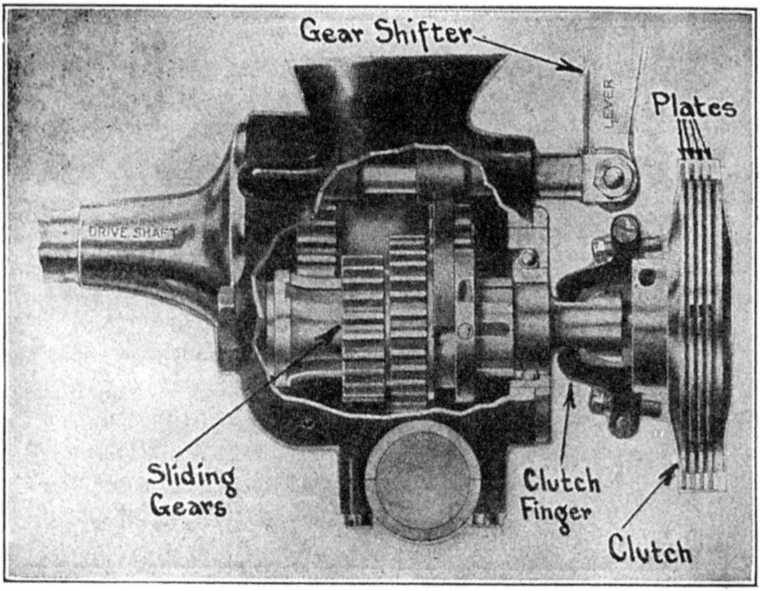

Fig. 187.—Pierce Two Speed Sliding Gear Transmission.

handled by expert mechanics, and the simpler the control system the more popular the motorcycle will be. In the individual clutch form, notably in the two-clutch planetary types, one cannot obtain a speed ratio without first declutching the engine. In the sliding gear, forms that are patterned after automobile practice, it is possible to shift gears whether the clutch is released or engaged.

A simple and effective sliding gear system which has been successfully used on Pierce motorcycles is shown at Fig. 187 with a portion of the gear case cut away to show the arrangement of the sliding members, and in section at Fig. 188 so that the method of actuating the sliding members and the friction clutch simultaneously may be readily ascertained. This sliding gear transmission does not have the main disadvantage to that form of gearing, because when the shifting member is moved from one gear ratio to the other, the clutch is released automatically by the double cone arrangement, and will not be fully engaged until the shifting member is completely in mesh with one or the other of the gears attached to the propeller shaft.

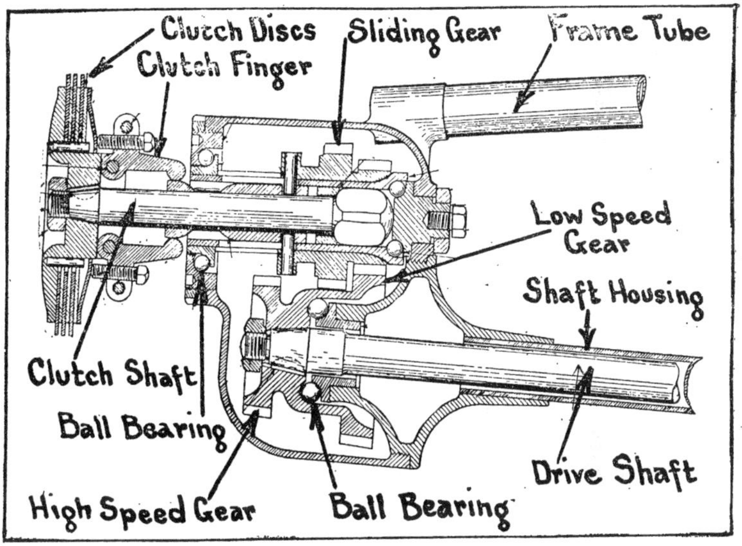

Fig. 188.—Plan View of Pierce Two Speed Sliding Gearset.

Power Transmission Methods.—A point on which considerable difference of opinion has always existed has been the best method of conveying the engine power to the traction member of the motorcycle. At the present time, belt, chain and gear drive are all used, and various combinations of these three forms are sometimes used in conjunction. Some systems of power transmission are more efficient than others, and, as a rule, those that are the most positive and that will transmit the engine power with minimum loss due to slipping are also apt to have other disadvantages which would tend to favor the forms where the drive was by more flexible means.

The two conventional methods of driving a motorcycle are outlined at Fig. 189. The first system to be applied, and the one that was formerly the most popular, is by leather belt, which may be any one of a variety of forms. The type illustrated is a flat belt of the form that has been so widely used in driving the machine tools of the mechanic, and practically all other forms of machinery for many years. The other, which is more positive, involves the use of chains and sprockets. The latter method of driving was used on the first automobiles, just as soon as it was definitely determined that the flat belt drive systems were not practical for the heavier forms of four-wheeled vehicles. These systems will be considered more in detail in proper sequence. Drive by gearing is general at the present time in automobile practice, and is followed to some extent by motorcycle designers. Either the bevel or worm gear drive may be used in connection with a shaft extending from the power plant.

The single-belt drive, either by means of flat or V-belt is the simplest power transmission system, because it is possible to obtain a degree of free engine action without the use of a clutch if a jockey pulley or idler is employed to tighten the belt. With a V-belt, it is necessary to use a free engine clutch of some form to obtain the free engine which is also true of the various positive driving means such as chains and gears. The system of transmission to use depends to a large extent on the individual preferences of the rider and designer, because each system has its advantages, and all have been proven practical. When it comes to a question of efficiency, the drive by single chain or V-belt is undoubtedly the one that will transmit power with the least loss. With a properly adjusted V-belt, there is practically no slipping, and a flexible drive is obtained. A certain amount of power is required to bend the belt over the pulleys, but this is probably no more than would be consumed by friction of the various members of the chain and the friction between the chains and sprockets.

The figures in the following table have been generally accepted by automobile designers, and apply just as well to similar driving systems used in motorcycle practice.

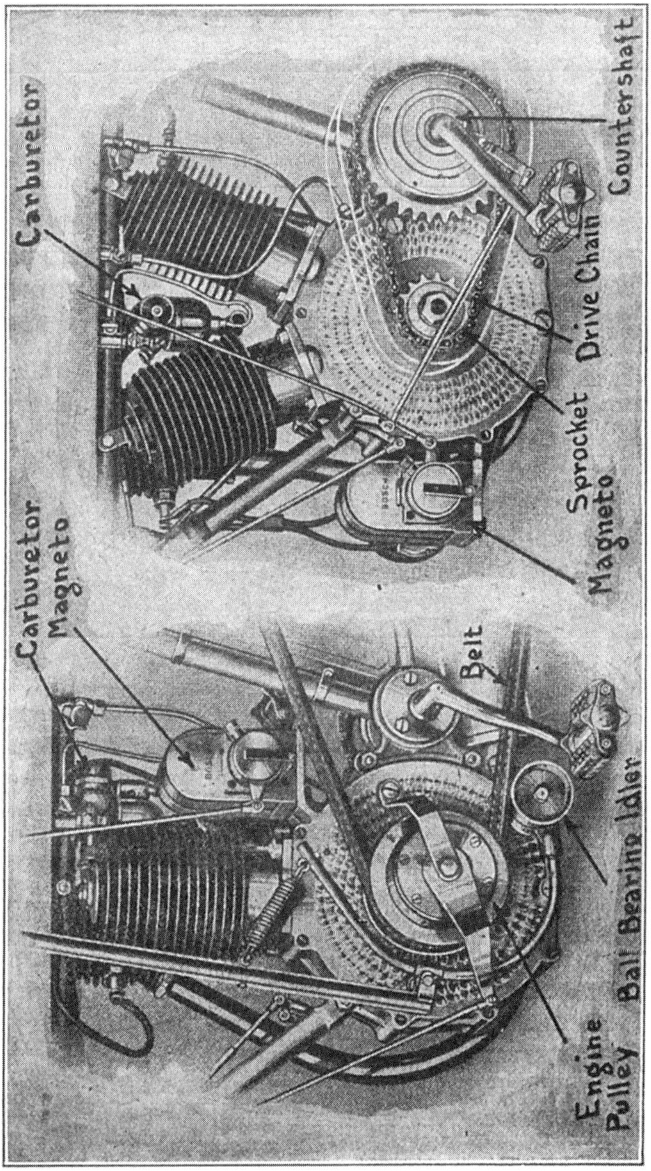

Fig. 189.—Illustration Showing Commonly Accepted Methods of Transmitting Engine Power to the Rear Wheel.

TRANSMISSION EFFICIENCY OF DIFFERENT TYPES OF MECHANISM (WORBY BEAUMONT)

Source of Loss of Power.	Amount of Loss Per Cent.	Efficiency Per Cent.
	....	100.0
When driving direct:		
One chain..............................	3.0	....
One and one-half pairs of bearings.......	7.5	89.5
With epicyclic speed gear in operation, add	15.0	74.5
When driving direct:		
One set of gear........................	5.0	....
Two pairs of bearings..................	10.0	....
Partially active bearings................	3.0	82.0
With change-speed reduction gear in operation, add............................	12.0	70.0

Carefully made brake tests have demonstrated that the power loss with a single-chain or V-belt drive is not greater than 10 per cent., whereas with a double-chain arrangement, which is the one generally used, about 20 per cent. of the power is lost in transmission. The type of change-speed gearing used also has some bearing upon the efficiency of the driving system. Gears of the planetary type will lose more power when on the low speed ratio than will either the sliding gear or sliding clutch forms, but at the other hand there is practically no loss when on the high speed because the assembly turns as a unit and the only power consumed is at the bearings. In either the sliding clutch or sliding gear forms, the countershaft is always in action due to the constant mesh gears, and some power is consumed at that point in addition to the main bearings.

While the positive driving systems are the most practical, some unconventional systems of propulsion have been devised and tried out in an experimental way. These are usually in the form of attachments intended for application to the ordinary foot-propelled bicycle to convert it into a power-propelled type. One of these, which was exhibited at the recent motorcycle shows, is shown at Fig. 190, and propulsion is obtained by an air propeller of the same type used in aeronautical practice. It is said that with the latest forms of air propellers, more power can be obtained with a given engine size than will be delivered by marine propellers working in water. It is also claimed that the efficiency of a marine propeller will rarely rise higher than 60 per cent., while aeroplane propellers working in air may be

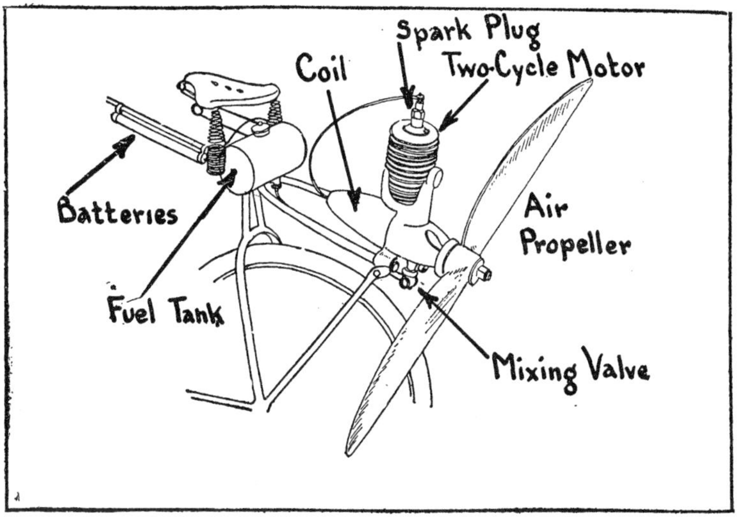

Fig. 190.—Unconventional Arrangement of Two-cycle Motor Driving Air Propeller for Bicycle Propulsion.

90 per cent. effective. The air propeller of the device shown at Fig. 190 has but little more spread than the span of the average bicycle handle-bars, and when used in connection with the small motor shown, the thrust is sufficient to push an ordinary bicycle 30 miles per hour over good roads. The engine is a three-port, two-cycle type, and with a bore of $2\frac{1}{2}$ inches and a stroke of $2\frac{1}{4}$ inches, at a speed of 2,500 revolutions per minute, develops power ample for the purpose. The engine weighs but 16 pounds, and the entire attachment, including propeller, ignition system and fuel tank is said to weigh less than

40 pounds. While this system of propulsion is practical in air and marine craft and may have some degree of merit, it does not appear to be anything more than freak construction, and is only illustrated to show an unconventional method of bicycle propulsion. Such devices cannot give the satisfactory service obtained from properly designed motorcycles as the average bicycle frame, tires, etc., are not built with the idea of attaching mechanical power.

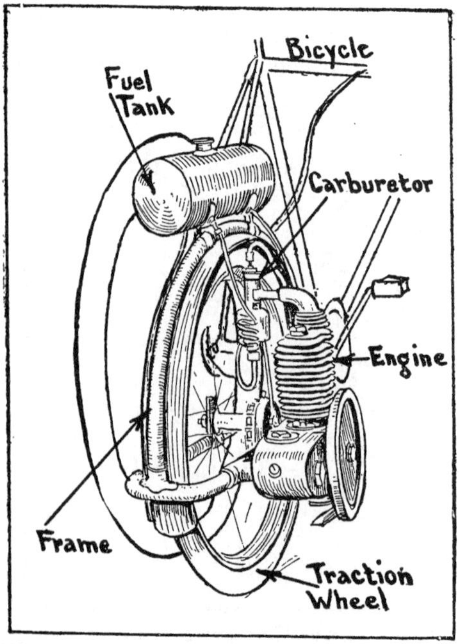

Fig. 191.—The Wall Auto Wheel, a Complete Self Propelling Power Plant Intended for Attachment to Ordinary Pedal Cycles.

The Wall Auto Wheel, which device is of English design, illustrated at Fig. 191, has considerably more merit than the air propeller, and has received practical application abroad. It consists of a separate wheel to which a miniature power plant is attached, and it is intended to be secured to the rear frame of a bicycle parallel with the rear wheel. The engine is air-cooled and has a bore and stroke of 2¼ and 2½ inches respectively. It is claimed that it will develop one horsepower, which is said to be ample to propel a bicycle at safe speed. The engine is of the four-cycle type, has an external fly-wheel, and includes a simple form of two-speed gear in an extension of the motor crankcase. The drive from the two-speed gear to a sprocket mounted on the wheel hub is by means of a short roller chain. The wheel is 22 inches in diameter and is carried in a substantial tubular framework to which the motor and fuel tank are secured.

This device has been produced for more than five years by the manufacturers, which have a factory in London, and, while it is not claimed that it will give the same results as a regularly designed motorcycle, still it permits of converting a pedal cycle into a self-propelled form, and on level roads and in practically all city work, it will undoubtedly be able to furnish power enough to drive the bicycle without any muscular exertion on the part of the rider. It is said that the two-speed gear makes it possible to climb all reasonable grades. An attachment of this kind can be used only on good roads and under favorable conditions, but the device is novel, thoroughly practical and probably will appeal to people of conservative temperament who will be satisfied with medium speed, and who do not intend to use the device in touring. The American rights have been acquired by a prominent manufacturer, and if it successfully stands the test that it is now undergoing it will be marketed in this country.

Belt Drive Systems.—Before describing the various systems of power transmission by belt, it may be well to review the advantages advanced by those who favor that form of transmission. One of the most important claims relates to the flexibility of belt drive and its power of absorbing the road shocks and machine vibration, which, it is contended, results in minimum depreciation of the power plant. It is also claimed that the reverse is true of the positive driving system which transmits the road shocks to the entire machine. The belt running over pulleys is silent because if a flat belt is used it is endless, and there are no metallic parts to strike and click. A V-belt may have a metallic coupling but this does not come in contact with the pulleys, and is therefore equally silent. Another feature of belt drive is said to be the absence of complicated parts. The conventional form of belt transmission consists of two grooved or flanged wheels, a connecting belt and a coupling, if a V-belt; or an idler or jockey pulley, if a flat belt. When a belt stretches, the rear wheel may be adjusted to compensate for the increase in length. It is said that the rider of a belt-driven machine experiences no discomfort from any irregularities of motor operation, as the flexible belt will take care of sudden changes of speed. Should a motor stop suddenly, as by breaking or sticking of some of the important internal parts, a belt will slip sufficiently to enable the rider to retain his place on the machine. A rigid form of drive would be apt to result in a sudden stop, and throw the rider.

The factor of cleanliness is also given some consideration by the belt enthusiast, and it is evident that belts are naturally more cleanly because they do not need the lubrication that is necessary with chain drive. With the various positive driving systems, it is imperative that the parts be maintained in absolute alinement or there will be considerable depreciation of the mechanism and loss of power. With

Fig. 192.—Harley-Davidson Five Horsepower Single Cylinder Motorcycle With Flat Belt Drive.

belt drive, any slight misalinement does not produce appreciable wear, and there is but little loss in transmission efficiency due to this condition. It is the belt that depreciates and not the pulleys, as these frequently outlast from three to five belts before they become worn enough to reduce the efficiency of the drive. If one considers the chain transmission, defective alinement means that the chain or sprockets, and in most cases both, will wear unduly, and have a material reduction of the useful working life. When a chain or its sprockets are worn, efficiency of drive can only be restored by renewing both members. It is a known fact among mechanics that a new chain will not work well on worn sprockets, nor will an old chain function properly on new sprockets. The following summary of the advantages of belt transmission is given by a prominent manufacturer of these elements: Belt transmission causes less trouble and is less expensive than other forms of drive, because it is not seriously affected by a loss of alinement, which causes other transmissions to wear appreciably and frequently results in costly replacements. The flexible transmission insures minimum wear of the power plant, because the elastic driving medium will transmit fewer road shocks than

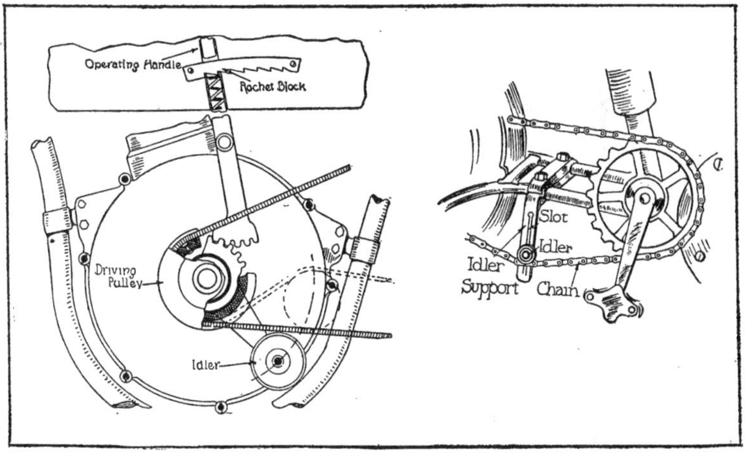

Fig. 193.—Showing Construction of Typical Idler Pulleys for Augmenting Tension of Driving Belts or Pedaling Chain.

the positive form. This means that there is less wear on bearings and gears because of the slipping under abnormal loads, such as quick starting, rapid acceleration, etc. These same features also contribute materially to the comfort of the rider because of smooth action. It is the least complicated, and therefore it is the least liable to get out of order. The feature of silence is also commendable, as drive is by leather to metal contact instead of metal to metal connections.

The application of flat belt drive to one of the Harley-Davidson models is shown at Fig. 192. The method of operating the belt idler or jockey pulley on this machine is clearly shown at Fig. 193. The idler is carried at the end of a bell crank which has a segment of a gear as its other member. These gear teeth engage with suitable members formed at the lower portion of the operating handle. As the handle is pulled toward the rider, the idler pulley moves on an arc of a circle having a radius equal to the center distance between the idler pulley bearings and the pulley center. The flat belt may be normally loose when the idler is in the position shown, but when the pulley is raised to the position indicated by the dotted line the

Fig. 194.—View of Power Plant and Drive of the Rudge-Multi Motorcycle, Showing V Belt Transmission.

belt is made to hug the engine pulley very closely, the effective arc of contact between the belt and the driving pulley is increased and a more effective drive obtained. The view at the right of Fig. 193 shows one method of compensating for the variation in pedal sprocket centers as the rear wheel is moved to allow for belt stretch. A small ball-bearing idler is mounted in a slotted support, and is moved down in the slot to tighten a loose chain, and moved up to loosen a tight chain. Many of the belt drive machines still retain the pedaling chain, and suitable provision must be made to keep that member in proper adjustment.

The V-belt drive which is used on the Rudge-Multi is shown at Fig. 194. The belt is a combination rubber and canvas form, and is utilized in conjunction with a variable pulley and friction clutch attached to the power plant.

Types of Driving Belts.—The various forms of belts that have been applied for motorcycle propulsion are outlined at Fig. 195. That at A is a twisted, round rawhide belt that was the first form to be used

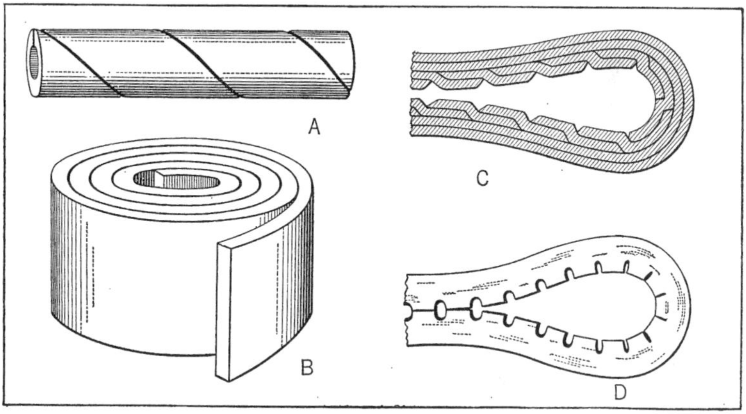

Fig. 195.—Forms of Motorcycle Driving Belts. A—Twisted Rawhide. B—Flat Leather Band. C—Duco-Flex Leather V Form. D—Shamrock Gloria, Rubber and Canvas Belt for V Pulleys.

in motorcycle service. It had one advantage, and that was that its tension could be increased when desired by twisting the belt more closely together. A grave disadvantage was that it was materially affected by changes in weather, and was apt to stretch very much when wet, and shrink very fast when drying. This form was soon succeeded by the flat belt depicted at B, which is the same form that has been widely used for power transmission in our workshops. The V-belts were the next to receive general application. These may be divided into two main classes, one of which comprises all belts made of leather, while the other includes those made of other materials, such as canvas and rubber vulcanized together. A typical leather V-belt, the Duco-Flex is outlined at C, and a rubber belt, the Shamrock-Gloria is depicted at D.

Various expedients are used by designers to secure flexible V-belts, as it is imperative that a belt bend easily in order that it may follow the contour of the small driving pulley attached to the engine crank-shaft. The special construction outlined at C involves the use of two continuous layers of leather to which are attached overlapping pieces that are to form the third and fourth plies of the belt. In the moulded rubber and canvas forms, shown at D, notches are cut in the bottom of the belt at frequent intervals, which permit the belt to describe a curve of small radius when the spaces close in as indicated, due to the bending of the belt.

The usual construction of a leather belt of the V-form is outlined at Fig. 196. The belt consists of two continuous plies of leather that are riveted together between leather blocks with tubular rivets. The leather block used on the bottom of the belt is not as long as that on the upper part, and this construction permits of considerable flexibility. The Wata-Wata, an English belt, is shown at Fig. 197. In this construction, the upper and lower plies of the belt are separated by spacer blocks of arch formation, which allow the belt to bend around a circle of small radius because the lower portion or ply of the belt will fill the space between the blocks and permit the belt to bend easily. The ends of V-belts are fastened together by metal hook members which are made in a large variety of forms, one of which is shown in this illustration.

Another English belt which is a distinctive construction, and which is said to give very satisfactory service, is shown at Fig. 198. This is known as the Whittle belt, and is a composite structure made of steel links carrying suitable bearing pins spaced between leather links. The two leather links are fastened together by a short regular pattern wood screw as indicated.

Some of the forms of belt fasteners that have received a ready market are shown at Fig. 199. That at A is a simple form consisting of a pair of hinges having downwardly extending prongs to grip the belt, joined together by a simple hook member. The form at B uses a quick detachable hook which permits of some adjustment by using hooks of different lengths. The form at C consists of a link of roller chain joining two simple duplicate V-shaped members carrying the screws for attachment to the belt. The wire hook depicted at D is the form of connector used with twisted rawhide belt. Another type of connector which provides some opportunity for adjustment is shown at E. When the belt stretches, the connecting member may be used to shorten the belt by changing its position. Instead of bearing at the extreme end one of the connecting members may be brought

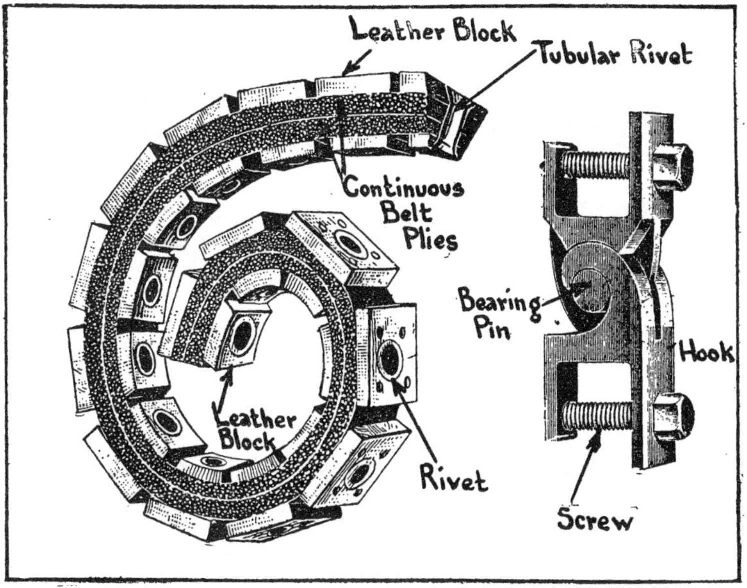

Fig. 196.—Typical Leather V Belt and Connecting Links.

nearer the other by placing it in the bearing at the upper portion of the connector ring.

Various tools are necessary to maintain belt efficiency. One of these, which is shown at A, Fig. 200, is employed to cut belting of the V-form smoothly and accurately. It consists of a suitable casting member carrying a sliding cutting knife guided by slots in the casing, which is forced down to sever the belt by a set screw bearing against the back of the cutting blade. The other set screw is utilized to clamp the belt tightly against the movable lower plate which may be raised when desired to accommodate smaller sizes of belts. Practically all of the connectors used with V-belts require that holes be made in the belts to permit of passing the screw that clamps the connector to the belt through it. A punch for making these holes is shown at Fig. 200, B. This is a double member, and the thumb-screw to which the punch is attached may be placed at either end. When in the position shown it will punch one-inch belt, and if the screw is reversed,

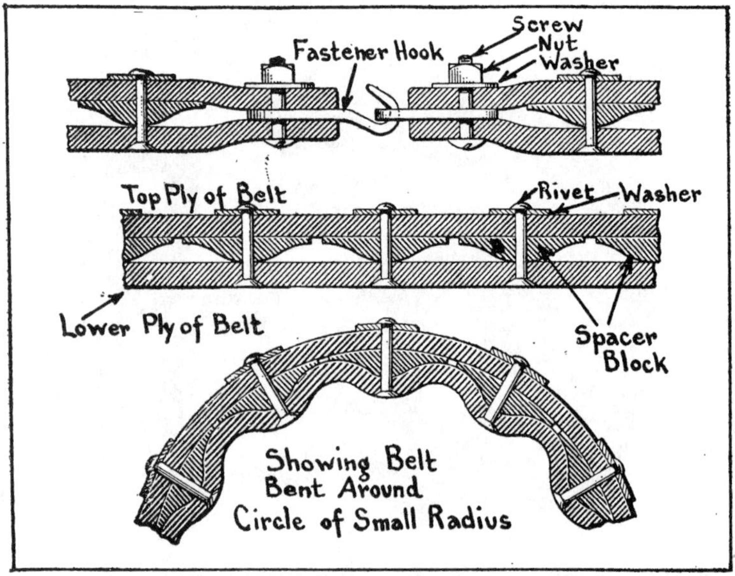

Fig. 197.—Showing Construction the Wata-Wata V Belt.

the device can be used for piercing seven-eighths-inch V-belt. After a belt has been shortened a number of times, a point will be reached where the ends will be too far apart to receive a standard connector of the simple form. In such cases, the links shown at C may be used to advantage because the center of the connector is composed of a block of rubber beveled off at the same angle as the V-belt. This grips the pulley and prevents slipping or noisy action which would be apt to result if a connector of the simpler form was used.

Standard Belts.—The regular pattern V-belt is made to run on pulleys that have the driving faces beveled so that the included angle between the flanges is 28 degrees. If trouble is experienced with slipping of a V-belt and the substitution of a new member for the old one does not cure the trouble, a gauge may be made of sheet metal and used as indicated at Fig. 201. If the pulley flanges are hollowed out, which would be apt to result after the pulleys have been in use for some time, this condition will be clearly indicated by the fit between the gauge and the flanges. Belts are made in a variety of

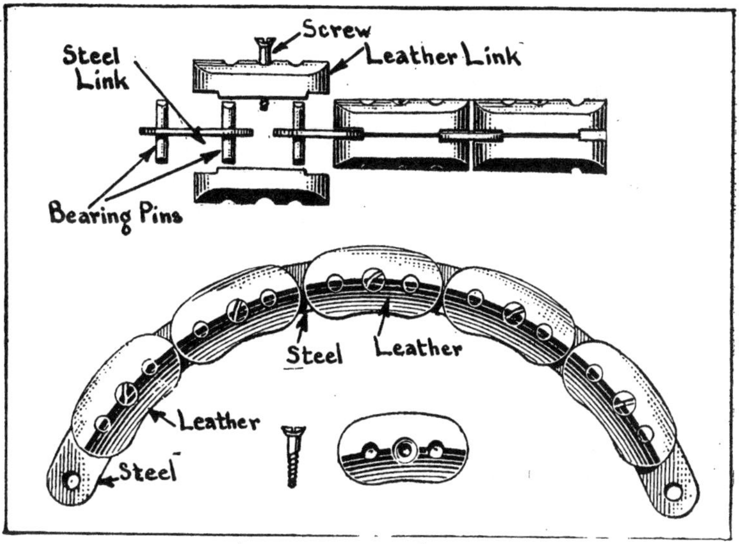

Fig. 198.—Unconventional Form of V Driving Belt of Whittle Design, in Which a Combination of Leather and Steel Links are Used.

widths, and are usually of special tannage because the ordinary oak-tanned leather used for belting in machine shops is absolutely unsuitable for the work demanded of a motorcycle drive. Chrome-tanned leather is generally used for belts because this produces a tough, sinewy material best adapted to resist oil, water and heat generated by excessive pulley friction. Chrome-tanned leather also has greater tensile strength than the oak-tanned and it will transmit more power. It is also more flexible, will not slip when wet, and is not apt to curl on the edges or stretch as much as the belting made by the other processes.

Flat belts are usually made in two plies and will range from 1½ to 2½ inches wide, the variations in size being by increments of one-eighth inch. Naturally, the greater the amount of power to be transmitted, the wider the belt must be to take the augmented pull. The plies are not only cemented together but, in some instances, they are also stitched at the edges. The cement used should be heat and water-proof, and it is also necessary to stretch the belts a number

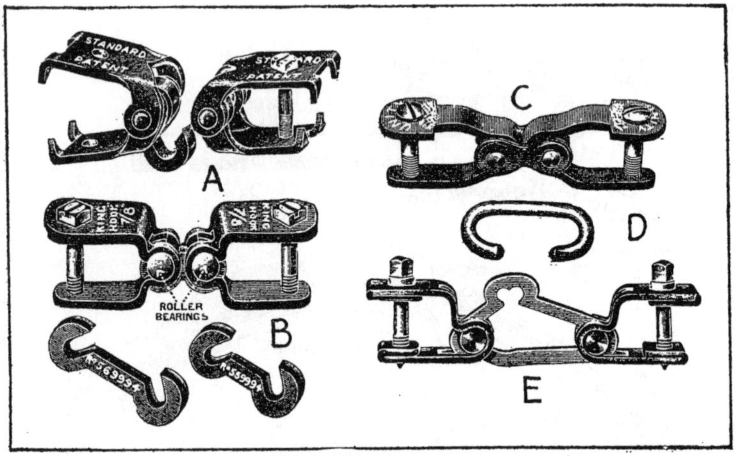

Fig. 199.—Various Forms of Connecting Links for Motorcycle Driving Belts.

of times after cementing before the belt is ready for use, to give them an initial permanent set.

In making V-belts, two continuous plies in the forms intended for medium-powered engines, and three continuous plies on the forms devised for larger power plants are cemented together, and then special two-ply blocks are riveted to the continuous plies with steel rivets to obtain the required depth of friction surface. The blocks are of special construction, in order to enable the belt to conform more readily to the small engine pulleys. All standard V-belts, whether made of rubber or leather have a 28 degree included angle.

Belts vary in length from 7 to 9 feet, and the average length is about

8 feet 6 inches. Leather belt is used almost exclusively in the United States, though the rubber and canvas V-belt is more popular abroad. The advantage of rubber belting is that it is not apt to be affected by water, but it is not as flexible as the leather belt, nor does it have the same amount of adhesion to the belt pulleys. Flat belt pulleys are usually made of cast iron covered with a layer of leather, or a lagging

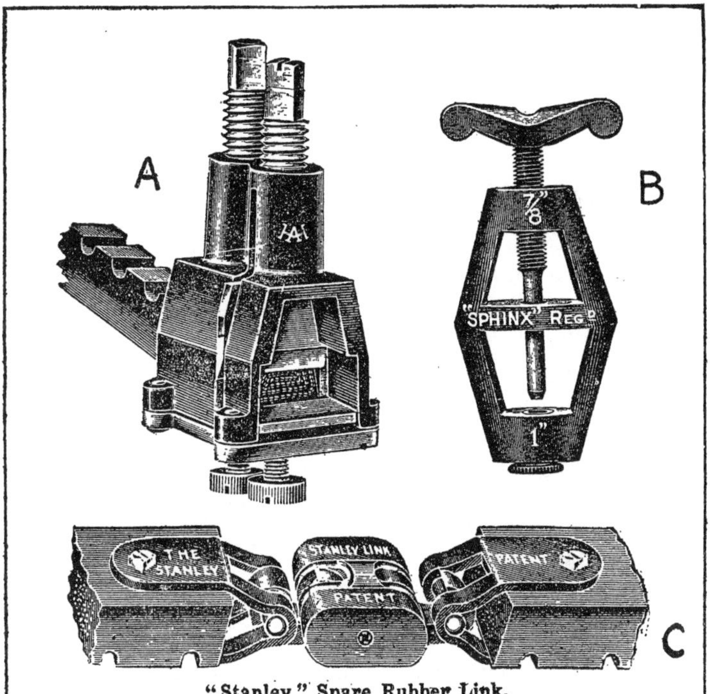

Fig. 200.—Useful Appliances for Repairing Rubber and Canvas V Belt.

of woven wire-asbestos fabric, in order to secure greater adhesion between the belt and pulley. Owing to the large amount of surface on the rear driving pulley, it is not customary to provide any lagging on that member, as sufficient adhesion is obtained without it.

Lagging is not necessary on V-belt pulleys, because the tendency of the belt is to wedge itself in the space between the flanges, and as the power developed by the engine increases, the adhesion augments proportionately because of a greater wedging effect. The four-ply V-belts vary in width from ¾ inch to 1¼ inches by increments of one-eighth inch, and the five-ply belt, which is intended for use with powerful twin motors will vary from 1⅛ inches to 1½ inches in width. There is no intermediate size between 1¼ inches and 1½ inches V-belt. The width of a V-belt is always measured at the top.

The writer has made a careful analysis of belt drive machines produced by American manufacturers for several years, in order to arrive at the average practice as relates to the sizes of belts used with various motor horse-powers. The following tabulation may prove useful for reference:

Single Cylinders, up to 2½ horse-power (Old Style Machines):	
Flat Belt	1¼ to 1½ inches wide
Twisted Rawhide	⅝ to ¾ inch dia.
V-Belt	¾ to ⅞ inch wide
Single Cylinders, 2½ to 5 horse-power:	
Flat Belt, 2-ply	1½ to 1⅝ inches wide
V-Belt, 4-ply	⅞ to 1 inch wide
Two Cylinder, up to 7 horse-power:	
Flat Belt, 2-ply	1⅝ to 1¾ inches wide
V-Belt, 4-ply	1 to 1¼ inches wide
Two Cylinder, up to 9 horse-power:	
Flat Belt, 3-ply	1¾ to 2¼ inches wide
V-Belt, 5-ply	1¼ to 1½ inches wide

Advantages of Drive by Chains.—The credit of being pioneers in the application of chain drive on motorcycles belongs to the Hendee Manufacturing Company in this country, and to Messrs Phelon & Moore in England. It was adopted by both of these makers on standard stock products in the year 1900, and both have been unusually loyal and have consistently advocated chain drive ever since. Other makers followed their example, but they either did not realize that in order to enjoy the real benefit given by the chains that the machine must be especially designed for them or else the majority of motorcycle engines in those days were not as smooth-running as the creations of to-day, because for a time, the chain transmission was not generally favored on account of the alleged harshness of the drive.

Other influences, however, were at work, and the consequent improvement and increase of power in the engine, and the use of side cars, showed that the belt drive was not always adequate for powerful motors pulling heavy loads unless made of excessively large size. Various cushioning devices were also evolved in order to relieve the mechanism of the shock, due to positive transmission of power and a review of current practice indicates that chain drive is standard on most of the best-known American machines, and is generally accepted as producing a moderately silent, smooth-acting and reliable transmission. In Europe, the belt is still the most popular form of power transmission, but indications point to a gradually increasing appreciation of chain drive in both England and France.

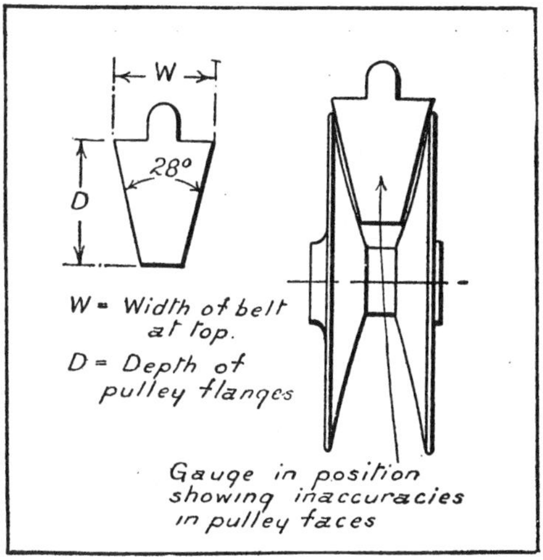

Fig. 201.—**Defining the Application of a Gauge for Testing Accuracy of Flanges of V Belt Pulleys.**

There has never been any question regarding the positiveness and efficiency of chain transmission. In fact, the first objections advanced against it was that it erred in being too positive. The early forms of motorcycle engines, especially the big single cylinder power plants did not deliver a very even turning moment as the power was applied as a series of violent shocks. As previously stated, the belt equalized the drive to some extent by slipping and stretching while the chain, as originally applied, transmitted the shocks to the machine, and thus not only caused considerable wear on the tires but promoted the discomfort of the rider. The introduction of better balanced engines and more especially of various compensating clutches and cushioning devices of one sort or another promoted the general adoption of chain drive.

An important advantage of chains is that these do not need to be tight to transmit power, which is absolutely necessary in connection with the use of belts, especially the flat belt. In order to reduce belt slip, it is necessary that they be tight, and the belt pull causes considerable unnecessary friction on the engine bearings, especially of the plain type. With the chain, no initial tension is necessary, and the frictional loss due to high bearing pressures is not as large as with a tight belt.

Fig. 202.—Side View of the Eagle Motorcycle Employing Single Chain Drive.

In order to use the chains successfully, the conditions under which they work to the best advantage must be fully realized. The removal of belt pulleys and the substitution of sprockets, and the use of a chain instead of a belt, does not mean that satisfactory chain drive will be obtained. On the contrary, essential conditions peculiar to chain drive must be properly taken into account. First, the nature of the load must be understood. The action of the four-cycle internal combustion engine consists of a series of power strokes due to the explosion of gases which are interposed between periods of neutral or even negative effort While the explosion forces the piston violently downward, during the other three strokes and especially on the compression stroke, the resistance is exactly reversed. A load of this nature is generally known as "impulsive," and is much more severe on the transmission system than the regular turning moment of an electric motor or the smooth action of a four-cylinder gasoline power plant. Consequently, if the chain drive is to be a thorough success, the shocks due to uneven power application must be reduced or absorbed as far as possible by some cushioning mechanism. Another thing that must be taken into consideration is that the speed of a motorcycle engine is very high, and, consequently, the chain speed is correspondingly fast. This is especially true of the first reduction or countershaft drive chain.

It is not generally realized that chain must travel at a velocity of 1,500 to 3,000 feet per minute, and that the impact between the rollers of the chain and the teeth of the sprockets is very severe and frequent. It is therefore important that the chains be kept thoroughly lubricated so the blows on the rollers may be softened by the interposition of a film of lubricant both on the outside of the roller—which is best attained by the use of an oil-bath gear case—and in the bush and rivet bearings. That the roller should be free to turn is also most important, since the wear is thereby distributed.

In view of this last consideration, it is very necessary to make sure that the sprockets are in perfect alinement. Otherwise, the teeth cut into the side plates of the chain, on which they wear a shoulder or ridge, which often causes the rollers to stick, with the result that the impact on the roller always comes in the same place, tending to break it. Correct adjustment also is of course necessary, as, if the chain is too slack, it tends to mount the wheel teeth and also "whips," which may have the effect of breaking the rollers, and in any case, intensifies the wear. The provision of a gear case, or at least some form of chain-guard, is highly desirable. Mud is not a satisfactory lubricant, and it is hopeless to expect the best results from a chain which is coated inside and out with slush and grit. The natural result is stiff joints, broken rollers, and rapid wear.

A point to be looked to in designing a drive is that the number of links in the chain from engine to countershaft should not be an even multiple of the number of teeth in the engine-shaft sprocket, as if this is the case the force of the explosion comes more often on certain rollers than on the rest. To sum up, the three essentials to be looked for in a motorcycle drive are: First, some species of slipping or cushioning device; second, efficient and thorough lubrication, and third, a reasonable chain speed.

On this last point, a compromise has to be aimed at. The chain speed may be reduced by reducing the diameter of the sprockets, i. e., the number of teeth. But, other things being equal, a small sprocket is more severe on the chain than a larger one, owing to the increased angle at which the wheel meets the chain. Normally speaking, the best results will be attained with driver or engine-shaft sprockets having from 15 to 17 teeth.

Single Chain Drive.—The simplest form of chain transmission and the most efficient is the single chain drive which, to date, has not been extensively applied in motorcycle practice. The method of using a single chain is clearly outlined at Fig. 202. This involves the use of an engine-shaft clutch, which also acts as a cushioning device, from which the drive is to a large sprocket mounted on the rear wheel hub. In the machine shown, the rear sprocket has 64 teeth and the engine sprocket from 16 to 18 teeth. The system of transmission is efficient, and about the only disadvantage that can be advanced against it is that the chain must be kept tight, because if loose it will be apt to flap or whip, owing to its length.

Another method of using a single chain is in combination with an undergeared drive and is outlined at Fig. 203. In this, the first reduction is by a spur pinion attached to the engine crankshaft which meshes with an internal gear that turns the driving sprocket. As practically all of the reduction in speed may be obtained between the gears, the front sprocket may be made nearly as large as the rear one, and the chain is operating under very favorable conditions, as relates to both chain speed and bending. The single-chain direct drive is, of course, the most efficient, as there is no bearing friction other than that of the engine shaft and rear hub to be overcome, while in the countershaft form its bearings consume power.

Double-Chain Drive.—The method of employing two chains for driving, used on the Alcyon (French) motorcycle, is shown at Fig. 204. A small sprocket is attached to a cushioning device carried on the engine shaft, and drives a larger sprocket mounted on a countershaft of the simple form. The drive to the rear wheel is from the small countershaft sprocket to a large member attached to the rear hubs. This provides a double reduction system, there being one reduction in speed between the engine sprocket and the member it drives on the countershaft, and another reduction between the smaller sprocket on the countershaft and the larger member on the hub. The original and as time has proven, the most practical system of double-chain transmission is illustrated at Fig. 205, which shows the transmission method employed on the Indian motorcycle. Even on the earliest forms, a compensating sprocket or cushioning arrangement was used

Fig. 203.—Undergeared Single Chain Drive of Reading-Standard Motorcycle.

on the countershaft, but in the modern types it is, of course, unnecessary to use any cushioning device other than the free engine clutch regularly provided on all these machines.

Types of Driving Chains.—The form of driving chain generally used at the present time for power transmission on both motorcycles and automobiles is a radical departure from the type of chain first used for the purpose. In order to reduce friction, and to insure easy running, rollers are used to come in contact with the sprocket teeth, and these roll instead of rub against the teeth as was the case with the block chain. A typical roller chain is shown at Fig. 206, A. Each roller is mounted on a bushing which joins a pair of side plates.

In this form, a link member is composed of two side plates, two bushings to hold them together, and two rolls that revolve on these bushings or hollow rivets. Each of these link assemblies is joined with its neighboring one by a simpler element composed of a pair of side plates and two solid rivets or bolts. The block chain which is shown at C is a simpler construction than the roller chain, as a link assembly is of the more simple form, i. e., two side plates and their retaining rivets is used to join the blocks. That shown at B is a roller chain

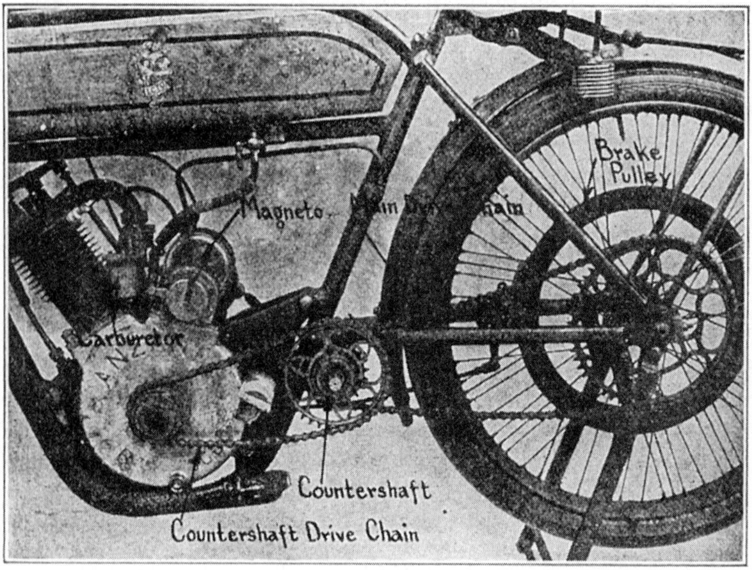

Fig. 204.—Application of Double Chain Drive to Alcyon (French) Motorcycle.

that can be used on block-chain sprockets. Block chains are seldom used for transmitting power at the present time, and when utilized are employed only for joining the pedaling sprocket to the corresponding member on the rear hub, or in connection with a step starter.

The parts of a typical roller chain are clearly shown at Fig. 207. At A, a connecting link which is used for repair purposes or to permit of taking the chain apart when it is necessary to remove it is shown. At B, the connecting link employed to join the roller link members C is outlined. The offset link at D is used in joining a chain together under conditions where the regular connecting link A cannot be employed, which is the case if the chain has an uneven number of links, such as 63, etc. At the lower portion of Fig. 207, the chain repair tool used for taking riveted chains apart is shown. It consists of a block member which supports a slotted piece having the slots separated by a distance equal to the pitch of the chain to be repaired. A guide member shown at the right can be placed over the head of the rivet which is driven out by means of the punch that is adapted

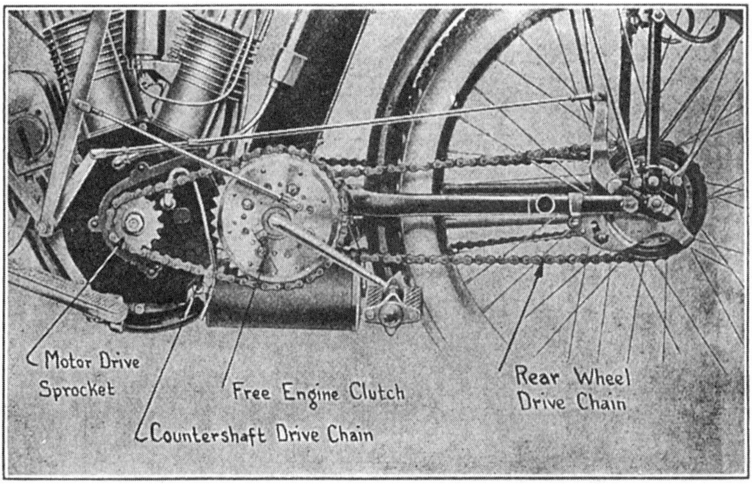

Fig. 205.—Double Chain Drive System Used on Indian Motorcycles on Which Machine This System of Power Transmission Originated.

to fit the guide piece. This arrangement is the only practical method of holding a chain for repairing, as it not only insures that the rollers or links will not be marred but it also provides the firm support that is necessary to drive out the rivets.

The popular motorcycle chain used in this country is a 5/8-inch pitch with a 1/4-inch width roll for engines below 5 horse-power, and 5/8-inch pitch with $\frac{5}{16}$-inch or 3/8-inch roll for engines of greater power. Two other sizes of chains are being used to some extent, these being $\frac{11}{16}$-inch and 3/4-inch pitch. The pitch of a chain is the distance between the center of one tooth space to the center of the neighboring one. In some cases where very low-powered engines are used, chains of ½-inch pitch with $\frac{3}{16}$-inch or ¼-inch wide rolls are sometimes employed. The breaking strain of chains used will range from 2,000 pounds to 3,000 pounds. Considerable useful information, in the form of formulæ for figuring chain length, sprocket sizes, etc., that will be of value to the designer or draftsman, or to the motor-

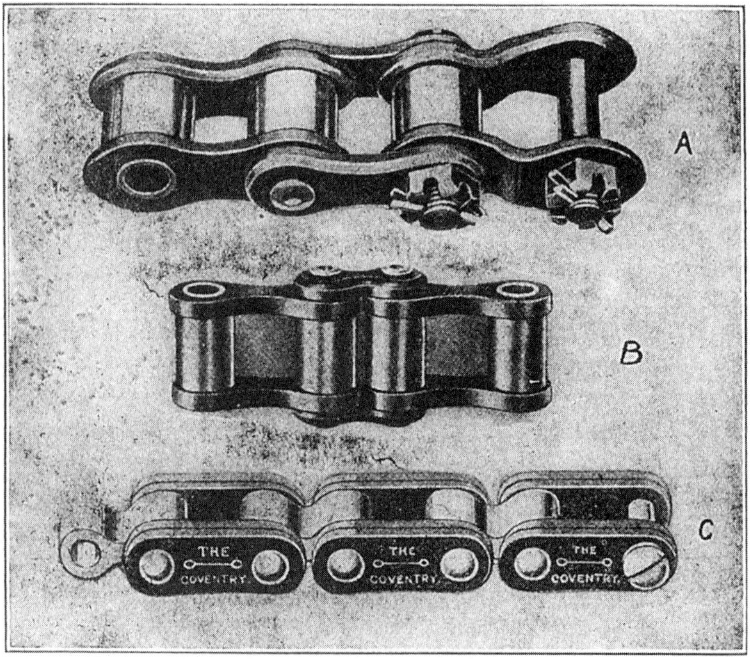

Fig. 206.—Types of Motorcycle Driving Chains.

cyclist who is mechanically inclined, are given in Figs. 208 to 210, inclusive.

Combination Chain and Belt Drive.—In an endeavor to obtain the advantages of both of the main systems of power transmission without the attendant disadvantages incidental to the use of either alone, combination drives are receiving considerable attention at the present time. The average composite drive consists of a chain or gear drive to a belt pulley, and from that member to a larger belt pulley on the rear wheel. The construction of the usual undergeared drive may be clearly grasped by referring to Fig. 211. While in this case the drive to the rear wheel is by chain, it is not difficult to substitute a belt pulley for the sprocket and drive by the more flexible means. The first reduction is obtained by the spur driving pinion attached to the engine crankshaft which meshes with an internal or ring gear mounted in a suitable extension from the engine base and revolving on ball bearings of generous proportions. The ring gear carries the final drive member.

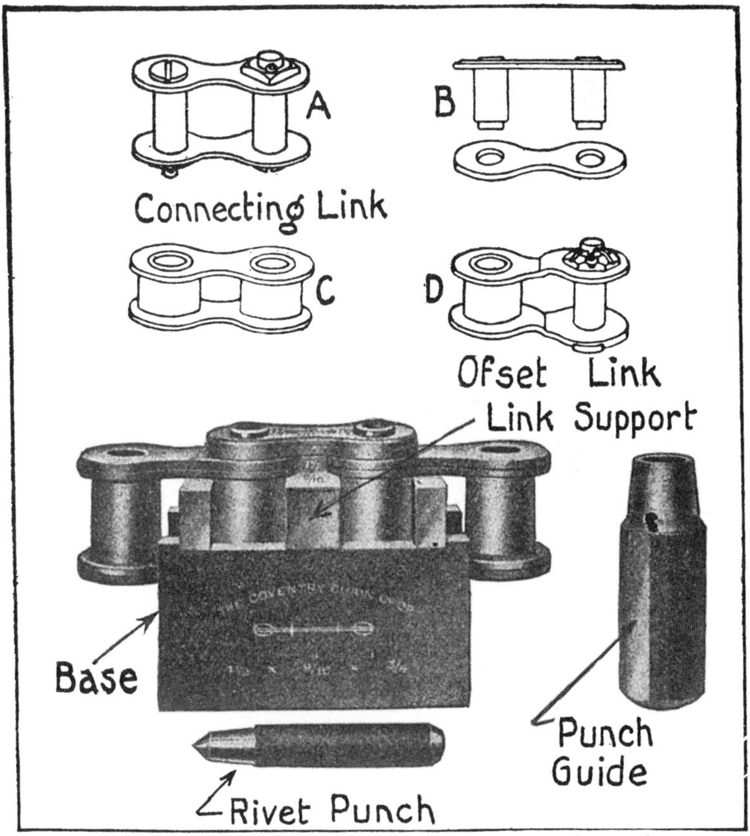

Fig. 207.—Roller Driving Chain Parts and Repair Tools.

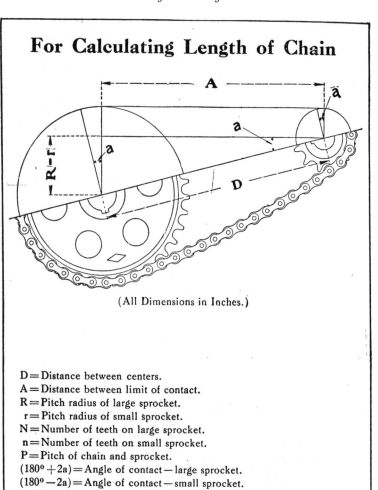

For Calculating Length of Chain

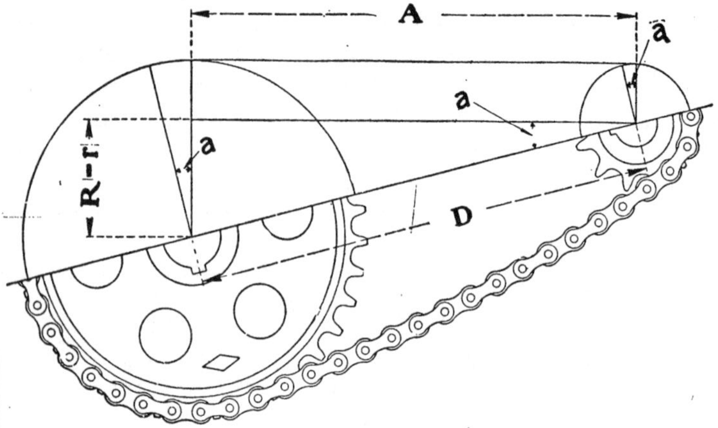

(All Dimensions in Inches.)

D = Distance between centers.
A = Distance between limit of contact.
R = Pitch radius of large sprocket.
r = Pitch radius of small sprocket.
N = Number of teeth on large sprocket.
n = Number of teeth on small sprocket.
P = Pitch of chain and sprocket.
$(180^\circ + 2a)$ = Angle of contact — large sprocket.
$(180^\circ - 2a)$ = Angle of contact — small sprocket.

$$a = \sin^{-1} \frac{R\text{-}r}{D}$$

$$A = D \operatorname{Cos} a$$

Total length of chain.

$$L = \frac{180 + 2a}{360} N P + \frac{180 - 2a}{360} n P + 2D \operatorname{Cos} a.$$

Fig. 208.—Useful Formulae for Obtaining Length of Driving Chain.

One of the disadvantages incidental to belt drive when used alone was that a small driving pulley which did not provide a sufficiently large contact surface had to be used on the engine shaft to secure the proper gear ratio. With the undergeared drive, which is shown at the top of Fig. 212, or with the combined chain and belt drive outlined at the bottom of the same illustration, it is possible to use a belt pulley of large diameter and obtain an arc of contact that will

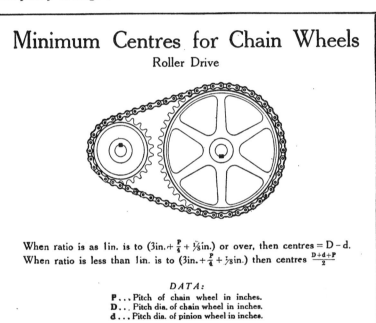

Minimum Centres for Chain Wheels

Roller Drive

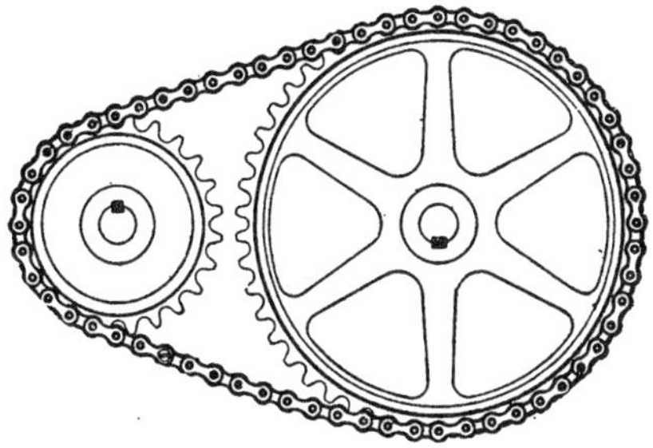

When ratio is as 1in. is to (3in. + $\frac{P}{4}$ + $\frac{1}{8}$in.) or over, then centres = D − d.
When ratio is less than 1in. is to (3in. + $\frac{P}{4}$ + $\frac{1}{8}$in.) then centres $\frac{D+d+P}{2}$

DATA:

P . . . Pitch of chain wheel in inches.
D . . . Pitch dia. of chain wheel in inches.
d . . . Pitch dia. of pinion wheel in inches.

Fig. 209.—Diagram Showing Calculation for Minimum Centre Distances for Sprockets.

insure positive drive and minimum flexure of the drive belt. The first reduction is obtained by positive means which are best adapted for this purpose, while the final drive is taken by the flexible member which provides the smooth and yielding transmission that is so desirable to relieve the power plant of road shocks. The view at Fig. 213 is that of a representative American motorcycle, the Reading Stand-

For Calculating Diameters of Sprocket Wheels for Roller and Built-Up Block Chains

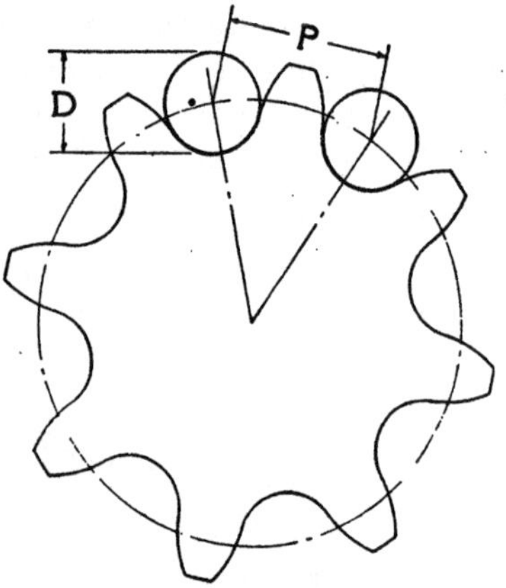

N = Number of teeth in sprocket.
P = Pitch of chain.
D = Diameter of roller.

$$a = \frac{180^\circ}{N}$$

$$\text{Pitch Dia.} = \frac{P}{\text{Sin. } a}$$

Outside Diameter = Pitch + D.
Bottom Diameter = Pitch − D.

For Calculating Diameters of Sprocket Wheels for Block Center and Twin-Roller Chains

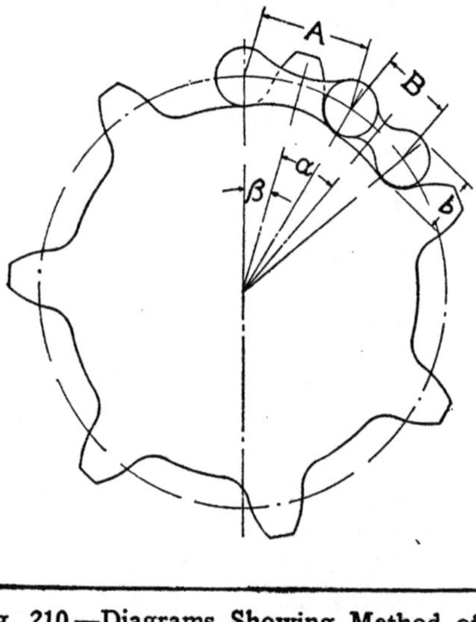

N = Number of teeth.
b = Diameter of round part of chain block (usually .325)
B = Center to center of holes in chain block (usually .4)
A = Center to center of holes in side links (usually .6)

$$a = \frac{180^\circ}{N}$$

$$\text{Tan. } \beta = \frac{\text{Sin. } a}{\frac{B}{A} + \text{Cos } a.}$$

$$\text{Pitch Diam.} = \frac{A}{\text{Sin. } \beta}$$

Outside Dia. = Pitch Dia. + *b*
Bottom Dia. = Pitch Dia. − *b*

In calculating the diameter of Sprocket wheels, the bottom diameter is the most important

Fig. 210.—Diagrams Showing Method of Calculating Sprocket Sizes for Roller and Block Chains.

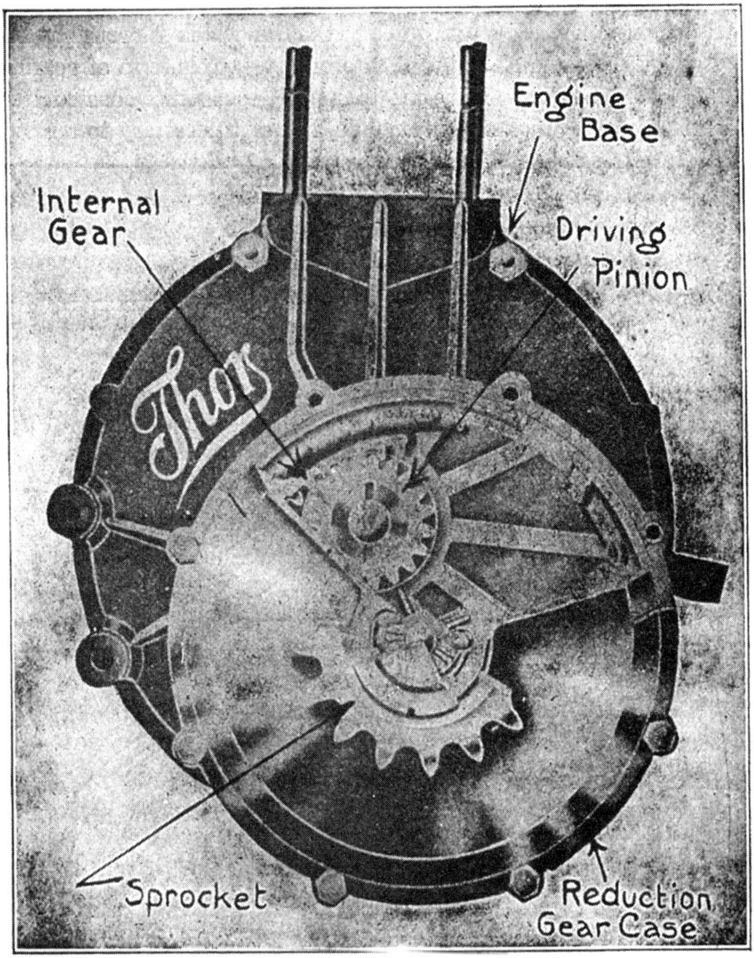

Fig. 211.—Undergeared Drive of Thor Design.

ard, employing the combination undergeared drive. The relative size of the front and rear driving pulleys may be readily ascertained and it is not difficult to understand how a combination drive of this nature is destined to become a very popular system, inasmuch as it will provide a positive drive and yet a flexible one.

Bevel and Worm Gear Final Drive.—The most popular system of driving automobiles is undeniably that in which thoroughly encased gearing is used. The problem of applying this form of gearing to motorcycles is not an easy one to solve, because the construction is difficult to apply. In an automobile, it is not necessary to remove

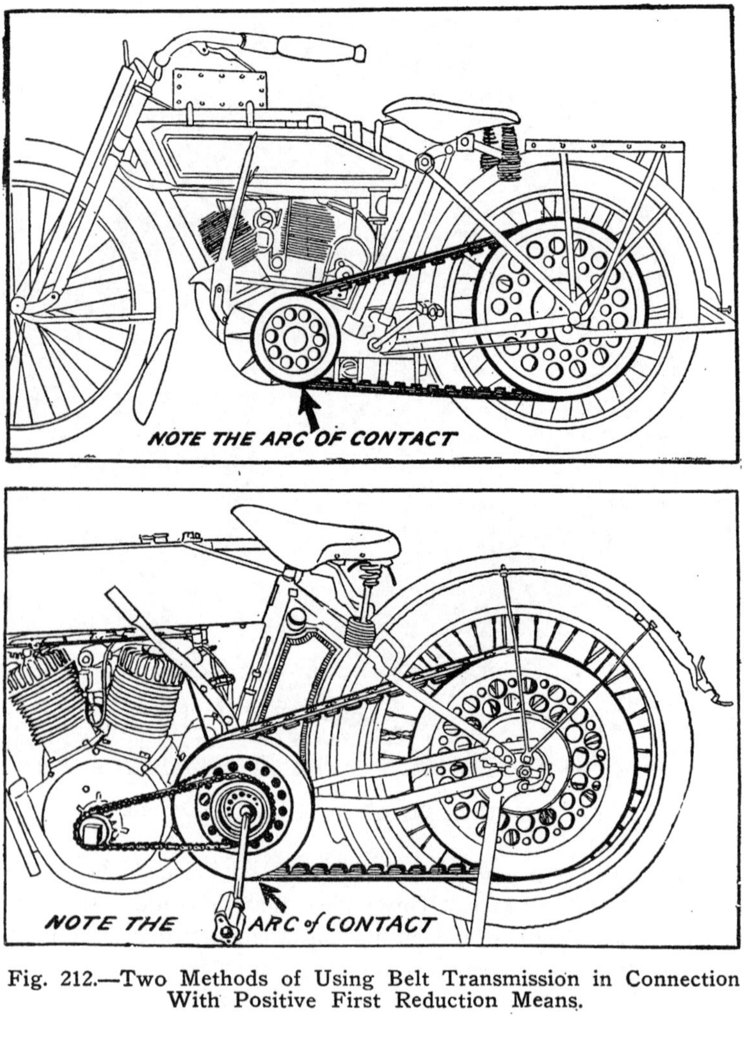

Fig. 212.—Two Methods of Using Belt Transmission in Connection With Positive First Reduction Means.

the rear axle every time a wheel must be reached to make repairs on the tires. In a motorcycle, it is necessary to take the rear wheel out of the frame before one can change a shoe or one-piece inner tube, and, whenever gear drive is used, it is somewhat of a job for an amateur to

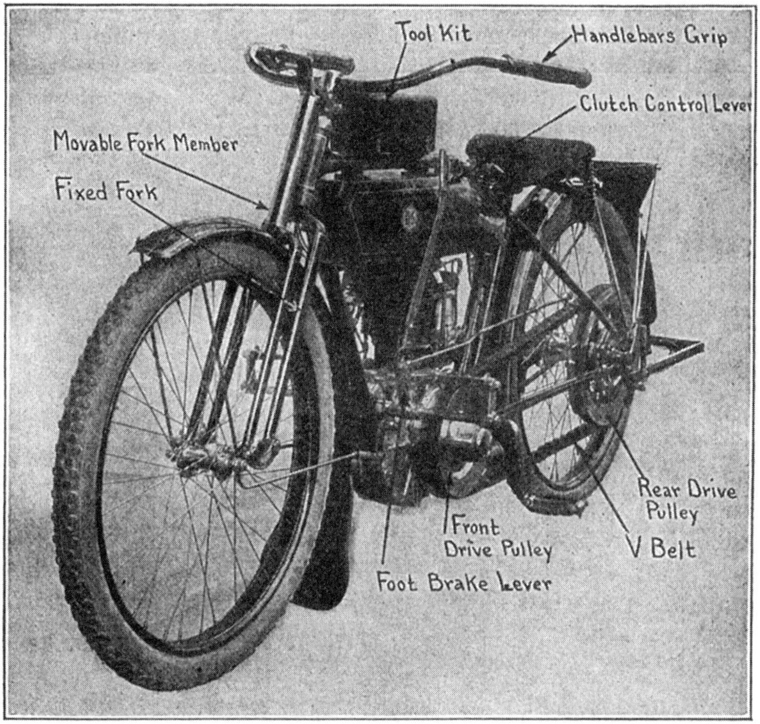

Fig. 213.—Three-Quarter Front View of 1914 Reading-Standard Single Cylinder Model, Showing Application of Undergeared V Belt Drive.

remove the wheel, and more of a proposition to replace it and secure proper adjustment of the drive gearing.

A bevel gear drive which has received successful application on the Pierce four-cylinder motorcycle is shown at Fig. 214. The rear hub member carries a bevel gear in place of the usual drive sprocket, and the power is transmitted to that member by a bevel drive pinion securely attached to a drive shaft that extends to the motor crankshaft. A worm gear drive used on an English motorcycle is shown at Fig. 215. The system is just the same as that previously described except that worm gearing is used instead of the bevel, for with either of these forms it is necessary to mount the engine in the frame in such a way that the crankshaft is parallel to the top frame tube.

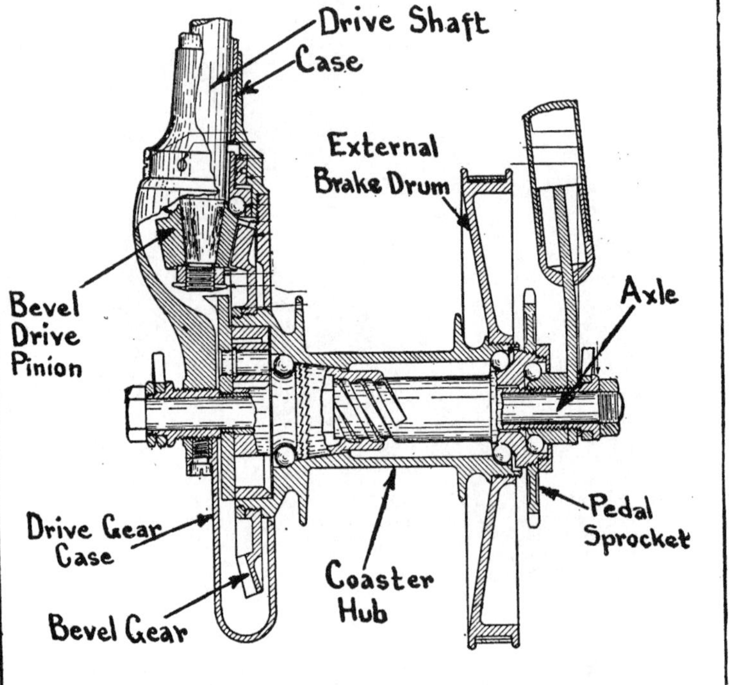

Fig. 214.—Bevel Gear Driving System of Pierce Four Cylinder Motorcycle.

The power transmission of the Fielbach motorcycle at Fig. 216 is distinctive, inasmuch as the twin-cylinder power plant is mounted in the frame in the conventional manner with its crankshaft at right angles to the frame tubes. The drive is by spiral gearing at the engine through a cone clutch and sliding gear transmission of the two-speed type to a worm gear carried on the rear axle. The view at the top shows the relation of the engine gearing, the clutch and the change-speed gearset. The drive from the gearset-driven shaft is to a worm mounted in a suitable casing which is shown in the longitudinal section in the lower left hand corner. The method of fastening the worm gear to the wheel hub is clearly outlined in the right hand corner. This system of gearing is more complicated and much more expensive to construct than the simpler two-chain or combination chain and

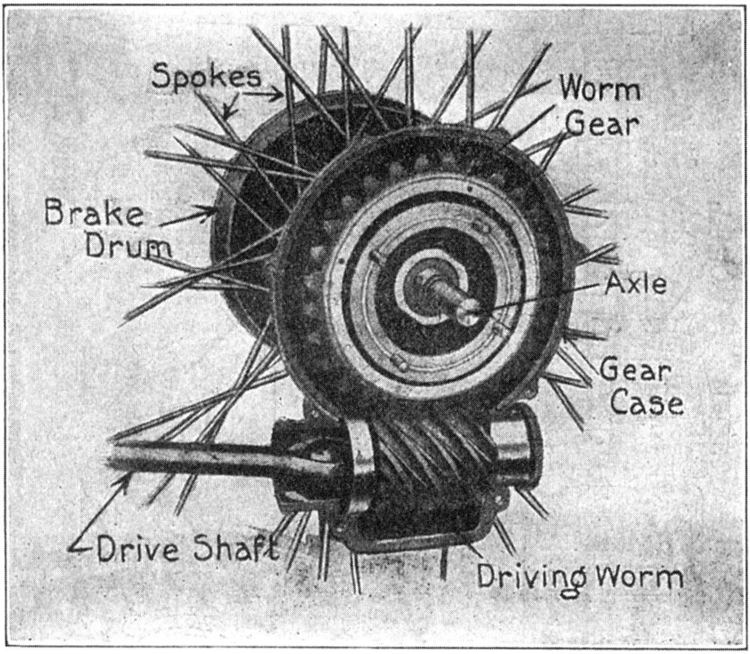

Fig. 215.—Worm Drive System of T. A. C. (English) Four Cylinder Motorcycle.

belt drive, but it has the important advantage of having all the driving elements thoroughly encased and protected from the abrasive effect of road grit, which cannot be said of any of the chain or belt drive systems. An important advantage of the positive encased gear drive is that the housings in which the gears are mounted may be filled with lubricant, and this not only cushions and silences the drive but it also reduces friction and wear, and promotes long life of the driving mechanism.

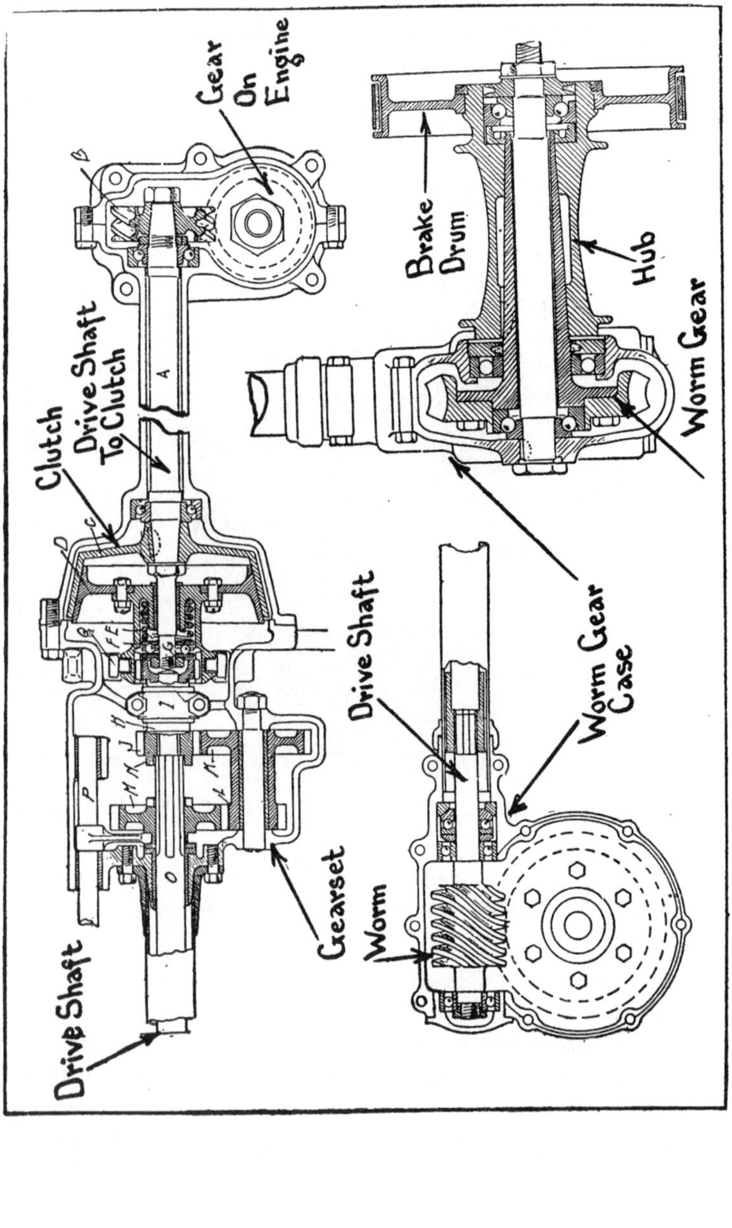

Fig. 216.—Application of Worm Drive System on the Fielbach Motorcycle.

Relation of Engine Power to Gear Ratio.—In one of the earlier chapters the reason for supplying various gear ratios has been considered in some detail, and the importance of selecting that best adapted so the power of the engine will be delivered most effectively is an important phase of motorcycle design. An engine may be geared too high, which means that it will have some difficulty in overcoming the resistance imposed by hills or bad roads but is very fast on the level. If a machine is geared too low, it will be a good hill climber but will not operate at satisfactory speeds under good conditions unless the engine is run excessively fast, which would produce more rapid depreciation of the power plant.

The two tables appended are given to show the gear ratios recommended by engine builders for their different motor types. It is, of course, understood that the designer of the motorcycle will select the power plant of the proper capacity for the machine to which it is fitted. The first table is given by the makers of the Precision (English) engines, various models of which have been illustrated in this work. The last table is especially valuable, as it shows not only the gear ratios but the road speeds obtained with various sprocket sizes and single and twin engines. This table has been compiled by the F. W. Spacke Machine Company who make the De Luxe motors. Other tables and formulæ to assist in figuring speed are also presented.

Riders will do well to remember that cycle engines are essentially high-speed engines, and should not be over-geared. The following table will be found to give best results both from the point of view of flexibility and average speed:

Engine Type.	Gear Ratio for Solo Riding.	Gear Ratio for Sidecars, Top Gear.
2½ horse-power..................	5½ to 1	....
2¾ horse-power..................	5 to 1	....
3¾ horse-power..................	4½ to 1	5½ to 1
3¾ overhead valves..............	4 to 1	5 to 1
4 horse-power twin..............	4½ to 1	5 to 1
Green model.....................	4 to 1	5 to 1
4¼ horse-power..................	4½ to 1	5 to 1
6 and 8 horse-power twin models...	4 to 1	4½ to 1

TABLE OF SPROCKET SIZES, GEAR RATIOS AND MOTORCYCLE SPEEDS FOR USE WITH DE LUXE ENGINES.

Size of Motor.	Motor Sprocket Number Teeth.	Eclipse Countershaft Sprockets.	Hub Sprocket Number Teeth.	Gear Ratio.	Speed with Motor Running 2,500 R.P.M. Miles per Hour.
4 and 5 horse-power singles	12	33 and 17	27	4.37 to 1	47.7
	12	33 and 17	29	4.69 to 1	44.4
	12	33 and 17	31	5.01 to 1	41.5
	12	33 and 17	35	5.66 to 1	36.8
7 and 9 horse-power twins	14	33 and 17	23	3.19 to 1	65.3
	14	33 and 17	25	3.47 to 1	60.1
	14	33 and 17	27	3.75 to 1	55.6
	14	33 and 17	29	4.02 to 1	51.8
	14	33 and 17	31	4.30 to 1	48.4

The point of highest efficiency and horse-power development is represented at approximately 2,500 revolutions per minute, on standard stock motors, and is, for that reason, taken as a basis for estimating gear ratios. The above does not, therefore, necessarily represent the extreme maximum of speed that may be obtained from any gear ratio.

SPEED FORMULA.

To reduce A miles in B seconds to miles per hour,

$$A \times \frac{3{,}600}{B} = \text{miles per hour.}$$

SPEED EQUIVALENTS IN AMERICAN AND FRENCH MEASUREMENTS.

1 mile per hour = 88 feet per minute.
= 1.46 feet per second.
= 27.8 meters per minute.
= 0.463 meter per second.
1 kilometer per hour = 0.624 miles per hour.
= 54.9 feet per minute.
= 0.914 meter per second.

RATE OF SPEED IN MILES PER HOUR FOR ELAPSED TIME OVER THE MEASURED MILE FROM ONE TO THREE MINUTES.

Time Over Measured Mile.		Rate of Speed in Miles per Hour.	Time Over Measured Mile.		Rate of Speed in Miles per Hour.	Time Over Measured Mile.		Rate of Speed in Miles per Hour.
Min.	Sec.		Min.	Sec.		Min.	Sec.	
1	0	60.00	1	27	41.38	1	54	31.58
1	1	59.00	1	28	40.91	1	55	31.30
1	2	58.06	1	29	40.45	1	56	31.03
1	3	57.14	1	30	40.00	1	57	30.77
1	4	56.25	1	31	39.56	1	58	30.50
1	5	55.38	1	32	39.13	1	59	30.25
1	6	54.54	1	33	38.71	2	0	30.00
1	7	53.73	1	34	38.29	2	3	29.26
1	8	52.94	1	35	37.89	2	6	28.57
1	9	52.17	1	36	37.50	2	9	27.90
1	10	51.42	1	37	37.11	2	12	27.27
1	11	50.70	1	38	36.73	2	15	26.66
1	12	50.00	1	39	36.36	2	18	26.08
1	13	49.31	1	40	36.00	2	21	25.53
1	14	48.65	1	41	35.64	2	24	25.00
1	15	48.00	1	42	35.29	2	27	24.49
1	16	47.37	1	43	34.95	2	30	24.00
1	17	46.75	1	44	34.61	2	33	23.53
1	18	46.15	1	45	34.28	2	36	23.07
1	19	45.57	1	46	33.96	2	39	22.64
1	20	45.00	1	47	33.64	2	42	22.22
1	21	44.44	1	48	33.33	2	45	21.81
1	22	43.90	1	49	33.03	2	48	21.42
1	23	43.37	1	50	32.72	2	51	21.05
1	24	42.85	1	51	32.43	2	54	20.69
1	25	42.35	1	52	32.14	3	0	20.00
1	26	41.86	1	53	31.86	..	..	.....

CHAPTER VI.

DESIGN AND CONSTRUCTION OF FRAME PARTS.

The Motorcycle Frame Structure—Foot-Boards—Rear Wheel Stands—Spring Forks—Spring Supported Seat-Posts—Spring Frames—Saddles and Tandem Attachments—Coasting and Braking Hubs, Why Used—Requirements of Pedal Drive Mechanism—What Brakes Should Do—Force Needed at Brake—Principle of Brake Action—Friction Co-efficient and Its Relation to Brake Design—Leading Types of Brakes—Operation of Typical Braking and Coasting Hub—How Rider's Effort is Multiplied—Motorcycle Tires—Side Car Advantages—Forms of Side Cars—Side Car Attachment and Control—Methods of Starting Motorcycles—Indian Electric Starting and Lighting System—Motorcycle Control Methods—Bowden Wire Control.

We have discussed at some length, in a previous chapter, the various forms of motorcycle frames and methods of power plant support in a general way. In view of the important functions of the frame structure, it may be well to describe this important component upon which the strength and endurance of the entire assembly depends more completely. A typical loop frame, such as used on the Indian motorcycle is shown at Fig. 217, and this shows clearly all of the parts, with the exception of the wheels and handle-bars that are generally considered as being part of the frame assembly.

It will be observed that in certain essential respects this frame differs materially from those used in bicycle construction. The looped member that supports the motor, the drop at the seat-post mast, and the elimination of the usual diamond construction at the rear end are all radical departures from bicycle frame design. In this construction, the effort is made not only to suspend the weight of the rider by resilient members other than pneumatic tires but by the use of the laminated leaf spring fork and the distinctive double cradle spring rear construction, the entire weight of the power plant and its auxiliaries as well as the rider are spring supported and protected from the undesirable influences of road shock. The complete frame assembly consists of the main frame member to which are attached the front fork at the steering head, a saddle over the seat-post tube, a luggage carrier, chain-guard, mud-guard, and suitable stand at the rear end.

The frame shown at Fig. 218 is representative of the form of construction in which the motor base is depended on to join the open portion of the frame when the power plant is in place. The important parts of this assembly are also clearly outlined. The frame

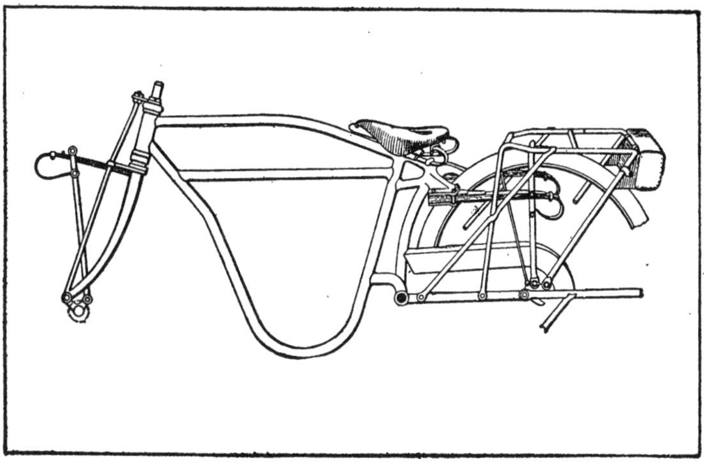

Fig. 217.—Complete Frame Structure of Indian Motorcycle.

at Fig. 219 is a loop design of merit, and shows the complete frame assembly minus the rear wheel. The motor supports are brazed to the frame loop and are in the form of brackets to which the lugs attached to the engine base are bolted. Attention is directed to the distinctive method of strengthening the rear end by means of vertical brace tubes that join the rear forks and rear-fork stays together. The form of the mud-guards, the design of the saddle and handle-bars, and the method of housing the tool compartment under the saddle, in the space between the seat-post mast and the rear mud-guards are also clearly depicted. Another open frame is shown at Fig. 220. This differs from that previously described, in that the motor casing is

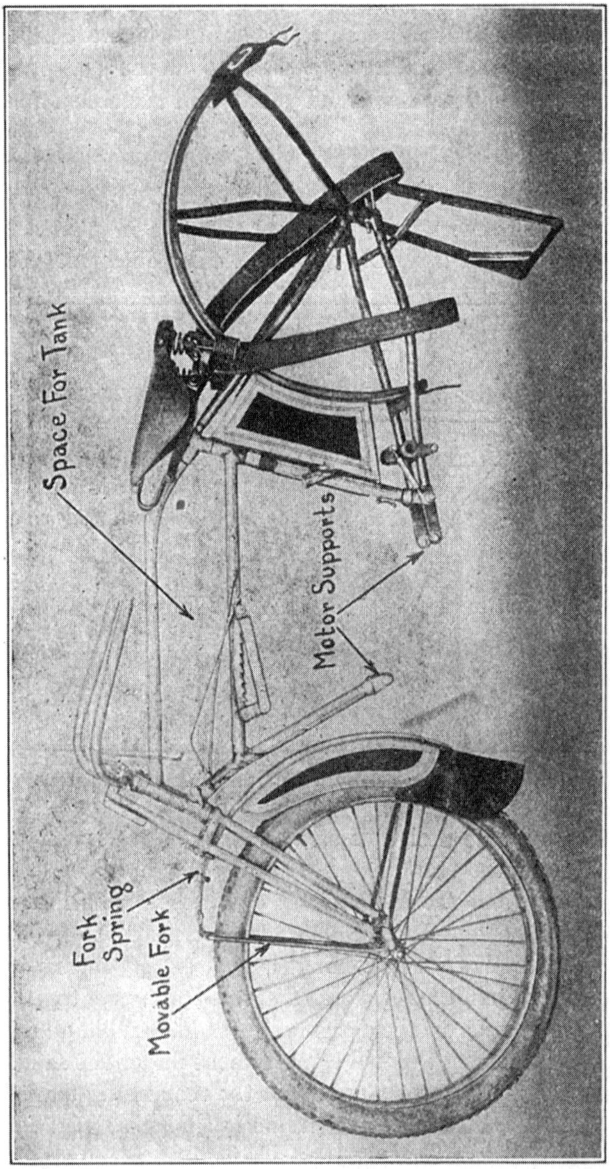

Fig. 218.—Frame of 1912 Eagle Motorcycle Showing Opening Left When Power Plant is Removed.

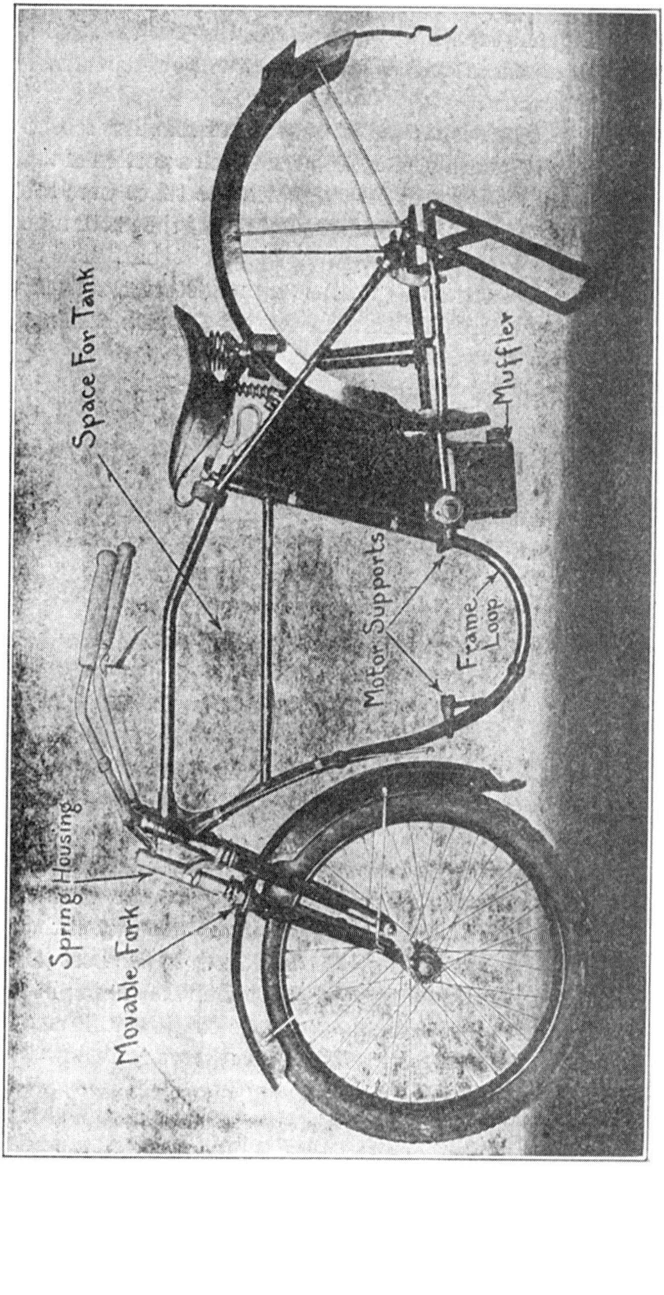

Fig. 219.—The Emblem Loop Frame With Reinforced Rear Construction.

secured to an extension of the crank-hanger by two bolts, and to the end of the diagonal tube with one bolt. Both of these members are forked so it is a simple matter to remove the power plant from the frame when necessary.

A motorcycle frame is generally built up of seamless steel tubing, though some designs have been evolved in which a portion of the frame is composed of a casting member to which the tubes were attached. The frames illustrated at Figs. 217 to 220 are of the pattern in which the various fittings are joined together by steel tubes. The Schickel frame which is depicted at Fig. 221 is a distinctive construction be-

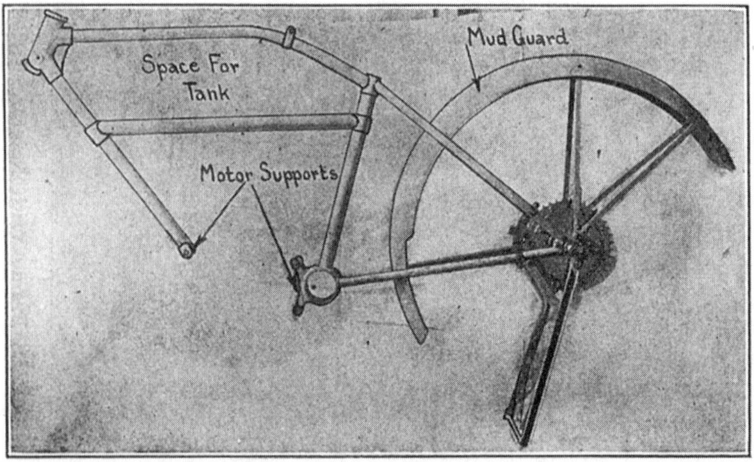

Fig. 220.—Frame of Excelsior Motorcycle Showing Motor Supports.

cause the main portion of the frame is a large aluminum casting which serves as a fuel container. The steering head and a portion of the seat-post tube retaining member are formed integrally with it. Another suitable projecting boss is employed to support the front diagonal tube. The rear fork assembly is built of tubing in the conventional manner. The Pierce motorcycle employs a frame made of large diameter tubing, which members also serve as fuel and oil containers, and which provide a frame of exceptional strength though unconventional in appearance.

When motorcycles were first made, light steel stamped reinforcements of the form used in bicycle frame construction were widely employed to hold the various parts of the motorcycle frame together. At the present time, stampings have been discarded for more substantial drop forgings and malleable iron castings. The steering head of practically all motorcycles is in the form of a forging or semi-steel casting provided with a substantial rib joining the two bosses to which the frame tubes are brazed. The seat-post cluster is also a forging and has four projecting bosses. One of these is intended to secure the seat-post tube, the one at the front is for attaching the upper frame member while the two at the rear form an anchorage for

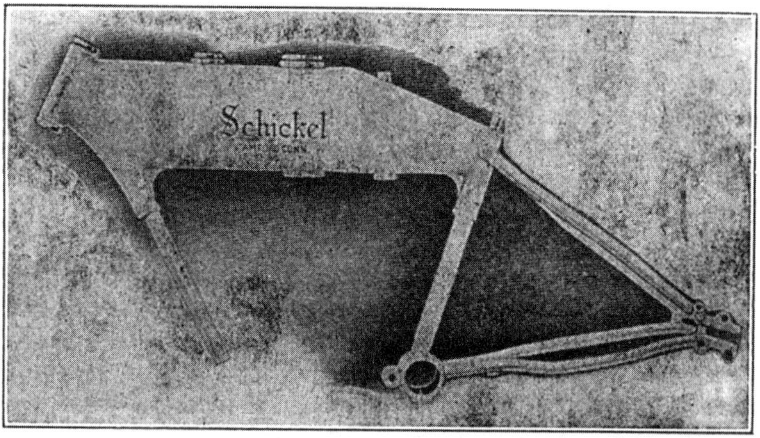

Fig. 221.—The Schickel Frame Construction.

the rear-fork tubes. The crank-hanger is still another member which varies according to the design of the frame to which it is fitted. The two common methods of brazing the frame tubes employed differ in one essential. The fittings are joined to the tubing in some frames by being pushed in the interior of the tube. This makes what is known as a flush joint because no evidence of the point of juncture between the frame and the fitting is noticed. The steering head forging of the Indian motorcycle, which is shown at Fig. 222 has internal reinforcement or flush joints, while the steering head fitting of the frame shown at Figs. 219 and 220 is attached by inserting the tube inside of projecting bosses that form part of the fitting. This method is often combined with an internal reinforcement and is said to be stronger, though not so neat in appearance, than the flush joint frame construction. The latter has survived from bicycle practice where it was desirable to eliminate all corners in which dirt or dust could collect, and also to have a smooth or finished appearance for the frame. In a motorcycle, the factor of strength is the most important consideration so that externally reinforced joints are used fully as much as the flush joint construction. The tubing used in motorcycle construction is not only of heavy gauge and of large diameter but is invariably provided with an internal reinforcement which in most cases is a vertical steel piece running through the center of the tube. This

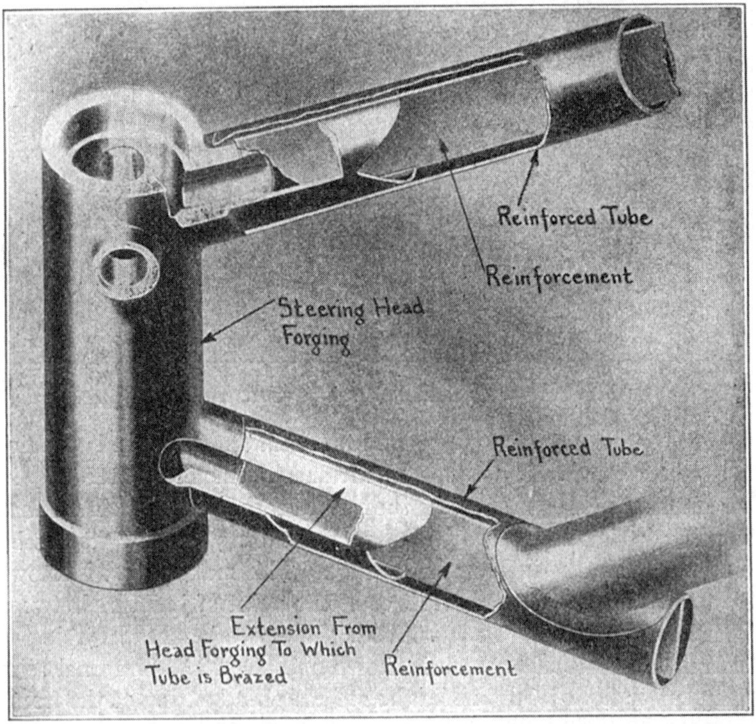

Fig. 222.—Steering Head Construction of Indian Motorcycle, Showing Internal Reinforcement and Method of Obtaining Strength While Using the Flush Joint Construction.

reinforcement is shown at Fig. 222. Another reinforcement which is even stronger than the single vertical member that bisects the tube into two D-shape or semi-circular sections is in the form of a triangular tube securely attached to the interior of the round frame tube. This tubing is used on the Emblem motorcycle, and is shown at Fig. 223.

The sizes of tubing used depends upon the character of the reinforcement and the strength it is desired to obtain in the motorcycle frame structure, which, of course, depends largely on the size of the power plant installed. A frame that may appear light when viewed from the outside on account of using tubing of small diameter may actually be stronger and weigh more than a more substantial looking frame of large diameter tubing, because it would have thicker walls and perhaps a more substantial internal brace member. The accepted method of fastening the frame components together is by a combination of pinning and brazing. When the frame is first assembled, it is placed in an alining fixture which insures that all the tubes will fit the various fittings to which they are attached properly, and that the center line of all the tubes comprising the main portions of the frame coincide. The next operation is to fasten the members together by drilling holes through the tube, and fitting and driving steel pins through these to hold the members together so the frame may be handled during the brazing operation. This process consists of heating the portion of the frame where the joint is to be made to a considerably higher point than the melting point of the spelter employed in joining the parts. The frame tube and fittings are raised to just below a white heat, and the binding material, which is a brass alloy in a molten condition is poured in the minute open space between

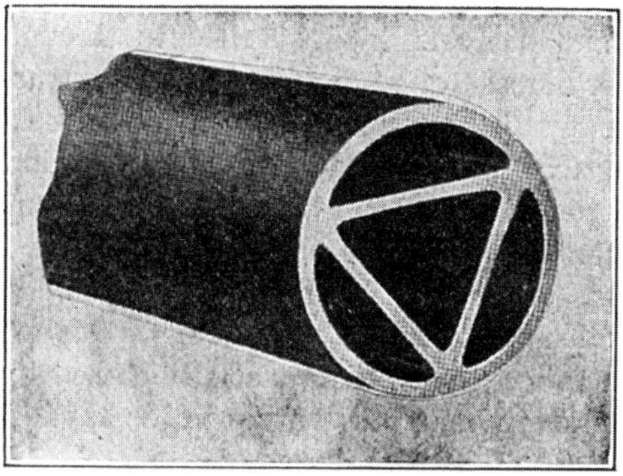

Fig. 223.—Tubing Used in Emblem Motorcycle Frame Has Triangular Reinforcement.

the frame tube and fitting at the joint. A flux, consisting of borax, is mixed with the spelter so it will flow readily between the tube and projecting member to which it is attached. When the joint is allowed to cool, the two members are held together by a thin layer of brass which forms a very strong joint that will give absolutely no trouble if it has been properly made.

There is also a tendency in modern motorcycle factories to use the oxy-acetylene flame in welding parts together, and this also makes a very strong joint. The process of electric butt welding or spot welding may also be used to advantage at various portions of the frame structure. Brazing is the method generally followed, because the process is well known and has been highly developed through many years of use in building bicycle frames. After the frame structure has been permanently assembled and all its components are held firmly together, the alining fixture is again brought into play and the frame straightened by suitable clamps if it has been knocked out of proper alinement by distortion due to the heat it was subjected to during the brazing process. After this, the frames are thoroughly cleaned, and all of the protruding spelter or flux at the joints is chipped or filed off. The frame tubes are then polished and smoothed by rapidly moving emery-coated cloth belts preparatory to the application of the enamel.

The size of the tubing employed averages about 1⅛ inches diameter for the seat-post mast and the diagonal tube extending from the steering head. The upper and lower frame members that join the steering head to the seat-post mast and between the seat-post mast are usually of 1-inch diameter tubing. The rear forks and rear fork stays will be of ¾-inch or ⅞-inch round tubing, though sometimes oval section tube may be employed for the rear forks. The front forks of most motorcycles are composed of oval section tubes which taper down from where it is brazed to the fork crown forging to the lower portion designed to carry the wheel hub, or the links to which that member is secured. Sometimes round tubing is used for front fork construction as shown at Fig. 218, though the general practice is to use the tapered section, flat oval tube. It is not considered good practice to use tubing much thinner than $\frac{3}{32}$-inch wall, and for the most part, even when it is well reinforced, tubing with a ⅛-inch thick wall is used for the principal frame members, such as the seat-post mast, the upper frame tube and the motor supporting loop member.

Foot Boards.—There is a growing tendency on the part of motorcycle designers, which has been fostered largely by the demands of the riders, to provide auxiliary foot-rests in addition to the usual pedals that have been used on motorcycles from the first. Foot-rests were first used on foreign machines, many of which have entirely discarded the pedaling cranks so widely used in this country. As these members are replaced by a simple starting crank or kick starter on motorcycles employing variable speed gears, it is necessary to provide some means for supporting the rider's feet. Naturally the simplest way was to braze extentions to the frame tube or attach foot-pads to the power plant in some way.

Some of the examples of foot supports used on American machines are shown in detail at Fig. 224. That at the top is the rigging used on the Excelsior motorcycle. The foot-rests are steel drop forgings of approximately the size of the average foot that are carried by a substantial auxiliary bracket member secured at its lower ends to one of the crank-case bolts and at its upper end to the diagonal frame tube by a substantial clip composed of two steel stampings held together by through bolts. The foot-rests are attached to suitable extensions by a hinge that permits of folding them up out of the way or to provide a safeguard against breaking them off or bending them, should the machine fall over. With the Excelsior assembly, a brake-operating pedal is included in order that the rider may work the brake as effectively when his feet are on the foot-rest as when they are on the pedal crank. The simple form shown in the lower left hand corner is used on the Schickel motorcycle, and consists of two simple cast aluminum members attached to a laminated leaf spring that is intended to provide a resilient support for the feet of the rider. The Iver-Johnson foot-rest also depicted at Fig. 224 is a folding type that offers a secure support for the rider's feet. It is carried by two hinges from a stamped steel member anchored to the frame.

In some machines, notably the Henderson and the two-speed Indian, the foot-boards are depended on entirely to support the feet of the rider, and no pedals are provided. There seems to be a tendency toward the elimination of the pedaling gear that has for so long been a feature of bicycles and motorcycles, and while it was formerly an essential part of the machine on the early types without two-speed gears or free engine clutches and equipped with power plants of low rating, it is no longer necessary to assist the motor up

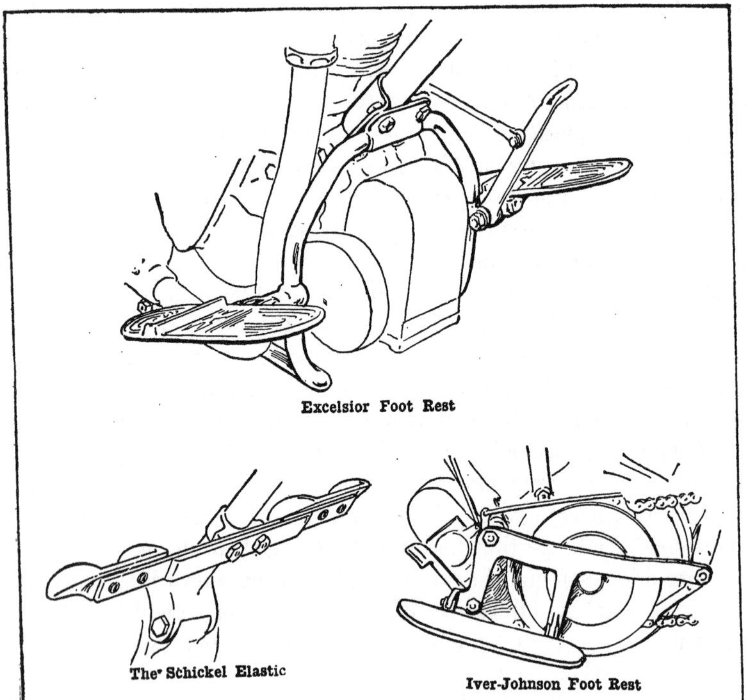

Fig. 224.—Examples of Foot Rest Construction Found on American Motorcycles.

a hill by vigorous pedaling or to constantly restart the motor after stopping it in traffic. The free engine clutch makes it possible for the rider to control his machine, and to bring it to a stop without affecting the motor, and the variable speed gear makes it possible to overcome all adverse conditions by the power of the motor alone. For this reason there is some talk about the elimination of the pedaling gear, and the substitution of foot-rests and suitable controlling levers that will permit of positive motorcycle control. There is considerable to be said in favor of the pedaling gear, however, and its value is clearly established in the mind of the rider who has tried to start a stiff motor on a cold day by a more or less positive kick starter which does not permit of spinning the motor, as is possible when the effort of the rider can be applied with both feet through a substantial chain and crank to the rear wheel of the machine, which in turn rotates the motor crankshaft very briskly through the driving gearing, and which induces an obstinate motor to start even when it is difficult to vaporize the gasoline. Another feature is that brisk pedaling produces a hot spark at the spark plug, because the current production from the magneto is of more value when that member is rotated briskly. While it is thoroughly practical to start a four-cylinder motor by a starting crank, it is conceded that it is more difficult to start a single cylinder to twin motor with a starting handle, unless conditions are favorable. The writer believes that the pedaling gear is a desirable fitting, because it provides a means of supporting the rider's limbs when they become cramped from maintaining a constant position on the foot-rest. Pedals also permit of considerably more comfortable riding on rough roads than foot-rests do, because it is possible for the rider to relieve the saddle of his weight when running on rough ground by using the pedals for support. They are also valuable in providing a positive control of the braking and coasting hub which forms an essential part of many American motorcycles of modern design.

Rear Wheel Stands.—The motorcyclist of to-day is fortunate in having many devices included as standard equipment on the motorcycle he purchases, that had to be bought as an accessory or that could not be obtained at any price with the early machines. No motorcycle sold at the present time would be considered complete without an integral stand by which the rear wheel can be raised from the ground and the machine kept upright when left by the rider. It is not more than six years ago that the portable stand which is now considered indispensable was unknown. If it was necessary to stand the machine up, it had to be leaned against some wall or tree which did not always prove to be as secure a backing as the rider wished, because the machine might slip from its upright position, and when the rider returned to his mount he was just as apt to find it lying on its side as in the upright position that he left it in. If it was necessary to raise the rear wheel from the ground, as in changing a tire or in making adjustments to the brake or hub, considerable ingenuity was necessary to improvise a suitable support for the rear end from a couple of boxes, odds and ends of boards, or even piles of bricks.

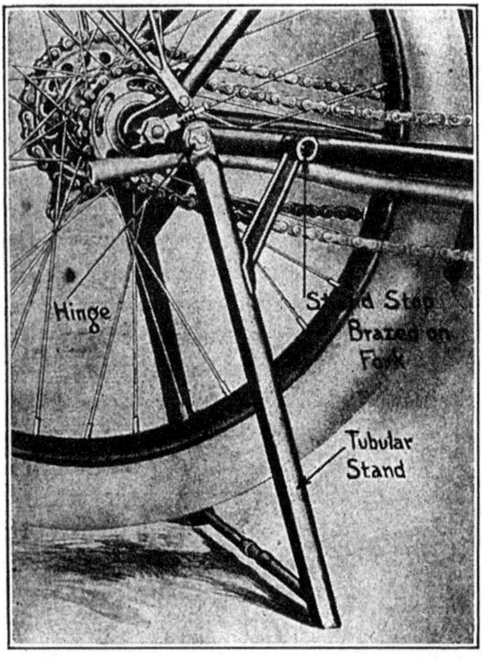

Fig. 225.—The Indian Rear Wheel Stand.

It is said that the first stand was offered by the Hendee Manufacturing Company for use in connection with the Indian motorcycles, during the early part of 1908. This consisted of two separate supporting members or legs fitted with clamps designed for attachment to the rear fork stays and hinged so the leg section could be folded up and away from the ground when the device was not in use. While this was a big improvement, it had the grave defect that it could not be used very well on soft ground, as the limited amount of contact at the lower portion of the legs would permit one or the other to settle into the earth, and either allow the machine to fall over or would permit the rear wheel tire to drag against the ground when the motorcycle was being tuned up on the stand.

At the present time, the stands are made with a cross piece at the bottom, which not only serves as a reinforcement but which provides an added means of support on soft ground. A motorcycle stand must be light, strong and rigid. It must be applied so it can be swung into place easily and securely fastened out of the way when not in use. The stand at Fig. 225 is a tubular construction employed on the Indian motorcycle. It is hinged at its upper end to the slotted plate member or rear hub carrier at the point of intersection between the rear forks and rear fork stays. Two arms or projecting members of T section are brazed to the stand tubes, and are of such form that

Fig. 226.—The Automatic Stand Used on Eagle Motorcycles.

they will rest against suitable stops on the frame. The stand at Fig. 226 is that used on the Eagle, and is an automatic type. Instead of tubing, channel section steel with substantial bracing members and forged arms is employed. The arms have a fork end at their upper portion that rests against the frame tube when the stand is in its operative position. A pair of tension springs are provided to return the stand to the position it occupies when not in use, automatically as the motorcycle is pushed off of the stand. The springs

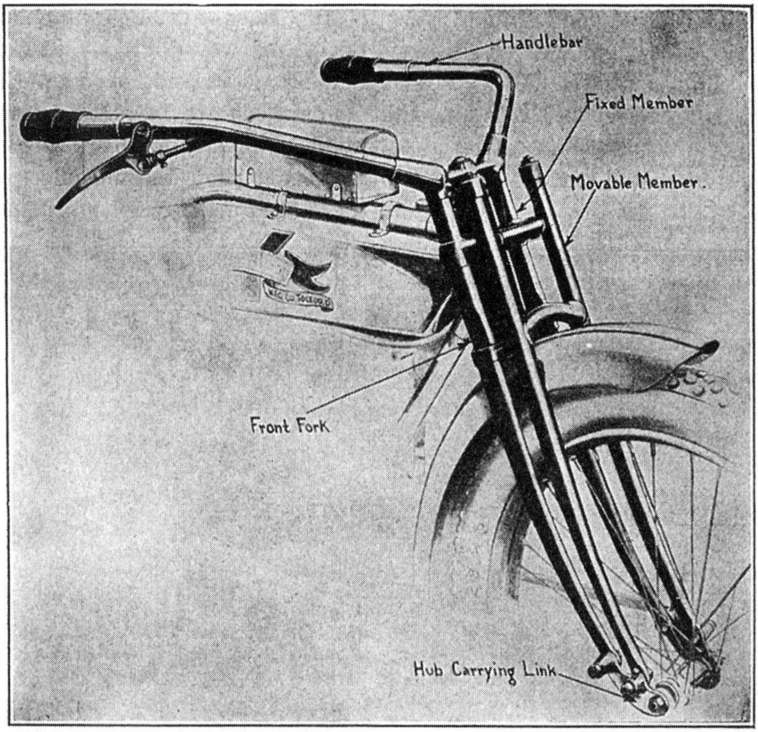

Fig. 227.—The Yale Spring Fork Construction.

draw the member into the stand retaining clip in the form of a piece of spring steel securely riveted to the lower portion of the rear mud guard. The front wheel stand which forms an item of equipment on many European machines and which has been previously illustrated is not supplied as a standard fitting on any of the American types, though some have been fitted to their machines by experienced riders familiar with the advantages obtained through its use.

Spring Forks.—One of the first concessions made for the comfort of the rider was the application of a resilient support for the front end of the frame in order that the shock incidental to operation over rough roads would be taken by springs instead of transmitted directly to the handle bars of the machine. This jarring promoted fatigue because of the shocks the rider's arms received. Even the earlier forms of saddles were comfortable, inasmuch as they were provided with fairly resilient springs or were well padded, so the attention of the designer was directed first to spring fork development on account of the complaints of the riders of the vibration at the handle bars. Spring forks have been made in infinite variety, though the object of all designers is to obtain the resilient feature without sacrificing strength unduly.

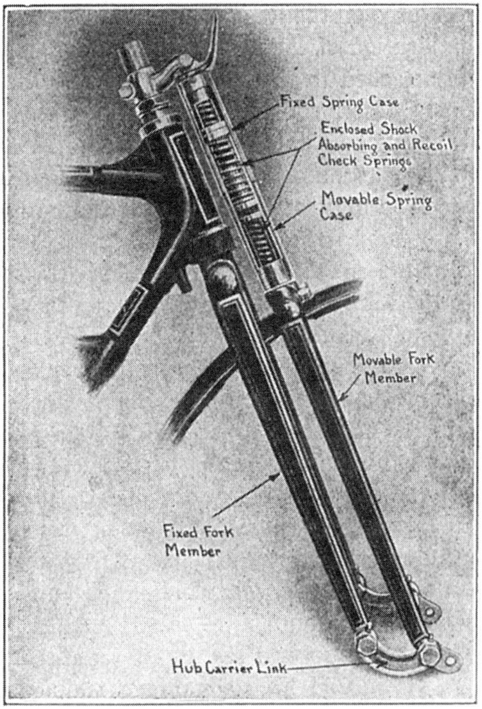

Fig. 228.—Sectional View of the Spring Case of Reading-Standard Spring Forks, Showing Load Carrying and Recoil Check Springs.

Two types of springs have been utilized to take the shock imposed on the front wheels. When coil springs are employed they are usually housed in casings of tubular form, though with leaf springs the resilient member is necessarily exposed. The fork used on the Yale motorcycle is shown at Fig. 227. It consists of two members, a fixed fork attached to the steering head in the usual way, and a movable fork. An extension piece carried from the fixed fork is mounted between springs at the upper end of the movable member, while the lower portion is attached at the center of the hub carrying link members. These are attached to the wheel hubs at one end and fulcrum on suitable bearing studs attached to the fixed fork end at the other. When the wheel encounters an obstacle, the hub carrying link will move on the supporting bearing, and will force the movable member upward. This motion is resisted by the extension forming part of the fixed fork and by a spring carried below the extension in the upper portion of the movable fork tube. Another spring is mounted above the extension in order to prevent rapid rebound. The sectional view of the spring fork used on the Reading-Standard shown at Fig. 228 shows another application of the spiral spring principle. The movable fork member is attached to the hub carrying links in the same manner as previously described, and carries two spring members inside of a movable spring case which is guided by a fixed spring case attached to the upper portion of the steering head. The shock absorbing and recoil check springs are clearly shown and both are thoroughly encased and protected inside of the spring casing.

The application of the laminated spring to secure resilient wheel support was first tried out on the Marsh-Metz motorcycles, and has been retained on the modern product manufactured by these interests which is known as the "Eagle" motorcycle. This construction is clearly shown at Fig. 229. The front hub is carried by links which fulcrum on suitable bearings at the end of the fixed fork assembly. Attached to the plate that takes the place of the usual fork crown is a six leaf spring, and from the eye at the forward end of this member a movable fork member composed of two steel rods passes to the front hub carrier. As the wheel is moved by irregularities on the road surface, it is apparent that the leaf spring will be raised and that the shock will be absorbed in this manner.

The cradle spring fork which is an important feature of design on the Indian motorcycles is shown at Fig. 230. The advantages claimed for this type of spring include maximum flexibility, which is said to be produced by the curved end of the lower leaves, and the quick dampening of the oscillations or absorbtion of rebound due to the friction between the spring leaves. The spring fork of the Indian motorcycle is of the trailing type, which means that the hub axle follows the forks instead of having the hub mounted ahead of the fork as is also common practice. The advantage of the trailing hub is not as clearly realized as it should be. With the forms in which the hub is carried ahead of the fork, when the wheel is raised, it is apt to produce an upward movement of the entire front end of the

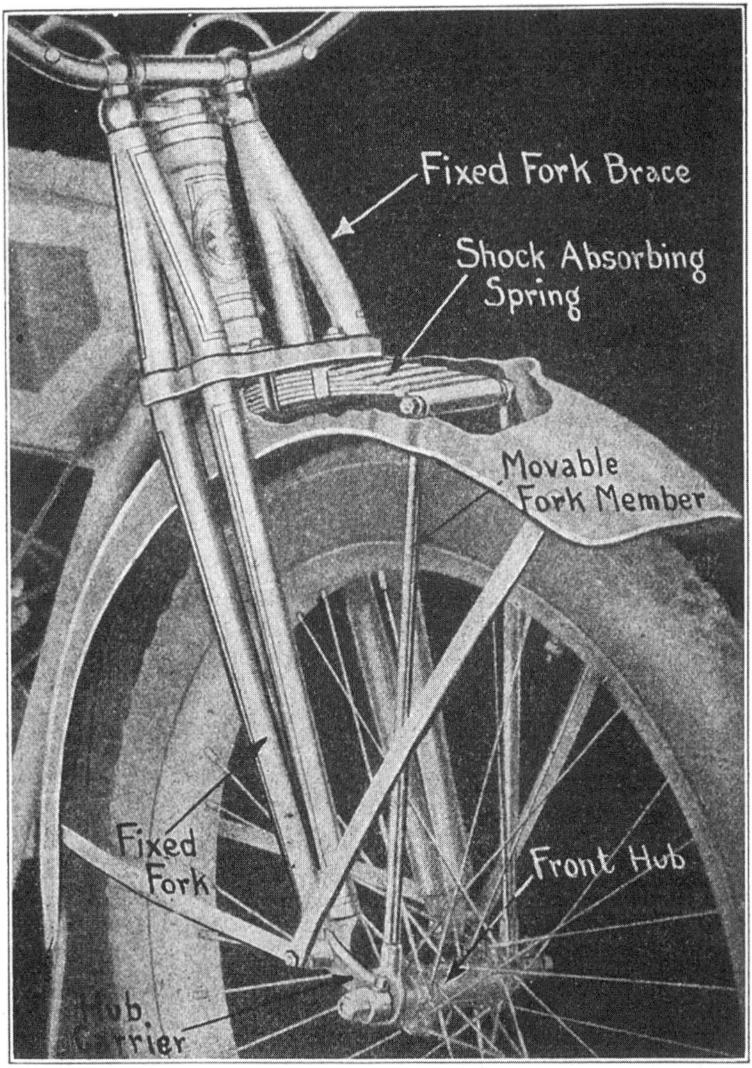

Fig. 229.—Leaf Spring Used on the Eagle Motorcycle to Control Movable Fork Member.

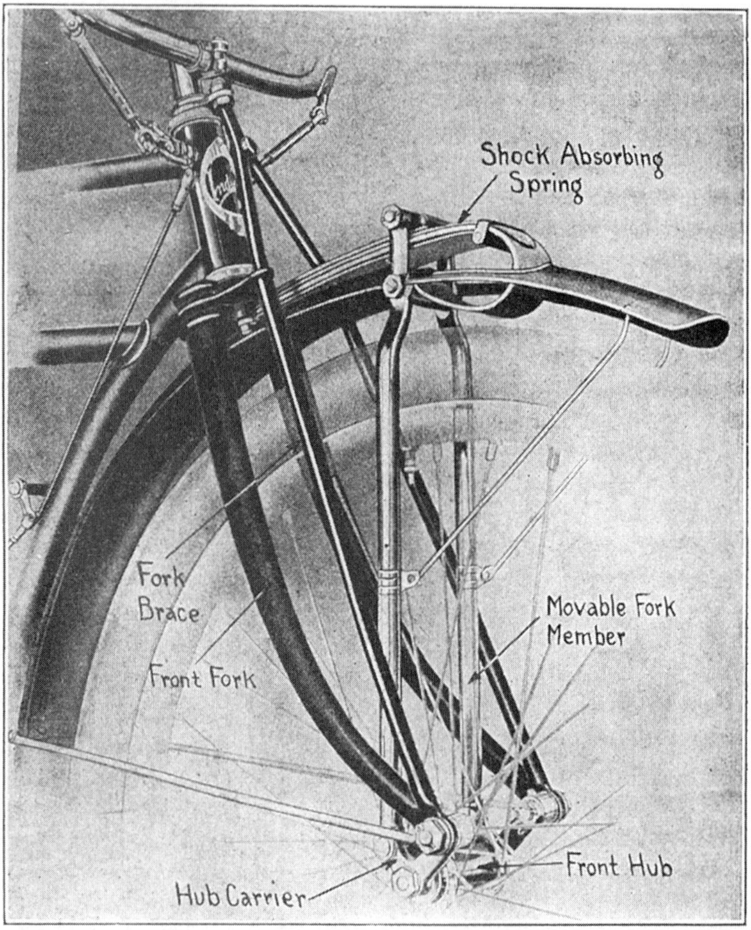

Fig. 230.—The Indian Cradle Spring Fork.

machine because a certain portion of the shock is transmitted by the hub carrier link directly to the fixed fork members as the wheel surmounts the obstacle. With the trailing hub construction, which is clearly outlined at Fig. 230, any movement of the wheel will affect only the shock absorbing spring.

The advantage of the trailing hub construction may be readily grasped by comparing its action to that of a wheelbarrow when it passes over a raised object. If a wheelbarrow is pushed against a curb, for instance, it will be found difficult to force it over the obstruction, whereas if it is pulled over it will surmount a high curb with comparatively little effort on the part of the person wheeling it. The usual method of supporting the front wheel ahead of the fork may be likened to pushing a wheelbarrow over; the trailing hub action is the same as when it is pulled over the obstruction.

The fixed fork member of the Indian machine is well braced by a tubular arch member extending from the top of the steering column to the lower portion of the fixed fork. The hub carrier links are attached at their front end to the fixed forks, carry the wheel hub at their center, and the movable forks at the back end. The curved lower leaf of the shock absorbing spring provides a certain degree of flexibility which makes the wheel respond to slight irregularities of the road surface, and when greater resistance is encountered the entire spring is brought in action because the movable fork member exerts its pressure against the lower leaf at a point calculated to bring the remainder of the spring leaves in action.

The foreign spring forks vary from the American designs, and the preference seems to be for coil springs as shock absorbing members, which are invariably exposed. A number of typical English spring forks are shown at Fig. 231. In the member outlined at A, the wheel is carried in a substantial movable fork member, that is secured to the member passing through the steering head by means of distance links which permit a certain amount of up and down motion, but which do not allow the wheel to move backward appreciably. In most American designs, the wheel may move backward as well as up and down. At the lower portion of the piece passing through the steering head a pair of spiral springs are mounted which are attached at their lower ends to extensions brazed to the fork tube. When the wheel meets an obstruction, its upward motion is resisted by the springs which are under compression while the violent rebound is checked by the tension resistance of the spring. In the form shown at B, the fixed fork member is fulcrumed on a pair of links which are attached to the piece passing through the steering head. The shock absorbing spring is also secured to the steering head member and

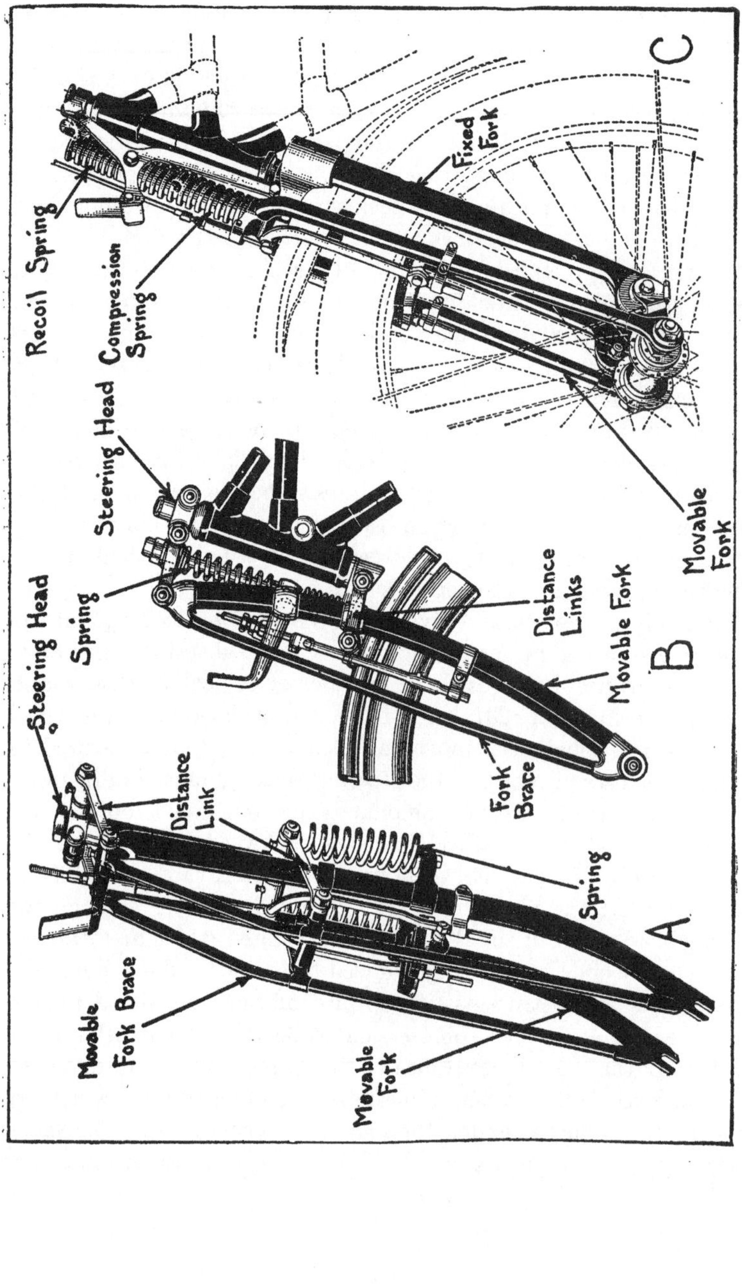

Fig. 231.—Spring Forks of English Design in Which Coil Springs are Employed Exclusively.

resists upward motion or vertical travel of the fork member, which can move in that plane as the distance links oscillate on their bearings. The upward motion is resisted by the upper coil spring while the recoil is checked by a suitable member at the lower part of the steering head. Both springs are under compression.

Another form which is very similar to the American design depicted at Fig. 228, without enclosed springs, is shown at C. In this, the lower of the two springs is a compression member that is provided to absorb the shock, while the shorter of the two or upper spring is used to check the recoil. The hub in this construction is carried in a movable fork member which is kept in proper relation with the fixed fork by suitable distance links. A point that should be noted by the reader is the system of applying a pair of brakes that act against the front wheel rim on all three of the forks shown at Fig. 231. This brake is actuated through the medium of Bowden wire control running to a suitable handle on the steering bar. The U-shape member carrying the brake blocks or contact shoes is guided at its lower ends by clips secured to the fork side, while it is steadied at the upper end by a bearing through which the wire or a lifting rod passes

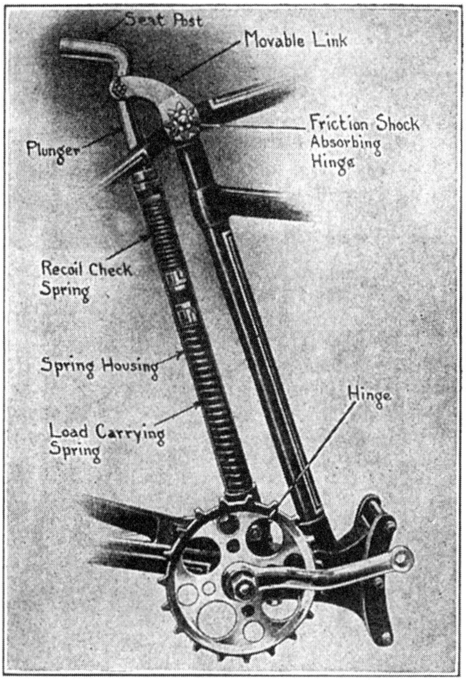

Fig. 232.—Spring Supported Seat Post of Reading-Standard Motorcycle.

Spring Supported Seat Post.—After the springing of the front

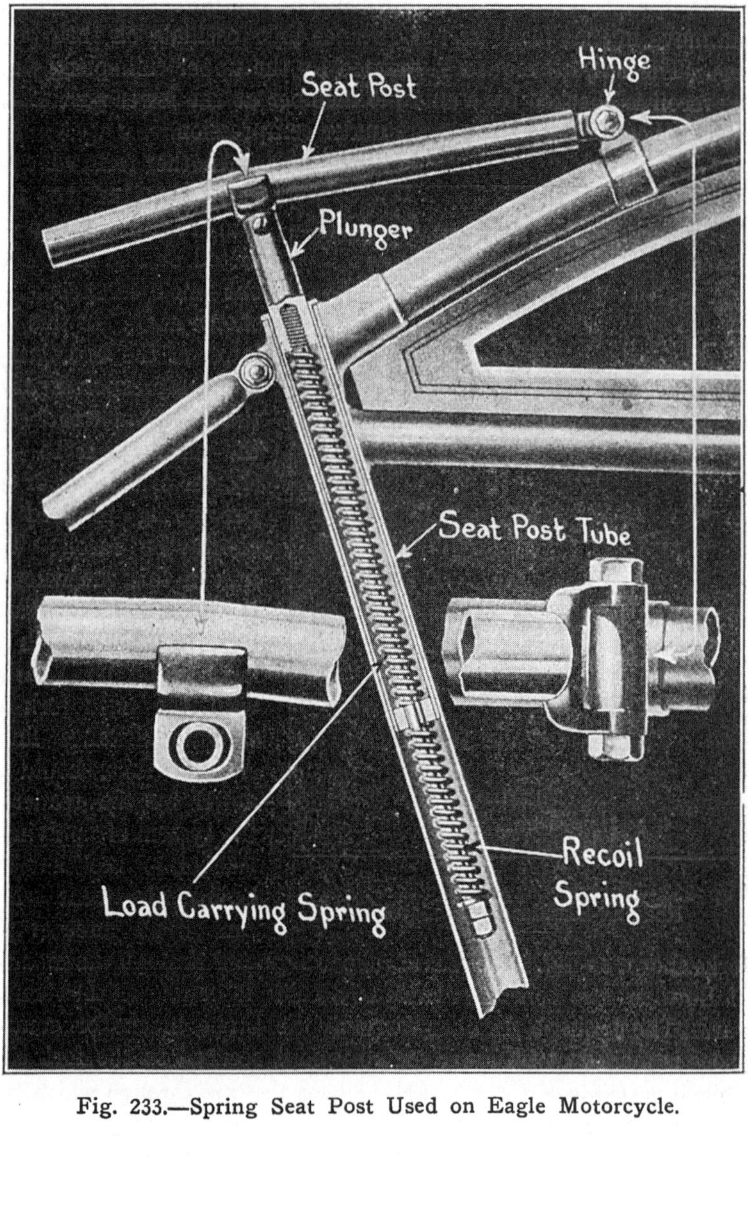

Fig. 233.—Spring Seat Post Used on Eagle Motorcycle.

end has been satisfactorily accomplished by the use of spring forks some of the designers began to consider the best method of eliminating the jar at the rear end of the machine. Some of the manufacturers have adopted a resilient frame construction with the idea that this would suspend the power plant on springs, as well as the rider. Other makers contend that the spring supported saddle coupled with a resilient spring fork is all that is needed to insure comfort of the rider, and reduction of shock on the machine.

The spring seat post attachment employed on the Reading-Standard motorcycle has demonstrated its efficiency and is very simple. As is true of the spring fork previously described, the resilient support of the saddle is attained by the use of coil springs protected by and housed in a tubular housing hinged at its lower portion just forward of the pedal crank hanger, and maintained in proper position at the upper end with a movable distance member or link. The seat post is extended to form a plunger that is guided by a suitable bearing at the upper end of the spring housing. The long coil spring is the load carrying member, while the shorter spring at the upper end is a recoil check. Another feature that tends to prevent too rapid movement of the seat post is the friction shock-absorbing hinge by which the movable link is held to the seat post tube.

The spring seat post used on the Eagle motorcycle, and illustrated at Fig. 233, is similar in construction to that just described, though it is different in detail and application. The seat post is hinged at its upper end to a clip attached to the upper frame tube. It is adapted to bear on a plunger member that projects through the seat post tube, which also serves to house the load-carrying and recoil spring. A simple application of a spring-supported seat post is shown at Fig. 234. The forward end of the seat post is hinged to the frame, while the rear end is secured to a conical spring that bears on a supporting member attached to the rear fork.

The method of mounting the saddle on the Yale motorcycle, shown at Fig. 235, is similar except that two springs are used, one at either side of the seat post tube in supporting the saddle. These are coil springs and are intended to supplement the action of the members with which the saddle itself is provided. Another application of a spring seat post is shown at Fig. 236, as applied to the Fielbach motorcycle. The saddle supporting member is in the form of a bell crank, the long arm of which carries the saddle, while the short arm is attached to a plunger that works through the lower of the two upper frame tubes which serves as a housing to retain the load-carrying and recoil-absorbing members.

Spring Frames.—There is a marked distinction between spring seat posts and spring frames, and this is well shown by comparing

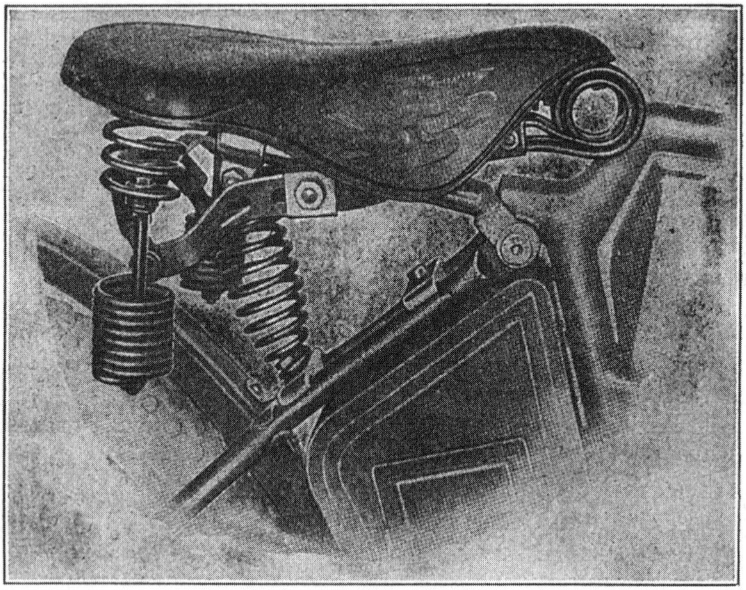

Fig. 234.—Application of Single Coil Spring to Support Seat Post of Thiem Motorcycle.

the two different methods shown at Fig. 237. That at A is a simple spring frame, which means that the weight of the rider is carried by a frame which in itself is capable of movement, and that the same frame to which the power plant is secured also directly supports the weight of the rider. The rear hub of the Pope motorcycle is mounted in simple forged yokes that are guided by plungers extending through bosses at the end of the U-shape brackets attached at the rear of the frame. The heavy coil springs are under tension and the tendency of

Fig. 235.—Double Coil Spring Supported Saddle Carrier of Yale Motorcycle.

the upward movement of the rear wheel when it strikes an obstruction is to extend rather than compress them. The spring-supported seat-post representative of the other construction, shown at Fig. 237, B, also includes a coil spring under tension. The seat post is guided by distance links, one end of the spring being attached to the frame, while the lower end is secured to the movable seat-post member.

The cradle spring frame utilized on the Indian motorcycle is conceded to be one of the biggest steps forward ever made in the development of the motorcycle frame. The construction is not unlike that of the spring fork except that two load-carrying springs are used, one at each side of the wheel. The wheel hub is carried in a movable rear fork stay hinged at its forward end to the lower portion of the tube

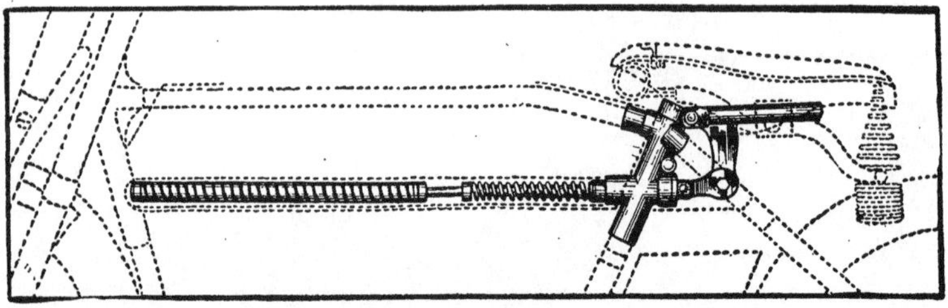

Fig. 236.—Method of Housing Spring Controlling Action of Fielbach Seat Post in Frame Tube.

that takes the place of the seat-post mast of conventional design frames. The load-carrying springs are attached to a semi-steel casting member in the form of a horseshoe that takes the place of the usual seat-post cluster. A movable rear fork member is attached to the springs in the same manner as the movable fork member of the spring fork assembly is, and is hinged at its lower portion to the hub-carrying plates. It will be evident that with this construction the rear wheel may move independently of the main portion of the frame that carries the weight of the rider and the power plant, and that the combination of this member with the effective spring fork should not

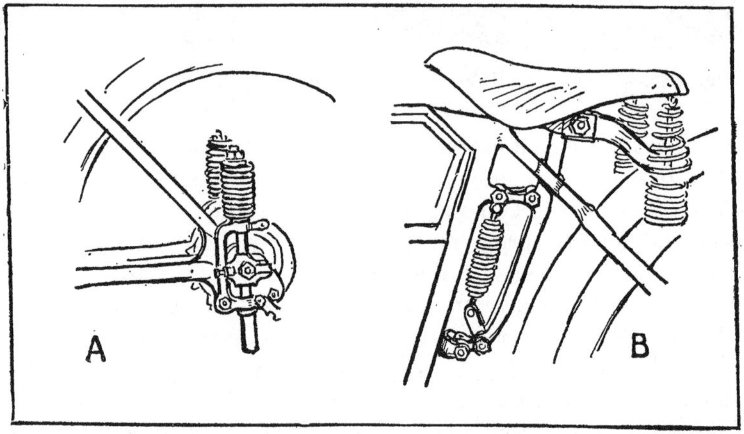

Fig. 237.—Examples of the Two Differing Methods of Providing Resilient Support for the Rider. A—The Pope Helical Tension Spring Frame. B—Tension Spring Supporting Movable Seat Post.

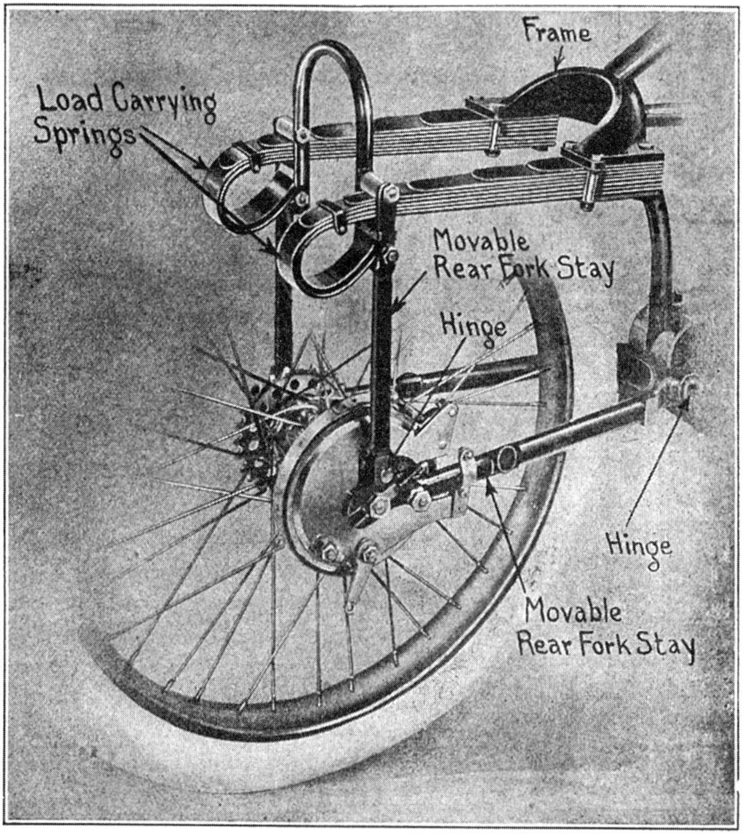

Fig. 238.—The Indian Cradle Spring Frame.

only provide for maximum comfort of the rider but contribute materially to the long life and endurance of the mechanism by insulating it from the destructive road shocks in a much superior manner to that which obtains in the conventional construction where the air-filled tire is the only resilient support.

Two spring frame constructions in which coil springs are used are shown at Fig. 239. That at A is the form used on the Merkel, and has been a feature of this machine for several years. The rear portion of the frame, which is comprised of the forks and rear-fork stays, operates in the same manner as the spring forks in which the enclosed coil springs are used. The rear-fork stay members are employed to house the coil springs, while the front end of the fork assembly is hinged to the crank hanger in order to permit free movement of the rear portion of the frame. The method of incorporating a heavy compression spring in the frame of the N. S. U. motorcycle, a foreign design, is shown at Fig. 239, B. The application of four laminated leaf springs to support the rear wheel of an English four-cylinder

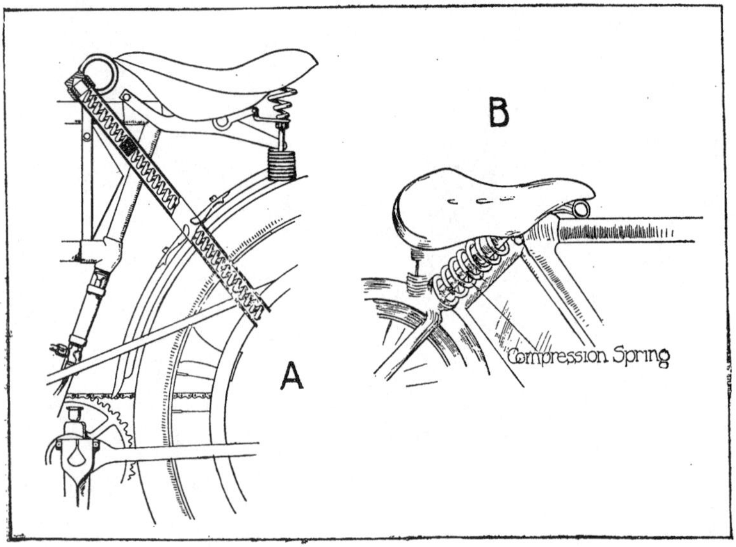

Fig. 239.—Two Methods of Incorporating Coil Springs in Spring Frames. A—Application in Merkel Rear Fork Stays. B—Compression Springs Used on N. S. U. Model.

motorcycle employing worm drive is shown at Fig. 240. In view of what has been presented before, and the complete explanations that have been given of spring fork and spring frame action, the method of operation of these various forms should be clearly grasped.

Saddles and Tandem Attachments.—The first motorcycle included practically all the parts of the bicycle without much change, and it was some time before some of the parts were altered or enlarged, even after considerable improvement had been made in motor design and in the construction of the mechanism. One of the fittings that was not changed for several years because the designers had all they could do to make the mechanism reliable was the support or saddle for the rider. The saddles that had been used in bicycles were of simple form, usually consisting of a light wooden or steel frame covered with leather; in some cases a padding would be interposed

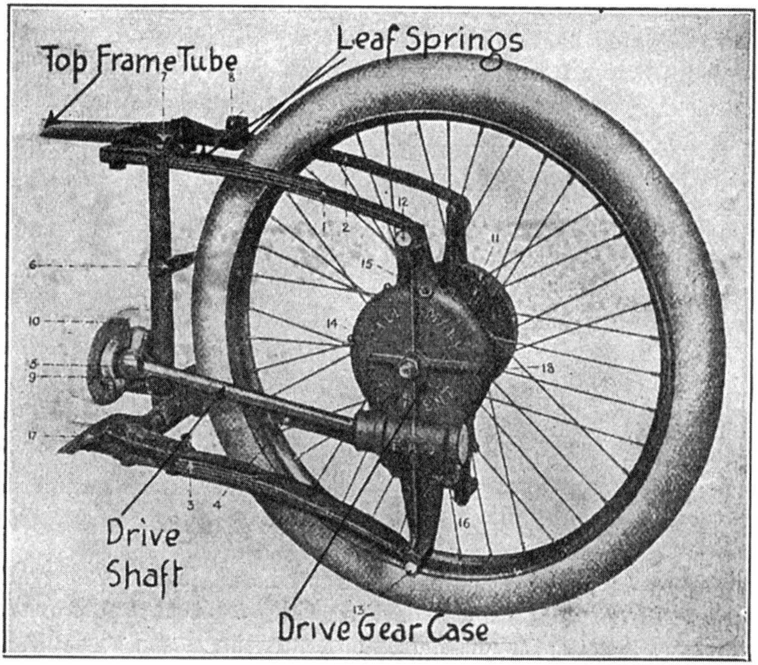

Fig. 240.—Method of Carrying Rear Wheel by Four Leaf Springs on T. A. C. Motorcycle.

between the leather covering and the base. Bicycle saddles were narrow, and they were very satisfactory on those machines where the riders weight was distributed to some extent on the crank hanger through the efforts made and pressure applied to the pedals to propel the vehicle. With the motorcycle, the rider did not have to pedal any more than was necessary to start the machine, which meant that practically all of his weight would rest on the saddle. Several forms of bicycle saddles were made that provided a wide support, but it was found that these materially interfered with the effective action of the rider's limbs when pedaling. This objection did not obtain in the motorcycle and the saddles were gradually increased in size, both in length and in width, until the forms used to-day provide a secure and comfortable seat. It was not desirable to have a very resilient saddle on a bicycle because the spring detracted somewhat from the effectiveness of the pedaling. On a motorcycle, however, it was soon learned that it was much more uncomfortable to sit on an inflexible non-yielding seat on a machine going 35 or 40 miles an hour than was the

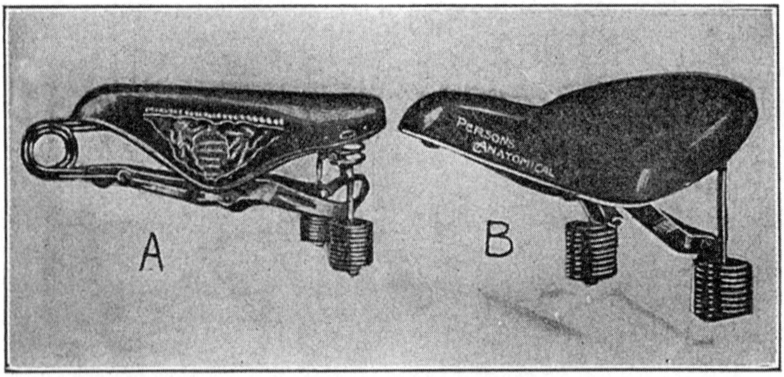

Fig. 241.—Typical Motorcycle Saddles.

case when traveling but one-third that speed on a bicycle. The saddle manufacturer was not slow in devising wide seats that were provided with substantial spring members in order to make them easy riding.

Two modern saddles are shown at Fig. 241. That at A consists essentially of a metal frame over which a leather seat is placed, the leather being kept under tension by the coil spring at the front end. This spring gives somewhat under the rider's weight, though the main reliance for easy riding is upon the coil springs at the rear of the saddle. The form shown at B is similar in construction as far as the frame work is concerned, except that the seat is formed to conform to the anatomy of the average rider and has a padded cushion interposed between the leather covering and the metal frame.

The arrangement of the springs used to support the rider in the

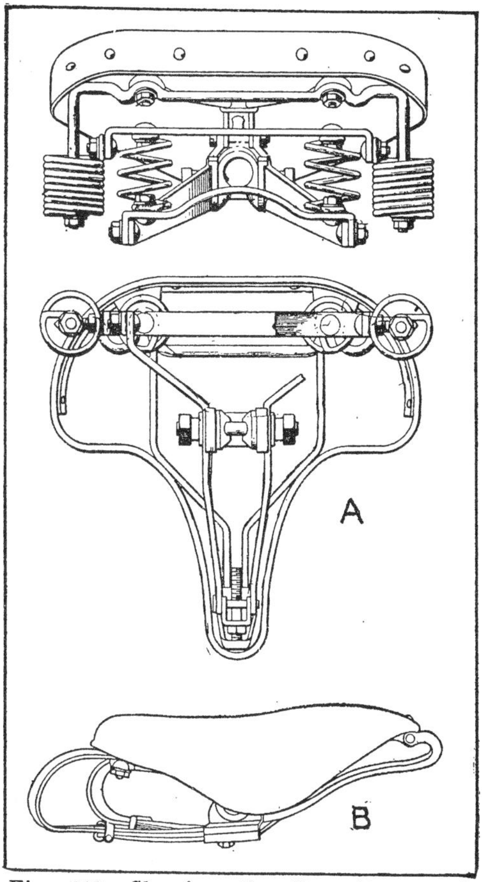

Fig. 242.—Showing the Two Forms of Springs Used in Supporting Motorcycle Saddles.

usual motorcycle saddle as well as the general construction of the form in which coil springs are used is clearly outlined at Fig. 242, A. The metal frame work with the leather coverings removed to show the arrangement of the parts of the Persons Champion Saddle is shown at Fig. 243. Coil springs are not the only type that have been adopted in saddle construction. A form in which leaf springs are used to support the rider's weight is shown at Fig. 242, B. Practically all saddles are provided with an adjustable clamp that permits of tilting the saddle to some extent and moving it back and forth on the seat post tube to adjust the seat member for different builds of riders.

While some of the early motorcycles were made in a tandem form, i. e., just the same as the two-passenger bicycles except for the addition of the power plant, this form of construction is now abandoned. The reason for discarding the tandem was that the machine was unwieldy and hard to handle if but one person was riding. For this reason, tandem attachments that would convert the ordinary form of one-passenger motorcycle so that two people can be carried effectively have been evolved. A typical tandem attachment removed from the machine is shown at Fig. 244, while a similar device attached is depicted at Fig. 245. The tandem attachment in its simplest form consists merely of a supplementary rear fork member carrying a pair of foot rests or pedals at its lower end, and a saddle at the upper part. A brace extends from the top of the fork to the seat post cluster of the machine, and in most cases this brace carries a pair of non-movable handle bars by which the passenger may steady himself.

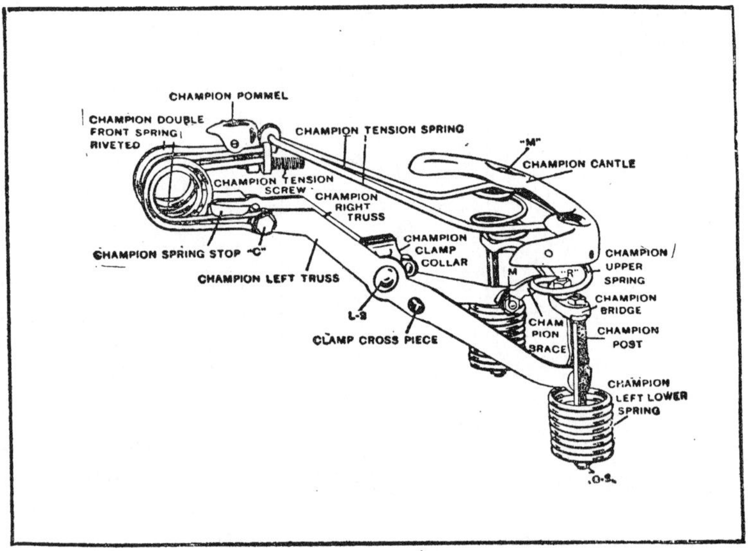

Fig. 243.—Steel Framework of Persons Champion Saddle.

Why Powerful Brakes are Necessary.—It is now generally conceded by manufacturer and rider alike that the motorcycle of to-day is practically a two-wheeled automobile capable of speeds rarely attained by the larger conveyance. Engines used are rated at from 7 to 9 horse-power, and these will usually develop twice their nominal rating. Larger motors call for heavier frames to carry them and the rider safely, more powerful transmission systems are fitted and spring frame and forks are also required to insure comfortable riding at high speeds over ordinary roads. All control elements must also be designed with a view of giving the rider positive mastery of the machine. When one considers the momentum it is possible to attain with a vehicle weighing, with average rider, nearly 400 pounds, and capable of a speed of 75 miles per hour in many cases, the need of a positive retarding member or brake can be properly realized. Brakes designed primarily for bicycle service and increased in size without due regard to the stresses obtaining in motorcycles, cannot work adequately or prove enduring. The brake as well as the other parts of the machine must be increased in size and capacity to correspond in efficiency to the larger power plants now fitted. The problem is therefore essentially one of automobile design, and can only be solved by a correct application of motor car engineering principles.

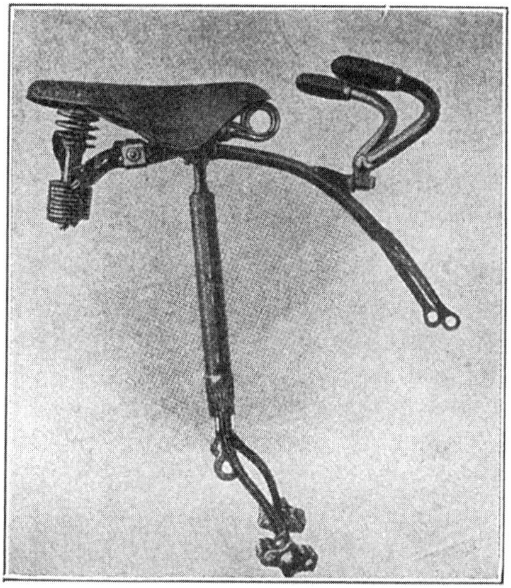

Fig. 244.—Typical Tandem Attachment.

Why Coasting, Driving and Braking Hub is Used.—One of the most important accessories developed for the bicycle trade, and one which has contributed materially to the expansion of that business by promoting the comfort and safety of the rider was the coasting and braking hub. In this device, the motorcycle manufacturer obtained a rear hub construction, already highly developed, that was just as well suited in principle to motorcycle use as it was to the bicycle, though applied in a slightly different manner. In bicycle service, it is provided to give the rider an opportunity to stop pedaling on down grades or smooth roads with favoring winds, and yet permits him to keep control of the bicycle, because a slight back pedal action applied a brake to the wheel.

On a motor-propelled cycle the motor does the driving normally, and the pedals are only brought in action when it is desired to propel the machine by foot power to start the motor. As soon as the engine starts, the coasting feature comes into play, and the action is just the same as though the rider of a foot-propelled cycle was taking advantage of down grade. The pedals provide a rest for the feet, and the back pedaling or reverse pressure begins to bring the brake in action any time it is necessary to retard the speed of the machine.

Fig. 245.—Application of Tandem Attachment on Henderson Motorcycles.

The rear sprocket of a chain-drive machine is attached directly to the hub shell; the belt pulley, if that system of transmission is used, can be secured to wheel rim or to hub shell, as desired. The only difference in principle between a coaster hub intended for motorcycle work and the similar device made for bicycles is that two methods of driving the rear wheel are provided, one by mechanical power to a member rigidly secured to the hub shell, the other by foot power through the medium of a friction clutch that automatically engages the hub shell interior as soon as the pedals are pushed forward.

Requirements of Pedal Drive Mechanism.—The requirements of the pedal drive mechanism are well known at the present time, and that employed has demonstrated its correctness in theory and practical application by years of actual use in millions of bicycles. The basic principle of the spirally threaded member and laterally shiftable connector to drive the hub, declutch to provide a free wheel and to apply the brake by further movement has been developed in this country to a state of practical perfection. The best argument in favor of this pedal drive mechanism is that a simple and successful coaster brake cannot be built without incorporating this system, and that all devices on the market embody this principle. The construction is such that the hub is driven smoothly and positively whenever the pedals are rotated forward, the hub is free to rotate independently of the pedal drive sprocket as soon as the feet cease rotating and a reverse motion of the pedals or back pedaling action will apply the brake without slipping. Coaster brakes have been made with ratchets, ball or roll clutches, etc., but these have not been as successful, reliable or enduring as the double taper cone principle of driving and brake actuation universally applied.

What Brake End Should Do.—While the requirements of the pedal drive mechanism were well understood, the principles making for efficient brake action of motorcycle hubs were not realized so completely, and it is on this portion of the mechanism that most manufacturers disagree. To begin with, the essential requirement is that the brake member be capable of retarding the cycle velocity to any degree from a simple and momentary slowing down to a quick, emergency stop. This condition is not hard to meet, almost any form of brake will do it, when new, clean and in proper adjustment. The successful and really practical brake must be one that will provide this essential prompt braking action but it must do it in a gradual manner, because a harsh acting brake will impose injurious stresses in the entire mechanism of brake and related wheel and frame parts. The practical brake should be a form that will not need constant adjustment, the essential mechanism should be thoroughly protected from the abrading influence of road dirt, the brake member should be housed in and supported in a manner that will preclude liability of rattling. The brake parts should be of material that will not only

Fig. 246.—External Constricting Band Brake Used on Harley-Davidson Belt Drive Model.

have a high degree of resistance to wear in service, but the members that come in contact to provide the braking action should also have a high degree of frictional adhesion because it is the absorption of power by the frictional contact that retards the momentum of the machine. The design of the brake end should be such that the parts will not drag or tend to engage each other when the brake is released, and the arrangement of braking members should be such as to provide immediate cessation of braking effort as soon as the pressure exerted by the rider on the actuating members ceases.

While the brake should be easy to apply so the maximum braking effect will be obtained without too much effort on the part of the rider, at the same time, the brake should not be so sensitive that it can be applied inadvertently through unconscious back pedaling. The ability of the brake end to function properly even though flooded with the oil or grease used in lubricating the hub bearings and interior mechanism is also essential.

Let us carefully consider the force needed to afford positive control of the modern motorcycle, then become familiar with the principle of braking action, and a careful analysis of the construction of various types of brakes will permit the rider to form his own conclusions regarding the type that best meets all of the requirements previously enumerated.

Force Required at Brake.—The most any brake can do is to skid the wheel to which it is applied. If it can accomplish this, it is adequate to cope with any of the normal operating conditions. The amount of force needed to lock the wheel depends upon the amount of the total weight of the machine supported by the wheel to which the braking effort is applied, and the relative diameters of wheel and brake member. Much less force will be needed to stop a wheel if the brake is applied near the tire than if it acts near the axle. Structural limitations make it necessary to locate the brake in the hub so it can be actuated positively by back pedaling mechanism that will be entirely protected and properly lubricated but at the same time it is possible to follow automobile practice and provide a drum for the brake to act against that will be of such diameter that the wheel may be controlled without too much exertion on the part of the rider, or producing undue stress on the brake members.

Assume that the machine we are to stop is a powerful twin weighing 250 pounds with tandem attachment and carrying a passenger load of 300 pounds, that being the weight of two average riders. This makes a total of 550 pounds, and we can justly assume that 450 pounds will be supported by the rear wheel. The amount of adhesion between the tire and the ground is generally taken as 60 per cent of the weight on the wheel, so we will have traction enough so a retarding force must be applied at the brake drum equivalent to the adhesive force of 270 pounds at point of contact between wheel tire and the ground. If the wheel is 28 inches in diameter, it will have a radius of 14 inches. The moment at the axle center due to the leverage factor would be the adhesive pressure times wheel radius which would give a value of 3,780 inch pounds at 1 inch from wheel center. If the brake had an effective diameter of but 3 inches, as would be the case if it was carried in the hub shell, we would be forced to apply a retarding effect of 2,520 pounds to lock the wheel. With a brake drum 6 inches in diameter, it would take only 1,260 pounds retarding

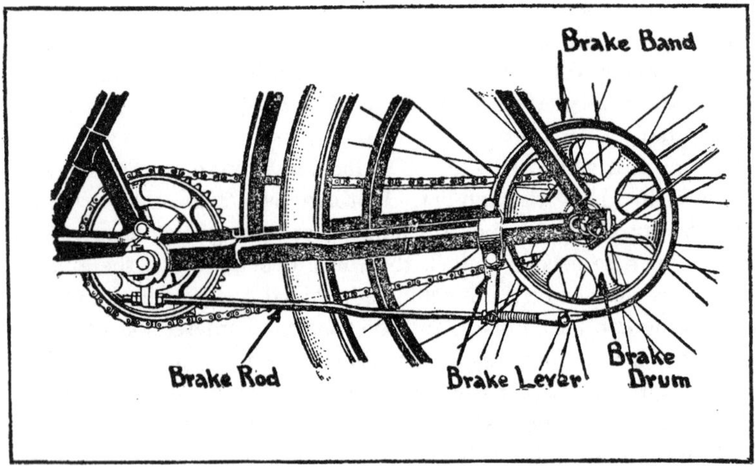

Fig. 247.—Application of Band Brake Actuated by Back Pedaling Ratchet Mechanism.

force to skid the wheel. If a brake block was applied directly to the tire, it would take but 270 pounds adhesive force, or the same amount as maintains traction, to stop the driving member.

It will be apparent that the larger diameter brake members require less effort to stop the wheel than those forms in which the braking effect is exerted near the axle. This use of a large brake drum not only makes for easier brake operation on the part of the rider but conduces to longer life of the parts because of the lessened stresses on the brake anchorage members and also lower unit stress on the materials in contact. While it is very desirable to have a compact brake assembly, still it is more important to use the requisite proportions that will insure positive braking under all conditions even if compactness and lightness are sacrificed by making the brake drum and brake shoes of adequate diameter, and all parts heavy enough so they will have an ample margin of safety over the actual requirements. Where human life and safety are concerned, it is best to err on the safe side, and the addition of a few ounces of metal is sometimes all that is needed to make a part of doubtful strength one with a large enough margin to guard against the weakening influence of hidden flaws or insure against breakage when subjected to abnormal stress. At the other hand, the brake parts require careful designing to keep the weight down and retain strength, and materials of construction must be selected intelligently to insure absolute reliability and endurance.

Principle of Brake Action.—The friction form of brake is that generally applied to all forms of vehicles. The principle of action may be concisely expressed by saying that if a fixed member is brought to bear against a rotating one, the friction between them will bring the one in motion to a stop. The time needed to stop a rotating body depends entirely upon the amount of friction present between the braking members. This in turn depends upon the co-efficient of friction existing, which varies with the nature of the materials in contact, the effective diameter of the brake members and the pressure holding the parts together. We have seen why large diameters are more desirable than small ones.

The amount of surface in the brake is not as important as effective diameter, because the braking effort depends primarily upon the diameter of the surfaces rather than their width. For example, there would be no difference in braking efficiency as relates to retarding power between a brake band ¼ inch wide or 2 inches wide if the diameter was the same. The wider brake band would provide an important advantage of having greater life because the braking pressure would be distributed over a larger area. It would not be any more effective as a brake, however, than the narrower member. It is generally believed that braking power depends upon the surface in contact, but this is not true. A brake of small diameter might have three times the surface of one of twice the diameter, yet the one with lesser surface would be twice as effective as a brake. The capable designer will always endeavor to provide surface enough to prevent undue depreciation, and will employ materials in contact that will have a high degree of resistance to deformation. In some forms of brakes, however, the large amount of surface provided is an actual detriment to efficient brake action and serves no useful purpose.

The materials employed for brakes depend largely upon the design, and in every case these should be chosen with two considerations in mind, the most important being the endurance of the material and ability to keep its shape under pressure as well as high degree of resistance to abrasion. The material should not be affected by the heat generated when the brake is used, nor should it become decomposed or its efficiency reduced materially by oil deposits. Another consideration, but one of secondary importance, if it calls for the sacrifice of the qualities previously enumerated, is to employ substances having a high degree of frictional adhesion.

Friction Co-efficient of Various Materials.—In brake design, engineers must seek to increase friction, whereas in bearing construction every effort is made to reduce it. The following brief notes on the characteristics of friction and a definition of the meaning of friction co-efficient will permit even the reader not thoroughly posted on mechanical subjects to understand clearly what is meant when the terms are used.

Friction acts on all matter in motion, and is present as a retarding influence that requires expenditure of power to overcome. As a rule, augmenting the pressure will increase the friction, while lessening the load will reduce it. Friction increases with the roughness of surfaces in contact and decreases as they become smoother. Friction tends to bring everything in motion to a state of rest, and, in so doing, mechanical energy is converted into heat which is dissipated and lost.

A simple experiment to show what coefficient of friction means can be made by anyone. This consists of drawing a block of iron or other metal across a wood table top by means of weights suspended by a cord passing over a pulley at the edge of the table, and then attached to the block, in order to avoid a sharp bend and eliminate lost energy as much as possible. Assuming the block is smooth, also the surface of the table, the first trial can be made with the surfaces absolutely dry. Weights are added to the cord until enough have been placed thereon to move the block on the table. The weight required to move the block divided by the weight of the block will equal the coefficient of friction for these surfaces. If the block of metal weighs 50 pounds, and the amount of weight necessary to move it is 25 pounds, the coefficient of friction is 25 divided by 50, or 0.50. If the surface of the table is greased with tallow, and the under surface of the block covered with oil, it will be found that considerably less weight will be needed to move the block, proving that the friction has been reduced by lubrication.

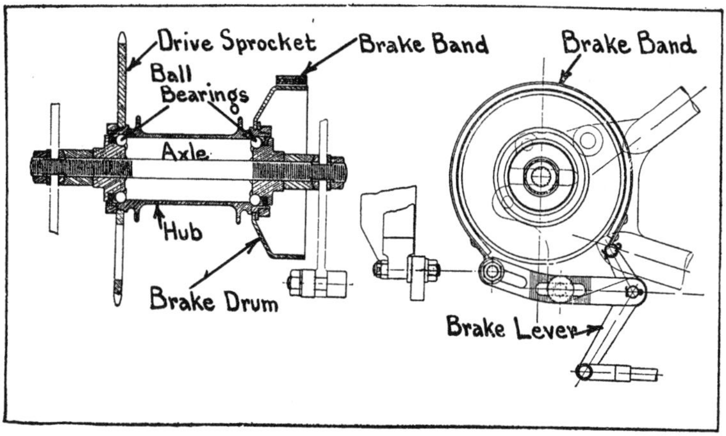

Fig. 248.—External Constricting Band Brake Used on Henderson Motorcycles.

This explains why it is desirable to lubricate bearings, whereas on first thought it would seem that the best braking effort would occur between perfectly dry materials. It would also appear that the softer and rougher materials which have greater friction would be better for brake construction than hard and smooth ones. This would be true if braking effect was all that was to be looked for, and if the factors of gradual application of retarding force and endurance of brake members could be disregarded. As it is important that depreciation be reduced to a minimum, and that all shock should be avoided when braking, one can see a logical reason for the use of materials that would have less friction adhesion though greater resistance to wear, and which provide smoother brake action.

The materials ordinarily used for brakes and their friction coefficients follow:

Asbestos Fabric on Dry Metal	0.30
Asbestos Fabric on Oily Metal	0.12
Metal to Dry Metal	0.15
Metal to Oily Metal	0.07

These values mean that if an asbestos fabric block or band bears against a dry metal drum, less than one-third or 30 per cent of the pressure maintaining the parts in engagement will be available for stopping brake drum rotation. If the asbestos fabric works against an oily surface, the frictional adhesion or braking force is reduced to but one-eighth of the pressure keeping the parts together.

Asbestos fabric is a soft, yielding material that is very effective if used as an external brake, but it is entirely unsuited for use where much oil is present. While it provides a gradual braking action, it is not capable of withstanding as high unit pressures as metal, so a larger surface must be provided to insure against untimely depreciation. As it is a rough-surfaced material that depreciates as used, constant adjustment and renewal will be necessary to keep the brake in a satisfactory condition. For this reason, this material is better adapted to external constricting band brakes than to other forms, because it can be easily reached for adjustment, and it will be free from oil deposits.

A metal is always used as one brake member, usually the rotating one, and sometimes it is used for both members, fixed as well as movable. While metal does not possess as much friction as the asbestos fabrics, it does not depreciate through action of oil, and it can be used with higher unit pressures than the softer fabric. The surface need not be so great if the metals are properly selected. When used in motorcycle brakes, the revolving metal drum is usually harder than the fixed shoes or retarding members, and in all cases efforts are made to use different metals in combination such as bronze against steel. The metals are much more enduring if lubricated, and the oil film serves to cushion the shock of braking by providing gradual application, as well as reducing the liability of dragging or heating, when brake members are released, should there be slight frictional contact between them. Metal brake shoes or discs are therefore better suited for internal brakes than asbestos fabric faced bands, if there is as much oil present as exists in motorcycle hubs.

Leading Types of Brakes.—The most common forms of brake are the various band or shoe types, and the braking members may act against either the inner or outer drum peripheries. The external

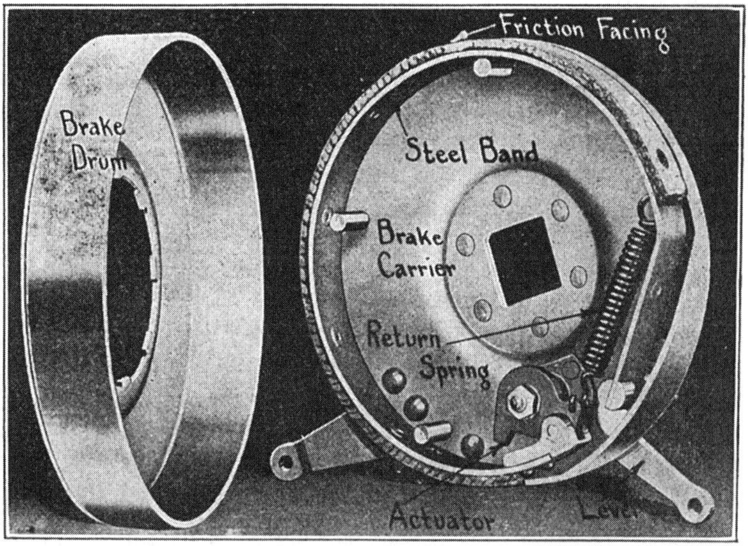

Fig. 249.—Internal Expanding Brake Used on Chain Driven Harley-Davidson Models.

band forms, shown at Figs. 246 to 248 inclusive, tighten around the drum, the internal form as Fig. 249 expands inside the drum or hub shell. There is still another form of external brake in which a friction block bears against the wheel rim or the belt pulley when that method of driving is employed. The external band is usually a flat steel strip faced with asbestos fabric which is sometimes made wedge shaped (Fig. 250) where it fits into the brake drum to provide greater frictional adhesion. The wedge-shape band offers an important advantage, in that it provides a positive grip, but it has an equally great disadvantage in that it is apt to engage too suddenly, and then again it may wedge in place so tightly that the spring provided to release it will not be effective, and it must be pried out of the V-groove in brake drum. The flat band provides more gradual braking, and if made of proper diameter is amply effective.

The brake block form shown at Fig. 252 has the fault that it cannot be easily operated through the pedals, or incorporated as a part of the hub. It is a separate attachment that is used in this country only for emergency brake service, being controlled by a separate pedal distinct from those utilized in driving the hub. The external brakes have a great disadvantage, inasmuch as they are exposed to dirt, and collect this matter which acts as an abrasive that promotes wear of friction material and drum. They are also liable to become loose and rattle, and they all have more small parts than the simple internal shoe forms. While these external brakes are good, they are not ideal by any means, and if only one brake member is fitted this should be preferably of the internal form. A combination of two brakes, one internal and one external, is provided on some machines, as shown at Fig. 251.

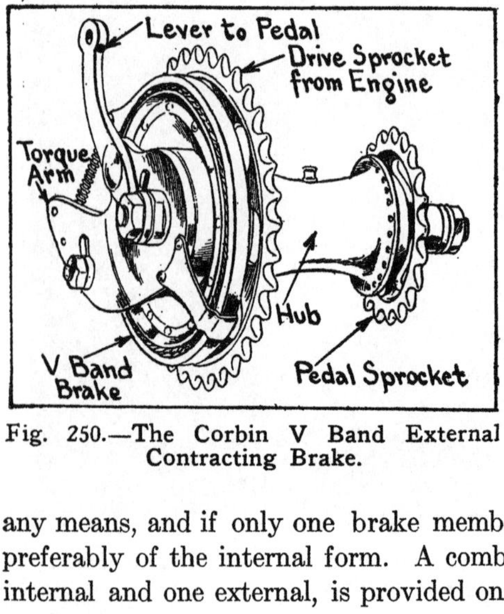

Fig. 250.—The Corbin V Band External Contracting Brake.

The internal brakes are offered in three classifications. The form using a pair of shoes expanded in a drum by a cam is the most popular. The internal ring form, in which the fixed member acts against the inside of the hub shell, is at a disadvantage on account of its small diameter and the great wear due to the excessive pressure necessary to have it grip the hub shell interior with sufficient force to stop the wheel positively. These also are a form that will not release promptly at all times, and are likely to stick if applied too suddenly.

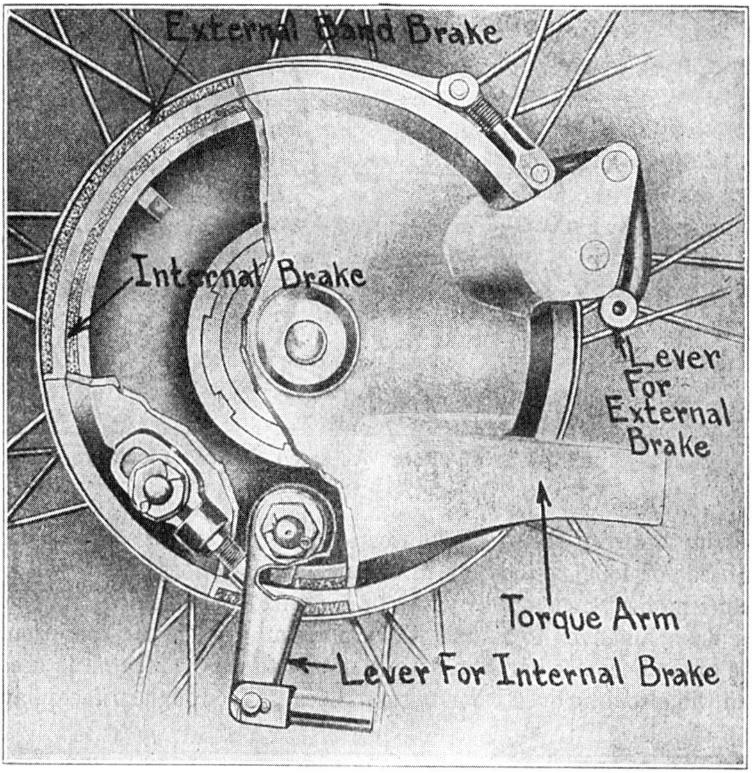

Fig. 251.—Double Brake Combination Used on Indian Two Speed Motorcycles.

The multiple disc brake (Fig. 255) is a form in which a large number of braking members are used, one-half being rotatable with the hub shell, the others being fixed to the axle. Suitable mechanism is interposed between the pedals and discs so the brake elements are brought together with considerable degree of pressure. This form of brake, if copiously lubricated, will provide smooth brake application, and also offers a large amount of frictional surface. It has the disadvantage of not always releasing promptly, because as the oil is squeezed from between the discs by the braking pressure, the plates tend to adhere together when pressure is released because of the partial vacuum

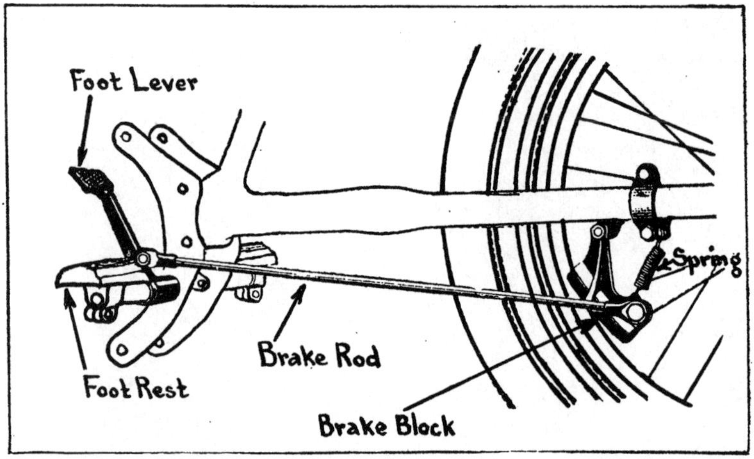

Fig. 252.—Application of Foot Actuated Brake Block to Belt Pulley Rim.

existing between them. If lubrication is neglected, or if the brake is used for long periods, as in mountainous sections, there will be sufficient heat generated by the braking friction to cut or roughen the discs, and even to actually deform them. Under such conditions, the brake becomes harsh in action, no matter how much oil is used, and will also drag even when released because the rough surfaces have

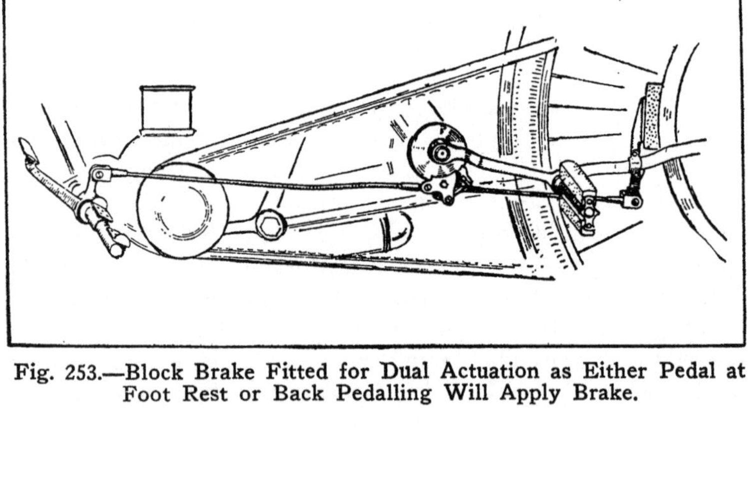

Fig. 253.—Block Brake Fitted for Dual Actuation as Either Pedal at Foot Rest or Back Pedalling Will Apply Brake.

myriads of microscopic projections that tend to interlock as the movable discs revolve by the fixed members.

The internal brake in which bronze shoes of ample size are brought into engagement with a hardened steel drum interior offers a large number of advantages. To enumerate these briefly, we have: First, utmost simplicity; second, strong parts; third, high retarding power; fourth, freedom from dragging; fifth, efficient braking with oil between the surfaces; sixth, gradual or immediate brake application as desired; seventh, all brake parts lubricated and kept clean; eighth, complete

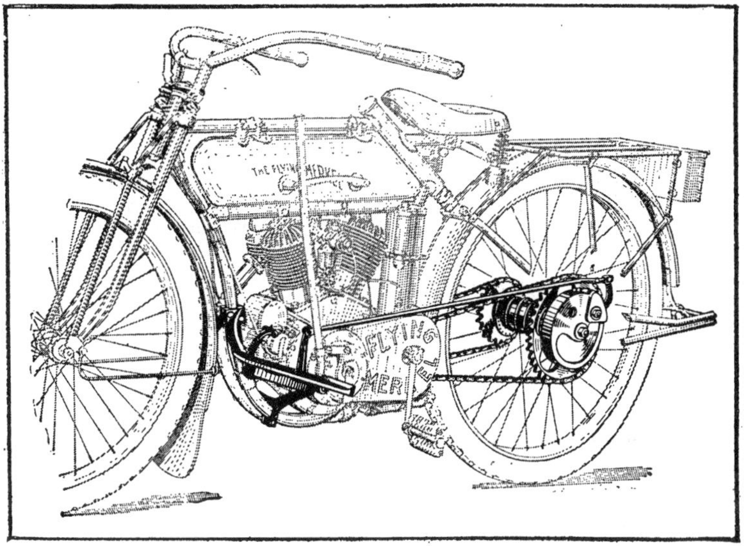

Fig. 254.—Showing the Application of Dual Brake Control on the Flying Merkel Motorcycle.

enclosure of brake members; ninth, absolutely prompt release of brake shoes; tenth, braking force obtained by minimum effort; eleventh, brake actuated directly from pedals by strong, simple mechanism; and twelfth, maximum endurance because of the ability of the bronze shoes to resist wear due to abrasion better than any other material and practical indestructibility of the hardened steel brake drum. This endurance is augmented by the oil always present between brake surfaces and the lessened strain on the parts, because the oil film absorbs the first shock due to brake application.

Operation of Typical Braking and Coasting Hub.—The New Departure, Model L, has been devised with special reference to the requirements of motorcycle service. As will be evident from inspection of illustration, Fig. 256, the general construction of the pedal drive mechanism follows the well-established practice except that all parts are heavier and stronger than anything devised to date. Beginning with a 5/8 inch diameter axle, the entire mechanism has been

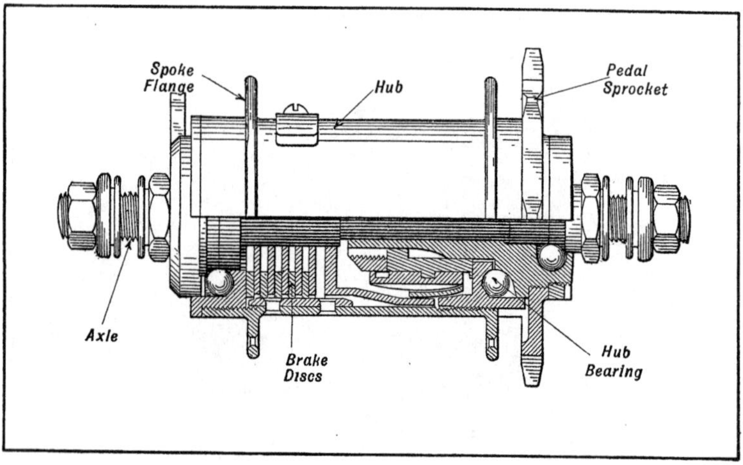

Fig. 255.—Typical Multiple Disc Coasting and Braking Hub.

augmented in size to conform to automobile rules of practice rather than adhering to bicycle construction. The ball bearings are large enough for the wheel of an automobile, and, in addition to the use of large balls, an automobile type or heavy separator is utilized.

Referring to the illustration, we see that the main portion of the device is a hub shell carrying a brake drum and flanges to which the spokes are secured. The outer ball races are formed in the hub shell, which is glass hard at the point where the balls run. The brake drum is a steel stamping 6 inches in diameter, and securely attached to the hub shell flange by a process of electric spot welding, which fuses the members at a number of points to form an intimate bond between

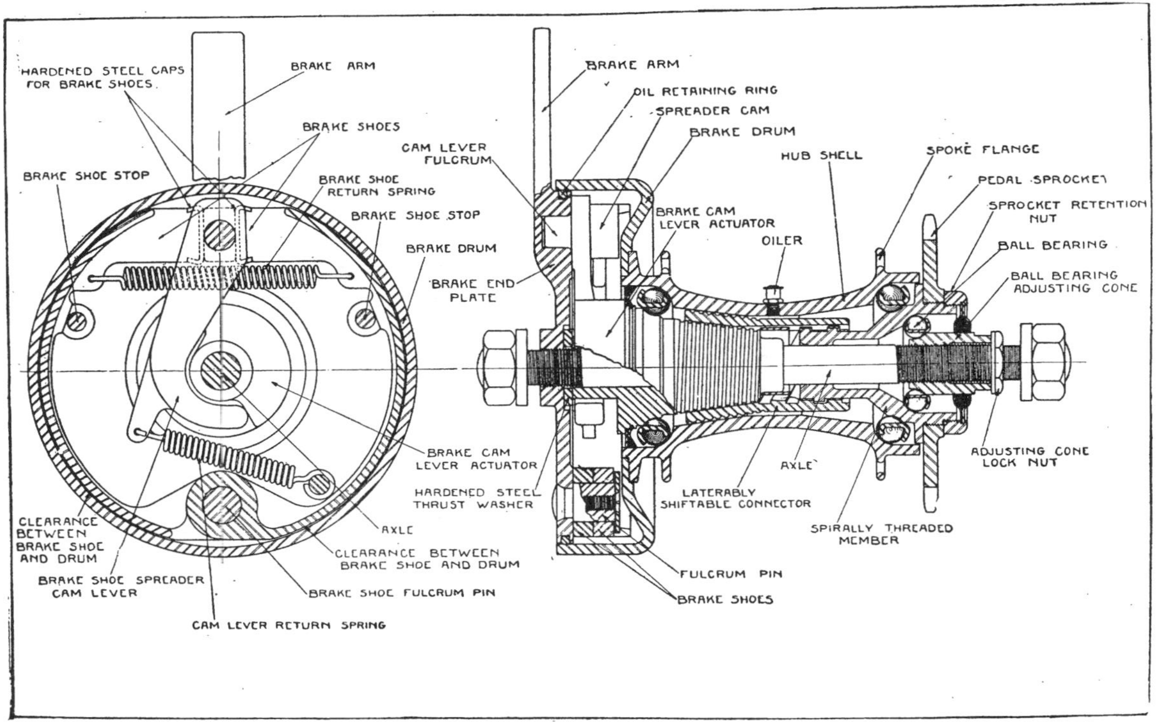

Fig. 256.—Sectional View, Showing Interior Construction of New Departure Model L Coaster Brake.

them. Contrast this to the usual method of riveting or keying such a member in place and it will be apparent that every precaution has been taken to avoid any trouble from loose fastenings. In the chain drive type the sprocket-retaining flange is secured to the brake drum by the same process.

The pedal-chain sprocket is attached to a rotatable member supported on an adjustable ball bearing, and at the inner end the member is provided with a spiral thread. This male thread fits into a corresponding female portion in the laterally shiftable member, and the angle of the thread is such that when the pedal sprocket is rotated forward, the spiral draws the shiftable member against the tapering female clutch member forming part of the hub shell. The clutching action connects the sprocket to the hub and rotates it. If the pedals are held from moving, the clutch releases automatically, and the hub shell can run independently of the foot pedal mechanism. If the foot action is reversed, or the pedal sprocket rotated backward, the female clutch member in the inner portion of the laterally shiftable connector will be forced tightly against the male taper of the brake cam-lever actuator, which can oscillate on the axle only in the direction necessary to apply the brake.

If one refers to sketch of brake end at Fig. 257, it will be seen that the oscillating motion of the actuator transmits a similar motion to the end of the lever of which the brake-shoe spreader cam forms a part. Any displacement of the cam will spread the brake shoes apart, and they will fulcrum on the supporting pin secured to the brake end plate. The brake shoes then take up the clearance existing between their outer surface and the inner surface of the drum, and exert a retarding effect in proportion to the amount of pressure applied by back pedaling.

As soon as the back pedaling pressure is released, the springs serve to bring the brake shoes out of engagement immediately. The upper one holds the brake shoes firmly against the cam, the lower one returns the cam lever back against its stop and also brings the oscillating actuator back in position ready for further brake application when the laterally shiftable member clutches it.

The brake shoes and spreader cam are carried by a drop forged steel plate which has an arm formed integrally that is intended to be

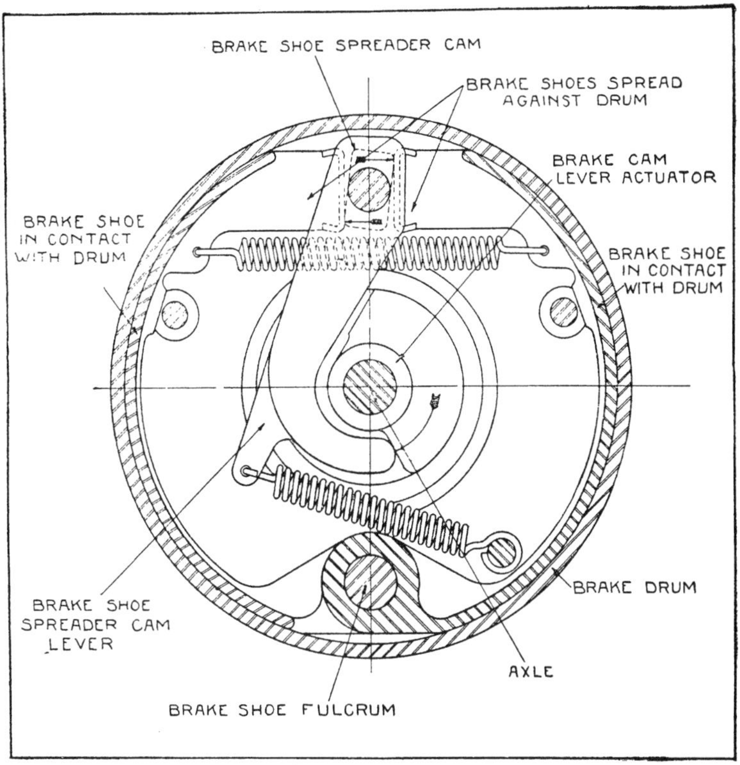

Fig. 257.—Showing Method of Brake Shoe Actuation by Cam Action in Internal Expanding Brake.

attached to the frame members and serve as an anchorage to prevent brake shoe rotation.

How Rider's Effort is Multiplied.—A diagram is presented at Fig. 258 for the benefit of those mechanically disposed, which demonstrates clearly how the pressure of the rider's foot on the pedal is multiplied, and how much pressure is available between brake shoes and drum to stop the wheel. This shows the effectiveness and correct design of the internal brake, and how positive control is obtained with but little effort.

In this case, we have assumed that the total weight of a heavy motorcycle, tandem attachment and two heavy riders is 600 pounds.

The amount of braking force required at wheel rim is equal to 36 per cent of the total weight, or 216 pounds, which represents the adhesion between tire and ground. This is not an extreme case, as the modern motorcycle and two large riders would easily weigh 600 pounds, and a brake must be designed with the abnormal service it may be subjected to in mind rather than the average if it is to be relied on to cope with the unexpected emergency.

Almost any rider can exert a back pedal pressure of 100 pounds. This is applied at the end of a 6-inch pedal crank, and if the front sprocket is 5.4 inches in diameter, a pull of 222 pounds is applied to the chain. This is directed to a sprocket having a radius of 2.2 inches, which is equivalent to a moment of 488-inch pounds at 1 inch from axle center. Owing to the point where the spreader-cam lever end bears against the brake shoes being less than 1 inch from axle center, we have an effective force of 601 pounds at the end of the lever. The difference in length between lever and spreader cam further compounds the pressure, and if we consider all the load concentrated against one brake shoe for simplicity, we find that we have an effective spreading force of 3,606 pounds at the end of the brake shoe. The brake shoe is really a curved lever, so at a point halfway between where the cam bears and the fulcrum pin, we find that it is possible to exert a pressure of 7,165 pounds. All of this is not available for braking, however, because if we consider the coefficient of friction, we will have an effective retarding force of 1,075 pounds at the brake drum, and this, in turn, is equivalent to a retarding force of 230 pounds at contact point of wheel tire and road surface, which is at 14 inches radius, or considerably more than is needed to skid the wheel. If a rider is alone, a back pedaling pressure of about 50 pounds would suffice to lock the wheel. It will be apparent that positive control with minimum exertion on part of the rider is possible, because the initial force is compounded many times by the simple and strong leverage provided. Obviously, the brake force can be varied at will and is entirely within the control of the rider.

Motorcycle Tires.—The single tube tires used on bicycles did not have sufficient resistance to perform satisfactorily on motorcycles, and also had the grave disadvantage of being difficult to repair. The double tube tire which was used to some extent in bicycle practice

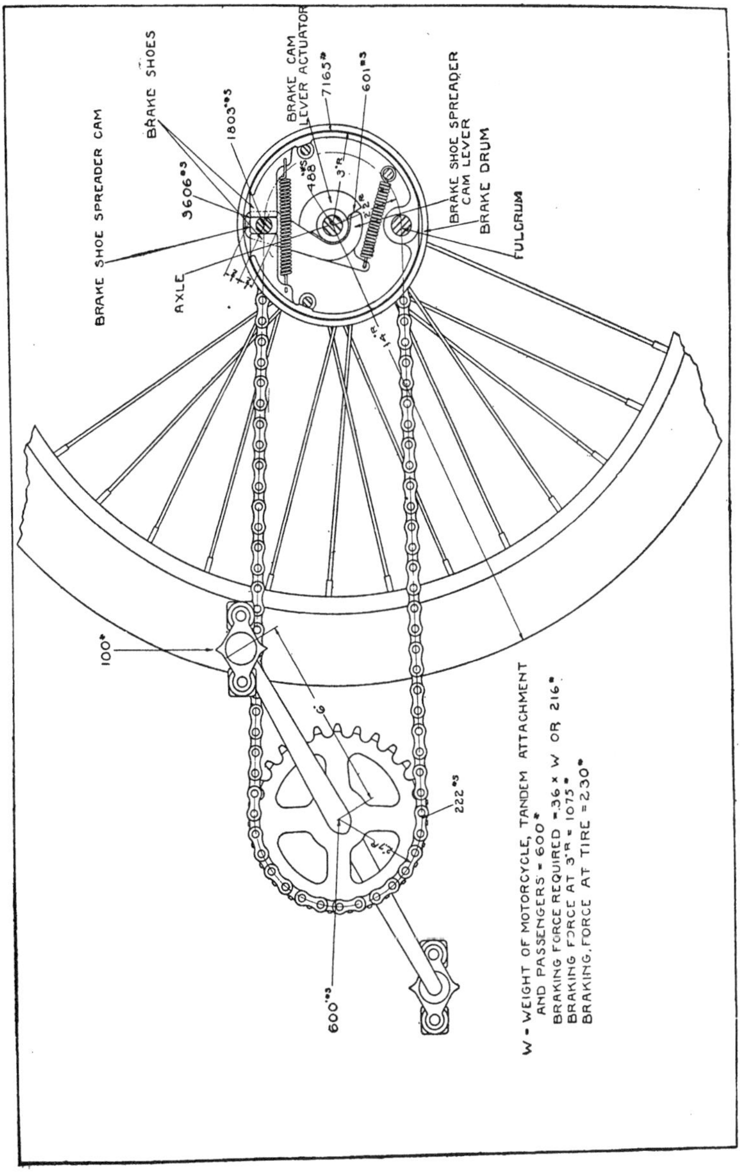

Fig. 258.—Diagram Showing How the Rider's Effort is Multiplied in Obtaining Effective Braking With Cam Actuated Internal Shoe Brake.

was strengthened and made larger, and adapted for the heavier vehicle. This construction consists essentially of two members, an outer casing or shoe, and an inner tube that is depended on to retain the air. The outer casing is attached to the rim in such a way that it may be easily removed to gain access to the inner tube. In event of a small puncture, the patch is applied to the inner tube member, and the outer casing need not receive attention until a more convenient time. A typical outer casing is shown at Fig. 259, A, and it consists essentially of a carcass or body composed of layers of Sea Island cotton fabric impregnated with rubber. A number of plies of this fabric are

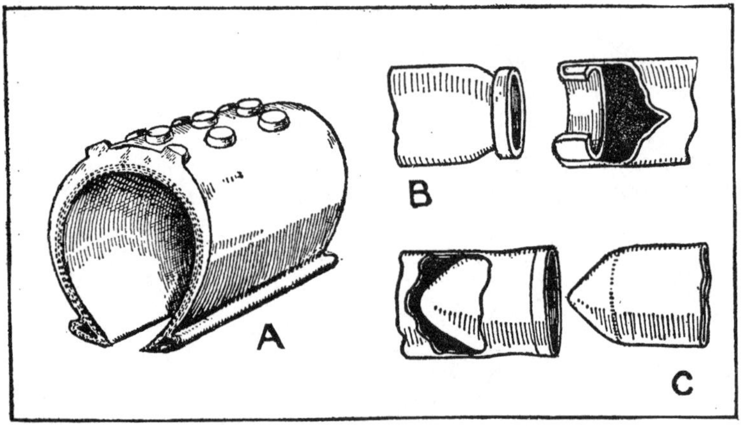

Fig. 259.—Construction of Motorcycle Tire Outer Casing and Inner Tube.

placed around a suitable iron core with vulcanizing cement between each layer, and over these are attached a number of layers of rubber composition that forms the tread of the tires. After being built up, the assembly is placed in a steam heater and vulcanized or cured until it is practically a solid mass. The casing is provided with beads around the inside which are intended to fit into channels in the rim. When the inner tubes are inflated, the beads will be forced tightly into the clincher rim and the tire will be held positively in place. To remove the outer casing, it is necessary to deflate the tire.

The outer or tread portion, which is the part of the tire that is in contact with the road surface, is made of exceptionally tough rubber compound which is not apt to depreciate rapidly. The inner tube, upon which the resiliency of the tire depends, is composed of practically pure rubber, and is therefore adapted for holding air, though the material of which it is composed is too soft to possess any strength or resistance to abrasion, which must be provided by the outer casings. Inner tubes are made in two forms, the continuous or one-piece type, which is the same as that so generally used on automobiles, and the jointed or butt end form as shown at Fig. 259, B and C. In the former, the joint is made by slipping one end of the tube into the other, and when the tube is inflated the collar member will be forced out tightly against the inner face of the retaining member on the other end, and an air-tight joint will be obtained. In the form shown at C, the inner tube is a closed end form, and has a tapering end that is intended to fit into a corresponding female member at the other. The advantage of the jointed inner tube is that it may be removed from the wheel without taking that member out of the frame which obviously is not possible with a one-piece inner tube. The form shown at B, however, is apt to leak to some extent, and if the jointed inner tube is used, the form shown at C is preferred. The ends of the tube in contact are also apt to chafe and leak.

Side Car Advantages.—While the tandem attachment is an inexpensive solution of the passenger-carrying problem, it is not the most satisfactory because it is not a really practical means of carrying an elderly person or one of the fair sex. The occupant of the tandem attachment may throw a machine out of balance by moving around, and may seriously interfere with the proper control of the machine by the rider, unless very careful and experienced. Then again, it is difficult to carry on a conversation between the motorcycle rider and the tandem passenger, so this device is not as sociable as the side car.

The side car is a simple one-wheel framework that may be readily clamped to the motorcycle, and which carries a seat of comfortable proportions that will provide thorough protection for the passenger. When a side car is used, it is imperative to employ a machine of ample power, and it is necessary to use a two-speed gear to secure proper results when touring. A typical side car attached to a motorcycle is shown at Fig. 260, and it will be apparent that the three-wheel vehicle thus provided is much more sociable than the tandem attachment, and also much more comfortable for the passenger. Owing to the three-point support, neither the rider nor the passenger need concern themselves with maintaining balance, as it is impossible for the machine to tip over. It costs but very little more to use the side car than it does to ride the machine without this attachment. An important advantage of the side car construction is that this member may be readily removed at such times that the motorcycle alone is to be used.

Fig. 260.—Application of Sidecar to Indian Motorcycle.

Forms of Side Car.—There are two main types of side cars, the rigid and the caster wheel, both forms being shown at Fig. 261. In the rigid wheel type at the top of the illustration, the outboard supporting member revolves on a fixed axle and is capable of only a rotary movement. In the caster wheel form below it, the outboard supporting member is carried in a fork supported by a ball bearing steering head so the wheel may turn automatically in the same

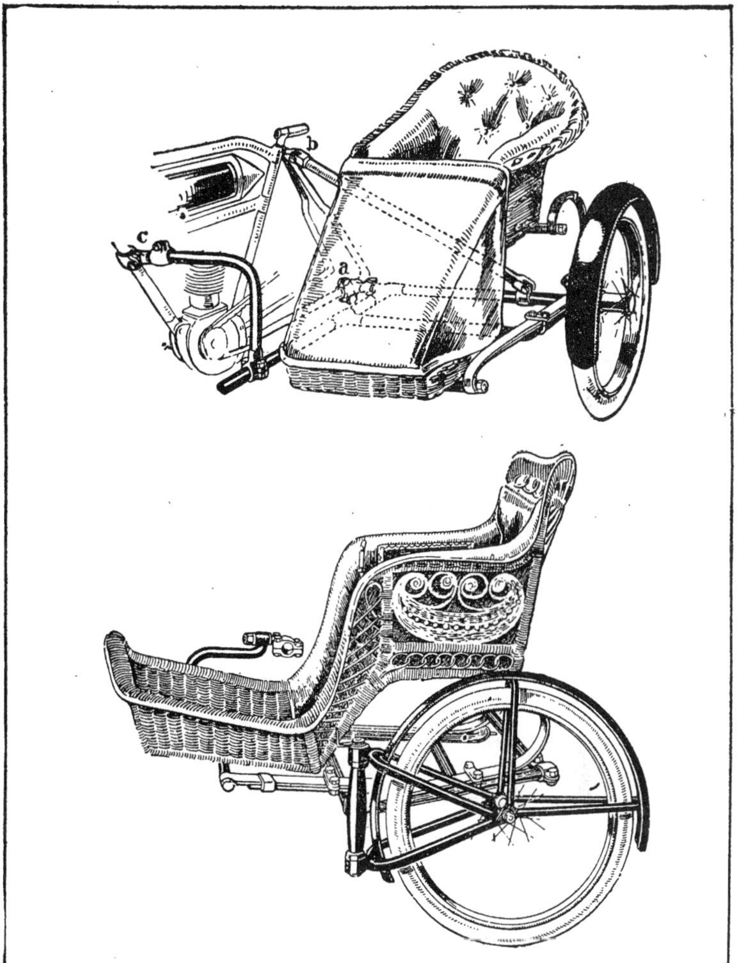

Fig 261.—Examples of Rigid and Castor Wheel Side Cars.

direction as the front wheel of the motorcycle. Experienced users of side cars are inclined to favor the rigid type, as it is claimed it is simpler, and if properly alined with the motorcycle frame there will be but little more wear on the tire than is evidenced in the caster wheel type. The form with the movable wheel is easier to steer however, owing to the wheel automatically assuming the angle required to describe the curve made when turning corners. A side car of American design which has attracted some attention on account of the novel construction is shown at Fig. 262. This is a flexible form in which it is possible for the rider of the motorcycle to lean when turning corners just as though the side car was not fitted to the motorcycle. The wheel of the side car is carried on an axle spindle supported by a hinged member from which the lever B extends. This is joined with lever A on the other end of the axle by a rod passing through the hollow tube forming the rear frame member. Any in-

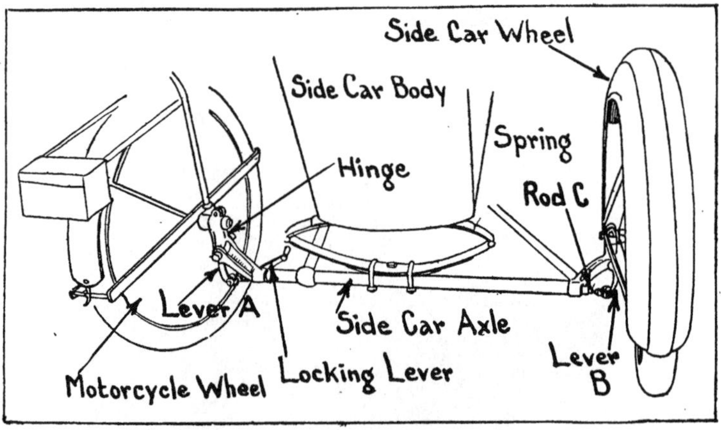

Fig. 262.—Flexible Side Car of American Design.

clination of the motorcycle wheel will produce a corresponding movement of the side car wheel, as lever A controlled by the motorcycle will transmit its motion to lever B that controls the side car wheel. A locking lever is provided so the wheels will remain vertical, and the same effect obtain as with the rigid type side car, if desired. It is claimed that the flexible feature makes the machine easier to steer than the usual rigid type. The side car frame may be fitted with a variety of bodies depending upon the preference of the purchaser, ranging from the simple chair form, shown at Figs. 261 and 263, to the more expensive coach-built body designs, such as shown at Fig. 260.

Side Car Attachment.—The chassis of a typical side car with the body removed is shown at Fig. 264 to outline the method of attachment ordinarily followed. Clamps are provided on the motorcycle frame at two points, one at the front end of the diagonal tube, just below the frame cross bar, and one on the rear fork stay, just a little ahead of the motorcycle rear wheel axle. The front end of the side car chassis is carried by a curved tube extending from the clamp on the frame tube to a similar clamping member at the front end of the side car. A yoke at the end of the side car axle attaches to the clamp at the rear end of the motorcycle, and a cross bar or brace

Fig. 263.—Inexpensive Form of Side Car.

extends from the seat post cluster of the motorcycle to a point on the axle of the side car adjacent to the supporting wheel. When the clamps are firmly secured a very stiff and rigid frame structure is obtained, and the motorcycle and its side car attachment are practically one structure.

Considerable care is needed in fitting a side car, because difficulty will be experienced in steering if the wheel of the motorcycle and that of the side car are not in proper alinement. This means that not only the wheel centers must coincide but that the front end of the side car wheel must be separated from a similar point on the motorcycle wheel by exactly the same amount of space as obtains at the rear end. In other words, the side car wheel must be parallel to the motorcycle wheel and a line drawn through the axle centers of both wheels must also coincide. The method of lining up a side car with a straight edge is shown at Fig. 265, A. If the wheel of a side car is set ahead of that of the motorcycle or if it is not parallel, steering will be very difficult because the wheel will not roll around on an arc of a circle but will move with a combined rolling and sliding motion as indicated by the dotted lines at Fig. 265, B.

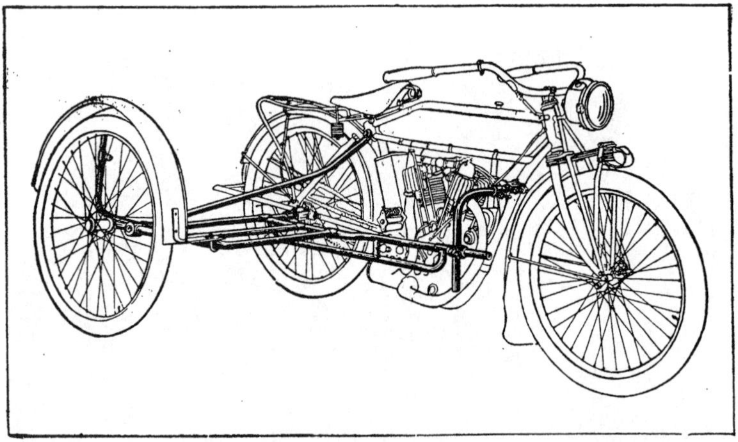

Fig. 264.—Typical Side Car Chassis With Body Removed, Showing Method of Attaching to Standard Motorcycle.

The diagrams presented at C will show a method of side car operation recommended by an English authority in order to secure easier steering. Even if the side car is perfectly lined up, some difficulty may be experienced in steering, though after a rider becomes proficient, it will not be a difficult matter to control the side car combination satisfactorily.

Methods of Starting Motorcycles.—The writer will now describe the common methods of starting motorcycles equipped with two-speed gear, as the accepted method of setting the power plant in motion in a single-geared machine by means of the pedals is generally understood at this time. The starting crank is a satisfactory means, if a multiple-cylinder engine is used and the crank can be applied to the driving gearing in such a way that the engine will be rotated faster than the starting handle. The starting arrangement used on the Henderson motorcycle, and illustrated at Fig. 266, is a distinctive design, because the handle may be folded out of the way after the engine is started. At A, the crank is shown extended for starting the motor, while at B the crank handle is shown in place in the clip

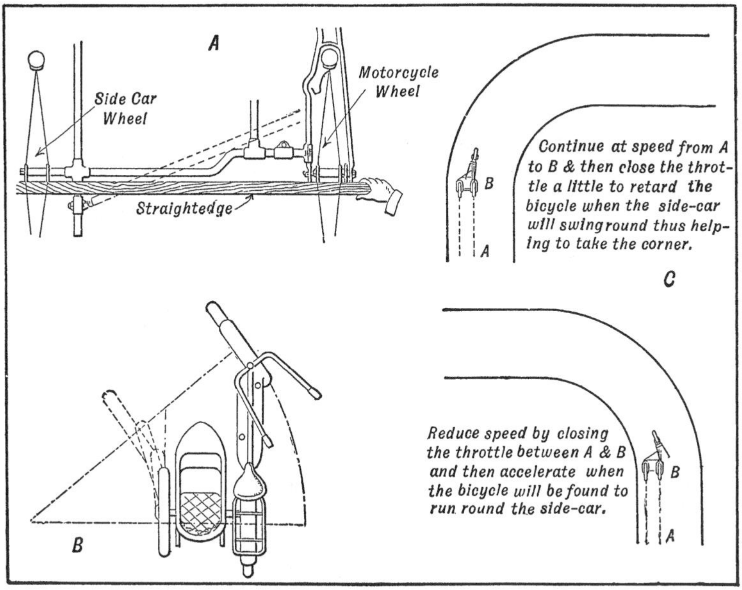

Fig. 265.—Diagram Showing Method of Attaching Side Car and of Controlling Motorcycle and Side Car Combination.

attached to the frame that holds it out of the way when the machine is in use.

A large and near view of the Indian kick starter, which is a thoroughly practical and simple device, is shown at Fig. 267. A large sprocket is mounted on a suitable bearing, and is adapted to be oscillated by a starter pedal carrying a suitable pad member against which foot pressure may be exerted. The large sprocket is joined to a much smaller starting sprocket that connects with the engine shaft when the pedal is pushed forward and which turns the interior mechanism of the engine fast enough to set the power plant in motion. It is said that the Indian was the first American motorcycle to depart from the conventional pedaling starting system and to introduce the foot starter. A forward thrust of the pedal crank engages the ratchet drive that connects the small starting sprocket to the engine shaft and at the end of the stroke the mechanism releases automatically, and permits the crank to return to its normal position. An automatic mechanism provides positive disconnection from the engine

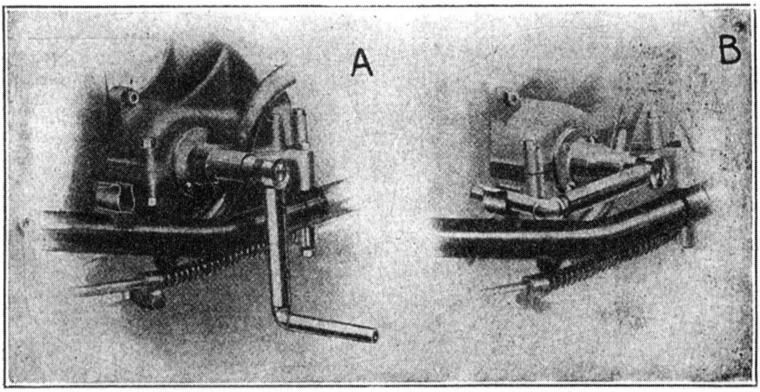

Fig. 266.—Folding Starting Crank Used on Henderson Four Cylinder Motorcycle.

should a back fire occur. The foot rest on the starting crank is hinged and can be folded out of the way when not in operation to allow unobstructed use of the foot board. With the foot starter, prompt starting is facilitated by priming the cylinders with gasoline, particularly when the motor is cold. This operation is made easy on the Indian machines by placing a small syringe or priming gun in the filler opening of the gasoline tank so a small amount of gasoline may be drawn out to fill the priming cups on the cylinders. It is said that when the engine has become heated it will be easily started without priming by one or two forward thrusts of the foot.

The step-starter used on the Harley-Davidson motorcycle is shown in some detail at Fig. 268. The arrangement is such that a pair of pedals are provided just as in the usual construction, though no chain extends from the pedal crank hanger to the hub. Instead, the engine is rotated directly from the pedals through an ingenious ratchet and pawl arrangement. The pawl-carrier plate is securely attached to the pedal crankshaft, and when that member is rotated forward, the

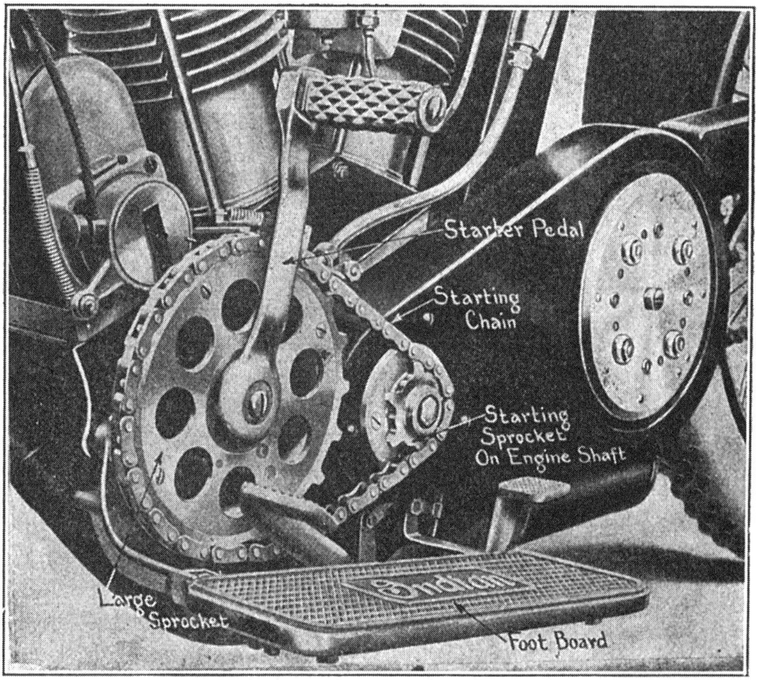

Fig. 267.—Outlining Construction of Indian Kick Starter Used on Two Speed Models.

pawls fly out and drop into suitable depressions in the ratchet ring which is attached to the first reduction sprocket, and which transmits the motion of the crank directly to the small sprocket on the engine shaft. The countershaft assembly includes a substantial ball-bearing carrying the member on which the first reduction sprocket and the rear wheel drive sprocket revolve. As soon as the engine is started,

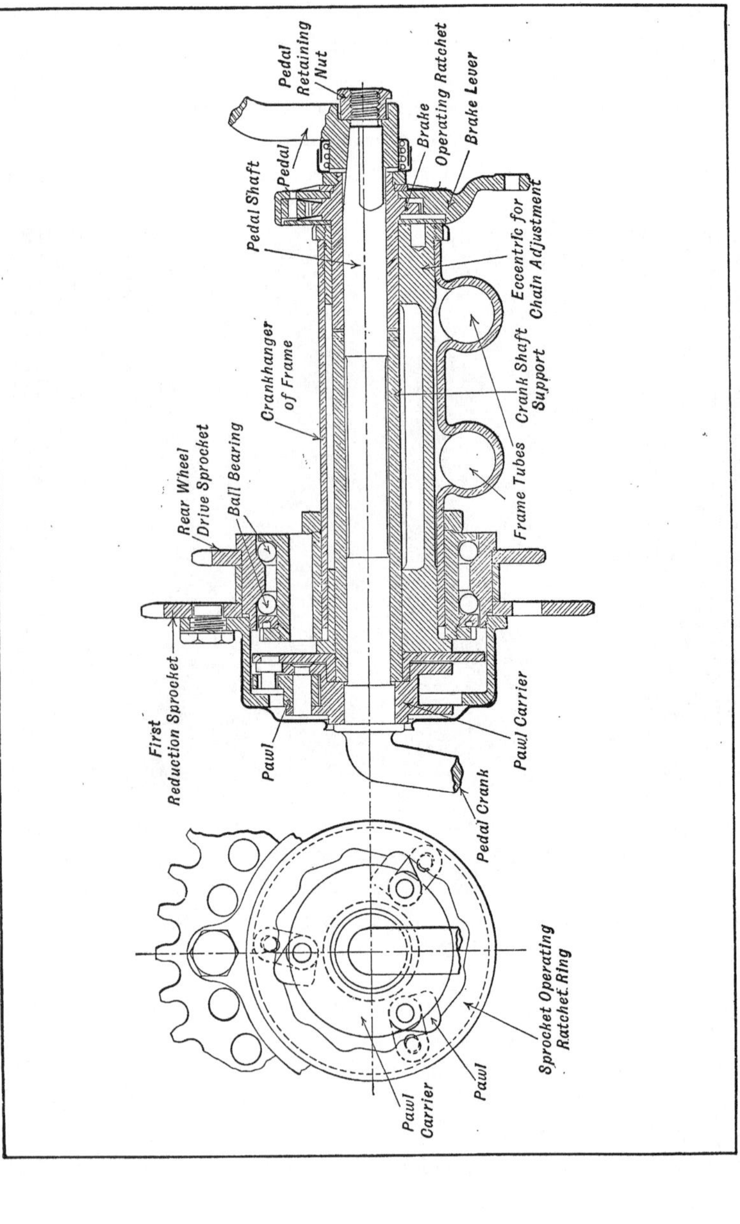

Fig. 268.—Sectional View Showing Construction of Harley-Davidson Kick Starter.

the pawls are released automatically and remain out of engagement as long as the ratchet revolves faster than the pawl-carrier plate. Another ingenious fitting is a ratchet which works only on back-pedaling carried at the other end of the countershaft which is used to operate the brake on the rear hub from the pedals when desired.

Electric Starting and Lighting Systems.—Electric lighting has long been recognized as an ideal illuminating system for motorcycles as well as motor cars, but it has been somewhat difficult to apply an electric lighting system successfully to rigid frame machines. The vibration encountered tended to rapid depreciation of the batteries, and if attempts were made to utilize current delivered directly from a small dynamo driven from the engine, other difficulties were encountered. Either the rider was experiencing continual trouble with the small round leather belts used in driving the generator or he was burning out a bulb, when the motor was suddenly accelerated and the generator produced an excess amount of current. If the motor was run slowly, the generator would not deliver enough current and the lights would burn dimly. In some models of the Indian motorcycle, two sets of batteries are furnished and are separately connected to the light. With reasonable precaution, the rider should never be without current for lights and electric horn operation. In the machines without the electric starter attachment when the lights become dim, the battery in service is cut out and the fresh battery carried in reserve is connected to the circuit. The batteries do not depreciate from vibration on account of being carried by the spring frame which insulates them from road shocks. A patented safety vent is used which permits the escape of gas from the battery interior, but which absolutely prevents the leakage of any of the electrolyte. Therefore, in passing over rough roads, or if a machine upsets in a fall, there is no weakening of the batteries by loss of liquid.

The Hendee special model, which is clearly the highest developed form of motorcycle ever offered, inasmuch as it not only incorporates full equipment including the various necessary accessories but also has a two-speed gear and electric self-starter, is shown at Fig. 269. On this model, the batteries are so connected that both of them discharge into the electric starting motor to secure the highest amperage for turning the engine over as fast as possible. It is said that it is

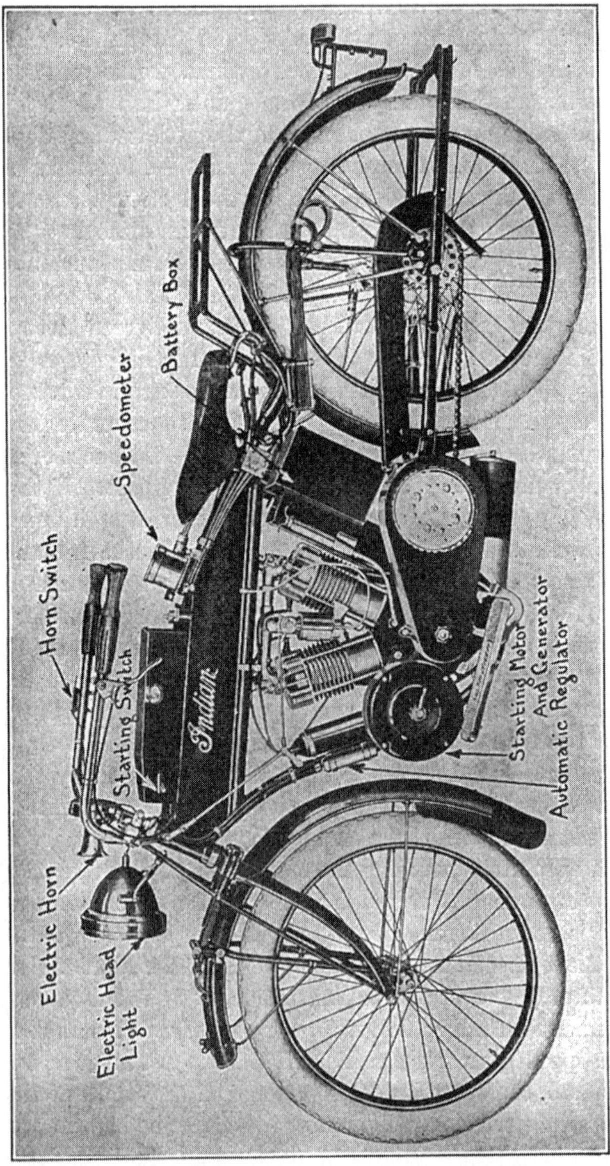

Fig. 269.—The Hendee Special Motorcycle With Electric Motor Starting Attachment.

possible to crank the engine over at the rate of 500 revolutions per minute, which is faster than any automobile starter. The nominal rating of the combined electric starter and generator is 1.5 horsepower, but the power actually developed is influenced by the energy necessary to start the engine. The starter has a high over-load capacity, and just as soon as the engine begins firing, the starter automatically becomes a generator and delivers a current that charges

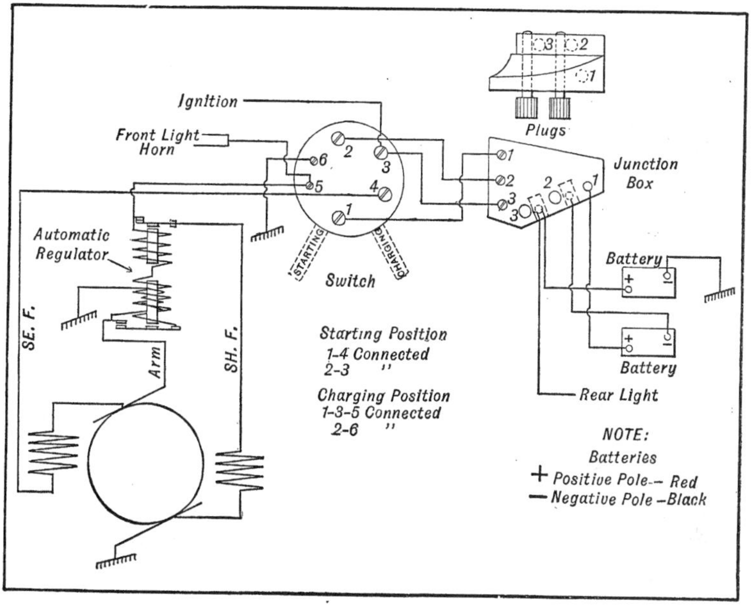

Fig. 270.—Wiring Diagram Showing Connections and Circuits for Electric Starting and Lighting System of Hendee Special Motorcycle.

the storage battery. The generator is always running while the engine is in operation, and an automatic regulator is included in the system so that when the batteries are fully charged the surplus electricity generated is dissipated. The current consumption of the lighting system is approximately two amperes. When the batteries are connected in multiple a current of 6 volts and 70 amperes is available, and when joined in series a current of 12 volts and 35 amperes is available for starting. The batteries are charged at a road speed of 12 miles per hour on the high gear, and the maximum charging current flows to the batteries when the machine is operated at 16 miles per hour.

As shown at Fig. 271, the electric starter is attached to the engine crankshaft by a roller chain, and is geared approximately 2 to 1. It is said that under ordinary operating conditions, it will start a cold motor in 12 or 15 seconds. When a motor is warm but 3 to 5 seconds

Fig. 271.—Showing Method of Driving Combined Motor-Generator of Hendee Special by Roller Chain From Engine Crankshaft.

will be necessary to start it. As the generator is constantly charging the batteries while the engine is running, the possibility of the cells becoming discharged is very slight. The current for ignition is derived from the batteries instead of from the usual high tension magneto, and as the batteries are kept fully charged, the main objection advanced against battery ignition, that of irregular and uncertain current supply, does not apply in this case. A wiring diagram showing the connections of the system is presented at Fig. 270.

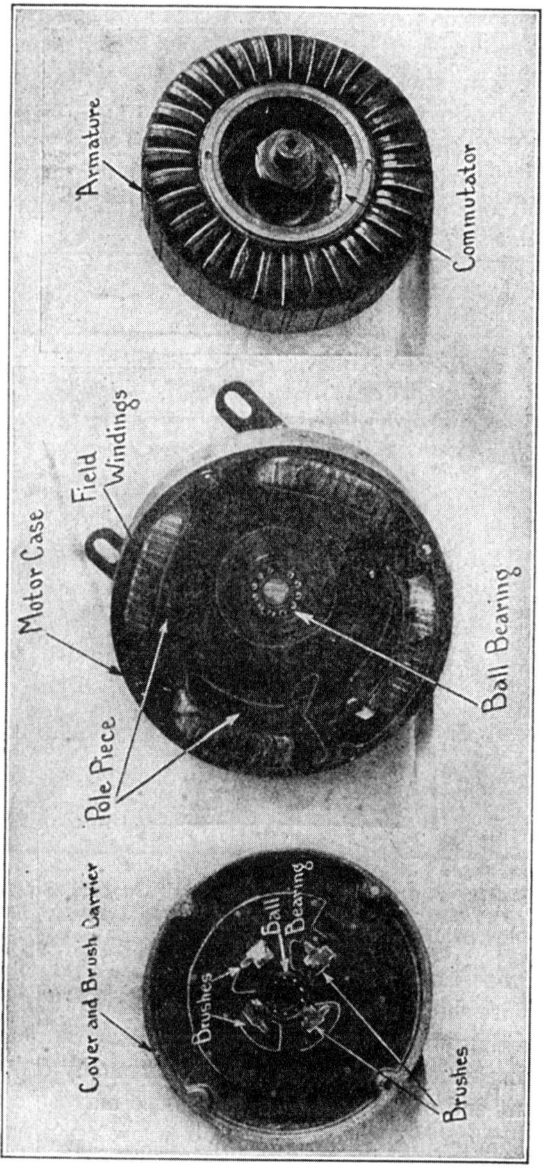

Fig. 272.—Parts of Combined Motor-Generator Used on Hendee Special Motorcycle.

The combination motor-generator used in connection with this system has been designed especially for the work, and as may be readily ascertained from the views at Fig. 272 it is a very compact and effective piece of electrical apparatus. In order to keep the device to the proper width, an internal commutator is used which is carried inside of the armature member. The brushes are supported by the cover plate, and project into the interior of the armature to make

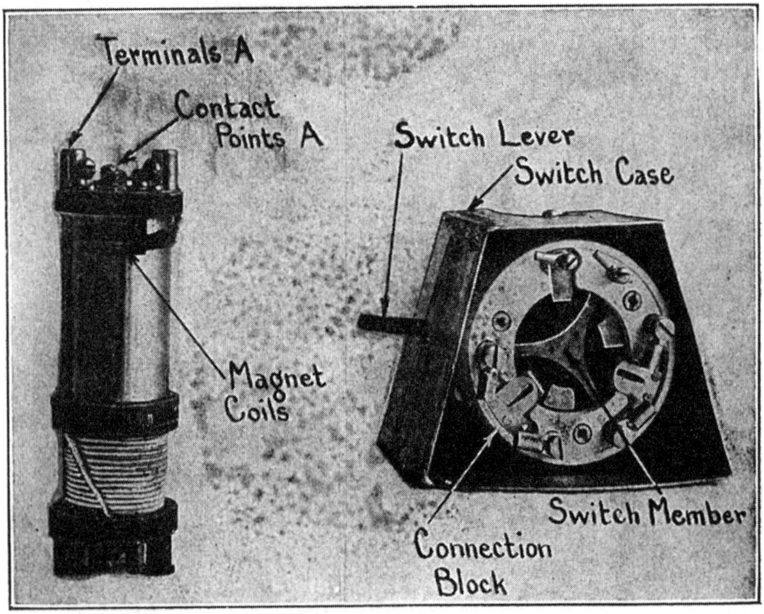

Fig. 273.—The Automatic Regulator and Control Switch Used in Connection With the Indian Electric Starting System.

suitable connections with the commutator segments placed therein. The armature shaft revolves on single row annular ball-bearings, and the device thus works with minimum friction. By a simple change of the wiring which is accomplished by a manually controlled switch at the front end of the tool box, the device may be converted into either a dynamo or a motor. The automatic regulator and switch member used in connection with the system are shown at Fig. 273.

When the switch is placed in the starting position, the circuits are arranged so that current is drawn from the batteries and directed to the starting motor fields. When the switch handle is moved back for the running position, the circuits are altered so that the current delivered from the generator armature is supplied to the batteries, first passing through the automatic regulator, which operates on a magnetic principle so that current is being supplied to the batteries only when it is of proper value for charging those members. As soon as the engine stops rotating, if the switch is left in the charging position, the automatic regulator will break contact and prevent the batteries discharging back through the windings of the motor-dynamo. The automatic regulator also functions and disconnects the windings from the batteries at such time that more than the charging current is delivered. The low current release portion of the automatic regulator also serves to break the circuit, when the power plant is running at rates of speed that would produce less than the proper amount of current for charging.

Motorcycle Control Methods.—When the motorcycle was first evolved, there was no attempt made to have the control arranged in a convenient manner, as the various levers by which the motor speed was varied were placed at any point on the frame that proved convenient for the designer in attaching regardless whether it was the best position for the person who would operate the machine. At the present time, every effort is made to locate the important and frequently manipulated control members where they can be easily reached, and very often the arrangement is such that the rider may have complete mastery of the machine without removing the hand from the handle bars. The control of American motorcycles is considerably simpler than that generally provided on the foreign mounts, as the common practice in this country is to regulate the motor speed through the medium of twisting grips. Of course, when a two-speed gear is used, an auxiliary control member is placed convenient to the rider to regulate the gear ratio desired, and on some machines still another lever is used to control the free engine clutch. Several of the American motorcycles employ grip control of the free engine clutch, prominent among which may be mentioned the Schickel, Excelsior and Eagle machines. For use in traffic, or operating under conditions that necessitate frequent use of the clutch, it is apparent that the most convenient method is by the grip because this does not require the rider to take his hands from the handle bars which insures positive control at a time that it is most needed. The free engine clutch is regulated on some machines through the medium of a pedal, and this control is very satisfactory on machines equipped with running boards to support the rider's feet and where the usual form of pedaling gear is dispensed with.

The first of the American manufacturers to utilize grip control, to

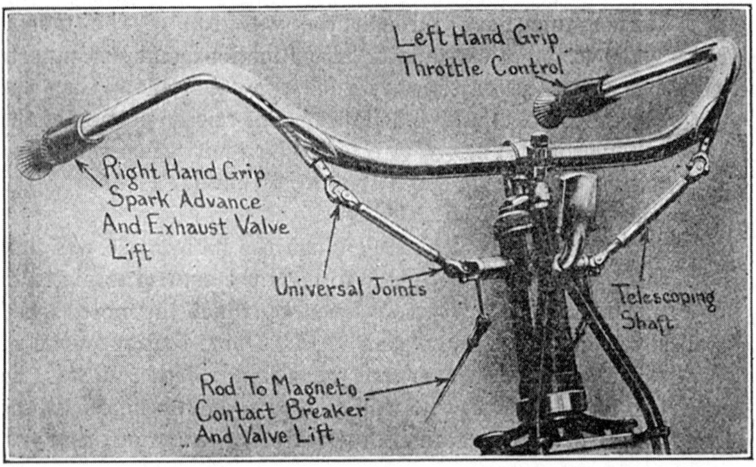

Fig. 274.—Handlebars of Indian Motorcycle, Showing Method of Motor Control by Twisting Grips.

regulate engine speed, were the makers of the Indian motorcycle, and this method was incorporated in even the earliest models of these machines. The method of regulating the motor speed and the construction of the universal joints and rods used in connection with practically all Indian models is shown at Fig. 274. The right hand grip controls the spark advance and the exhaust valve lift. The valves are lifted to relieve the compression and to make it possible to turn the engine over easily for starting. The left hand grip is used to control the throttle. The twisting movement of the grips is transmitted by means of a flexible shaft running from the grip through the hollow tube comprising the handle bar to a bearing from which the end of the shaft projects. A universal joint attached to this shaft transmits its motion to a compound member consisting of one shaft telescoping into another, that is secured to the actuating lever attached to the steering head. The reason for using the telescope shaft arrangement is that it is necessary to have some flexible connection other than the universal joint to permit the handle bars to be turned when steering the machine.

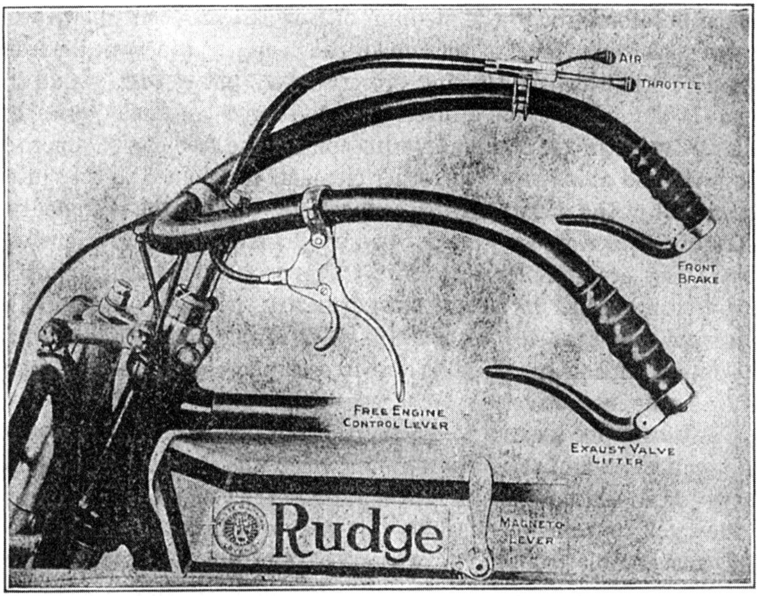

Fig. 275.—Control System of the Rudge Motorcycle, Typical of Foreign Practice.

If one compares this simple and direct control with that shown at Fig. 275, which is an illustration of a representative English construction, it will be apparent that the American design is considerably neater. Of course, on the single-speed Indian models it is necessary to have a lever to actuate the free engine clutch which is carried at the side of the machine and an auxiliary pedal is provided near the footboard to operate the hub brake. On the two-speed machines, a lever is provided to shift the positive change speed clutch and a foot-controlled member supplied to release the master or free engine clutch. In addition to the control members shown at Fig. 275, there is another lever which is not illustrated, provided to operate the variable speed pulley. The control of the ignition is by a small lever at the side of the tank connected with the magneto contact breaker.

The speed of the motor is controlled by the magneto lever and by the air and throttle levers mounted on the handle bars and connected to the carburetor through the medium of Bowden wire control. At the end of each grip, a lever is fulcrumed, one being used to work the front wheel brake, which is a fitting prescribed by law abroad, while the other is the exhaust valve lifter. On the same bar that carries the exhaust valve lifter, a hand lever to control the free engine clutch is mounted and as is true of the other elements it is joined to the clutch member by the flexible wire connection. From the handle bar assembly shown, five of the Bowden wires extend to the various elements they are intended to control. One goes to the air slide of the carburetor, another to the throttle regulating the supply of gas. The third member goes to the exhaust valve-lifting arrangement, while the fourth and fifth extend to the free engine clutch and the front wheel brake respectively.

Bowden Wire Control.—While the Bowden wire control is used on practically all of the foreign motorcycles, and is employed to some extent on American machines as well, there is a general lack of understanding of its principle of action on the part of the American rider, and considerable trouble is experienced from time to time in fitting up or making repairs to this system. The Bowden wire mechanism consists mainly of two parts, one which, termed "the outer member," is a closely coiled and practically incompressible spiral spring while the "inner member" is an inextensible wire cable passing through the outer member which acts as a casing. The usual mechanical method of transmitting power in other than a straight line in this country is by means of universal joints, small bell crank levers and suitable connecting rods. The Bowden wire mechanism is considerably simpler and is easily fitted. The principal requirement is that the outer member or casing shall be anchored to a stop at each end, while the inner member is attached to an operating lever at one end and to the object to be moved at the other.

A diagram showing the method of operation is shown at Fig. 276, and the reader should have no difficulty in understanding the action of this control system. A line of Bowden wire mechanism sufficient to reach from the point where the object is to be moved to the point where the necessary power is to be applied is represented by D D D. The outer cable of the mechanism is passed around any intervening corners or obstacles. At C C the inner member of the mechanism will be seen emerging from the outer case being attached at one end

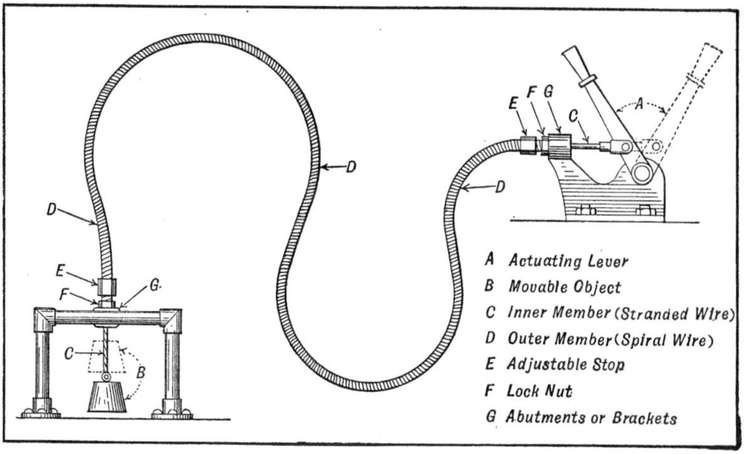

Fig. 276.—Diagram Explaining Action of Bowden Wire Mechanism.

of the actuating lever A and at the other to the object to be moved B. The outer member is anchored to fixed abutments G G. If the lever A is moved, the motion is at once imparted to the other end. When being actuated, the mechanism will exhibit a wriggling movement at the curves because the inner member attempts to reach the straight line of pull, but is resisted by the outer casing which cannot shorten its length inasmuch as it is anchored at both ends. The movement should not be restrained, as the mechanism functions best when the curves are free. The dotted lines show the lever A in its actuated position, and the weight B, or object to be moved, correspondingly raised. E E are adjustable screws or stops, the screwing out of which is equivalent to lengthening the outer member, and are held in position by the lock nuts F F.

Various examples of the levers used in connection with Bowden wire mechanism are shown at Fig. 277. The hand lever with ratchet retaining lever shown at A is widely used for clutch actuation, brake application and lifting the exhaust valves. The assembly shown at B consists of two levers carried above the clamp, and a lifting lever below it. One of the upper members may be used to control the spark

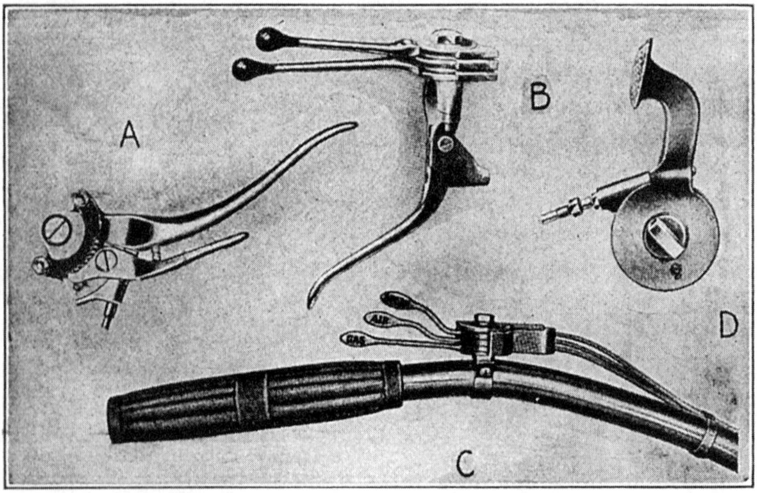

Fig. 277.—Showing Various Forms of Levers Used in Connection With Bowden Wire Mechanism.

time and the other connected to the throttle, or both may be used to regulate the carburetor. The handle at the lower part of the assembly may be connected to brake, clutch, or exhaust valve release. A group of three control levers, each being plainly marked to show the functions performed, designed for handle bar attachment is shown at C. The pedal at D is adapted for brake actuation.

The Bowden wire control is also sold in connection with complete control devices, two popular fittings being outlined at Fig. 278. At A a front wheel brake assembly is shown. The contact blocks which bear against the wheel rim are carried by a U-shaped member that is held at its lower portion by clips attached to the fork sides. The upper portion may be guided by any suitable bracket and is connected with a hand lever intended to be attached to the handle bar by a length of the Bowden wire mechanism. An auxiliary air fitting and suitable controlling means are shown at B, while the usual method of rigging up to a magneto contact breaker is shown at C.

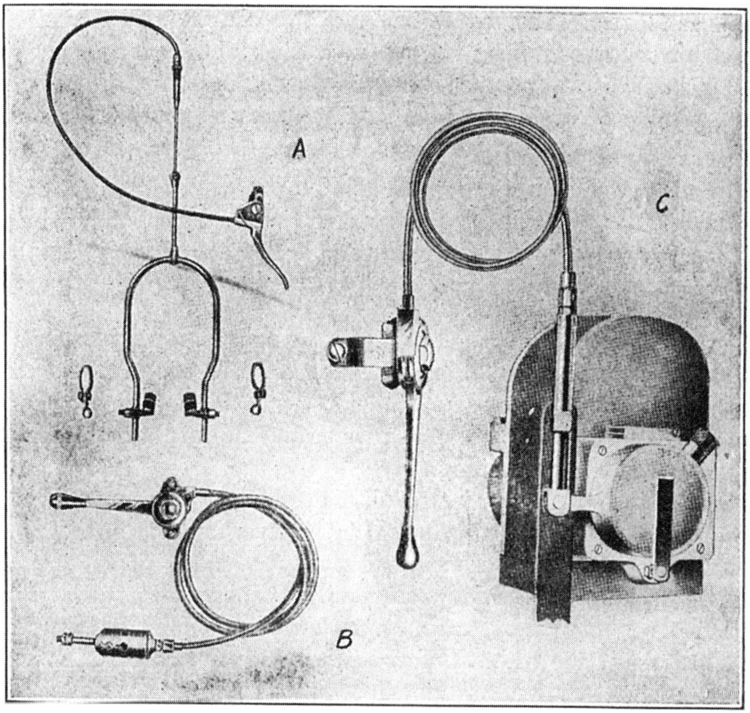

Fig. 278.—Showing Practical Application of Bowden Wire Mechanism for Controlling Front Wheel Brake, Auxiliary Air Intake and Magneto.

The following hints on fitting the Bowden wire mechanism, given by the makers, will undoubtedly be found of value by riders and repair men who are not thoroughly familiar with the application or maintenance of this system of control.

It is important that the inner member of the mechanism should be soldered before it is cut, as it is composed of a number of fine strands which are liable to become untwisted unless this precaution is taken. With the smaller sizes, up to No. 3, a pair of pliers or a spoke-cutting machine will suffice for cutting, but larger sizes will require a file or cold chisel to sever the strands.

The brass nipple supplied for the purpose should be carefully attached to the end of the inner member. A good method of effecting this is as follows: The wire, after being soldered and cut, should be passed through the nipple, the end then being nipped flat for about 1/16 inch. This will prevent it drawing out again during the process of soldering the wire and nipple together, which should be done in combination with a non-corrosive soldering fluid (on no account should killed spirit be used), care being taken that the soldered joint extends the full length of the nipple. The nipple should then be held in the vise, and the wire burred over and finished off with a blob of solder. It will then be found impossible to remove the nipple by any fair means.

For the varieties of the mechanism known as Bowdensilver, Bowdenbrass, and Bowdenite, special metal caps are provided for encasing the ends. These serve the purpose of finishing the ends off neatly, and, in the case of Bowdensilver and Bowdenbrass, prevent the protecting cover uncoiling.

When a single-pull lever is used, it is necessary to have a spring at the opposite end of the wire to which the lever is fixed, in order to ensure prompt recovery. This spring may be made either to pull the inner member back through the outer member, after pressure has been relieved from the operating lever, or it may be inserted between the stop holding the outer member and the end of the inner member, in which case, of course, it will be in compression. In the latter case, it will generally be found that the simplest method of fixing is to fit the device up minus the spring, and to wind the spring on afterward, as one puts a key on a split ring. But when a double-pull lever is used, a spring is not necessary, as the separate mechanisms so balance each other that while the lever is pulling on in one direction it is pulling off in the other.

Care should be taken that the inner member, on leaving the stop in which the outer member terminates, should be kept in an absolutely straight line, as should it be otherwise, it will rub on the edge of the stop, and be gradually worn away in consequence.

The inner member should be thoroughly smeared with motor grease or vaseline before being passed through the outer member.

CHAPTER VII.

CONSTRUCTION, EQUIPMENT AND OPERATION OF MODERN MOTORCYCLES.

Features of 1920 Models—Harley-Davidson Sport Model—Indian Scout Model—Indian Scout Frame—Modern Motor Wheel Design—Motorcycle Equipment—Lighting Systems—How Acetylene Generator Works—Alarms, Tools and Supplies—Harley-Davidson Tool Outfit—Useful Spare Parts—Carrying Tools and Supplies—General Instructions—Learn to Control Motor Operating Motorcycles—Motor Control Rules—Handling Spark Lever—To Start Motor of 1920 Harley-Davidson Models—To Start the Motor in Cold Weather—Difficult Starting—Keep Your Eyes on the Road—To Start the Machine on the Road—Suggestions for Smooth, Quiet Starting—To Stop the Machine—To Use the Motor as a Brake—To Change Back to Lower Speeds—To Shift from High Gear to Intermediate—To Shift from Intermediate Gear Into Low—Instructions for Use of Hand Pump—Use of Muffler Cut-out—Simple Rules of the Road.

In Essentials, the motorcycles for 1920 do not differ radically in design from those of previous years but there has been considerable refinement of detail. The modern motorcycle is just as reliable as the automobile, they are better balanced than the old types and are more easily controlled. There is a tendency noted to the use of a unit power plant such as found in automobiles in which the engine, clutch and change speed gearing are combined in one, this making a very compact and cleanly assembly.

Pedals have been eliminated on all machines, their place being taken by running boards and a kick starter is used to start the engine. There are fewer makes of machines on the market, a number of manufacturers having discontinued production on account of the competition of the large producers.

There are only a few active makers left in the industry, the prominent ones being the makers of the Harley-Davidson, Indian,

Excelsior, Henderson, Reading Standard and Cleveland. The latter is a new comer that is deservedly popular and that has a number of good features, such as a worm gear reduction drive gear and a two-cycle, single cylinder engine. Roller bearings are used in practically all new engines and valve sizes have been increased, making for greater efficiency. The three speed gearset is widely used and several new models are doing away with the double chain

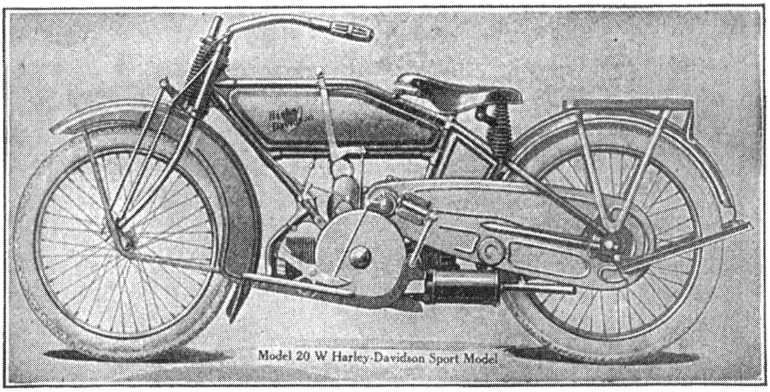

Fig. 279.—Harley-Davidson Sport Model.

drive and using a single chain from the unit power plant. The coaster brake is no longer used, its place being taken by a free wheel hub with pedal applied brake working on the hub brake drum. The coaster brake is found on only the early type machines.

The accompanying illustrations show the new type machines and complete instructions are given that will enable the motorcyclist to care for and operate the new models, especially those equipped with electric lighting systems. The operating principles of motors, clutches and change speed gearing have not been altered, so the subject matter relating to the old machines applies just as well to the operation of the new units.

Harley-Davidson Sport Model.—One of the new models that is attracting considerable attention is the Sport Model Harley-Davidson which is shown at Fig. 279. In addition to the usual features, this model has an unusual type of power plant as shown at Fig. 280.

The motor in the Harley-Davidson Sport Model is a balanced opposed four-cycle twin cylinder motor, with a 2¾″ bore and a 3″ stroke. This is a piston displacement of 35.64 cubic inches. Ex-

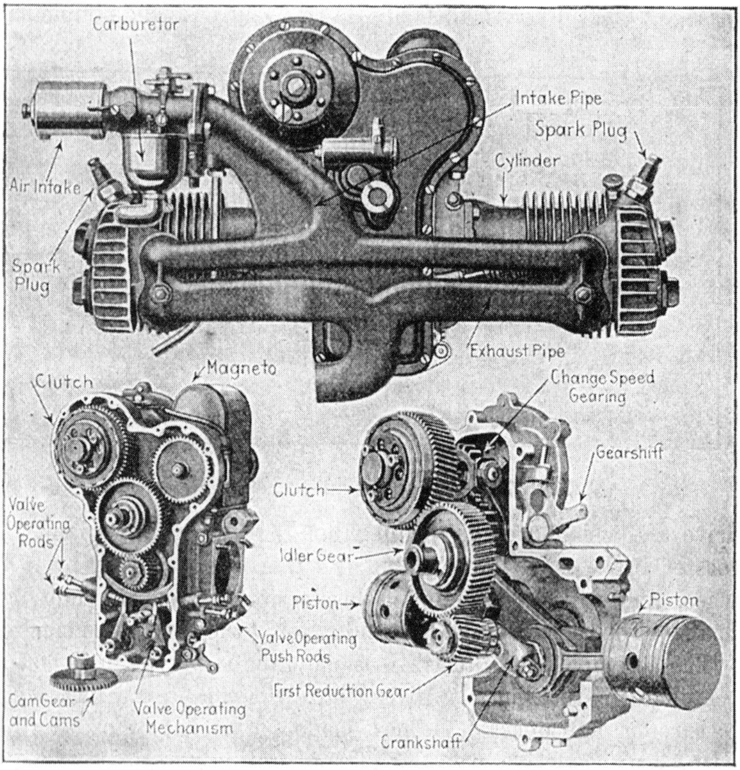

Fig. 280.—Details of Motor Used in Harley-Davidson Model 20 Sport Model.

pressed metrically, the bore is 69.84 millimeters, the stroke 76.20 millimeters, and the piston displacement 584.02 cubic centimeters. This motor is a high speed high efficiency motor conservatively rated at 6 horsepower, but developing considerably more by actual dynamometer test. The motor is roller bearing throughout, even to the crank pin bearings, which is an unusual construction, to say the least, for an opposed twin cylinder motor. The crank shaft is carefully balanced by means of large counterweights. The outside flywheel is built up of pressed steel discs, and is completely enclosed by a neat guard, so that water, sand or mud will not be thrown on to the rider's clothing.

Having in mind the low grade fuels sold under the guise of gasoline, Harley-Davidson engineers designed the new opposed twin motors so as to operate satisfactory on present day fuel. The twin-cast superheated manifold will, indeed, meet with the approval of experienced motorcycle riders.

This manifold is a single casting which serves for both the intake and exhaust passages. By means of a bi-pass from the exhaust pipe, that part of the intake pipe where condensation is most likely to occur, is heated to a temperature high enough to prevent manifold "loading."

A careful inspection of this rather ingeniously designed manifold discloses the fact that the use of this construction has eliminated all nipples, jam nuts, packing bushings and flanges which might cause trouble. A simple gasket insures a gas-tight joint where the manifold meets the cylinder casting proper. The carburetor is a standard 3/4″ Schebler, but it features a very unique attachment in the form of a neat, cylindrical dust baffle. This is an air filtering device which prevents road dust or sand from entering the carburetor air valve and reaching the inside of the motor.

Indian Scout Model.—Another interesting machine is the Indian Scout which is shown at Fig. 281 A and B. The motor is shown at Fig. 282 and the three speed transmission is clearly outlined in the sectional view given at Fig. 283. With motor, clutch and three-speed gear in one unit and all moving parts enclosed, the Indian Scout is remarkable for cleanliness and silence in operation. The mechanism is positively oil-tight, eliminating splash on rider and the machine itself. All gears and shafts run in oil and the valves are completely housed in, making for the utmost silence in operation. This oil-bathing of the working parts gives the maximum of life to the parts and guarantees the rider the longest possible service from the machine. Smooth surfaces on the unit powerplant, combined with its position above the lower framework of the motorcycle, further emphasize the factor of cleanliness.

In the Indian Scout, the L-head, one-piece cylinders with side-by-side valves having the Powerplus characterization of maximum

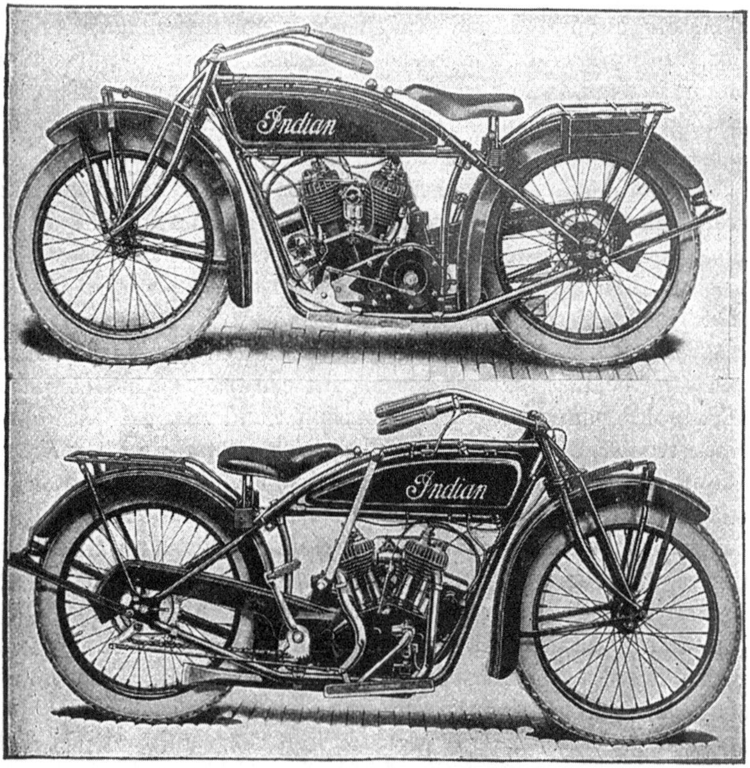

Figs. 281A and B.—Views of the Indian Scout Motorcycle.

power per cubic inch of piston displacement are used. The bore is 2¾ inches and the stroke 3$\frac{1}{16}$ inches, giving a piston displacement of 36.38 inches. Although rated at 5 horsepower, the Indian Scout motor develops over 11 horsepower on actual dynamometer tests, sustaining high power output for a remarkable period of time. This ensures the rider getting the best from his machine under all conditions; reduces gear shifting to a minimum and enables him to travel with speed and comfort where other motors would employ a lower gear.

The powerplant combines motor, clutch and transmission in a single compact unit, although any of these important members can be got at independently of the others. The power is transmitted to the clutch through spiral gears of great strength, running in

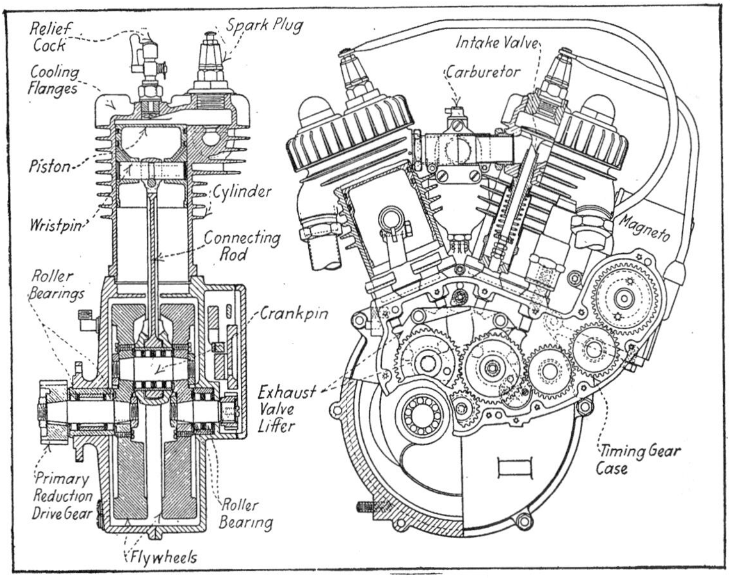

Fig. 282.—Motor of Indian Scout Motorcycle.

a separate oil bath. The clutch is mounted on the main shaft of the transmission and runs entirely in oil. The transmission is in a separate casing directly behind the motor and is effectively lubricated by its own oil bath. It is firmly attached to the motor by studs, while the spiral gears are housed in a casing which is bolted to both transmission and motor base. Thus the three members form one unit. Each member is individually cooled, keeping the lubricant at the proper working temperature and eliminating all possibility of carbonized oil from the cylinders reaching and injuring the gears and bearings.

The powerplant unit is carried at three points on the motorcycle frame. This suspension prevents strains being transmitted from the frame to the powerplant and ensures absolute alignment of all bearings. It also permits the quick removal or replacement of the complete powerplant when such course is necessary, and with the minimum of labor.

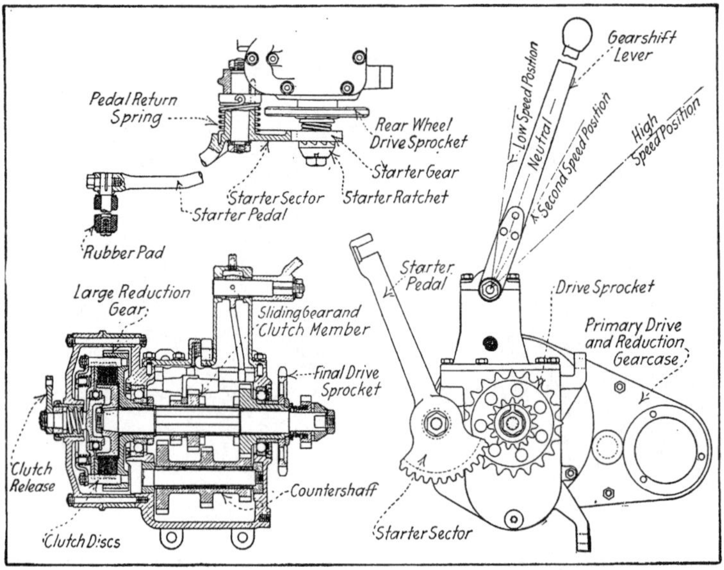

Fig. 283.—Change Speed Gearing of Indian Scout Motorcycle.

Indian Scout Frame.—Constructed to give the utmost in stress-resistance both laterally and longitudinally with a remarkable lightness in weight, the double tube frame embodies the highest form of motorcycle engineering construction. Two large alloy steel tubes diverge from the steering head drop-forging and form a cradle for the unit powerplant, continuing parallel to the rear of the structure. The unit powerplant attaches by a lug to each of the frame tubes at the front and to a cross-member at the rear, giving a three-point suspension. The form of the frame tends to absorb vibrations, thus conducing to easy riding and protecting the powerplant from strains and shocks.

The steering head is provided with large ball-bearings, giving more than ample strength and ensuring long life under the most arduous service. The lines of the frame give evidence of great strength yet in no way detracting from the graceful appearance of the machine as a whole. One-piece mud guards of scientific form and simple construction amply protect rider and mechanism from road dirt. The front guard is fitted with flat stays fastened in place by rivets. The rear guard is stayed to the frame and to a luggage carrier which performs the double function of carrier and guard brace.

Both gasoline and oil tanks are in one unit. The forward part of the tank contains the oil in a special compartment in which is situated the hand oil pump, within easy reach of the rider. This pump has a simple device for locking the plunger so that it only can be operated at the will of the rider. Two large oil pipes lead from the oil compartment, one going to the mechanical oiler and the other from the discharge end of the pump to the motor base. The gasoline compartment of the tank has a capacity of three gallons and is provided with a priming syringe in the filler cap and a needle valve for controlling the flow to the carburetor. The tank is in one piece and rests on lugs on the lower top tube of the frame.

Modern Motor Wheel Design.—The motor wheel of American design and construction, which is shown at Figs. 284 and 285, is a thoroughly practical, self-contained power plant that can be attached in about five minutes to any bicycle, either open or diamond frame, and is held by clamps at three places. If it is desired to remove the wheel and use the bicycle alone, the attaching frame need not be unclamped from the bicycle, but the wheel may be released by undoing one lock nut. The maintenance and operating cost is extremely low as figures have been given showing an expense of about $2.50 for 1,000 miles use.

The engine is a one cylinder air cooled form, and develops 1½ horsepower. The bore is 2⅜ inches, the stroke, 2¼ inches. A high tension magneto supplies ignition current. The crankcase is of aluminum and an outside flywheel is used to insure smooth run-

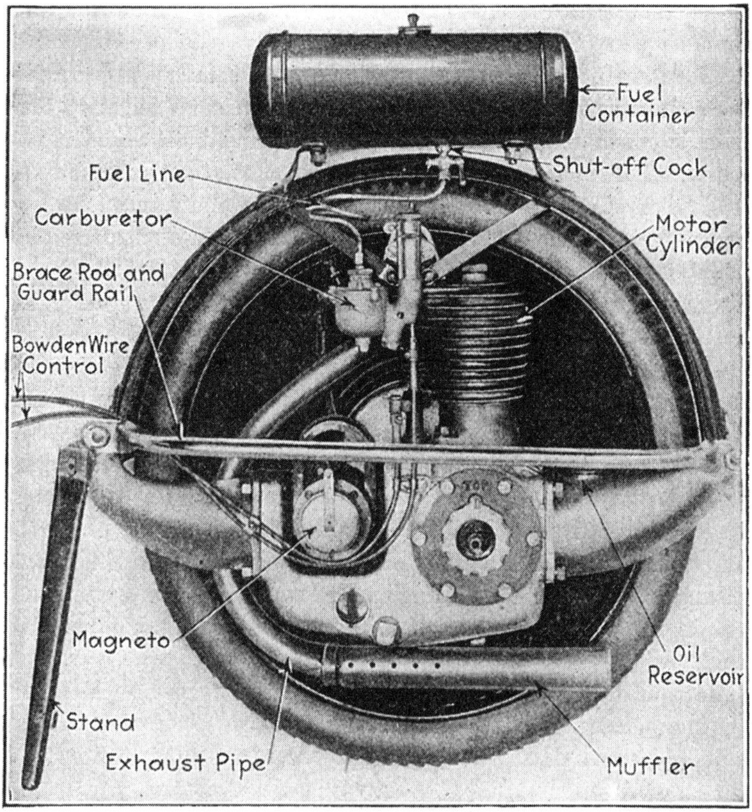

Fig. 284.—Modern Motor Wheel of American Design for Bicycle Propulsion.

ning. The bearings are improved anti-friction members of the roller type. The gasoline tank is 2 quarts capacity, which is enough for 50 to 60 miles, and is supported by the mudguard. Lubricating oil is carried in the engine base and enough is supplied for 50 to 75 miles. The attaching frame is of strong steel stampings and tubing, brightly nickelled. The tire is a double tube clincher, non-skid tread, 20 inches by 2 inches. Completely equipped for attaching to the bicycle, the attachment weighs about 60 pounds. Control is by throttle and compression release operated by levers on the handle bars through Bowden wire cables.

Motorcycle Equipment.—Of the innumerable accessories that have been devised for use of the motorcyclist, either for his personal benefit or to be used in connection with the machine, fully three-quarters are unnecessary, and can be easily dispensed with. It is not the writer's purpose to describe all of the various articles of equipment because the opinions of the various riders differ as to what should be considered necessary and what may be just as well omitted. Assuming that the rider has received a bare motorcycle without any auxiliary fittings whatever, it will be well to enumerate briefly some of the accessories that are really necessary in order to insure safety and comply with the law.

The first thing needed is adequate lighting equipment, and in most states a tail light is required as well as a head light. The next fitting prescribed by law is some form of signal or alarm by which the motorcyclist may notify other users of the highway of his approach. There is always a certain number of tools and spare parts that can be carried to advantage and that are not furnished with the machine. The equipment of a motorcycle does not include a speedometer unless one purchases a special model that is sufficiently expensive to have the cost of the accessories included in the purchase price.

The speedometer, which indicates the speed attained, and which also includes a mileage recorder, is a very necessary fitting. One is not only able to keep the speed in accordance with the legal requirements, but a reliable speed indicating device forms a good check on motor action and when to oil. The mileage recorder enables the rider to keep track of the service given by tires or other parts, and the amount of gasoline and oil consumed in covering a given mileage. The cost of the average motorcycle speedmeter will

Fig. 285.—Modern Motor Wheel of American Development formerly known as the Smith and now as the Briggs and Stratton wheel attached to latest model truss frame and fork bicycle.

be exceeded by a substantial margin if fines are paid for just one violation of the speed law, so it is much better to insure against arrest and obtain all the other advantages by investing in a speedometer than it is to pay more than the cost of one of the devices to swell the bank account of some rural constable. Another article of equipment is a watch and holder designed for attachment to the handle bars. Weed chains should be provided for the tires to minimize skidding; they are light and easily carried as they occupy but little space when not in use.

Lighting Systems.—The kerosene burning lamps used on the bicycle do not provide sufficient illumination for the motorcycle, on account of the greater speed of the power-propelled form. The

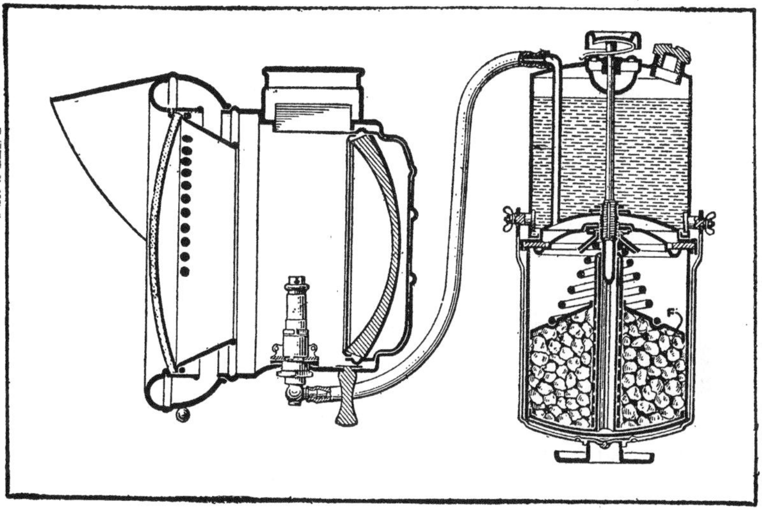

Fig. 286.—Diagram Showing Construction of Gas Lamp and Acetylene Generator.

various forms of lamps that are widely employed utilize acetylene gas as fuel and throw a brilliant light which will illuminate the road for several hundred feet ahead of the motorcycle. The lamp that is most popular in bicycle work is combined with the gas generator, which is a simple device for producing acetylene gas by the chemical action of water on calcium carbide. While the generator has been widely used, it is being superseded in all cases by the Prestolite tank for motorcycles in which the gas is stored under pressure, and from which it may be taken as needed by a simple operation of the tank valve. The searchlight shown at Fig. 286 is a separate type which can be used in connection with either the separate generator shown or the gas tank with which all are familiar. A small gas burning lamp designed for attachment to the rear mud guard is also used when a Prestolite tank is fitted.

How Acetylene Generator Works.—The method of operation of a generator may be clearly understood by referring to Fig. 286. As will be apparent, the device consists of two parts, an upper chamber to hold water and a lower portion divided in two compartments, one of which holds carbide while the other provides space for the gas to collect in. The carbide in the lower chamber surrounds a central tube in which measured quantities of water from the upper chamber are allowed to drip. The water is controlled by a needle valve, and the more water admitted the more energetic the liberation of gas becomes. The gas passes through a cooling chamber at the bottom of the upper portion that holds the water, and from there it passes to the burner in the lamp, through a length of rubber hose. After the carbide has been used up, which is evidenced when it has turned from the state of crystals or lumps to dust, the lower portion of the generator must be removed and thoroughly cleared out and fresh carbide inserted before one will obtain any more gas.

The latest types of motorcycles are provided with electric lighting systems similar to those used in automobiles in which an engine driven generator charges a storage battery which supplies current for lighting and in some cases for ignition as well. These systems and their care are described fully in proper sequence.

Alarms, Tools and Supplies.—On machines that are provided with electric lighting, it is not difficult to use electric alarms in the form of vibrating diaphragm horns which are set in action by a simple pressure on a push button. When a machine is not provided with batteries and a loud alarm is desired, a mechanical horn such as shown at Fig. 287, A, will produce a louder tone than the usual electric buzzer arrangement. This is a diaphragm form, and is similar to the type that is so widely used on automobiles. A downward pressure on the plunger extending from the back of the horn casing sets the train of gears in motion which, in turn, actuate the diaphragm at a rapid rate. The simpler forms of bulb operated horns such as shown at B and C are also adapted for the motorcycle, but these do not provide the best alarm when touring, inasmuch as their note does not have a very great carrying

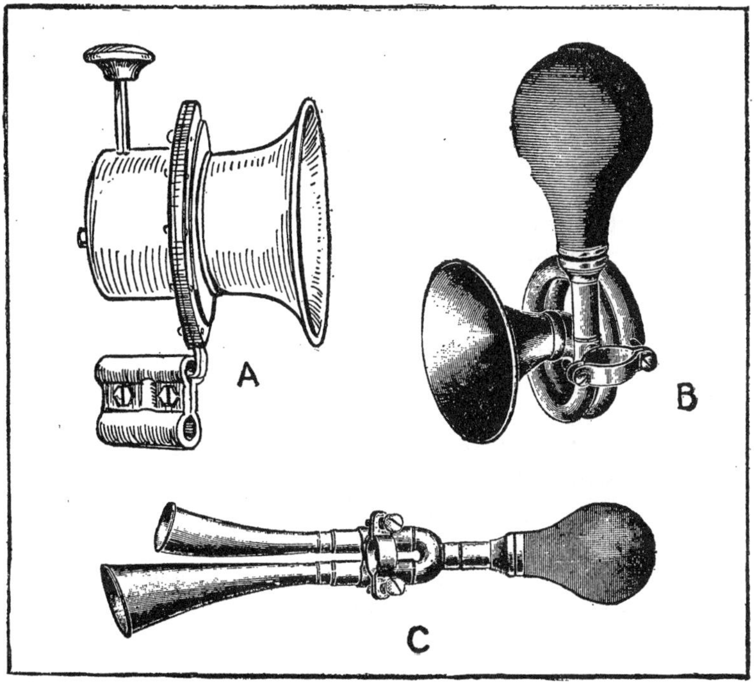

Fig. 287.—Popular Forms of Motorcycle Alarm Signals.

power. The shriek of the mechanical horn can be heard for many hundred feet.

It is difficult to outline the tools that should be provided because so much depends upon the character of the machine and its equipment. Most motorcycle manufacturers provide the special tools that are needed to get at any adjustments or nuts and bolts that would not be accessible with the ordinary tools obtained in the open market, so it will not be necessary to describe the special socket wrenches or spanners that fit only certain makes of machines. The main item of the average tool kit is a monkey wrench of special, light, thin form that still has a large enough opening to take the largest nut on the machine. For instance, if the inlet-valve cage screws into the cylinder, or if valve chamber caps are used the wrench should be large enough to move either of those members, which are usually the largest of the parts that must be handled by the wrench. A small size wrench of the bicycle type is also convenient and does not occupy much space. Two screw drivers should be provided, one small one with a blade that will permit removal of the smallest screws on the machine (such as those on the magneto) and one a little larger in size, preferably short and stubby with a strong blade for handling the other members that are screwed in tighter, and which could not be very well removed with a light screw driver.

A pair of combination pliers are usually part of the equipment, but if these are not provided by the maker the rider should see that they are included in the tool outfit. The best all around form for motorcycle use is that which is provided with a joint of such form that the opening between the jaws may be varied. The jaws are provided with a flat portion at the extreme end and below this part, which is used for gripping flat stock, a semi-circular, serrated opening is provided in each jaw for gripping pipe or round objects. The lower portions of the jaws near the hinge are usually sharpened to a cutting edge and move over each other with a shearing action. This portion serves as a wire cutter. One or two small files are also desirable, as many occasions arise where they will prove useful. Other tools should be provided depending upon the transmission employed. If the V-belt is used, as on some old type machines, a belt punch or awl as well as several spare connectors may be included. If drive is by chain a chain tool for removing the rivet from the links, and a number of spare connecting links are necessary.

Harley-Davidson Tool Outfit.—A complete tool outfit as supplied by the makers of the Harley-Davidson motorcycle is shown at Fig. 288. The various pieces are indicated by numerals and their use is indicated in the following key:

1. Envelope containing the registration card, which should be filled out and sent to the factory immediately upon delivery of your machine.

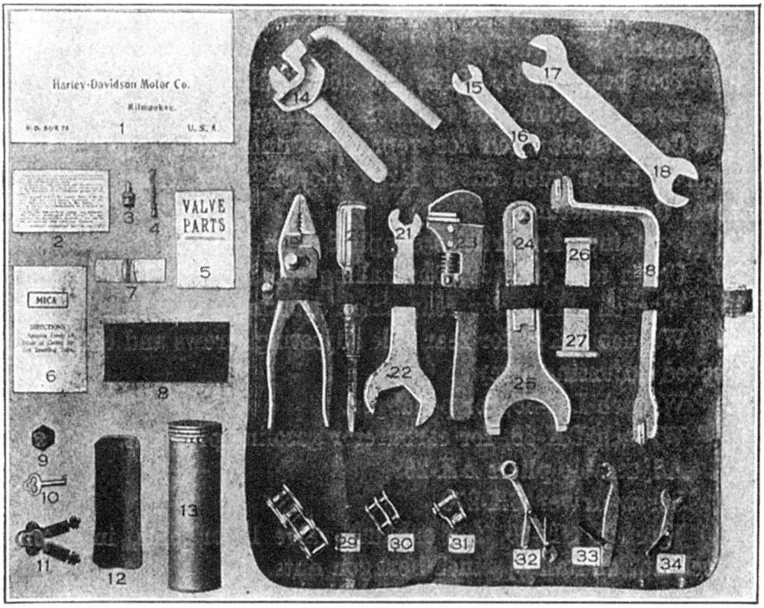

Fig. 288.—Tool Outfit Furnished on Harley-Davidson Motorcycles.

2. Envelope containing four washers for changing the adjustment of the mechanical oiler, as given in the instructions. Two thick washers BO-320. Two thin washers BO-280. Spark plug adjusting gauge EK-1091 is also in this envelope.
3. Extra inner tube valve cap DX-146.
4. Extra inner tube valve plunger DX-148.
5. Envelope containing valve parts.

6. Envelope containing powdered mica. Mica to be spread over repair after repair is completed to prevent tube or casing from sticking to repair.

7. Inside blowout patch for temporary repair of casings. To repair a small cut in the casing, cut a large enough piece from the roll.

8. Emery paper for cleaning the inner tube when a repair is necessary.

9. Cap EO-747 to screw on oil tank nipple when feed pipe is disconnected.

10. Tool box key DJ-721B, for electrically equipped model.

11. Keys AJ-505A, for tool box on magneto model.

12. Cementless patch for repairing inner tube. To repair a punctured inner tube cut a large enough piece from the patch to cover the puncture.

13. Container for articles supplied with tire kit.

14. Chain tool GK-739, for making repairs to the drive chain.

15. Wrench AK-2, for rear axle adjusting screw lock nuts.

16. Wrench AK-2, for rear axle adjusting screws and carburetor low speed adjusting screw.

17. Wrench DK-38, for pedal pin.

18. Wrench DK-38, for carburetor gasoline pipe nut.

19. Adjustable pliers AK-269.

20. Screw driver CK-270.

21. Wrench GK-65, for exhaust valve lifter pins, inlet push rod lock nut and all $\frac{7}{16}$ inch hexagon nuts.

22. Wrench GK-65, for exhaust valve spring cover.

23. Monkey wrench DK-809, for general use.

24-25. Wrench FK-822, for inlet housing clamp nuts and crank case stud nuts.

26-27. Wrench DK-805, for clutch pull rod adjusting nut and lock nut.

28. Wrench DK-807, for nuts holding the transmission onto frame.

29. Double repair link DK-316, for repairing the drive chain.

30. Coupling link DK-712, for use when only a coupling link is broken.

31. Half link DK-315, to be used when chain does not require a full link.

32. Bosch Magneto Wrench AK-424, supplied with those models equipped with a Bosch magneto.

33. Berling Magneto Wrench GX-1621, supplied with those models equipped with a Berling magneto.

34. Wrench DK-815, the flat steel strip is a gauge to be used when adjusting the circuit breaker points, as mentioned in the instructions covering the care of the Remy generator. The notched blade is used to tighten the nuts holding the cables to the coil. The wrench is for adjusting the circuit breaker points.

Useful Spare Parts.—Among the spare parts that may be carried to advantage may be mentioned a small spool of copper wire about No. 16 gauge, a length of high tension cable, and a number of assorted bolts, split pins, nuts and washers that conform to those used on the machines. If a single cylinder engine is employed as a power plant two spare spark plugs should be carried, while if it is a twin cylinder, three extra spark plugs should be included. To insure against breakdowns when away from the source of supplies, a few spare magneto parts such as the high tension carbon brush holder, a platinum pointed contact screw and a contact breaker bell crank will be found of advantage.

A roll of tire or insulating tape, and a complete tire repair outfit should figure in the equipment. The average outfit for inner tube restoration consists of a piece of emery cloth, a tube of cement, and some patches of assorted sizes. Patches may be obtained that do not require any cement as it is already incorporated with them, and a couple of these may be provided for an emergency where the regular cement would not work properly. Small tire irons to remove the casing from the rim and an air pump, as well as a number of spare valve insides, complete the outfit for repairing the inner tube. In case of a blow out, or a serious cut in the outer casing, it will be well to have an inside blow out patch and a tire gaiter handy. The inside patch is a piece of heavy canvas, 5 or 6 inches long and wide enough to conform to the curved interior portion of the tire completely when doubled over. The outer sleeve is made of leather or rubber and fabric, and is provided with a lacing by which it may be tightly drawn in place around the injured portion of the casing. If going on a tour of any magnitude, a complete inlet and exhaust valve assembly and several extra inner tubes will complete the kit.

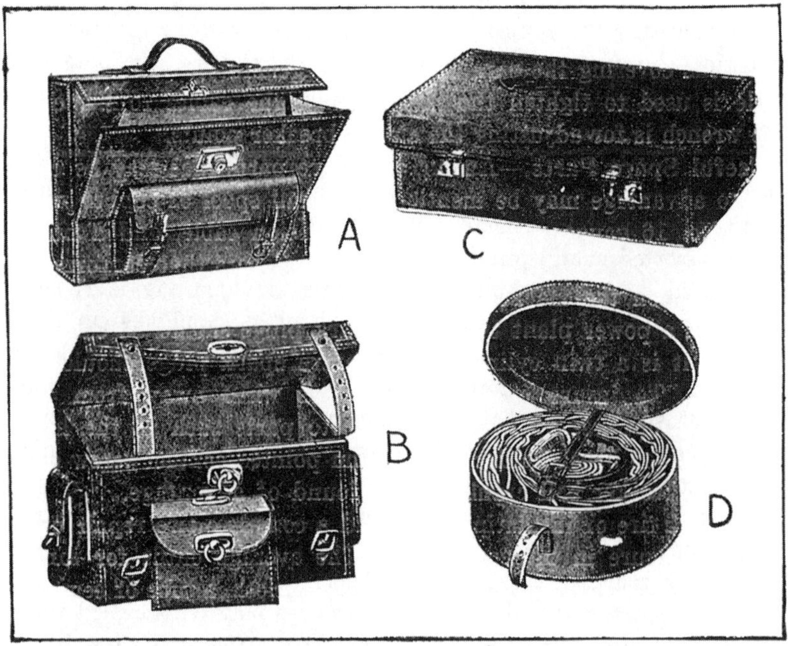

Fig. 289.—Examples of Cases Adapted for Carrying Tools or Supplies on Motorcycles.

Carrying Tools and Supplies.—The problem of carrying tools and supplies is not an easy one to solve on a motorcycle, though many very practical bags and carrying cases have been designed that will fit the top of the luggage carrier, or that are adapted to be carried one on either side of that member. These provide room for considerable material and enough equipment for a trip of some magnitude may be easily stowed away. The bag shown at A, Fig. 289, is intended for attachment to the side of the luggage carrier, and not only provides a large amount of storage space inside but has a smaller tool bag attached as well as a pocket to carry the oil can. The form at B is intended to be carried on top of the luggage carrier and is considerably larger than that designed for attachment to the side. The bag shown at C is also intended for the top of the luggage carrier, and when flanked on either side with a bag of the form shown at A much storage space is available. Where machines are driven by belt, if one undertakes a long tour and the belt has seen considerable service, it may be well to carry a spare member in a special casing such as shown at D. The interior of this case is divided into two concentric compartments, the outer one serving for the belt, the inner one to carry the spare inner tube. If a side car is fitted, an opportunity for carrying considerable luggage may be taken advantage of by fitting a luggage carrier or rack, as shown at Fig. 290, to the back of the side car body. Modern motorcycles have a good sized tool box included in the standard equipment.

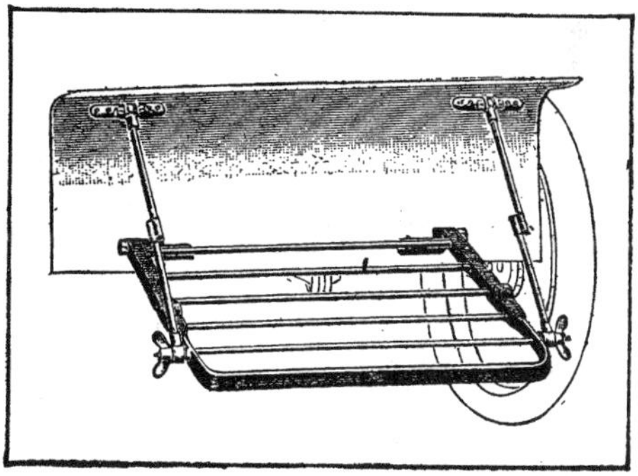

Fig. 290.—Application of Luggage Carrier at Rear of Side Car Body.

General Instructions for Starting Motor.—Assuming that the rider has just received a machine, and that it has come crated, and also that he is not familiar with motorcycle operation, we may give the following general instructions: After the machine has been uncrated, and the handle bars, saddle and pedals attached in their proper places, the first step is to see that the tanks are filled with gasoline and oil. As a rule, the filler caps are very plainly marked to indicate the purpose of the container to which they are fitted. In filling the tank with fuel, filter the gasoline by passing through a chamois skin which insures positive removal of all dirt and water. Be sure to fill the oil tank with the proper grade of lubricant, which must be a good air-cooled engine cylinder oil, and preferably of the brand recommended by the maker of the machine. Before attempting to start the motor, become familiar with the various parts of the controlling apparatus. In most American machines the gas supply is regulated by one of the movable grips on the handle bar, and which one it is can be easily ascertained by moving both of them in turn and seeing which oper-

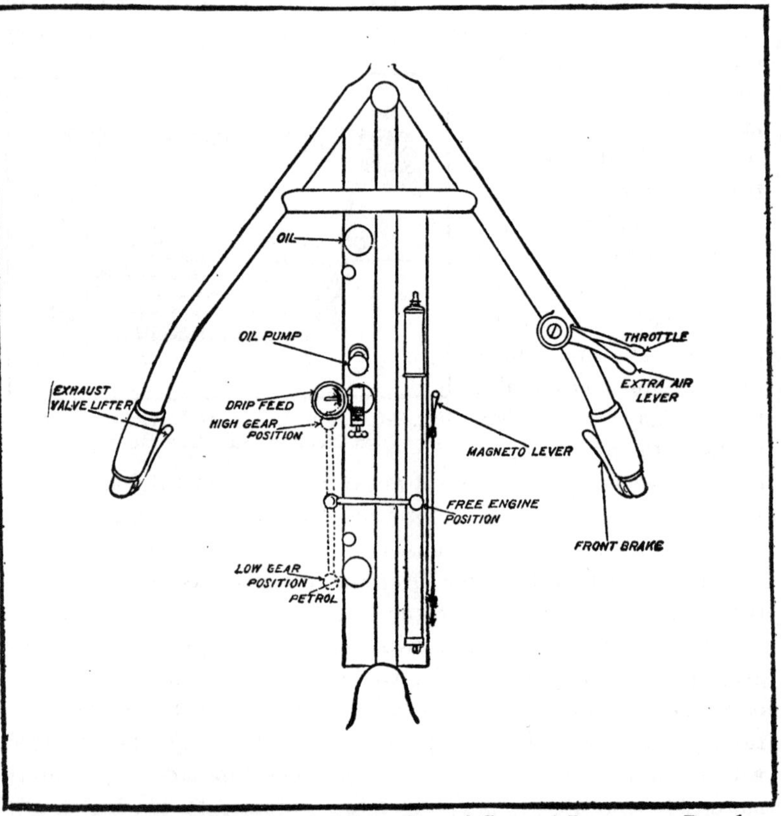

Fig. 291.—Diagram Showing Location of Control Levers on Royal Enfield, an English Motorcycle Design.

ates on the throttle lever at the top of the carburetor. In some machines, the grip is turned in one direction to close the throttle which would be just the same as that to open the throttle in other motorcycles. The proper mode of procedure can only be determined by experiment. The grip on the other handle bar is used for advancing the timer or contact breaker of the magneto when turned in one direction and for raising the exhaust valves if turned to the other extreme position. In some motorcycles, the exhaust valves are raised by a special lever carried by the handle bars. The clutch of most motorcycles is operated by a hand lever at the side of the tank, and in some machines a smaller lever will be mounted at the side of the tank that is connected directly with the contact breaker of the magneto. When a two-speed gear of the planetary type is used, a single-control lever usually serves to control both high and low speeds, and this member corresponds to the usual free engine clutch actuator. When an individual or shifting clutch, two-speed gear is used, the master or friction clutch is often shifted by a foot lever, while the speed changing is effected by a suitable lever carried on the upper frame tube.

Learn to Control Motor.–The first thing to do is to learn to control the motor. To do this, raise the rear wheel of the machine from the floor by the stand provided for that purpose, open the valves in the gasoline line so the fuel will flow to the carburetor and supply a couple of pumpfuls of oil to the engine base. Prime the carburetor by pressing the priming pin and holding that member down until gasoline flows from the bottom of the device. This shows that the spray nozzle has overflowed which indicates that it is clear of dirt. Set the spark about half way advanced, open the throttle slightly, and raise the exhaust valves by whatever means are provided for that purpose. Pedal briskly and turn the motor over at a fair rate of speed, and then drop the exhaust valves and the motor should start. After the motor has been started, become familiar with the action of the spark and throttle levers or control grips by moving them back and forth, and noting the effect of the various positions on the behavior of the engine. Do not run the engine unnecessarily fast when on the stand.

Instructions for Operating Motorcycle.—After having learned to manipulate the motor and control its speed on the stand, the motor may be started and allowed to run slowly, and the high-speed or free-engine clutch lever may be set in the free engine position. This may be clearly noted by pressing on the brake pedal with the engine in motion. If the rear wheel stops rotating without affecting the engine speed, it indicates that the clutch is free and functioning properly. If applying the brakes stops the motor as well as the rear wheel, it shows that the clutch is not properly released, which may mean that the lever is not in the proper position or that there is some defective condition in the clutch itself. The machine is then dropped off of the stand with the clutch lever in the off position, and, after the rider has mounted, the engine may be speeded up and the clutch lever moved gradually until the motorcycle acquires a certain momentum, after which the clutch may be engaged positively.

If the machine is a two or three speed form, the start may be made on the high speed without any trouble if the ground is level, as the friction clutch will provide gradual application of power if it is controlled properly. When starting on a hill or in sand, it will be well to start on the low gear and throw into the high only when the top of the hill is reached, or road conditions become more favorable. Do not slip a clutch of any type unnecessarily, because this will produce wear of the friction surfaces, so it is best to start on the low speed under any conditions. In operating change-speed gears of the shifting clutch type or of the sliding gear pattern, always be sure that the master clutch is completely released before endeavoring to shift gears. When shifting from high speed to lower speed, always slow down the engine or wait until the speed of the motorcycle drops to the point that will correspond to the gear ratio obtained by the reduction gearing. In changing from the low to the high gear, accelerate the engine slightly to speed up the machine before the shift is made.

Motor Control Rules.—All motorcycle motors have a certain degree of flexibility, i.e., they may be run slow or fast, and the speed may be accelerated or cut down as desired within a range from 200 revolutions per minute to the maximum, 2,500 or 3,000, which will vary with the type of motor. This is an important advantage, inasmuch as it permits one to regulate the cycle speed on most occasions by a touch of the throttle grip alone. The engine speed of practically all motorcycles is controlled by two ways, though usually these are employed in conjunction. One of these consists of varying the time of the spark in the cylinder, the other regulating the amount of gas supplied. The spark and throttle levers, while designed to be manipulated independent of each other, usually move with a certain definite relation. It would not be good practice to run an engine with the spark lever way advanced and gas supply throttle nearly closed; nor would good results be obtained if the spark lever was retarded and the throttle opened, as it is desired to increase the motor speed. It is not difficult to understand the function of the throttle lever and how the admission of more gas to the cylinders would act in creating more power, just as augmenting the steam supply to a steam engine will increase its capacity.

The rules for manipulation of the spark lever are not so well understood. In order to make clear the reason for intelligent manipulation of the spark handle, there are certain points that must be considered. On most motorcycles, there is a position of the spark lever at some point of the arc over which it moves which corresponds to the normal firing point. If the spark lever is not advanced beyond this position, and the motor is turning over slowly, the gas in the cylinders is being exploded when the pistons reach the end of their compression stroke. When the gas is fully compacted, the explosion or power obtained from combustion is more powerful than of the spark fired gas which was not compressed properly. The electric spark is not produced at the exact time that the motor should be fired at all speeds, and if the spark was supplied the very instant of full compression, irrespective of the speed of rotation, there would be no need of moving the spark lever.

Not only is the current apt to lag, but it takes a certain definite amount of time to set fire to the gas. It requires the same amount of time to ignite the gas, of given composition, regardless of the speed of the motor. If the motor is only turning at a few hundred revolutions per minute, there is ample time to ignite all gas charges positively, but if the motor speed increases and the explosions occur oftener, then one must compensate for the more rapidly occurring combustion periods by arranging to start igniting the gas earlier so the explosion will occur when the piston is at its highest point in the cylinder. The compensation for lag is made by advancing

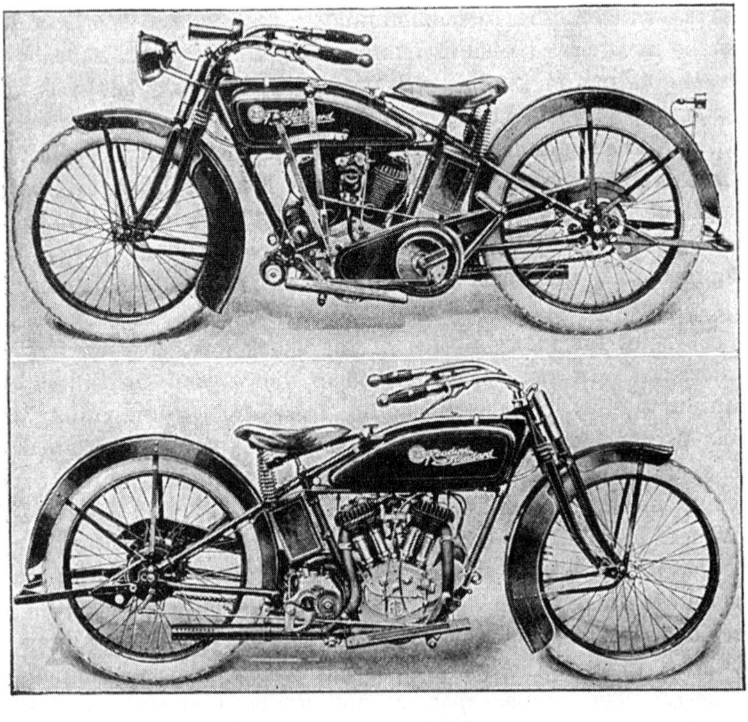

Figs. 292 and 293.—Views of Reading Standard Motorcycle Showing Control Levers and Kick Starter.

the spark. The spark lever on the handle bar or tank moves a commutator, if battery system is employed, or the magneto contact breaker box, if that form of current producer furnishes the ignition energy. The amount of spark advance needed depends on engine speed and the greater the piston velocity the more the spark should be advanced.

Handling Spark Lever.—It is possible to advance the spark lever too far, and, when this occurs, the gas is exploded before the piston reaches the top of its stroke, and premature explosion takes place. As a result of this, the upwardly moving piston is forced to overcome the resistance exerted by the expanding gas of the ignited charge in completing the remainder of the compression stroke, and before it will return on the power stroke. The in-

Fig. 294.—Side View of Indian Power-Plus Model Showing Control Levers.

jurious back pressure on the piston reduces the capacity of the motor and a pounding noise similar to that produced by loose motor parts gives positive indication of premature ignition due to excessive spark advance.

At the other hand, if the spark lever is not set as far forward as it should be, the explosion may be late because of the "retarded spark." If the spark occurs late in the cycle, the charge is not fired until the piston has reached its highest point and after it has completed a small portion of its downward movement. As the point of maximum compression is passed and the piston moves down in the cylinder, the size of the combustion chamber augments and the gas begins to expand again before it ignites. Owing to the moderate compression, the power resulting from explosions is less than would be the case with a higher degree of compression. To secure power, it is necessary to supply more gas to the cylinders. Driving with a retarded spark produces heating of the motor and is wasteful of fuel.

For ordinary running, the spark lever is usually placed about midway of its travel on the sector, and as a general rule an engine with magneto ignition does not require the frequent manipulation of the spark necessary when current is produced by chemical means.

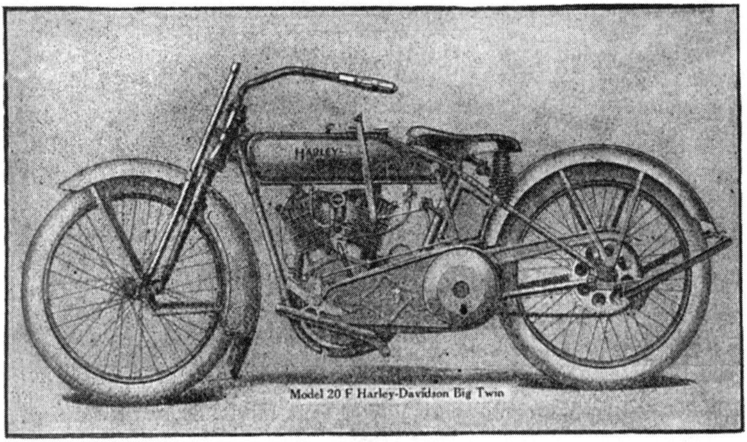

Fig. 295.—Model 20F Harley-Davidson Big Twin.

As the engine speed increases, the current produced by the magneto is proportionately augmented, and the spark lever need not be advanced from the center position except under conditions which permit of exceedingly high engine speeds.

Summing up, it will be patent that the greatest economy of fuel will result when the motorcycle is operated with as little throttle opening as possible, and with the greatest spark advance the motor speed will allow. To obtain maximum power, as in hill climbing on the direct drive, the spark lever should never be advanced beyond center and the throttle should be opened as wide as possible.

For extreme high speed, the spark is advanced as much as possible and the throttle opened wide.

To Start the Motor of 1920 Models F and J Harley-Davidson.—The beginner may find it easier to start the motor with the machine on the stand. He does not have to balance the machine this way. However, be sure to put the gear shift lever into neutral position or disengage the clutch by pulling the hand lever shown in Fig. 295 way back before taking the machine off the stand.

1. Release the clutch by pulling the clutch hand lever back all the way, or by pressing the heel of the foot down on the rear part of the clutch pedal.

2. Put the gear shift lever in the position marked "Neutral." The lever will generally go into this position very easily if the

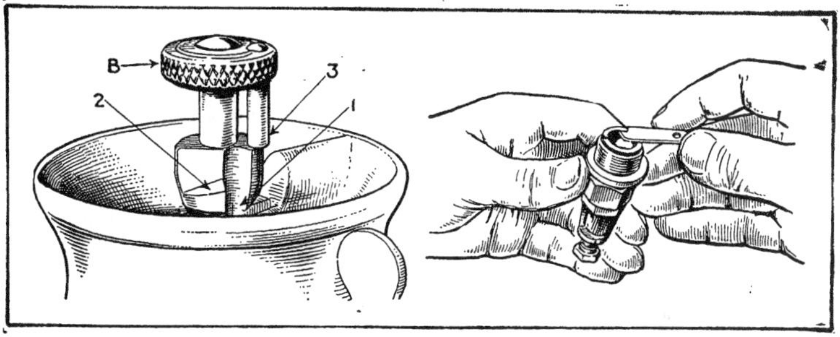

Fig. 296.—How to Close Carburetor Air Valve.
Fig. 297.—Gauging Spark Gap.

clutch lever is all the way back, but if the transmission gears happen to stop so that the teeth are opposite each other, it will be necessary to turn the gears over by giving the starter pedal a stroke, or by turning the rear wheel slightly. Do not under any circumstances try to force the gear shift lever because damage will result. The gears will always shift easily if the shifting mechanism is properly lubricated at the various places provided for oiling.

3. After the gear shift lever is in neutral position, engage the clutch by pushing the clutch hand lever forward all the way, or by pushing down on the forward part of the clutch foot pedal.

4. To facilitate starting, close the carburetor air valve by pulling out the bottom "B" (see illustration Fig. 296) and give it a slight turn to the left. There are three positions that this button can be put into to readily control the tension of the air valve spring. In very cold weather pull the button way out as in position marked "3." After the motor is started, turn the button still further to the left until the pin drops into position marked "2." Then start the machine in the regular way. Leave the stem here until the motor starts to miss, then release the stem entirely by turning the button still further to the left, until the pin drops into position marked "1." This is the position the button should always be carried in after the motor has warmed up.

5. Close the throttle by turning the right handlebar grip to

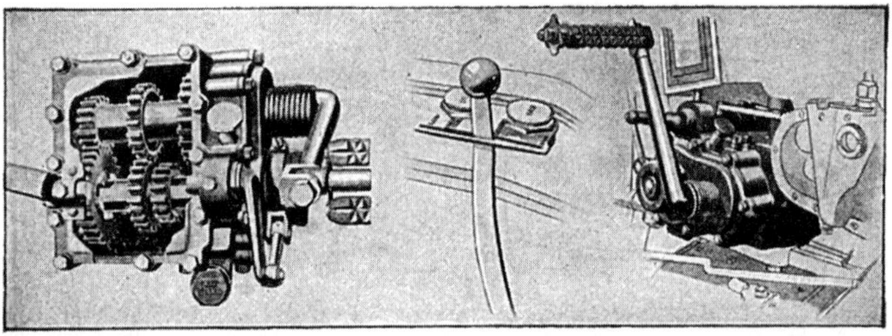

Fig. 298.—The Harley-Davidson Change Speed Gear at Left, the Shift Lever at Center and the Enclosed Kick Starter Mechanism at Right.

the extreme right and then open it slightly by turning the grip slightly to the left.

6. Turn the left grip to the left as far as possible, raising the exhaust valves, thereby relieving the compression in the cylinders.

7. Give the step starter pedal a vigorous stroke downward, at the same time turning the left grip to the right one-half or two-thirds of the way, thereby dropping the valves and advancing the spark. After the motor is running, advance the spark fully by turning the left grip all the way to the right, release the air valve stem and close the throttle.

In starting the electrically equipped model 20-J, care should be taken that the left grip is not advanced more than one-half or two-thirds of the way. If it is advanced more than this, the motor may backfire. Sometimes the magneto model 20-F will start more easily if the spark is advanced all the way. The exact spark advance necessary to start the motor quickest and easiest will be ascertained after a few trials.

8. If the motor is warm, it should start on the first attempt. If it does not, repeat the operations as mentioned above. Do not race the motor on the stand.

Some motors will start more easily if the throttle is not quite closed.

Some experienced riders prefer to start the motor "against compression." This is done by advancing the spark about half way and closing the throttle either all the way or almost all the way and then using the starter pedal. Which ever way is selected by the owner after he gets accustomed to his mount is a matter of preference or individual knack.

9. To stop the motor in model 20-F, or 20-J, turn the left grip all the way to the left. On the electrically equipped model 20-J, also try to sound the horn as soon as the motor has stopped, to make sure that the centrifugal switch has opened the battery and generator clutch. If the horn can be sounded with the motor idle, disconnect the ground wire from the battery box cover screw to prevent discharging the battery and then apply the instructions under "To Adjust the Centrifugal Switch" in the chapter on Electric Lighting.

After you have started the motor a few times on the stand, learn to start it with both wheels on the ground, either by straddling the machine or standing alongside of it. The starter crank describes a very large arc, turning over the motor with sufficient momentum to generally start it on the first stroke. Of course, until you acquire the knack of using the starter crank, you may have to make a few trials. Start the motor as naturally as possible.

To Start the Motor in Cold Weather.—To facilitate starting in cold weather the motor should be primed; that is, gasoline introduced directly into the cylinders through the cylinder priming cocks. The reasons why a motor does not start readily in cold weather are these:

Gasoline does not vaporize readily when mixed with cold air. The term "raw" is applied to a mixture of gasoline and cold air. It is advisable to use higher test gasoline in winter than in summer.

Oil congeals or becomes practically solid in cold weather. If a machine is standing in the cold, the oil congeals between the cylinders and pistons and in the bearings. This makes it difficult to crank the motor. By priming the cylinders with gasoline, the thick oil is immediately turned into liquid form allowing easy cranking. For this reason the following recommendations are offered for cold weather starting:

1. Unscrew the knurled button of the primers located on the left side of the cylinders near the top, about two turns.

2. Charge the priming gun, which is a unit with one of the gasoline tank caps, by drawing the plunger button out to its full extent.

3. Place the point of the priming gun into the opening of the primer and give it the charge of the gun. Prime the other cylinder in the same way.

4. Close the primers.

5. Hold down the carburetor float primer until the carburetor overflows.

6. Tighten the easy starting tension spring of the carburetor auxiliary air valve by pulling out the button "B" and giving it a slight turn to lock it. Start the motor.

After the motor is warmed up, loosen the tension spring on the carburetor. If the carburetor chokes, do not release the stem entirely. Drop it into recess number "2," illustration Fig. 296, and leave it here until the motor misses, due to the rich mixture, then release it entirely by dropping it into recess marked "1."

Difficult Starting.—Frequently difficult starting is due to nothing more than dirty or poorly adjusted spark plugs. As soon as difficulty in starting is experienced remove the plugs, inspect and clean. Clean the points and polish with very fine sand paper or emery cloth. Adjust the clearance of the points with the gauge furnished with the machine for that purpose. The gauge measures .022 inch in thickness and its use is shown at Fig. 297.

Keep Your Eyes On the Road.—One thing the beginner must bear in mind at all times is that under no circumstances must he take his eyes from the road ahead. The gears must be shifted or the clutch released or engaged by the sense of touch, and the sooner the rider learns to operate these controls correctly, the sooner he will be safe on the road. It is true that many old riders are negligent on this score, and often take their eyes off the road, but it is a careless act and many accidents can be traced directly to this cause.

To Start the Machine On the Road.—Assuming that the motor is started as per previous instructions, the first thing to do is to release the clutch by pulling back the clutch hand lever or pressing on the rear part of the clutch foot pedal, and then shift the gears into first or low speed, by moving the gear shift lever into position marked "Low." If the motor was started on the stand, the gears must be in neutral or the clutch released before the machine is taken off the stand. (See Fig. 298.)

Next, let in the clutch very gradually by pressing the toe on the forward part of the clutch foot pedal, or, if preferred, by moving the clutch lever forward by hand.

For the first ride or two, do not be afraid to run in low gear for 100 feet or so. After the machine is under way and you have it in good balance, release the clutch all the way, quickly close the throttle and move the gear shift lever through neutral into position marked "Second."

Then engage the clutch again slowly, as before, at the same time, opening the throttle slightly. After running 50 feet or so, it will be easy to shift into high speed or direct drive by again releasing the clutch, closing the throttle and setting the gear shift lever into position marked "High." Then again open the throttle while engaging the clutch, allowing the machine to get away smoothly and quietly. During this time the spark is being carried practically fully advanced.

Suggestions for Smooth, Quiet Starting.—With a little practice the beginner will learn just how far the throttle should be opened while engaging the clutch, enabling him to get away as smoothly and quietly as the highest class cars.

Never race the motor while running idle. To say that this practice is to be condemned is putting it mildly for these reasons: The motor will sooner or later show the effects of having been abused. If the motor is raced while starting the machine, the clutch is being slipped unnecessarily, meaning friction and wear, and the rear tire is under a terrible strain. Another objection is the noise of the motor while the machine is getting under way. Take a pride in making a smooth, quiet get-away and you will command the respect of your fellow riders and the general public. The Harley-Davidson motorcycle is practically noiseless. Why incur criticism, giving yourself and machine a black mark?

Never let your rear wheel spin under any conditions. When starting, use extreme care to see that the clutch is engaged gradually enough so that there is no grinding of the rear tire on the road. Owing to the tremendous power transmitted to the rear wheel when low or second gear is being used, it is an easy matter to spin the wheel. This places a terrific strain on the tire and the practice, if persisted in, will rapidly wear out the tire.

To Stop the Machine.—In learning to operate a motorcycle one of the most important things to bear in mind is that the ability to stop the motorcycle quickly is occasionally of great importance. After a few weeks' use the rider will find that the actions necessary to bring the motorcycle to a stop, come about almost unconsciously at the first sign of an obstruction ahead or other necessity for a quick stop.

Possibly the brake is subject to more abuse than any other part of the motorcycle, simply because many riders seem to take delight in seeing how close they can come to the stopping point at high speed, before they shut off the motor and apply the brake. Do not form the habit of applying the brake suddenly and bringing the motorcycle to a standstill in a short distance. The rider who can shut off his motor at some distance from the point where he desires to stop and coasts up to it, applying the brake gradually, thereby bringing the motorcycle to a graceful stop, shows good judgment from every standpoint. No one who takes pride in keeping his machine in tiptop condition will stop suddenly except in case of emergency.

The proper way to stop the motorcycle is to release the clutch, closing the throttle at the same time, and then stopping by careful and gradual use of the brake pedal. Never jam the brake on, if it can be avoided. To stop the motors of all 1920 models turn the left grip to the left as far as possible, thereby raising the valves and relieving the compression.

It is not uncommon to hear riders complain that they are not getting the right kind of service from their tires. They will even claim that a casing has been ruined in three or four hundred miles of riding. Invariably this is the rear casing and investigation will demonstrate that almost without exception, riders making complaints of this nature have been abusing the tires and the braking mechanism by sudden stops or quick starts.

Excessive tire wear can oftentimes be traced to fast riding over rough roads, which give the rear wheel an opportunity to spin. Every time such spinning takes place a certain amount of rubber is worn off the tread of the tire.

To Use the Motor As a Brake.—In riding down long steep hills it is sometimes advisable, in order to save the brake and keep it from getting heated, to use the motor as a brake.

To do this does not require stopping the machine and a new rider will soon adopt this method. Just before descending a hill, disengage the clutch, close the throttle and at the same time shut off the motor. As soon as the motor is stopped, both grips should be turned inward so as to get as much compression as possible in the cylinders. Then push the clutch lever forward just far enough *not* to turn the motor over. Having this slight drag at the clutch will greatly retard the momentum of the machine and will naturally save the brake considerably. Before descending extremely long steep hills put the gear shifter lever in low gear position and apply the above instructions. Under this condition wonderful braking power is received, only care should be taken that the clutch is not engaged far enough to turn the motor.

To Change Back To Lower Speeds.—All ordinary grades can of course be negotiated on high gear without trouble if the machine is traveling at a fair speed. If it is necessary to slow up on a grade for traffic, or for some other reason, and the motor begins to knock, the spark should be retarded a trifle. If this does not remedy the knocking, the spark should be retarded still further; then if the motor continues to knock, the transmission gears should be shifted from high into intermediate or low. A sectional view of the gearset is given at Fig. 298 and also at Fig. 299.

The knowledge of the correct time to make this shift will come to the rider only through experience. Not only is it an easy matter to stall the motor by attempting to negotiate a hill on high gear, when the laboring of the motor indicates that intermediate or low gear should be used, but it is a tremendous strain on the entire power plant.

To Shift from High Gear Into Intermediate.—When it becomes necessary to us intermediate gear, the clutch should be released and the gear shift lever moved from high gear position straight through into intermediate or second speed position with a quick firm movement, after which the clutch should be engaged again as quickly as possible but without any perceptible jerk.

The change from high gear into intermediate is generally made after the rider has retarded the spark, therefore it is necessary to advance the spark when the intermediate gear is engaged. It will not take the rider long to become acquainted with the control of the machine, so that he will know just when to throttle the motor to prevent it from racing while shifting gears.

To Shift from Intermediate Gear Into Low.—Occasionally you will encounter a hill so steep that the machine will not negotiate it, even on intermediate gear, without the motor slowing down. In this case, low gear or first speed must be called into action. To make this change, it is only necessary to release the clutch, shift the lever forward from second into low and again engage the clutch, similar to the manner in which the shift was made from high gear into intermediate. It must be remembered that it is necessary to have the spark advanced after a shift into a lower gear. This is an important point because an advanced spark tends to keep a motor cool, while a retarded spark will soon cause a motor to heat up unnecessarily. For this reason the rider should never attempt to run the motorcycle for any distance with a retarded spark.

A little difficulty may be encountered at first in shifting gears, especially on a hill. A little practice will enable the rider to become expert so that gears may be shifted easily and without a sound.

Under no circumstances run a new motor at high speed until it has covered several hundred miles and is thoroughly "run in."

Instructions for Use of Hand Pump.—When climbing a long hill, or pulling through long stretches of sand or mud it is often advisable to give the motor a little extra oil with the hand pump. A third of a pumpful or a half pumpful is enough if the hill or bad stretch is not a very long one. On a very long hill or bad stretch it is better to give the motor this extra supply of oil a little at a time, say, one-third of a pumpful, than it is to give it an entire pumpful at one time. This is true especially if the machine is carrying a loaded sidecar.

To Turn Corners.—The confidence necessary to turn a corner nicely comes only with experience and the new rider should turn all corners very slowly and cautiously to avoid falling, especially if the road is wet.

Skidding.—There is absolutely no excuse for skidding under ordinary conditions, but skidding may occur on slippery surfaces or in rounding turns at high speed, even on dry surfaces, if the rider is careless. Not only is skidding dangerous, but it causes excessive tire wear. Sometimes on a road which has a high crown the machine may show a tendency to skid if the surface is very wet, even when running straight ahead. This tendency will be minimized if the rider keeps to the middle of the road or where the road is the highest. When traffic conditions prevent this, great caution should be exercised to ride at a moderate pace or a fall may result.

Sometimes the rider may feel the machine starting to skid. An experienced rider can sometimes stop a skid by turning the front wheel in the same direction in which the rear wheel is sliding, but it is only an experienced rider who can do this, and the better plan to follow is to take precautions to prevent a skid in the first place.

Use of the Muffler Cutout.—One thing which has given motorcycles and motorcycle riders a great amount of undesirable publicity is the fact that some riders persist in riding with the muffler cutout open. This may have been excusable in the early days of the sport when some motors were not powerful enough for even ordinary touring conditions, and the rider because of this fact opened the cutout to relieve the back pressure caused by the inefficient mufflers of those days. The Harley-Davidson muffler is a very efficient piece of mechanism and causes no appreciable back pressure in the motor.

It has been proven by dynamometer tests at the factory that the difference in power between using a closed muffler and an open cutout is less than one per cent. Therefore, there is no reason whatever for the rider opening the muffler cutout unless it is desired to locate a miss in the motor.

Simple Rules of the Road.—When meeting any vehicle from the opposite direction, it is the rule of the road in the United States for both vehicles to keep to the right. In no place is courtesy more appreciated, or a better indication of good manners, than on the road. If a motorcycle rider wants to pass another vehicle, it is often easier for him to turn out of the way, than for the other vehicle to turn out. The motorcycle will negotiate a bad piece of road better than any other vehicle, and motorcycle riders as a rule are always glad to accommodate more cumbersome conveyances.

In overtaking a slower going vehicle traveling in the same direction, pass the vehicle on the left.

No considerate rider will annoy or frighten pedestrians by improper use of the horn of warning signal. It has become the accepted rule in many localities to hold one's left arm to the left when turning to the left, or when turning to the right to extend one's right arm in that direction.

It is a good plan to look up the local traffic laws or ordinances governing motorcycles; then you will be on the safe side.

CHAPTER VIII

MOTORCYCLE MAINTENANCE

What To Do Every Day—What To Do Every Week—Lubrication Hints—What To Do Every Two Weeks—What To Do Every Month—What To Do Every Two Months—What To Do Every Year—Handling Brake and Clutch—To Adjust the Foot Brake—To Adjust the Hand Brake—To Adjust the Clutch——Care and Lubrication of Hubs—To Clean Your Motorcycle—Care of Three Speed Transmission—Proper Adjustment of Drive Chains—Drive Chain Repairs—Operation of Automatic Oil Pump—How to Adjust Automatic Oil Pump—What To Do When Oiler Overfeeds—Flushing Motor with Kerosene—Advice on Lubrication—Care of Indian Magneto—Care of Electric Generator—Care of Electric Wiring—Operation of Lamp and Horn—Amperemeter Indications—General Maintenance of Indian Motorcycle—What Spares to Carry—Where to Oil and When—Tips That Save Trouble—Operation and Care of Cleveland Motorcycle—Engine Action—Transmission Gear and Clutch—Control System—Kick Starter—Lubrication and Fuel—Adjustment of Model ''A-G'' Schebler Carburetor.

What To Do Every Day—Wipe off all motor parts, including the exhaust pipes.

Oil the inlet valve rocker arm bearings. To do this, turn the hinged cap on the inlet lever bolt backward, so that the oil hole is exposed, as shown in the illustration, Fig. 300. After oiling, be sure to turn the cap back to keep out dirt. Put a drop of oil in the hole on the end of the inlet lever to lubricate the end of the push rod, and place a few drops of oil around the inlet valve collar so as to lubricate the inlet valve stem and prevent premature wear. Oiling the inlet valve stem is not recommended in very sandy country.

Give the grease cups on the fork rocker plates a half turn.

See that you have enough gasoline and oil in the tanks for your trip.

What To Do Every Week.—Put a drop or two of oil on all bearings in the clutch operating and gear shifting mechanism.

Every week put a drop or two of oil on the adjusting plunger on the starter, where the plunger enters its bushing, and also put a little oil on the black spring on the starter crank. Put the oil just back of the washer, next to the pedal crank itself, where it will work in and lubricate the bearing.

See that the oil in the transmission is at the proper level.

Add distilled water and test your storage battery, if your machine is electrically equipped.

Look over both wheels carefully and tighten any loose spokes taking care to see that the wheels run true.

Go over all the nuts and bolts including engine clamp bolts and nuts to see that they are tight; do this before taking any long trip.

Look over the tires for cuts. Sometimes a tack or small nail which has not punctured the inner tube may be found in the casing. If it is removed in time, a puncture may be avoided.

If your machine is a 20-J, give the grease cup on the right side of the generator one-half turn.

What To Do Every Two Weeks.—Flush the motor with kerosene.

Clean your drive chains and treat with Harley-Davidson chain compound.

Fill the grease cups on the front fork rocker plates and inject a few drops of oil at the oil cups in the front and sidecar wheels.

Examine the adjustment of the head fitting bearings and tighten the lock nut if necessary.

What To Do Every Month.—Have your battery inspected and tested by our dealer, or at the nearest Exide service station. On request, your dealer will furnish you with a card entitling you to this service free of charge. Be sure to take advantage of it. If you cannot have the battery inspected and tested, do so yourself. If you find that any solution has been spilled, be sure to remove the battery and clean both battery and box.

Lubricate the magneto with a few drops of good oil placed in the oil cups.

What To Do Every Two Months.—Pack the bearings of the front and rear wheels, as well as the bearings of the sidecar wheel with good cup grease.

Inspect, clean and, if necessary, adjust the contact points of the ignition unit. Also inspect and reseat the brushes and clean the commutator if necessary.

Inspect and, if necessary, readjust the exhaust valve tappets and push rods.

What To Do Every Year.—Take the muffler apart and clean it thoroughly.

Remove the seat post and lubricate the springs thoroughly with heavy grease.

Have your dealer take the motor apart for cleaning and inspection. It is advisable, even though the motor has regularly been flushed with kerosene, to have it taken apart and all carbon scraped from the cylinders and pistons, especially from the more or less inaccessible parts. The valves should be cleaned, and, if necessary, reseated and ground. The motor parts should be inspected carefully, especially the pistons, rings, piston pins, crank case and connecting rod bearings. Any worn parts should be renewed. This attention is sure to mean a smooth running motor for the next season.

Handling of the Brake and Clutch.—The amount of "set" or wear on the brake lining depends entirely on the care used in handling the brake. A careless rider may find it necessary to adjust his brake every 500 miles. On the other hand, a careful rider, one who uses his brake properly, may not be obliged to adjust it inside of 4000 or 5000 miles.

What is true of the brake is also true of the clutch. The rider who is not afraid to use intermediate gear and low gear when occasion demands it, will not have to adjust his clutch as often as the rider who attempts to negotiate every hill on high gear or to pull through a long stretch of sand or mud without shifting into intermediate gear, or low gear. A hard pull causes a certain amount of "set" in the clutch, and only an occasional adjustment is necessary if the clutch is used as it should be. Some riders find

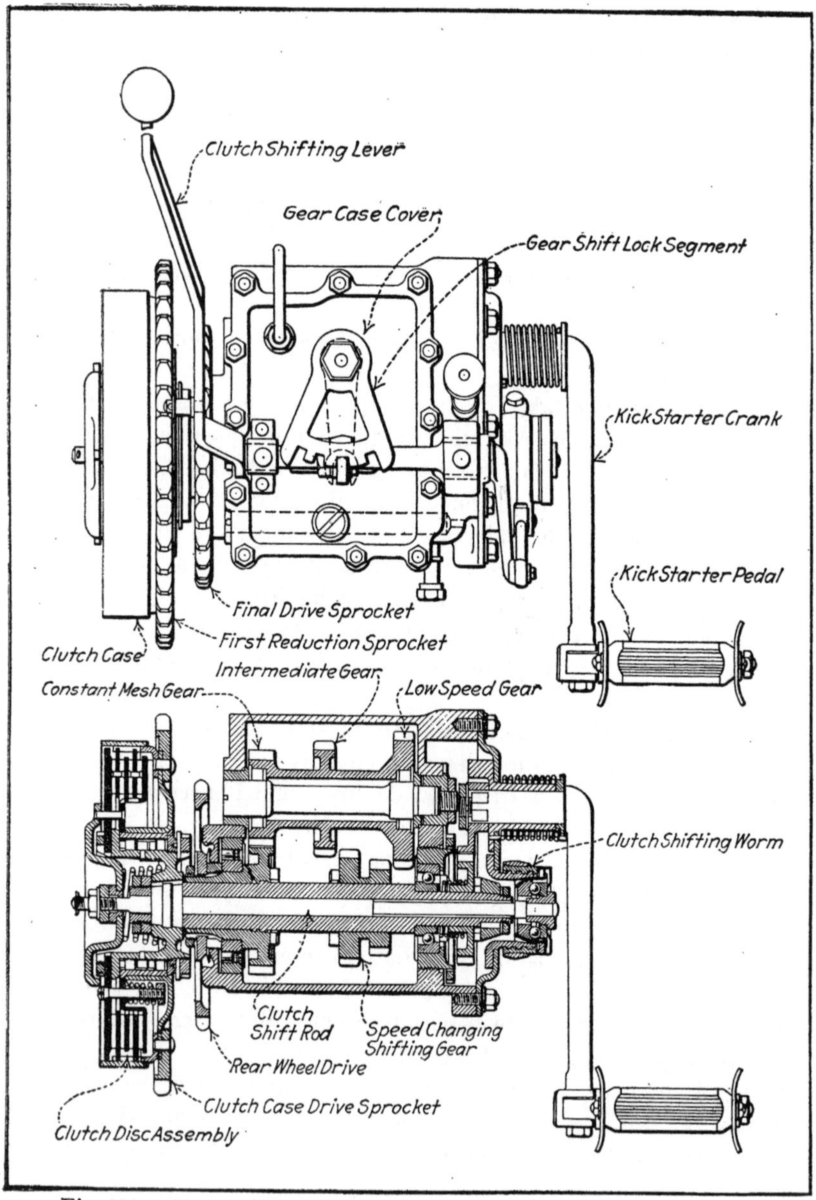

Fig. 299.—Change Speed Gearing and Clutch Assembly of Harley-Davidson Motorcycle.

it necessary to adjust the clutch every 800 or 1000 miles. Other riders will go through an entire season without tightening the clutch more than once or twice. The Harley-Davidson Clutch is shown at Figs. 299 and 301, the latter showing its important parts as they appear when clutch is dismantled.

To Adjust the Foot Brake.—If the foot brake does not hold and the foot pedal can be forced down to the foot board, the brake rod should be shortened. To shorten the brake rod, remove the pin "E" connecting the clevis of the brake rod to the brake arm shown at Fig. 302. Loosen the clevis lock nut "F" and screw the clevis "G" farther on the brake rod until the desired adjustment is obtained. Caution: Do not set up the brake too tight or overlook replacing the cotter pin in the brake clevis pin. With the machine on the stand the wheel must turn as freely as before the brake was adjusted. If the brake does not hold and the pedal cannot be pushed way down, inspect the pedal to see whether it is stuck or whether the various joints along the braking mechanism need lubricating.

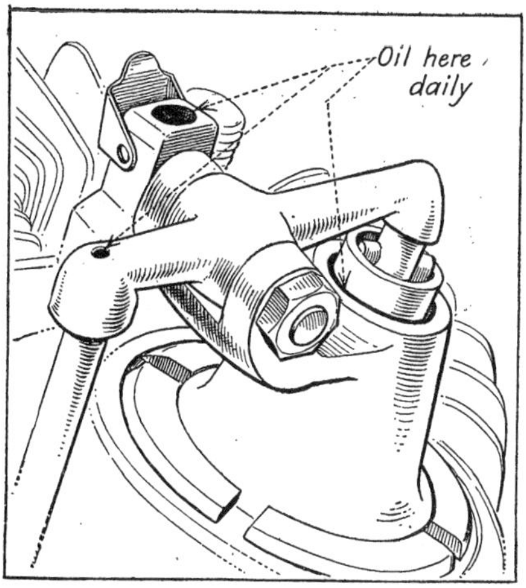

Fig. 300.—Points on Inlet Valve Rocker That Need Daily Oiling.

To Adjust the Hand Brake.—The hand brake (which is only furnished as special equipment) requires adjusting from time to time due to natural wear, as well as when the position of the rear wheel has been changed to adjust the chain. The proper adjustment can in most cases be obtained by merely adjusting the brake band eye bolt "A" and clamp "D."

Before making any adjustment it is advisable to remove the long drive chain and set the machine on the stand. If the brake will not hold properly, loosen nut "C" in illustration, a few turns; then tighten nut "B." Be careful that the brake is not set tight enough to drag, by turning the wheel while making this adjustment. The wheel must turn perfectly free after the adjustment has been made, and the brake lever must bear against the stop when released. If the lever will not bear against this stop, brake action will be lost. In this case readjusting of the frame clamp "D" on the stay will be necessary.

To Adjust the Clutch.—If it is noticed that the clutch is slipping and will not hold properly when pulling hard, it should be adjusted at once.

Fig. 301.—Parts of Harley-Davidson Motorcycle Clutch.

Before turning the adjusting screws make sure that the adjustment of the clutch lever is correct as explained in the following paragraphs.

If the clutch lever has no free motion when in the extreme forward position the clutch will slip. Therefore see that this adjustment is correct before tightening the adjusting screws. The clutch will not hold even though the adjusting screws are tightened, if the adjustment of the clutch lever is not correct. On the other hand, the clutch will not release if the hand lever has too much play. To insure that the clutch holds and releases properly the clutch hand lever must have ½ inch to ¾ inch free motion at the top end when it is in the extreme forward position.

If the clutch lever of a three-speed model has no free motion when it is in the forward position, turn the nuts off the clutch pull rod until this free motion is obtained. One-quarter turn of these nuts will make a decided difference in the clutch lever adjustment. These nuts are reached through the large hole in the chain guard, without removing the latter. A special wrench, No. DK805 in illustration Fig. 288, is provided for this purpose. After turning the adjusting nut, tighten the lock nut.

If the clutch slips and it is seen that the adjustment of the clutch lever is correct, it is generally possible to tighten the clutch suffi-

Fig. 302.—How to Adjust Harley-Davidson Motorcycle Brake.

ciently by giving each of the six clutch adjusting screws one-half turn to the right. These screws can be reached through the small hole in the chain guard, without removing the latter. Care should be taken to see that the six screws are given the same number of turns regardless of how hard some may turn. One-half turn is generally sufficient, but if this does not tighten the clutch enough, a second half turn, making one full turn for each screw, should prove to be ample. The adjusting screws are self-locking, therefore be sure that each screw drops into its seat properly after each half turn.

Sometimes the rider may find that the clutch engages too quickly, or that there is too much free motion when the clutch lever is all the way forward. In this case the clutch will not release. This can be remedied by turning the adjusting nuts farther onto the clutch pull rod.

Care of the Hubs.—The only attention required by the hubs is lubrication with cup grease every 3000 miles, and occasional inspection to see that the bearings are properly adjusted. To test the adjustment of the hub bearings, turn the wheel slowly to see whether it spins easily and rolls freely. Then see if there is any shake to the wheel, that is, any great amount of side play or lost motion. A very slight shake indicates proper adjustment.

To Adjust and Lubricate the Front Hub.—To overcome shake in the front wheel it is best to remove the wheel from the machine. Remove the cotter pin in the castellated lock nut and then the nut. Remove the axle which is of the knock-out type and take out the wheel. Loosen either one of the cone lock nuts. Remove the lock washer from the pin in the cone; then turn the cone to the right until nearly all shake is eliminated. Fit the lock washer and firmly draw up the lock nut. See that there is a very slight shake in the bearing. Replace the wheel in the forks and draw up the castellated lock nut; then replace the cotter pin. Try the wheel once more for play. Make sure that there is a very little play as an indication that the bearing is not being clamped.

To lubricate the front wheel bearings, the cones must be taken apart and removed from the wheel. Wash the cones, balls and ball races with gasoline. Inspect carefully for wear. If the parts are O. K., pack the races with good cup grease and reassemble. An oil cup is also provided. Inject a few drops of oil every two weeks.

To Adjust and Lubricate the Rear Hub.—Remove the wheel from the frame. Remove the left axle clamp nut, left axle clip, spacer washer, left cone lock nut and left cone. Draw out the axle to the right. Wash the axle, cones, balls and ball races with gasoline. Inspect for wear. If the parts are O. K., pack the races with good cup grease and reassemble. Adjust the bearings with the left cone. The right cone is locked stationary. The adjustment is O. K. if the axle can be turned perfectly free before the wheel is placed in the frame.

Caution: Never use a thin lubricant, such as oil or vaseline, in the rear wheel bearings. Such a lubricant will in time work past the oil retainers, get into the brake and cause slipping.

To Clean Your Motorcycle.—It pays to keep your motorcycle clean. A clean machine is attractive. There is a pleasure in driving it. To keep your motorcycle clean will also keep your clothes clean. Many parts of your motorcycle are easily damaged by allowing dust, grit and dirt to get into the working parts.

When it is necessary to wash your motorcycle use cold water and a good grade of soap—Ivory Soap is recommended. Be sure to rinse off all traces of soap with clean water, because soap is injurious to the fine enameled finish.

After washing, be certain that all parts are thoroughly dried to prevent rust. The enameled parts may be dried readily with a good clean chamois skin which has first been thoroughly soaked and then wrung out as dry as possible. Chamois skin will not absorb water readily unless it has been thoroughly moistened.

To prevent scratching, never attempt to clean any part of the machine, whether nickeled or enameled, with a dry rag. Gasoline may be used to clean the motor parts and other nickeled fittings. Care must be used to see that the gasoline does not come in contact with any enameled parts, because gasoline is injurious to the fine finish. A good way to clean the motor is to use a brush to apply the gasoline, after which the parts are wiped with a piece of cheesecloth.

When washing the motorcycle, cover up the magneto or generator.

If your motorcycle is badly covered with mud, better turn a hose on the parts covered with the most mud, giving the latter a chance to soak before attempting to remove. When using a hose, take off the nozzle and just let the water run over the parts, taking care to see that the water is only turned on part way. This helps to prevent injury to the finish.

To polish highly finished nickel plated parts, use nothing except a piece of cheesecloth moistened with kerosene, or a high-grade metal polish such as can be purchased of any Harley-Davidson dealer.

Lubrication and Care of the Three-Speed Transmission.—The only care or attention the three-speed transmission, shown at Fig. 299, requires is that the proper oil level be maintained. Under no circumstances should so-called transmission grease, such as is used in many automobile transmissions, be placed in the Harley-Davidson gear box. We recommend Harley-Davidson motor oil for transmission lubrication, the grade of oil depending on the season. Use the heavy oil in summer and the light oil in winter.

The transmission oil lever should be inspected at least once every 500 miles, or, say, once each week. Keep the level up to the top of the filler opening, and be sure the machine is standing level when the box is filled. Oil should be put in very slowly as it takes time to reach all low parts of the transmission.

There are several small oilers provided for lubricating the shifting device, clutch crank, etc. These should be taken care of with a drop of oil every week. A nice, smooth, easy working control makes it a pleasure to drive a motorcycle, while a difficult operating control will prove to be a constant source of annoyance.

Too much emphasis cannot be laid on the fact that liquid oil *only* should be used in lubricating the three-speed transmission. Hard oil or grease should not be placed in the transmission, even for emergency use, either in winter or summer. If Harley-Davidson oil cannot be obtained, use some other good motor oil for transmission lubrication.

Proper Adjustment of Drive Chains.—When the chains are properly adjusted they should be fairly tight, that is to say, they must not "hang" to any appreciable extent. On the other hand, they must not be tight in the strict sense of the word. There should be a little play. The average rider does not give his chain adjustment enough attention and it is such a simple matter to take proper care of the chains on the Harley-Davidson, that there is no excuse for this neglect at all.

Adjusting Front Chain.—Loosen the four nuts beneath the three-speed gear box with wrench No. DK807, Fig. 288. Loosen the lock nut on the adjusting screw which is exposed on the right rear side. A few turns of the adjusting screw will effect a decided tightening in the front chain. The chain should be watched carefully while the adjusting screw is turned.

Be sure to tighten the four nuts on the bottom of the transmission and also the adjusting screw lock nut after adjusting the front chain. This is extremely important.

Adjusting the Gear Shift and Clutch Rods.—If, after adjusting the chain, it is found that the gears do not engage readily, it will be necessary to readjust the three-speed shifter lever or the bracket on the frame loop, on account of the change in the position of the gear box. It will be difficult to shift into high gear if the shifter shaft comes in contact with the frame loop. If the shaft touches the frame, loosen the two cap screws that clamp the shifter bracket onto the frame a few turns, and tap the shifter bracket to the right and upward as may be needed. It should be possible to insert one thickness of paper between the shifter shaft and frame loop when the gear shifter lever is in high gear. After adjusting, tighten the cap screws.

It may also be necessary to adjust the clutch lever rod leading to the foot lever, to compensate for the new chain adjustment. When the clutch hand lever is way forward, the foot pedal must be in the same direction. If it is not, lengthen or shorten the foot clutch pedal rod as may be necessary.

To Adjust the Rear Chain.—The rear drive chain is adjusted by sliding the rear wheel backward or forward in the frame. To tighten the rear chain, loosen the axle clamp nuts, adjusting screw lock nuts and the brake arm clamp bolt a few turns, and turn the adjusting screws farther into the axle clips.

To loosen the rear chain, the wheel will have to be pushed forward after the adjusting screws have been turned farther out of the axle clips.

When adjusting the rear drive chain, be sure that the screws in both axle clips are given the same number of turns. This will facilitate correct adjustment without the necessity for testing the wheel alignment a number of times. Under no circumstances attempt to operate the motorcycle with the rear wheel out of alignment. This may result in a broken chain at any time, besides causing rapid chain and tire wear. Be sure that the chain runs true. Line up the rear drive sprocket properly with the countershaft sprocket. See that all nuts are again securely tightened.

As a matter of precaution always carry one or two chain repair links in your tool box besides the chain tool, for the unexpected

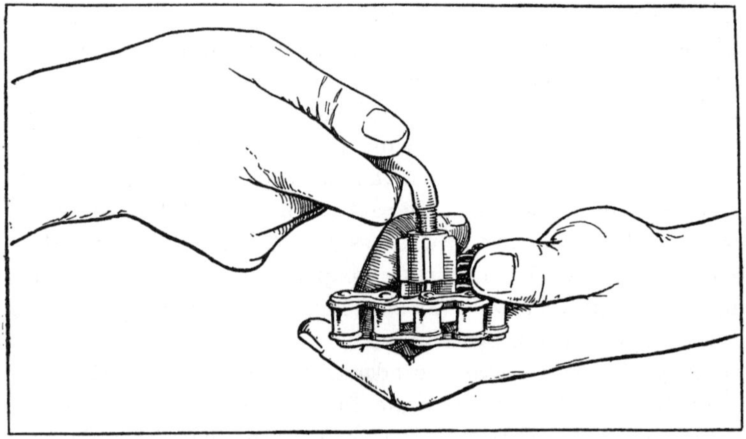

Fig. 303.—How to Use Special Chain Tool.

may happen in the form of a stick or stone being thrown between the drive chain and sprockets, resulting in a broken chain. With a repair link and a chain tool a quick repair can be effected.

To Repair a Drive Chain.—Examine both chains carefully every week or two. If a broken roller is found, fit a complete new link at once, because a broken roller is very hard on the sprockets and is likely to make the chain jump a sprocket, thereby breaking the chain or doing more serious damage.

How the Chain Tool Is To Be Used.—If a chain is to be repaired, refer to the illustration, Fig. 303, showing how the chain tool is to be used. Be sure that the roller pin or rivet of the chain is exactly beneath the point of the repair tool handle. If the chain has been properly placed in the tool, it is an easy matter to screw in the handle, thereby forcing the pin from the chain. Whenever a chain is taken apart, it will be found necessary to remove at least two rivets or pins.

After fitting a new chain link, be sure to put a few drops of oil between the rollers and the sides of the chain, taking care that the oil works in below the rollers. It is important to keep every roller properly lubricated.

Operation of Harley-Davidson Automatic Mechanical Oil Pump.—The Harley-Davidson oil pump has no check valves to stick, no ball valves to "float," no valve springs to break and no small parts to go wrong. In illustration Fig. 304 the rotary valve member R rotates in a left hand direction, looking at it from the top.

After the cam H has raised the plunger P to its highest point, the spring Y returns the plunger, drawing a change of oil from the tank through the supply pipe S, and through the intake system as follows:

Through the channel L, oil reaches the intake port I, in the valve chamber. The port I is connected with the hollow center C of distributor R. From C the oil passes through the opening A into the distributor channel X, then through channel B to pump chamber T.

Just after the completion of the intake stroke of the plunger P the intake port I closes and the discharge port D opens, lining up with channel E. As soon as the plunger is raised by the cam H, the oil in chamber T is discharged through the channels B, X, A, C, D (D is now opposite E), E and F to the sight feed. From the sight feed the oil is forced to the motor through opening G.

Although the highest crank case pressure registered to date in any Harley-Davidson motor tested was 4 pounds to the square inch, the Harley-Davidson oil pump will operate against a pressure of 70 pounds if necessary. It is absolutely infallible in its operation. There are no small parts to break. The pump has but two moving parts, the plunger "P" and the distributor valve member "R," rotated by a worm gear made integral with one of the gears.

To Adjust the Automatic Oil Pump.—When each motor is tested at the factory the mechanical oiler is adjusted so as to give the proper oil supply at speeds up to 45 miles per hour. With this adjustment a half pint of oil will average approximately 45 miles (720 miles to the gallon), if Harley-Davidson cylinder oil is used. This adjustment, as it leaves the factory, is such that plenty of oil will be fed to the motor and should not be changed excepting for good reason.

When the machine leaves the factory the mechanical oil pump is not fitted with any definite number of washers at "K." The number of washers varies, depending on the amount required to give the plunger $\frac{1}{32}$ inch stroke.

If for good reason it is desired to decrease the oil supply, remove one thin washer. The adjusting screw "J" regulates the stroke of the oil pump plunger and should be securely tightened after adjusting.

When all the washers have been removed the plunger has no stroke, and nothing can be gained by counterboring the cover or adding to the length of the screw.

In the tool box will be found two thin washers, each .013 inch thick and two washers each .065 inch thick. To increase the oil supply, add one of the thin washers at a time to the standard washers with which the machine comes from the factory, until the proper oil supply is obtained. Be very careful not to reduce the oil supply below the safety margin. It is better to feed a trifle too much oil than to run the chance of underoiling, but an absolutely correct adjustment can be made and should be.

What To Do When Oiler Overfeeds.—It may happen in a rare case that the motor receives too much oil with the adjusting screw raised as far as possible. In that event make the following adjustment: Fill the oil tank. Remove the operating shaft chamber cap vent screw "N." If the oil does not overflow readily, the oiler ports are not in line and the motor should be turned slowly until the oil overflows. Let a reasonable amount of oil overflow and replace the screw firmly. Then remove the plunger chamber cap vent screw "M" and let the oil overflow in the same manner as before. Replace the screw firmly.

After venting the oiler as just explained, regulate the oil supply by placing the same washers on the adjusting screws with which the machine was received from the factory. Drain the motor and fill with 1½ pumpfuls of oil with the hand pump.

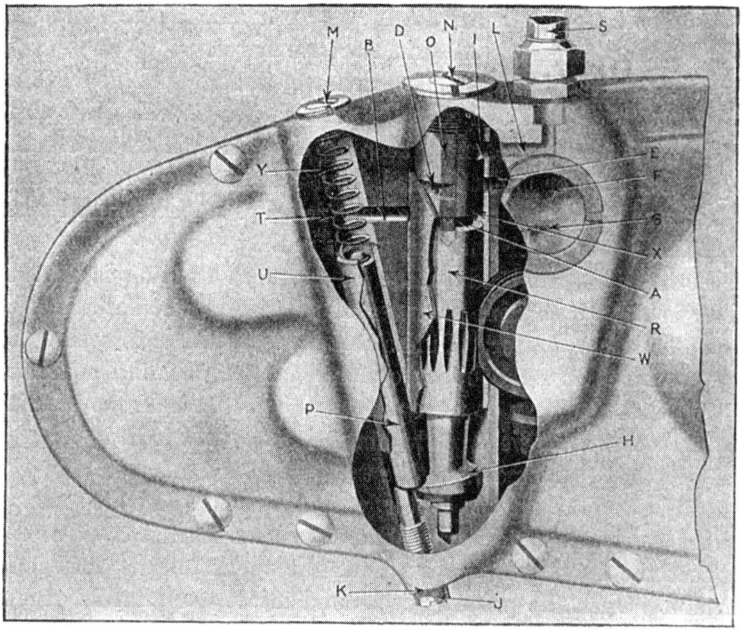

Fig. 304.—Construction of Harley-Davidson Mechanical Oil Pump.

Use Good Oil.—For the protection of Harley-Davidson owners, genuine Harley-Davidson oil is put up in one gallon and five gallon cans that are sealed and bear the name and trade mark lithographed on the tin. By purchasing this oil in original sealed containers, Harley-Davidson owners are assured of getting the genuine Harley-Davidson oil.

Harley-Davidson oil is sold by most Harley-Davidson dealers and for convenience we advise the rider to get his oil from the dealer directly. If your dealer does not sell Harley-Davidson oil he will obtain it for you. If you are so situated that you cannot buy oil from a dealer, write the factory. Take no chances. Use only the genuine.

Flushing the Motor With Kerosene.—Flush your motor every 750 miles. The purpose of flushing the motor is to loosen up and remove the carbon which may have accumulated in the combustion chambers, to keep the piston rings free and also to thoroughly clean out all the old oil and grit from the motor.

Frequent flushing is recommended even though Harley-Davidson oil is used, because all oil contains some carbon and frequent cleaning is the simplest means of keeping the motor in sweet running order. If a motor is not flushed from time to time, the carbon becomes hard and scraping is the only remedy. A carbonized motor overheats, loses power and will knock readily.

Another important advantage of frequent flushing is that the motor is kept free from particles of dust and grit that will work through the carburetor. Unless this foreign matter is removed, it will combine with the burnt oil and carbon, forming a mixture that will act as emery on the cylinder, the pistons, and the bearings, and cause excessive wear. Flushing with kerosene is an inexpensive way of keeping the motor in fine trim the year round.

It is best to flush the motor while it is hot. Do not run the motor on the stand to heat it but always flush after a ride. Disconnect the spark plug cables from the spark plugs. This is important. Open the priming cocks and inject five gunfuls of kerosene into each cylinder. The kerosene striking the hot motor is vaporized, loosening the carbon from all surfaces. If the kerosene were injected in a cold motor, this advantage would be sacrificed, for the kerosene would only reach the piston heads.

After having injected the kerosene, fill the crank case with kerosene. Disconnect the hand pump oil pipe at the lower connection; then remove the nipple from the crank case and pour in a quart of kerosene. Replace the nipple and connect the oil pipe. Of course, the spark plug cables must be disconnected as already instructed, for if an explosion occurred while the motor were filled with kerosene vapor, serious damage might result.

Turn the motor over briskly 10 or 15 times to distribute the kerosene and to thoroughly clean the crank case, remove the crank case drain plug as quickly as possible, and the burnt oil, carbon and kerosene will drain out before the solid matter has had time to settle. Be sure to turn over the motor a few times while draining, because this will materially assist the removal of all solid matter. Tilt the machine over to the left slightly and do not replace the crank case drain plug before you are sure that all kerosene has drained off.

Replace the drain plug and pump two pumpfuls of oil into the crank case with the hand pump. Crank the motor a few times to distribute the oil to the bearings, cylinder and piston surfaces before running the machine.

Advice on Lubrication.—One of the most important considerations, making for efficient action and promoting long life of the mechanism, is to provide proper lubrication. The lubrication of the power plant is the most serious proposition. The best oil is the only kind that should be used, as more good motors have been ruined by the use of lubricant of improper quality or insufficient quantity than have been destroyed by accidents. If a drip sight feed is used, as in early models, a medium grade oil may be employed in warm weather, but a light grade will be necessary in cold weather. If the supply is by mechanically operated pump, a heavier bodied lubricant may be used than when the drip feed system is employed. When oil is introduced to the engine crankcase by means of a hand-operated pump as on very early models, such as built prior to 1913-14, which means that lubrication is directly under the control of the rider, one pumpful of oil, every 8 or 10 miles, at speeds of 20 miles per hour will be sufficient. For a speed of 30 miles per hour, it will be necessary to inject a pumpful every 5 or 6 miles. It is better to over-lubricate a machine than not to supply enough, so any time that the rider is in doubt it will be well to inject another pumpful on general principles. If the engine is over-lubri-

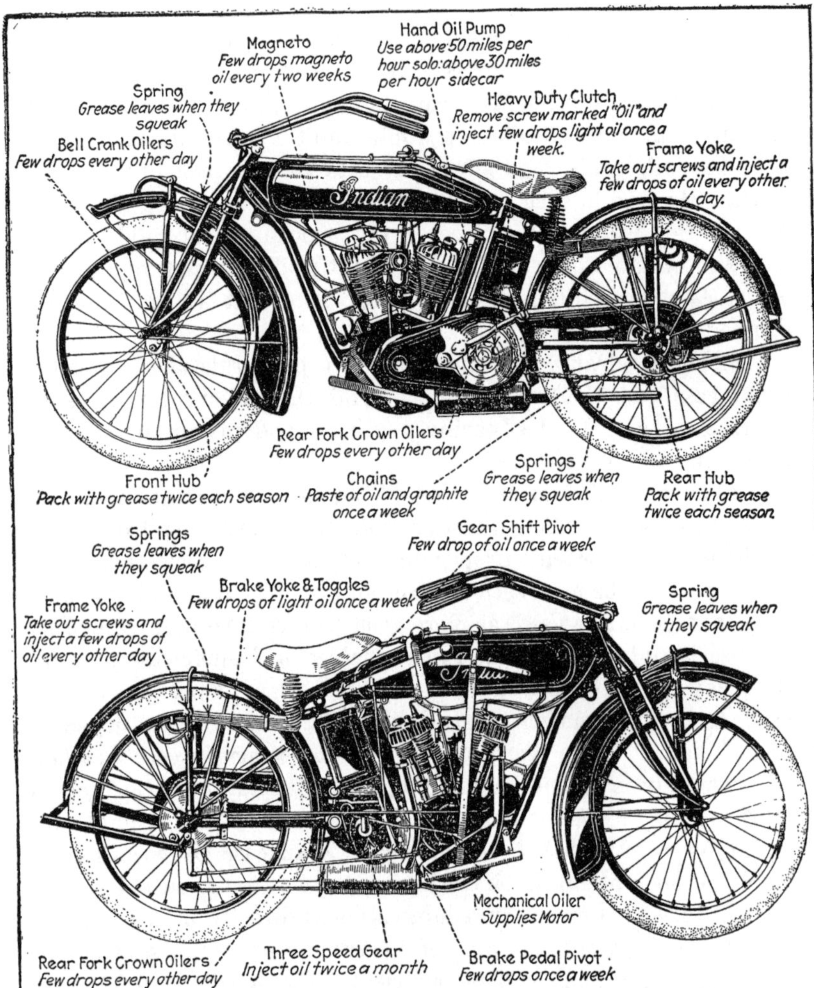
Magneto
Few drops magneto oil every two weeks
Hand Oil Pump
Use above 50 miles per hour solo: above 30 miles per hour sidecar
Spring
Grease leaves when they squeak
Heavy Duty Clutch
Remove screw marked "Oil" and inject few drops light oil once a week.
Bell Crank Oilers
Few drops every other day
Frame Yoke
Take out screws and inject a few drops of oil every other day.
Rear Fork Crown Oilers
Few drops every other day
Springs
Grease leaves when they squeak
Front Hub
Pack with grease twice each season
Chains
Paste of oil and graphite once a week
Rear Hub
Pack with grease twice each season
Springs
Grease leaves when they squeak
Gear Shift Pivot
Few drop of oil once a week
Brake Yoke & Toggles
Few drops of light oil once a week
Spring
Grease leaves when they squeak
Frame Yoke
Take out screws and inject a few drops of oil every other day
Mechanical Oiler
Supplies Motor
Rear Fork Crown Oilers
Few drops every other day
Three Speed Gear
Inject oil twice a month
Brake Pedal Pivot
Few drops once a week

Fig. 305.—Views of Indian Power-Plus Twin-Cylinder Motorcycle. Showing Points Needing Periodical Lubrication.

cated, the exhaust will be smoky. If a mechanically operated oil pump is used and the hand pump is provided only as an auxiliary, it will not be necessary to supply oil except at such times that the engine is run exceptionally fast.

Among some of the points that should receive oil every time the machine is used may be mentioned the valve lifters, or rocker arms, the free engine clutch, the steering head, and the various hinges and joints on the spring frame or spring fork. If a two-speed gear is provided the supply of lubricant should be renewed every 300 miles. Planetary gearing requires more lubricant and a lighter semi-fluid grease than either the sliding clutch or sliding gear forms. It is well to put a few drops of oil in the front hub and coaster brake oilers every day. About the only point on the motorcycle that can receive too much oil beside the engine interior is the magneto, and only a few drops are required every two or three months to insure adequate functioning of this device. A special light oil is necessary for the magneto, and a good grade of sewing machine or 3 in 1 oil will be found satisfactory for this purpose. The hand oil-can may be filled with cylinder oil which can be used on all points of the machine, because if it is good enough for the engine interior, it is much better than needed for the various external parts. The ball bearings in the hubs, countershaft, and steering head may be packed with grease once or twice a season which will be adequate. Specific instructions are given for oiling leading motorcycles in proper sequence. The principal points calling for lubrication on the Indian Powerplus model is shown at Fig. 305.

Care of Indian Magneto.—The Aero Magneto is used on all twin cylinder Powerplus models. It should be oiled every 1,000 miles with magneto oil or 3-in-1 and the contact breaker points should be looked at and cleaned at least once a month. Use sand-paper, 00 grade, for dressing the points. Emery cloth should not be used, it leaves small particles in the platinum which cause trouble. Full instructions for the adjustment and care of this instrument are found in the chapter on ignition. Do not put grease or other lubricant in the timing gear casing, as the motor automatically takes care of the lubrication of all the gears in the train.

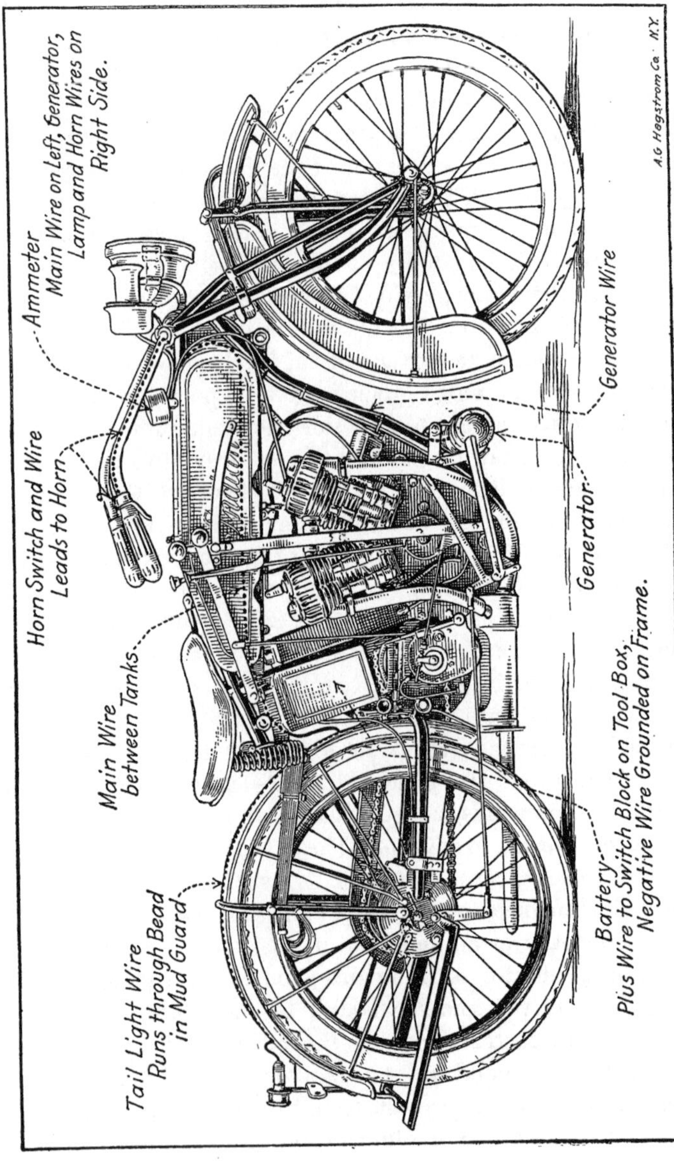

Fig. 306.—Electrical System of Indian Power Plus Motorcycle.

Care of Electric Generator.—The Splitdorf DUI generator, shown in Fig. 306, supplies current for the battery and lights. It is driven by a coiled wire belt from a pulley attached to the motor shaft sprocket. It is independent of the magneto and is carried in front of the motor. An instruction book for this generator is found in the tool box of every electrically-equipped Powerplus motorcycle. Write the Splitdorf Electrical Company for additional information.

Care of Electric Wiring.—All ignition wiring is heavily insulated and thoroughly waterproof. The cable from the front of the magneto leads to the rear spark plug, while that from the rear leads to the front cylinder spark plug. Keep all connections tight and inspect cables occasionally for chafing. If chafing occurs, tape worn places and fasten cable to prevent recurrence of trouble.

The wiring for the lighting system is heavily insulated, also. Keep the connections tight. Watch the ammeter and lights as a check on the condition of these cables.

Operation of Lamp and Horn.—The headlight has two bulbs, a main and a pilot. The small or pilot bulb is above the main bulb; it is used when riding in cities and towns and other places where a bright light is prohibited. It is also used when the motorcycle is standing at the curb.

The main bulb is of 21 candle power and is provided with a focussing attachment. Both bulbs are controlled by a push-button and a bayonet-joint switch. The latter is connected to a wire from the ammeter. When the bayonet-joint switch is pushed in and turned to the right, one of the two bulbs is on. To light the other, use the push-button switch. One pressure changes the light from one bulb to the other. Both lights are extinguished when the bayonet-joint switch is turned to the left.

An electric horn is of the vibrator type, mounted on the handlebar close to the head. A wire leads from the ammeter to the horn socket, while a second goes from the horn to the horn switch on the right handle-bar. Pressing the horn switch blows the horn.

What the Ammeter Indicates.—The Indian ammeter, fitted

to electrically-equipped Powerplus models, gives an indication of what is going on in the entire electric system. It is also a first-class trouble detector, when any arises.

The ammeter shows a range of 5 amperes charge and discharge. The zero of the scale is at the center; all marks to the right indicate that the battery is charging. All marks to the left of the zero indicate discharge. The long marks are whole amperes while the short marks are half amperes.

When motor is stopped and lights not being used, the pointer should cover the zero on the scale. When the motor is running and the lights are off, the pointer will indicate the amount of current sent into the battery. Normally this will be between 2 and 3 amperes, according to the speed of the motor and the condition of the storage battery.

When tail light and pilot bulb are on and the motor stopped, the pointer will indicate half an ampere discharge. With main headlight bulb and tail light on, motor stopped, the pointer will show 2 amperes on discharge side. When motor is running and lights are on the ammeter will show the difference between the amount of current the generator is giving and what the lamps are taking. This will be shown on the charge side of the scale. Horn blowing is shown on the discharge side of the scale, as the horn takes 2-2½ amperes.

As Trouble Detector.—With motor stopped and lights off, if the pointer shows a discharge, there is a short circuit in the system. Hunt for it. With motor running, if the ammeter pointer jumps quickly or moves continually from side to side, there is a loose connection. If the pointer moves to the charge (right) side, the loose connection is between generator and battery. If it moves to the discharge (left) side, the trouble is between the battery and lamps or horn.

If there is an open circuit between battery and generator (very rare), the ammeter will indicate normal discharge for the lamps which are lighted, whether the motor is running or not. Trace the broken wire and repair immediately. If the open circuit is between the battery and lamps or horn, the ammeter will show excessive discharge when the lamps are on. If this is not corrected, the lamps may burn out. With motor stopped and lamps switched on, if the pointer shows zero and the lamps do not burn, there is a break between battery and lamps.

A break or open circuit between the main wire and any lamp will be indicated by that lamp not burning, and the ammeter will indicate the discharge for the remaining lamps only.

If when the motor is running and no lights on, the ammeter pointer stays at zero, the driving belt may be found to be loose or broken.

General Maintenance of Motorcycle.—Keep it clean. Give it this attention regularly, as it will keep the mechanism at its best working point. The appearance of the machine also reflects on the rider.

Use kerosene on enamelled parts, not gasoline. Use gasoline to remove grease and oil from the motor base, motor, etc. Gasoline will dim the lustre of the enamelled surfaces, hence it should not be used on them. Do not use either gasoline or kerosene in the presence of an open flame, or a fire may result.

The use of a good nickel polish will prevent rusting of plated parts. Kerosene can also be used on these parts if polish is not available. A clean motorcycle adds to the pleasure of operating it and also makes it worth more when offered for sale.

Try all bolts and nuts at least once a week. Any loose parts will be detected by regular inspection of this kind and prevent trouble on the road.

What Spares To Carry.—For average riding, carry the regular tire and tool kits, spare chain links and connectors, a spark plug, an extra valve, a roll of tire tape, some copper wire.

For long trips, in addition to the above, carry a spare inner tube well wrapped and *not* placed in the tool box, a few cotter pins, miscellaneous nuts and washers, a valve inside or plunger (tire valve), and an inside blow-out patch. It is not necessary to load the machine with enough parts to rebuild it. Genuine Indian parts can be obtained from Indian dealers in every important city and town.

Where to Oil Indian Motorcycle and When.—Study the Oiling Diagram in Fig. 305 and follow the directions carefully.

To remind you:

ONCE A WEEK.—Oil shackle pins of rear springs and front fork link. Oil clutch. Oil working joints of brake, clutch and gear shift linkage. Oil hinge of rear fork crown.

500 MILES.—Put on a paste of oil and graphite. See Care of Chains.

1,000 MILES.—A few drops of light oil in magneto and electric generator.

HUBS.—Pack with grease twice a season.

THREE-SPEED BOX.—See Oiling directions under Three-Speed Gear.

BELL CRANKS.—Give a turn on the lubricator handles at frequent intervals. Refill with cup-grease when empty.

Tips Which Save Trouble.—Don't race the motor on the stand. This abuse has ruined more motors than road use.

Don't use inferior oil; use the oils recommended. They keep the motor new.

Don't neglect to oil all parts needed, as indicated in the Oiling Diagram.

Don't oil electrical apparatus any oftener or anywhere than when directed to.

Don't forget that the motorcycle will serve you in proportion to the way you operate it and care for it.

Don't forget to keep the motorcycle clean; inspect it regularly and make necessary adjustments in the garage. It is more convenient and pleasant than having to do it on the road.

Don't forget you can obtain service from over 2,800 Indian dealers. You Don't have to carry a repair shop with you.

Don't expect to get from the battery more than 90 per cent of the current you put in it.

Don't use counterfeit parts. They are made of poor material, wear out rapidly, require frequent replacement and void the guarantee. Genuine parts are better and cheaper in the long run.

Don't fail to keep tires properly inflated at all times.

Don't spin the rear wheel when starting. Let the clutch engage gently. Each time the wheel spins, rubber is worn off the tire, cutting down its mileage and rendering it more susceptible to puncture.

Don't daydream while riding. Keep your eyes on the road at all times.

Don't look at the control levers every time you operate them. Get the habit of locating them instinctively.

Don't open and close the throttle suddenly. It injures the motor and makes enemies for motorcycling.

Don't force the machine to climb a hill on high gear when the motor is laboring. It strains the motor and transmission. Change early to a low gear.

Be sure to see that your registration card is filed with the factory at the earliest possible opportunity.

Keep your tires pumped up to proper pressure.

Keep lighted matches and flames away from your motorcycle.

Never run the motor more than a few seconds at any time on the stand.

Keep all control parts properly oiled and working easily.

Keep your chains properly adjusted, clean and well lubricated.

Never take your machine apart unless it is a matter of urgent necessity.

Never ride through a town with your muffler cutout open.

Never exceed the speed laws of your locality.

See that the three-speed transmission is kept properly filled with oil.

Keep your small gasoline or emergency tank filled and closed for all ordinary riding. This will insure an emergency supply when you need it.

Three Basic Principles of Efficient Motor Service.—Use good oil and flush your motor with kerosene every 750 miles.

Do not run your motor on the stand more than absolutely necessary and never at high speed.

Let a new motor work in gradually before running it at high speed on the road. Do not run faster than 35 miles per hour during the first 300 miles.

Operation and Care of Cleveland Motorcycle.—Broadly speaking, the mechanism of the Cleveland Motorcycle, shown at Fig. 307, may, for convenience in explaining the functions of the various parts, be considered as consisting of three general groups or units. The first will include all of the parts corresponding to an ordinary bicycle, such as the frame, front fork, wheels, handle bar, etc., all of which are so generally understood that no further comments regarding them should be necessary.

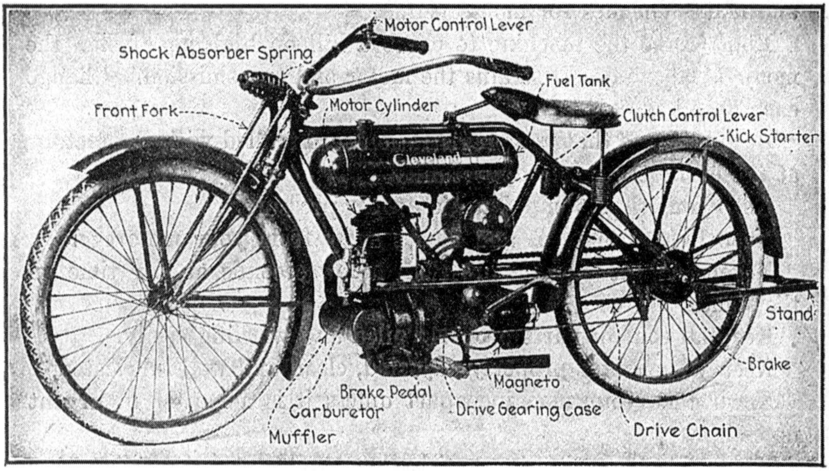

Fig. 307.—The Cleveland Lightweight Motorcycle, Showing Principal Parts.

The second group, or power unit, includes the motor with its carburetor, muffler and ignition apparatus, the transmission or speed changing device and the clutch, while the third group or control system consists of the various pedals, levers, and other mechanism by means of which the motorcycle is operated.

The simplest practical form of gasoline motor in use at the present time is known as the three port, two stroke type, this being the design which is used on the Cleveland.

Figs. 308 to 310 inclusive show a motor of this type with its outer walls cut away and its moving parts in the positions which they occupy at different times during the cycle of operations.

Referring to Fig. 308 the various parts may be identified as follows:

"A" represents the cylinder, inside of which the closely fitting piston "B" may be made to move up and down. The connecting rod "C" is furnished with a bearing at its upper end through which wrist pin "D" passes to hinge it to the piston. At its lower end, crank pin "E" passes through another bearing into flywheel "F" which turns in the air tight crank case "G." At "H" is the inlet port or opening through which gas is admitted to the motor, with the exhaust port "K," through which the burned gas escapes, directly above it. By-pass "L" is a passage which connects the crank case with the cylinder through the transfer port "M." "R" is the spark plug, between the points of which the spark for igniting the gas takes place, and "S" is the compression release valve, the object of which will be explained later.

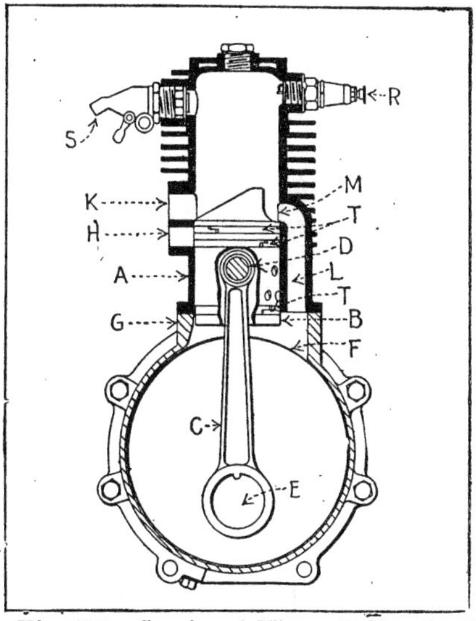

Fig. 308.—Sectional View of Cleveland Motorcycle Engine.

Having identified all of the essential parts of the motor, we will now consider what takes place when it is in operation.

Starting with the piston at the bottom of the cylinder as shown by Fig. 308, assume that the fly-wheel is being slowly turned around by hand, moving always in the same direction.

As the flywheel turns, the piston, pushed up into the cylinder, by the connecting rod, acts as an air pump, creating a partial vacuum in the crank case, which, as previously mentioned, is air-tight. As the piston moves up to the position shown in Fig. 309A its lower edge begins to uncover the inlet port, leaving an opening through which the gas passes, drawn in by the vacuum in the crank case.

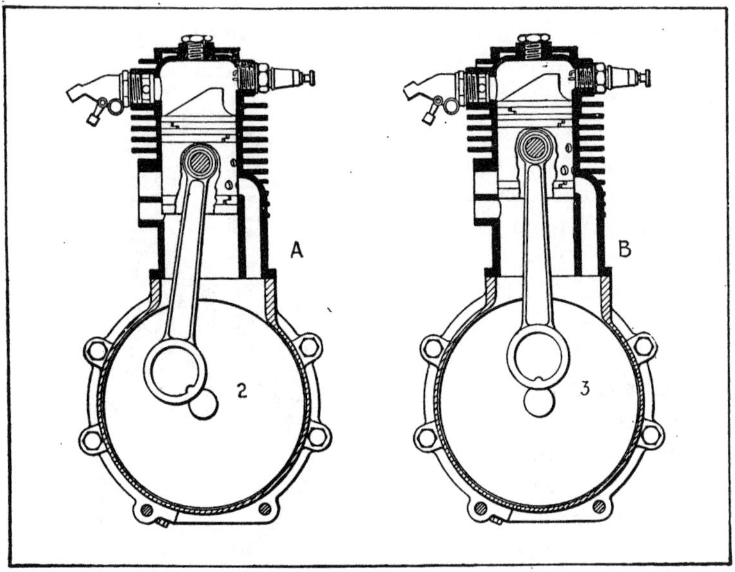

Fig. 309.—Diagrams Explaining Action of Cleveland Motorcycle Engine.

By the time the piston reaches the top of the cylinder (Fig. 309B) the inlet port is entirely uncovered, and the motor has taken in a full charge of gas. Continued movement of the flywheel causes the connecting rod to pull the piston back toward the lower end of the cylinder, closing the inlet port and preventing the escape of the gas which has just been drawn into the crank case. Further downward travel of the piston compresses this gas, until, in the position shown in Fig. 310A, its upper edge begins to uncover the transfer port, allowing the compressed gas to pass from the crank case through the by-pass into the cylinder.

When the piston reaches the bottom of the cylinder and is back in the position shown by Fig. 308, the transfer port is wide open, and the full charge of gas has passed from the crank case to the cylinder.

It will be noted that at this time the exhaust port is also wide open, and it might be expected that the incoming gas would pass directly over the piston and out of the exhaust port without doing

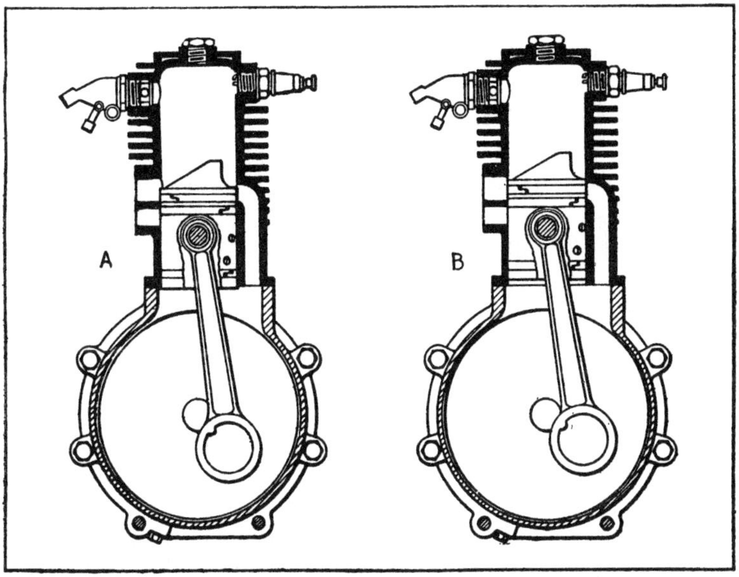

Fig. 310.—Diagrams Explaining Action of Cleveland Motorcycle Engine.

any useful work. However, this is avoided by means of a projection or baffle plate on top of the piston, the object of which is to deflect the incoming gas toward the top of the cylinder and away from the open exhaust port.

The piston now starts once more on its upward travel, closing the exhaust and transfer ports and again compressing the gas, which, however, is now in the cylinder instead of the crank case. In the meantime another vacuum is being created in the crank case and the inlet port opened to admit another charge of gas, exactly as was done during the first upward stroke. At the instant when the second upward stroke is completed and the piston is once more in the position shown by Fig. 309B, the compressed gas above it is ignited by a spark at the spark plug, driving the piston down on its power stroke, and at the same time compressing the fresh charge in the crank case. Nearing the end of this stroke the top of the piston uncovers the exhaust port (see Fig. 310B) allowing the burned gas to escape through the muffler and outlet pipe.

Immediately after the opening of the exhaust port, the transfer port is again opened to admit fresh gas (Fig. 310A) thus completing the cycle of operations which, after the motor is started, is repeated at every revolution of the flywheel or "two strokes" of the piston.

In order to prevent leakage of gas past the piston, it is provided with three grooves into which cast iron piston rings "T," Fig. 308, are closely fitted. These rings are made slightly larger than the inside diameter of the cylinder and split so that they spring out against the cylinder wall, thus forming a gas-tight joint.

On account of the rapidity with which the successive charges of gas are ignited in the cylinder, it is evident that a great deal of heat is generated, which, if not dissipated in some manner, would interfere seriously with the operation of the motor. This is taken care of by providing the cylinder with a number of fins or flanges which greatly increase the area of its outside wall, and provide a large surface which the relatively cooler air blows against when the machine is running. The Cleveland unit power plant construction is clearly shown in Fig. 311 which outlines all important parts as they actually appear in the engine.

Transmission Gear.—Every bicycle rider is familiar with the fact that it is much easier to propel a low-geared bicycle up hill or through sand than is the case when a high-geared machine is used. The terms "low-geared" and "high-geared," as used in this connection, refer to the ratio between the number of times which the rear wheel will revolve during a given number of turns of the pedals. For instance, if the rear wheel on one machine makes two revolutions to one of the pedals, it would be low geared as compared with one on which the wheel makes three revolutions while the pedals are making one. Assuming that a certain pressure on the pedals is required to turn them, it is evident that in traveling a given distance, this pressure can be exerted more frequently with a low-geared machine than is possible with a higher gear. The same explanation applies to the gearing of a motorcycle; the power stroke

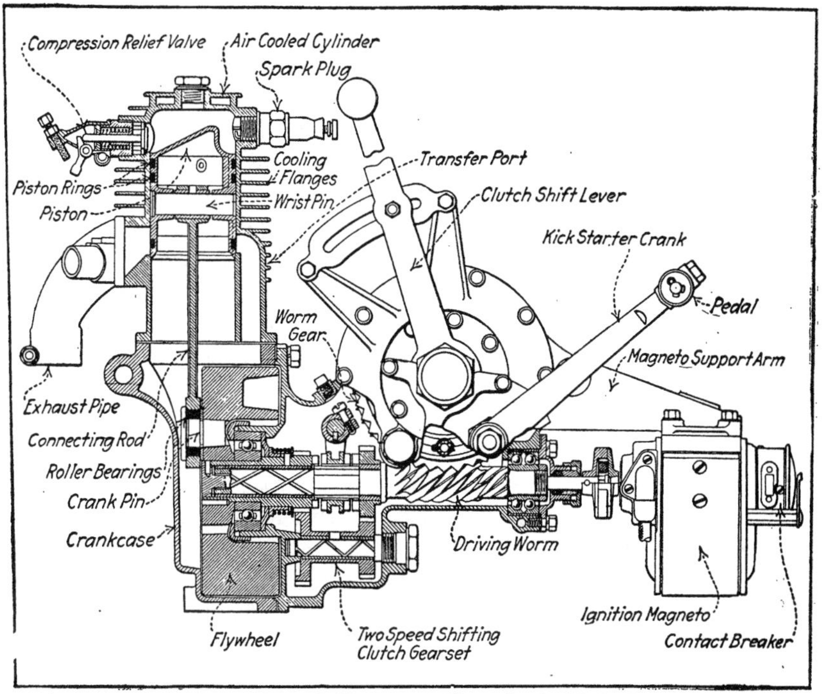

Fig. 311.—The Simplicity of Cleveland Two-Cycle Unit Power Plant Is Clearly Shown in Sectional View.

of the piston corresponds to the pressure which the rider exerts on the pedals, and any variation in the gear ratio affects the number of power strokes delivered by the piston while the machine is moving a given distance.

On a bicycle, one gear ratio is usually sufficient and ordinarily no provision is made for changing it except by substituting larger or smaller sprockets. On a motorcycle, however, some means for quickly and conveniently changing to a low gear is very desirable, and this is accomplished by the transmission or two speed gear, which, in addition to the high gear or "direct drive," provides a much lower ratio for starting, hill-climbing, etc.

On the Cleveland motorcycle, the power is transmitted from the motor through a hardened steel worm to a bronze worm gear mounted on the shaft which carries the front or driving sprocket. From this point, the drive is by chain to another sprocket on the rear wheel.

The transmission gear is located between the flywheel and the worm, as shown in Fig. 311, and is so arranged that when the high gear is in use, the worm is driven at the same speed as the motor. With the low gear in operation the speed of the worm is relatively much slower. The manner in which this is accomplished is shown by Figs. 312 and 313A and B, which represent the various parts of the transmission gear and driving mechanism as they would appear if removed bodily from their case or housing and viewed from the side of the machine.

Referring to Fig. 312, "A" is the connecting rod and "B" is the flywheel. These parts, together with the worm "C" and worm gear "D" should not be considered as a part of the transmission gear, but are illustrated in connection with it in order to show its action more clearly. The transmission consists of the flywheel gear "E," countershaft "F," worm gear "G" and transmission clutch "H" with its shift yoke "K." The flywheel gear has a long hub or extension which is pressed into a hole in the center of the flywheel and fastened so that when the latter is turning the flywheel gear rotates with it, driving the countershaft through gear "L." The countershaft revolves on countershaft pin "M," and at its rear end a small gear "N" drives the worm shaft gear "G." The front end of the worm is made in the form of a shaft which passes through the center of the worm shaft gear and into the hub of the flywheel gear. The transmission clutch is mounted on the worm shaft between these gears, and may be moved back and forth by rocking the shift yoke. This yoke is attached to the shift yoke shaft "R" which projects through the side of the worm gear housing and is connected to the operating mechanism. The hole through the clutch and the section of the worm shaft between gears "E" and "G" are shaped so that although the clutch is free to slide back and forth on the shaft, it must rotate with it.

Each end of the clutch is provided with four jaws or projections,

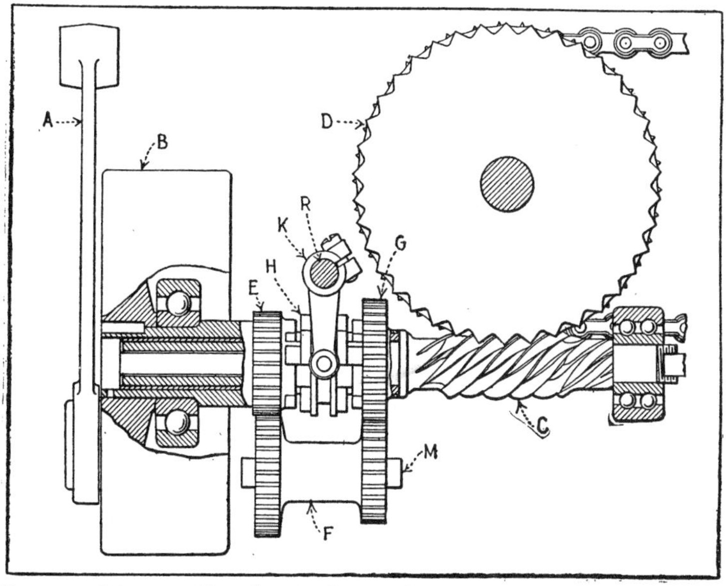

Fig. 312.—Diagram Showing Action of Change Speed and Transmission Gear of Cleveland Motorcycle.

equally spaced around the hole through which the worm shaft passes. Corresponding jaws are formed on the rear end of the flywheel gear and on the front end of the worm shaft gear.

Assuming that the motor is running, and the clutch is in its neutral position, or midway between gears "E" and "G," as shown by Fig. 312, gear "E," countershaft "F" and gear "G" will all rotate, but as gears "E" and "G" are free to turn on the worm shaft without driving it, no power is being transmitted to the rear wheel. As gear "E" is attached to the flywheel its speed in

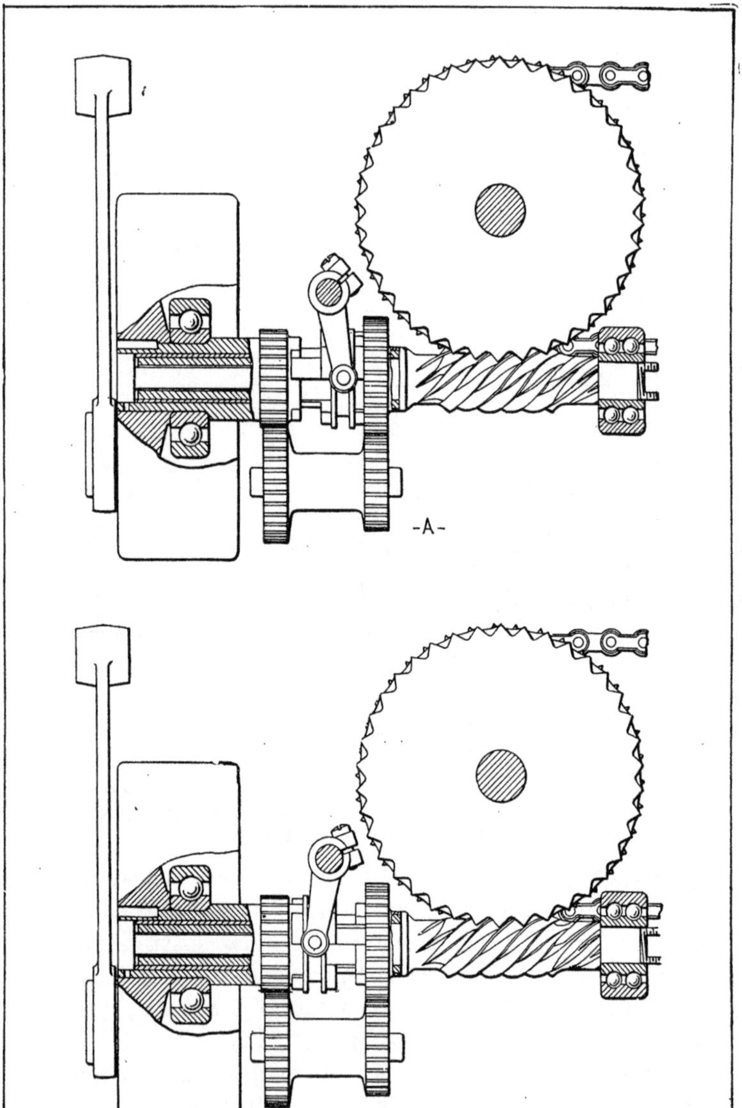
-A-
-B-

revolutions per minute is, of course, exactly the same as that of the motor, but the speed of gear "G" is very much slower, this being due to the fact that when a large gear is driven by a smaller one, the speed of the larger gear is lower than that of its driver, the difference being proportional to the difference in size. Consequently as gear "L" is larger than flywheel gear "E," the speed of the countershaft will be slower than that of the motor, and gear "N," driving the large gear "G," causes the latter to rotate at a still lower speed. When the clutch is moved back until its jaws engage those on this gear, as shown by Fig. 313A, the low gear is in operation, and the clutch, gear, and worm rotate as a unit. To bring the high gear into action the clutch is moved forward until it engages flywheel gear "E" (Fig. 313B), which turns the worm at motor speed.

Clutch.—On account of overheating, waste of fuel, and unnecessary wear and tear which would be sure to result, it is inadvisable to operate the motor for any considerable length of time while the machine is at a standstill. However, it is permissible and very convenient to run it during short stops, such as are frequently necessary in driving through congested traffic, etc., and the clutch now under consideration it fitted to enable this to be done. It is of the friction type, and should not be confused with the positive or jaw clutch which is used in the transmission, as the functions of the two are entirely different. Its action depends upon the friction between two sets of steel discs, one set of which is attached to the worm gear in such a manner that its discs alternate with those of the other, the second set being attached to the shaft on which the driving sprocket is mounted. When the discs are pressed tightly together by springs which are provided for the purpose, the worm gear and sprocket revolve together, and when the spring pressure is released, the discs in the two sets separate so that the worm is free to rotate without turning the sprocket shaft.

Fig. 314A shows the clutch engaged, with the plates pressed together as they appear when the machine is in motion, and in Fig. 314B it is shown in the released position, with the discs separated to permit the worm gear to turn without driving the sprocket.

Referring to Fig. 314A, "A" is the clutch body, which, together with clutch cover "B," is bolted to worm gear C, forming what may be considered a large hub. Around the outer edges of the clutch body discs "D" are a number of lugs or projections which fit into corresponding slots cut around the inside of the clutch body in a direction parallel to its center hole. This arrangement permits a slight endwise movement of the discs, but at the same time prevents them from turning independent of the clutch body. A hole in the center of each of these discs allows the enlarged central portion of clutch countershaft "E" to pass through them without touching.

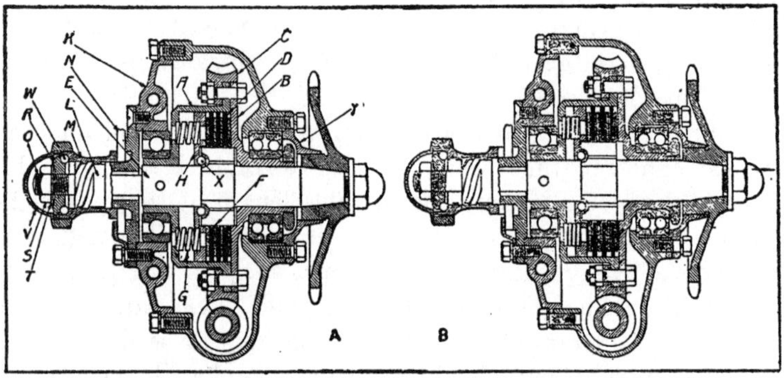

Fig. 314.—Action of Cleveland Motorcycle Clutch.

The shaft discs "F" are similar to the body discs except that the outer edges have no projections, the lugs being located around the central hole and fitting into slots cut in the enlarged portion of the countershaft. Consequently when the clutch is released these discs are free to turn inside of the clutch body but must rotate with the countershaft. Springs "G," acting against pressure plate "H," press the discs together against the clutch cover. In order to simplify the drawings, Figs. 314A and B show only seven discs, but thirteen is the number actually used. However, the principle is the same, regardless of the number of discs. The clutch is operated by means of a screw and nut mechanism which is mounted on the outside of the worm gear cover "K." The parts consist of a clutch screw "L," attached to the cover in such a manner as to prevent it from rotating. A coarse thread on the outer end of this piece fits a corresponding thread in clutch nut "M," to which clutch lever "N" is attached. Countershaft pin "O," which forms an extension of the countershaft, passes out through a hole in the center of the clutch screw and carries a thrust bearing "R" on its outer end. This bearing may be adjusted by screwing in or out

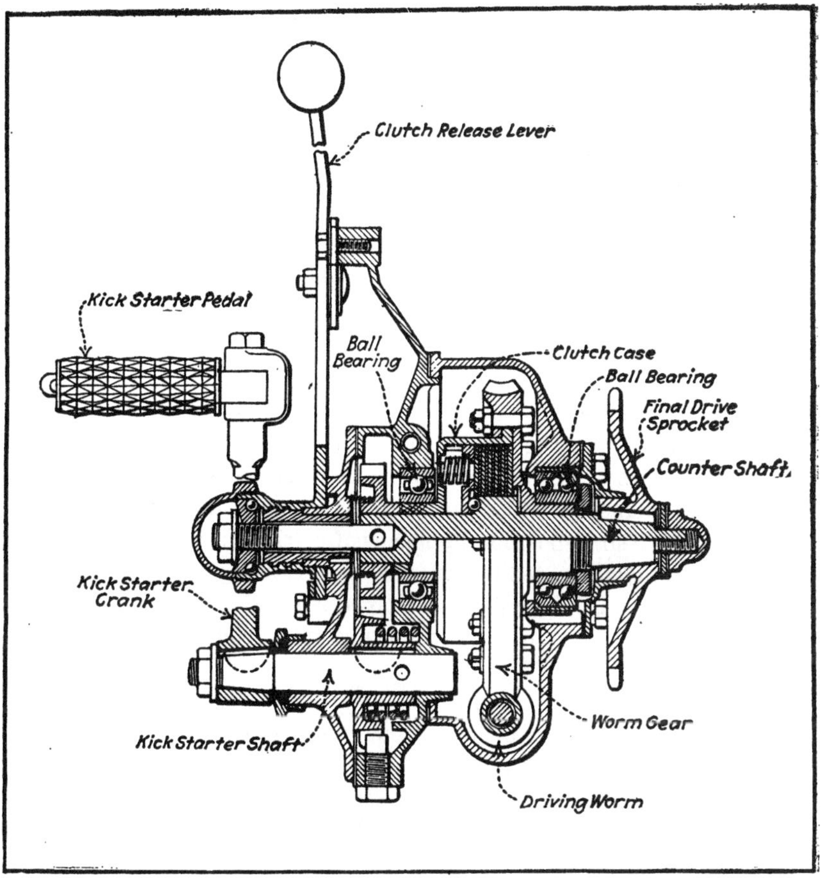

Fig. 315.—Clutch of Disc Type. Mounted on Countershaft of Cleveland Motorcycle Which Is Driven by Worm Gearing from Engine Crankshaft.

as may be necessary, and locked by tightening lock nut "S" against lock washer "T." A dust cover "V," which screws on the end of the clutch nut, protects the mechanism from dust and dirt. When the clutch nut is screwed out by pulling back on the clutch lever, its motion is transmitted to the countershaft through ball bearing "W" and from the countershaft to the pressure plate through another ball bearing at "X." This compresses the springs and allows the clutch to release. The clutch and kick starter assembly are shown in Fig. 315.

Control System.—This includes the mechanism for operating the compression release, air and throttle valves and clutch, shifting gears, and also the brake and kick starter.

The throttle and air valves are controlled by means of two small levers which are clamped on the handle bars just forward of the right-hand grip, and connected with the valves by flexible wire cables. The shorter or top lever operates the air valve, and the longer one the throttle. By moving either of these levers to the right, the valve which it operates is opened; when they are moved to the left the valves are closed. A friction device in the hubs of these levers retains them in any position in which they may be set.

The clutch lever, the upper end of which swings along the left-hand side of the gasoline tank, releases the clutch when it is pulled back, and engages it when pushed forward. The clutch lever is held in any desired position by means of a friction device consisting of a quadrant, supported by arms from the worm gear cover, against which the lever is held by a star-shaped spring. Fibre washers between the lever and quadrant increase the friction and prevent wear.

Gears are shifted by means of a double or "heel-and-toe" pedal, which is mounted just inside of the right-hand foot-rest, near the bottom of the power plant. When the rear end of this pedal is pushed down, the low gear is engaged, and by depressing the front end the high gear is put in action. The neutral position, in which neither gear is engaged, is midway between these two points. In order to hold the clutch in its high gear, neutral or low-gear position, as may be desired, a device known as a "detent" is used. It consists of a small shell or cup which screws into the worm gear housing just below the shift yoke shaft and contains a blunt pointed steel plunger which is forced out against one side of the shift yoke by means of a spring. On the side of the shift yoke are three shallow cone-shaped depressions spaced so that when the shift yoke is moved to bring the clutch to any one of its three positions the corresponding depression comes opposite the point of the plunger,

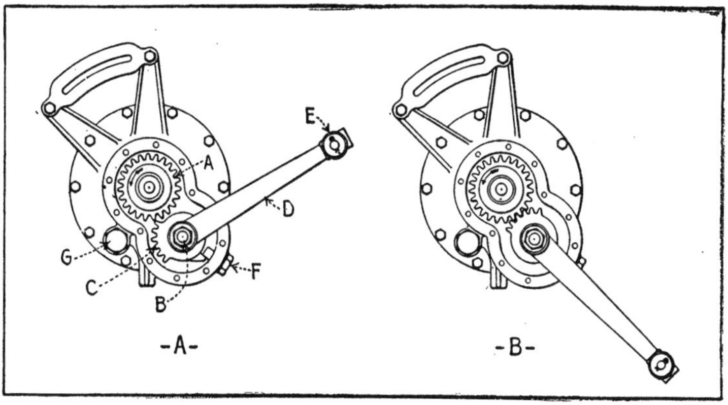

Fig. 316.—Kick Starter of Cleveland Motorcycle.

which, pushed out by the spring, snaps into the depression and holds the clutch in place.

The brake is of the band type, and its construction is very similar to those used on automobiles. Surrounding the drum, which is mounted on the left-hand end of the rear hub, is a steel band, lined with a fabric composed of asbestos, brass wire, etc., which has high frictional and wear-resisting properties. The ends of this band are attached to the brake bell-crank, from which a rod runs to the brake pedal. When this pedal, which is mounted beside the left-hand foot-rest (see Fig. 307 for illustration of control), is pushed down, it applies the brake by tightening the band around the drum. When pressure is removed from the pedal, a spring pulls it back and releases the brake.

Kick-Starter.—As was mentioned in explaining the action of the motor, no gas is drawn into it and compressed, and no sparking current is generated except when it is revolving. Consequently, it is necessary to revolve it by power derived from some other source until at least one charge of gas has been drawn in, compressed and ignited. Model A-2 is started by means of a foot pedal or "kick-starter," which, when pushed down, rotates the motor and automatically returns to its original position. In Figs. 316A and B, the starter parts, which are enclosed in a compartment formed on the worm gear cover, are shown as they would appear with their cover plate removed. On this model, the left-hand end of the clutch countershaft is made slightly longer than on the other models and carries a starter pinion "A," Fig. 316A, which, however, is not fastened to the shaft, the extension simply forming a support for the pinion. The inner end of the hub on this pinion and the end of the clutch hub which is in contact with it are provided with ratchet teeth so arranged that when the pinion is rotated in the direction of the arrow, its teeth engage those on the clutch hub and cause the latter to turn also. The two are held together by a spring which is coiled around the outer hub of the pinion, one end bearing against the pinion, and the other end against the inside of the cover plate. The ratchet permits the pinion to be held stationary or turned in a direction opposite to the arrow without interfering with the rotation of the clutch body or the worm gear which is attached to it. The starter shaft "B," which projects through the cover below the pinion, has a sector or portion of a gear "C" keyed to it in such a position that when the shaft is turned, the sector teeth engage those on the pinion. A starter lever "D," carrying a hinged pedal "E," is attached to the projecting end of the shaft. When the starter is not in use, this lever is held in the position shown in Fig. 316A by means of a spring which is coiled around the sector hub, one end being attached to the worm gear cover and the other to the sector. Its action, which is similar to that of a clock spring, tends to hold a lug on the sector in contact with the stop "F."

The starter is operated by engaging the high gear, releasing the clutch, and pushing down on the starter pedal. This causes the sector to swing into engagement with the pinion as shown by Fig. 316B, and revolve the motor by driving it through the worm gear and worm. When the pressure on the pedal is released, the coiled spring on the sector hub brings the parts back to their former position, the ratchet on the pinion hub permitting it to revolve independent of the clutch body until the sector swings out of engagement with it.

Lubrication and Fuel.—As has been previously mentioned, the lubrication of the motor is effected by mixing oil with gasoline, consequently the gasoline supply and motor lubrication will be considered together.

This system, which is remarkably simple and effective, requires practically no attention from the rider, but if the best results are to be obtained, a suitable oil must be used and the proportions of the mixture must be correct. Over-lubrication, or the use of an oil which is not adapted to this system, will invariably cause trouble on account of its tendency to burn and form a deposit of carbon on the piston, cylinder head, spark plug, muffler pipes, etc.

While there are a number of oils which work well in connection with this system, we particularly recommend a heavy lubricant such as Gargoyle-Mobiloil "B" or Texaco Heavy Motorcycle Oil, either of which will give excellent results if properly used.

As the correct mixture depends to a certain extent upon the conditions under which the machine is operated, it is practically impossible to lay down a hard and fast rule which will cover all cases. However, in a general way it may be said that the mixture need never be any heavier than eight parts of gasoline to one of oil, or one pint of oil per gallon. This proportion is permissible on a new machine, or when the motor is to be worked very hard, but a ten to one mixture will usually be more satisfactory for ordinary service. An even lighter mixture, say, twelve or thirteen parts of gasoline to one of oil, may be advantageous if the machine is used only for short runs, or at a moderate speed. The rider should experiment until he determines what proportion is correct for his particular requirements, always remembering that while the heavier mixtures are necessary for severe service, the motor, spark plug and exhaust line will require less attention if a smaller quantity of oil is used whenever possible. Instead of preparing a fresh supply of gasoline and oil each time the tank requires refilling it will usually be more convenient to mix a considerable quantity (say, five gallons of gasoline with the proper amount of oil), from which the tank can be replenished when necessary. As the oil, being slightly heavier than the gasoline, has a tendency to settle to the bottom, the mixture should be thoroughly stirred before filling the tank.

The cap over the opening through which the tank is filled is provided with a small hole, the object of which is to admit air as the gasoline flows out to the carburetor. Do not allow this opening to become stopped up, as this may cut off the gasoline supply.

The capacity of the gasoline tank is seven quarts, which under ordinary conditions is sufficient to run the machine approximately 125 miles.

Any dirt which may accidentally find its way into the tank is prevented from entering the carburetor by a wire gauze which is soldered to the upper end of the shut-off cock. To clean this strainer, it is necessary to drain the tank and unscrew the shut-off cock. As an additional precaution, another small piece of gauze is placed in the gasoline line at the point where it enters the carburetor. In order to avoid evaporation and leakage, the filler cap should always be screwed down tightly, except when filling the tank, and the shut-off cock should be closed when not using the machine.

Do not attempt to improve the lubricating system by pouring oil into the crank case or using drip oilers, pumps, etc. If the proportions of the mixture are correct, the oil which enters with the gasoline vapor is ample for all the working parts of the motor, and any quantity in excess of this amount may cause trouble on account of carbonization, etc. The crank case is provided with a drain plug, located at its lowest point, which should be removed every ten days or two weeks to allow any surplus oil to drain out. Do not neglect to replace the plug after draining the case.

Lubricating Transmission, etc.: The other parts of the power unit, including the transmission gears, worm and worm gear, clutch, etc., are lubricated by partially filling the worm gear housing with oil, which, when the motor is running, is splashed over the working parts.

Keep worm gear housing well filled with oil at all times. Use Mobile "B" or Texaco Heavy Motorcycle Oil. Refill with a pint of oil every 500 miles. To fill housing, remove plug on top of housing to rear of cylinder. Also remove stop screw. Put oil in plug hole until it runs out of stop screw hole.

Power Plant.—In taking down the Cleveland Power Plant it will be found most convenient to remove parts in the general order named below: 1—Magneto. 2—Kick starter assembly, housing cover group and clutch assembly. 3—Cylinder and piston. 4—Crank case. 5—Stuffing box and nut and bearing, flywheel assembly. NOTE—Both the crank pin and flywheel gear are a press fit in flywheel. Do not attempt to remove these parts without using an arbor press. First press out flywheel gear, magneto shaft, bearing, etc., and then from the bearing side of flywheel press out crank pin. 6—Gear shifter shaft, yoke, bushing and shifter lever. 7—Worm and transmission clutch. 8—Transmission countershaft and pin.

Timing.—To time the Cleveland Motor, adjust the Magneto Coupling on its shaft so that the platinum points in the magneto interrupter "break" when the piston is 7/32″ from the top of its stroke—on the up-stroke.

Instructions for Adjustment and Operation of the Model "A-L" Schebler Carburetor.—The Model "A-L" Carburetor used on the Cleveland motorcycle is shown at Fig. 317 and is manufactured in the 3/4-inch size and has a clamp type of manifold connection. This carburetor is made with a two-piece piston throttle, one being used as a throttle and the other as an air choke for starting and warming up the motor. To adjust the Model "A-L" carburetor: First turn on the main needle, which is located on the top of the carburetor, three or four turns; then open low speed needle, which is on the bottom of the carburetor, about $1\frac{1}{4}$ turn from closed position. Start the motor by flushing the carburetor, and after the motor has become thoroughly warmed up, adjust the main or high speed needle on the top of the carburetor, cutting down the fuel supply until the motor back-fires; then turn on a little more gas, a notch at a time, until the motor runs smoothly and the

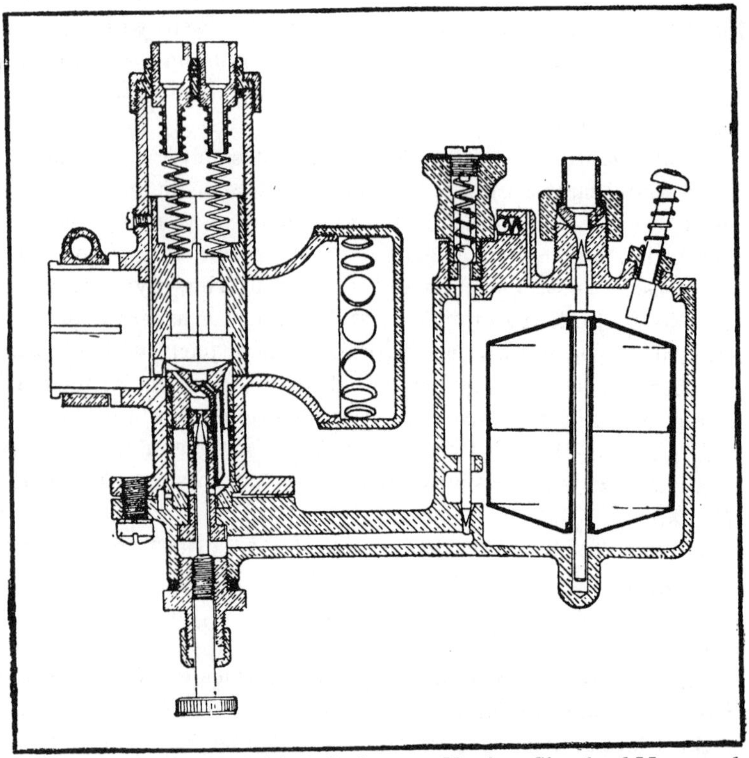

Fig. 317.—Schebler Model A-L Carburetor Used on Cleveland Motorcycle

proper adjustment will have been secured for high speed. Next adjust the low speed needle, located at the bottom of the carburetor, until the desired low speed is secured. No further adjustments are required. Strain fuel in order to remove any particle of dirt or water and also be sure that you have no air leaks between the carburetor and the motor.

"Don'ts" for the Cleveland Rider.—1. Don't fail to keep spark plug clean. 2. Don't keep clutch lever pulled back when machine is not running. 3. Don't fail to put oil in tank at same time you put in gasoline. 4. Don't use anything but heavy oil. 5. Don't fail to keep machine clean. 6. Don't race motor on stand. 7. Don't tamper with magneto. 8. Don't take motor apart until you are sure that it is necessary. 9. Don't fail to remove carbon from piston-cylinder and muffler every 1,000 miles. 10. Don't fail to keep housing filled with oil.

CHAPTER IX.

HARLEY-DAVIDSON-REMY ELECTRIC LIGHTING AND IGNITION SYSTEM.

Function of Automatic Switch—The Lighting System—Headlight Should Be Carefully Focused—Care of Electrical System—Lamps Do Not Burn, Motor Is Idle—One Lamp Fails to Burn—If Neither Headlight Will Burn—Fluctuating Lights—Faulty Lighting Switch—Faulty Ignition Switch—To Get at Centrifugal Switch—To Adjust the Centrifugal Switch—The Warning Signal—To Run with Discharged Storage Battery—Hard Starting—To Recharge a Dead Battery—If Battery Discharges Without Apparent Cause—How to Test a Suspected Battery—To Adjust and Clean Circuit Breaker—To Clean and Resear Brushes and Commutator—Ignition Mechanism of Type 235 Generator—Lubricating the Generator—Battery Requires Reasonable Care—To Gain Access to the Battery—Add Distilled Water Regularly—Why Distilled Water Must Be Used—Keep Battery and Battery Box Clean—What Specific Gravity Indicates—Normal Charging Rate—How to Distinguish "Positive" and "Negative" Terminals—Explanation of Storage Battery Action—Care of Battery in Cold Weather—Specific Gravity Table—What To Do When Machine Is Taken from Service—Placing Battery Back in Service.

The Harley-Davidson-Remy Electric Lighting and Ignition System.—This remarkably efficient system consists of a compact direct current generator, storage battery, head light with two bulbs, tail light, warning signal, and switch. An illustration of the electrically equipped motorcycle is given at Fig. 318. The generator furnishes low tension 6 volt direct current for the lights, signal system, and for charging the battery. This current is "stepped up" or transformed into high tension current for ignition by the coil on top of the generator. It should be understood that the battery is not provided as an independent system for lighting and ignition, although the storage battery will provide ignition current for a short time when the generator itself is not generating.

Function of Automatic Switch.—A simple automatic switch controls the ignition current. When the starter is put into action, this switch automatically closes the ignition circuit. When the motor stops, this switch automatically breaks the circuit, breaking the

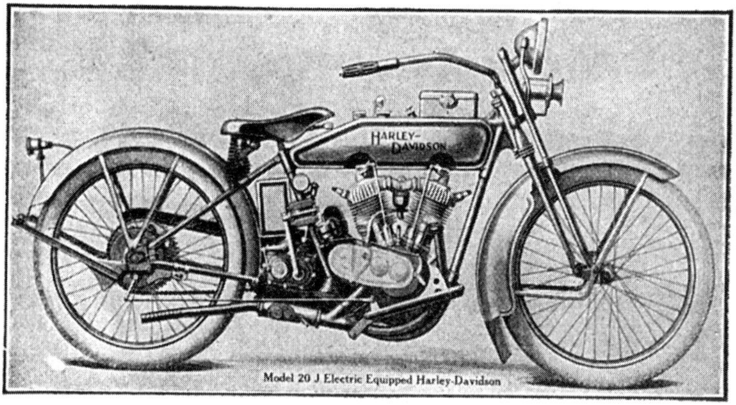

Fig. 318—Model 20-J Electric Equipped Harley-Davidson Motorcycle.

warning signal circuit at the same time, thereby making it impossible for a meddlesome person to sound the warning signal while the machine is left standing. The generator supplies current directly to the lamps, horn, and for ignition, the surplus current going to the battery and keeping it properly charged. This provision is necessary, for the battery in turn provides current for the lights when the motor is not running and for ignition when starting the motor. A complete wiring diagram is given at Fig. 319.

The battery acts as an accumulator and governor, holding the voltage down to 6 volts. The voltage produced by the generator at 60 miles per hour, with the battery out of circuit, is above 35 volts. The high voltage produces a serious overload on the generator and will burn and pit the breaker points in a short time. Other serious damage may result. Therefore, even though the storage battery should be exhausted and not capable of giving off current it must be left connected up. Never overload the electrical system by equipping with accessories of any kind or by in-

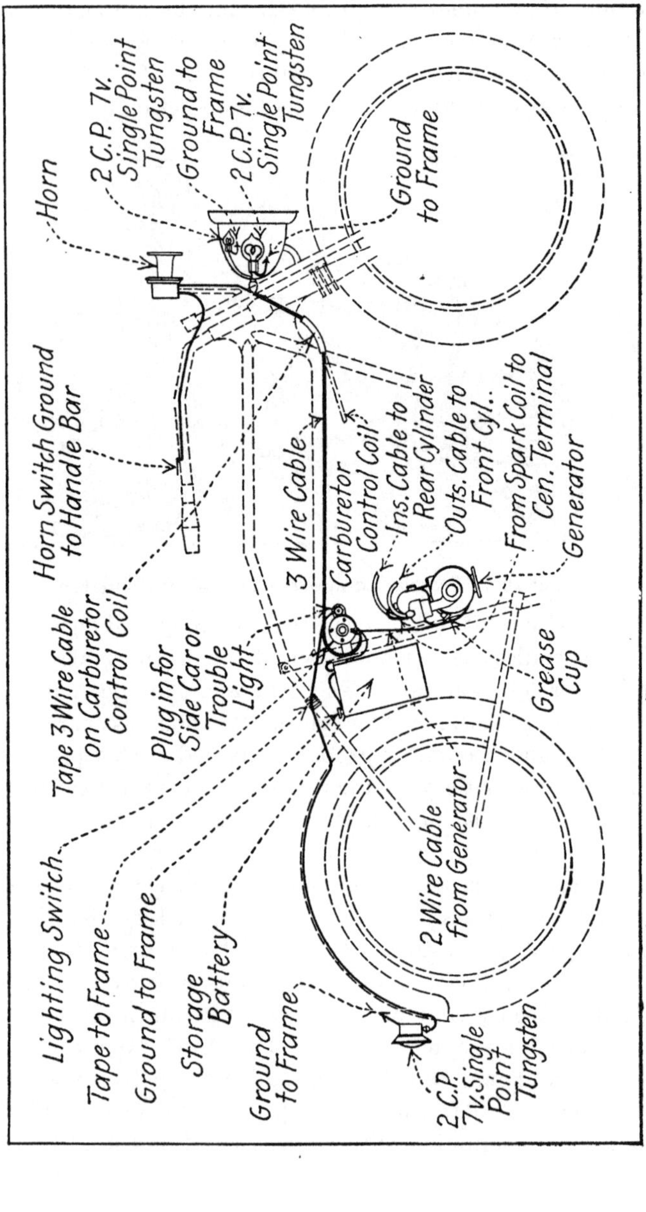

Fig. 319.—Diagram Showing Location of Electrical Units of Harley-Davidson Motorcycle.

stalling a larger headlight than the one regularly used, because the system is designed for a definite load.

The Lighting System.—The headlight contains two bulbs—the bright bulb a twenty-one candle power nitrogen, and the dimmer a two candle power tungsten. The tail light carries a two candle power bulb also. The lighting switch has three positions; all off, bright headlight and tail light, and dim headlight and tail light.

Never leave the machine standing with the bright headlight turned on as the battery will be discharged in a short time. Do not add any lamps, with the exception of one for the sidecar. This bulb must not be over two candlepower. If any of the lamp bulbs need renewal, replace with lamps of the same candlepower and voltage. This is extremely important. Six to 8 volt bulbs should be used. In ordering, specify single point bulbs. The trouble lamp or the sidecar lamp connection is made by plugging in at the hole in the center of the switch clamp bolt, as indicated in illustration Fig. 319. In order to light either the trouble lamp or the sidecar lamp, the lighting switch must be turned *on* because this plug socket is in circuit with the tail lamp circuit.

Headlight Should Be Carefully Focused.—The bright headlight is equipped with means for readily adjusting the focus of the light. It is necessary to focus the light after dark of course. The adjustment should be made with the large bulb turned on and pointed at a wall about 30 feet from the lamp. To focus the lamp, turn the slotted screw on the back of the lamp to the left or right with a screw driver. It will be found that by turning the screw to the left, a dark or blind spot will show in the center of the illuminated portion. By turning it to the right from this, a place will be found where the beam of light is uniform and the field brilliantly illuminated.

Care of Electrical System.—The electrically equipped model requires reasonable attention. It is advisable to have your dealer or repairman make any necessary inspections, tests and adjustments because extreme accuracy is, of course, essential. For the rider who cannot conveniently take his machine to a dealer for inspec-

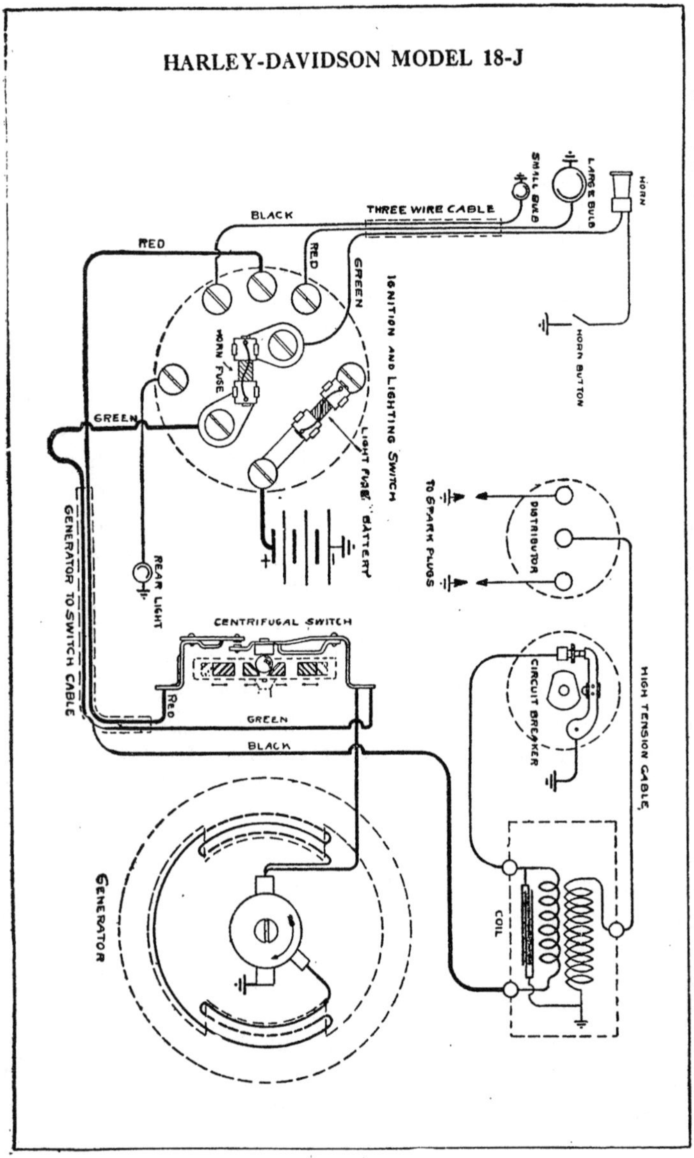

Fig. 320.—Wiring Diagram Showing Electrical System of Harley-Davidson Model 18-J.

tion, or who has mechanical skill, the care of this model is covered in the following pages. If the instructions are closely followed, and care is exercised, the adjustments can be made successfully.

Lamps Do Not Burn, Motor Is Idle.—Failure of the lamps to burn while the motor is not running generally indicates that the battery is discharged, or the lighting fuse is burned out due to a short circuit in the lamp circuit. In the latter case, remedy the short circuit before replacing the fuse. See that the fuse is held

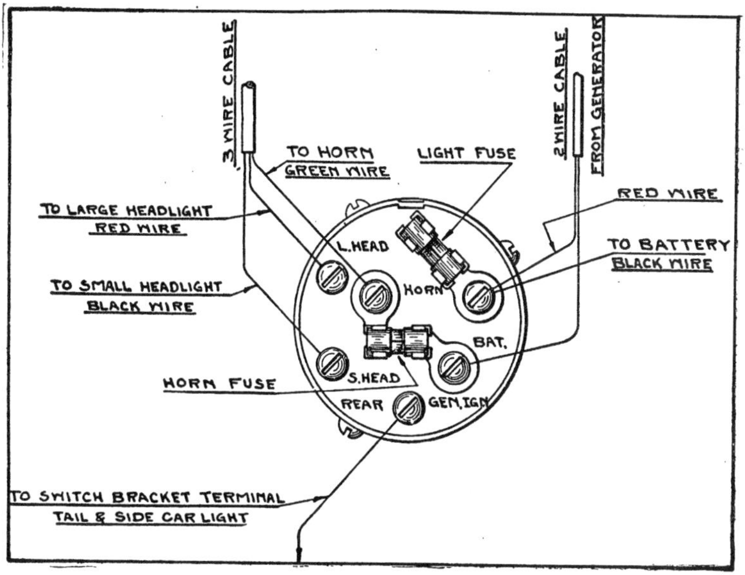

Fig. 321.—Fuse Block of Harley-Davidson Electrical System.

firmly in the holder. Examine the contact spiders and connections of the lighting switch to make sure that a good contact is made. To ascertain whether or not the battery is discharged test it as explained under battery instructions. If the fuse and battery are found to be in good condition, the trouble lies in the lamps or in the wiring. Inspect the bulbs and examine the wiring for a break. Also look over the lamp connections to see if any are loose or broken. If the battery is discharged, have it recharged immediately. If the trouble is due to a loose or broken connection, or a short circuit in the wiring, apply the proper remedy.

Two fuses are mounted in the switch box (one for the horn circuit and one for the lighting circuit) to prevent discharge and possible injury to the battery should a short circuit occur in the horn or lamp wiring.

In case a fuse burns out do not use a piece of wire or any other substitute. Locate and remedy the cause of the trouble and replace the fuse with a new Harley-Davidson fuse. By using a substitute, the short circuit that was responsible for the fuse burning out may cause serious injury to the switch or wiring, and discharge the battery. In an emergency, if the fuse in the lighting switch is burned out, and the short circuit has been remedied, the horn fuse can be used safely in the lighting circuit.

If One Lamp Fails to Burn.—If all the lamps but one burn, the fault lies in that particular lamp, or in the wiring thereto. It may be that the contact spider for that particular lamp is making a poor connection with the insert contact in the switch. In that case see switch instructions. The failure of a lamp to burn may be due to a burnt out bulb, and the test of inserting a good bulb in place of the suspected one immediately suggests itself. If the good bulb fails to burn, the wiring and connections to the lamp should be carefully examined.

If Neither Headlight Will Burn.—If neither head lamp bulb lights, but the tail lamp bulb does, the trouble must lie either in the headlight bulbs, wiring, lighting switch or the double connector in the headlight. Sometimes trouble with the dimmer bulb is caused by failure of the reflector to make a good connection or ground to the lamp body, especially if the entire interior of the lamp is covered with enamel. If the enamel is the cause of the trouble, scrape the lamp at the point of contact with the reflector with a scraper or screw driver. If it is necessary to remove the reflector, use the greatest care not to touch the reflecting surface. To open the lamp for replacing a bulb, loosen the screw in the bottom of the front flange about ¼ inch. Remove the glass retainer, glass and packing washer.

Fluctuating Lights.—If the lamps burn brightly when the motor is running at moderate speed, but vary and flicker when the motor is running slowly, the cause is a discharged battery or a poor circuit between the battery, generator and the lights, at one or more of the following points:

Carefully inspect the ground wire which is clamped under the cover clamp screw of the battery box, and which leads to the negative pole of the battery. In like manner examine the positive wire leading from the battery to the terminal block on the battery box, and to the lighting switch. See that the lighting fuse is O. K., that it is held securely, and that the wire connection on the switch clamp screws are clamped firmly. Examine the spider contacts of the lighting switch as explained under "Faulty Lighting Switch." Examine the wiring leading to the lamps and the connection on the inside of the lamps. A circuit diagram of the complete system is given at Fig. 320.

Faulty Lighting Switch.—Remove the two hexagon nuts which clamp the entire switch box assembly to the studs of the switch base. Take hold of the black switch box cover and remove the entire assembly from the switch base. If the cover sticks, it can be forced off easily by placing a screw driver against the edge of the cover from the left side of the machine, and then striking the screw driver with the fist or palm of the hand. Remove the two round head screws which clamp the block switch box cover to the switch assembly and remove the cover. If an inspection proves that the wires are connected firmly and properly as per illustration, Fig. 321, showing switch wiring diagram, the fibre switch base to which the wires are attached should be removed from the cover and spider assembly. These two assemblies can be taken apart after the three screws which pass through the side of the spider cover have been removed.

Inspect the four spider contacts inside of this cover. Make sure that they bear against the contact inserts in the fibre base with sufficient pressure to insure a closed circuit, and that they cannot slide beyond the insert contact. If you are doubtful whether or not they bear with sufficient pressure, bend the spider contacts slightly outward. To see whether the spider contacts slide beyond the insert contacts, turn them to the various positions, and with a pencil mark the exact location of the contacts on the metal cover of this assembly. Then put the fibre switch base assembly into the switch cover assembly, and note whether or not each mark lines up with its respective clamp screw. If they do not line up properly, bend the spider contacts as may be found necessary.

Fig. 322.—Harley-Davidson Centrifugal Switch.

Faulty Ignition Switch.—The centrifugal switch is entirely automatic. If trouble is experienced, and the centrifugal switch is suspected, the following symptoms can be traced directly to this switch. The centrifugal switch is out of order when: 1. The horn can be sounded when the motor is idle. 2. The horn can be sounded for a period of a few seconds after the motor stops. 3. The horn cannot be sounded when cranking the motor vigorously.

To Get at the Centrifugal Switch.—If the horn is O. K. when the motor is running, and any of the mentioned symptoms exist, the motor will be hard starting. In this case inspect the centrifugal switch. To gain access to the centrifugal switch it is necessary to remove the left foot board, short chain guard and chain. Under the cover on the lower left end of the generator is a set screw. With a screw driver, loosen this screw a few turns. This cover, which is held by a bayonet type connection, is then removed by taking hold of it with the hands, turning it to the left as far as it will go, and pulling it from the generator. The centrifugal switch blades are now exposed and should be inspected.

To Adjust the Centrifugal Switch.—Make sure that the clearance "A" between thrust button "B" and cover of the centrifugal switch shown at Fig. 322 does not amount to more than a few thousandths of an inch. If there is too much clearance at this point, ball action will be lost which will not allow a good contact, if any, at the points "D." If the thrust button does not clear the centrifugal switch cover, the button will be worn off due to the friction with the cover. If the blades require adjusting, disconnect the ground wire from the battery box cover screw to prevent short-circuiting the battery. Adjust the long blade first. If the thrust button is too far away or too close to the cover, bend it as may be necessary to obtain the proper adjustment. When bending the long blade, care must be taken to bend it so that the steel insert in the thrust button is in line with the thrust ball in the switch housing. This is very important, because, if the ball comes in contact with the bakelite of the button, it will wear a pit into the button in a short time. This pit will then produce the same result as having the blade adjusted so that the button is too far away from the thrust ball, thereby causing a loss of action.

After the large blade has been properly adjusted, obtain the proper clearance at the contact points by bending the lower or short blade. A definite clearance for these points cannot be given because of the variation in the stiffness of some of the blades. It is, however, safe to assume that $1/32$ inch clearance is about right. Bend this blade accordingly, making sure that the points line up and make a good square contact.

The switch should now be tested to see whether or not the adjustment is correct. Replace the short chain and battery ground wire. Raise the valves, press firmly on the handlebar horn button, and give the starter crank a vigorous stroke. If the centrifugal switch blades are properly adjusted, and the circuit between the generator and battery and the battery itself are O. K., the horn will sound for just a fraction of a second. If the switch does not seem to be correctly adjusted, whether the horn sounds too long or not at all, do not change the adjustment immediately. Test the switch several times to make sure that a different adjustment is required. If the test proves that the switch is O. K., again remove the short chain and put the cover in place on the generator before assembling the machine.

If the horn does not sound while making this test, watch the action of the centrifugal switch blades. See if they make contact. Then if the horn does not sound while pressing the horn button, one of the following must be the reason: 1. Battery is discharged. 2. Loose wire connections. 3. Faulty horn or the wire itself is broken at one or more places.

The Warning Signal.—One feature much appreciated by owners of Harley-Davidson electrically equipped models, is the fact that the warning signal or horn can be sounded only while the motor is running. This feature discourages meddling; thereby preventing useless discharge of the battery. It is well to get into the habit of attempting to sound the horn after stopping the motor, to make sure that the automatic ignition switch has opened the circuit between the generator and battery.

If the horn can be sounded constantly when the motor is idle, prevent complete discharge of the battery by removing the battery ground wire from the battery box cover. This wire is, of course, to be re-connected whenever the motor is run for reasons already explained. If the horn can be sounded even for only a short time after the motor has stopped, the centrifugal switch is out of order and instructions under "Faulty Ignition Switch" should be applied or the machine should be referred to the dealer at once. If the horn cannot be sounded, examine the fuse in the horn circuit. Of course with a burnt out or a loosely held fuse, the horn cannot be sounded. The cause of the short circuit must be found and remedied before the fuse is replaced. If the fuse is not held tight, remove it from the holder and bend the holder clips together. If the horn cannot be sounded while the motor is running, remove the horn cover and make sure that the armature is not stuck and revolves freely. If the armature is free, see that the wiring from the switch box to the horn, and from the horn switch to the horn is not damaged or loose. If the horn sounds continually without pressing the horn button, while the motor is running, there is a short circuit either in the horn switch on the handlebar, in the wire from the horn switch to the horn, or in the horn itself.

The only attention that the horn requires is to lubricate the bearings with a few drops of 3 in 1 oil every 2 months. Access to the bearings is gained by removing the rear cover.

To Run with a Discharged Storage Battery.—The motorcycle can be run with a discharged or disabled battery, but it is very important to have the battery recharged or repaired immediately, because if the battery is left in a discharged or disabled condition for any length of time it will be ruined. If the storage battery is disabled, turn off all lights before attempting to start the motor. Prime the motor as per instructions given for starting the motor in cold weather. See that the spark plug points are properly adjusted and clean.

Put the gear shifting lever in either low or second gear, engage the clutch, raise the exhaust valves and push the machine at a good pace by running alongside, drop the valves, and jump on or quickly disengage the clutch as soon as the motor starts. If the machine will not start, disconnect the battery ground wire on the outside of the battery box and repeat the above instructions. After starting the motor, be sure to reconnect the battery ground wire at once or the generator may be ruined. See that the battery ground wire is connected while the motor is running, because the battery acts as a safety valve and protects the generator. It is possible to ruin the generator if the motor is driven at a speed greater than 15 miles per hour unless the storage battery remains connected.

Caution.—Before disconnecting any of the wires other than the spark plug wires to make a repair, disconnect the battery ground wire from the battery box cover to prevent burning out a fuse, or short-circuiting the battery. The battery ground wire must be reconnected before the motor is started, and also after the repair is completed, for the reason already explained.

Hard Starting.—Hard starting of the motor of model 19-J can generally be traced to a discharged storage battery or failure of the ignition switch to make a good connection between the generator and battery. In the case of a discharged battery refer to instructions under "To Run with a Discharged Battery." If the switch is suspected refer to instructions under "To Test and Repair a Faulty Ignition Switch." Instructions relative to "Hard Starting," should also be consulted.

To Recharge a Dead Battery.—A discharged battery can be recharged by sufficient daylight riding at a reasonable speed, although the best way to charge an exhausted battery is from an outside source, as explained under battery instructions. The output of the generator is greatest at a speed of from 20 to 30 miles per hour. After riding a reasonable distance, see that the battery is really charging by turning on the lights while the motor is not running. If they do not light, the battery is charging very slowly or not at all. In such event there is a leakage of current, the generator output is low, or the centrifugal switch is not making good contact. If the switch is suspected refer to instructions under "Faulty Ignition Switch."

If the storage battery is exhausted and it is suspected that the generator is not charging, have the battery recharged and start the motor in the regular way. Then disconnect the ground connection from the battery box cover screw. If the motor continues to run, the generator is furnishing current. If the motor stops, the generator is faulty and the matter should be referred to your dealer. During this test the motor must not be run at a speed exceeding 15 miles per hour.

If Battery Discharges Without Apparent Cause.—If the battery discharges with normal use of the lamps, and inspection of the ignition switch proves it to be O. K., and, provided the generator is charging according to the previous test, one of the following conditions applies: There may be a short circuit between the battery and the generator. This short circuit may be due to a saturated battery and box. If so, refer to instructions on keeping the battery and battery box scrupulously clean. Be sure that the insulation of the wire is not damaged.

Test for a short circuit between the generator and battery as follows: Have the lighting switch turned to the OFF position and the motor idle, making sure that the horn cannot be sounded; then disconnect the ground wire from the battery box cover screw and rub it against some metallic part of the machine. If sparking occurs, there is a short circuit. To find out where this short circuit is, inspect all connections and wire leading from the positive battery connection to the generator.

How to Test a Suspected Battery.—If this test and the above explained conditions do not apply, the battery itself may be at fault. Take the battery out of the box and have it charged. After charging, tape the ends of the wires. Take a hydrometer reading and make note of the specific gravity of each cell. Set the battery in a cool, clean and dry place for twenty-four hours; then take a second hydrometer reading of each cell. If the battery is O. K., the readings will be practically the same. If there is a decided difference, the battery is at fault, and should be referred to the nearest Exide battery service station.

If the above tests prove that the generator is charging, that the circuit between the generator and battery is closed, that there is no short circuit, and that the battery is not at fault, the output of the generator most likely is not normal due to a dirty commutator and brushes. In that case, clean and reseat the commutator and brushes as explained under that heading.

Caution.—After stopping the motor, try to sound the horn to make sure that the circuit between the generator and battery is open. If the horn can be sounded, disconnect the battery ground wire. This will prevent the discharge of the battery due to the centrifugal switch failing to work.

To Adjust and Clean the Circuit Breaker.—The fibre block on the circuit breaker arm is subjected to a certain amount of wear in service, and after several thousand miles it may be necessary to readjust the contact points to make up for this wear. The

Fig. 323.—Showing Breaker Box and Distributor of Harley-Davidson Motorcycles Using Storage Battery Ignition.

circuit breaker and distributor mechanism is shown at Fig. 323. As a matter of precaution, an inspection and adjustment, if necessary, should be made, say, every 1500 miles. It is necessary when adjusting these points that the fibre block is resting on the center of one of the steel cams so that the circuit breaker points are separated as far as they will go. If the high side of one of the steel cams is not in contact with the fibre block, it will be necessary to turn over the generator slowly by means of the rear wheel (transmission must be in high gear and the clutch engaged) until the steel cam hits the fibre block and separates the contact points as far as they will go. The lock nut "11" should then be loosened with the generator wrench, and the adjusting screw "10" should be turned out or in by turning the hexagon head until it is just possible to insert the flat steel gauge on the wrench between the points at "9." After the points are correctly adjusted, carefully tighten the lock nut and measure the clearance again to be sure that the adjustment is correct. To get at the circuit breaker points, it is only necessary to remove the bakelite cap of the distributor and the distributor segment. If the circuit breaker points at "9" are slightly pitted or burned, they should be cleaned with No. 00 sandpaper. Never use emery cloth or paper.

To Clean and Reseat Brushes and Commutator.—Inspect the commutator and brushes every month or every 1500 miles. If the commutator is found blackened—not dark brown—it should be cleaned by burnishing with No. 00 sandpaper. Never use emery cloth or paper. Ordinarily the commutator requires no attention. To clean the commutator, cut a piece of No. 00 sandpaper into strips about 3/8 inch wide. Run the motor slowly and hold the sandpaper with the coarse side against the commutator until the latter is bright. Be careful not to get a finger caught in the drive chain during this operation. When cleaning the commutator, see that the brushes have a good clean bearing surface against the commutator. If they have not, insert a strip of the same sandpaper between the commutator and the brush, with the sanded side towards the brush. Be sure to pass the strip of sandpaper around the commutator as far as possible, and when drawing it out, follow the radius of the commutator to prevent trimming off the edges of the brushes. It is extremely important to have the entire surface of the brush bear against the commutator, to receive full efficiency from the generator. Bear down lightly on the brush holder and withdraw the sandpaper. After cleaning the brushes and commutator, remove any particles of sand with a gasoline moistened cloth. This is important, for sand will cut the commutator. Do not take for granted from the above instructions that it is necessary to clean and trim the commutator and brushes every 1500 miles. Clean these parts only when conditions warrant. If the commutator is found cut or worn by the brushes, even though the damage seems to be only slight, refer your machine to the dealer immediately.

Ignition Mechanism of Type 235 Generator.—1.—Distributor cap locating lug, or stop, should interlock with the slot at "6" whenever the distributor cap "3" is replaced. (See Fig. 323.) Failure to fit the distributor cap properly may mean a damaged generator; 2.—High tension terminals which alternately collect the ignition current from segment "5" and carry it to the spark plug wires. These high tension terminals clear the segment by about 1/64 inch and should never be adjusted; 3.—Distributor segment contact spring which carries the ignition from carbon contact "14" to segment "5"; 5.—Distributor segment distributes the ignition current from the distributor segment contact spring "4" to the high tension terminals at "2"; 6.—Slot in timer head casting lines up with lug "1" when the distributor cap "3" is properly fitted; 7.—Circuit breaker lever; 8.—Circuit breaker cam; 9.—Circuit breaker points; 10.—Adjusting screw with which the gap at the circuit breaker points "9" is adjusted; 11.—Adjusting screw lock nut; prevents adjusting screw "10" from turning automatically. The lock nut must be loosened before an adjustment is made and must be securely tightened after adjusting; 12.—Primary wire, connects primary winding of coil "16" to ground through circuit breaker points at "9"; 13.—Distributor cap spring (2 used) securely holds the distributor cap "3" in position; 14.—High tension carbon contact insert which carries the ignition current from wire "15" to distributor segment contact spring "4"; 15.—High tension wire which carries the ignition current from the secondary winding of the coil to the carbon contact insert "14" in the distributor cap; 16.—Coil, only one used. The construction is clearly shown in Fig. 323.

Lubricating the Generator.—Never use thin oil on any part of the generator. Once a year put a little vaseline about half the size of a pea on the top of the fibre block on the interrupter lever, and keep the cup on the right side of the generator filled with good cup grease. Give the grease cup ½ turn every 500 miles. This is important.

Battery Requires Reasonable Care.—Read the following instructions very carefully and once they are understood apply them as needed.

The three important points in battery care are these: 1.—Add distilled water regularly each week. 2.—Test the specific gravity of each cell before filling. 3.—Keep the battery and battery box clean. If you give your battery this care you can forget about battery trouble. Your battery will stand a certain amount of neglect or abuse but neglect or abuse it continually and you will experience trouble. The battery, unlike the motor, may not give any symptoms of needing attention until it is very badly damaged. For this reason constant vigilance is called for in battery care. As is explained further on, the care of the battery is very simple and there is no good excuse for neglect. If you will take the above facts into consideration, you will not neglect your battery. We advise you to invest in a hydrometer. This is the one instrument you need to keep close watch on the condition of your battery. Do not use an ammeter to test your battery.

To Gain Access to the Battery.—To gain easy access to the battery with a hydrometer, the saddle must be raised from the riding position. In order to do this quickly, remove the cotter pin in the seat bar clamp pin. Withdraw the clamp pin and the saddle can be raised with the seat bar as per illustration, Fig. 324. Do not attempt to test or fill the battery without raising the saddle.

Add Distilled Water Regularly Each Week.—Having raised the saddle from the riding position, as shown in Fig. 324, take out the two knurled screws clamping the battery box cover and ground wire. Remove the cover, rubber mat and three filler plugs. To remove the filler plugs give them one-quarter turn to the left and lift them out. For safety and convenience, always use a battery hydrometer for filling, as shown in Fig. 325.

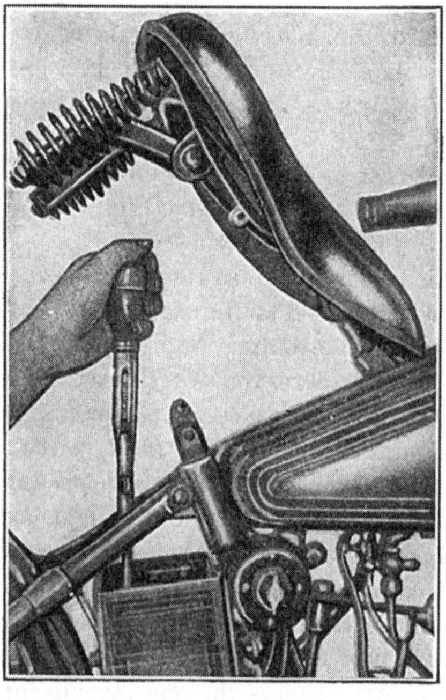

Fig. 324.—How to Reach Storage Battery in Harley-Davidson Motorcycle.

It is easy to see that with this little instrument, the battery can be filled in a minute. Do not get the impression that the battery requires a large amount of distilled water each week and that a jar of distilled water and a funnel are needed. Nothing could be further from the actual facts. The only reason distilled water is needed, is to replace the water lost by evaporation, which is naturally very little. If distilled water is added regularly, only a few drops are needed weekly in each cell.

It can easily be understood why distilled water only must be added to the battery regularly each week. The battery solution is composed of acid and distilled water. As the distilled water evaporates, the solution naturally becomes stronger and eventually will eat up the material in the plates. This will mean complete ruin of the battery in a comparatively short time. Therefore, by adding distilled water regularly, the solution is always kept at the right strength. The acid does not evaporate. Another reason why distilled water must be added to the battery regularly is the fact that if the plates of the battery are exposed to the air they will be ruined in a short time. These plates must be kept immersed in the electrolyte. as the solution of acid and distilled water is called.

It is just as important not to add too much water as it is to add any at all. The correct level of the solution is ½ inch above the wood separators. This is very clearly shown in the sectional cut of the battery, Fig. 326. Remember that the battery may not be

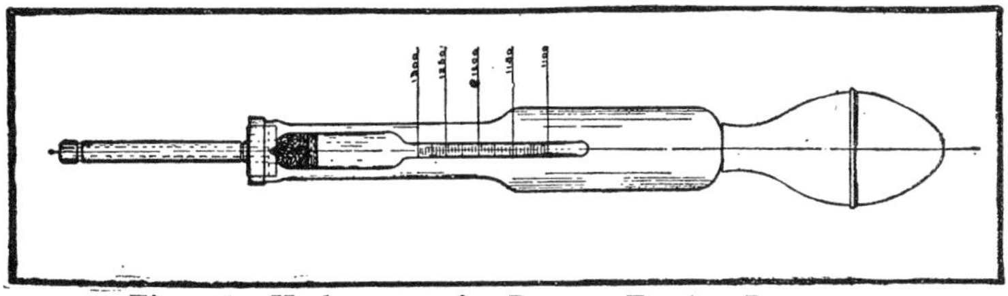

Fig. 325.—Hydrometer for Battery Testing Purposes.

filled clear to the top, not only because of the danger of flooding, but because the battery will be internally injured and eventually ruined if it is continually overfilled.

Only Distilled Water Used.—Practically all water contains traces of minerals or chemicals which are injurious to the plates of the battery. For this reason, use nothing but distilled water. Never store distilled water in a metal vessel or fill the battery with a priming gun, a tin funnel or any other metal container, for the water will absorb some of the mineral properties and become as unfit for the battery as ordinary water. Store the water in a glass bottle and use a storage battery hydrometer for filling.

Never Use Acid or Electrolyte.—In the process of evaporation no acid is lost. For this reason it is imperative that no acid be added to the solution at any time unless part of the electrolyte itself has been lost by spilling or through a leak. If it is believed that some of the solution has been spilled, refer the battery to the nearest Exide service station for refilling. Do not attempt to refill the battery yourself, because it is essential that the proportion of acid and water be exactly right.

It is absolutely necessary that the filler plugs are in place and secure. Lock them by a quarter turn to the right. Should there be a leak between the filler plug rubber bushing and the battery when the plug is properly closed, remove the plug and wrap several thicknesses of rubber bands around it between the soft rubber bushing and the head of the filler plug.

Keep Battery and Battery Box Clean.—The battery and box should be so clean and dry that one's hands are not soiled by handling. The acid in the solution is a destructive liquid and will eat through the metal of the battery box in a short time. The simplest way to save the trouble of cleaning the battery and box is to exercise care in filling when using a hydrometer. If the battery and box must be cleaned, disconnect the wire from the terminal block on the battery case and the battery ground wire. Loosen the battery box stud nuts, and remove the left front bolt holding the box in place. The box can then be removed to the right, after the pedal crank has been pushed downward. In raising and removing the battery from the box, do not pull on the cables. Lift out the battery by means of the connecting links. Thoroughly clean the inside of the metal battery box with a clean rag which has been dipped in liquid household ammonia, or moistened with water, and then sprinkled with household ammonia in powdered form, or with baking soda. If a formation of electrolysis collects around the sealing nuts or vent plugs, clean immediately or the battery will be short-circuited. If the rubber mats or the wood liners are acid soaked or soggy, discard and fit new ones. Obtain these from your dealer or directly from the maker. Do not place a blotter or anything across a battery to absorb moisture. Place the rubber mats in the box in such a position that the corrugated side of the mats are toward the battery.

Coat the Battery Connections with Vaseline.—The terminals and connections within the battery box should be kept coated with a thin film of vaseline to prevent corrosion. If solution is spilled upon the terminals of a battery, it will set up a very destructive process of corrosion, which is likely to entirely destroy the connections or materially decrease the properties of conductivity. This will prevent a proper charge coming from the generator to the battery, and likewise make it impossible to draw the necessary current from the battery for the lamps and for ignition. Do not make the mistake of coating the rubber insulated cables with vaseline nor of applying too much of this lubricant.

Why the Battery is Tested Each Week.—It may happen that your battery runs down because you forget to turn off your large headlight for several hours while the machine is standing idle, or because you do more night running than daylight riding. If you take a weekly hydrometer reading of each cell, you will know that the battery is showing a discharge and will naturally apply the proper remedies, namely, use your lamps and horn sparingly or run more during the day than at night until the battery has fully recuperated. If you find the battery wholly discharged, you will have it charged from an outside source. Do not attempt to restore a discharged battery by running the motor on the stand, as the damage done to the motor will be out of all proportion to the charge gained by the battery.

What the Specific Gravity Indicates.—The specific gravity of a fully charged battery averages 1.275 to 1.300 in each cell. A specific gravity of between 1.250 and 1.200 indicates that the battery is more than half charged, between 1.200 and 1.150 less than half charged, and below 1.150 completely discharged. It is easy to use the hydrometer correctly. Press the bulb and place the end of the rubber tube in the cell. Release the bulb without withdrawing from the cell and sufficient solution will be drawn into the chamber to float the hydrometer proper. The hydrometer proper is made with a thin neck which is marked with a scale of graduated specific gravity readings. The point at which the hydrometer floats in the solution indicates the specific gravity of the cell. In other words, if the hydrometer floats at 1.275, the specific gravity of the solution is 1.275. After taking a reading, be sure to return the solution to the cell from which it was removed.

Always take the hydrometer reading before filling the battery; never after. If the reading were taken after filling, the distilled water that would be on top of the solution would be drawn into the chamber and a faulty reading obtained. Keep a record of the successive hydrometer readings of each cell, so that by comparison,

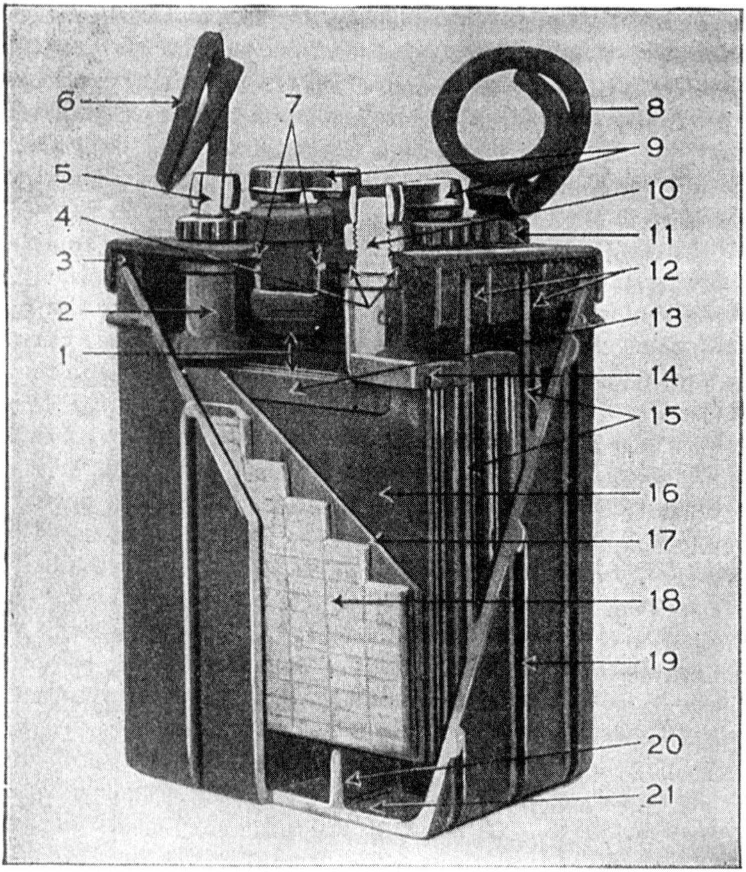

Fig. 326.—Internal Construction of Storage Battery. Space 1 Must Always Be Kept Filled with Liquid by Adding Water Periodically; 2, Connecting Post; 3 and 4, Seal; 5, Terminal; 6, Wire Lead; 7, Gas Vents; 8, Wire Lead; 9, Connecting Straps; 10, Terminal Post; 11, Plate Support Nuts; 12, Cell Jars; 13, Wood Separator; 14, Plate Element Strap; 15, Cell Jar Walls; 16, Plate; 17, Wood Separator; 18, Plate; 19, Cell Jar; 20, Plate or Element Supports; 21, Sediment Space.

the slightest discharge will show. This is especially important in cold weather. If the specific gravity of one cell falls below that of the others and successive readings show the difference in the specific gravity to be increasing, if the specific gravity does not rise, or if the battery continues to show a discharge although the lamps and horn are used sparingly, the instructions to correct such condition should be consulted and followed. Also see instructions under Remy Generator.

If a single hydrometer reading shows the gravity in one cell 25 or 30 points lower than in the others, there may be nothing seriously wrong with the battery. However, if successive readings show the difference to be increasing, the cell is not in good order. Also, if one cell regularly requires more water than the others, a leaky cell may be indicated, especially if it is noticed that the successive hydrometer readings show a gradual lowering of the specific gravity. The best way to determine whether a battery jar leaks is to place the battery on a clean piece of glass and leave it for a few hours. If no moisture collects on the glass, it is safe to assume that the battery does not leak. If a leak is indicated, refer the battery to your dealer or Exide service station. If an examination shows that there is no leak, but if the specific gravity falls 50 or 75 points below that in the other cells, trouble within the cell is indicated. This trouble, if neglected, may seriously injure the battery, if it does not ruin it altogether. This is a very rare occurrence and should be referred to your dealer or the nearest Exide service station.

Should your battery need charging from an outside source, refer it to your dealer or through him to the local Exide service station. However, most dealers are now equipped to charge batteries. If you cannot refer the battery to your dealer or to the Exide service station, take it to some other reliable battery station or to a garage where first class battery charging is done.

Normal Charging Rate Is One Ampere.—Do not allow any one to give your battery a full charge at a higher rate than one ampere. The normal charging or finishing rate is one ampere and direct current only must be used. It has come to our attention a number of times that motorcycle batteries have been brought to a complete charge on the same line with automobile batteries. Naturally, large batteries require a higher charging rate than a motorcycle battery, meaning that a big charge was put through the small motorcycle battery. This is a serious form of abuse, because it means greatly shortened battery life. When you have your battery recharged remember that the correct finishing rate is one ampere, and that the battery should never be started at a higher rate than two amperes. The two ampere rate should be cut down to one or even one-half ampere as soon as the battery begins to gas.

Another important fact in connection with outside charging is that the positive of the charging circuit must be connected with the positive lead or cable of the battery. The positive battery lead is painted red, and marked ''Pos'' and + at the binding post. There is therefore no excuse for making an error. The negative of the charging circuit must be connected with the negative lead of the battery, marked ''Neg.'' If the cables are connected in reverse for charging, the polarity of the battery will be reversed, and the battery ruined.

How to Distinguish "Pos" and "Neg".—If there is any doubt about whether a connection is positive or negative, a simple test is to dip both wires in a glass of water in which a tablespoonful of salt has been dissolved. Bubbles will form on the negative wire. When reconnecting your battery in the machine, the lead marked ''Pos'' is to be connected on the terminal block with the wire leading from the switch, while the wire marked ''Neg'' is to be grounded on the battery box cover.

Referring again to outside charging, the charge is complete when, and only when, with a charging current of one ampere flowing, all cells are gassing, bubbling freely and evenly, and when the gravity of all the cells has risen to a maximum (as far as it will go) and has shown no further rise for ten hours following. This does not mean that the battery should be charged for a total of ten hours, but that it should be charged for ten hours after the maximum or highest specific gravity readings are obtained.

Explanation of Storage Battery Action.—The popular idea in connection with a storage battery is that when a current of electricity is passed through the storage battery, the current is "stored" in the battery. This is not the case at all. A "fully charged" battery does not contain any electricity. What actually takes place is this: When a current is passed through the battery, certain elements in the storage battery plates are combined with the solution or electrolyte in the battery, by a purely chemical process. This is why the hydrometer reading of the solution in a fully charged battery is much higher than that of a discharged battery, because the solution is heavier, having in it some of the elements which were in the plates of the battery before the charging took place. When the battery is discharged, the action which takes place is that the chemicals in the solution or electrolyte are again combined with the plates of the storage battery, through another chemical action. This is the reason why the hydrometer reading of a discharged battery is materially lower than that of a fully charged battery. As mentioned, there is no electrical energy stored up in a fully charged storage battery. The current which is taken from a fully charged battery is generated through the chemical action described, and is generated only at the time it is being taken from the battery.

When a battery is charged, certain elements in the solution are constantly striving to again combine with the elements in the plates, or to return to the condition which they were in before the battery was charged. This explains the reason for the storage battery gradually discharging itself when it is not in use. On the other hand, when a storage battery is discharged, and is left in that condition, it will ruin itself in a short time due to an action called "sulphating."

A storage battery will last longer and can be kept in good condition most easily when it is in constant use, that is to say, when it is being charged and used and recharged right along. A writer once described a storage battery very aptly when he said it was "a nervous proposition" and that it needed constant "excitement."

This is really the stiuation in a nutshell. To keep your storage battery in good shape it should be kept in service. It should also be remembered that a battery will wear out in time. It is not a body that will give service forever without rebuilding. The Exide battery is long lived, and with reasonable care according to the preceding instructions will give a long term of service.

Care of the Battery in Cold Weather.—With the coming of cold weather the storage battery requires some special attention, whether kept in service or laid up temporarily. If the battery is looked after according to the following instructions, there is no danger of damaging it in the severest cold weather.

Add the distilled water once each week as per instructions previously given, but in cold weather be sure to add the water just before the battery is charged, or before running the motor. If the temperature is very low, run the machine for a while before adding the water; then add the water and run again. This will thoroughly mix the distilled water and electrolyte, preventing freezing of the battery. It is a very important point to run the motor immediately after putting distilled water in the battery in cold weather, but do not run the motor on the stand or idle. Run the machine on the road under normal conditions. Do not add water while the machine is standing idle in the cold or after a ride, because the water may freeze on the surface before it is mixed with electrolyte and seriously damage the battery.

Keep Battery Fully Charged in Cold Weather.—It is, of course, important to keep the battery as fully charged as possible at all times, but this is particularly true in cold weather. Do not burn the lights unnecessarily while the machine is standing. Take frequent hydrometer readings and if the specific gravity falls below 1.200, have the battery charged from an outside source. From the table given below it will be seen that the electrolyte in a fully charged storage battery will not freeze even in the coldest weather. On the other hand, the electrolyte in a discharged battery will freeze at about 18 degrees above zero. The importance of taking frequent hydrometer readings and of keeping the battery fully charged can therefore be appreciated.

SPECIFIC GRAVITY TABLE

Specific Gravity	Freezing Point
1.100	18° F.
1.150	4° F.
1.200	—17° F. (below zero)
1.250	—60° F. (below zero)
1.300	—94° F. (below zero)

What to Do if Machine is Taken from Service Less than Two Months.—Many riders now use their motorcycles practically the year round so that the following suggestions may not fit your case. If you do not use your machine continually in cold weather, read carefully. If the battery is to be placed out of commission for less than two months, it is only necessary to add water to the cells just before running the motor the last time, and to make sure that the battery is as near fully charged as possible. The specific gravity should read 1.250 or over. If lower than this, have the battery charged from an outside source. Disconnect the charging wire from the terminal block on the outside of the battery box, because often a slight leak in the wire will cause the battery to discharge. Disconnect the battery ground wire as well, and tape the ends of both wires so that they cannot make connection on the machine.

What to Do if Machine is Taken from Service Longer than Two Months.—It is best to refer your battery to your dealer, to the local Exide service station, or to a reliable garage or battery service station for attention, if the machine is to be laid up more than two months. If this is not practical, fill the battery to the required level and have it charged. Remove it from its case and place it where it will be dry, cool (not freezing) and free from dust. Once every two months during the period it is out of service, renew the freshening charge, that is, charge the battery as explained previously. If it is not possible to have the battery charged, it can be allowed to stand for a period not to exceed six months, provided it has been fully charged first. Better results, however, will be obtained if the freshening charge is given every two months as mentioned.

Placing the Battery Back Into Service.—Always add distilled water and have the battery charged before putting it back into service, even though it has been out of service less than two months. If it has been out of service more than two months and the periodic charges have not been given, have the battery charged for at least 50 hours at one-half ampere charging rate. With the exception of this point, follow carefully the instructions given under directions for charging the battery.

CHAPTER X.

MOTORCYCLE TROUBLES AND SIDE CAR ATTACHMENT.

Motorcycle Troubles—Classification of Engine Defects—Testing Ignition System—Common Faults in Carburetor System—Causes of Lost Compression—Causes of Irregular Motor Operation—Conditions Producing Overheating—Some Causes of Noisy Operation—Chart to Trace and Correct Trouble—Motor Does Not Run—Motor Starts Hard—Motor Stops Shortly After It Is Started—Motor Misses—Valve Removal and Grinding — Removing Carbon Deposits — Grinding Harley-Davidson Valves — Accurate Valve Tappet Adjustment — Adjusting Exhaust Valve Lifter Pins and Inlet Push Rods—To Clean Spark Plugs—Adjust Spark Plug Points—To Test Spark Plugs—The Schebler Carburetor Easy Starting Device—Air Valve Spring Adjustment Instructions for Adjusting Carburetor—Needle Valve Adjustment—Low Speed Adjustment—High Speed Adjustment—Remedy for Flooding—Clogged Gasoline Line—Strain Gasoline When Filling Tank—When Machine Does Not Run Right—Motor Misses at High Speed—Motor Misses When Running Slowly—Motor Misses at Medium Speeds—Motor Refuses to Run—Loss of Power—Defects in Power Transmission Elements—Testing for Chain Alignment—How to Adjust Chains—Slipping Belt Drive—Care of Leather Belts—Care of Wheels—Defects in Clutches and Gearbox—Adjustment of Brakes—Repairing Inner Tube Punctures—Outer Casing Repairs—Tire Inflation Pressures—Advice to Purchasers of Second Hand Motorcycles—To Assemble and Attach Harley-Davidson Side Car—To Attach Side Car to Motorcycle—Attaching and Lining Up Indian Side Car—Driving Pointers—Gear Ratios of Indian Models.

Motorcycle Troubles.—When the motorcycle was first evolved, it was a composite structure of two distinct assemblies, neither of which was adapted to the other. The gasoline motor could not be placed in the ordinary bicycle frame to advantage, and therefore gave continued trouble. As light bicycle frame construction was not sufficiently strong to withstand the vibration incidental to the motor, and greater speeds made possible by mechanical power, the early motorcyclist was confronted with two radically different species of troubles. While the most important of these were undoubtedly due to power plant defects, the annoyances caused by structural weakness of frame, wheels and tires were almost as numerous.

The individual peculiarities of the different machines preclude any specific outline of all derangements apt to occur, but a general outline of the common troubles may prove of value to the novice rider, regardless of the make of machine he rides. Motorcycle troubles may be divided into three main classes: those incidental to the power plant, the derangements of power transmission units and the difficulties encountered with the frame structure. In the first-named classification the defects in the engine itself, and the auxiliary groups such as carburetion, ignition and lubrication, may be included. Troubles arising from belts or chains, sprockets or pulleys, clutches or two-speed gears are properly part of the second class, while frame, wheel, coasterbrake, spring fork and tire troubles are assigned to the third classification. It is with the first two that we have to deal mostly, because there are practically no structural defects in the modern machine, therefore of the third classification, we are limited almost entirely to tire troubles.

Classification of Engine Defects.—It is not difficult for one familiar with motorcycle construction and operation to make suggestions intended to assist the motorcyclist in locating troubles that may materialize with his power plant. The expert, as a rule, recognizes the symptoms of derangement, and usually has no difficulty in tracing the trouble to its source by well-known methods. The novice is often at loss to know how and where to begin to look for trouble and a safe rule for one with little mechanical experience to follow is to search systematically for derangements and discover the fault that the expert would find through its symptoms by a patient process of elimination. The motorcycle power plant is really composed of several groups, each of which includes a

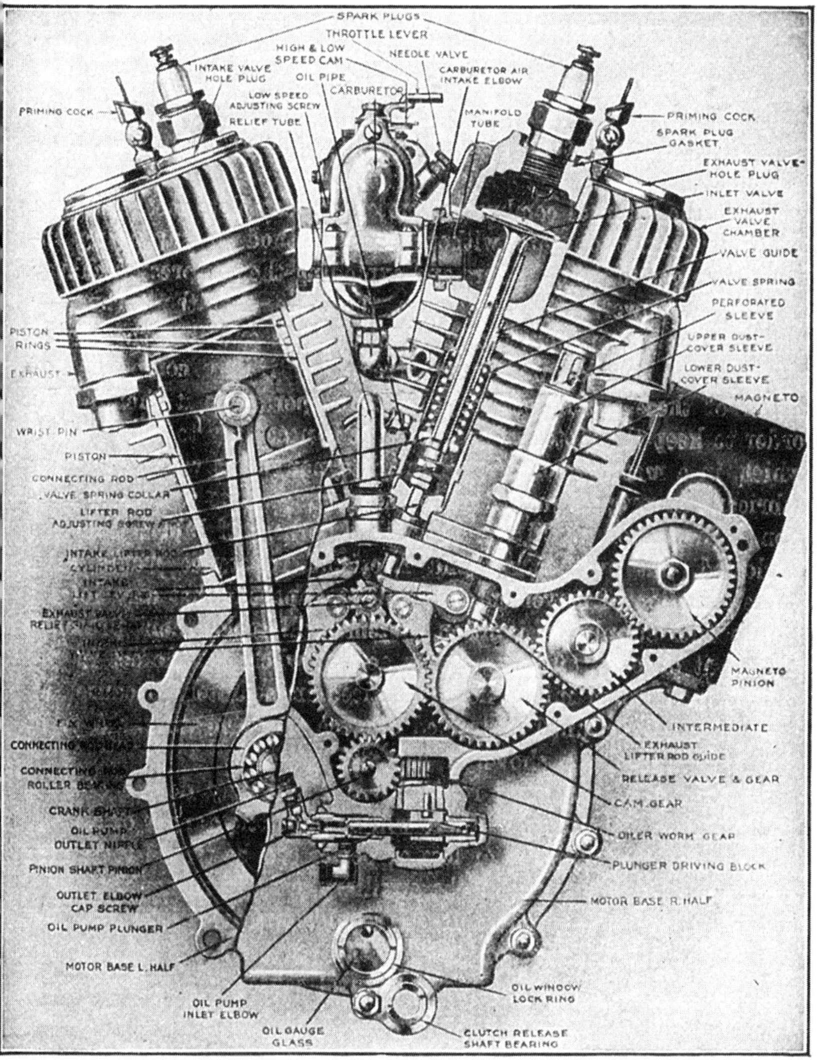

Fig. 327.—The Indian Power-Plus Twin-Cylinder Motorcycle Power Plant.

series of distinct components. These are related so closely to each other that the failure of any one of the devices will affect the operation of the others and thus break the continuity of power production. Some auxiliary groups are more important than others, because the motor often continues to operate for a time after the failure of some essential parts in the group of lesser importance.

While the internal combustion motor is a complete mechanism in itself, it cannot operate without some method of supplying inflammable gas to the cylinders and exploding the compressed charge to produce power. It will be seen, therefore, that the carburetor and ignition systems are really essential parts and that the engine will stop at once or work very irregularly if any component of either of these auxiliary groups fails to operate as it should. In order to keep the motor in operation, it is necessary to keep it cool, which, in a motorcycle power plant, is synonymous with supplying lubricant in proper quantities to the moving parts to reduce friction. The motor would run for a time perhaps if lubrication was neglected, but overheating and frictional resistance would soon cause cessation of movement. It will be apparent that any defects in the fuel supply or ignition systems will make their presence known at once by affecting motor action, whereas a defect in the lubricating system might not be noticed immediately because the engine would run until it stopped because of overheating. A typical modern engine is shown at Fig. 327.

If a motor be inspected regularly and with any degree of care before a trip is commenced, there will be but little danger of serious trouble and any skipping or loss of power can be traced to failure of one of the components of the auxiliary systems rather than to a defect in the power plant itself. Irregular operation is seldom due to the actual breaking of any of the parts of the mechanism. Fortunately, depreciation, due to natural causes, comes slowly and deterioration of any of the mechanical parts always gives sufficient warning so that satisfactory repairs may be made before serious troubles occur. One of the most annoying troubles, and one that invariably denotes wear of the mechanism is continued noisy operation. The sharp metallic knocking that is so annoying to both experienced driver and novice, when not due to carbon deposits or preignition due to overheating or too highly advanced spark, indicates wear at either the main bearings or at the upper or lower end of the connecting-rod where the bushings may be worn so that considerable play exists between them and the shaft they encircle. A grinding noise accompanied by a knocking sound generally means that the lubrication system is not functioning properly or that the motorcyclist has neglected to inject the proper quantities of oil in the engine crank-case.

Before discussing the failures that may obtain in any particular part of the power plant, we will consider a case of engine failure, and, for the guidance of the novice, outline the main steps constituting a practical process of locating the trouble by systematic elimination. If the engine stops suddenly, the two main causes may be either failure of the gasoline supply or trouble in the ignition system. A sudden stop, when not due to overheating and seizing of the piston in the cylinder, which, as we have seen would be evidenced by a pronounced knocking long before the overheating became sufficiently great to cause binding, is generally due to a broken wire or a defective spark plug. It can be caused also by the stoppage of the spray nozzle in the carburetor or the main fuel supply pipe with a particle of foreign matter.

Testing the Ignition System.—In a motorcycle, the simplest thing to test, in event of engine failure, is the ignition system, then the amount of motor compression, and lastly the fuel supply system. If the ignition system is working properly, as may be determined by laying the spark plug on the cylinder head and connecting it with the large wire leading from the magneto or coil and then pedaling briskly to see if there is any spark between the points of the plug, one should test the compression, and if this is satisfactory, the carburetor demands attention. The compression is tested by pedaling the engine over with the exhaust valve lift down, and if there is a decided resistance to turning at a certain point in the engine rotation, it is safe to say that there is no undue loss of gas.

Let us assume that in making our test with the spark plug on the cylinder that there has been no spark between the points of the plug. The first thing to inspect is the spark plug itself, where the following points should be carefully considered. First examine the gap between the points of the plug. This should be about $\frac{1}{64}$-inch, if a magneto system is installed, or about $\frac{1}{32}$-inch, if a spark coil and batteries are utilized to produce the spark. With a battery ignition system, one should examine carefully all the wires to see that they are tight on their terminals, and that none of the wires have become short-circuited by burning away of the insulation, which may have been in contact with a hot exhaust pipe or cylinder head flange. The vibrator or contact spring at the timer may be adjusted poorly, which would mean that contact would not be established properly, while the spark plug might become short-circuited because of cracked procelain insulation or carbon deposit. Short-circuiting will also occur in mica plugs if the insulator becomes oil-soaked.

With dry battery ignition, now used only on old types that are practically obsolete, the source of current should be tested with an ammeter to determine if the dry cells have sufficient amperage to insure regular ignition. If they indicate less than 5 amperes a cell, new ones should be used. A good way to see if current is present at the timer is to bridge the insulated contact screw on the timer case to the crankcase by means of a screw-driver, with the switch plug in place, and observe if there is any spark as the screw-driver end is rubbed over the engine base. If a spark is present at this point, it is reasonable to assume that the trouble is due to defective spark plug or to a defective secondary wire leading from the coil to the plug.

If a magneto be used, it is possible also for troubles to exist at the spark plug as previously enumerated, or the ground wire may make contact with the metal of the frame before it reaches the cut-out switch. The platinum contact points in the breaker box, which is the part rocked back and forth as the timer lever is moved, may be out of adjustment; the carbon contact brushes that convey the current from the revolving armature to the terminal by which the device is connected to the spark plug may be broken or not making contact, or the insulation of the secondary wires may be defective.

Common Faults in Carburetion System.—If the trouble is not due to the ignition system, and there is good compression in the motor, the carburetor demands attention. The first thing to look for is to see that there is plenty of gasoline in the tank, as many a novice has exerted himself unduly trying to make an engine start

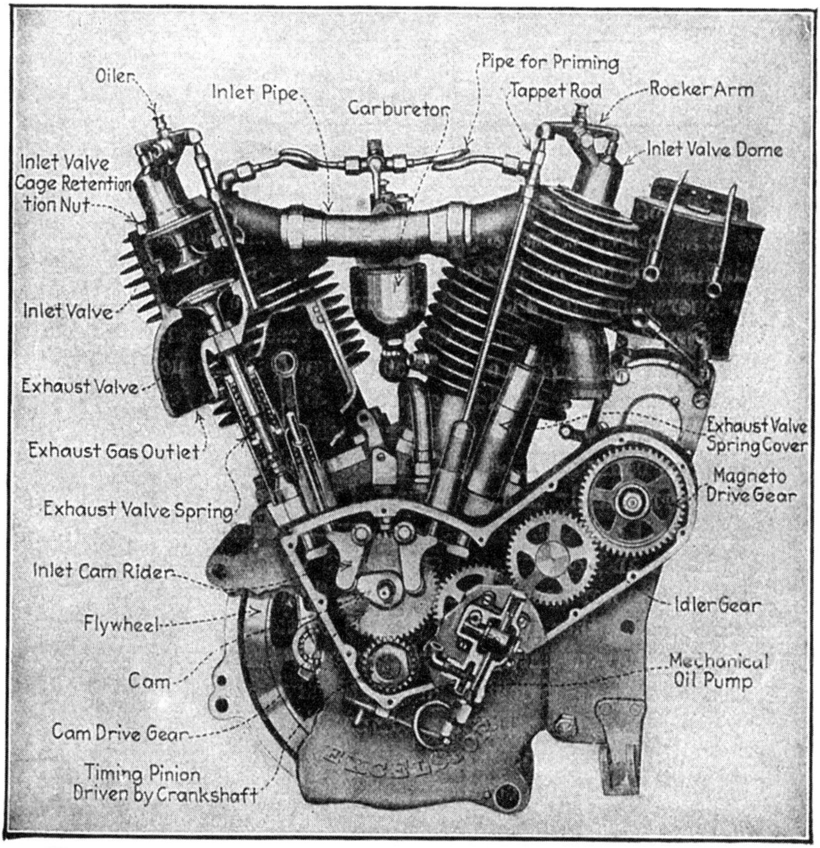

Fig. 328.—Part Sectional View of Twin-Cylinder Motor of Excelsior Design with Timing Gear Case Cover Removed.

when there was no fuel in the container. If the tank is found to hold a sufficient supply of fuel, the next thing to do is to make sure that the pipe line is clear to the carburetor. This may be ascertained easily by shutting off the gasoline at the tank, uncoupling the gasoline pipe at the carburetor, and then turning the supply on to see if any issues from the pipe. If the gasoline runs out in a full stream when the valve is opened, the pipe is clear; whereas, if it trickles out but slowly, one may assume that the bore of the tube is constricted by becoming dented or by dirt.

One may often determine if the gasoline supply is all right by pressing on the little priming pin on the carburetor float bowl until gasoline drips out of the bottom of the carburetor or the air intake. This is called flooding the carburetor. If, on the other hand, the carburetor floods continually without the priming pin being depressed, it constitutes a defect that will produce other troubles, though not always stoppage of the motor. Among other causes that might cause engine to stop one should see that the throttle has not become closed through the failure of a connecting link or operating wire and that the shut-off valve in the feed pipe has not jarred closed. The gasoline may reach the carburetor all right and yet there may not be enough liquid in the float chamber of the device. This would happen if the action of the float-controlled needle valve was interfered with by dirt or binding, if the float was badly adjusted or if the float valve operating mechanism was worn unduly in some forms of carburetor.

Causes of Lost Compression.—Assuming that we have found both ignition and carburetion systems to be functioning properly and that the motor has no compression, then the trouble is due to some condition either inside or outside of the motor. As the external parts may be inspected with greater ease, one should look for the following: Sticking or bent valve stem, broken valve spring, leak through spark plug compression release cock or valve dome, valve plunger stuck in its guide, keeping valve open, lack of clearance between valve stem end and operating plunger or tappet-rod and in very rare instances a cracked cylinder head or leaky cylinder head gasket where the head is separate from the cylinder.

Among some of the defective conditions that may exist inside of a motor are: a broken valve, a warped valve head, foreign matter under valve seat, piston rings broken or gummed in the piston grooves or scored or worn cylinder. The parts of typical engines

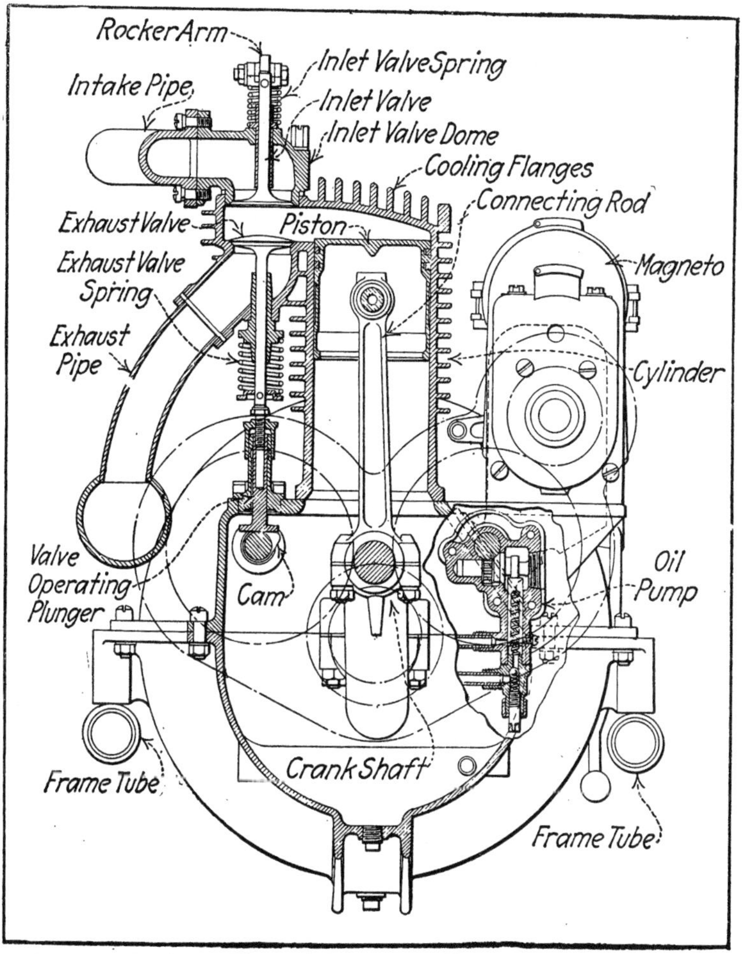

Fig. 329.—Sectional View of Henderson Four-Cylinder Motorcycle Engine.

are clearly shown in Figs. 327, 328, 329 and 330 and should be easily recognized.

Causes of Irregular Motor Operation.—If the engine works irregularly or skips, the cause may be harder to locate because many possible conditions may exist that must be eliminated and checked over one by one. In addition to the troubles previously enumerated, a very common cause is an air leak around the induction manifold, dirt in the carburetor or improper mixture. The gasoline needle may be set improperly or may have jarred out of adjustment or the air valve spring may have been weakened or broken. The air intake dust screen may be so full of dirt and oil that not enough air will pass through the mesh. There may be water or sediment in the gasoline which would cause irregular operation because the fuel supply would vary at the nozzle.

Where a magneto ignition system is employed, it is seldom that one finds defects in the magneto, but when batteries are used just as soon as they become weakened the engine will begin to miss fire. Another thing that must be done very carefully is adjusting the contact screw at the timer, as many puzzling cases of irregular ignition with battery systems have been corrected by cleaning the oil out of the timer, washing the interior out thoroughly with gasoline, and then readjusting the points while the engine was running. Points may be screwed nearer together, and if this does not correct the trouble they may be separated very gradually. When the proper adjustment is reached, the engine will accelerate and run smoothly. (See instructions in chapter on ignition for magneto contact breaker adjustment.)

Conditions Producing Overheating.—Overheating is usually caused by carbon deposits or derangement of the lubrication system. It is sometimes caused by carburetor troubles as well as insufficient oiling. The lubricating system of the modern motorcycle is extremely simple, consisting of a simple hand pump by which oil may be injected into the crank-case when desired, as an auxiliary, and the regular oil feed to the cylinders by means of a mechanical oiler on the engine base. The conditions that most commonly result in poor lubrication are: Insufficient supply of oil in engine base, use of poor quality oil, clogged oil pipe, defective check valve or worn plunger at the pump, clogged sight feed fitting, and if a mechanical oiler be employed, a broken pump, or a defective drive.

Any condition that will cause too rich mixture will also result in overheating. These may be enumerated briefly, as follows, too much gasoline in the mixture due to improper needle valve regulation, level in float chamber too high or auxiliary air valve spring

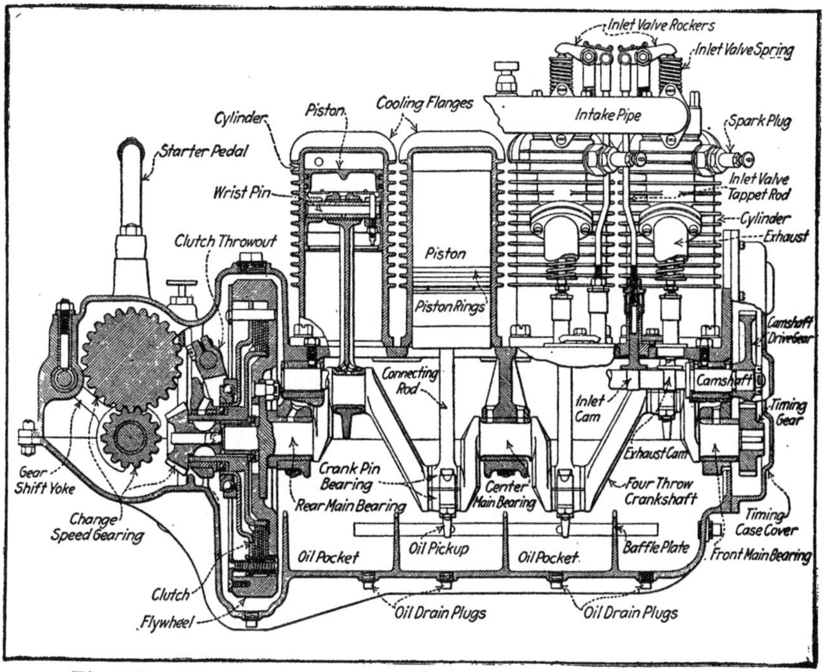

Fig. 330.—The Henderson Four-Cylinder Unit Power Plant for Motorcycles Incorporates Many Distinctive Features.

too tight. A cork float may be fuel-soaked, or a hollow metal float may leak and be full of liquid which increases the weight and causes the carburetor to flood. Dirt will also keep the float-controlled needle valve from seating, and the level be too high at the standpipe, or, as previously outlined, the air screen may become clogged with dust and not enough air reach the mixture. If there is an excessive amount of carbon present in the combustion chamber and on top of the piston, this will also produce overheating and pre-ignition. These deposits should be removed from the piston top and combustion chamber wherever present. Many cases of lost power which also causes overheating have been corrected by merely grinding in the valves to a correct seating. Overheating has been caused also by a worn or poorly adjusted valve plunger which did not raise the exhaust valve from its seat sufficiently, or by altered spark timing which meant operating the motor on a late or retarded spark or late exhaust valve opening. The illustration at Fig. 331 shows how a feeler gauge is used to test the clearance between valve lifter and valve stem.

Some Causes of Noisy Operation.—There are a number of power-plant derangements which give positive indication because of noisy operation. Any knocking or rattling sounds are usually produced by wear in connecting rods or main bearings of the engine, though sometimes a sharp metallic knock, which is very much the same as that produced by a loose bearing, is due to carbon deposits in the cylinder heads, or premature ignition due to advanced spark-time lever. Squeaking sounds invariably indicate dry bearings, and whenever such a sound is heard it should be immediately located and oil applied to the parts thus denoting their dry condition. Whistling or blowing sounds are produced by leaks, either in the engine itself or in the gas manifolds. A sharp whistle denotes the escape of gas under pressure, and is usually caused by a defective packing or gasket that seals a portion of the combustion chamber or that is used for a joint as the exhaust manifold. A blowing sound indicates a leaky packing in crank-case. Grinding noises in the motor are usually caused by the timing gears, and will obtain if these gears are dry or if they have become worn. Whenever a loud knocking sound is heard, careful inspection should be made to locate the cause of the trouble. Much harm may be done in a few minutes if the engine is run with loose connecting-rod or bearings that would be prevented by taking up the wear or looseness between the parts by some means of adjustment.

In the Henderson engine shown at Figs. 329 and 330, the connecting rods and main bearings are adjusted the same as those of automobiles, as the bearings have caps that may be removed and carefully fitted by removing shims and scraping. In roller bearing engines, such as the Harley-Davidson and Indian, special care is taken in fitting these bearings as outlined in a following chapter on engine overhauling.

Fig. 331.—How to Test Clearance Between Valve Stem and Operating Plunger.

Chart to Trace and Correct Trouble.—This Chart, compiled by the Harley-Davidson Motor Co., forms a comprehensive basis to locate and correct motor trouble. In connection with the causes of trouble as indicated under the respective headings, the proper instructions in the manual should be consulted.

If it is impossible to turn the motor over with the starter, the trouble is most likely due to the fact that the machine has been run without oil or run without sufficient oil, until the pistons or piston rings have become seized in the cylinders. The only effective remedy is to have the motor taken down and any damage repaired. All of the points outlined can be easily inspected and the points at fault can be corrected by systematic search. The charts given on pages 576, 577 and 578 are very valuable to permit the motorcyclist to locate his motor troubles in a logical manner.

Valve Removal and Grinding.—The operation of valve grind-

- **Motor Does Not Run**
  - **No Spark**
    - **Magneto**
      - Circuit Breaker Lever Is Stuck
      - Circuit Breaker Points Out of Adjustment
      - Circuit Breaker Points Are Pitted
      - Circuit Breaker Points Are Worn Badly
      - Brushes Oil Soaked
      - Spool Oil Soaked
      - Brush Holders Cracked
      - Brushes Worn
      - Magneto Water Soaked
      - Magneto Faulty, consult manufacturer
      - → See Instructions Under Care of Magneto
    - **Generator**
      - Circuit Breaker Points Are Out of Adjustment
      - Centrifugal Ignition Switch Is Out of Order
      - Battery Is Discharged
      - Loose Primary Connections on Coil
      - Breaker Lever Is Stuck
      - Breaker Points Worn
      - Breaker Points Pitted
      - Breaker Lever Coil Spring Broken
      - Generator Faulty, consult nearest United Motors Service Inc. Service Station
      - → See Instructions Under Care of Generator
  - **Spark Plug**
    - Cracked Core
    - Points Set Wrong
    - Electrodes Oxidized
    - Oil Soaked
    - Sooted
    - → See Spark Plug Instructions
  - **Good Spark**
    - **Timed Wrong**
      - Were Gears Removed?
      - No Key in Pinion
      - No Key in Generator Gear
      - No Key in Magneto Gear
      - → See Dealer for Timing Instructions
    - ……
      - Carburetor Out of Order
      - Carburetor Out of Adjustment
      - Sediment in Carburetor
      - Gasoline Pipe Is Clogged
      - Gasoline Tank Is Clogged
      - Water in Gasoline
      - No Gasoline
      - → See Carburetor Instructions
    - **No Compression**
      - **Valves Do Not Seat**
        - Poor Lifter Pin and Push Rod Adjustment
        - Valve Stem Bent, Seat Warped
        - Seats Pitted
        - Valve Key Sheared Off
        - Valve or Cylinder Seat Cracked
        - Valve Spring Broken
        - Lift Mechanism Sticks
      - **Valves Do Not Lift**
        - Roller Arms Broken
        - Lifter Pins and Push Rods Loose
        - Pinion Key Sheared
        - Gears Stripped
      - **Valves Timed Wrong**
        - Were Gears Removed?
        - No Key in Pinion
        - Were Any New Gears Fitted?
        - → See Dealer for Timing Instructions
      - **Valves Seat O. K.**
        - Motor Worn from Service
        - Cylinders Scored
        - Piston Rings Worn
        - Piston Rings Burnt—No Life
        - Piston Rings Fit Too Loose
        - Sand Hole in Piston
        - Sand Hole in Cylinder
        - Inlet Housing Clamped Loosely
        - Inlet Housing Warped

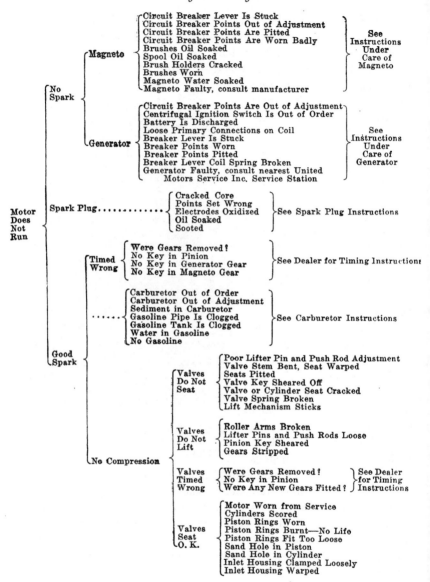

- lotcr Starts Hard
  - Magneto
    - Good Spark
      - Poorly Adjusted Carburetor
      - Water in Gasoline
      - Poor Gasoline
      - Poor Compression
    - Poor Spark
      - Plug Points Set Wrong
      - Plugs Faulty
      - Poorly Adjusted or Pitted Circuit Breaker Points
      - Dirty Distributor Spool
      - Dirty Brushes
      - Sticking Circuit Breaker Lever
      - Magneto at Fault
  - Generator
    - Good Spark
      - Poorly Adjusted Carburetor
      - Water in Gasoline
      - Poor Gasoline
      - Poor Compression
    - Poor Spark
      - Discharged Battery
      - Plugs Faulty or Set Wrong
      - Poorly Adjusted or Pitted Circuit Breaker Points
      - Oil on Circuit Breaker Points
      - Poor Circuit Between Generator and Battery
      - Sticking Circuit Breaker Lever
      - Centrifugal Switch Out of Adjustment
      - Generator at Fault
- lotor Stops Shortly After It Is Started
  - Magneto
    - No Gasoline
    - Gasoline Pipe Clogged
    - Poorly Adjusted Carburetor
    - Carburetor at Fault
    - Float Set Too Low
    - Motor Runs Tight
  - Generator
    - No Gasoline
    - Gasoline Pipe Clogged
    - Poorly Adjusted Carburetor
    - Carburetor at Fault
    - Float Set Too Low
    - Discharged Battery and Generator Dead
    - Motor Runs Tight

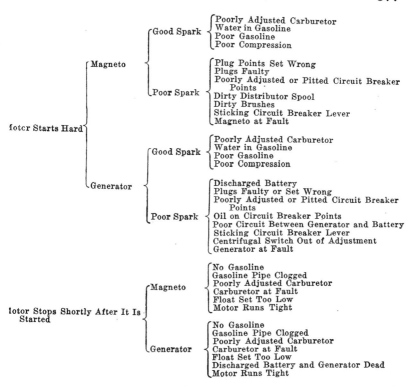

ing is a simple one provided that the valve seat is not too badly pitted or scored. The first step is to remove the valve from the cylinder, which is not difficult with the usual forms of inlet valves, as it is merely necessary to remove the dome in which they are housed. To facilitate the removal of the exhaust valve, tools such as shown at Fig. 332 may be employed to compress the valve spring and permit the removal of the pin or key at the bottom of the valve stem. With the form shown at A, it is necessary to hold the exhaust valve down as the spring is raised, which may be easily done by interposing a small block of wood, belt connector, chain link or other object between the valve cap and the valve head or

- If Motor Runs Normally and . . . .
  - Clutch Slips
  - It Is Difficult to Stop the Machine
  - It Is Hard to Shift Gears
  - Battery Discharges
  - Over Oils
  - Machine Runs Jerky

- Motor Misses
  - Plugs Spark Regularly
    - Carburetor at Fault
      - Readjust Carburetor
      - Water in Gasoline
      - Poor Gasoline
      - Gasoline Line Clogged Up
      - Sticking Needle Valve Lift Lever
      - Auxiliary Air Valve Loose on Bushing
      - Auxiliary Air Valve Spring Worn
    - Poor Compression
      - Valves Do Not Seat
      - Lifter Pins Adjusted Improperly
      - Push Rods Adjusted Improperly
    - Air Leaks—Test with Gasoline While Motor Is Running Slowly
      - Around Inlet Housings
      - Around Inlet Manifold Nuts and Nipples
      - Around Spark Plugs
      - Around Cylinder Plugs
      - Around Priming Cocks
  - At All Speeds
    - Faulty Spark Plugs
    - Dirty Gasoline or Clogged Line
    - Poorly Adjusted Carburetor
    - Poor Compression
    - Sticking Valves
    - Weak or Broken Valve Spring
    - Valve Key Sheared Off
  - At Low Speed
    - Readjust Carburetor
    - Faulty Spark Plug
    - Poor Compression
      - Poor Lifter Pin Adjustment
      - Poor Push Rod Adjustment
      - Valves Do Not Seat
      - Leaks Past Piston Rings
      - Sand Hole in Piston or Cylinder
    - Air Leaks—Test with Gasoline While Motor Is Running Slowly
      - Around Inlet Housings
      - Around Inlet Manifold Nuts and Nipples
      - Around Spark Plugs
      - Around Priming Cocks
      - Around Cylinder Plugs
  - At High Speed
    - Faulty Spark Plug
    - Dirty Gasoline or Clogged Line
    - Readjust Carburetor
    - Weak Valve Springs
    - Sticking Lift Mechanism
    - Sticking Valves
    - Sticking Circuit Breaker Lever
  - Plugs Spark Irregularly
    - Magneto
      - Faulty Spark Plug
      - Sticking Circuit Breaker Lever
      - Brushes and Distributor Spool Oil Soaked
      - Oil on Circuit Breaker Points
      - Pitted Circuit Breaker Points
      - Poorly Adjusted Breaker Points
      - Bruised Spark Plug Cables, Causing Short Circuit
    - Generator
      - Faulty Spark Plug
      - Sticking Circuit Breaker Lever
      - Oil on Circuit Breaker Points
      - Poorly Adjusted Circuit Breaker Points
      - Poor Primary Connections
      - Poor Circuit Between Generator and Battery
      - Bruised Spark Plug Cables
      - Faulty Generator, consult dealer

by holding the head down against the seat with the screw-driver or other tool. With the valve lifter shown at B, the hook member supporting the fork or lever that raises the spring holds the valve against the seat. If the valve face is badly scored or pitted, it may be found desirable to reface that member before endeavoring to grind it in. This may be done by a simple tool as shown at Fig. 333. A cutting blade is carried by a casting which also serves

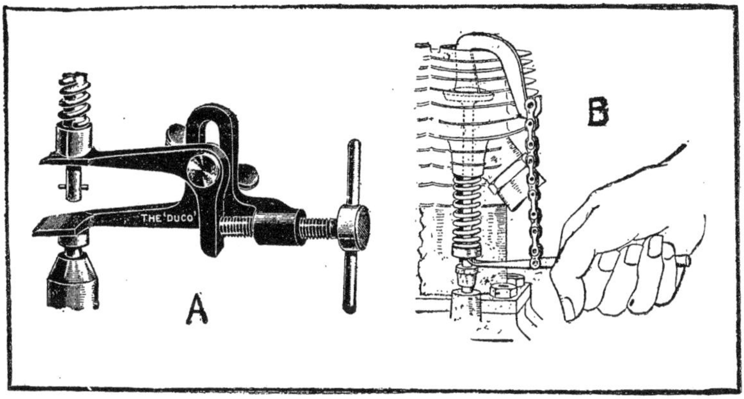

Fig. 332.—Two Methods of Raising Exhaust Valve Spring to Permit Valve Removal.

to support the valve stem at one end and a screw at the other by which the valve head may be brought in contact with the angularly disposed shaving cutter. As the valve is rotated by the dog attached to the valve stem, the seat will be trued off to the proper angle. Valve grinding consists merely of smearing the face of the valve and the seating with a mixture of emery and oil, and rotating the valve against the seat by a screw-driver as hereinafter described.

Removing Carbon Deposits.—If the motor is of a detachable head form, it is a comparatively simple matter to remove the combustion head which will expose the piston top as well as the combustion chamber. The carbon deposits, which are a fertile source of trouble, may be removed by positive mechanical means, such as indicated at Fig. 334, A, in which a screw-driver, chisel or scraper is employed to scrape them off. As the combustion head is removed, it will not be difficult to relieve it of carbon deposits in the same manner. If a one-piece cylinder is employed, that member may be removed, which will expose the piston top and the combustion chamber interior for mechanical scraping.

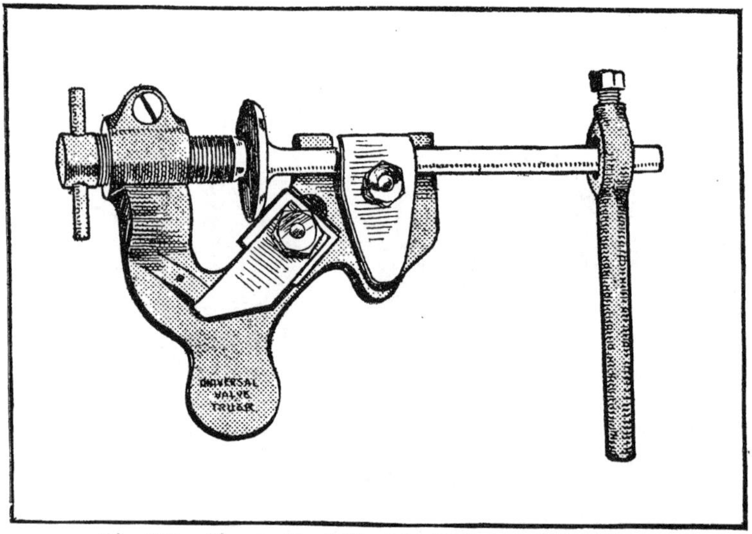

Fig. 333.—Simple Tool Used in Refacing Valve Seat.

A new process of carbon removal which is meeting with success is shown at Fig. 334, B. This calls for the use of a small torch burning ordinary gas or an ordinary match to start combustion, and another member that will supply oxygen to the interior of the combustion chamber. The stream of oxygen permits combustion of the deposit and the carbon is burnt out at all points where the flame touches, passing out of the cylinder in the form of a gas, and leaving only a fine residue or dust in the combustion chamber, which is blown out with the exhaust as soon as the engine is started. As the application of the oxygen process does not necessitate dismantling the engine, it may be used to considerable advantage, especially with the one-piece cylinder construction.

To insure continued good motor service, it is advisable to have your motor taken apart, the carbon removed by scraping, and, if necessary, the valves reground once each season. This is recommended in addition to the periodic flushing. Have your dealer do the work if possible, since he has the wrenches and tools necessary for a first-class job. For the rider so situated that a dealer's services are not available we cover the subject fully in the following pages.

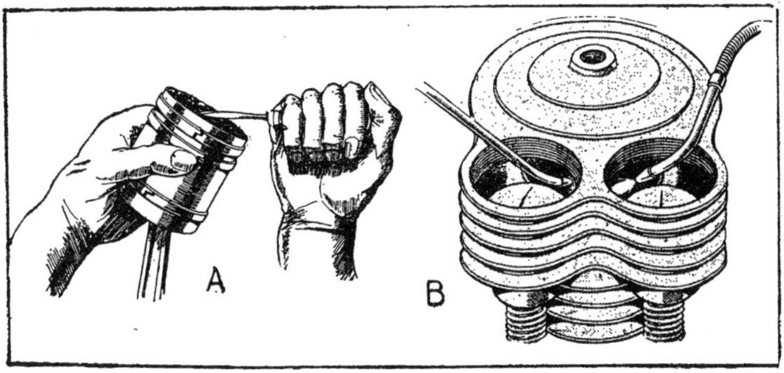

Fig. 334.—Methods of Removing Carbon Deposits from Piston Top or Combustion Chamber Interior.

Removing Carbon from Harley-Davidson Motor.—Remove the motor from the frame. It is advisable to clamp the motor in a vise at the front crank case lug. The bottom of the crank case should rest on the bench or on a board fastened to the bench for that purpose. Loosen both manifold packing nuts, screw out the manifold nipples and remove the carburetor and manifold complete. Loosen the push rod spring covers and remove the inlet push rods from the inlet lever sockets.

Unscrew the exhaust valve spring covers with the wrench provided in the tool kit.

Remove the cylinder stud nuts and then the cylinders, being careful that the pistons do not strike the connecting rods sharply. Bring the crank pin to the upper position. Place a clean rag under the pistons to prevent dirt falling into the crank case. Scrape the carbon from the pistons, remove the carbon, if any, from the piston ring grooves under the rings, and look at the underside of the piston heads for carbon. If no carbon scrapers are available use a screw driver, or a file bent hook-shaped so as to obtain easy access to all carbon. Flush the crank case and wash the pistons carefully with gasoline; then drain and cover the whole assembly with a clean rag and set aside.

Next, place one of the cylinders in the vise. Lay the cylinder flat between the jaws and screw up the vise. There is no danger of breaking the cylinder flanges if the jaws are four inches or more in length. Remove the inlet housing clamp nut and cap. A wrench to fit the clamp nut is furnished with the tool kit. Remove the inlet housing lock screw and take out the inlet housing. If the housing sticks, it can easily be removed after the exhaust valve spring has been taken off, as follows: Raise the exhaust valve spring collar, withdraw the key and remove the collar, spring and spring cover. The inlet housing can then be easily pushed out of the cylinder with the exhaust valve. If necessary tap the exhaust valve squarely and lightly with a small hammer or block of wood.

Remove the cylinder plug with a large monkey wrench. Then take out the priming cock. After having removed all fittings, the cylinder is ready for scraping. Take the cylinder from the vise and with a set of carbon scrapers remove all the carbon from the combustion chamber and all corners of the exhaust port. Also clean out the priming cock.

Grinding Valves.—Clamp the cylinder in the vise again and clean the carbon from the exhaust valve and stem. Place a reasonable amount of grinding compound on the seat of the exhaust valve, drop the valve back into the cylinder and with a screw driver or breast drill, turn the valve first one way and then the other. It is necessary to turn the valve back and forth and not press too hard, or the seat may be badly "ringed." When the face of the valve seat and the seat in the cylinder present a smooth uniform appearance, it may be taken for granted that the valve is seating properly.

After the valve has been ground to the operator's satisfaction, it should be given a simple but accurate test by marking the valve seat and the seat in the cylinder with pencil marks about 1/8 inch apart. Put the valve into the cylinder, give it about one-quarter turn, take it out and see whether the marks have been erased equally. If the marks are only erased in places, the valve or cylinder seat is warped, and it may be necessary to fit another valve or take off a light cut in a lathe or a grinder, or re-ream the seat in the cylinder after which, of course, the valve must be ground again.

Harley-Davidson dealers are furnished with a special tool for reaming exhaust valve seats in cylinders and the operation of refacing should be referred to the dealer when possible.

After grinding both exhaust valves, inspect the inlet valve seats. Compress the inlet valve spring, remove the key and the assembly can be taken apart. If the seats are pitted, they should be reground. A convenient method is as follows: Fit the valve in the housing and place a small quantity of grinding compound on the seats; then clamp the upper end of the valve stem in the vise. Turn the housing by hand first one way and then the other until the seats present a smooth, uniform appearance.

In this connection it is advisable to inspect the inlet and exhaust valve springs. The 1920 inlet valve springs and exhaust valve springs are 2½ inches in length. If the springs are found set (shrunk) considerably, replace them. Good valve springs make for quiet running, and smooth and flexible motor action.

Before assembling the motor wash all parts thoroughly in clean gasoline to remove all particles of carbon and grinding compound. Apply a little oil to the pistons, working it well under the piston rings. Replace the cylinders, making sure that the paper gaskets between the cylinders and crank case are in good condition. Replace the carburetor and intake manifold assembly in such a way that the manifold is clamped centrally between the packing nuts.

Readjust the exhaust lifter pins as shown in Fig. 331. Replace the inlet push rods, adjusting them to the proper clearance.

Fit the motor in the frame, making sure that the cylinder and crank case connections are secure. The corrugated lock plates are to be placed one each under the bolt heads, and one each under the lock washers, with the oblong holes upward. If one connection is left loose, the resultant excessive strain placed on the other connection may cause the breaking of a frame fitting. The controls should be given very careful attention. See that the spark can be advanced and retarded the full travel of the interrupter. The throttle should open fully and close entirely without placing any strain on the throttle shaft.

Give the motor two hand pumpfuls of oil. Run it slowly. Test for a possible leak around both inlet housings, manifold ends, cylinder plugs, spark plugs, and priming cocks, using a priming gun and gasoline. If the running of the motor is affected during one of these tests, a leak is indicated. This leak must be eliminated before the motor will run satisfactorily, especially at low speed.

Grinding the Valves Without Removing Motor.—The above instructions cover the grinding of the valves when the motor is removed from the frame and, as explained, every motor should be given this attention annually. During the season it may be desired to grind the valves. This can be done without removing the motor from the frame as follows:

Wrench FK822 in illustration Fig. 288 is provided to handle the inlet housing clamp nut. After removing this nut and the set screw in the cylinder, the housing can be removed. If the inlet housing sticks in the cylinder, it can easily be forced out by the motor itself. This is accomplished by removing the inlet housing set screw, loosening the housing clamp nut about two turns and running the motor slowly. The force of the explosion and compression will loosen the housing. Do not remove the housing clamp nut entirely or the housing may be blown out with sufficient force to do considerable damage.

Before the exhaust valve can be removed, it is necessary to loosen the exhaust valve spring cover. After removing the inlet housing and spark plug, put a wedge of some kind through the spark plug hole against the exhaust valve, so as to hold the latter in place while raising the exhaust valve spring collar to remove the key in the exhaust valve stem. The spring, of course, must be compressed before the key can be withdrawn.

Before grinding in the valve, be sure that the cam which raises the exhaust valve is all the way down, so that the exhaust valve is resting on its seat, and that the exhaust valve is free from carbon. Place a reasonable amount of grinding compound on the seat of the exhaust valve, distributing it evenly over the surface and grind the valves per instructions previously given.

It is seldom necessary to grind in the inlet valve, inasmuch as it is not subject to as much heat as the exhaust valve. It is, however, a simple matter to grind the inlet valve.

The Importance of Accurate Valve Tappet Adjustment.—After grinding the valves, it is necessary to readjust the exhaust lifter pins and inlet push rods, or tappets, as termed hereafter. The method of adjusting the tappets is covered in connection with the subject of valve grinding, for convenience, although it is advisable to inspect and adjust the tappets of a new machine after the first 200 miles of service and every two months thereafter, because it is essential that the adjustment be correct. This holds true after the valves are ground as well as when the motor is new. If the gap between the valve stem and lifter pin is too small, the valve may be held open after expansion under heat, since the expansion of the cylinder and valve mechanism vary. The result will be a pitted and eventually burnt valve. On the other hand, if there is too much clearance, the valves will be late in opening and early in closing, resulting in sluggish motor action and overheating.

INCHES TO MILLIMETERS

Inches $\times$ 25.4 =millimeters.
Inches $\div$ .03937=millimeters.

It can be understood from the foregoing that accuracy in the adjustment of the tappets is essential. For example, if an inlet lever has 1/16 inch clearance when the motor is cold, instead of the correct clearance, .004 inch, the inlet valve timing will be changed from about 1/4 inch before top center, the correct timing, to top center. We recommend that your dealer make the adjustments, since he most likely has a feeler gauge as shown in the accompanying illustration, Fig. 331, and the necessary wrenches. However, for the rider who cannot conveniently refer his machine to a dealer we cover the subject thoroughly in the following paragraphs.

To Adjust Exhaust Lifter Pins and Inlet Push Rods.—When adjusting an exhaust lifter pin be sure that the pin is in its lowest or bottom position, by turning the motor until the exhaust valve of the other cylinder is raised. To make sure that the lifter pin is in its bottom position, force it down with a screw driver before adjusting. The motor must be cold when making these adjustments.

The correct clearance between the exhaust lifter pins and exhaust valve stems for both cylinders on the 1920 models, with the valves closed is .008 inch to .010 inch. For accuracy, we advise using a feeler gauge such as shown. This gauge has blades of various thicknesses and can very conveniently be used to gauge different clearances, such as spark plug points and circuit breaker points. If a gauge is not available, a piece of ordinary writing paper will do the job. An ordinary piece of writing paper is about .003 inch thick, therefore, by doubling the paper to obtain the required thickness an accurate adjustment can be made.

If a larger gap is required, hold the hexagon head of the lifter pin with one wrench and with another wrench turn the screw to the right or into the lifter pin. The reason we do not advise loosening the lock nut first, is because if the lifter pins were set with a .010 inch gap with a loose lock nut, the gap would not remain the same after the lock nut were tightened, since there is always a slight give in the threads and metal. Also turn the lifter pin while adjusting to insure against high spots, and give the required clearance. Do not loosen the lock nut unless the screw is so tight that there is danger of twisting off the screw. Then loosen it only slightly so as to keep a pulling tension on the screw, pin and threads.

If the lifter pin clearance is too great, hold the lock nut with one wrench and with another wrench turn the screw outward or to the left. Even though it was not necessary to loosen the lock nut to adjust the lifter pin, make sure that this nut is absolutely tight after the adjustment has been obtained. Then check the clearance again with the feeler gauge or a piece of paper doubled to the required thickness.

Both inlet valve tappets should be adjusted so that there is .004 inch play between the inlet valve stem and inlet lever. The motor must be cold when making this adjustment. When adjusting, do not release the lock nut entirely. Keep a strain on the threads so that the adjustment can not vary while tightening the lock nut. To increase the clearance, hold the push rod end with one wrench and turn the push rod into the end with another wrench. To decrease the clearance, hold the lock nut and turn the push rod out of the end. Make sure that the valve is closed before adjusting and again measure the clearance after the lock nut has been tightened.

For convenience, remove the cover and spring while adjusting the push rod. Unscrew the cover from the lifter pin bushing and bear down on the inlet lever directly above the inlet valve stem to open the inlet valve. Do not attempt to remove the push rod from the inlet lever socket, but raise the cover and spring slightly and remove the lower end of the push rod from the inlet lifter pin. Remove the cover and spring. Replace the push rod in the same manner that it was removed and make the required adjustment. Remove the push rod again, fit the spring and cover and refit the push rod. This method is more satisfactory than to try to adjust the push rods without removing the covers and springs.

To Clean Spark Plugs.—If possible, take the spark plug apart, wrap a small strip of fine sandpaper or emery cloth around the core, and revolve the core several times with the fingers. It is a good plan to lightly sandpaper the spark plug points or electrodes, because they get coated with a substance that tends to insulate them, causing hard starting and missing. After the plug has been fitted to the cylinder, test for leaks by running the motor slowly and squirting gasoline over the plug. If the running of the motor is effected, the plug leaks. If tightening the clamp nut does not help, fit a new plug.

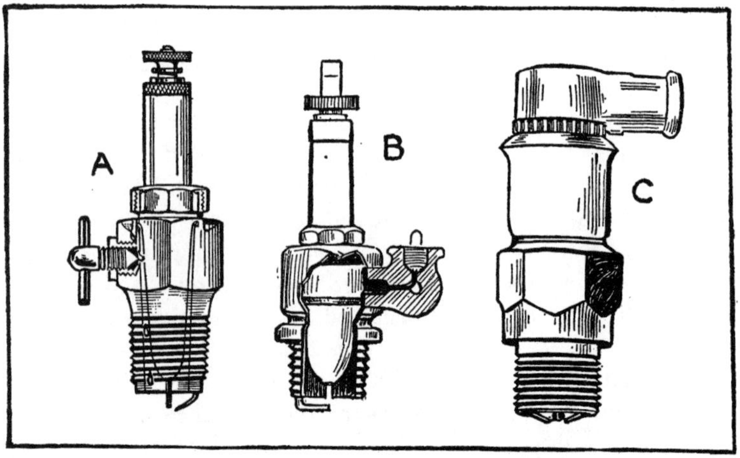

Fig. 335.—Combination of Spark Plugs and Priming Arrangements at A and B Facilitates Starting on Types of Motors Not Equipped with Compression Relief Cocks. Spark Plug with Waterproof Terminal Shown at C.

To Adjust the Spark Plug Points.—The spark plug gauge in envelope No. 2 in illustration Fig. 288 is supplied to enable the rider to keep the spark plug points in perfect adjustment at all times. When the sparking points are the correct distance apart, it should just be possible to insert the gauge between the points, as shown in the illustration. It is a good plan to carry the spark plug gauge on your key ring. Properly adjusted points and clean spark plugs contribute greatly to a smooth running motor. The spark plug gauge is just .022 inch thick. The Harley-Davidson engineers have proved that this gap is best for most efficient performance of the Harley-Davidson motor and it will also be satisfactory on most engines used in motorcycles.

To Test the Spark Plugs.—If the motor does not fire evenly on both cylinders or skips on one cylinder, and a spark plug is suspected, it is advisable to reverse the plugs. For example: If the miss is in the front cylinder and reversing the plugs transfers the miss to the rear cylinder, it is clear that the spark plug is faulty. In that case the spark plug should be cleaned or if necessary replaced with a new one.

When a machine has been left in a damp place for some time and the motor is found difficult to start, it may be that the spark plugs have absorbed moisture. Heating them will materially assist in starting the motor easily.

A spark plug may be tested by holding it against the cylinder and turning the motor over. If a good spark appears, it may generally be taken for granted that the spark plug is O. K. This is not an absolute test, however, for a plug may spark in the open air but not under compression in the cylinder.

The one sure way of testing a suspected plug is to try another plug which is known to be good, in its place.

It is always advisable to carry a spare spark plug for emergency use. To buy a cheap plug is poor economy. Get a good plug, if possible one of the make with which your machine was equipped when you received it.

THE SCHEBLER CARBURETOR.

Do Not Change the Carburetor Adjustment Unless Necessary.—The carburetor on each machine is properly adjusted when it leaves the factory, and under ordinary conditions of service should not require any readjustment. Occasionally, however, a change in adjustment becomes necessary for some reason or other and when you are absolutely sure that the carburetor does require readjusting take your machine to your dealer. If this cannot be done conveniently, apply the directions under instructions for adjusting carburetor.

How the Carburetor Works.—The gasoline is converted into a gas by the suction formed in the cylinder when the piston is on its downward intake stroke. This suction draws a fine spray of gasoline from the nozzle "N," see Fig. 336, and also draws a quantity of air into the carburetor through the hot air connection "V" and the auxiliary air valve "A." The gasoline and air are then thoroughly mixed while passing through the mixing chamber, manifold and into the cylinder.

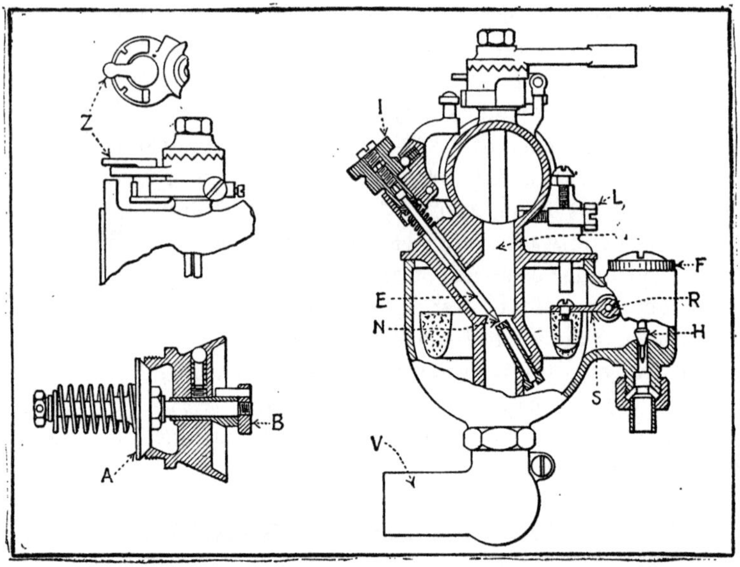

Fig. 336.—Schebler Carburetor Used on Motorcycle Engines.

Easy Starting Device.—To facilitate easy starting of the motor, pull out the knurled bottom "B," see illustration at Fig. 336, and give it a slight turn to the left. This tightens the spring of the auxiliary air valve, preventing a large quantity of cold air rushing past this valve. The cold air admitted to the carburetor will then come in only at the bottom of the carburetor, directly past the spray nozzle, insuring a rich mixture which will facilitate ready starting. After the motor starts, the knurled button "B" should be turned back so as to release the spring tension.

Just after the motor starts, it will often be inclined to backfire, which is caused by the parts being cold. In that case the knurled button "B" should be dropped into recess marked "2," Fig. 296, which will apply only a slightly increased tension on the spring. The motorcycle can be run this way until the motor gets warm enough to miss, after which the button should be entirely released. Do not readjust the carburetor, but simply wait until the engine is warmed up, when the motor will run smoothly.

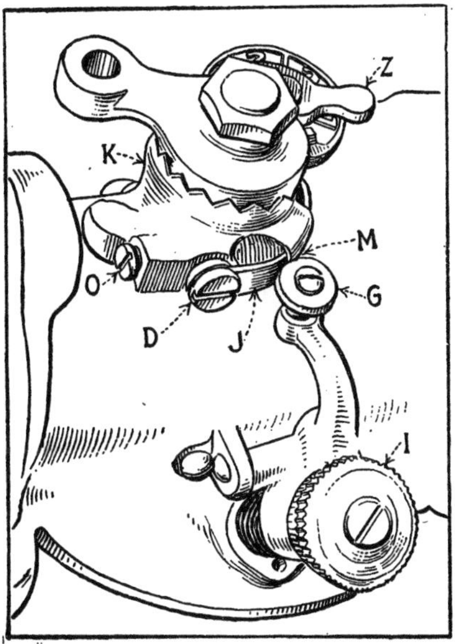

Fig. 337.—Showing Mixture Adjustments on Schebler Motorcycle Carburetor.

Air Valve Spring Adjustment.—The auxiliary air valve is equipped with an adjusting device, which allows taking up the set in the spring, and also the end wear of the air valve parts. Sometimes, slightly tightening or loosening the air valve spring tension, which is done by turning button "B" without pulling it outward, will improve the running of the motor. Under normal conditions the pressure of the air valve against the seat should be seven ounces when the starting stem is entirely released. To tighten the spring tension, turn the button "B" to the left without pulling the button out. To loosen the spring tension, turn button "B" to the right.

Pulling out button "B" and then turning it, which is done before starting the motor, does not affect the air valve spring adjustment.

Instructions for Adjusting the Carburetor.—The needle valve should not be turned to obtain the low or high speed adjustment. The only time when the needle valve should be turned is when the roller of the needle valve lift lever has traveled about $\frac{3}{16}$ inch over the length of the cam, measuring from the closed position. Refer to "M" in Fig. 337 indicating this position. This is the highest point of the cam and is the only part which is not adjustable. Both ends are adjustable and therefore control the position of the needle valve without the need of turning the valve itself.

In some cases a better adjustment can be obtained when the roller is not exactly 3/16 inch from the closed position. Therefore, do not take for granted that one position, that is, 3/16 inch from the end of the cam, will give best results from all carburetors.

Before changing any adjustment, run the motor until it is warm to make sure that a change in adjustment is absolutely necessary, also because the carburetor can only be adjusted properly when the motor is warm. If all adjustments, including the low, intermediate, and high speed, seem to be a little too rich or too lean and this effect is the same for all throttle positions, the needle valve can, of course, be turned as may be necessary. See that the leather air valve "A" seats firmly but lightly and that the brass hexagon nut firmly clamps the valve onto the bushing.

Obtain the Proper Needle Valve Adjustment First. —Open the throttle far enough so that the cam "J," which is on the cam casting "K," moves about 3/16 inch under the roller "G" of the lift lever. Refer to arrow "M," illustration 29, showing this position. Be sure to measure this distance from the closed throttle position; then turn the knurled nut "I" of the needle valve "E" to the left or right, as may be necessary to make the motor fire evenly. Have the motor running idle with a fully advanced spark while making this and the low speed adjustment.

To Make the Low Speed Adjustment.—Turn the low speed adjusting screw "L" out of the carburetor 1/16 inch. Then turn the large grooved screw "D" into which the end of the cam is hooked, inward or outward, as may be necessary, to make the motor fire evenly with a closed throttle. Turning the screw inward increases the amount of gasoline, while turning it outward decreases it. Do not turn the small jamb screw "O" which is turned into the casting.

To Make the High Speed Adjustment.—The carburetor is now ready for the high speed adjustment. Do not make the adjustment with the motor running idle. The machine should be run at high speed on the road. The throttle and spark should be fully advanced. The adjustment is now made by the pointer "Z" (see illustration Fig. 337), which as it moves from "I" forward "3" increases the supply of gasoline. Moving the indicator until it reaches the right point, the motor will run without missing or backfiring.

Extra Air Port for High Speed.—The air lever on the side of the mixing chamber should be opened when extreme high speed is desired. Be sure to shut this port before the motor is stopped, because you will find it difficult to start the motor with this port open. Harley-Davidson riders in high altitudes, where the air is thin, find the extra supply of air made possible by this port of great value.

How to Remove the Carburetor.—Disconnect the throttle control and gasoline pipe from the carburetor. The carburetor can then be removed readily by taking out the three screws with which it is fastened to the intake manifold. Do not lose or damage the paper gasket between the carburetor and the manifold in this operation.

Remedy for Flooding.—If the carburetor floods and the carburetor primer is not sticking, thereby holding down the float, which will of course cause flooding, the carburetor should be inspected as follows:

Remove the carburetor as just explained. Remove the hot air connection and the bowl clamp nut. Take off the bowl with the float assembly. Turn the bowl bottom end up and try to blow through that part to which the gasoline pipe connects. If there is an air leak, the float valve is not seating firmly; then try to force the float valve onto its seat by raising the float and repeat the test. If the float valve still leaks, remove the threaded float lever pin "R," then the cap "F" and the nut clamping the float valve "H" to the float lever "S." Remove the float valve and then the float with the lever. Inspect the seat of the float valve and remove all dirt and other foreign matter. Fit the float lever pin in the float lever and see that the fit is free.

If the test above referred to, namely, to force the float valve onto its seat, proved that the flooding was not due to a faulty float valve or dirt, inspect the float carefully. See that the shellac with which the float is coated has not cracked or peeled, allowing the gasoline to saturate the cork. A gasoline logged float will not close the float valve at the correct gasoline level and will cause flooding. A gas logged float must be dried out, thoroughly sandpapered and reshellacked.

If these suggestions do not apply, measure the distance from the top of the float in its raised position at a point opposite the float valve, to the top of the bowl. The correct distance is $^{19}/_{32}$ inch. If necessary, bend the float lever to get the correct level.

Clogged Gas Line.—Great care should be taken to keep the tanks, vent holes in filler caps and feed pipes free from dirt and foreign matter that will interfere with the flow of gasoline.

A clogged gas line means that the motor will not run at all, will run for a while and then stop or, if the flow is only slightly retarded, the motor will slow down, and it will be impossible to adjust the carburetor satisfactorily, especially for high speed.

Strain Your Gasoline.—On account of the large amount of sediment and water which si in all gasoline, and which causes most so-called carburetor trouble, we advise the use of a fine brass strainer in the funnel with which the gasoline tank is filled.

Prior to 1916, gasoline dirt traps or strainers were fitted beneath the tanks. On the later models, the gasoline strainers are fitted within the tanks. The screening surface is so large that the strainers can never become clogged, doing away with the necessity for cleaning.

Attention is called to the gasoline strainers here, because some old riders may conclude from the absence of the strainers below the tanks, that the gasoline is not strained before it enters the carburetor.

Never fill your gasoline tanks near an open flame. If your machine is equipped with any lights other than electric, be very careful to have the lights out when filling the tanks. If any gasoline is spilled when the tanks are being filled, be careful to wipe off all the parts which the gasoline reached and wait a full ten minutes before starting the motor.

Go over the gasoline pipe and shut off valves carefully from time to time to see that there is not the slightest gasoline leak. Sometimes the gasoline line becomes damaged without the rider's knowledge, causing a small leak, and it is best to be on the safe side and examine these parts as recommended.

Carelessness may cause a gasoline blaze. Never use water in attempting to put it out. A fire extinguisher using a liquid or a powdered composition is best for the purpose. Sand, dust or fine dirt will generally put a small blaze out quickly.

When Machine Does Not Run Right.—Remember there is a definite reason for every form of trouble. When your machine does not run right, investigate, and you will most likely find that there is one simple cause responsible.

In connection with the following suggestions the proper instructions in the foregoing part of this manual should be consulted.

If the Motor Misses At High Speed.—Gasoline pipe or shutoff valve may be partially plugged. Inspect carefully and clean thoroughly. Often a clogged gasoline line may be cleared by closing one shutoff valve, and then taking the filler cap off the other tank and blowing into the tank while the carburetor primer is held down. After blowing into one tank, reverse the operation, that is, close that shutoff valve, open the other one and blow into the other tank.

The air vent in the gasoline filler cap may be plugged. This can generally be cleared by removing the cap and blowing through it.

The carburetor may be improperly adjusted.

The spark plug points may not be properly adjusted or the spark plugs may be dirty or faulty.

There may be water or impurities in the gasoline. The only remedy is to completely drain both gasoline tanks and carburetor and refill the gasoline tanks with gasoline which you know to be clean and of a good grade.

The gasoline supply may be running low. Sometimes a low gas supply causes a miss at certain speeds.

The valves may be in bad condition and need grinding.

Weak valve springs are frequently the cause of a miss.

If the motor of an electrically equipped model misses only at high speed; it may be due to a loose wire or connection between the generator and battery. The centrifugal switch points may be making a poor contact.

The magneto or generator circuit breaker points may be improperly adjusted or in poor condition.

The interrupter lever may be sticking.

If the Motor Misses When Running Slowly.—Apply the tests described under, "If the Motor Misses at High Speed." If those tests do not apply, test the manifold for a leak. To locate a leak take the priming gun and squirt gasoline around the manifold packing nuts and connections while the motor is running slowly. If there is a leak, the result will be misfiring, or the motor may possibly stop altogether.

To remedy this trouble, go over the manifold connections very carefully, tightening the manifold packing nuts and nipples, and replacing any parts which may have been damaged from some cause; also test around both inlet housings, spark plugs, cylinder plugs, and priming cocks with gasoline. Leaks at any of the above places will cause poor running of the motor, especially at low speed, and can generally be overcome by tightening with proper wrenches.

If the missing is not due to one of these causes, test the compression by cranking the motor by hand, with transmission in high gear and clutch engaged.

If the Motor Misses at Medium Speeds.—One or more of the remedies given in the two previous headings will correct a misfire of this nature, although an improperly adjusted carburetor is the most likely cause.

If the Motor Refuses to Run.—See if you can locate any faults mentioned under the above headings. See that there is gasoline and oil in the respective tanks and that gasoline is reaching the carburetor. See if gasoline drips from the carburetor after priming.

See that the oil pipes are properly connected.

See that the carburetor is secure on the intake pipe.

See that there is a good spark at the end of the spark plug cables.

See that the spark plugs are clean and properly adjusted.

See that no wires are broken, loose or disconnected, also that the insulation has not been damaged, thereby causing a short circuit.

Examine the circuit breaker points on the magneto or generator. See that the interrupter lever works freely, and the points separate properly.

See that the controls work properly.

If it is impossible to turn the motor over with the starter, the trouble most likely is due to the fact that the machine has been run without oil or run without enough oil until the piston rings have become seized in the cylinders.

Under these conditions it is generally possible to loosen the motor by injecting a half cup of kerosene into each cylinder. A motor that has seized, should be referred to a competent repairman at the first opportunity.

If it is Difficult to Start the Motor.—Look for trouble as outlined in previous instructions and the difficulty will most likely be overcome. It is necessary to give the starter pedal a vigorous stroke in order to start the motor with any consistent regularity.

This sharp starting stroke is generally developed by the rider only after a week or so of practice. If hard starting is experienced with electrically equipped Harley-Davidson model 20-J, test the centrifugal switch and storage battery before applying the above instructions. To test, try to sound the horn while cranking the motor vigorously, first making sure that the horn will sound when the motor is running. If the horn will not sound, the battery is discharged or the centrifugal switch does not make contact and instructions in Chapter IX should be referred to.

If the Motor Stops on the Road.—Generally when your motor stops, you can ascertain the cause by referring to previous instructions and the charts on pages, 576, 577, 578.

If the Motor Shows Loss of Power.—Occasionally a rider will complain that his motor has lost some of its power, and investigation will show that the spark does not advance all the way.

Loss of power is often due either to improper carburetor adjustment or to excessive carbon deposits in the combustion chambers.

Sometimes loss of power is caused by loss of compression. This generally points to worn out or damaged piston rings, scored pistons, and cylinder walls, or the valve may need grinding or adjusting.

Pre-Ignition.—Sooner or later excessive carbon deposits will cause pre-ignition, due to the particles of carbon which get red hot by the compression of the gas in the combustion chamber and increase the compression by naturally decreasing the area of the combustion chamber.

Pre-ignition is sometimes mistaken for a miss in the motor. If the trouble is due to pre-ignition, it will not be noticeable until the machine has been run possibly a quarter of a mile or more. The remedy, of course, is the very careful removal of the carbon deposits.

Pre-ignition may be caused by improper adjustment of the circuit breaker or spark plug points, or by a poor circuit between the generator and storage battery.

Sometimes it will be necessary to put a different type spark plug into a motor, the plug itself being the cause of pre-ignition.

Back-Firing or Popping in the Carburetor.—This is due to the fact that either the carburetor or inlet push rods are not properly adjusted, the spark is advanced too far, or the intake valve lift mechanism is sticking, or is out of adjustment.

If the Motor Overheats.—Overheating of the motor may be caused by an over or insufficient oil supply, by a loss of compression, by a large carbon deposit, by a clogged or dirty muffler, by a retarded spark, or by an improperly adjusted carburetor.

Sometimes in extremely cold weather, unless kerosene is mixed with the lubricating oil, the oil may partially freeze, preventing sufficient oil from reaching the motor, which, of course, will cause the motor to overheat.

Proper attention to the motor will generally insure satisfactory service. If any trouble develops, refer to the previous instructions. Locate the trouble and apply the suggestions before taking anything apart.

Defects in Power Transmission Elements.—If the drive is not positive when chains are employed, the trouble is invariably due to a slipping clutch or compensating sprocket which may be easily remedied by adjusting these devices. If chains break frequently, it is because they are either worn unduly, sprockets are not in proper alinement, or the sprockets have depreciated to such a point that the teeth are hooked and do not permit the chains to ride smoothly over them. Chains should be kept clean and thoroughly lubricated in order to obtain silent driving. Lubrication does not consist of indiscriminate application of oil over the chain surface, but should be done by removing the chains, cleaning them thoroughly in gasoline or kerosene, and then boiling them in tallow or a mixture of grease and graphite. After the chains have been allowed to soak in this hot mixture, they are taken out and the surplus lubricant wiped off the outside. Oil on the chain surfaces merely serves as a basis for accumulations of dirt which act as an abrasive and produces rapid wearing of both chains and sprockets.

Testing for Chain Alinement.—There are two ways in which alinement may be at fault. The sprockets may be in line, but the shafts may be out of parallel. On a well-designed machine, this should not happen, but cases have been known. The second possibility is that the shafts may be parallel, but one sprocket further in or out on the shaft than the other.

In order to discover if the alinement is correct, the inside of the side plates of the inner links of the chain should be examined after the chain has been in use some little time. If the side plates on one side of the chain are worn much more than those on the other, with ridges or shoulders cut in them by the wheel teeth, the probability is that one of the shafts is a little out of parallel. Should both sides of the chain be unduly worn and cut, probably one wheel is further out on its shaft than the other. A straight edge,

Fig. 338.—Chain Drive of Indian Scout Model.

or even a piece of string stretched tightly across the faces of both wheels, will often indicate the error. Generally speaking, errors in alinement are best corrected by the expert, i.e., the machine should be taken to the agent for examination. The chain drive of the Indian Scout model is shown at Fig. 338.

How to Adjust Chains.—If the chain is too slack, it is apt to "whip," which intensifies the wear and tends to break the rollers. If, on the other hand, it is too tight, a crushing effect is produced on the rollers, and the whole chain is strained unduly. A chain should be adjusted, and kept adjusted, so that it can be pressed down with the finger from 1/8 inch on the short drive from engine to countershaft, to, say, 1/2 inch on the back chain.

Adjustment of the first reduction drive is generally provided for by an eccentric on the countershaft, or by sliding the gear box. The slack in the back chain is taken up in the same manner as on the pedal cycle by drawing back the rear wheel. Of course, the tension of all chains should be looked to at the same time.

Slipping Belt Drive.—Flat belt drive was well thought of on early machines but has the defect of slipping at times. It is imperative that the belt be kept soft and pliable at all times with applications of neatsfoot oil, and that the lagging on the small pulley be maintained in proper condition. When the lagging wears off, the belt will not have sufficient adhesion with the small metal pulley, and slipping is unavoidable. Various special laggings composed of woven asbestos materials impregnated with rubber are marketed at the present time which give much more satisfaction than leather, as they are more enduring and have a greater degree of friction. The V-belt transmits power positively and only slips when the pulleys are worn so that the belt does not contact properly with the pulley sides. The design of the V-belt is such that it has a certain wedging action in the pulley and is not apt to slip as is the flat belt. If the clutch is at fault as is the case if the belt or pulleys are not worn unduly, it can be taken up until it transmits power without slipping.

Care of Leather Belts.—Clean your belt thoroughly and often, once a week, or at least after every hard run. Carefully scrape off all dirt or sand. After each cleaning, apply motorcycle belt dressing. This dressing will increase the life and efficiency of your belt —keep it soft and pliable, and prevent unnecessary slippage, which will wear out any belt.

It is important that the screws in pulley lagging do not

project; if they do, they will cut the belt and shorten its life.

Be sure to release the idler when machine is not in use, and apply carefully when in service—this insures minimum stretch of belt, and enables it to retain its elasticity and wear longer.

Care of Wheels.—The important point to observe in regard to the wheels is that these are adjusted so that they revolve freely. If the cones of the hubs are screwed up too tightly, the ball-bearings will have considerable friction and will wear out rapidly. The hub bearings should always be kept properly lubricated, and the cones should never be tightened up beyond the point where the wheel will revolve freely and yet have no side-play or shake. Where the drive is through the hub, as is the case in all chain-driven machines, one should inspect the rear wheel carefully from time to time for loose spokes. With a belt-driven machine, this precaution is not so necessary because the power is applied to a large belt pulley attached directly to the rim and not through the medium of the hubs and spokes. The front hub, if properly adjusted, is not apt to give any trouble, but the rear wheel which has a coaster-brake hub needs more attention. It not only demands more oil and careful adjustment of the hub bearing, but the braking mechanism must be looked at from time to time to make sure that the brakes will function properly when needed. If the coaster brake does not engage promptly, it indicates that the brake end is filled with an accumulation of old, gummed-up lubricant. If the brake takes hold too quickly, it indicates lack of lubrication in brake end. If hub runs hard, it indicates that adjusting cone is too tightly screwed in; if hub wabbles, it means that bearings are adjusted too loosely. If forward pedaling does not engage hub and rotate it promptly or back pedaling does not apply brake positively, examine transfer spring to see that it is not broken and that it is in place correctly.

Defects in Clutches and Gearbox.—Considering first the member of the transmission system that will affect the efficiency of the entire assembly when deranged, it will be well to discuss the troubles common to the various types of clutches. The defective conditions that most often materialize are too sudden engagement which causes "grabbing," failure to engage properly, slipping under load, and poor release. Clutches utilizing a leather facing will cause trouble after a time, because of natural wear or some defect of the friction facing. The leather may be charred by heat caused by slipping, or it may have become packed down hard and have lost most of its resiliency. The asbestos-wire combinations do not give this trouble. The clutch spring may be weakened, or broken; this will cause the clutch to slip even if the leather facing of the cone is in good condition. The two troubles usually met with by the motorcyclist are harsh action, as one extreme condition, and loss of power through slippage as the other.

On motorcycles fitted with multiple-disc clutches, as practically all modern machines are, the same troubles may be experienced. If a multiple-disc clutch does not release properly, it is because the surfaces of the plates have become rough and tend to drag. The plates of a multiple-disc clutch should be free from roughness, and the surfaces should always be smooth and clean. Harsh engagement also results by the absence of oil in those types where the discs are designed to run into an oil bath. Spinning or continued rotation of a multiple-disc clutch often results from seizing due to gummed oil, the presence of carbon or burned oil between the plates and sometimes by a lack of oil between the members. When a multiple-disc clutch slips, it is generally caused by lack of strength of the clutch springs or distortion of the plates or wearing of friction facing in the dry plate types. To secure the best results from a multiple-disc clutch, it is imperative that only certain grades of oil be used. If one uses a cheap or inferior lubricant, it will gum and carbonize, because of the heat present when the plates slip or it will have such viscosity that it will gum up between the plates. Most authorities recommend a good grade of light or medium cylinder oil in multiple-disc clutches where lubricant is required. In some cases, faulty multiple-disc clutch action is due to "brooming," which is the condition that exists when the sides of the keyways or the edges of the disc become burred over and prevent full contact of the plates. Clutch plates with friction facing, such as Raybestos, are intended to be run without lubricant in most cases and will be apt to slip if oil is put in the clutch case. When the frictional material wears, it must be replaced with new. New facings or discs may be obtained from the motorcycle builder much cheaper than from other sources. The disc clutch used on the Indian Scout is shown at Fig. 339-A.

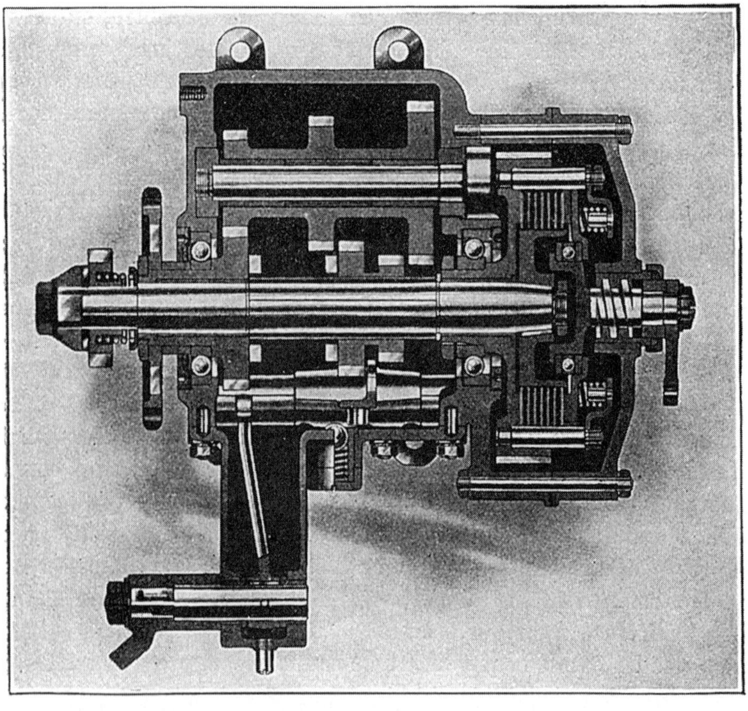

Fig. 339-A.—Clutch and Gearbox of Indian Scout Motorcycle.

When sliding-gear or shifting clutch transmissions as shown at Fig. 339-B are used, the most common defect is difficulty in shifting gears and noisy operation. The trouble met with in gear shifting is usually caused by the edges of the teeth of the shifting members having burred over so that they do not pass readily into the spaces between the teeth of the gears they engage with. Another cause of poor gear shifting is deterioration of the bearings which may change the center distances of the shafts to a certain degree and the relation of the gears may be changed relative to each other so they will not slide into mesh as freely as they should. Noisy operation is usually due to a defective condition of lubrication, and if the gears are not worn too much it may be minimized to a large extent by filling the gear case with oil of sufficient consistency to

Fig. 339-B.—Three Speed Gearbox of Reading Standard Motorcycle.

cushion the gear teeth and yet not be so viscous that it will not flow readily to all bearing points. A difficulty in shifting is sometimes due to binding in the control levers or selective rods, and these should always work freely if prompt gear shifting is required. If considerable difficulty is experienced in meshing the gears and the trouble is not found in the gear-set, it will be well to examine the clutch to make sure that the driven member attached to the gear-set main shaft does not "spin" or continue to revolve after the clutch is released.

Adjustment of Brakes.—The means of adjusting brakes may be easily ascertained by inspection. If brakes do not hold properly, and the friction facing is in good condition and free from oil, the failure to grip the drum is probably due to wear in the operating

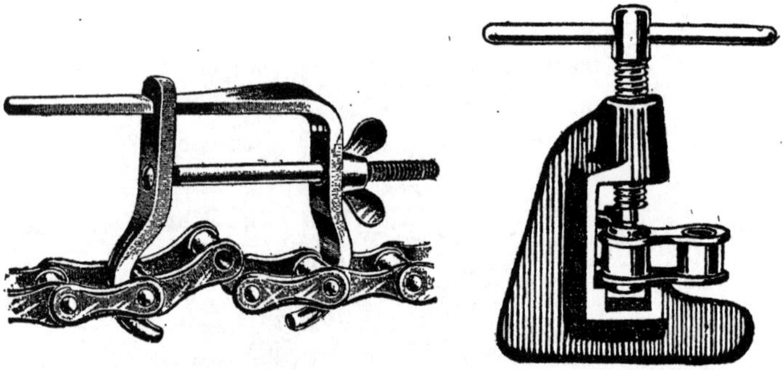

Motor Cycle Chain Puller with Fly Nut. **Chain Rivet Punch.**

Fig. 340.—Tools Used to Facilitate Repair of Motorcycle Drive Chains.

leverage. On some form of brakes, notably those which are expanded by a cam motion, compensation for wear of the brake shoes is often made by shortening the rods running from the brake to the operating lever. External brakes are usually provided with an adjustment on the brake band, which permits one to draw the ends of the band closer together and take up much of the lost motion between the band and the brake drum. After the brakes are adjusted, it is well to jack up the machine to make sure that the wheel turns freely and that there is no binding between the brake members and the drum on the hub. If the brake is adjusted too tightly the friction will cause heat after the motorcycle has been run a short distance, and this increase in temperature is a very good indication of power loss by friction between the brake and the drum. If the brakes are not adjusted sufficiently tight, a full movement of the pedal or hand lever will prove inadequate to apply the brakes tight enough to stop rotation of the wheels. When the friction facing is worn, it must be renewed. Slipping of metal-to-metal brakes is often due to accumulation of gum or old oil. This is a common fault with multiple disc types. If a disc brake heats up, the surfaces of the plates are rough and do not pass each other freely. Complete instructions for brake adjustment of Harley-Davidson motorcycles are given in Chapter V.

Repairing Inner Tube Punctures.—The first thing to do is to locate the hole through which the air is escaping. If it has been caused by a nail or other large object, it may be easily found by examining the tube, but in some cases it may be a very small puncture that cannot be discovered readily. After removing the inner tube blow it up until it is distended to its normal size. Do not put enough air in the tube to stretch it; if the pressure is too high it may enlarge the hole. If a bucket or trough of water is at hand, immerse the tube in the water a little at a time, at the same time slightly stretching the tube. If this is done carefully, air bubbles will be seen rising from the leak, no matter how minute it is when the injured portion of the tube is under water. If it is impossible to get enough water to immerse the tube, dampen the hand and pass it along the tube surface. The wet hand is very sensitive to even the slightest air current, and the leak can be found very readily in this manner. Another way to locate a leak is to blow the tube up and then pass

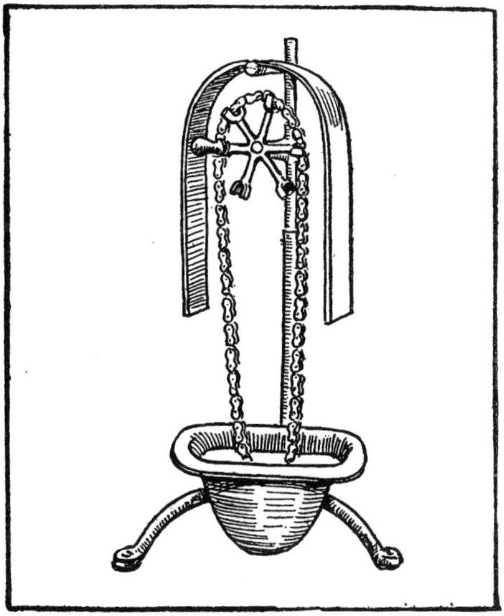

Fig. 341.—The Noonan Chain Bath, a Handy Device for Cleaning Motorcycle Drive Chains.

it close to the ear, revolving it slowly so that all parts of the tube are passed before it. The leak will be evidenced by a hissing noise which is in proportion to the size of the leak. A good way of marking the leak positively is by means of an indelible pencil which will leave a mark on the rubber when moistened that will not come off.

A piece of sandpaper or emery cloth is usually provided in a repair kit, and with this all of the gray deposit from the rubber should be cleared from an area around the puncture, somewhat

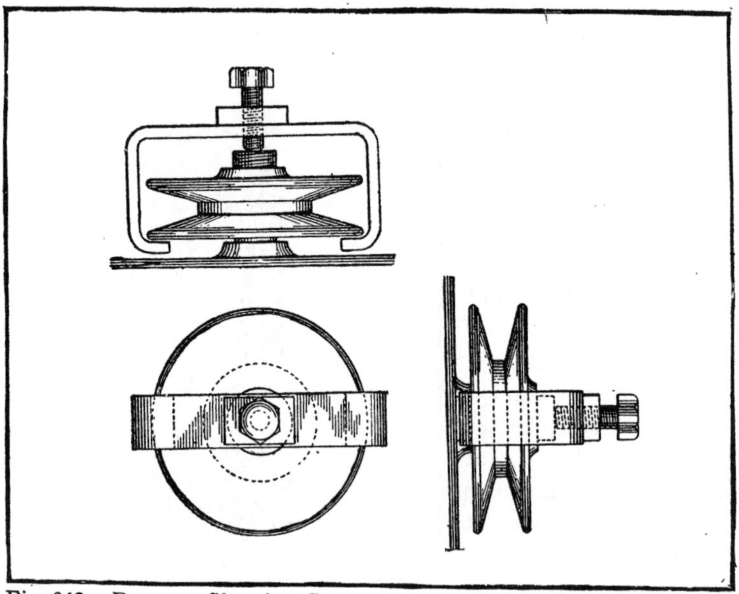

Fig. 342.—Diagram Showing Construction of Simple Puller for Removing V Pulleys or Sprockets from the Taper on End of Engine Crankshaft.

larger than the patch to be fitted. This talc and powdered rubber may also be washed off with gasoline or scraped off with the blade of a jack-knife if the sandpaper is not available. It will be well to treat the surface of the patch in the same manner, and to roughen up the clean surfaces of both tube and patch with sandpaper or a wire scratch brush. A light coat of cement is then applied to both patch and inner tube, and is allowed to dry for five or six minutes. Then the operation is repeated and more cement is spread over the surface. This is also allowed to dry, and, when the surface is sticky, the patch is pressed firmly in place and held in position by a clamp or some other means that will produce pressure. The patch should be allowed to set for ten or fifteen minutes before replacing the tube. Powder the patch and tube freely with soapstone or talc to prevent the tube sticking to the causing, due to heat produced by tire action.

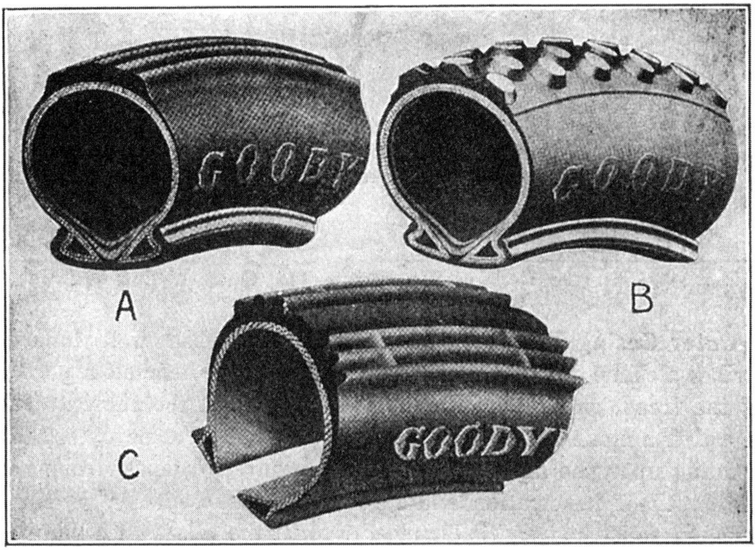

Fig. 343.—Conventional Forms of Motorcycle Outer Casings That Have Been Generally Applied. A—Corrugated Tread. B—Studded Tread. C—Combination Tread.

It is well to examine the casing before replacing the tube to be sure that the cause of the puncture is removed. This may be done by passing the hand around on the inside. The puncturing object often becomes imbedded in the rubber, and while it is not visible from the outside it may stick through the casing and protrude on the under side. Temporary repairs to the casing should be made from the inside. A piece of fabric three or four times the width of the hole and long enough to reach from edge to edge of the casing should be cemented in place. This is done by cleaning the lining of the casing and applying two coats of cement, while the prepared fabric which is already coated with rubber should be wet with a little gasoline before it is pressed in place in the inside of the shoe.

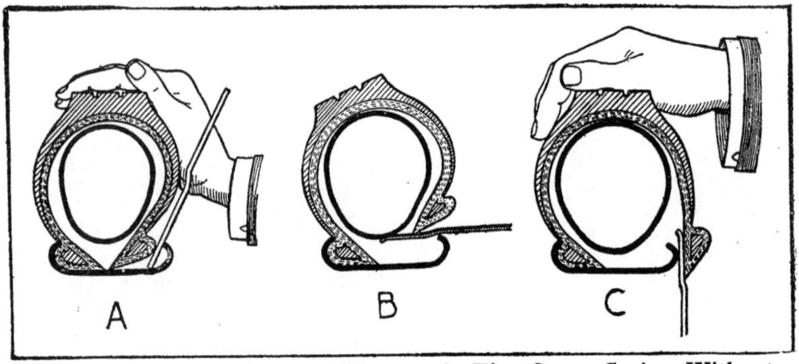

Fig. 344.—How to Remove Motorcycle Tire Outer Casing Without Pinching Inner Tube.

Outer Casing Repairs.—If a tire, even when well inflated, strikes a sharp stone at high speed this is apt to tear off a portion of the tread, and often injures several plies of the fabric. This is called a stone bruise and weakens the shoe to some extent, depending upon the amount of material removed from the casing or the depth of penetration and its location. The shoe is weakened much more if the tread is damaged than if the side wall is scraped. If a stone bruise or other cut penetrating the tread is neglected, sand or road gravel is apt to work into the tire as it revolves and this material soon accumulates between the tread and fabric or between the layers of farbic until it forms a protuberance of some size. This is called a sand blister. The action of this compacted material is to break down the layers of fabric between it and the tube and the casing inevitably blows out if the defective condition is not remedied.

Rim cutting is usually caused by running the tire flat or not inflated sufficiently. It is sometimes due to rusty or rough rim edges or to poorly fitting rims or improperly designed beads on the tire casing.

Cuts in casings allow water to enter and rot the fabric even if they are not sufficiently large to weaken the shoe appreciably. They may be easily filled up by using special repair pliers to spread out the rubber and open the cut sufficiently to clean it out with gasoline and insert special cement and repair gum. When the

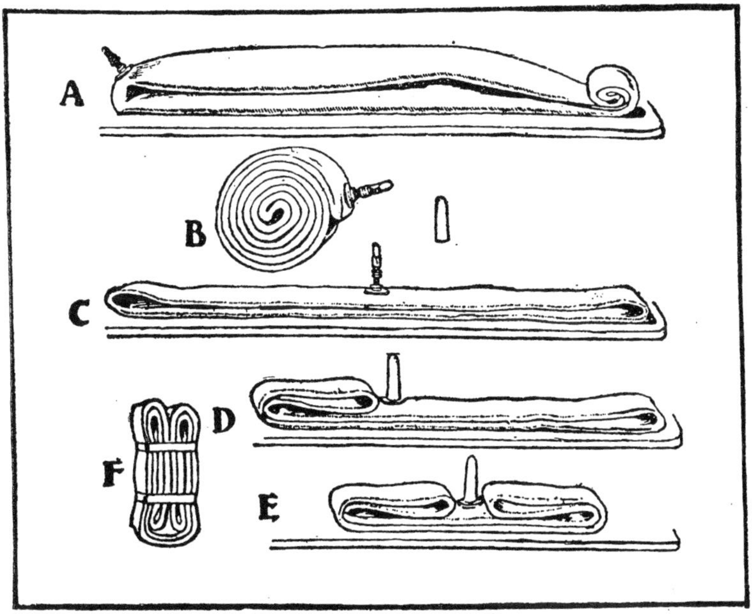

Fig. 345.—Defining Methods of Folding Inner Tubes for Transportation.

pliers are withdrawn, the rubber closes around the repair material, and when the gum hardens it fills the hole thoroughly.

Weakened casings can be used for some time by the insertion of a reliner of fabric which strengthens it and presents a solid, unbroken surface for the inner tube to bear against. An outer casing or leather protector may also be employed.

A good temporary repair of a burst casing can be made by using an inside and an outside blowout patch. A new inner tube should

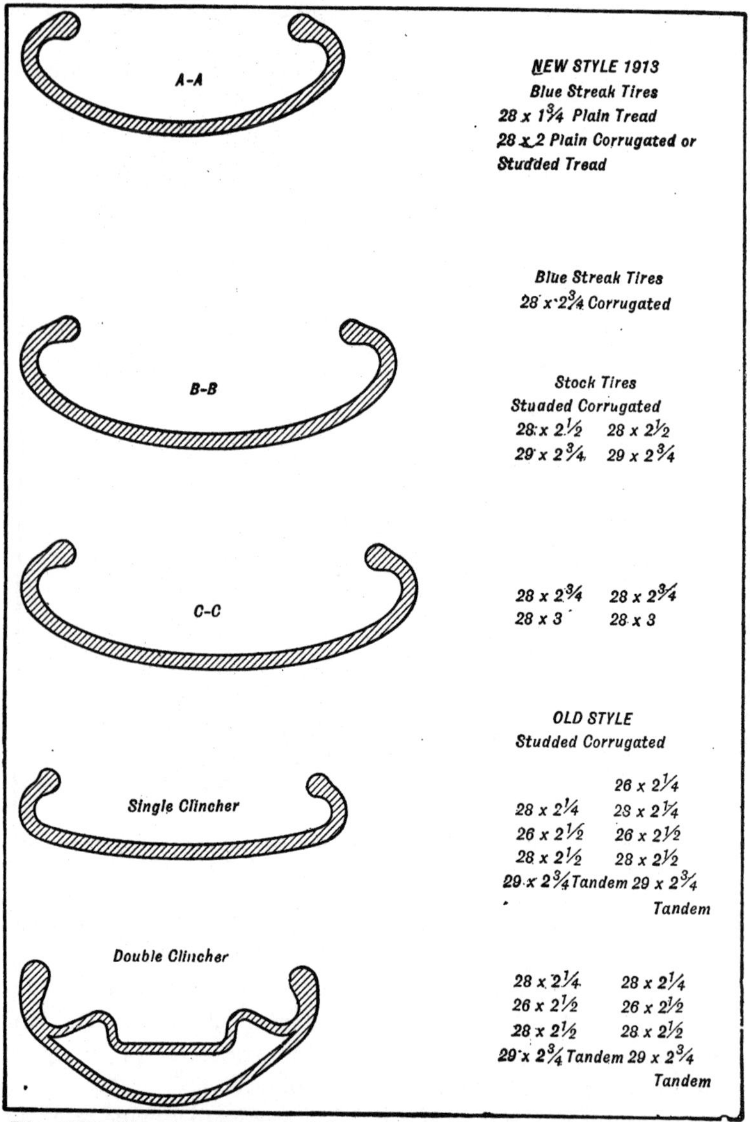

Fig. 346.—Showing Forms of Rims That Have Been Used in Motorcycle Wheel Construction and Sizes of Tires Adapted for Them.

never be inserted in a burst casing without first taking some precautions to close the hole or rent, both from inside and outside, or the tube will blow through at the weakened spot of the shoe before it had been in use for any length of time. The inner patch is composed of several layers of frictioned fabric (fabric impregnated with rubber compound) and the larger sizes are provided with hooks which engage the rim if a clincher type is used. It is from six to eight inches long for small tires. The strength of fabric used also varies with the size of the tire the patch is made for. This is placed in the casing in such a way that the rent comes at a point approximately at the center before the inner tube is inserted. After the casing is replaced and is partially inflated, the outer shoe or patch is laced tightly in place around tire and wheel rim and then inflation of the tire is completed. A repair made in this manner is reliable enough so the tire remains in service for some time without attention, though the temporary patches should be replaced by a permanent repair at the earliest opportunity. Winding the casing with tire tape will help if no blowout patch is available.

To repair a badly cut or rent outer casing, it is usually necessary to rebuild the casing at the injured part. The injured fabric is cut out and replaced with new, and new tread rubber is also applied to the outside of the casing. The layers of fabric or rubber are well cemented with special material adapted for curing, and are thoroughly vulcanized together and amalgamated with the remainder of the shoe. In cutting out the old fabric, the first inside layer is cut out at least six inches each side of the blowout. The next layer is stripped off for five inches each side of rent, then two or three of the succeeding layers are taken off for the same distance, say, four inches each side of the injury. In replacing the layers with new fabric, it is cut to fit the steps left when the injured material has been removed. Building up in this manner makes a much stronger repair than just replacing the injured material would, because each layer applied reinforces the others beneath it, and when the last ply is in place and all firmly joined together by the curing process, the shoe is practically as good as a new one.

Tire Inflation Pressures.—Improper inflation is responsible for much of the tire trouble that comes to motorcyclists. Under-inflation makes rim-cutting easy. The continued flexing of partially filled tires tends to break down the fabric in the side walls. Careful, scientific tests—trials of actual service—have shown conclusively the air pressure best suited for each tire size. The following table is offered by the Goodyear Company:

Regular Tires.	Racing Tires.
2¼ inches, 30 pounds	1¾ inches, 45 pounds when cool
2½ inches, 32 pounds	2 inches, 50 pounds when cool
2¾ inches, 35 pounds	2¼ inches, 55 pounds when cool
3 inches, 40 pounds	

Advice to Purchasers of Second-Hand Motorcycles.—In the present state of efficiency of motorcycle manufacture, no machine can be said to be worn out for several years, but styles change very rapidly and there will always be those who want to be right up to the minute regardless of the expense entailed. In consequence, there is on the market to-day a large number of excellent second-hand machines. But in no other business, except perhaps the gold-brick and green-goods line, it is so easy for the novice to make a poor bargain. It is very difficult to tell the real condition of a motorcycle at a glance, and even a trial cannot always be depended on. Furthermore, a machine may run nicely for a few miles, and yet, in a few weeks, require endless repairing. On the other hand, one often finds motors which, through bad handling or lack of tuning, run very badly or not at all, though for a small outlay of time and money, properly applied, they could be made to give excellent results.

The first thing to consider is whether the machine in question is worth purchasing at all. With the large selection offered one can afford to be particular; there are some faults which it is not worth while to attempt to remedy. The question of age resolves itself entirely into a question of make. for, if the machine was a good one in the beginning, it will be good much longer than one which was originally of a lower grade; but the matter of design is also important. Be sure its maker is still in business. Do not buy orphan motorcycles, as you will not be able to get spare parts. A machine of short wheel-base, high saddle, high-hung engine, and short handle-bars will never be comfortable, and it would be wiser to wait for an opportunity to obtain one of a more modern build. Transmission must also be considered. The type is entirely a matter of personal preference; but block chains, roller chains too small for their work, a narrow flat belt with an idler, "V" pulleys not cut to twenty-eight degrees, or too small an engine pulley, can never be made to give efficient service. A cracked frame lug, cylinder, crank-case, or piston, or a buckled wheel, also mean repairs that had better be left for the buyer with mechanical skill.

Not less important is the condition of the engine. This is the heart of the machine, and, if it has been seriously injured, the cycle will be part of the repair shop furniture for some time to come. Jack up the rear wheel, and stand on the pedal with the exhaust valve dropped. A high compression engine in good condition will hold your weight almost indefinitely in this manner, but if the pedal does not fall for several seconds, the cylinder and rings may be considered to be in good condition. If it goes down rapidly, the engine should be examined further. Have the cylinder taken off and run your finger carefully all over the inside surface. If you find any cuts, scratches, grooves, or rough spots, it must be replaced. If, however, it is all bright and smooth, you may turn your attention to the rings. Examine carefully the surface which rubs against the cylinder. It should be all brightly polished, but there will probably be dark spots. If these spots are very frequent, you had better steer clear, but if only a few it simply means new rings. First, however, be sure that you can obtain new rings for that particular make of model, as it is an expensive job to have them especially made.

While you have the cylinder off, glance at the bearings. Run off the belt or remove the chain and try to move the pulley or engine sprocket up and down. A tiny amount of play is to be expected here, but if it is at all great, new main bushings will be needed, the cost of which must be added to the price you are to pay. The same is true of the crank and wrist-pin bushings. The former can be tested by moving the connecting-rod up and down while the pulley is held still, and the latter by holding the connecting-rod with one hand and moving the piston up and down with the other. If the motor is a ball or roller bearing form and the bearings are worn, remember that these cost money, in fact, several times as much as plain bearings. Better let some one else buy them unless you are getting the machine cheap enough to warrant your assuming the cost of repairs.

Next to motor repairs the tires are probably the most expensive parts to renew. These are often overlooked in buying a second-hand mount, because they can be obtained anywhere, but it should be remembered that they cost a great deal. A flat tire means a puncture or rotten tube, although the owner may tell you that he just let it down "to keep it from stretching." Chains or belts are also large items and their condition should be noted. Do not forget to examine the sprockets, as, if they are worn, it will be useless to replace the chains unless they are replaced also. Damaged pedaling gear, broken brake, dented tanks or rims, run-down batteries, bent spokes, and broken mud-guard stays or control levers, are of less importance, as they are easily repaired, but they should all be looked for and taken into consideration.

TO ASSEMBLE AND ATTACH THE HARLEY-DAVIDSON SIDECAR AND PARCELCAR.

Use the Proper Sprocket Combination.—If a machine is used with a sidecar, see that it is geared for sidecar service. The standard gear for solo riding is not satisfactory, since for sidecar service the motor is naturally called on for more power, and with standard gear, will labor, overheat, lose power and wear prematurely.

Use a 4.91 to 1 gear ratio for sidecar service. For very hilly country a lower gear, obtainable with a smaller motor sprocket, can be used to advantage.

To Assemble the Axle and Wheel.—Remove the lock pin from the sidecar axle and release the axle tube clamp bolt. Lubricate the axle with graphite or grease before fitting, to keep it free and allow easy changing of tread when desired.

Insert the axle in the tube and turn it until the lock pin holes line up when the mud guard clip is upward. Insert the lock pin

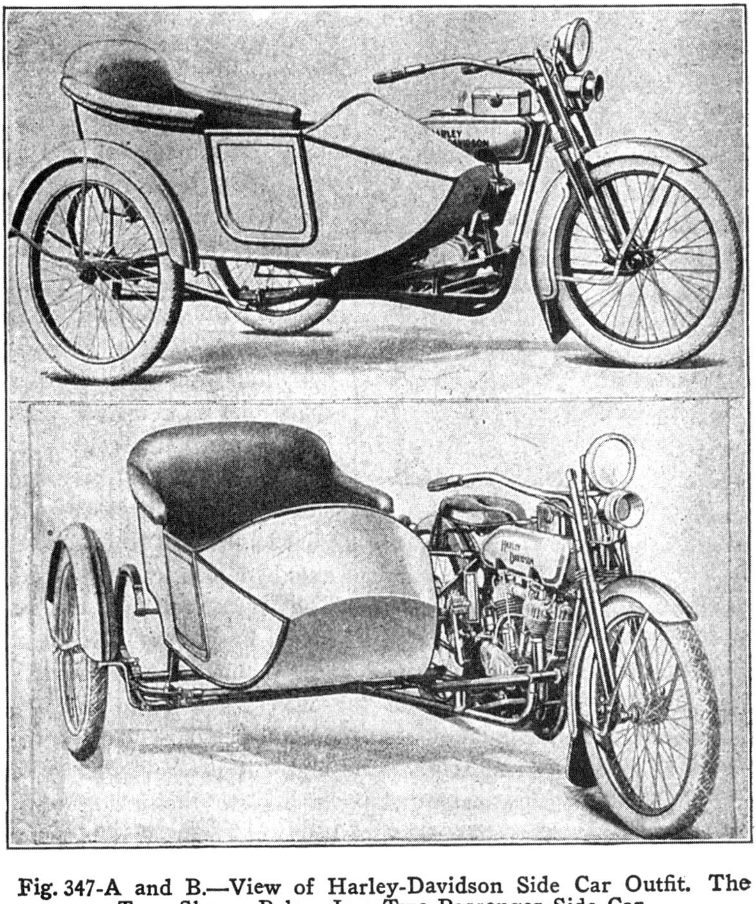

Fig. 347-A and B.—View of Harley-Davidson Side Car Outfit. The Type Shown Below Is a Two-Passenger Side Car.

and fasten it on the under side by means of the spring, washer, and cotter pin. Tighten the axle tube clamp bolt nut. Do not try to move the axle after removing the lock pin without loosening the clamp bolt.

See that the hub is packed with good cup grease and assemble the wheel on the axle. Adjust the cone carefully to the point where the wheel has no appreciable shake. The wheel will not run absolutely free at the outset because of the felt washers provided as oil retainers. These washers will wear in in a short time. Do not set the cone up tight enough to bind, or the bearing surface will be injured. Fit the lock washer, nut, and cotter pin, and again try the hub adjustment. Remember that the bearings should not be cramped, then screw on the hub cap.

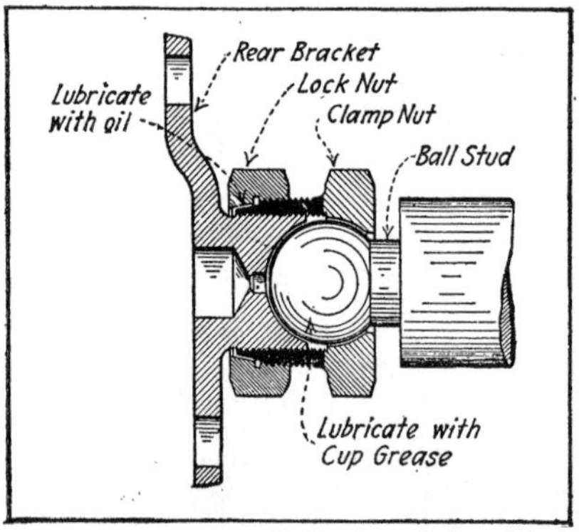

Fig. 348.—Ball and Socket Joint Used in Attaching Side Car to Motorcycle.

To Assemble Mud Guard and Braces.—Fasten the inner mud guard brace to the inner shoulder of the axle flange by means of the provided bolt, nuts, and lock washers. Place one lock washer under the bolt head, insert the bolt, fit the clamp nut, lock washer, and lock nut. The outer mud guard brace is held to the axle by a lock washer and nut. The forward part of the mud guard is securely held on the support rod by a lock washer and nut. Connect the brace, which is attached to the axle tube of the sidecar frame, to the inner rear mud guard brace, passing it over the lower part of the spring. Adjust the support rod so that the wheel is in the center of the mud guard, and tighten the support rod to the inside of the frame by means of a set screw and lock nut.

Instructions for Lubricating and Assembling Ball and Socket Joints.—The front and rear sidecar connections are ball and socket joints and should be packed with graphite grease or cup grease before assembling. The joints are flexible and give to the thrusts of the motorcycle and of the sidecar, therefore must be lubricated. Both the clamp nuts and the lock nuts have tapered shoulders which clamp the threads when the lock nuts are tightened. The clamp nuts are also split, allowing contraction. Place a little oil on the lock nut threads, enabling drawing up the lock nuts securely on the taper shoulders and locking the split end of the clamp nuts. The lock nuts will not take as firm a hold if assembled dry. Care should be taken to see that no oil gets on the inside clamp nut threads or on the threads of the sockets because oil will permit the clamp nuts to loosen.

If the ball studs are assembled dry or are not lubricated regularly, they will rust in place, become rigid and lose their usefulness as flexible joints. When in a rigid condition, an uncalled for strain will be placed on the studs, connections and motorcycle frame that may result in breakage. The ball joint construction is clearly shown in Fig. 348.

Do not draw the clamp nuts up tight on the ball studs, for the connections must be flexible enough to give easily under the weight of the sidecar. The lock nuts are, of course, to be drawn as tight as possible. A good way is to back the clamp nuts off one-half turn after having drawn them way up, and then to tighten the lock nuts securely and test the adjustment by shaking the motorcycle sideways.

To Attach Sidecar to Motorcycle.—Remove the eye bolt from the frame brace and fit it in place of the seat post pinch bolt. The eye bolt should be a tight fit in the frame. Remove the front clamp connections and the rear bracket connection from the sidecar frame. Temporarily fasten the front clamp to the loop of the frame about one-half inch above the engine lug with the four lock washers and nuts. Remove the nuts, lock washers and plain washers from the rear axle clip studs. Discard the plain washers. Fit the rear frame bracket with the short offset to the top, and draw up the nuts securely. This is important because if the machine is used with this bracket loose, the threads on the frame studs will be damaged.

Lubricate both front and rear ball and socket joints with thick cup grease. Support the sidecar along side of the motorcycle with boxes or blocks. Attach the front end of the sidecar frame to the frame clamp. Then make the rear connection.

Connect the frame brace clevis to the eye bolt. Securely draw up the four front clamp nuts. The lower connection and clevis should be so adjusted that the motorcycle leans slightly away from the sidecar, depending on the average sidecar load. A sidecar that carries a heavy load will exert more pull on the motorcycle than one that carries a light load. Consequently, the frame brace connection must be backed off the frame brace, or screwed on further until the correct adjustment is obtained. Draw up all the ball joint clamp nuts reasonably tight and tighten the lock nuts as explained previously. To enable lining up the sidecar properly, the motorcycle frame and forks must be in line.

When a sidecar is properly lined up, the machine will travel in a straight course for one hundred feet, or more, without guidance. Make this test at medium speed and on a level road.

When attaching or disconnecting the sidecar, be careful not to let the whole weight rest on one clamp nut, and under no condition remove the lock nut from the clamp nut, because the weight of the sidecar can easily break off a piece of the milled clamp nut.

To Detach the Sidecar.—When disconnecting, remove the frame brace clevis bolt, loosen the lock nuts of the front and rear ball joint connections, support the sidecar in some convenient way and then remove the front and rear clamp nuts, taking care not to damage the threads. All nuts have tight threads.

To Attach the Brake Lock.—The brake lock furnished with the sidecar is fitted as follows: Remove the front nut clamping the right sidecar to the footboard support rod. Fit the brake lock with the ratchet facing the driver. Replace the lock washer and clamp nut.

General Instructions.—Wrench GK853 fits the ball joint nuts and lock nuts. This wrench also fits the 1915 to 1920 inlet manifold nuts and nipples.

Go over the connections from time to time. Do not allow them to get dry and keep them properly tightened. This attention will mean perfect sidecar service, easy handling of the machine, comfortable riding and absence of strain on the motorcycle frame.

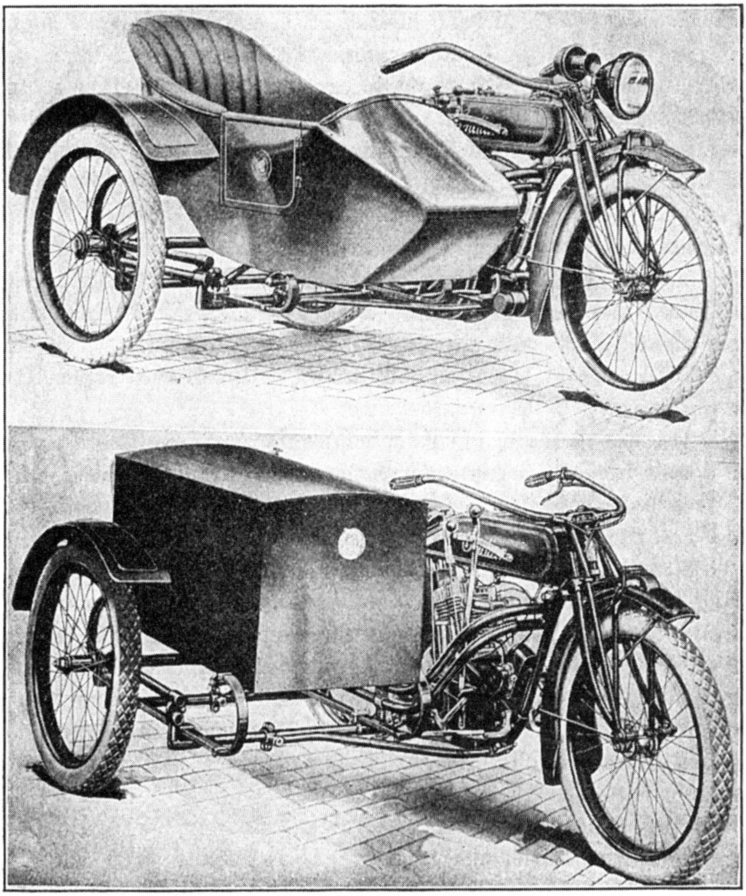

Fig. 349-A and B.—Indian Side Car Type for Passenger Work Shown in Upper View. Delivery Box Shown Below It.

The sidecar wheel should be tested for end play once a week. If any shake is noticeable, the bearings should be adjusted by drawing up the cone until the end play has been eliminated.

The Indian Sidecar.—The Indian sidecar, which is shown in Fig. 349A and B, should be lined up with the motorcycle so that the sidecar wheel is parallel to the rear wheel of the motorcycle and both wheels are vertical. If the sidecar leans away from the motorcycle, the tires will be worn on the side of the tread and their life materially shortened. If the side car leans in toward the motorcycle, the tires will be worn on the side of the tread instead of on the center and steering will be interfered with. Misalignment of the sidecar may result in bent connections, in addition to causing rapid wear on the tires.

Attaching and Lining Up.—Have the motorcycle perpendicular. Insert the studs in the sidecar lugs (in steering head forging, seat post cluster and above three-speed bracket). Put in the studs from right to left and put the nuts on the left side. Turn the studs so that their joints will be in line. Be sure to tighten the nuts.

See that the clamp on the short connection (the one which clamps the double tube at the left side of the sidecar frame) is loose. Put the front connection on the stud; then put the short connection in place and tighten the clamp nut with the fingers.

Tighten the nuts on the front and short connections at the studs. Bring the sidecar wheel vertical and with its track approximately parallel to that of the rear wheel. Prevent the wheel from moving out of this position; then put on the rear long connection (from the lug under the seat post cluster to the sidecar rear frame tube). Set up the nuts and clamps. Put on the long front connection and set up its nuts and clamps. Go over all nuts and see that they are tight before using the sidecar outfit.

Driving Pointers.—In taking a right hand turn with a sidecar combination approach the turn at reduced speed, and with the clutch disengaged. At the turn, move the bars to the left and let in the clutch. The outfit will pivot on the sidecar wheel and will go off smoothly in the new direction when the throttle is opened.

To make a left turn, approach at reduced speed with the clutch disengaged. Keeping the clutch disengaged, move the bars to the right and when the turn has been completed, engage the clutch and proceed. If these directions are not complied with the sidecar will tend to rise off the ground when making a right hand turn and will tend to skid to the right in making a left hand turn. Neither of these are good for tires or frame.

Don't do monkey stunts with a sidecar, such as riding with the car in the air. The sidecar is meant to ride with the wheel on the road. Lifting it puts an enormous strain on the tires and on the frame for which they were never intended.

Don't forget to use the hand oil pump when driving with a passenger aboard the sidecar.

GEAR RATIOS FOR TYPES N-20 and NE-20.

Motor Sprocket	Countershaft Sprocket	Clutch Sprocket	Rear Wheel Sprocket	High	Ratio Inter.	Low
15	21	38	36	4.34	6.80	10.60
15	21	38	40	4.73	7.43	11.69
16	21	38	36	4.08	6.50	10.07
16	21	38	40	4.55	7.15	11.23
17	21	38	36	3.82	5.99	9.45
17	21	38	40	4.24	6.65	10.47

CHAPTER XI.

COMPLETE INSTRUCTIONS FOR OVERHAULING ENGINE.

Removing the Motor from the Frame—To Support the Motor While Making Repairs—Tools Required for Motor Overhauling—Stripping the Motor—Removing the Pistons—Stripping the Crank Case—Removing Cylinder Fittings—Stripping the Flywheels—Removing the Connecting Rods—Washing and Cleaning the Parts—Inspection and Repair of Motor Parts—Cylinder Dimensions—Piston Dimensions—To Fit a Cylinder with a Piston—Inspecting and Fitting Piston Rings—Inspecting and Repairing Exhaust Valve Seats—To Inspect and Repair Inlet Valves—Fitting Inlet Housings into Cylinders—To Inspect, Adjust or Replace Secondary and Roller Arm Studs—To Inspect and Repair Roller Arms—Inspecting Gears—Pinion Gear Shaft and Gear Side Crank Case Bushing—Flywheel Washers—Connecting Rod Piston Pin Bearing—Sprocket Shaft, Bearing, Bushing and Rollers—To Line Up Left Crank Case—To Line Up Right Crank Case—Connecting Rod Crank Pin Bearing—To Assemble and Fit Crank Pin Bearing—Assembling the Flywheels—To True Flywheels—Assembling the Motor—To Fit Pistons to Connecting Rods—To Center Pistons—To Round Pistons—To Square Pistons—To Fit the Cylinders—To Fit the Gears and Time the Motor—When New Gears Have Been Fitted—To Fit the Magneto or Generator—To Place Motor in Frame—To Test the Motor.

The instructions and recommendations offered in this chapter are based on Harley-Davidson factory standards, and are presented in such a way that they can easily be adopted and applied by any competent repair man. The material is reproduced by special permission and is taken from the Motor Repair Manual of the Harley-Davidson Motor Co., Milwaukee, Wis. The motor is divided into assemblies and parts. The instructions follow the operations of overhauling in natural order, beginning with the removal of the motor from the frame; then taking it apart, inspecting the parts for wear, making repairs and renewals when necessary, reassembling and testing.

This text should be preserved and kept handy in every motorcycle repair shop as an authoritative guide to doing first class repair work. Dependable and efficient repair work is impossible without the right equipment and tools. Wherever reference is made

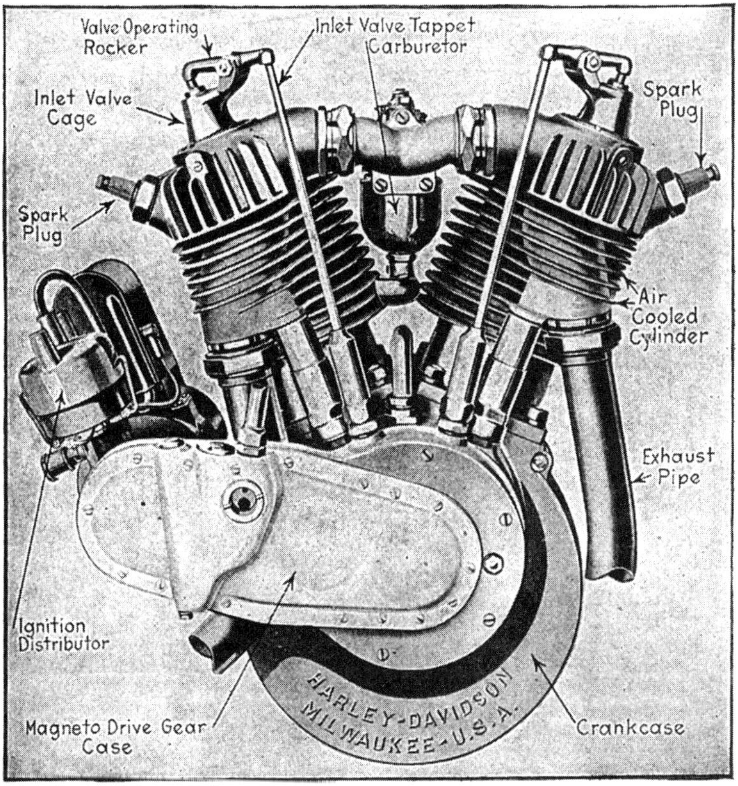

Fig. 350.—Harley-Davidson Motorcycle Engine.

to a wrench or tool, that piece of equipment has been found most practical for the job by expert factory workmen and can be used advantageously by the repairman. While the instructions which follow consider the Harley-Davidson motor specifically, much of the matter can be considered as applying to any high grade motorcycle engine. The appearance of the Harley-Davidson motor when removed from the frame is given at Fig. 350. The sectional drawing at Fig. 351 shows all the important parts clearly. When the engine is partly dismantled it looks like Fig. 352, which has the

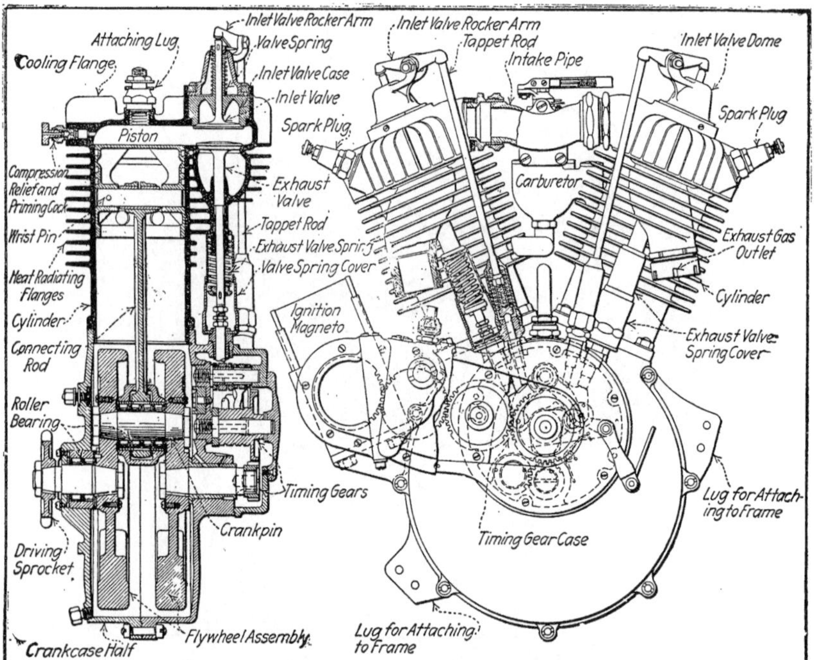

Fig. 351.—The Harley-Davidson Twin-Cylinder V Power Plant, an Excellent Example of Engine Design Commonly Used for Motorcycle Propulsion.

carburetor and piping removed and the cam case and cam case cover lifted from the motor base.

Removing the Motor from the Frame.—1. If the machine is equipped with a front stand disconnect the front stand only from the right side bar, after removing the cotter pin and washer. With "S" wrench AK-435 take off the two nuts on the support rods which clamp the right sidebar. Remove the right footboard assembly with sidebar complete. This assembly should not be detached from the brake rod. Lay it under the machine until the motor is removed, and then again place it on the support rods temporarily to be out of the way. Remove both spark plugs. Shut off both gasoline cocks, and with "S" (open end) wrench CK-803 disconnect the right gasoline pipe clamp nut. This is all

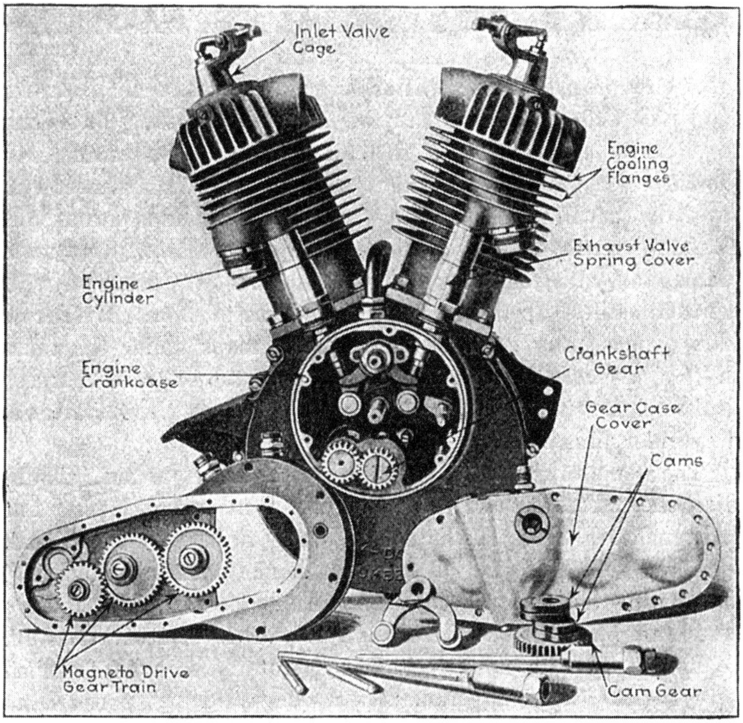

Fig. 352.—Harley-Davidson Motor Partially Dismantled.

that should be disconnected from the right side at this time, and is reached while the repairman is at that side of the machine.

2. Disconnect the following from the left side of the machine: Remove the cotter pin in the stud which is on the clutch hand lever, and remove the foot clutch lever rod. Remove the two nuts on the footboard support rods with wrench AK-435 and take off the left

footboard assembly complete with sidebar and front stand. Remove the two 8x32 screws with lock washers clamping the front and rear chain guards together. With socket wrench AK-430, remove the nut clamping the rear end of the front chain guard to the frame clamp, and the two nuts clamping the front end of the guard to the crank case.

3. Disconnect the front chain connecting link and chain. Remove the nut clamping the ball stud to the gear shifter lever, and the nut clamping the gear shifter lever to the tank bracket with "S" wrench CK-804. Withdraw the lever through the gear shifter gate. Remove the cotter pin fastening the magneto control rod to the three way bell crank, and remove the rod. Disconnect and remove the gasoline pipe from the left tank and carburetor. With "S" wrench CK-803 disconnect the drive case oil pipe from the tank, and with the brass hexagon cap EO-747 furnished with each machine close up the oil tank to stop the oil flow. Withdraw the long spark plug cable from the three loops under the tank. With "S" wrench CK-804 remove the nut on top of the carburetor and take off the throttle lever. With "S" wrench CK-435 remove both cylinder plug nuts.

4. The remaining parts accessible from the right side should be disconnected as follows: Remove the front exhaust pipe nut with wrench DK-810. If the nut is found to be very tight, soak it with kerosene. If the pipe sticks in the muffler connection, twist the pipe and withdraw. With socket wrench AK-430 remove the nut clamping the relief lever, and pry the lever from the stud.

5. Loosen the rear exhaust pipe clamp nut and with "S" wrench CK-804 remove the clamp nuts, lock washers and lock plates from the muffler stud. With the rawhide mallet EK-327 strike the muffler downward, and after it is lower than the supporting brackets, strike it backward while holding the rear exhaust pipe. This will remove the exhaust pipe from the muffler connection. If care is taken to strike only the muffler ends, there will be no danger of damaging the muffler.

6. Wind the spark plug cables around the inlet push rods to have them out of the way and save them from possible injury when

removing the motor. Remove the cylinder plug nuts with "S" wrench CK-425; then remove the front cylinder plug washer.

7. With socket wrench AK-432 remove the four casing (crank-case) clamp bolt nuts. If the bolts have a tendency to turn while removing the nuts, hold them with socket wrench CK-801. Knock out the engine clamp bolts. Hold the motor in place while driving out the bolts so that it cannot fall out and be damaged. From the left side of the machine take hold of the front and rear cylinders, lift the bottom part of the motor outward, drop it slightly and at the same time tip it forward so as to disengage the front cylinder plug from the front cylinder clamp. Allow the gear bracket boss of the crank case to rest on the loop of the frame. Remove the bell crank bracket with the intermediate control rod assembly from the rear cylinder plug, and put it out of the way by passing it along the inside of the clutch hand lever, and hanging it on the rear fork or some other part of the machine. Lift the motor out of the frame. Replace the right side footboard assembly on the support rods.

To Support the Motor While Making Repairs.—1. Support the motor properly while stripping or assembling it, to avoid breaking cylinder ribs or damaging any nuts as would happen with a loosely held motor. Fasten a strip of wood (about one inch thick, four inches wide, and eight inches long) to the bench with one bolt close to the vise. This strip is to be used as a rest for the motor when the front crank case lug is clamped in the vise jaws. Only one bolt is recommended to hold the strip so that the latter can then readily be swung aside when not in use, allowing other work to be done in the vise without interference.

2. To hold the crank case while removing the casing studs, make a box of 1 inch lumber about 8 inches square and 4 inches deep. Pad the open end with cloth to prevent scratching the enamel of the crank case.

3. Lay out the tools necessary for motor work and secure a tight box to receive the parts. In loosening tight nuts and tightening loose nuts, be careful not to break off the crank case lug. All nuts fitting studs in a horizontal position should be tightened or

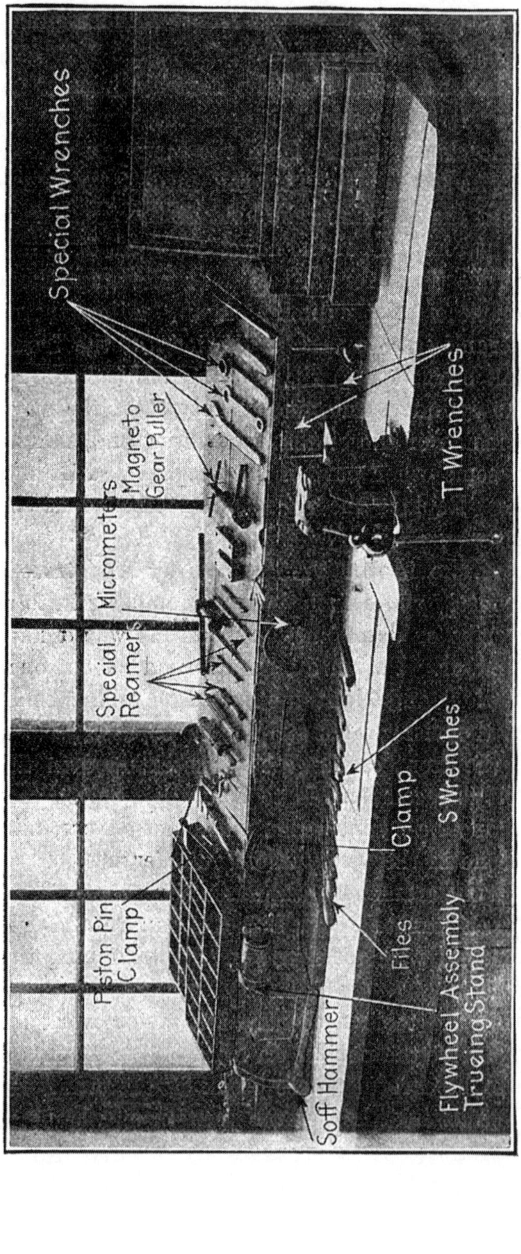

Fig. 353.—Special Tools and Appliances Designed by Harley-Davidson Experts to Facilitate Motor Repair Processes.

loosened by pulling the wrench in line with the vise jaws. When turning the inlet manifold packing nuts or nipples, always brace the motor with the other hand.

4. Whenever clamping motor parts in a vise, use copper jaws FX-790 to protect the parts from damage.

TOOLS REQUIRED FOR MOTOR OVERHAULING *

Where Wrench Will Fit

Part Number	
	OPEN END WRENCHES
CK803	Gasoline pipe nuts, drive case oil pipe nuts, Bosch, Dixie, and model 250 generator shaft nuts, cylinder stud nuts.
AK435	Side bar clamp nuts, inlet pushrod spring covers, relief pipe nut.
CK804	Shifter lever stud nuts, throttle shaft nut, muffler stud nuts, priming cocks.
GK866	Relief pipe connection.
CK435	Cylinder plug nuts.
GK65	1918 lower exhaust valve spring covers.
CK65	Earlier than 1918 lower exhaust valve spring covers.
	SOCKET WRENCHES
AK430	Front chain guard nuts, relief lever stud nut, gear stud plate screws.
AK432	Casing clamp bolt nuts.
CK801	Casing clamp bolts.
	SPECIAL WRENCHES
DK810	Exhaust pipe nuts and nipples, head cone lock nut.
GK853	Later than 1914 manifold nuts and nipples, sidecar nuts.
GK854	Crank pin nuts.
FX748	10″ monkey wrench, to straighten connecting rods.
GK865	Closed (socket) cylinder plug wrench.
GK861	Open end cylinder plug wrench.
AK59	Sprocket nut, gear shaft nut, and sprocket shaft nut.
	Magneto wrench, or generator wrench, depending on type magneto used or model machine.
	SPECIAL TOOLS AND FIXTURES
FK824	Cylinder exhaust seat and guide reamer.
GK864	Inlet housing (seater) lapping tool.

* These tools are listed in the Harley-Davidson accessory catalog. Copy will be furnished upon request to Service Department, Harley-Davidson Motor Company, Milwaukee, Wis. The various special tools and fixtures that will be found useful are shown at Fig. 353.

GK862	Crank case lining bar and bushing.
FK828	Connecting rod lower bushing lapping arbor.
GK850	Flywheel truing device.
GK855	Piston squaring plate.
GK859	Pinion gear puller.
EK332	Sprocket puller.
FK831	Magneto gear puller.
EK335	39/64″ expansion reamer for piston pin bushing and piston.
EK336	15/16″ expansion reamer for gear side bushing.
FK799	Piston pin removing tool.
EK328	Copper hammer for flywheel truing.
EK325	Yankee screw driver, drive case screws and cover screws.
EK330	Feeler gauge to use when adjusting tappets, spark plug points, breaker points, etc.
EK329	6″ scale, to measure piston positions, etc.
FX790	Copper jaws for vise.
EK326	6″ screw driver.
	3½″ "C" clamp.
	3″ x 4″ outside micrometer.
	3″ x 4″ inside micrometer.
GK833	Model 235 generator cam puller and drive gear puller.
FK832	Pinion lock screw and oiler wrench.

Stripping the Motor.—1. With wrench GK-853 loosen both manifold packing nuts, screw both nipples out of the cylinders, and remove the manifold and carburetor assembly. Remove both inlet push rod spring covers from the inlet lifter pin bushings with "S" wrench AK-435. Press down on the inlet lever so that the inlet valve opens, raise the spring cover, and remove the push rod which is also held to the lifter pin with a shallow ball and socket joint. Disconnect the drive case oil pipe. Remove both inlet lifter pins. With a Yankee screw driver EK-325 remove the drive case cover screws, and with the screw driver EK-326 pry off the cover which may be sticking lightly on the gear studs. Place the screw driver over the relief lever stud and hook it under the edge of the cover. Be careful not to damage or mar the perfect fit between the cover and drive case during this operation, or an oil leak may develop.

2. With "S" wrench CK-803 remove the nut clamping the

magneto drive gear. With magneto gear puller FK-831 remove the gear from the taper magneto shaft or tap the outside rim of the gear with brass hammer EK-331. Remove both the intermediate and intermediate worm gears, after removing the stud rings. With the Yankee screw driver remove the six screws clamping the drive case to the crank case. The drive case may be found to stick slightly, but no trouble or damage will result while prying it off, if the tool is put between the front inlet lifter pin bushing and the exhaust lifter pin bushing. Now remove the following: Secondary gear, inlet and exhaust lifter arms, relief lever stud, lifter cam, and the crank case relief valve with gear. Remove the three studs and lock washers clamping the magneto to the bracket of the crank case with "S" wrench CK-803, and take off the magneto.

3. Remove the left hand pinion lock screw with wrench FK-832, and with pinion puller GK-859 pull the pinion from the shaft. Be careful not to lose the key. With 1917 and earlier motors use wrench CK-65, and with 1918 motors use wrench GK-65 to unscrew both exhaust valve spring covers. With "S" wrench AK-435 disconnect the relief pipe nut and with "S" wrench GK-866 remove the nipple. With special wrench AK-59 remove the sprocket clamp nut. This nut is drawn up firmly and it may be necessary to use a hammer on the wrench before the nut can be turned. With sprocket puller EK-332 remove the motor sprocket. If the sprocket is wedged tight on the shaft, strike the screw handle squarely in the center with a hammer after the puller screw has been drawn up tight. With wrench CK-803 remove all cylinder clamp nuts and take off the cylinders.

Removing the Pistons.—4. If the pistons are to be removed for renewal or for repairs to the rod, they should be taken from the connecting rods immediately after the cylinders have been removed. For repairs to the motor other than these, do not remove the pistons. With a screw driver straighten the split end of the piston pin lock pin. Drive the lock pin from the piston and pin with a small drift and hammer. Scrap the lock pin. Never use it a second time. Place the piston pin removing tool FK-799 over the piston so that the end of the screw fits against, and is in line with, the piston pin. Turn the handle and the piston pin is easily pressed out. See illustration Fig. 356 for method of using this tool.

Fig. 354.—Motorcycle Supported by Special Stand to Facilitate Overhauling.

5. Often punches or undersize piston pins are used to drive piston pins from pistons. This practice while answering the purpose will generally bend or twist the connecting rods slightly, and also put the piston badly out of round. Very often the piston pin bushing is burred and damaged during this operation, requiring rereaming of the bushing and piston and the fitting of an oversize piston pin to obtain a good fit again. Tool FK-799 is therefore recommended.

6. If the pistons are to be used again, be very careful that they are not mixed, that is, do not place the piston which was in the rear cylinder on the front connecting rod. The piston which is stamped with letter "F," should be placed on the front rod.

Cylinders vary slightly; that is, the diameters of the bore of the front and rear cylinders may not be alike; this also holds true of the pistons; the outside diameters vary, and to obtain the right clearance between the cylinder and piston each cylinder and piston are measured carefully at the factory. Therefore, if the pistons were accidentally reversed when overhauling the motor, there would be no fit.

7. Remove the exhaust lifter pins. Drain the oil from the crank case by removing the base of the motor from the vise and turning it bottom end up.

Stripping the Crank Case.—8. Lay the crank case with the sprocket side on the box, and with wrench CK-35 remove the casing stud nuts from the end of the studs facing upward. The short studs can readily be removed, while the three long studs are light press fits and can easily be removed with a drift made out of an old inlet push rod. After all the casing studs are removed, strike the supporting lugs lightly, while pulling the gear side crank case upward with the other hand, to take the two halves apart. Never put a wedge between the casings to pry them apart, because this will damage the good machined fit and cause an oil leak. Remove the gear or right side crank case, then the fly wheels. When removing the latter, be careful not to lose any of the rollers.

Removing Cylinder Fittings.—9. If a cylinder clamping plate such as T2-6492 is not available, clamp the cylinder securely in the vise, by laying it on its side with the valves upward. Clamp the horizontal ribs firmly. There is no danger of breaking any ribs if the top horizontal rib is not clamped in the vise jaws.

10. Remove the inlet housing set screw. With wrench DK-808 or FK-822 remove the inlet housing clamp nut and take out the inlet housing cap assembly. If the inlet housing cannot be removed easily, it can be forced out of the cylinder by means of the exhaust valve by striking the stem of the valve squarely after the exhaust valve key has been removed.

11. To remove the exhaust valve key, put a wedge through the spark plug hole to hold the exhaust valve on its seat; then with a screw driver or some other suitable tool compress the exhaust

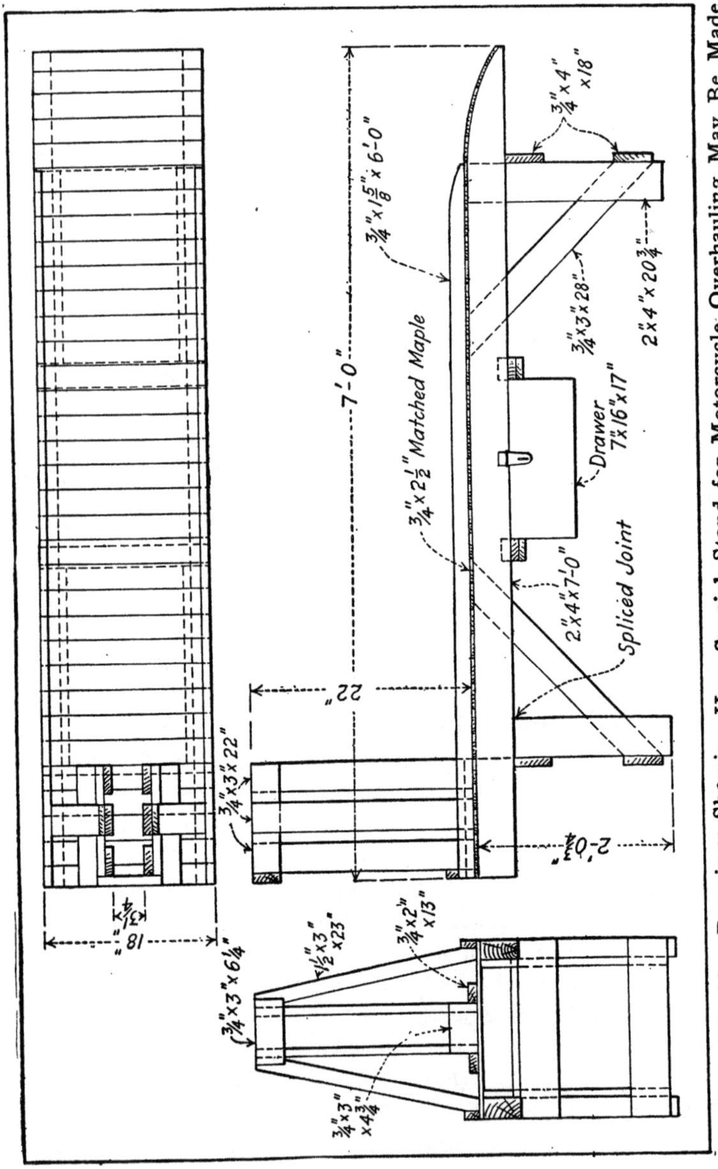

Fig. 355.—Working Drawings Showing How Special Stand for Motorcycle Overhauling May Be Made.

valve spring and withdraw the key. Remove the collar, spring and cover.

12. With special wrench GK-861 or GK-865 remove the cylinder plug. If the plug fits very tight, use a hammer on the wrench. With wrench CK-804 remove the priming cock, and with wrench DK-810 remove the exhaust pipe nipple.

Stripping the Fly Wheels.—13. Clamp the sprocket shaft of the fly wheels in the vise. Remove the lock washer screw and the lock washer from the crank pin nut; then with special wrench GK-854 remove the crank pin nut. If the nut is very tight and the fly wheels have a tendency to turn, hold them by placing a wedge of some kind, such as a large wrench, between the spokes of the fly wheels and the vise jaws. With copper hammer EK-328 sharply strike the outside rim of the upper fly wheel sideways, while the fly wheels are still clamped in the vise, and at the same time brace the lower wheel with the other hand. Always use this hammer for fly wheel work, and avoid striking the fly wheels between the spokes as much as possible because this may crack them.

Removing the Connecting Rods.—14. With the top fly wheel removed, the connecting rods can be slipped over the rollers and retainers, but care should be taken not to drop or lose any of the rollers. To safeguard against this, place the lower half of an exhaust valve spring cover over the crank pin before trying to remove the rods. Bear down on the exhaust valve spring cover and at the same time slip the connecting rods over the rollers. If the roller bearing is not worn badly, the rods will not slip over the rollers easily. In that case, do not hesitate to use a pry of some kind to force them off. Never use a hammer for this operation. The appearance of the pistons and connecting rods removed from the stripped fly wheel assembly is shown at Fig. 357.

Washing and Cleaning the Parts.—1. Having stripped the motor as far as is necessary for inspection, all parts should be washed and cleaned carefully preparatory for accurate checking up.

2. Gasoline cannot be equalled for cleaning, because the parts will be cleaned thoroughly and the gasoline will evaporate quickly. With the present need of economy it would be wasteful to use a

fresh supply of gasoline for each job. Therefore, two gasoline wash cans, as illustrated in Fig. 358, each of about five gallon capacity and with tight fitting covers are recommended. Put four or five gallons of gasoline into each can so as to have a sufficient quantity to wash the largest parts of the machine. Drop the cover when not using the gasoline and thereby avoid unnecessary evaporation and danger of fire.

3. One of the cans should be used for the first washing, which should remove all dirt. After the gasoline has been allowed to drip

Fig. 356.—How to Remove Harley-Davidson Wristpins from Pistons.

off, the parts should be rinsed in the other (clean) can of gasoline. This practice will permit using the gasoline in the rinsing can for an indefinite period, while the gasoline in the washing can can be strained through cheesecloth and be used over again after it gets too dirty.

4. Do not use waste or rags to wash the parts, because they

fill the gasoline with fuzz. Use a brush which is about two inches wide and wash all parts thoroughly. After drying, the parts are ready for inspection.

5. Carefully scrape all shellac from the step joints of the crank cases and drive case. Be sure to remove all the shellac, but be careful that the scraper does not dig into and cut away the aluminum, or an oil leak is very apt to develop. If the paper gasket which is shellacked to the drive case cover is not torn, do not remove it.

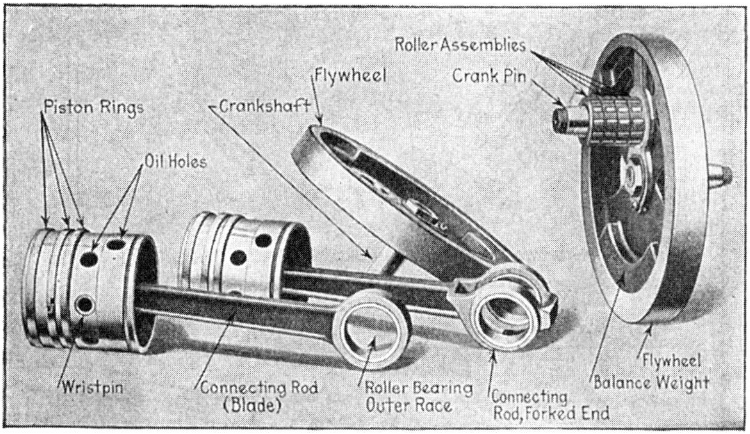

Fig. 357.—Pistons, Connecting Rods and Flywheels of Harley-Davidson Motor.

6. Before washing the cylinders, scrape all carbon from the cylinder head, valve chamber and exhaust port. The carbon which has accumulated on top of the piston head, under the head, and in the ring grooves should also be removed if the pistons appear to be in good condition.

Inspection and Repair of Motor Parts.—1. A thorough inspection of all parts is an essential part of first class repair work. Any part requiring repairs should be taken care of as it is inspected. These subjects are thoroughly covered in the proper sequence in this chapter.

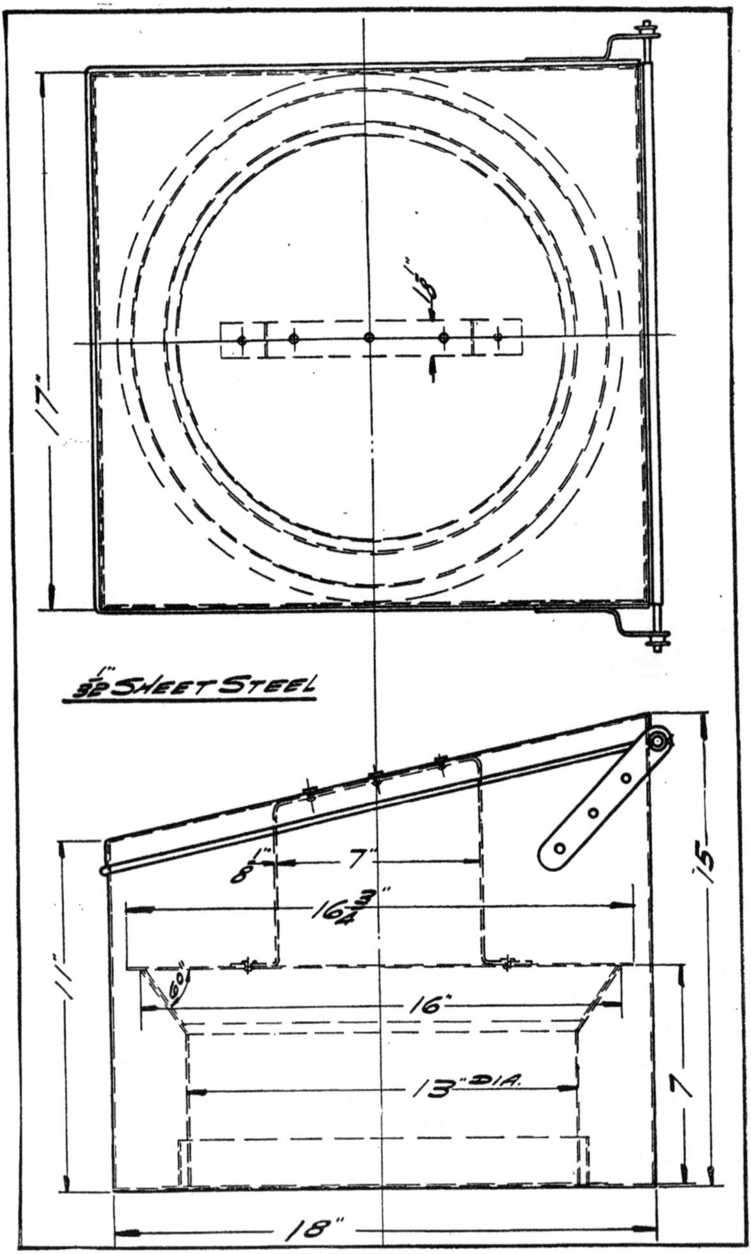

Fig. 358.—Drawings for Wash Rack to Handle Motor Parts.

Cylinder Bore Dimensions.—2. A cylinder in good condition is perfectly smooth with possibly a few grinder marks visible. The bore of the cylinder tapers .003 inch. The diameter of the bore decreases gradually toward the upper end. The small diameter of the bore of a new cylinder will be found to be between 3.307 inches and 3.308 inches. This measurement can be taken about 1/4 inch from the upper end of the bore in the cylinder.

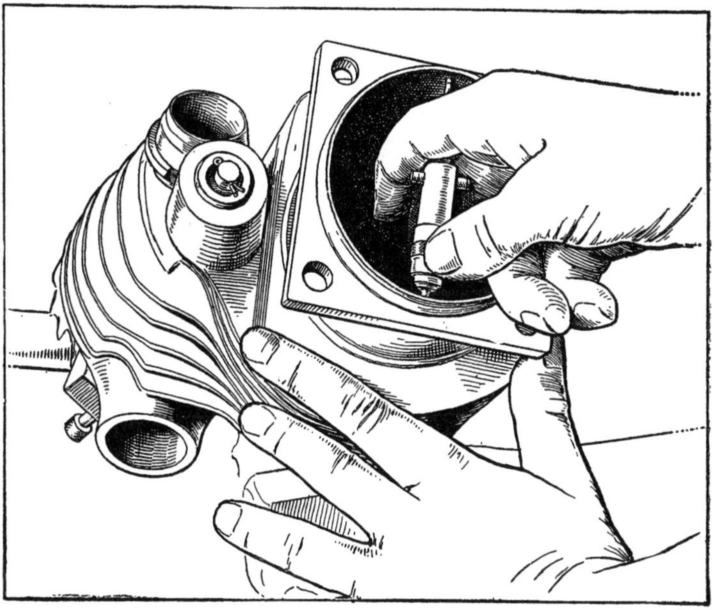

Fig. 359.—Measuring Cylinder Bore with Inside Micrometer to Determine Wear.

3. If the cylinders appear O. K., that is, not scored or grooved, measure them for wear with micrometers, as shown at Fig. 359. The wear cannot be measured with calipers or gauges, because the cylinders always wear taper, that is, get larger at the upper end of the cylinder than at the lower. Measure the cylinders at about four different places along the length of the bore, and also try them for roundness. Make note of the different sizes. These

sizes will be referred to after measuring the diameter of the piston to determine the piston and cylinder clearance.

4. If the cylinder is scored (cut), measure the depth of the scores with a micrometer. If the scores are not more than .002 inch deep, the cylinder can be placed in fair shape again by lapping. This, of course, should only be done if the cylinder is not worn A cylinder which is scored more than this should be reground. Unworn cylinders of standard diameter (3.307 inches) which are scored more than .060 inch should be scrapped, as well as cylinders which have been reground repeatedly until they have a bore diameter of 3.380 inches.

Piston Dimensions.—1. Pistons are ground straight only from the bottom (bell end of the piston), to and including the shoulder between the bottom and center ring grooves. Between the center and upper ring grooves the diameter of the piston is relieved .0015 inch. Above the upper ring groove the diameter of the piston is .008 inch smaller than at the extreme bottom. Between the lower bearing of the piston and the shoulder between the two lower ring grooves, the piston is relieved .028 inch. The piston pin bosses are reamed to .609 inch and the piston pin diameter being .610 inch gives the piston pin a .001 inch press fit. The large diameter of the piston (which is at the lower end as just explained) is 3.305 inches to 3.3055 inches.

To Fit a Cylinder With a Piston.—1. It is a difficult matter to state a definite and accurate clearance for a piston on account of the method employed in the grinding of cylinders and pistons. Shop practice is to refer to a .003 inch loose piston fit if the small (upper) bore diameter of a cylinder is .003 inch larger than the large diameter of a piston, which is at the bell or skirt end. This rule or method of referring to piston clearance, although not accurate in actual measurements, can safely be followed, and is therefore recommended.

2. If the motor has been stripped only for inspection, removal of carbon, and grinding of valves, measure the diameter of the piston at the lower end with micrometers. No attention should be paid to the other dimensions unless the piston is scored. Always

measure the piston about ½ inch from the bottom, and be sure to take measurements from different positions. If the piston is out of round, round it up by striking the high spots with a hammer handle or a piece of wood. Sometimes a 3½ inch or a 4 inch "C" clamp will have to be used to press the piston before it can be trued up accurately.

3. Compare the large diameter of the piston with the diameter of the upper end of the cylinder bore. If the piston is more than .010 inch smaller than the upper end of the bore, or if the cylinder is worn so that the diameter of the upper end of the bore is larger than the lower end, the cylinder should be reground and refitted with the necessary oversize piston.

4. If a cylinder has been reground, it will have to be fitted with an oversize piston to obtain the proper clearance. Oversize pistons are furnished by the Harley-Davidson Motor Co. in any size, or if the shop includes a grinder, the turned pistons can be carried in stock and can be ground to size as needed.

5. At the factory the fit is made with a difference in size, or piston clearance as it will be termed hereafter, of .00175 inch to .00225 inch. After selecting a piston and fitting piston rings, the cylinder and piston are clamped in a lapping machine and lapped for twenty minutes with a number 00 quartz sand and oil mixture. This lapping operation is generally not applied in a repair shop, and a clearance of .003 inch is therefore recommended.

6. Cylinders should be reground at the factory of the Harley-Davidson Motor Co. The price is very reasonable considering the quality of the work. Because of the need of absolute accuracy, which can only be attained with special machinery, a factory job is recommended.

Inspecting and Fitting Piston Rings.—1. Inspect the piston rings carefully. The upper and center ring should show an unbroken bearing surface over the entire circumference of the face of the ring. If there are any dull spots across the face of the ring, if the ring is burned or if it is scored, it should be replaced. A ring which fits loosely sideways in the groove of a piston should be removed and measured for width. If the ring is not .2175 inch wide, it should be replaced. If the ring is of the right width, the piston groove is worn and the piston should be replaced.

2. In some cases cylinders, rings and valves are O. K., yet the motor will have little compression. Trouble of this kind can generally be traced to too large a gap at the ring slot. Measure the gap after removing the ring from the piston and after placing it squarely into its cylinder. The gap should be no more than .050 inch. If the gap is more than this, fit an oversize ring. The diameter of a standard ring is 3.309 inches. However, oversize rings are made to .090 inch oversize, each size varying .005 inch.

3. When fitting an oversize ring, select one that will have a gap of .015 inch to .025 inch when the ring is placed squarely into its cylinder without it being necessary to file the slot. If only slight filing is necessary, be sure to file both ends of the ring equally and squarely. The gap at the ring when entirely compressed should be closed, to prove that the ends were filed equally. If a ring of too large a diameter is selected, and the slot is filed until the ring has the proper gap, the ring will not bear properly against the walls of the cylinder and will allow the compression to leak into the crank case.

Inspecting and Repairing Exhaust Valve Seats.—1. After the bore of the cylinders has been attended to, the valves, valve seats, and inlet valve assemblies are to be inspected and repaired. Inspect the exhaust valve stem and the guide in the cylinder.

2. The exhaust valve stem is .003 inch to .004 inch smaller than the guide hole. If the stem of the exhaust valve is worn enough to give it about .010 inch clearance, the exhaust valve should be replaced with a new standard valve. If the guide in the cylinder is worn so that a fair fit (between .003 minimum and .010 maximum clearance) cannot be obtained, the guide in the cylinder should be reamed with the $\frac{1}{32}$ inch oversize reamer furnished with tool FK-824.

3. When reaming the guide, never ream the large diameter any deeper than $1\frac{3}{8}$ inches. If the oversize guide reamer is used, it will of course be necessary to fit an exhaust valve which has a $\frac{1}{32}$ inch oversize stem.

4. If the guide does not appear to be worn, remove the carbon from it with the standard size reamer furnished with tool FK-824. Attention is again called to ream the large diameter of the guide just 1$\frac{3}{8}$ inches deep.

5. Inspect the exhaust valve seat in the cylinder. If it is burned, pitted, or warped it should be rereamed with exhaust reamer FK-824. Never lap or grind in a valve to obtain a good seat, if either valve seat or the cylinder seat it pitted, burned, or warped, because excessive grinding would be required which would make the seat considerably lower in the cylinder. A low seat would naturally cut down the opening and interfere with the free escape of exhaust gases, resulting in lack of power, loss of speed, and overheating.

6. After the guide has been reamed, select the pilot which is a good snug fit in the cylinder, and force it into the cylinder by hand as far as possible to hold it firmly; then place the seat reamer over the pilot. If the reamer is allowed to "wobble" while the seat in the cylinder is being reamed, an uneven and poor job will be made. The exhaust valve must seat squarely and firmly; otherwise the motor will not be flexible, and the burning gases passing by will burn the seat in a very short time.

7. The fact that the reamer will not cut at the first attempt to ream the seat, does not indicate that the reamer is dull. It is due to the hard scale which the heat forms on the exhaust seats. To save the cutting edges of the reamer, do not attempt to force the reamer through this scale by pressing squarely. Instead, exert a slight pressure on one end of the wrench handle (being careful not to press hard enough to spring the pilot); then give the wrench one complete revolution, and the hard scale should be cut through. After the scale has been cut through, the seat should be trued up. This is done by pressing lightly and squarely on the center of the reamer, while giving the wrench about three or four complete turns depending on the condition of the seat.

8. Care should be exercised when rereaming the seat not to remove too much stock, because the exhaust valve may at no time be below the bottom of the valve chamber. If the seat is deep

enough to allow the valve to rest too low, the bottom of the valve chamber should be turned down, or the same trouble will be experienced as just explained. Care should be taken when reaming a cylinder seat never to turn the reamer in the reverse direction, because this will quickly dull it.

9. Generally when rereaming of the seat in the cylinder is necessary, the exhaust valve seat is in poor condition, and should be cleaned or trued up in a grinder or in a lathe. If the valve is burned so that the taper seat will come flush with the top of the valve, it should be scrapped.

10. A new or repaired valve should be ground just as little as possible to obtain a good seat. Excessive grinding or lapping will ruin the straight face of the valve and cylinder seat, and allow only a very narrow seat. This can be understood if it is considered that during the operation of grinding, the compound is forced away considerably more from the center of the seats than from the outer edges. The greater amount of compound on the outer edges naturally will remove more stock and make the seats oval instead of a straight 45° taper.

11. Test the valve seats to see whether or not they seat accurately by marking the seats of the valve and cylinder across the faces with pencil marks about $1/8$ inch apart. Place the valve in the cylinder and with a screw driver give it one quarter turn. Remove the valve and inspect the marks. If the erasure of the marks is alike all around the seats, the valve is seating properly.

12. After the exhaust valve has been properly fitted, inspect the exhaust valve spring. The spring should be $2\frac{1}{2}$ inches long when it is not compressed. When the spring is compressed to $1^{15}/_{16}$ inches, it should have a pressure of thirty pounds to thirty-five pounds. If the spring is set and does not give the required pressure when compressed to $1^{15}/_{16}$ inches, it should be shimmed up by placing one washer $1/8$ inch thick between the cylinder and spring or the spring should be replaced. After thoroughly washing the seats, test the exhaust valve stem to see whether or not it is bent, by turning it several times. If it is straight, fit the exhaust valve with cover, spring, collar, and key.

To Inspect and Repair Inlet Valves.—1. Scrape all carbon from the inlet valve and housing. Strip this assembly and inspect the fit of the inlet valve stem in the inlet housing. If the clearance between the guide and the stem is too great, it will be difficult to get a good carburetor adjustment, and impossible to throttle the motor down to a slow space. New and repaired motors are fitted with a .002 inch clearance for the inlet valve stem. This clearance is necessary to prevent the inlet valve stems from sticking in the housing guides when the motor gets hot.

2. If the guide of the housing is worn so that the valve stem is more than .006 inch loose, the housing and valve should be referred to the Harley-Davidson Motor Co. for repairs by replacing the guide with a steel guide or bushing. If a lathe is available the repair can be made as follows: Place the housing in a lathe, cut off the entire guide, bore a $^{33}/_{64}$ inch hole centrally through the housing, tap this hole with a $^{9}/_{16}$x24 tap, and firmly screw in the new guide. These guides can be obtained from the Harley-Davidson Motor Co. at very small cost. If the inlet valve stem is worn, several light cuts should be taken off and a bushing or guide with $^{1}/_{64}$ inch undersize hole be used. Standard and undersize bushings are furnished for 1916 to 1918 models inclusive. The shortage of material makes it necessary to repair worn inlet housings and valves whenever possible.

3. Pay special attention to the condition of the seats. If the seat in the housing is worn so that the bottom of the valve fits beyond the bottom of the lower housing flange, the flange should be turned off. Never turn the flange off so that it is less than $^{3}/_{16}$ inch deep.

4. Grind the inlet valve into the housing whether the housing was repaired or new parts selected.

5. Inspect the inlet valve spring. A good spring is $2\frac{1}{2}$ inches long when it is not compressed. When compressed to $1^{17}/_{32}$ inches, it should show a pressure of twenty to twenty-eight pounds. Thoroughly clean the housing parts and assemble.

Fitting Inlet Housings Into Cylinders.—1. It is as important to have the inlet housing seat perfectly in the cylinder as it is to have the inlet valve seat perfectly in the inlet housing. Invariably the housing must be ground into the cylinder to obtain a tight fit, even if the housing were only removed to do other motor work. When grinding a housing into a cylinder, use very little grinding compound and grind the housing only as much as is necessary to obtain a perfect fit. Tool GK-864 is especially made for this grinding operation. Very often a good fit can be obtained by grinding the housing into the cylinder without using any grinding compound whatever.

2. After grinding, wash the housing and cylinder thoroughly. Make a paste out of plumbago (powdered graphite) and cylinder oil. Put just a little of this mixture on the shoulder of the housing which rests on the cylinder. Put the housing into the cylinder and give it several turns to distribute the mixture evenly; then line up the housing with the set screw, and tighten the screw. Be sure to tighten the set screw before tightening the clamping nut and make sure that the set screw does not jam the housing out of center. Do not use too much of this mixture or it may drop from the housing, bake onto the exhaust seats when the motor gets hot, and cause the exhaust valve to burn, pit, and warp; also put just a little of this mixture on the base of the inlet housing cap and clamp nut threads. Fit the cap, being careful to line it up with the dowel pin in the housing and to line up the inlet lever properly when a push rod is fitted. Draw the clamp nut down tight with wrench DK-808 or FK-822.

3. To have a quiet inlet valve action, the inlet lever should be a free running fit on the bushing. See whether or not the inlet levers are worn and have a lot of up and down play. If they are loose, remove them and inspect the clamp bolts, levers, and bushings for wear. Replace all worn parts. When fitting new parts, be sure that the bushing is a snug fit in the clevis of the inlet cap and that it is also a few thousandths of an inch wider than the inlet lever. While assembling, lubricate all parts thoroughly and have the oil cup end of the bolts toward the cylinder plugs.

To Inspect, Adjust, or Replace Secondary and Roller Arm Studs.—1. Inspect the studs to see whether or not they are loose or worn. To test either stud to see if it is loose, strike it lightly with a small hammer. A loose stud can be felt and will make a dull thud when struck. If a loose stud is found, tighten it securely as explained hereinafter.

2. If the stud is tight, inspect it for wear. Try the secondary gear on the secondary stud, and both inlet and exhaust roller arms on the roller arm stud for shake. These parts are assembled with just a free running fit, the inside diameter of the roller arm bushing or the hole diameter of the secondary gear being .0005 inch larger than the diameter of its respective stud. Secondary gear studs are ground to $\frac{1}{2}$ inch diameter, while roller arm studs are ground to $\frac{7}{16}$ inch diameter.

3. If the exhaust or inlet roller arm or the secondary gear clears its respective stud by more than .0015 inch, the studs or stud plate assembly, secondary gear, or the roller arm bushings should be replaced. Too much clearance at any of these places reduces valve lift and delays valve action, cutting down the efficiency of the motor and also making the motor extremely noisy.

4. Two methods of fastening gear studs into plates were used during 1917. The first and prior to 1917 method was to hold the studs with threads and then to rivet them, while the other method was to make the studs a .002 inch press fit in the plate, and then to rivet them after a $\frac{1}{8}$ inch dowel pin was wedged between the stud and the plate. The dowel pin is used on the secondary stud only.

5. The first method was used on all motors prior to 1917 and all 1917 motors up to motor No. 17T-17916. All twin cylinder motors assembled after this number, including all 1918 motors, are fitted with a stud plate assembly in which the studs are a press fit (not threaded) in the plates. All single cylinder motors have threaded studs.

6. To tighten the threaded studs, turn them into the stud plate as far as possible and then rivet them on the threaded end. To turn the gear stud tighter into the stud plate, clamp the stud firmly in a vise (protecting the stud with sheet copper or copper jaws), then turn the crank case to the left. This stud has a left

thread. Thoroughly rivet the threaded end. To tighten a threaded roller arm stud, turn the crank case to the right. This stud has a right thread. Then rivet the threaded end.

7. If the gear stud is tight but is found badly worn, it should be replaced with a new one.

8. To remove a worn gear stud, cut off the riveted end of the stud with a ½ inch drill. Clamp the other end of the stud in a vise and turn the crank case to the right. If the stud is very tight in the plate, and constantly slips in the vise jaws, a flat spot should be ground on the stud with an emery wheel. Clamp this flat spot of the stud in the vise jaws, and the stud can be turned out of the plate.

9. If a threaded secondary gear stud is broken off flush with the shoulder and not sufficient stock remains to clamp it in a vise, the threaded end can easily be removed with a drill and square punch. Cut off the riveted end of the gear stud with a ½ inch drill; then with a 11/32 inch drill, drill all the way through the stud; drive the square or four cornered punch into the hole, and the stud can in most cases be turned out without trouble.

10. When fitting a new stud be sure to turn it as tightly as possible into the stud plate before riveting.

11. If a roller arm stud is to be replaced, the same instructions can be applied that are used in removing a worn gear stud with these exceptions: The roller arm stud has a right thread, is 7/16 inch in diameter, and a 5/16 inch drill should be used when drilling it out.

12. After a roller arm stud or gear stud has been replaced or tightened, always test to see whether or not the oil passages in the stud are open. Do this by putting a drop of oil on the oil holes; then blow air through the studs from the riveted end. Bubbles will indicate open passages.

13. If one of the press fit studs is loose, try to tighten it by riveting. If a satisfactory job cannot be made, the stud plate assembly should be replaced as explained under next heading.

14. If a press fit stud is worn, do not remove the stud and fit

another in its place, because the boss in the plate in which the original stud was fitted is damaged and another stud cannot be tightened to hold permanently with any safety.

To Remove and Fit Gear Stud Plate Assembly.—15. The stud plate, regardless of the method used to hold the studs, is a light press fit in the crank case and is held secure with five 1/4 inch clamp bolts. The clamp bolts are turned firmly into the stud plate from the inside of the crank case and then riveted over into the countersunk holes of the plate.

16. To remove the plate, cut away the riveted part of the clamp bolts with a 1/4 inch drill, and with socket wrench AK-430 turn the bolts out of the plate. The plate can then be removed by alternately striking the riveted end of the studs.

17. When fitting another stud plate, use new clamp bolts. Draw them up tight and rivet them carefully into the countersunk holes of the stud plate.

To Inspect and Repair Roller Arms.—1. The fit of the roller arm bushings on the stud should be the same as explained under To Inspect, Adjust or Replace Secondary and Roller Arm Studs. The roller arm bushing should just be free on the stud. This also holds true of the fit of the front exhaust roller arm on the bushing, the fit of the rear inlet roller arm on the bushing, and the fit of all four rollers on their respective bushings.

2. If the exhaust roller arm bushing is loose on the stud and the stud is O. K., the bushing is worn and should be replaced. If the front exhaust roller arm is too loose on the bushing, inspect the bushing for wear. A worn bushing should be replaced, while if the roller arm is worn, a front roller arm which is just a free fit on the bushing, should be fitted. The rear exhaust roller arm is a .002 inch press fit on the bushing and no trouble with wear should be experienced.

3. Inspect the fit of the rear inlet roller arm on the bushing. This should be free without any perceptible shake, while the front inlet roller arm is a .001 inch press fit on the bushing. If sufficient wear has developed, replace which ever part is worn.

4. Try the fit of the two inlet and two exhaust rollers on their bushings. If any play has developed, the roller should be removed and all worn parts replaced.

5. To remove a roller from a roller arm, the riveted pin will have to be driven out. Rest the roller on a piece of pipe or tubing which has a 5/8 inch or a 11/16 inch hole, and the riveted pin can be driven out by means of a small drift and hammer. It is not necessary to cut away the riveted part of the pin before the pin can be removed.

6. Examine the fit of the roller on the bushing. If the roller can be shaken, even only slightly, both roller and bushing may be worn and should be replaced. When selecting another roller and bushing, make sure that the bushing is a few thousandths of an inch wider than the roller, or the roller, instead of the bushing, will be clamped by the head of the pin when the pin is riveted in place.

7. When assembling the roller arms, new pins should be used. Rest the roller arm assembly on the pin head and rivet the pin carefully. After riveting, grind the riveted end off flush with the side of the roller arm. Test the fit of the roller. If it sticks, even if only slightly, the roller should be loosened up so that it turns perfectly free. To loosen the roller, clamp it in the chuck of a lathe, cover the roller with thin grinding compound, hold the roller arm stationary, and run the lathe at high speed until the roller loosens sufficiently to turn freely; then wash the assembly thoroughly.

Inspecting Gears.—1. To determine whether or not a gear is worn enough to warrant fitting a new one, put the gear on a new stud and try it for shake. A properly fitted secondary gear has no appreciable shake, and is just a free running fit. This fit requires about .0005 inch clearance. If the gear clears the stud by .0015 inch, it should be scrapped.

2. The fit of the intermediate gear and intermediate worm gear on their respective studs can be looser than the fit of the secondary gear on its stud. If, however, the clearance of either intermediate gear is more than .006 inch, the gear, or stud, or both the gear and the stud should be replaced.

3. Examine the teeth of all gears for wear. The proper clear-

ance or back lash of this type gear is .004 inch, but to have the gears run as quietly as possible they should be fitted as closely as possible without binding, and the .004 inch back lash should be disregarded. If only one tooth binds slightly, the gears will howl; for that reason the fit of every gear tooth should be tried.

4. Only in emergencies should the gear studs be sprung, by striking them with a hammer and piece of brass to bring the teeth closer together. Gears cannot line up and run true on studs which stand at an angle. The secondary gear may also run tight on the stud due to the stud having been bent, while, if the intermediate studs are struck with a hammer, the bosses in the drive case will be damaged, allowing the studs to work loose continually.

Pinion Gear Shaft and Right Crank Case (Gear Side) Bushing.—1. Inspect the fit of the gear side bushing by placing the crank case over the pinion gear shaft. Very little shake will indicate a good fit, the proper clearance being .002 inch to .003 inch. If the shaft is over .005 inch loose in the bushing, the bushing, or the shaft, or possibly both should be replaced. Too much play at this bearing will cause the motor to knock and the gears to run noisily and click, because the distance or the back lash between the pinion and secondary gear teeth is constantly changed.

2. Measure the diameter of the shaft to see whether or not it is worn. The diameter of the pinion gear shaft is .9375 inch. If a shaft is worn, replace it. It can be driven out of the fly wheel after the lock washer and nut have been removed. Before fitting a new shaft, make sure that the key is placed into the shaft, that the shaft keyway is clean, that the key is not too high, and that the shaft and taper hole of the fly wheel are free from all dirt and grit.

3. To gauge the amount of wear of the bushing, use a new pinion gear shaft as a size plug. If the shaft is .005 inch loose or looser, fit another bushing. With an arbor press or a drill press, press the worn bushing from the crank case. If a press is not convenient, a drift and hammer can be used. Rest the crank case on an old piston to avoid springing it while changing bushings. Lay the inside of the crank case on the open end of the piston.

Place a piece of shafting or pipe about $1\frac{1}{8}$ inches wide on the end of the bushing, and the bushing can be forced from the crank case, as shown at Fig. 360.

4. To fit a new bushing, rest the other side of the crank case boss on a surface plate or on a square block of wood and press the bushing in place. Be sure to place the bushing into the crank case

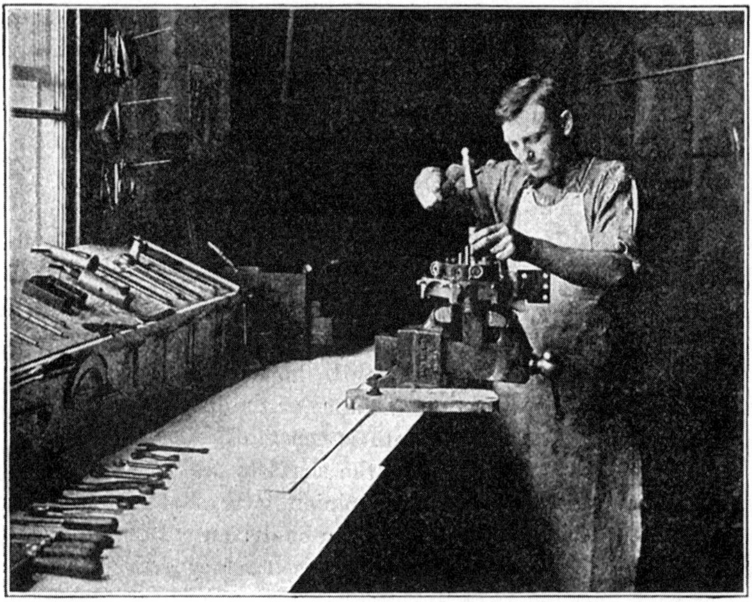

Fig 360.—Method of Driving Gear Side Bushing from Motor Crankcase.

so that the part where the spiral oil grooves cross, is toward the top of the crank case. This is important because the oil holes will meet both of these grooves after they are drilled. With a $\frac{3}{16}$ inch drill, drill the two oil holes through the bronze bushing, using the original oil holes as guides for the drill.

5. The pinion gear shaft bushing is a .0025 inch press fit in the crank case, but to prevent the bushing from turning in the

aluminum crank case, should the bushing and shaft seize, the bushing is doweled to the crank case with a 3/8 inch x 1/8 inch steel dowel pin. For this reason lock the new bushing permanently in the same manner that the original bushing was locked.

6. The same dowel pin that was used with the original bushing can be used again. Before the pin can be fitted, the crank case boss and the bushing must be drilled 1/2 inch deep with a No. 31 drill. Do not use the original hole in the crank case but drill a

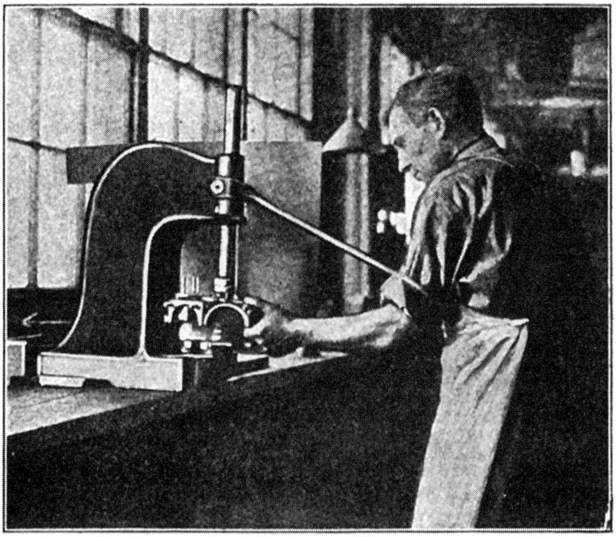

Fig. 361.—How Arbor Press Is Used to Replace or Remove Bushing from Crankcase.

new hole at least 1/4 inch from the original hole. The hole should be drilled in the center between the crank case and bushing in the same way as the original hole. However, trouble may be experienced in keeping the drill in the center, because the drill will have a tendency to work toward the aluminum. To prevent this trouble, it is advisable to drill a 3/64 inch hole in the bushing first as close to the outside edge of the bushing as possible to guide the

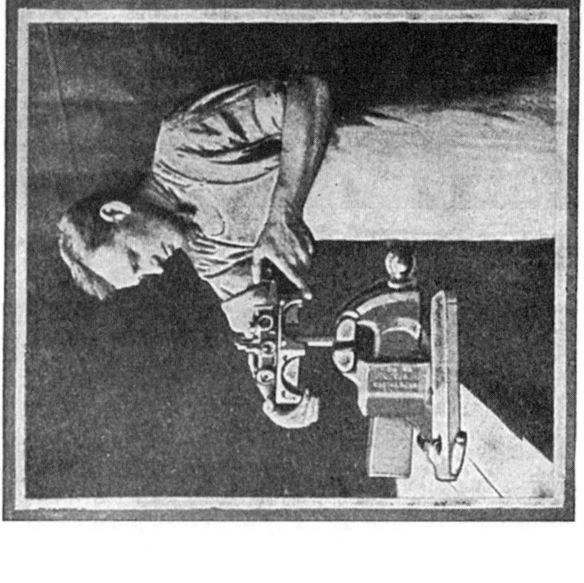

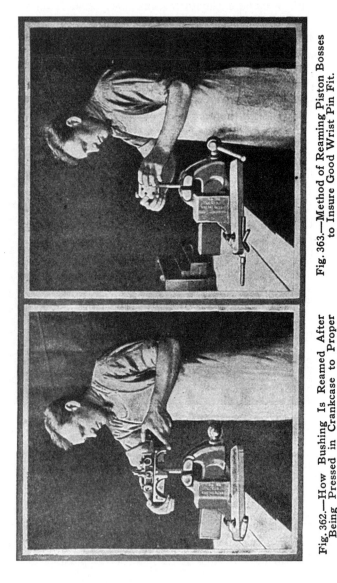

Fig. 362.—How Bushing Is Reamed After Being Pressed in Crankcase to Proper Size.

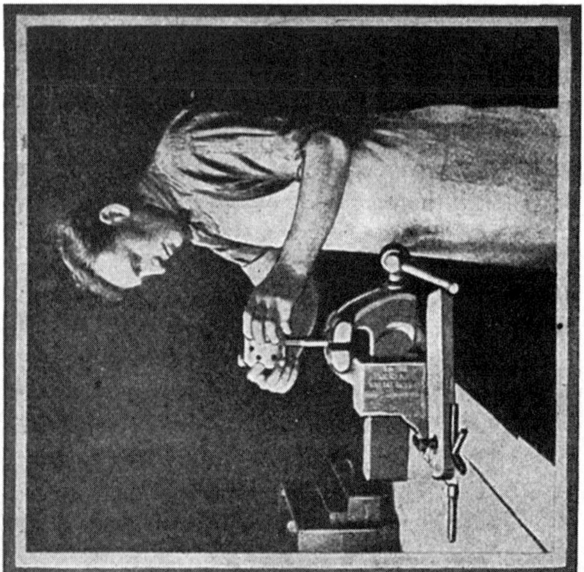

Fig. 363.—Method of Reaming Piston Bosses to Insure Good Wrist Pin Fit.

larger drill. After the dowel pin hole has been drilled, drive the pin in as far as it will go and pean the opening of the dowel pin hole to prevent the pin from dropping out.

7. Bore or ream the bushing to size in a lathe or with the $^{15}/_{16}$ inch expansion reamer EK-336. If a lathe is available use this method, because a more accurate job can be made. Bolt the crank case squarely to the face plate and bore the bushing to .940 inch.

8. When using the expansion reamer do not attempt to ream the bushing to size with one operation, because the reamer will contract and not remove sufficient stock from the center of the bushing. The result will be that the shaft will run tight in the bushing when the motor is run at high speed. Therefore, be sure to cut off as little stock as possible with each adjustment of the reamer until the shaft has .002 inch to .003 inch clearance.

9. After the hole has been turned to size, face off the end of the bushing in which the dowel pin has been fitted until it is flush with the crank case. A facing reamer or a lathe should be used for this operation. The shoulder of the bushing will also have to be turned down until it is between $^{3}/_{32}$ inch and $^{7}/_{64}$ inch thick.

10. The machine may have been in an accident, and the crank case sprung; in that case, it is best to lay a depth gauge or straight edge across the wider face of the step joint of the crank case, and to turn down the shoulder until the space between the lower edge of the depth gauge or straight edge and the bushing is $1^{3}/_{4}$ inch. Relieve the straight edge so that it will clear and not rest on the face of the narrow step joint, because the height of this step varies and cannot be used as a standard.

11. After all machining operations on the bushing are completed, remove all sharp edges with a scraper and thoroughly clean all grit and dirt out of the oil grooves and oil holes.

Flywheel Washers.—1. Inspect the flywheel washers which protect the flywheels from the crank pin roller bearing and connecting rod end thrust. It very seldom is necessary to replace these washers, but it is advisable to do so if they show only a little wear.

2. These washers fit snugly in the recess of the flywheels and

are securely held in place by peaning the edge of the flywheel at four different places with a prick punch.

3. If a washer must be removed to be replaced by another, place the point of a prick punch or the cutting edge of a small chisel 1/32 inch to 1/16 inch from the edge of the recess, hold the tool at about a 45° angle and drive it carefully into the flywheel. If the washer is only slightly and evenly worn, it can be reversed, otherwise it must be renewed. When fitting a washer, be careful that no grit or dirt remains in the flywheel recess, otherwise the washer will not fit squarely. When the washer has been properly fitted, lock it securely by prick punching the flywheel about 1/32 inch from the outer edge of the recess at four equally spaced places.

Connecting Rod Piston Pin Bearing.—1. Examine the fit of the piston pin in the piston pin bushing. This fit requires 1/16 inch end play with the pin nearly a free fit in the bushing.

2. If a slight up and down play has developed, a good fit can be obtained again by truing the bushing up with the 39/64 inch expansion reamer EK-335 and then fitting an oversize piston pin. These oversize piston pins are made in sizes varying .002 inch, up to .010 inch oversize. When using an oversize piston pin, be sure to ream the bushing first, so that a good bearing is again obtained. To hold the reamer, clamp the shank in the vise and turn the rod on the reamer. Adjust the reamer to take off very light cuts, or the bushing will not be reamed accurately. Do not ream the bushing until the pin is a free fit, but ream it so that the weight of the piston will be just enough to turn the pin in the bushing when this assembly is held in a horizontal position.

3. If an oversize pin has been fitted to the connecting rod bushing, it will be necessary to ream the piston also. To ream the piston, clamp the reamer in the vise in the same manner as in reaming the bushing, and turn the piston by hand. Always be sure to take off only a very light cut at a time because it is important to have the piston pin fit with a .001 inch press in the piston.

4. If the piston pin bushings are to be renewed, they can easily be pressed out of the connecting rods and replaced. After a new

bushing has been fitted, it will of course be necessary to file or cut a $\frac{1}{16}$ inch oil groove in the top of the bushing, slot the top of the bushing with a hack saw for lubrication, ream the bushing to fit the piston pin, and trim off both sides of the bushing to obtain proper end play for the piston.

Sprocket Shaft, Casing Bearing Bushing and Rollers.—1. The proper clearance for the sprocket shaft in the roller bearing is .001 inch. To measure this clearance, use a .001 inch oversize shaft as a size plug. If considerable shake has developed, measure the diameter of the original sprocket shaft where the rollers bear. The diameter should be 1 inch. If the shaft is worn .001 inch, fit a new one. If the shaft and bushing are O. K., a good fit can be obtained by fitting the proper oversize rollers.

To Change Sprocket Shaft.—2. To remove the sprocket shaft, take off the lock washer screw, lock washer and the clamp nut; then with a hammer force the shaft from the flywheel.

3. Before fitting the new shaft, be sure that the shaft and flywheel tapers and keyways are perfectly clean. This is important because if dirt or grit is allowed to remain here, it will be impossible to properly line up the flywheels. Before placing the shaft into the flywheel, fit the key into the keyway of the shaft, making sure that the key is not too high. Draw the clamp nut tight, fit the lock washer and washer lock screw. If the hole in the lock washer does not line up with the threaded hole in the flywheel, do not loosen the flywheel shaft nut to line up the holes, but tighten it still more or reverse the lock washer, that is, turn it bottom end up.

To Replace Casing Bearing Bushing.—4. If the casing bearing bushing is only very slightly ringed, showing where the rollers bear, it is O. K. A bushing which shows that it is worn by the rollers and on which the grooves can be felt, should be replaced.

5. The casing bearing bushing can be removed after heating the crank case, or can be pressed out Since heating the case destroys the enamel, pressing out the bushing is recommended.

6. To press the bushing from the crank case requires a special set of fixtures. This set is identified by number GK-834, and con-

sists of three separate pieces; viz., one a piloted pin guide, the other two fixtures fitted with four pins each, the pins of each fixture being of different length and placed so as to line up with the 4 screw holes for the felt washer retainer.

7. When a bushing is to be pressed out of a crank case, remove the felt washer retainer, put the piloted pin guide over the fixture with the short pins, and place the pins through the 4 felt washer retainer screw holes. Support the inside of the crank case on an old piston to prevent springing the crank case out of line, and the casing bearing bushing can be pressed out as far as is possible with this fixture. Remove the guide from the fixture, and place it on the fixture with the long pins. With this fixture the bushing can then be pressed all the way out of the crank case.

8. Never attempt to press out a casing bearing bushing without using the piloted pin guide, or without using the fixture with the short pins first, because the bushing is a .0025 inch press fit in the crank case and would cause the pins to bend.

9. Examine the casing bearing end plate, which is placed between the bushing and crank case. If it is worn, replace it.

10. When pressing another bushing into the crank case, be sure that the casing bearing end plate is in position, that the crank case is supported squarely, and that the bushing is pressed absolutely straight into the crank case.

To Line Up Left Crank Case.—11. After a new bushing has been pressed into the sprocket or left side crank case, the crank case should always be tested to see whether or not the bearings are still in line. It is very important to have the crank cases exactly in line; otherwise the flywheel shafts will bind and run tight, the motor will always be stiff and not give maximum power and speed.

12. To test whether or not the crank cases are in line, force the bushing of the lining bar GK-862, into the casing bearing bushing by hand as far as possible. Clamp the crank cases together with two long and two short casing studs evenly spaced. Pass the crank case lining bar through the lining bar bushing (in

the left side of the crank case), and through the pinion shaft bushing in the right crank case. If the lining bar can be turned perfectly freely, the crank cases are in line. If the lining bar sticks, or cannot be passed into the gear side bushing, although it will just fit into the bushing without passing the bar through the left side crank case first, the crank cases are out of line.

13. To line up the left side crank case, pass the lining bar

Fig. 364.—How to Line Up Crankcase Halves with Mandrel.

through the lining bar bushing up to the pinion shaft bushing. Look through the pinion bushing and locate the point where the lining bar comes closest to the bushing. Turn this part of the crank case directly upward, draw the lining bar out of the crank case far enough to only extend through the lining bar bushing, keep the bar in this position, raise the crank cases and lining bar, and strike the outer end of the bar against the bench. This will spring the left crank case boss so that the bearings will line up properly. If the crank cases do not line up at the first attempt, repeat the operation as often as necessary.

To Line Up Right Crank Case.—14. If the right crank case bushing was bored to size in a lathe as has been explained on page 24, the bushing must be in line, but if the bushing was reamed to size with a $^{15}/_{16}$ inch expansion reamer EK-336, the right crank case will have to be lined up with the left crank case. To line up this bushing, apply the instructions in the preceding paragraph. Of course, instead of keeping the bar in the left crank case, it should be kept in the right crank case so that that boss can be sprung.

To Line Up Both Crank Cases.—15. If both crank cases need lining up, start by lining up the left crank case first until the lining bar will just come to the center of the inside hole of the pinion shaft bushing. Line the right crank case in like manner, and do not stop until the crank cases are as near in line as it is possible to make them. The left crank case can be sprung easily, while the right is quite a bit stiffer on account of the thickness of the stock.

Connecting Rod Crank Pin Bearing.—1. Good judgment must be used when overhauling crank pin bearings. This bearing should not be overhauled as soon as a little side shake has developed at the upper end of the rod, nor is it advisable to neglect this bearing when the motor is being overhauled. This bearing need not be overhauled unless the upper end of the connecting rods can be moved sideways over $^{3}/_{16}$ inch. The best way to determine the condition of this bearing is to try the rod for up and down play when the crank pin is on top center, and when the rod is in line with the crank pin and flywheel shafts. If any up and down play can be felt, the bearing should be overhauled.

Overhauling Crank Pin Bearing.—2. If, according to the foregoing, the crank pin bearing is too loose and the flywheels have not been taken apart, refer to instructions for stripping the flywheel and removing the connecting rods previously given. Care should be taken not to drop any of the rollers while removing the connecting rods.

3. If the connecting rods are too loose, do not discard the crank pin, bushings, retainers and rollers at once, but inspect the parts for wear. If the crank pin, retainers and connecting rod bushings appear O. K., a good fit can be obtained again by fitting a larger size set of rollers.

4. In some cases the crank pin is worn badly and the connecting rod bushings are only slightly worn. A bearing in this condition can be put in good shape again by fitting a new crank pin and rollers, and lapping the bushings with the connecting rod lapping arbor FK-828 to true up the bushings.

5. Before lapping a bushing, adjust the lap so that the rod can just be passed over it. Place the lap in a lathe, run the lathe at about 200 r.p.m., put some fine grade grinding compound on the lap, and lap the bushing for a few seconds. While lapping the rod, slide it back and forth on the lap to make an accurate job and also to save the lap from being ringed and grooved. Hold the rod squarely and lap the bushing only as much as is necessary to true it up. Be careful when lapping the front (yoke) rod that one bushing is not lapped more than the other. To lap both bushings alike, turn the rod after lapping it slightly, so that the bushing which was to the left will be to the right. It is also important to place the rod over the lap as quickly as possible or one end of the bushing will be lapped more than the other.

6. The wear of a crank pin can readily be determined either by measuring the diameter or holding a small straight edge against the pin while holding the pin up to the light. The most accurate way, however, is to measure the diameter at various points. The crank pin diameter should measure just 1 inch. A crank pin which is worn more than .001 inch should be replaced.

7. The closed end of the roller retainers should be inspected for wear. If the closed end is less than .025 inch thick, the retainer should be renewed. If the retainers are O. K., they should be used again whether or not new rollers, crank pin, and bushings are being used.

8. If the crank pin is to be replaced, it can be removed from the flywheel in the same manner that the pinion gear shaft is re-

moved. The only difference is that the crank pin is not keyed to the flywheels.

9. Rollers that have to be replaced on account of the fit being too loose, should be scrapped, because they are worn unevenly. To measure the diameter of a roller, do not use a micrometer which is graduated to only .001 inch. Micrometers which are graduated to .0001 inch and only those which are in perfect mechanical condition should be used to measure rollers. If through accident or carelessness different size rollers should become mixed even though the difference in the size of the mixed rollers is only .0001 inch, the rollers should be carefully measured and again assorted according to sizes.

10. The diameter of the standard roller is .250 inch, but to get a perfect bearing fit, whether the shaft or bushing is standard or not, the rollers are made in twenty sizes, from .001 inch oversize to .001 inch undersize, each size varying .0001 inch.

To Assemble and Fit Crank Pin Bearing.—11. When it is necessary to fit another crank pin, it is common practice always to assemble the crank pin into the sprocket (left) side flywheel. This assembly is then held secure by clamping the sprocket shaft in a vise to facilitate fitting the connecting rod bearing on the crank pin.

12. While selecting the proper size rollers and testing the bearing fit, always keep the yoke (front) rod to the left. This is important, because the yoke rod must be to the front on account of lubrication.

13. Whether renewing the whole bearing, or only fitting a new set of rollers and crank pin and lapping the connecting rod bushings, the bearing fit should, of course, be made so that the rods have no shake and can be turned perfectly freely. If one size of rollers allows the rods to have a little shake at the upper end, and the next size, which is .0001 inch larger, causes the rods to climb or bind, the rods should be lapped to fit the larger size rollers. Under no conditions should the bearing be allowed to climb, or bind, even if only slightly, when the rods are spun in either direction.

14. To select the proper size rollers, if the rods have been re-

bushed and a new crank pin is to be used, put a set of standard size rollers on the crank pin. If the rods can be passed over the rollers easily the rollers should be removed, and a larger size should be tried. The proper size rollers will be found when the rods can just be forced over them by hand. Never use a hammer or any other kind of a tool to pound the connecting rods on or off the crank pin, because this seriously damages the bearing. If

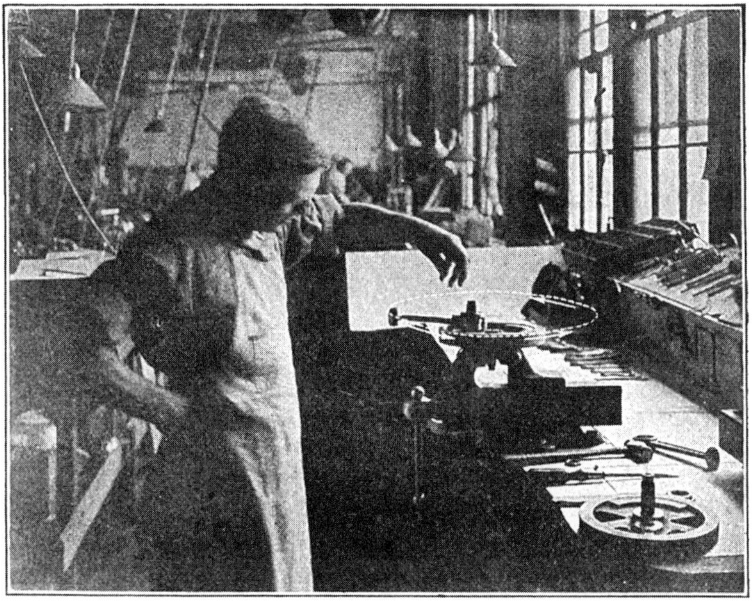

Fig. 365.—How to Test Fit of Crankpin Roller Bearings.

the connecting rods cannot be forced over the rollers by placing one's entire weight on the lower end of the connecting rods, the bearing fit is too tight and a smaller size roller should be used, or the bushings should be lapped until they are large enough for that size roller. To remove tight fitting rods pry them off and place the wedge as close as possible to the crank bearing end.

15. While trying the various size rollers, do not use both rods at the outset. Try to find the proper size roller by using the yoke

rod. After the proper yoke rod fit has been obtained, remove that rod and try the rear rod on the bearing. If the fit is too tight, lap the rod as may be necessary, but bear in mind that a very little lapping has a decided effect on the fit of the bearing.

16. If the fit of the bearing seems O. K., but the rods climb slightly when spun, do not strike the rod to loosen the bearing but remove the rod and reverse the retainers with the rollers. To re-

Fig. 366.—How to True Up Flywheel Assembly

verse them, remove the retainers from the crank pin and replace them in such a manner that the retainers and rollers which were on the top are on the bottom. If this will not give the desired effect, the bushings which are smallest should be lapped slightly.

17. If the yoke rod has been fitted properly on a set of rollers and the rear rod is entirely too loose on this set of rollers, try another rod in place of this one or select a set of rollers for the inside rod which will give a satisfactory fit. After a good fit has

been obtained, it will of course be necessary to place the rollers with retainers in the connecting rods, after the rods have been put together, and then slip this entire assembly over the crank pin. The method of spinning a connecting rod to test its bearings is clearly outlined in Fig. 365.

Assembling the Flywheels.—1. After the flywheel shafts, crank pin bearing, and thrust washers have been properly fitted, the flywheels can be assembled. Before assembling them, make sure that the yoke rod will be to the front and that the taper hole in the flywheel and taper end of the shaft are perfectly clean.

2. Place the gear side flywheel over the crank pin which is assembled with the rods and sprocket side flywheel. With a scale or straight edge line up the outside faces of both flywheels, and with wrench GK-854 draw the crank pin nut tight. If the flywheels have a tendency to turn in the vise while pulling the nut tight, place a wedge of some kind between the spokes of both flywheels and the vise.

3. After tightening the crank pin nut, test the connecting rod crank pin bearing for end play on the crank pin. Test the play by prying the lower end of the rods, first from one side, and then from the other. If the rods can be moved between .006 inch and .012 inch, the end play is correct and the lock washer can be fitted.

4. If the end play is .030 inch the crank pin nut can be tightened until the maximum end play is obtained. If the end play is more than .030 inch, another crank pin should be tried, because the flywheels would crack if it were attempted to overcome more than this amount of play by tightening the crank pin nut. Never put oil on the shafts, or in the taper holes of the flywheels when assembling.

5. If the connecting rods have no end play after the crank pin nut is drawn up tight, do not loosen the nut, because the shafts in the flywheels must be clamped securely. In this case try another crank pin. If another shaft will not give the proper end play, the taper holes in the flywheels are undoubtedly too large and the only remedy, although not urged by us, would be to grind off the outside of the yoke connecting rod bushings and to grind

off the open end of each retainer with the rollers. Before grinding the yoke connecting rod bushing, measure the distance between the outer edges of both bushings with a 2 inch micrometer. Then grind off one bushing with a disc grinder or on the side of a perfectly true emery wheel, again measure the diameter of the bushings and grind off the other bushing the same amount. When preparing to grind off the open ends of the retainers and rollers, do not mix the retainers, because trouble may be experienced with the bearing fit when again assembling. Be careful not to lose any rollers and to grind each set squarely and the same amount.

6. After the retainers have been ground, place them together including the spacer washer and measure the width. This width should be .005 inch to .010 inch less than the distance between the outside ends of both yoke connecting rod bushings.

To True Flywheels.—1. To true a set of flywheels does not refer to lining up the face of one flywheel with the face of the other, but refers to truing up the sprocket shaft and pinion gear shaft. This can only be done successfully as follows: Support the flywheel assembly on its main shafts between centers, and move or slip the crank pin in the flywheel (depending, of course, which shaft is out of line) by striking that part of the rim which is in line with the high spot of the shaft. Flywheel truing device GK-850 is recommended to support the flywheels in preference to a lathe, because the hammering required in some cases would ruin a lathe in time. In addition to the flywheel truing device, copper hammer EK-328 should be used to strike the flywheels, because if a steel hammer were used, the wheels would be badly marred and possibly broken. (See Fig. 366.)

2. When supporting the flywheels between centers, care must be taken not to clamp them too tight, nor to hold them too loose. Clamp them so that they have no play and still can be turned perfectly freely. If the truing device is equipped with Brown and Sharp indicators, adjust them so that they bear against the shafts as close to the flywheels as possible. If the truing device is equipped with the standard indicators, also adjust them to come in contact with the shafts as close to the wheels as possible.

3. Turn the wheels by means of the rods and watch the action of the indicator pointers. If the pointers of the indicators do not move more than .001 inch, which is from one graduation to the other, the flywheels need not be lined up any better, although, if possible, they should be lined up absolutely true.

4. If the truing device is used with the standard indicators, lay a piece of white paper under the flywheel assembly and try to look through between the indicators and the shafts while the flywheels are turned. If light can be seen through at certain positions, the shafts are out of line and the flywheel rim should be struck downward at that part which is in line with the high part of the shaft until the shaft runs absolutely true.

5. Under no conditions should flywheels which are more than .001 inch out of line be placed into a motor. If the flywheel shafts are a few thousandths inch out of line, find the point where the shafts are furthest out of line, turn the wheels to bring this point to the top, hold them in this position, raise the indicators, and with the copper hammer strike the wheel in which the shaft is clamped squarely on top. If the point where the wheel is to be struck is between two spokes, do not strike the wheel there, because it may crack. Strike the wheel at two places, that is, directly over the spokes, on both sides of the point where the wheel should be struck.

6. Do not true up one shaft so that it runs absolutely true before starting truing the other, because the first shaft generally would be knocked out of line again. The best and quickest way to true flywheels is to true both at the same time, that is, to find the high spots of the pinion gear shaft and the sprocket shaft, mark the flywheels accordingly, release the indicators and strike the wheels in the proper places.

7. If the flywheels stick very tight on the crank pin, trouble may be experienced in lining them. In this case, tightly clamp the flywheel rims together at the crank pin with a "C" clamp. Place the clamp against the sides of the rim and turn it up tight, then proceed to line the wheels as explained.

8. After the flywheels are properly lined, handle them with care.

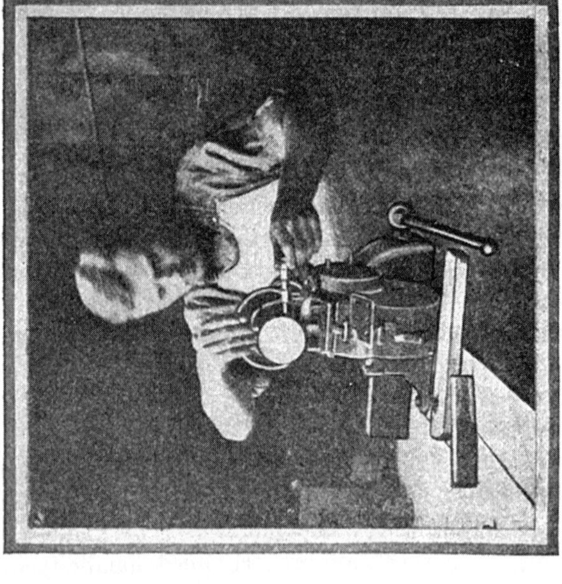

Fig. 367.—How to Check Piston Diameter with Micrometer.

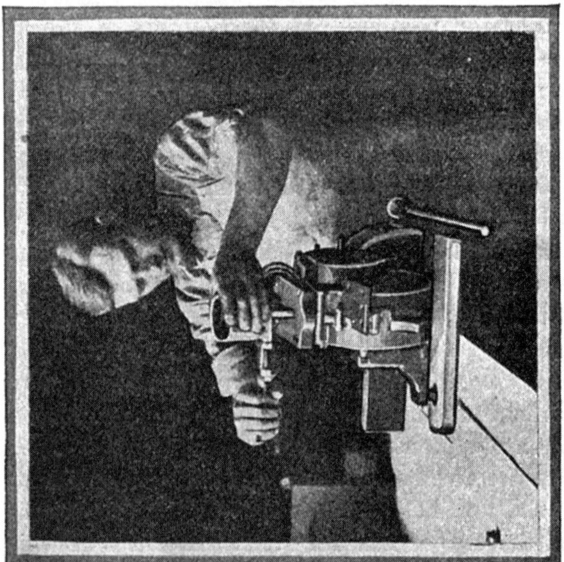

Fig. 368.—How to Straighten Connecting Rod After Assembly.

Do not give them a sudden jar or they may require realigning again.

Assembling the Motor to Fit Flywheels Into Crank Case.—1. Lay the left side crank case on the 8x8 inch box. Place the two sets of rollers and retainers in the sprocket bearing bushing with the open end of the retainers toward the flywheel. Lay the flywheel assembly in position in the left side crank case. Put some lubricating oil on the pinion gear shaft and place the right side crank case in position over the left crank case. Bolt both halves together with two of the short casing studs. Test the flywheels for end play in the crank case.

2. If the play is considerably over .003 inch, measure the excessive amount; then take the crank cases apart, remove the sprocket shaft collar, measure the thickness of the collar, add this thickness to the amount of end play, and select a collar of the combined thickness minus .003 inch. Since sprocket shaft collars are made in forty sizes ranging from .062 inch thick to .102 inch thick, any needed clearance can be obtained. Place the selected collar on the flywheel and again clamp the crank cases together with two short studs. If the flywheels have about .003 inch end play when the crank cases are bolted together with two bolts, this .003 inch end play will generally disappear when all the casing studs are drawn up tight.

3. If the flywheels have no end play and do not bind when all the casing studs are fitted, the fit is O. K., even though the flywheels did not have .003 inch end play with only two studs clamping the crank cases. When a motor is overhauled, fit the flywheels in the crank cases so that they are a free running fit, to .003 inch loose endwise.

4. If the flywheels are held tight sideways in the crank case, the spacing collar should be replaced with one which will give the proper fit. Never let a job go out if the flywheels cannot be turned perfectly freely, thinking that the wheels will loosen up properly, as is often the case with automobile motor repairing. Harley-Davidson motors must not bind anywhere; they must be perfectly

free, yet not too loose, on account of the extremely high speed at which these motors are generally run.

5. Do not overhaul a motor just because the flywheels have developed end play. Generally when 1/64 inch end play has developed, some other part of the motor requires attention. However, if everything else about the motor seems O. K., do not overhaul it just because the flywheels have 1/64 inch end play. When checking up end play, be sure to measure it carefully. Do not guess at it because this cannot be done with any accuracy.

6. After the flywheels are properly fitted in the crank case, take the crank case apart and cover both surfaces where they are joined together with a thin coating of shellac; then bolt the crank cases together securely with the casing studs, by drawing the nuts up tight. If any shellac has squeezed out at the joint, it can easily be removed with an alcohol soaked rag.

To Fit Pistons Onto Connecting Rods, Center, Square, and Round Them.—1. Before putting a piston onto a connecting rod, support the motor in a vise. Make sure that the right piston is used for the right cylinder, because the diameters of the front and rear cylinders and pistons generally are not alike. If a new piston, pin, or upper connecting rod bushing has been selected, refer to instructions previously given covering the reaming of the piston and connecting rod bushing. Do not let a piston pin have any up and down shake in the bushing, nor let a job go out in which the piston pin is not a .001 inch press fit in the piston.

2. After the proper piston pin fit has been obtained and the proper piston has been selected, put the piston pin into the right piston boss in such a position that the lock pin holes in the piston and in the pin will line up when they are assembled. Place the piston on its respective rod and hold it in place with the pilot furnished with the piston pin tool FK-799. Place the piston pin tool over the piston, put the screw against the piston pin, turn the handle, and the pin will be forced into the piston, see illustration on page 8. While pressing the pin in place, look through the piston and do not press the pin any farther when the lock pin holes line up. Remove the tool and fit a new lock pin, being sure

to spread it to prevent its falling out. Under no conditions use a lock pin twice and never use an ordinary cotter as a substitute.

To Center Pistons.—3. Turn the flywheels until the crank pin is on lower center and test the pistons to see whether they are central between the crank case. It is not necessary to have the pistons so central that there is the same clearance on both sides when the pistons are removed from side to side. It is, however, important to have the pistons center exactly between the crank cases without rubbing against either side of the piston pin bushing.

4. If the pistons do not center within the limits and the connecting rods are straight, that is, if the pistons bear properly on the squaring plate, the pistons should be removed and that side of the piston pin bushing where the least clearance is obtained should be faced off, or the bushing should be pressed toward the other side of the rod slightly. Do not put an offset bend in the rods to center the pistons.

To Round Pistons.—5. After the pistons have been centered, they will have to be rounded, because they are forced out of round when the piston pins are pressed in place. With micrometers, measure the diameter of the pistons for high spots at various places at the bell end. Very often the pistons can be rounded up accurately by just striking the piston pins from one side or the other with a drift and hammer. In some cases a "C" clamp will have to be used to press the pistons into shape, while some pistons can be rounded by striking the high spots with a hammer handle. True the pistons within at least .0005 inch of being round to avoid overheating and unnecessary loss of power and speed due to friction. Handle this assembly with care after the pistons have been trued up, because they are easily knocked out of round by letting them strike the connecting rods.

To Square Pistons.—6. Square the pistons up with piston squaring plate GK-855 by either bending or twisting the rods until the pistons rest squarely on the squaring plate, regardless of whether the crank pin is in the forward or backward position. Before placing the squaring plate on the crank case, remove all grit or burrs which may be on top of the crank case because the squaring plate must rest squarely on the crank case.

7. Put the plate on the crank case, turn the flywheels so that one of the pistons is resting on the squaring plate, hold the motor in this position without pressing the piston too tight against the plate, and strike the top of the piston on both sides to see whether or not it is resting squarely on the plate. If the piston does not rest squarely, turn the flywheels in the opposite direction and see

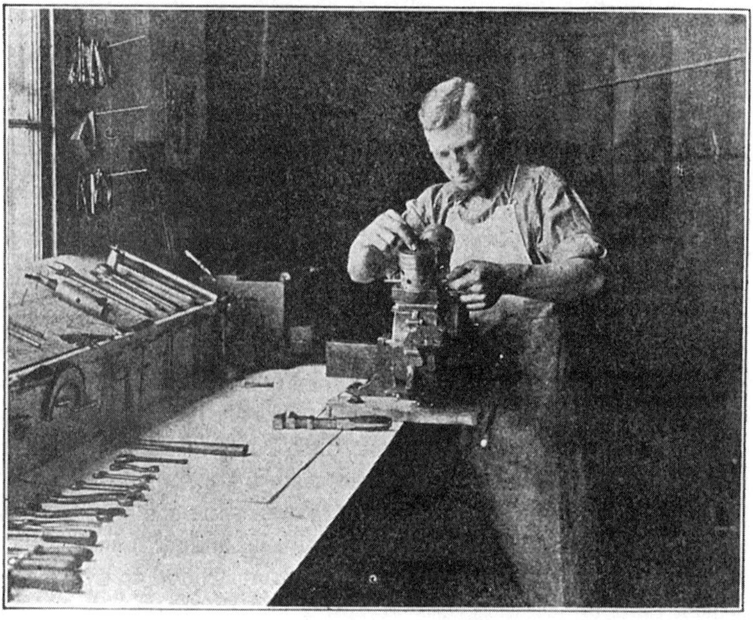

Fig. 369.—How to Test Pistons for Correct Alignment.

if the piston is just as crooked in this position. If it is, the connecting rod is bent and should be straightened by bending with monkey wrench FX-748.

8. If the right side of the piston does not bear on the plate when the crank pin is forward, but bears on the right side when the flywheels are turned so that the crank pin is backward, the connecting rod is twisted. In this case, it is best to twist the

rod backward slightly while standing at the right side of the motor and using the wrench with the right hand. Again test the condition of the rod by resting the piston on the squaring plate with the crank pin in both the forward and backward positions. If some of the twist has been taken out but not enough, pull the rod still more. If the distance between the piston and plate with the crank pin forward is greater instead of less the rod was pulled in the wrong direction. The connecting rod is straight when the piston bears evenly on the squaring plate with the crank pin both forward and backward.

9. A good way to test whether the connecting rods are absolutely straight is to lay two pieces of thin paper about 2 inches long and 1/4 inch wide on both sides of the squaring plate and then bear lightly on the piston with one finger while pulling the pieces of paper out with the other hand. It should be just as difficult to draw the paper from under one side of the piston as it is to draw the other piece from the other side. See illustration Fig. 369.

10. Screw the relief pipe nipple into the crank case. Examine the exhaust lifter pins and if they are O. K. try the fit of the pins in the exhaust lifter pin bushings.

To Fit the Cylinders.—1. If the paper cylinder gaskets were torn, fit new ones. Place one on each side of the compression plates (if the motor is of the sidecar type), without shellacking them. Wipe all grit from the pistons and cylinders, put a thin film of powdered graphite and oil mixture on the pistons and in the cylinders. Set the piston rings so that the slots are evenly divided around the pistons, place the cylinders over the pistons, and clamp the cylinders secure with the clamp nuts. When tightening the nuts, do not draw one tight all the way before starting the other. Draw them all nearly tight, before giving them the final tightening.

To Fit the Gears and Time the Motor.—1. To fit the gears, clamp the front cylinder of the motor in the vise with the gear side upward and support the crank case end of the motor by placing a 2 inch piece of wood about 8 inches long between the rear crank case lug and the bench. Place the exhaust and then the inlet roller arms on the roller arm stud with the yoke arms toward the rear. Place the secondary gear on the stud and raise the exhaust valve spring covers. Turn the secondary gear so that the exhaust roller arms are in their lowest position, and adjust the exhaust lifter pins, so that there is between .008 inch and .010 inch clearance between the exhaust valve stems and the exhaust lifter

Fig. 370.—How to Trace Piston Movement in Timing Valves of Harley-Davidson Motor.

pins. Note whether or not the rollers of the roller arms ride centrally on their respective cams. If they do not, and all rollers bear too far toward the crank case, shim them up by placing a 1/64 inch thick fibre washer on the stud under the roller arms.

2. Remove the secondary gear, and fit the lifter cam and relief lever stud without the spring. Again fit the secondary gear and turn the relief stud to see whether or not both exhaust valves

start to lift at the same time, and whether or not the exhaust roller arms are kept from resting on the low side of the cams on the secondary gear by the lifter cam. If one valve lifts considerably sooner than the other, locate the points of contact between the lifter cam and exhaust roller arms, and grind the high side of the lifter cam down so that both exhaust valves raise simultaneously. If the lifter cam does not let the exhaust roller arms rest on the gear cams, grind the lifter cam off as may be necessary.

3. If no new gears have been fitted, place the pinion gear and key on the shaft. This gear should be a .001 inch press fit on the shaft. If the pinion gear is a loose fit, select another, because the key is very apt to shear off. Note whether or not the pinion and secondary gear teeth line up evenly. If the secondary gear is higher than the pinion, place a $\frac{1}{64}$ inch thick fibre shim under the pinion gear. Clamp the pinion secure with the left threaded pinion lock screw.

4. Remove the roller arms and test the secondary and pinion gears for back lash. If the back lash or play between the teeth is considerable, remove the secondary gear and with a hammer and piece of brass, spring the stud toward the pinion. Be sure to put the piece of brass bar against that end of the stud which is toward the stud plate, because if the stud were sprung by striking it on the outside end, it would be very apt to bend and cause the secondary gear to run tight. After springing the stud, try every gear tooth to see whether or not any bind. The best fit is obtained when the gears do not bind and when they have the least bit of back lash.

5. Turn the motor so that the mark on the pinion gear is in line with the secondary and roller arm studs; after this do not turn the motor again. Put the relief valve assembly into the relief valve casing bearing bushing so that the mark on the relief valve gear is in line with the "U" mark stamped in the boss of the crank case next to the relief valve bushing.

6. Remove the secondary gear, put the roller arms on the stud and replace the secondary gear on the stud in such a position that

one of the marks on this gear is in line with the mark on the pinion gear, while the other mark of the secondary gear is toward the rear of the motor.

When New Gears Have Been Fitted.—7. If all new gears have been fitted, or only another secondary, or another pinion gear, it will, of course, be necessary to retime the motor according to piston position. If another pinion gear has been fitted, time the breather valve first. Turn the motor until the front piston is on top center; then place the breather valve in the bushing so that the port is open from $1/16$ to $3/32$ inch. Place the valve in the bushing in such a position that the port will gradually open if the motor is turned in the direction that it runs, and again closes when the piston reaches bottom center. After the breather valve has been properly timed, see whether or not the mark on the breather gear is in line with the "U" mark in the crank case when the mark of the pinion gear is in line with the secondary and roller arm studs. If the mark of the breather gear does not line up right, another wider mark can be ground into the gear, after which the original mark can be ground off.

8. If another secondary gear, or another pinion gear, or both have been fitted, turn the motor until the front piston is between $3/4$ inch and $9/16$ inch before bottom center. Place the secondary gear on the stud so that the opening side of the front exhaust cam is just starting to lift the valve. The exhaust valves should open within these limits, and close when the pistons are between $1/32$ inch to $3/32$ inch past top center. It will not be necessary to time the rear exhaust valve or either inlet valve, because these cams are mounted on the same gear with the front exhaust cam, and all cams are machined together. After timing the secondary gear, see that the marks line up properly and turn the exhaust valve spring covers in place.

9. If no $1/64$ inch thick fibre washer was placed under the roller arms, place one on top of them. Place a $1/64$ inch thick fibre washer on the cam end of the relief lever stud, and place a $1/32$ inch thick fibre washer on the drive case end of the stud. Put the stud in position and fit the drive case temporarily with two screws. Test

the roller arms and relief lever stud to see that neither is clamped tight sideways, and that there is not over $\frac{1}{64}$ inch end play. If the roller arms or stud are too tight, entirely remove or file off the $\frac{1}{64}$ inch thick washers as may be necessary. If any part has sufficient play to allow the fitting of another fibre washer, do so. The roller arms and relief lever stud are good fits when they have no end play and are perfectly free.

10. After a good fit has been obtained, remove the drive case,

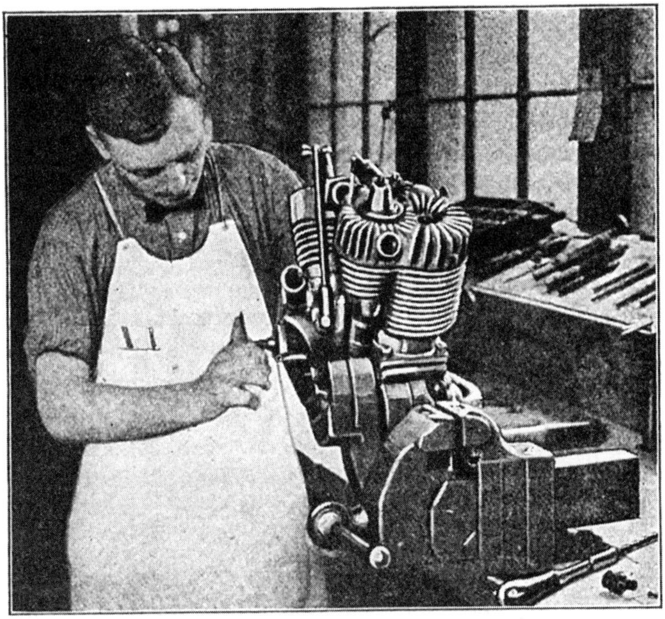

Fig. 371.—How to Use Gear Puller.

fit the coil spring in the end of the relief lever stud, and return the stud into the crank case, holding it in place by turning the motor until the front exhaust roller arm is raised. Put a few drops of oil over the moving parts, give the crank case and drive case stepped faces a thin coating of shellac, and assemble the drive case to the crank case, clamping it secure with the six drive case clamp screws. Be sure to place the two cover screw separators over the two rear drive case clamp screws before turning the screws in place. If any of the shellac is forced out when these parts are clamped together, it can readily be removed with an alcohol soaked rag.

To Fit the Magneto or Generator.—11. Examine the felt shaft washer on the drive end of the magneto. If the washer is not in good shape, fit another and prevent it from turning with the shaft by shallacking it to the side of the magneto. Place the tin washer on the magneto shaft and put the magneto on the magneto bracket, holding it temporarily with the three base screws and lock washers. Temporarily clamp the magneto drive gear to the magneto shaft and put the intermediate worm gear on its stud. Remove the motor from the vise, set it up and again secure it in the vise by clamping the front crank case lug. Draw the magneto toward the drive case as tightly as possible, making sure that the magneto base screws are not preventing the magneto from coming up tight against the drive case. If the screws are preventing the magneto from coming up close against the drive case, remove the magneto and with a rat-tail file, file the screw holes in the bracket accordingly, or an oil leak will develop between the magneto and drive case. While pulling the magneto squarely toward the drive case, also push it forward so as to get the teeth of the magneto gear and the intermediate worm gear as close together as possible without having them bind. Hold the magneto in this position while tightening the three base screws securely.

12. After the magneto is clamped securely on its bracket, again test the fit of the gears. A good way to test whether or not the gears bind if they have no back lash is to slide the intermediate worm gear back and forth on its stud while turning the gears slowly. If a spot is found where the gears bind, even if only slightly, the magneto should be moved backward slightly on its bracket. After the magneto is set and tightened properly on the bracket, remove the magneto drive gear. If the gear sticks, use puller FK-831.

13. To time the magneto according to gear marks it is only necessary to have all gear marks in line (with each other), with the exception of the breather gear, and then to tighten the mag-

neto gear clamp nut, being sure that the key is placed in the magneto shaft.

14. If the motor is fitted with another than the original magneto, set all gear marks in line (with each other), with the exception of the breather valve gear, and have the magneto gear held loosely without a key. Turn the motor until the front piston is between 1/4 inch and 5/16 inch before top center on the compression stroke, fully advance the interrupter, turn the circuit breaker to the left until the fibre breaker lever is touching the lower interrupter shoe sufficiently to just cause the circuit breaker points to start to break contact. Hold the magneto in this position while marking the magneto gear and the intermediate worm gear with a pencil. Remove the gear, fit the key into the magneto shaft, replace the gear just as it was removed and tighten the clamp nut. To make sure that the magneto is timed correctly, again check over the timing as previously explained.

15. If the motor is equipped with a generator in place of a magneto, the preceding instructions can be applied with the exception that the method of timing is different; and with model 235 generator a piece of blotter paper and two screws with separators are used to draw the generator snugly against the drive case, while the generator gear is lined up with the generator intermediate gear instead of with the intermediate worm gear.

Caution.—Care should be taken when turning the two screws through the drive case and into the generator, that in addition to placing the separators on the screws, a 1/16 inch thick washer is placed on the screw which goes toward the rear.

16. To time a generator according to gear marks, it is important to turn the generator gear to the left until the small (front) cam is just touching the fibre block of the circuit breaker lever, with the interrupter fully advanced, and with all gear marks with the exception of the breather valve gear exactly in line with each other. The reason for this is that the generator gear and the circuit breaker cam are geared three to one, respectively.

17. If a generator is used to replace the original one, do not refer to gear marks to time the generator, but set all gear marks in

line. Loosen the circuit breaker cam with puller GK-833 after the nut has been loosened, insert a scale through the front cylinder plug hole and turn the motor until the front piston is between 7/32 inch and 9/32 inch before top center on the compression stroke. Fully advance the circuit breaker, turn the small cam to the right until it is just touching the fibre block, hold the cam in this position and securely draw up the clamp nut.

18. After the gears and ignition unit have been properly fitted, place the gear stud collar and split rings on the intermediate gear studs and again clamp the motor in the vise by clamping the front cylinder. Put the 1/8 inch thick fibre washer on the secondary gear stud and lay a straight edge across the drive case next to the stud to see whether or not the fibre washer is too thick or too thin. If the washer is too thick, file it off as may be necessary, or if another 1/64 inch thick washer can be put on the stud without clamping the secondary gear when the drive case cover is fitted, put it on.

19. Pour one-half pint of good engine oil over the gears, and fit the drive case cover after making sure that the paper cover gasket is O. K. If another gasket must be fitted, scrape off every bit of the old gasket and shellac, and shellac the new gasket to the cover only. To soften the paper gasket and to prevent it from sticking on the drive case, give the gasket a film of oil after it has been shellacked to the cover. Use Yankee screw driver EK-325 to turn the screws in place.

20. Set up the motor and hold it in the vise by clamping the front crank case lug. Inspect the cylinder plug gaskets and discard them if there is the slightest chance for a leak. Select new ones and with wrench GK-865 or wrench GK-861 turn the plugs into the cylinder heads. If necessary, use a hammer on the wrench to thoroughly tighten the plugs. Put the inlet lifter pins into their bushings, and make sure that they do not stick. Connect the breather pipe to the nipple in the crank case. With the later type 1918 motors also clamp the lower end of the pipe to the crank case with the small clip and screws. Connect the drive case oil pipe to the nipple in the drive case cover.

21. Fit the inlet push rods without the springs or covers, ad-

just them so that there is .004 inch clearance between the inlet valve stems and inlet levers, again remove them from the motor, and fit the push rod springs and covers.

22. Before connecting the inlet manifold and carburetor assembly to the motor, inspect the copper gaskets, manifold and packing bushings. If the manifold has been bent by the packing bushings, another manifold and another set of packing bushings should be used, because the manifold would leak and it would be impossible to get the motor to run satisfactorily. If the carburetor has been removed, make sure that the paper gasket between the carburetor and manifold is in good condition, that there are no burrs which might prevent a tight fit and that the three screws are drawn up firmly.

23. When connecting the manifold assembly to the motor, be sure to get the manifold in the center between the two cylinders or a leak will develop. Turn both inlet nipples as tightly as possible into the cylinders, set the manifold central, and while holding the carburetor square, tighten the manifold clamp nuts.

To Place Motor in Frame.—1. When placing a motor back into the frame, reverse the operations of taking it out. Be sure to put the bell crank bracket and intermediate control rod assembly over the rear cylinder plug, before placing the motor in its final position. Make sure that all casing clamp bolt nuts, as well as all other nuts, bolts, and screws, are drawn up as tightly as it is safe to draw them.

2. Inspect the spark and throttle controls after they are connected up. Make sure that the throttle can be fully opened and closed, that the spark can be fully advanced and retarded, and that the exhaust valves can be lifted by turning the left grip to the extreme left after the spark has reached the retarded position.

3. To prevent overoiling, vent the oiler before running the motor. This is covered on page 40 of the 1918 manual. The oiler is very likely to become air bound whenever the drive case oil pipe is disconnected.

To Test the Motor.—1. To test the motor does not require taken it out on the road and running it at its maximum speed. This is abuse to which no motor should be subjected.

2. The most important test can be made right in the repair shop if an electric fan or some other means of cooling is available.

3. Before starting the motor, inject one pumpful of oil with the hand-pump. Start the motor in the usual way, and adjust the carburetor so that the motor will fire regularly and fairly slow with an advanced spark and closed throttle. For instructions covering carburetor adjustments, refer to the proper manual.

4. Under no conditions turn the low speed adjusting screw way into the carburetor, because it will then be impossible to adjust the carburetor, to have the motor fire nicely for all throttle positions. If the motor will not throttle down to a fairly slow speed unless the adjusting screw is turned way in, the carburetor is worn, or there is a leak between the carburetor and cylinders. To test for a leak, squirt gasoline along these places with the priming gun, while the motor is running slowly. If there is a leak, the running of the motor will be affected.

5. The inlet housings, manifold connections, cylinder plugs, and priming cocks, should be tested in like manner for leaks. If a leak is found, make the necessary repairs.

6. After the motor has warmed up, carefully look at the joints between the crankcases, drivecase, and drivecase cover for oil leaks. The presence of oil indicates a leak which should be repaired immediately, because the motor may run dry and a considerable amount of oil be wasted.

7. After the motor has been running well for about 15 minutes on the stand, the machine should be taken out for a short road test. If the motor is quiet, fires evenly, has a good pickup, etc., it can be taken for granted that it is O. K. and can be put back into regular service.

8. If the cylinders were reground and several bearings replaced it is advisable to inform the rider to run the machine in as though it were new, to avoid the danger of running it tight.

INDEX

A CATALOG OF SELECTED

DOVER BOOKS

IN ALL FIELDS OF INTEREST

A CATALOG OF SELECTED DOVER BOOKS IN ALL FIELDS OF INTEREST

CONCERNING THE SPIRITUAL IN ART, Wassily Kandinsky. Pioneering work by father of abstract art. Thoughts on color theory, nature of art. Analysis of earlier masters. 12 illustrations. 80pp. of text. 5⅜ x 8½. 23411-8

ANIMALS: 1,419 Copyright-Free Illustrations of Mammals, Birds, Fish, Insects, etc., Jim Harter (ed.). Clear wood engravings present, in extremely lifelike poses, over 1,000 species of animals. One of the most extensive pictorial sourcebooks of its kind. Captions. Index. 284pp. 9 x 12. 23766-4

CELTIC ART: The Methods of Construction, George Bain. Simple geometric techniques for making Celtic interlacements, spirals, Kells-type initials, animals, humans, etc. Over 500 illustrations. 160pp. 9 x 12. (Available in U.S. only.) 22923-8

AN ATLAS OF ANATOMY FOR ARTISTS, Fritz Schider. Most thorough reference work on art anatomy in the world. Hundreds of illustrations, including selections from works by Vesalius, Leonardo, Goya, Ingres, Michelangelo, others. 593 illustrations. 192pp. 7⅛ x 10¼. 20241-0

CELTIC HAND STROKE-BY-STROKE (Irish Half-Uncial from "The Book of Kells"): An Arthur Baker Calligraphy Manual, Arthur Baker. Complete guide to creating each letter of the alphabet in distinctive Celtic manner. Covers hand position, strokes, pens, inks, paper, more. Illustrated. 48pp. 8¼ x 11. 24336-2

EASY ORIGAMI, John Montroll. Charming collection of 32 projects (hat, cup, pelican, piano, swan, many more) specially designed for the novice origami hobbyist. Clearly illustrated easy-to-follow instructions insure that even beginning papercrafters will achieve successful results. 48pp. 8¼ x 11. 27298-2

THE COMPLETE BOOK OF BIRDHOUSE CONSTRUCTION FOR WOODWORKERS, Scott D. Campbell. Detailed instructions, illustrations, tables. Also data on bird habitat and instinct patterns. Bibliography. 3 tables. 63 illustrations in 15 figures. 48pp. 5¼ x 8½. 24407-5

BLOOMINGDALE'S ILLUSTRATED 1886 CATALOG: Fashions, Dry Goods and Housewares, Bloomingdale Brothers. Famed merchants' extremely rare catalog depicting about 1,700 products: clothing, housewares, firearms, dry goods, jewelry, more. Invaluable for dating, identifying vintage items. Also, copyright-free graphics for artists, designers. Co-published with Henry Ford Museum & Greenfield Village. 160pp. 8¼ x 11. 25780-0

HISTORIC COSTUME IN PICTURES, Braun & Schneider. Over 1,450 costumed figures in clearly detailed engravings–from dawn of civilization to end of 19th century. Captions. Many folk costumes. 256pp. 8⅜ x 11¾. 23150-X

THE CLARINET AND CLARINET PLAYING, David Pino. Lively, comprehensive work features suggestions about technique, musicianship, and musical interpretation, as well as guidelines for teaching, making your own reeds, and preparing for public performance. Includes an intriguing look at clarinet history. "A godsend," *The Clarinet,* Journal of the International Clarinet Society. Appendixes. 7 illus. 320pp. 5⅜ x 8½. 40270-3

HOLLYWOOD GLAMOR PORTRAITS, John Kobal (ed.). 145 photos from 1926-49. Harlow, Gable, Bogart, Bacall; 94 stars in all. Full background on photographers, technical aspects. 160pp. 8⅜ x 11¼. 23352-9

THE ANNOTATED CASEY AT THE BAT: A Collection of Ballads about the Mighty Casey/Third, Revised Edition, Martin Gardner (ed.). Amusing sequels and parodies of one of America's best-loved poems: Casey's Revenge, Why Casey Whiffed, Casey's Sister at the Bat, others. 256pp. 5⅜ x 8½. 28598-7

THE RAVEN AND OTHER FAVORITE POEMS, Edgar Allan Poe. Over 40 of the author's most memorable poems: "The Bells," "Ulalume," "Israfel," "To Helen," "The Conqueror Worm," "Eldorado," "Annabel Lee," many more. Alphabetic lists of titles and first lines. 64pp. 5$\frac{3}{16}$ x 8¼. 26685-0

PERSONAL MEMOIRS OF U. S. GRANT, Ulysses Simpson Grant. Intelligent, deeply moving firsthand account of Civil War campaigns, considered by many the finest military memoirs ever written. Includes letters, historic photographs, maps and more. 528pp. 6⅛ x 9¼. 28587-1

ANCIENT EGYPTIAN MATERIALS AND INDUSTRIES, A. Lucas and J. Harris. Fascinating, comprehensive, thoroughly documented text describes this ancient civilization's vast resources and the processes that incorporated them in daily life, including the use of animal products, building materials, cosmetics, perfumes and incense, fibers, glazed ware, glass and its manufacture, materials used in the mummification process, and much more. 544pp. 6⅛ x 9¼. (Available in U.S. only.) 40446-3

RUSSIAN STORIES/RUSSKIE RASSKAZY: A Dual-Language Book, edited by Gleb Struve. Twelve tales by such masters as Chekhov, Tolstoy, Dostoevsky, Pushkin, others. Excellent word-for-word English translations on facing pages, plus teaching and study aids, Russian/English vocabulary, biographical/critical introductions, more. 416pp. 5⅜ x 8½. 26244-8

PHILADELPHIA THEN AND NOW: 60 Sites Photographed in the Past and Present, Kenneth Finkel and Susan Oyama. Rare photographs of City Hall, Logan Square, Independence Hall, Betsy Ross House, other landmarks juxtaposed with contemporary views. Captures changing face of historic city. Introduction. Captions. 128pp. 8¼ x 11. 25790-8

AIA ARCHITECTURAL GUIDE TO NASSAU AND SUFFOLK COUNTIES, LONG ISLAND, The American Institute of Architects, Long Island Chapter, and the Society for the Preservation of Long Island Antiquities. Comprehensive, well-researched and generously illustrated volume brings to life over three centuries of Long Island's great architectural heritage. More than 240 photographs with authoritative, extensively detailed captions. 176pp. 8¼ x 11. 26946-9

NORTH AMERICAN INDIAN LIFE: Customs and Traditions of 23 Tribes, Elsie Clews Parsons (ed.). 27 fictionalized essays by noted anthropologists examine religion, customs, government, additional facets of life among the Winnebago, Crow, Zuni, Eskimo, other tribes. 480pp. 6⅛ x 9¼. 27377-6

FRANK LLOYD WRIGHT'S DANA HOUSE, Donald Hoffmann. Pictorial essay of residential masterpiece with over 160 interior and exterior photos, plans, elevations, sketches and studies. 128pp. 9¼ x 10¾. 29120-0

THE MALE AND FEMALE FIGURE IN MOTION: 60 Classic Photographic Sequences, Eadweard Muybridge. 60 true-action photographs of men and women walking, running, climbing, bending, turning, etc., reproduced from rare 19th-century masterpiece. vi + 121pp. 9 x 12. 24745-7

1001 QUESTIONS ANSWERED ABOUT THE SEASHORE, N. J. Berrill and Jacquelyn Berrill. Queries answered about dolphins, sea snails, sponges, starfish, fishes, shore birds, many others. Covers appearance, breeding, growth, feeding, much more. 305pp. 5¼ x 8¼. 23366-9

ATTRACTING BIRDS TO YOUR YARD, William J. Weber. Easy-to-follow guide offers advice on how to attract the greatest diversity of birds: birdhouses, feeders, water and waterers, much more. 96pp. 5$\frac{3}{16}$ x 8¼. 28927-3

MEDICINAL AND OTHER USES OF NORTH AMERICAN PLANTS: A Historical Survey with Special Reference to the Eastern Indian Tribes, Charlotte Erichsen-Brown. Chronological historical citations document 500 years of usage of plants, trees, shrubs native to eastern Canada, northeastern U.S. Also complete identifying information. 343 illustrations. 544pp. 6½ x 9¼. 25951-X

STORYBOOK MAZES, Dave Phillips. 23 stories and mazes on two-page spreads: Wizard of Oz, Treasure Island, Robin Hood, etc. Solutions. 64pp. 8¼ x 11. 23628-5

AMERICAN NEGRO SONGS: 230 Folk Songs and Spirituals, Religious and Secular, John W. Work. This authoritative study traces the African influences of songs sung and played by black Americans at work, in church, and as entertainment. The author discusses the lyric significance of such songs as "Swing Low, Sweet Chariot," "John Henry," and others and offers the words and music for 230 songs. Bibliography. Index of Song Titles. 272pp. 6½ x 9¼. 40271-1

MOVIE-STAR PORTRAITS OF THE FORTIES, John Kobal (ed.). 163 glamor, studio photos of 106 stars of the 1940s: Rita Hayworth, Ava Gardner, Marlon Brando, Clark Gable, many more. 176pp. 8⅜ x 11¼. 23546-7

BENCHLEY LOST AND FOUND, Robert Benchley. Finest humor from early 30s, about pet peeves, child psychologists, post office and others. Mostly unavailable elsewhere. 73 illustrations by Peter Arno and others. 183pp. 5⅜ x 8½. 22410-4

YEKL and THE IMPORTED BRIDEGROOM AND OTHER STORIES OF YIDDISH NEW YORK, Abraham Cahan. Film Hester Street based on *Yekl* (1896). Novel, other stories among first about Jewish immigrants on N.Y.'s East Side. 240pp. 5⅜ x 8½. 22427-9

SELECTED POEMS, Walt Whitman. Generous sampling from *Leaves of Grass*. Twenty-four poems include "I Hear America Singing," "Song of the Open Road," "I Sing the Body Electric," "When Lilacs Last in the Dooryard Bloom'd," "O Captain! My Captain!"–all reprinted from an authoritative edition. Lists of titles and first lines. 128pp. 5$\frac{3}{16}$ x 8¼. 26878-0

MY BONDAGE AND MY FREEDOM, Frederick Douglass. Born a slave, Douglass became outspoken force in antislavery movement. The best of Douglass' autobiographies. Graphic description of slave life. 464pp. 5⅜ x 8½. 22457-0

FOLLOWING THE EQUATOR: A Journey Around the World, Mark Twain. Fascinating humorous account of 1897 voyage to Hawaii, Australia, India, New Zealand, etc. Ironic, bemused reports on peoples, customs, climate, flora and fauna, politics, much more. 197 illustrations. 720pp. 5⅜ x 8½. 26113-1

THE PEOPLE CALLED SHAKERS, Edward D. Andrews. Definitive study of Shakers: origins, beliefs, practices, dances, social organization, furniture and crafts, etc. 33 illustrations. 351pp. 5⅜ x 8½. 21081-2

THE MYTHS OF GREECE AND ROME, H. A. Guerber. A classic of mythology, generously illustrated, long prized for its simple, graphic, accurate retelling of the principal myths of Greece and Rome, and for its commentary on their origins and significance. With 64 illustrations by Michelangelo, Raphael, Titian, Rubens, Canova, Bernini and others. 480pp. 5⅜ x 8½. 27584-1

PSYCHOLOGY OF MUSIC, Carl E. Seashore. Classic work discusses music as a medium from psychological viewpoint. Clear treatment of physical acoustics, auditory apparatus, sound perception, development of musical skills, nature of musical feeling, host of other topics. 88 figures. 408pp. 5⅜ x 8½. 21851-1

THE PHILOSOPHY OF HISTORY, Georg W. Hegel. Great classic of Western thought develops concept that history is not chance but rational process, the evolution of freedom. 457pp. 5⅜ x 8½. 20112-0

THE BOOK OF TEA, Kakuzo Okakura. Minor classic of the Orient: entertaining, charming explanation, interpretation of traditional Japanese culture in terms of tea ceremony. 94pp. 5⅜ x 8½. 20070-1

LIFE IN ANCIENT EGYPT, Adolf Erman. Fullest, most thorough, detailed older account with much not in more recent books, domestic life, religion, magic, medicine, commerce, much more. Many illustrations reproduce tomb paintings, carvings, hieroglyphs, etc. 597pp. 5⅜ x 8½. 22632-8

SUNDIALS, Their Theory and Construction, Albert Waugh. Far and away the best, most thorough coverage of ideas, mathematics concerned, types, construction, adjusting anywhere. Simple, nontechnical treatment allows even children to build several of these dials. Over 100 illustrations. 230pp. 5⅜ x 8½. 22947-5

THEORETICAL HYDRODYNAMICS, L. M. Milne-Thomson. Classic exposition of the mathematical theory of fluid motion, applicable to both hydrodynamics and aerodynamics. Over 600 exercises. 768pp. 6⅛ x 9¼. 68970-0

SONGS OF EXPERIENCE: Facsimile Reproduction with 26 Plates in Full Color, William Blake. 26 full-color plates from a rare 1826 edition. Includes "The Tyger," "London," "Holy Thursday," and other poems. Printed text of poems. 48pp. 5¼ x 7. 24636-1

OLD-TIME VIGNETTES IN FULL COLOR, Carol Belanger Grafton (ed.). Over 390 charming, often sentimental illustrations, selected from archives of Victorian graphics–pretty women posing, children playing, food, flowers, kittens and puppies, smiling cherubs, birds and butterflies, much more. All copyright-free. 48pp. 9¼ x 12¼. 27269-9

LITTLE BOOK OF EARLY AMERICAN CRAFTS AND TRADES, Peter Stockham (ed.). 1807 children's book explains crafts and trades: baker, hatter, cooper, potter, and many others. 23 copperplate illustrations. 140pp. 4⅝ x 6. 23336-7

VICTORIAN FASHIONS AND COSTUMES FROM HARPER'S BAZAR, 1867–1898, Stella Blum (ed.). Day costumes, evening wear, sports clothes, shoes, hats, other accessories in over 1,000 detailed engravings. 320pp. 9⅜ x 12¼. 22990-4

GUSTAV STICKLEY, THE CRAFTSMAN, Mary Ann Smith. Superb study surveys broad scope of Stickley's achievement, especially in architecture. Design philosophy, rise and fall of the Craftsman empire, descriptions and floor plans for many Craftsman houses, more. 86 black-and-white halftones. 31 line illustrations. Introduction 208pp. 6½ x 9¼. 27210-9

THE LONG ISLAND RAIL ROAD IN EARLY PHOTOGRAPHS, Ron Ziel. Over 220 rare photos, informative text document origin (1844) and development of rail service on Long Island. Vintage views of early trains, locomotives, stations, passengers, crews, much more. Captions. 8⅞ x 11¾. 26301-0

VOYAGE OF THE LIBERDADE, Joshua Slocum. Great 19th-century mariner's thrilling, first-hand account of the wreck of his ship off South America, the 35-foot boat he built from the wreckage, and its remarkable voyage home. 128pp. 5⅜ x 8½. 40022-0

TEN BOOKS ON ARCHITECTURE, Vitruvius. The most important book ever written on architecture. Early Roman aesthetics, technology, classical orders, site selection, all other aspects. Morgan translation. 331pp. 5⅜ x 8½. 20645-9

THE HUMAN FIGURE IN MOTION, Eadweard Muybridge. More than 4,500 stopped-action photos, in action series, showing undraped men, women, children jumping, lying down, throwing, sitting, wrestling, carrying, etc. 390pp. 7⅞ x 10⅝. 20204-6 Clothbd.

TREES OF THE EASTERN AND CENTRAL UNITED STATES AND CANADA, William M. Harlow. Best one-volume guide to 140 trees. Full descriptions, woodlore, range, etc. Over 600 illustrations. Handy size. 288pp. 4½ x 6⅜. 20395-6

SONGS OF WESTERN BIRDS, Dr. Donald J. Borror. Complete song and call repertoire of 60 western species, including flycatchers, juncoes, cactus wrens, many more–includes fully illustrated booklet. Cassette and manual 99913-0

GROWING AND USING HERBS AND SPICES, Milo Miloradovich. Versatile handbook provides all the information needed for cultivation and use of all the herbs and spices available in North America. 4 illustrations. Index. Glossary. 236pp. 5⅜ x 8½. 25058-X

BIG BOOK OF MAZES AND LABYRINTHS, Walter Shepherd. 50 mazes and labyrinths in all–classical, solid, ripple, and more–in one great volume. Perfect inexpensive puzzler for clever youngsters. Full solutions. 112pp. 8⅛ x 11. 22951-3

PIANO TUNING, J. Cree Fischer. Clearest, best book for beginner, amateur. Simple repairs, raising dropped notes, tuning by easy method of flattened fifths. No previous skills needed. 4 illustrations. 201pp. 5⅜ x 8½. 23267-0

HINTS TO SINGERS, Lillian Nordica. Selecting the right teacher, developing confidence, overcoming stage fright, and many other important skills receive thoughtful discussion in this indispensible guide, written by a world-famous diva of four decades' experience. 96pp. 5⅜ x 8½. 40094-8

THE COMPLETE NONSENSE OF EDWARD LEAR, Edward Lear. All nonsense limericks, zany alphabets, Owl and Pussycat, songs, nonsense botany, etc., illustrated by Lear. Total of 320pp. 5⅜ x 8½. (Available in U.S. only.) 20167-8

VICTORIAN PARLOUR POETRY: An Annotated Anthology, Michael R. Turner. 117 gems by Longfellow, Tennyson, Browning, many lesser-known poets. "The Village Blacksmith," "Curfew Must Not Ring Tonight," "Only a Baby Small," dozens more, often difficult to find elsewhere. Index of poets, titles, first lines. xxiii + 325pp. 5⅝ x 8¼. 27044-0

DUBLINERS, James Joyce. Fifteen stories offer vivid, tightly focused observations of the lives of Dublin's poorer classes. At least one, "The Dead," is considered a masterpiece. Reprinted complete and unabridged from standard edition. 160pp. 5³⁄₁₆ x 8¼. 26870-5

GREAT WEIRD TALES: 14 Stories by Lovecraft, Blackwood, Machen and Others, S. T. Joshi (ed.). 14 spellbinding tales, including "The Sin Eater," by Fiona McLeod, "The Eye Above the Mantel," by Frank Belknap Long, as well as renowned works by R. H. Barlow, Lord Dunsany, Arthur Machen, W. C. Morrow and eight other masters of the genre. 256pp. 5⅜ x 8½. (Available in U.S. only.) 40436-6

THE BOOK OF THE SACRED MAGIC OF ABRAMELIN THE MAGE, translated by S. MacGregor Mathers. Medieval manuscript of ceremonial magic. Basic document in Aleister Crowley, Golden Dawn groups. 268pp. 5⅜ x 8½. 23211-5

NEW RUSSIAN-ENGLISH AND ENGLISH-RUSSIAN DICTIONARY, M. A. O'Brien. This is a remarkably handy Russian dictionary, containing a surprising amount of information, including over 70,000 entries. 366pp. 4½ x 6⅛. 20208-9

HISTORIC HOMES OF THE AMERICAN PRESIDENTS, Second, Revised Edition, Irvin Haas. A traveler's guide to American Presidential homes, most open to the public, depicting and describing homes occupied by every American President from George Washington to George Bush. With visiting hours, admission charges, travel routes. 175 photographs. Index. 160pp. 8¼ x 11. 26751-2

NEW YORK IN THE FORTIES, Andreas Feininger. 162 brilliant photographs by the well-known photographer, formerly with *Life* magazine. Commuters, shoppers, Times Square at night, much else from city at its peak. Captions by John von Hartz. 181pp. 9¼ x 10¾. 23585-8

INDIAN SIGN LANGUAGE, William Tomkins. Over 525 signs developed by Sioux and other tribes. Written instructions and diagrams. Also 290 pictographs. 111pp. 6⅛ x 9¼. 22029-X

THE WIT AND HUMOR OF OSCAR WILDE, Alvin Redman (ed.). More than 1,000 ripostes, paradoxes, wisecracks: Work is the curse of the drinking classes; I can resist everything except temptation; etc. 258pp. 5⅜ x 8½. 20602-5

SHAKESPEARE LEXICON AND QUOTATION DICTIONARY, Alexander Schmidt. Full definitions, locations, shades of meaning in every word in plays and poems. More than 50,000 exact quotations. 1,485pp. 6½ x 9¼. 2-vol. set.
Vol. 1: 22726-X
Vol. 2: 22727-8

SELECTED POEMS, Emily Dickinson. Over 100 best-known, best-loved poems by one of America's foremost poets, reprinted from authoritative early editions. No comparable edition at this price. Index of first lines. 64pp. 5$\frac{3}{16}$ x 8¼. 26466-1

THE INSIDIOUS DR. FU-MANCHU, Sax Rohmer. The first of the popular mystery series introduces a pair of English detectives to their archnemesis, the diabolical Dr. Fu-Manchu. Flavorful atmosphere, fast-paced action, and colorful characters enliven this classic of the genre. 208pp. 5$\frac{3}{16}$ x 8¼. 29898-1

THE MALLEUS MALEFICARUM OF KRAMER AND SPRENGER, translated by Montague Summers. Full text of most important witchhunter's "bible," used by both Catholics and Protestants. 278pp. 6⅝ x 10. 22802-9

SPANISH STORIES/CUENTOS ESPAÑOLES: A Dual-Language Book, Angel Flores (ed.). Unique format offers 13 great stories in Spanish by Cervantes, Borges, others. Faithful English translations on facing pages. 352pp. 5⅜ x 8½. 25399-6

GARDEN CITY, LONG ISLAND, IN EARLY PHOTOGRAPHS, 1869–1919, Mildred H. Smith. Handsome treasury of 118 vintage pictures, accompanied by carefully researched captions, document the Garden City Hotel fire (1899), the Vanderbilt Cup Race (1908), the first airmail flight departing from the Nassau Boulevard Aerodrome (1911), and much more. 96pp. 8⅞ x 11¾. 40669-5

OLD QUEENS, N.Y., IN EARLY PHOTOGRAPHS, Vincent F. Seyfried and William Asadorian. Over 160 rare photographs of Maspeth, Jamaica, Jackson Heights, and other areas. Vintage views of DeWitt Clinton mansion, 1939 World's Fair and more. Captions. 192pp. 8⅞ x 11. 26358-4

CAPTURED BY THE INDIANS: 15 Firsthand Accounts, 1750-1870, Frederick Drimmer. Astounding true historical accounts of grisly torture, bloody conflicts, relentless pursuits, miraculous escapes and more, by people who lived to tell the tale. 384pp. 5⅜ x 8½. 24901-8

THE WORLD'S GREAT SPEECHES (Fourth Enlarged Edition), Lewis Copeland, Lawrence W. Lamm, and Stephen J. McKenna. Nearly 300 speeches provide public speakers with a wealth of updated quotes and inspiration–from Pericles' funeral oration and William Jennings Bryan's "Cross of Gold Speech" to Malcolm X's powerful words on the Black Revolution and Earl of Spenser's tribute to his sister, Diana, Princess of Wales. 944pp. 5⅜ x 8⅜. 40903-1

THE BOOK OF THE SWORD, Sir Richard F. Burton. Great Victorian scholar/adventurer's eloquent, erudite history of the "queen of weapons"–from prehistory to early Roman Empire. Evolution and development of early swords, variations (sabre, broadsword, cutlass, scimitar, etc.), much more. 336pp. 6⅛ x 9¼. 25434-8